D11232284

ENCYCLOPEDIA
of
PERENNIALS

ENCYCLOPEDIA *of* PERENNIALS

A GARDENER'S GUIDE

Christopher Woods

Facts On File
New York • Oxford

ENCYCLOPEDIA *of* PERENNIALS: A GARDENER'S GUIDE

Copyright Photos and Text © 1992 by Christopher Woods

All rights reserved. No part of this book may be reproduced or utilized in any form or by any means, electronic or mechanical, including photocopying, recording, or by any information storage or retrieval systems, without permission in writing from the publisher. For information contact:

Facts On File, Inc.	Facts On File Limited
460 Park Avenue South	Collins Street
New York NY 10016	Oxford OX4 1XJ
USA	United Kingdom

Library of Congress Cataloging-in-Publication Data
Woods, Christopher.
Encyclopedia of perennials: a gardener's guide / Christopher Woods.
p. cm.
ISBN 0-8160-2092-2
1. Perennials—Encyclopedias. 2. Perennials—Pictorial works.
I. Title.
SB434.W66 1992
635.9'32—dc20 91-15280

British CIP data available on request from Facts On File.

Facts On File books are available at special discounts when purchased in bulk quantities for businesses, associations, institutions or sales promotions. Please contact our Special Sales Department in New York at 212/683-2244 (dial 800/322-8755 except in NY, AK, or HI) or in Oxford at 865/728399.

Text design by Ron Monteleone
Jacket design by Catherine Hyman
Composition by the Maple-Vail Composition Services
Manufactured by Mandarin Offset
Printed in Hong Kong

10 9 8 7 6 5 4 3 2 1

This book is printed on acid-free paper.

To my father, Arthur Woods,
with love

Contents

Acknowledgments

No book is ever written by just one person, although this work has been produced from my own personal experience in growing and observing plants in Great Britain and in the United States. I would like to thank the following, without whom I would not have undertaken this often exasperating enterprise.

My special thanks go to Judy Zuk, who got me into this and has supported me, despite several reasons not to, through thick and thin; Rick Darke, who provided me with a great deal of technical help, especially about ornamental grasses; Maggie Oster, who talked me through the many mood swings and convinced me not to give up my day job; the late Adolph Rosengarten, Jr., who gave me the precious gift of time; and the board and the staff of the Chanticleer Foundation, who, whether they knew it or not, supported this project with patience and understanding.

INTRODUCTION

This book is an encyclopedia written in nontechnical language with the interested but not necessarily experienced gardener in mind. I have tried to translate botanical terms into everyday language with the hope that the reader will not be intimidated by the often overwhelming complexity of plant descriptions. In any work such as this, a substantial amount of generalization must take place. I have had to generalize in my attempt to keep it simple, and I apologize to my colleagues in the garden world if I have simplified too much. But this book is not written for botanists and taxonomists; it is written for those who love plants and gardens and who spend much of their valuable time cultivating herbaceous perennials for their own pleasure and for the pleasure of others.

The world of herbaceous perennials is one of richness and diversity. With this book I have attempted to describe this world and how we can grow and propagate the plants that delight us. Millions of words have been and will continue to be written about plants. This book was written out of a love of nature and of the green commonwealth of plants. It is my hope that this book will not only educate the novice but also stimulate the sophisticated plant lover to look for plants outside his or her experience. As the world turns in its ever-increasing complexity, we should remember that plants not only feed us, they delight us, softening the harshness of daily life and making our existence joyful. This book was written as an expression of passion for plants and a passion for life.

WHAT'S IN A NAME

The names of plants are often confusing to the uninitiated. In fact, plant nomenclature is quite simple. We owe the botanical naming of plants to a Swedish botanist, Carl Linnaeus (1707–78), who divided the names of plants into two parts. The first is the genus, for example, ***Coreopsis,*** which denotes a closely related group of plants; the second is the name of the species within that genus, for example, ***verticillata,*** which describes common characteristics. Thus the botanical name of a specific tickseed is ***Coreopsis verticillata.*** Often the species name is followed by other names. These further identify the plant and can be varieties (var.), which are slightly different; subspecies (subsp.), which are often geographical variants; or forma (f.), which differ only slightly, usually in flower color or leaf form. Other identifying names can and often do follow. A cultivar is a cultivated variety and is listed within single quotation marks; for example, ***Campanula alliariifolia*** 'Ivory Bells' is a cultivated variety of ***Campanula alliariifolia.*** Since 1959 cultivars must be listed in nonbotanical language. For example, 'Ivory Bells' is correct, but naming this particular cultivar 'Alba' would be incorrect. Hybrids between one species and another are written with a multiplication sign. For example, ***Aconitum × cammarum*** is a hybrid between ***A. napellus*** and ***A. variegatum.*** The multiplication sign denotes that this is a sexual cross between two species. Sometimes two or three species of different genera are crossed; in this case a multiplication sign is written in front of the genus name; for example, **× *Heucherella*** is a cross between species of ***Heuchera*** and ***Tiarella.*** Finally, the family name, ending in *-aceae,* denotes plants that are grouped together according to their floral characteristics.

Plant nomenclature is a botanical minefield governed by *The International Code of Nomenclature for Cultivated Plants* and *The International Code of Botanical Nomenclature.* Plant names are constantly revised to reflect new understanding of common characteristics. At times the revision of plant names seems an obtuse way of confusing even the most knowledgeable gardener. I have attempted to name the plants described in this book as accurately as possible. Recent changes have been incorporated; for example, ***Zauschneria*** is now placed in the genus ***Epilobium, Polygonum*** has become ***Persicaria*** and ***Fallopia,*** and ***Chrysanthemum*** has been dismantled and divided into a number of genera, including ***Dendranthema*** and ***Leucanthemum.*** So active are the minds and deeds of taxonomists that undoubtedly there will be changes of nomenclature after this book was written. Fortunately, the plants themselves do not change so rapidly.

The botanical names are our key to recognizing and understanding plants. Botanical Latin is an international language immune from the diversity of vernacular language. Despite the apparent complexity, it is a language in which we can all communicate.

HARDINESS

The hardiness zones included in the descriptions of each species, hybrid or cultivar, refer to the U.S. Department of Agriculture (USDA) Hardiness Map published in 1990. The zones are based on the annual average minimum temperatures recorded throughout the United States. They are as follows:

Zone 1	Below −50°F (below −45° C)
Zone 2	−50° to −40° (−45° to −40°)
Zone 3	−40° to −30° (−40° to −34°)
Zone 4	−30° to −20° (−34° to −29°)
Zone 5	−20° to −10° (−29° to −23°)
Zone 6	−10° to 0° (−23° to −17°)
Zone 7	0° to 10° (−17° to −12°)
Zone 8	10° to 20° (−12° to −7°)
Zone 9	20° to 30° (−70 to −1°)
Zone 10	30° to 40° (−1° to 5°)
Zone 11	Above 40° (above 5°)

Hardiness zones in Great Britain and Ireland are far less complex: The central and eastern regions are Zone 8 and the western coasts are Zone 9.

There is currently so little scientific information on the performance of herbaceous plants throughout the United States that hardiness zones should be regarded as only an approximate measure of plant hardiness. When calculating whether a particular plant is hardy, gardeners should consider a number of mitigating factors. In much of North America, winter snow is common. Dormant plants are protected from the often fierce continental climate by this "mulch." For example, according to the USDA hardiness map, a large portion of the Rocky Mountains receives average annual termperatures of −30° to −20° F. However, under several feet of snow, soil temperatures in the mountain town of Vail, Colorado are often much higher, reaching up to 32° F. This temperature ensures that many plants unable to tolerate air temperatures of −30° F, survive unharmed.

Without consistent snow cover plants are vulnerable to fluctuating temperatures. In Pennsylvania minimum winter temperatures average 0° to 10° F, and yet bursts of warmer weather are common in February and March. These warm periods are often followed by blasts of cold arctic air. Such volatile temperatures can cause unprotected plants to be pushed out of the soil, often exposing the crown and roots. This common occurrence is referred to as "heaving." Unless the plants are pushed back into the ground and covered with a protective mulch of straw or woodchips, heaving can be fatal to herbaceous perennials supposedly hardy to much colder temperatures. In my own garden in Pennsylvania snow is rare, and because they are unprotected by the blanket of snow, it is common for plants listed as hardy to Zone 7 to be killed by cold temperatures.

High summer temperatures can be just as harmful. Much of North America experiences summer temperatures over 90° F. The southern United States is particularly prone to hot and often humid summers. Many herbaceous perennials cultivated in gardens are native to mountainous regions or maritime provinces, or to countries where the winters are mild and the summers cool. Taking these plants from the cooler regions and growing them in the furnace of a southern summer is often a highly frustrating occupation. Many plants react dramatically to high temperatures, particularly when the night temperature remains above 70° F. Often herbaceous plants cease to bloom as the temperature exceeds 80° F. As the temperature increases, many perennials fail, weaken, and finally die, unable to tolerate this heat. While plants can be protected against the ravages of winter temperatures by mulching or covering, summer temperatures cannot be moderated. Gardens do not possess air-conditioners to cool plants. In Pennsylvania ***Geranium endressii*** 'Wargrave Pink,' a plant noted for its extensive floral display, ceases to bloom and becomes weak and unattractive in the heat of the summer but resumes growth and flowering when the temperatures begin to cool in September. In England this plant blooms throughout the summer and into the autumn, making it one of the finest herbaceous plants for the summer border. In the last few years members of the genus ***Diascia*** have become increasingly popular. In the United States they were first widely cultivated in the Pacific Northwest, a region with cool summers and mild winters. In the eastern half of the United States, *Diascias* are especially susceptible to the ravages of high temperatures, flowering well in early summer but declining rapidly as the temperatures rise, often dying altogether by late summer.

One of the best ways to ensure that plants sensitive to high temperatures survive the summer is to cut them down to the ground in midsummer. This often forces the plants to respond with a flush of new growth, which often results in a fresh crop of flowers as the temperatures cool in late summer and early autumn.

In this book species are described as requiring varying degrees of sunlight. In my experience of cultivating plants on both sides of the Atlantic, I have learned that many of the species described in English gardening books as sun-loving need protection from the North American midday and afternoon sun. As we know, sunshine in the British Isles is more rare than gold, and British gardeners do not generally need to consider the heat of the afternoon sun. But in North America the afternoon sun can wilt and wither plants more adapted to more clement climates.

This problem can be quickly remedied by growing sun-loving plants in areas that are lightly shaded in the afternoon. It is fortunate that there are enough herbaceous plants native to the open fields and meadows, mountains and marshes of North America and other continents to satisfy even the most rabid collector of sun-loving and heat-tolerant plants.

The nature of the planting site often can determine whether a species survives the winter. While most herbaceous perennials perform best in climates with mild temperatures, very few can survive water-logged soils. If the soil consists of a heavy clay that remains sodden throughout the winter months, plants rot. This is particularly true of species native to the drier parts of the world, or those plants native to the mountainous regions, where, even if there is considerable winter precipitation, the rocky soil remains well drained.

While good drainage is extremely important for most cultivated herbaceous plants, excessively dry soils can be equally damaging. Plants not specifically adapted to dry conditions often enter the winter months in a considerably weakened state. These weakened plants then undergo substantial winter stress and are killed.

Certain areas in any garden are warmer or colder than other sites. At times somewhat tender plants will survive the winter if they are planted in a sheltered site against a south-facing wall, or if they are protected from frosts by shrubs and trees. Conversely, cold temperatures frequently kill even hardy plants if the planting site is susceptible to continual frost and freezing. This is common in valley bottoms, where the cold air does not become warmed by the winter sun. Only by close observation and continuing experience of growing plants in different sites can gardeners become aware of the different microclimates in their gardens.

Despite the difficulties climate presents, there is no need to be discouraged. Herbaceous plants are tough and adaptable, often requiring far less care than we give them. The best method to determine whether a plant is hardy or whether it can stand up to high temperatures is to grow it. We can know whether a plant will grow in our garden only if we can see it with our own eyes and touch it with our own hands.

Soil and Fertilizer

In general, herbaceous plants grow at their best in well-cultivated, reasonably fertile, moist but well-drained soil that neither remains wet throughout the winter nor becomes too dry in the summer. The ideal soil contains about 20% clay, 40% silt, and 40% sand. Many soils need additions to accommodate plant needs. The main ways to adjust soil include adding organic matter, adjusting pH, adding fertilizer, and mulching.

Incorporating organic matter, such as well-rotted manure, compost, or leaf mold improves clay soils by increasing the soil pore space and thus increasing aeration and drainage capabilities. A quick-draining sandy soil is also improved with the addition of organic matter, which increases the soil's ability to retain water and nutrients. Organic matter should be dug into the soil on a yearly basis, either before the perennials are planted or, in an established planting, around the plants during the spring clean-up. The soil should be turned and organic matter incorporated in an established perennial bed carefully so that plants are not disturbed.

Before planting, a soil test should be taken. This can be done by purchasing a soil test kit or by contacting the local Cooperative Extension Service, which will provide details of how to send soil samples for testing. A soil test determines both the pH and the amounts of major nutrients in the soil.

The pH scale determines the acidity or alkalinity of a soil. The scale ranges from 1.0 to 14.0. Levels below 7.0 indicate an acidic soil; levels above 7.0 indicate an alkaline soil. A reading of between 6.0 and 7.0 is best for most plants cultivated; however, plant requirements may vary widely. Soil requirements for specific plants are described in the notes on cultivation in the main part of this encyclopedia. Do not assume that because your soil pH range is between 6.0 and 7.0 all plants will grow at their best. Many perennials suitable for a rock garden are native to limestone soil and require soils with a high pH, while a great number of woodland plants require a soil with a pH below 6.0.

Adjusting pH is a simple task. Adding sulfur to the soil will lower the pH. Adding lime to the soil will increase the pH. The soil sample adjustment charts included with the soil tests specify the amount of sulfur or lime to be added per 100 square feet of ground.

Adding fertilizer to established plants has become a spring ritual. At the first signs of warm weather we rush out to the nursery and return with bags of high-potency fertilizers. We blithely scatter pounds of granules throughout our garden, ignorant of soil nutrition and plant needs. I believe we add fertilizer to our gardens because it makes us feel good rather than because it helps the plants.

Plants need at least 16 essential elements to grow. They use hydrogen, oxygen, and carbon from air and water. Major nutrients available from the soil and fertilizers are nitrogen (N), phosphorus (P), and potassium (K). Nitrogen is available as manure or compost, liquid seaweed, fish emulsion, and blood meal. Phosphorus is commonly found in bonemeal, and potassium is found in wood ash. Secondary and micronutrients needed are calcium, magnesium, and sulfur, chlorine, copper, boron, iron, manganese, molybdenum and zinc. These can be found in varying degrees in the soil or in fertilizers. Plants remove nutrients from the soil, and replenishment of these nutrients is essential for good growth. However, adding organic material to the soil can provide a broad range of nutrient needs. Commercially available inorganic fertilizers provide varying amounts of major, secondary, and micronutrients, mainly N, P and K.

Many herbaceous perennials require little or no fertilizer. *Achilleas,* for example, tend to produce fewer flowers and more leaves if the soil is too rich. However, *Paeonies* and *Delphiniums* are hungry feeders often requiring two or more applications of fertilizer in the growing season.

Fertilizers in liquid form used as foliar sprays make nutrients quickly available to the plant. Applications of fish emulsion to plants that are clearly in need of nitrogen can rapidly turn poorly growing plants into lush and healthy ones. These nutrients are fast-acting but not long-lasting.

Mulching with organic material, such as salt hay or wood chips, not only provides a weed-suppressing cover but also shades the soil and helps reduce water loss. Mulch also provides organic material that becomes incorporated into the topsoil. It is important to remember that fresh wood chips will use nitrogen in the decomposing process, making it unavailable to plants that need it. Composted or aged wood chips used infrequently as a mulch have been found to be beneficial, but gardeners should be aware that large quantities of wood-chip mulch applied to the soil frequently may, over a long period, change the pH and do more harm than good.

Pests and Diseases

Herbaceous perennials are susceptible to damage from insects and to fungal, bacterial, and viral diseases. The key to managing pests and diseases is to provide the plant with the best possible growing conditions. Natural resistance is little understood, but observation and good sense tell us that well-grown plants are able to tolerate pest and disease damage better than plants that are in poor health. Sometimes even the healthiest plants can be attacked by insects and disease. In the past we have been quick to spray with insecticides and fungicides. This nozzle-happy attitude is no longer tolerable. Using poisons to wipe out insect populations kills beneficial insects, birds, and mammals, and the tide of poisons reaches us, ending up in the food we eat.

No gardener will deny that there are times when something has to be done about an insect infestation or a spreading disease. However, a commonsense approach is required. Integrated pest management (IPM) is a way of dealing with insects and disease without first resorting to noxious chemicals.

IPM begins with the gardener deciding whether controlling the pest is really necessary. Often a plant can tolerate a small degree of insect activity without being damaged. Determinations must be made as to whether the insect damage goes beyond what can be tolerated, either on an aesthetic or an economic basis. A small cluster of aphids on a foxglove may not cause any appreciable damage. Thousands of aphids sucking the sap of that foxglove, weakening the plant and transmitting disease, will undoubtedly require some degree of control.

Once we have determined that the level of insect population is causing damage, we must then attempt to predict what level of injury is tolerable if we decide to do nothing. If the small cluster of aphids is left alone, will the insects multiply and begin causing substantial damage or will the population decline, perhaps with the aid of beneficial insects or inclement weather? If the population does decline, we need not implement control measures.

If we believe that the insect levels will reach an intolerable level, the next phase is to calculate what treatment should be selected. There are a number of options, including selecting species or forms that are resistant to pest and diseases; for example, many ***Phlox paniculata*** cultivars are highly susceptible to spider mite damage and powdery mildew damage.

We can look for cultivars that are less susceptible and plant them in the garden, thus averting the need for pest and disease control.

Altering our horticultural practices can often prevent or control damage. Irrigating plants in the early evening ensures that water remains on the leaves throughout the night and into the early morning. The wet leaves are vulnerable to fungal spores carried in the air. By watering in the early morning and allowing the sun to dry the leaves rapidly, we can often avoid providing a favorable environment for the spread of disease. Overhead watering often aids the spread of disease and should be replaced by ground-level watering. Leaves are not splashed with water and remain dry, making it more difficult for diseases to take hold.

The control of a pest outbreak can be dealt with in a variety of ways. The manual picking and destroying of insect pests is a frequently used but often underrated method of control. Japanese beetles feeding on herbaceous perennials can be picked off and crushed between the fingers or dropped into a jar of soapy water and left to drown. We cannot expect to control a large outbreak of pests with this method, but we can often control pest damage by grooming the plants and removing the offending insects.

Biological controls, such as introducing natural enemies of the offending pest or providing an environment in which pest enemies prosper, is an increasingly important method of pest control. Green lacewings and ladybugs are voracious consumers of spider mites. These beneficial insects can be purchased and released into the garden. Ladybugs have a particular appetite for aphids, and while they will not control every one, their feeding will have a substantial effect on the aphid population. When we spray with broad-spectrum insecticides, we also kill the natural enemies of the pest we really want to control. Having removed the pest's natural enemies, we are forced to continue spraying to keep pest populations down. We then find ourselves in an ever-tightening spiral that ends up with us having to spray more and more powerful insecticides increasingly frequently.

If species selection, proper cultivation techniques, and the introduction of beneficial insects do not solve the problem, we are forced to use chemicals. Chemical control should be the good gardener's last resort. Moreover, chemical pest control does not mean that we find the strongest chemical available and spray indiscriminately. We should choose the chemical control that suppresses the pest but causes the least damage to the pest's natural enemies. We should also find a chemical that breaks down rapidly after it has been sprayed, and we should find one that kills the insect simply yet effectively. Horticultural oils kill insect pests by covering them in oil, effectively suffocating them. Oils do not kill insects that are not covered, and the oils are broken down into harmless compounds relatively quickly. *Bacillus thuringiensis* (Bt) is a chemical that kills only caterpillars. It is used increasingly for controlling caterpillar damage on ornamental as well as economic crops. By killing only caterpillars, beneficial insects, such as parasitizing wasps, are left unharmed and are allowed to continue to kill caterpillars missed by spraying.

The following list describes common insect pests, the damage they cause, and how they can be controlled.

Insects

Aphids: Aphids are small, pear-shaped insects that suck the juices from plants causing leaf curl, weakened growth, and damaged flowers and buds. Aphids transmit virus diseases from plant to plant and secrete a sticky substance called honeydew that encourages sooty mold disease. Aphids can be controlled by being blasted from the plant with sharp bursts of water or by being sprayed with insecticidal soap. Ladybugs are the aphid's natural enemy.

Caterpillars: Many caterpillars feed on plants and cause only minimal damage. When caterpillar populations reach damaging levels, they should be handpicked and destroyed or sprayed with *Bacillus thuringiensus.* A number of parasitic wasps lay their eggs in the caterpillars' bodies, killing the caterpillar. The introduction of these commercially available wasps, such as Trichogramma and braconid wasps, can be an effective method of control.

Cutworms: Cutworms are the larvae of nocturnal moths. They are chewing insects that feed at night on the stems of plants near or below ground level. Trichogramma wasps and beneficial nematodes are an effective control. A flat paper saucer used as a collar around seedlings will prevent cutworms from feeding.

Flea Beetles: These shiny black insects weaken plants by chewing many tiny holes in the leaves. They can be controlled by spraying with pyrethrum or by introducing beneficial nematodes that kill the larvae.

Japanese Beetles: These shiny, metallic-looking betles begin feeding after midsummer and cause considerable damage to ornamental plants. The adults eat the leaves while the grubs chew the roots. Manual control by handpicking is effective against small populations. Pyrethrum and insecticidal soaps are useful in controlling larger populations. Milky spore disease *(Bacillus popillae)* is a disease that kills only the grubs. It is commercially available in granular form and can be applied to turf throughout the growing season. The bacillus infects the grubs, killing them.

Leafhoppers: These are tiny, hopping insects that suck the sap from many plants. They can be controlled by using insecticidal soap.

Leafminers: These are small caterpillars that eat the insides of leaves. Control methods include the picking and destroying of spoiled leaves as well as spraying the emerging larvae with insecticidal soap or pyrethrum.

Scale: There are numerous species of scale insects. They are round and waxy and are often found on the underside of the leaf and along the stem. They can be controlled by applying horticultural oil when the plant is dormant in late winter, or by spraying the young mobile insects (nymphs) with insecticidal soap. The chalcid wasp is a natural enemy.

Slugs: These common garden pests generally feed at night, leaving a slimy trail from plant to plant. Beer traps are highly effective. Shallow saucers of stale beer will attract slugs and snails, which will come to drink. They will then fall into the beer and drown.

Spider Mites: These tiny, eight-legged, spiderlike mites suck the sap from plants, often stippling the leaves. Sharp bursts of water will deter spider mites, while spraying insecticidal soap is also effective. Green lacewings and ladybugs are their natural enemies.

Thrips: These are tiny insects that feed on the plants' sap. Pyrethrum or insecticidal soaps are effective sprays.

Whiteflies: These are tiny, white, flying insects that suck the sap of plants. They can be controlled by spraying with insecticidal soap or pyrethrum.

Diseases

Controlling plant diseases is less easy than restricting insect populations. Good horticulture is probably the most effective way of preventing diseases from becoming established and spreading. As previously mentioned, eliminating overhead watering is an effective method of disease prevention. Removing and destroying infected plants as soon as the disease is apparent can help prevent its spread, as can avoiding working with plants in wet weather. Cleanliness is the watchword for disease prevention. Removing debris, pruning dead flowers, and not overcrowding plants goes a long way toward preventing disease. However, there are times when even the most diligent gardener will have to spray for disease. It is very important that the chemicals selected be the correct ones for controlling the problem. Read the label on the chemical container to find out whether the particular fungicide is the right one. Spray in the early morning to avoid the heat of the day, and wear protective clothing, especially rubber gloves and an agricultural respirator, to avoid poisoning yourself. Fungicides are strong and effective controls for many plant diseases, but they are toxic chemicals that need to be treated with a great deal of care.

Maintenance

Gardening with herbaceous plants should be a pleasurable and rewarding experience, but no one should grow plants who cannot spare the time to look after them. In recent years there have been a spate of books on low-maintenance gardening. While professional horticulturists and garden writers may try to seduce us with the idea that work and horticulture are not necessarily related, gardening is hard work, and it takes more than a few minutes a day to create and maintain a good garden. Working with herbaceous plants is not a low-maintenance activity. I am not even sure whether there is such a thing as a low-maintenance garden, or whether it is particularly desirable. We garden to get away from the more jarring aspects of the modern world. We garden because we love plants and enjoy working with them. To be constantly conscious of time limits for this particular recreational activity seems contrary to our needs.

To maintain herbaceous plants we need to spend time watering, staking, deadheading, pinching, fertilizing, mulching, hoeing, digging, and preparing for the changes in season.

Watering is necessary whenever we plant something new, when the soil is too dry and plants are stressed, or when we have received plants from a nursery or garden center and must leave them in their containers until we are ready to plant them out. The one important rule for watering is to give the plants a thorough soaking where it matters, at the roots. Watering foliage, either with irrigation systems or by hand, is not only wasteful, it often creates a favorable environment for disease. As time consuming as it often is, watering around the base of the plant is the only effective method.

The popularity of container growing of herbaceous perennials allows us to buy plants in containers and plant at our convenience. We can plant at any time of the year as long as the ground is not frozen. Container-grown perennials should be removed from the pot before planting. The potting soil surrounding the roots of the plant should be gently disturbed to allow the roots to grow into the natural soil. Not doing this forces the roots to grow only within the container soil, eventually stressing the plant, weakening it, and often killing it.

Staking the taller perennials is a time-consuming but essential activity, especially when the planting is new and is yet to be established. Stakes can be made of many materials, such as wood, pea-sticks, metal or plastic rods. They can be as simple as a single bamboo cane stuck in the ground, or as sophisticated as a series of interlinked plastic-coated metal stakes. It is important to stake early, because gathering tall stems of a plant, wrapping them in string, and tying them to bamboo canes is very difficult. Stakes—as unobtrusive as possible—should be placed around the plant after the first flush of growth but before the full spurt of growth takes place in summer. Badly staked plants advertise poor horticulture.

PROPAGATION

Division

Most herbaceous plants are easily divided during the dormant season by lifting them from the soil and, in the case of large clumps or crowns, breaking them apart into several pieces, either by inserting two garden forks into the clump back to back, with the clump levered apart, or by gently separating the roots with hands or a trowel. Discard the older, central portions and plant the outer, newer parts.

Plants with fleshy roots, such as daylilies, can be divided by digging the plant out of the ground and cutting the roots with a knife or, in the case of a large plant, chopping it into sections with an ax. Be sure that each piece has two to six buds showing signs of upward growth before replanting.

For most herbaceous perennials early spring and early autumn are the best times for division. In climates with mild winters, successful division may be accomplished throughout the dormant period. In the Midatlantic United States, late summer and early autumn are the best times to divide many perennials. Although the newly divided perennials often appear to suffer, plants divided at this time rapidly recover and are partially if not fully established before the onset of winter cold.

There are, of course, certain perennials that should be divided only in the spring. Most ornamental grasses should be divided as the temperatures warm toward the summer months, rather than in autumn when temperatures are declining.

Containerized perennials bought in the spring or autumn can often be increased by dividing before planting out. If a plant appears overcrowded in its pot, it is likely to be pot-bound and can be divided into two or three plants.

Many perennials need to be divided frequently, while others should not be touched for many years. The notes on propagation in the main part of this book include greater detail concerning when and how often to divide.

Layering

Layering is an infrequently used but not ineffective method of summer propagation of plants with lax or ground-hugging shoots. Young sideshoots that are still attached to the parent plant are wounded by cutting a small sliver from the stem and are then pinned to the surrounding soil and covered. The shoot is severed from the parent plant after it has rooted sufficiently.

Cuttings

Propagating herbaceous perennials by taking softwood cuttings in late spring or mid- to late summer can dramatically increase the number of perennials available to the gardener. The stems of herbaceous perennials used for cuttings should not be so soft that they do not remain erect when cut or so hard that they cannot be bent. With a sharp knife cut 2 to 4 inches (5–10 cm) below the tip of the shoot. Cut about 1/4 inches (0.6 cm) below a leaf or pair of leaves (node). Remove all but the top pair of leaves and insert the cutting to about one-third of its length into a moistened and sterile medium, such as one of the many soilless cutting or potting compost commercially available.

Cuttings can be rooted easily in a mist bench or in pots with the pot covered in clear plastic. The plastic should be suspended over the cuttings and periodically opened to allow for air movement. Once the cutting has rooted, carefully transplant the cutting to a larger pot, grow on and then plant out into the garden.

Sowing Seed

the average gardener, propagating herbaceous perennials by seed is the fastest way to produce large quantities of desirable plants. Although many seeds can remain viable for many years, in general, freshly ripened seed provides a higher percentage of germinated seedlings.

Seed flats or pots should have drainage holes in the bottom. If not, holes should be punched in the base of the containers to allow water to drain. The sowing medium, preferably a mix of peat or sphagnum moss with the addition of perlite or vermiculite, should reach to about ¼ inch (0.6 cm) from the top of the containers. It should be moistened before the seeds are sown, preferably by soaking water up from the bottom. Sow the seed in rows to the depth described on the seed packet. If seed-depth information is unavailable, a rule of thumb is that the seed should be covered to one to two times its own thickness. Very fine seed should not be covered but rather pressed into the surface of the growing medium. Some seeds need light to germinate; these too should be pressed into the surface of the medium. Once the seed is sown and a label written and placed at the end of the seed row, the flat should either be wrapped in a plastic bag or covered with a sheet of glass. This ensures that the medium will remain damp enough and not need watering until the seeds have germinated.

Except for seed that germinates in darkness, the seed flat should be placed in a light area but away from direct sun. Temperature requirements for seed propagation are highly variable. Often temperature information is given on the side of the seed packet. Some seeds need periods of alternating warm and cold temperatures before germinating. Other seeds have hard seed coats that may need to be scratched (scarified) to disturb the hard coating and make the seed permeable to water. Again, this information is often available on the seed packet.

Gardeners propagating perennials from seed must be patient. Germination may take several weeks or even months. Once the seeds have germinated, the plastic or glass cover should be removed and the seedlings lightly watered. Once the first pairs of leaves have been produced, light applications of liquid fertilizer are recommended. After the seedlings have developed two pairs of leaves, they should be gently transplanted to pots and grown on. They should be watered and fertilized and kept away from strong sunlight. Once the weather warms the young plants should be hardened off gradually until the temperature is warm enough to put the plants outside. It can take up to two years before young herbaceous perennials are big enough to go out into the garden.

Sowing Ferns from Spores

Ferns can be propagated easily by dividing them in the same way other herbaceous perennials are divided. Sowing spores, though less easy, is a fascinating way of propagating ferns in larger numbers. To sow spores, first collect the mature fertile leaves that have dark-green or dark-brown spore capsules (sori) underneath the leaves. Place the underside of the leaves on white paper and leave for two or three days. At the end of this period the spore capsule should have released its tiny spores, which can be collected on the paper. Spore viability varies, but fresh spores generally germinate more successfully than older ones. Sterile conditions are essential for fern propagation. The medium, a mixture of coarse sand, peat moss, and humus, and the container should be free of harmful organisms. Spores can be tapped from the white paper onto the surface of the medium. The container should be covered in plastic or glass and placed in indirect light at a temperature of about 65° to 70° F. After three or four days or up to several weeks, a green mossy substance will appear. This is the prothallia, the first phase in the life cycle of the fern. After several months, young, recognizable ferns will appear. When the ferns are about 1 inch (2.5 cm) high, pot them into larger containers and grow on for up to a year before planting out.

Whether you are taking cuttings, sowing seed, or growing young plants, cleanliness is required. Good hygienic practices will help ensure successful propagation.

ACAENA

(New Zealand Burr)

FAMILY: Rosaceae

Acaena nova-zelandiae

A genus of about 100 evergreen plants native to the mountainous regions of Australia, New Zealand, and South America. The name cames from the Greek *akaina*, "a spine," referring to the spines on the fruiting heads. Most species commonly grown are generally vigorous, mat-forming groundcovers with brownish green foliage. The flowers are inconspicuous, appearing in summer, followed by spiny, brightly colored burrs. In general, members of this genus perform best in areas with cool summers.

CULTIVATION: Grow in well-drained, average to poor soil in full sun or partial shade. Prune flower heads back to ground level in spring. In areas with cold winters, plant in a sheltered location and provide winter protection.

LANDSCAPE USE: Evergreen mat-forming plants with attractive foliage for use in rock gardens, between paving stones, or as an edging plant. Sometimes invasive.

PROPAGATION: Sow seeds in autumn or divide in early spring.

A. buchananii. New Zealand, Height 2 in.; spread 24 in. (5 × 60 cm). A spreading groundcover with 1–2-in.- (2.5–5-cm-) long, silvery green, sharply toothed leaves with seven to 13 leaflets. Pale-green, globular flowers about 1 in. (2.5 cm) in diameter appear in summer, developing later to yellow to brown spiny burrs. Zones 6–9.

A. caesiiglauca (A. microphylla 'Glauca'). New Zealand. Height 2 in.; spread 24 in. (5 × 60 cm). A spreading groundcover with blue-gray leaves up to 2 in. (5 cm) long, divided into seven to nine leaflets and softly hairy underneath. Round heads of brown-green flowers in summer develop into reddish brown, spiny burrs in autumn. 'Blue Haze,' which may well be a hybrid, has gray-blue foliage and dark red burrs. Zones 5–8.

A. microphylla. New Zealand. Height 2 in.; spread 24 in. (5 × 60 cm). A widely grown species with green leaves with purple-bronze tinge up to 1 in. (2.5 cm) long, divided into many leaflets. Rounded, green flowers appear in summer and develop into dull red, spiny burrs in late summer and autumn. 'Copper Carpet' has copper-colored foliage and green-red burrs. Zones 6–9.

A. nova-zelandiae. New Zealand. Height 6 in.; spread 24 in. (15 × 60 cm). A vigorous, mat-forming plant with silver-green leaves 2–4 in. (5–10 cm) long divided into as many as 15 leaflets. Rounded heads up to 1½ in. (3.8 cm) in diameter of dark-purple flowers with long spines are produced in summer. Zones 8–9.

ACANTHOLIMON

(Prickly Heath)

FAMILY: Plumbaginaceae

Mostly evergreen, tufted plants with cushions of sharp, needlelike leaves on crowded stems. Pink-and-white flowers appear in summer. Native to desert and semidesert areas of the eastern Mediterranean and Asia Minor. They are difficult, almost impossible, to cultivate in areas with wet winters and humid summers. The generic name is derived from the Greek *akanthos,* "thorn," and, *limon,* "sea lavender."

CULTIVATION: A difficult genus to grow outside of the alpine house. Those species available prefer steep, well-drained walls or rock gardens in a warm, sunny location. All the species require lime. They resent being moved and are best established from pot-grown plants.

LANDSCAPE USE: Dry walls, south-facing rock gardens, and scree gardens.

PROPAGATION: Difficult. Take cuttings in mid- to late summer. Peg down layers in early spring and separate from parent plant the following year.

A. glumaceum. Caucasus. Height 6 in.; spread 12 in. (15 × 30 cm). A mounded species with narrow, rigid, dark-green leaves about 2 in. (5 cm) long and with 4-in. spikes of starry, deep-pink flowers in summer. Foliage turns bronze in late autumn. The easiest of the species to grow in the garden. Zones 7–9.

A. venustum (A. olivieri). Asia Minor. Height 6 in.; spread 12 in. (15 × 30 cm). A slow-growing, tufted cushion with silvery green leaves and arching sprays of deep-rose flowers appearing in late spring to early summer. The flowers are larger and more abundant than ***A. glumaceum.*** Needs a hot, dry, well-drained site. Zones 7–9.

ACANTHUS

(Bear's Breeches)

FAMILY: Acanthaceae

A genus of some 20 species native to a wide range of areas from the tropics to the steppes. Those cultivated in gardens are somewhat invasive, evergreen plants of great architectural quality with large, opposite, lobed or toothed basal leaves with spiny edges and stiff spikes of tubular and lipped flowers often surrounded by sharp bracts. The curled and lobed leaves of ***A. mollis*** are said to have inspired the decoration on Corinthian columns.

CULTIVATION: Plant in the spring in fertile, well-drained soil in full sun to partial shade. Afternoon shade is of benefit in hot climates. Mulching before the onset of winter greatly prevents cold damage. Cut the stems down after flowering.

LANDSCAPE USE: Excellent plants for herbaceous borders, where the dramatic foliage and imposing

Acanthus mollis

flower spikes should be displayed without competition. Particularly impressive when planted en masse, they do not flower well in climates with cold winters.

Propagation: Sow fresh seed and grow in a nursery bed for two to three years before planting out. Divide the heaviest of clumps in early spring. Root cuttings taken in early spring produce strong plants the following year.

A. balcanicus (A. longifolius). Balkans. Height 3–4 ft; spread 2–3 ft (90–120 × 60–90 cm). A clump-forming plant with up to 3-ft- (90-cm-) long, deeply lobed and wavy, dull-green leaves. The leaf lobes are almost egg-shaped, narrowed at their base and spiny. Tall spikes of mauve to lilac flowers are borne above the foliage in late summer. Zones 6–10.

A. dioscoridis var. ***perringii.*** Asia Minor. Height 12 to 18 in.; spread 18 in. (30–45 × 45 cm). Rarely available but worth cultivating, with grayish greeen, stalkless leaves often without spines. The flowers are rich pink or purplish red on spikes held just above the foliage in mid- to late summer. Spreads by suckers and may be slightly invasive where established. A prize for a sunny wall or rock garden. Zones 8–10.

A. mollis. Bear's breeches. Mediterranean. Height 4 ft; spread 3 ft (120 × 90 cm). A variable species with up to 2-ft- (60-cm-) long, glossy green, oval leaves that are deeply cut, wavy, and spineless. Hooded, funnel-shaped, white-and-purple flowers are borne on tall spikes in early summer. Zones 8–10. The variety ***latifolius*** is larger and more robust than the species and is more widely found in cultivation. It is often listed as being hardy to Zones 8–9 but with winter mulching may be grown successfully in Zones 6–9, although it flowers poorly in Zone 6. In areas with mild climates, this species is quite invasive, rapidly forming a dense thicket. It performs poorly in hot and humid climates.

A. spinosus. Spiny bear's breeches. Southeastern Europe. Height 4 ft; spread 3 ft (120 × 90 cm). Approximately 2-ft- (60-cm-) long and 10-in.- (25-cm-) wide, dark-green and glossy, deeply divided, thistlelike leaves with strong spines along the edges of the leaf. Abundant spikes of mauve-and-white flowers appear in summer. More tolerant of heat and cold than other species, it is hardier and more free-flowering than ***A. mollis.*** A form with more deeply divided leaves and greater spines on the leaf edges is often listed as a separate species, ***A. spinosissimus,*** but there is substantial doubt that this is a separate species; rather it should be regarded as a variety. Zones 6–10.

ACHILLEA

(Yarrow, Milfoil)

Family: Compositae

Achillea 'Coronation Gold'

Achillea millefolium 'Fire King'

Achillea x *taygeta*

A large genus of hardy plants with alternate, aromatic, mostly fernlike leaves and colorful flowers in open clusters of dense, flat heads. The generic name commemorates the Greek hero Achilles, who was taught the healing properties of the plant by his teacher Charin. "Yarrow" is a corruption of the Anglo-Saxon name, while "milfoil" refers to the finely divided, ferny foliage, or thousand leaves. ***A. millefolium*** was widely used to heal wounds and as an ingredient in salads in the 17th century.

CULTIVATION: Cultivated since medieval times, *Achillea* does best in a sunny, well-drained site in average to poor soil. They are tolerant of hot summers and dry conditions but intolerant of wet conditions. The larger species and cultivars often need staking, especially if the soil is heavily fertilized. Planting is best in spring. Powdery mildew and other fungus diseases may be a problem in humid climates.

LANDSCAPE USE: The dwarf species and varieties are colorful plants for the rock garden; the taller ones are useful for the border, wild garden, or meadow. Many are excellent for cut or dried flower arrangements.

PROPAGATION: Division in spring is the easiest method. Stem cuttings taken in midsummer are also usually successful.

A. chrysocoma. Eastern Europe. Height 6 in.; spread 10 in. (15×25 cm). A compact plant with golden yellow flowers in sumemr over mats of aromatic gray-green, ferny leaves about 1 in. (2.5 cm) long. An excellent rock-garden plant that requires good drainage. Zones 5–9.

A. clavennae (A. argentea). Silvery milfoil. Eastern and southern Alps. Height 6 in.; spread 8 in. (15×20 cm). A spreading plant that blooms in late spring to early summer with ¾-in.- (1.8-cm-) wide clusters of yellow-eyed white flowers, over mats of silvery green, lobed and hairy elliptic leaves. A hybrid, ***A×kellereri,*** grows to a height of 6 in. (15 cm) and has finely cut, gray-green leaves and yellow-centered creamy-white flowers. Zones 5–8.

A. clypeolata. Balkans. Height 18 in.; spread 12 in. (45×30 cm). Feathery, silvery green hairy leaves about 12 in. (30 cm) long and up to 2 in. (5 cm) wide, with flat heads of clear yellow flowers throughout the summer. Responds well to annual division. Zones 3–8.

A. filipendulina. Caucasus. Height 4 ft; spread 2 ft (1.2 m×60 cm). A good border plant with feathery, mid-green leaves and 5-in.- (12.5-cm-) wide, upward-facing heads of light-yellow flowers on leafy stems in summer. 'Coronation Gold' is a popular hybrid produced from the crossing of this species with ***A. clypeolata;*** it grows to a height of about 3 ft (90 cm) and has mustard-yellow flowers and silver-gray leaves. It rarely needs staking. 'Gold Plate,' height 4 ft (120 cm), has bright-yellow flowers 6 in. (15 cm) across. 'Parker's Variety' is 4 ft (120 cm) high with 4-in.- (10-cm-) wide golden yellow flowers and gray-green foliage. All are excellent plants for dry, sunny borders, and benefit from division every three to four years. Zones 3–9.

A. millefolium. Yarrow. Europe. Height 2 ft; spread 15 in. (60×37.5 cm). A common European meadow plant with feathery green leaves 6–8 in. (15–20 cm) long and clusters of small white or pink flowers in summer. The following cultivars are far better than the type, although they often need staking. 'Cerise Queen': height 30 in. (75 cm), flowers intense pink-red; 'Fire King': height 2 ft (60 cm), flowers red fading to pink; 'Red Beauty': height 20 in. (50 cm), flowers dark red. 'White Beauty': height 2 ft (60 cm), flowers white. Zones 3–8.

A series of hybrids produced from ***A. millefolium*** and ***A. taygeta*** named 'Galaxy Hybrids' have been introduced over the last few years from West Germany. All have large clusters of flowers, ferny foliage, and reach heights of 30–36 in. (75–90 cm). The flower colors are of considerable variety: 'Appleblossom,' medium pink; 'Beacon,' crimson; 'Great Expectations,' amber; 'Paprika,' red with a white eye; 'Salmon Beauty,' salmon pink. However, their growth is often thin, the flowers tend to fade in summer heat, and they fall over when in flower, which means they require staking. It is to be hoped that more compact forms will soon be available. Zones 3–8.

A.* × 'Moonshine.'** Height 2 ft; spread 18 in. (60×45 cm). A beautiful hybrid produced from the crossing of ***A. clypeolata and ***A. taygeta,*** with sulfur-yellow flower heads up to 3 in. (7.5 cm) wide throughout the summer over mounds of ferny, gray foliage. An excellent border plant although highly susceptible to leaf diseases in hot and humid summers. Spraying does help as does cutting the plant back hard after flowering to stimulate new growth in late summer. It flowers well if divided every two to three years and grown in lean, well-drained soil. Zones 3–9.

A. ptarmica. Sneezewort. Europe. Height 2 ft; spread 2 ft or more (60×60 cm). An invasive and untidy plant with glossy, narrowly lance-shaped, toothed leaves and clouds of rounded white flowers in early to midsummer. The varieties with double white flowers bloom for a longer period but are no less invasive. 'Perry's White': height 2½ ft (75 cm); 'The Pearl': height 20 in. (50 cm) with double, white flowers smaller than 'Perry's White'; 'Snowball': height 14 in. (35 cm), a dwarf form, less invasive than the others. All are tolerant of moist soil but are rampant invaders of good soil. The name "sneezewort" refers to the dried leaves and flowers once being used as snuff. Zones 4–9.

A. tomentosa. Woolly milfoil. Europe, Asia. Height 6 in.; spread 12 in. (15 × 30 cm). Flat yellow flowers are borne over gray-green, woolly foliage. A good rock-garden plant for dry soil and full sun but a poor performer in hot and humid climates. Cultivars include 'Maynard Gold' ('Aurea'): height 6 in. (15 cm), rich golden yellow flowers; 'Nana': height 4 in. (10 cm), deep-yellow flowers. Zones 3–9. A hybrid, 'King Edward,' is a spreading plant with pale-yellow flowers on 10-in. (25-cm) stems. Zones 3–9.

A. × wilczeckii. Height 6 in.; spread 9 in. (15 × 22.5 cm). A mat-forming plant with silver-gray rosettes of gray-woolly leaves about 2½ in. (6.2 cm) long and drooping white flower clusters in early summer. Zones 3–9.

ACONITUM

(Monkshood, Wolf's Bane)

Family: Ranunculaceae

Aconitum carmichaelii 'Arendsii'

Aconitum lycoctonum var. *neapolitanum*

A large genus of more than 100 species of summer- and fall-flowering perennials of great importance to the garden. Those species useful for the herbaceous border have alternate, divided leaves and mostly blue, purple, or yellow hooded flowers arranged spirally on strong stalks from clump-forming plants. They have been sadly forgotten in American gardens and are in need of a renaissance. Their native habitat is wide, ranging from the Asiatic mountains to the Appalachians.

The common name, monkshood, refers to the distinctive cowllike or helmet shape of the flowers. Several ***Aconitum*** are sources of alkaloids used as drugs, and the name wolf's bane alludes to the wolf-killing poison manufactured from the toxic leaves and roots of ***A. vulparia.*** All species are poisonous.

Cultivation: Grow ***Aconitum*** in moist but well-drained soil in full sun to partial shade. They will suffer in full sun if the soil is too dry. Annual mulching and feeding is beneficial for most species. They resent root disturbance and should be left alone to prosper. In general, this genus does not grow well in hot and humid climates.

Landscape Use: Useful plants for shady areas, the larger herbaceous border, or wild garden. They are commonly tall plants providing much-needed blue tones in summer. With their dark Delphinium-like leaves and dramatic flowers, they are worth growing singly mixing with strong yellows or vivid whites, or massed together in a partly shady corner.

Propagation: Division is best in spring. The roots are poisonous and care should be taken when propagating or handling in any way. Seeds should be sown as soon as ripe, generally in late summer and autumn, but they take many months to germinate.

A. anthora. Europe. Height 1–2 ft; spread 18 in. (30–60 × 45 cm). A sturdy species with strong stems and up to 5-in.- (12.5-cm-) long, deep-green leaves finely divided into linear segments. Spikes of hooded, yellow or occasionally bluish flowers are produced in summer. Zones 5–8.

A.* × *cammarum (A.* × *bicolor). Height 3 to 4 ft; spread 18 in. (90–120 × 45 cm). A hybrid between ***A. napellus*** and ***A. variegatum,*** a number of good garden plants are derived from this cross. All have dark-green, glossy, hand-shaped leaves about 3 in. (7.5 cm) long, with five to seven toothed segments. The large, generally dark-blue, strongly hooded flowers appear in summer. 'Bicolor': height 3–4 ft (90–120 cm), flowers white with blue edges; 'Bressingham Spire': height 3 ft (90 cm), erect spikes of deep violet-blue flowers; 'Ivorine': height 3 ft (90 cm), flowers ivory white; 'Newry Blue': height 4 ft (120 cm), navy-blue flowers often appearing earlier than those of the other cultivars; 'Night Sky': height 4 ft (120 cm), large deep-violet flowers. Zones 5–8.

A. carmichaelii. Eastern Asia. Height to 6 ft; spread 18 in. (180 × 30 cm). An upright plant with thick, leathery dark-green leaves. The round, hooded, rich-blue flowers appear on 6-in. (15-cm) open spikes in early autumn. Variety ***wilsonii*** is a 6-ft- (180-cm-) tall variety with spikes of violet-blue flowers. Var. ***wilsonii*** 'Kelmscott' has lavender-blue flowers. 'Arendsii' is perhaps the best cultivar, becoming increasingly available in North America, growing to a height of 4 ft (120 cm) with amethyst-blue flowers. All may need staking. Zones 3–8.

A. columbianum. Blue monkshood. Western North America. Height 4 ft; spread 18 in. (120 × 45 cm). Flowering in midsummer, this native of open woodland has lobed, hand-shaped leaves up to 6 in. (15 cm) across, and spikes of blue flowers. Zones 3–8.

A. henryi. Autumn monkshood. Asia. Height 4 ft; spread 18 in. (120 × 45 cm). Flowering from midsummer to early autumn with open, branching spikes of blue, lilac, or white flowers on slender stems. The leaves are glossy and dark green with five to seven lobes. 'Spark's Variety' is 4–5 ft (120–150 cm) tall with violet-blue flowers on branched spikes and is similar to ***A. carmichaelii*** but flowers earlier in the season. Zones 5–8.

A. lycoctonum var. ***neapolitanum (A. lamarckii).*** Europe. Height 5 ft; spread 2 ft (150 × 60 cm). A robust plant with dark green and deeply divided leaves. The flowers are creamy yellow on branching spikes in summer. Needs staking. Wolf's bane, ar. ***vuplaria (A. vulparia),*** is similar in that it has densely clustered spikes of creamy yellow flowers carried in summer. The dark-green leaves are deeply divided, toothed, and lobed. Zones 4–8.

A. napellus. Common monkshood. Europe, Asia. Height 4 ft; spread 18 in. (150 × 45 cm). A parent of the garden hybrids listed under ***A.* × *cammarum,*** this stately perennial has the deeply divided, hand-shaped, three-lobed, glossy, dark-green leaves common to much of the genus. The erect, leafy stems terminate in branched spikes of indigo-blue flowers with hoods broader than tall; blooms in mid- to late summer. Forma ***album*** has white flowers. Zones 5–8.

A. unciniatum. Eastern monkshood. Eastern North America. Height 3 ft; spread 12 in. (90 × 30 cm). Kidney-shaped leaves up to 4 in. (10 cm) wide and deeply lobed. The stems are slender, bearing hooded blue flowers in late summer. Found in moist soils. Zones 6–8.

ACORUS

(Sweet Flag)

Family: Araceae

Two or three species of semievergreen, irislike plants with creeping rhizomes. Native to boggy areas, they have grasslike foliage and insignificant greenish flowers. The variegated forms are attractive plants for wet areas. In the past sweet flag was strewn on the floors of castles and manor houses to freshen them. The leaves and rhizomes emit a spicy odor when crushed.

Cultivation: Grow in soil that is constantly moist or wet, in full sun to partial shade.

Landscape Use: Grown for ornamental foliage in bog gardens and water gardens either as specimen plants or in mass.

Propagation: Easily propagated by division.

A. calamus. Sweet flag. Asia, North America. Height 3 ft; spread 12 in. (90 × 30 cm). An aromatic plant with mid-green, sword-shaped leaves. The flowers are insignificant. A more interesting, variegated form, 'Variegatus,' has striped green-and-white leaves often flushed pale pink in spring. Plant in up to 10 in. (25 cm) of water. Zones 4–9.

A. gramineus. Japanese sweet flag. Asia. Height 12 in.; spread 6 in. (30 × 15 cm). A small, tufted evergreen plant with dark-green, linear leaves up to 12 in. (30 cm) tall. 'Pusillus' is smaller than the species, growing to about 10 in. (25 cm); 'Variegatus' has creamy white striped leaves. The variegated form tends to become open in the center in soils that are too dry. If this happens, divide and replant in wet soil. Zones 6–9.

ACTAEA

(Baneberry)

Family: Ranunculaceae

Actaea alba

Temperate woodland plants with large divided leaves and feathery flowers in spring followed by white, red, or purplish-black berries in late summer into autumn. The fruits are attractive but poisonous.

CULTIVATION: Grow baneberries in moist, acid woodland soil in partial shade.

LANDSCAPE USE: Handsome plants for the woodland garden or shady rock garden. Useful foils for astilbes and hostas.

PROPAGATION: Division in autumn or spring. Sow fresh seed in autumn; germination will occur in spring.

A. alba (A. pachypoda). White baneberry. Eastern North America. Height 2–3 ft; spread 18 in. (60–90×45 cm). This woodland native has large toothed leaves divided into threes and fluffy white flowers on 4-in. (10-cm) spikes in spring. The berries are a striking ivory with a dark-purple spot and are borne on thick red stalks in autumn. Zones 3–9.

A. rubra. Red baneberry. Eastern North America. Height 18 in.; spread 12 in. (45×30 cm). In late summer and autumn ½-inch- (1.2-cm-) long red berries in clusters on thin stalks appear, after white flowers in summer. Subspecies ***arguta*** is a western North American native with spherical red berries. Zones 3–9.

A. spicata. Black baneberry. Europe, Asia. Height 18 in.; spread 18 in. (45×45 cm). Similar to the American species except that the fruits are glossy purplish black borne on black stalks. Zones 3–9.

ADENOPHORA

(Ladybells)

FAMILY: Campanulaceae

About 40 species of summer-blooming plants similar to ***Campanula,*** although those species cultivated in gardens are somewhat weedy. The basal leaves are often disc shaped while the leaves farther up the branched stems are alternate, long, and narrow. The flowers are mostly pale blue, nodding, and bell-shaped.

CULTIVATION: Plant in well-drained fertile soil in full sun to light shade.

LANDSCAPE USE: Summer flower border or large rock garden. Some species can be invasive.

PROPAGATION: Seed or stem cuttings. Ladybells resent being moved and do not propagate well from division.

A. confusa. China. Height 3 ft; spread 18 in. (90×45 cm). In midsummer ¾-in.- (1.8-cm-) long deep-blue bells appear on stiff, erect, heavily leafy stems. The leaves are toothed, lance-shaped to egg-shaped, up to 3 in. (7.5 cm) long. Zones 3–8.

A. liliifolia. Lilyleaf ladybells. Europe. Height 2–3 ft; spread 12 in. (60–90×30 cm). Stout stems with egg-shaped to lance-shaped, toothed, 3-in.- (7.5-cm-) long leaves and flower clusters of pale blue or white, fragrant, ½-in.- (1.2-cm-) wide, nodding, bell-like flowers produced from mid- to late summer. Spreads rapidly. Zones 3–8.

A. tashiroi. Japan, Korea. Height 4–12 in.; spread 2–4 in. (10–30×5–10 cm). A low-growing, clump-forming species with blue-violet flowers either single or a few to a spike on thin stems. The coarsely toothed, mid-green leaves are up to 1½ in. (3.8 cm) long and broadly egg-shaped. Zones 3–8.

ADIANTUM

(Maidenhair Fern)

Family: Adiantaceae

Adiantum pedatum var. *aleuticum*

A large genus of ferns, most of which are native to the tropics. The few species that are hardy in temperate zones are prized for their delicate foliage. Their fronds are divided two to three times and rise on black stalks from creeping rhizomes. They are frequently found along streams, in crevices around waterfalls, and in limestone rocks and chalky soils.

Cultivation: Maidenhairs prefer a soil rich in organic matter, well drained but not too dry. They should be grown in areas with dappled, high shade, preferably receiving some morning sun but little, if any, strong sunlight. The foliage will suffer from sun scorch if subjected to too much sun. Those species listed, other than ***A. pedatum,*** need to be planted in a protected site.

Landscape Use: Grow in woodland gardens with a high canopy or by waterfalls, pond gardens, and rock gardens. A large planting of maidenhair ferns is particularly impressive. Autumn color is often a good yellow.

Propagation: Divide rhizomes in spring or sow spores when ripe in late summer.

A. capillus-veneris. Venus-hair fern. Subtropical and temperate areas. Height 12–24 in.; spread 12 in. (30–60 × 30 cm). Common in subtropical regions but able to grow to *Zone 7*. Delicate soft-green fronds with fan-shaped segments (pinnae) are borne on glossy, black, arching stems. 'Banksianum' has less of an arching growth habit and is hardy to Zones 7–10.

A. hispidulum. Rosy maidenhair. Australia, Asia. Height 12–18 in.; spread 8–12 in. (30–45 × 20–30 cm). A spreading fern with branched fronds that are bright pink when first produced in spring. Requires good drainage. Zones 9–10.

A. pedatum. Northern maidenhair. North America, Asia. Height 12–20 in.; spread 12 in. (30–50 × 30 cm). This is the most commonly grown garden plant of the genus. It is a semievergreen fern with finely textured, light to mid-green, twice-branched fronds on glossy, black stems. ***A. pedatum*** var. ***aleuticum*** is a very cold-hardy form with fewer individual segments. Subspecies ***calderi*** is an upright plant with smaller leaf segments. 'Japonicum' has fresh new fronds of a bronze color. 'Miss Sharples' has new growth of a yellow-green color. Zones 3–8.

A. venustum. Himalayas. Height 12 in.; spread 8 in. (30 × 20 cm). The fronds are large, with small, pale-green, and triangular leaf segments carried on purplish black stems. They have a blue tint in midsummer and turn yellow-brown in autumn. Zones 3–8.

ADONIS

(Pheasant's Eye)

FAMILY: Ranunculaceae

Low-growing, clump-forming plants with feathery foliage and buttercuplike yellow or white flowers in early spring. The name commemorates Adonis, favorite of Venus, who was turned into a flower upon his death.

CULTIVATION: ***Adonis*** require a position in sun to partial shade in soil that does not get excessively dry.

LANDSCAPE USE: ***Adonis*** are low-growing plants for combining with spring bulbs along a path edge, rock garden, or sunny bank. Because they die down to the ground in early summer, later-flowering plants should be used to cover the bare area. A mass planting of ***Adonis*** flowering in very early spring is guaranteed to drive the winter blues away.

PROPAGATION: Not easy to propagate. Division in late spring after flowering is possible if roots are not allowed to dry out. Seed, if fresh, will germinate, but plants grown from seed are slow to flower.

A. ***amurensis.*** Amur adonis. Eastern Asia. Height 12–18 in., spread 8–12 in. (30–45 $\times$ 20–30 cm). Often flowering at the same time as the Snowdrop, this is a delightful plant with golden yellow buttercuplike flowers rising out of the ground before the leaves develop. While flowering, large collars of ferny leaves are produced, only to die down in early summer. The double form 'Pleniflora' blooms a little later and lasts longer. Many forms grown in Japan seem to be unavailable in the West. Zones 4–8.

A. ***brevistyla.*** Tibet. Height 12 in.; spread 8 in. (30 $\times$ 20 cm). Bluish gray buds produce buttercuplike white flowers flushed blue in midspring. Zones 4–8.

A. ***pyrenaica.*** Pyrenees. Height 12 in.; spread 8 in. (30 $\times$ 20 cm). Similar to ***A. vernalis*** but with smaller, golden yellow flowers and stalked lower leaves. Zones 3–8.

A. ***vernalis.*** Europe. Height 12–18 in.; spread 12 in. (30–45 $\times$ 30 cm). Large golden yellow flowers are produced at the ends of the stems in early spring. The green leaves are delicate and finely cut. Blooms slightly later than ***A. amurensis.*** Zones 3–8.

Adonis amurensis

AETHIONEMA

(Stonecress)

FAMILY: Cruciferae

About 60 species of generally short-lived, evergreen, spreading, shrubby perennials native to the Mediterranean, with small, blue-gray, stalkless leaves and tight clusters of cross-shaped flowers of pink, white, or lilac. They can be attractive adorning rock gardens or walls.

CULTIVATION: Stonecress need full sun, good drainage, and a sandy soil that is alkaline or neutral. Deadhead after flowering for compact plants.

LANDSCAPE USE: Excellent plants for the sunny rock garden or dry stone wall. Use the taller ones for the front of the border.

PROPAGATION: Take tip cuttings either before flowering or from growth produced after deadheading. Sow seeds in spring. Often self-sows.

A. coridifolium. Turkey. Height 8 in.; spread 12 in. (20 × 30 cm). An erect, woody subshrub with bluish green linear leaves about ½ in. (1.2 cm) long and rose-pink, cross-shaped flowers in late spring. Zones 5–9.

A. grandiflorum. Turkey, Iran. Height 12 in.; spread 18 in. (30 × 45 cm). A spreading, variable, loose-stemmed plant with blue-gray linear to lance-shaped leaves about 1 in. (2.5 cm) long and masses of clustered salmon-pink flowers in late spring to midsummer. 'Warley Rose,' often listed as ***A. × warleyense,*** is a selection or probably a hybrid of ***A. grandiflorum*** and ***A. coridifolium*** and has bright-pink flowers and steel-blue foliage. 'Warley Ruber,' also a hybrid, has deep rose-pink flowers. Zones 4–9.

Aethionema grandiflorum

A. iberideum. Turkey. Height 6 in.; spread 12 in. (15 × 30 cm). A cushion of gray-green, lance-shaped leaves is covered in compact clusters of small white, fragrant flowers in late spring. Zones 6–9.

AGAPANTHUS

(African Lily)

FAMILY: Liliaceae

A subtropical genus of about nine species, the majority of which are grown as container plants in cold areas. Those that have proved hardy in temperate zones are listed here. They are elegant clump-forming plants with fleshy roots and strap-shaped leaves. The funnel-shaped flowers, in shades of blue, are borne in clustered heads on smooth, long stalks in summer. The generic name is derived from the Greek *agape,* "love," and *anthos,* "flower."

CULTIVATION: Grow in full sun in a rich, well-drained soil in a sheltered site. Protect from winter cold with 6 to 9 in. (15–22.5 cm) of salt hay or mulch in late autumn. Can be grown in containers and stored in a cool, dry place over winter. Zone 8 except where noted.

LANDSCAPE USE: Excellent border plants in frost-free areas. In colder areas they should be planted in a sheltered border at the base of a south-facing wall, protected patio, or poolside garden. The dark-blue flowers go very well with light-yellow companions. They are also excellent cut flowers.

PROPAGATION: Divide and replant the fleshy roots in spring.

A. africanus. South Africa. Height 3 ft; spread 18 in. (90 × 45 cm). An elegant clump-forming, evergreen species with ½-in.- (1.2-cm-) wide, strap-shaped, dark-green, leaves up to 18 in. (45 cm) long. Long stems bear round clusters of deep-blue flowers in late summer. Variety ***albus*** has beautiful white flowers; 'Blue Giant' has large trusses of deep-blue flowers; 'Peter Pan' is a floriferous dwarf form with deep-blue flowers on 18-in. (45-cm) stems. Zones 8–10.

The *Headbourne Hybrids.* Height 2 ft; spread 18 in. (60 × 45 cm). A large group raised in England in the 1950s with colors ranging from deep to light blue. Notable named cultivars are 'Alice Gloucester,' with white flowers; 'Bressingham Blue,' with deep-blue blossoms; 'Profusion,' with mid-blue flowers; and 'Loch Hope,' with violet-blue flowers. They are generally hardier than the species and can be grown with protection in Zones 7–10 and possibly to Zone 6.

AGASTACHE

(Giant Hyssop)

FAMILY: Labiatae

A genus of about 30 species native to North America and Mexico, with one native to Japan. The name comes from the Greek *aga,* "very much," and *stachys,* "ears of wheat," referring to the many flower spikes. The coarse leaves are aromatic, rounded at the base, and pointed at the end on square stems.

Agastache foeniculum

Slender spikes with lipped, tubular flowers are arranged in tiers.

CULTIVATION: Plant in ordinary soil with good drainage in full sun to partial light shade. They are short-lived plants that should be propagated frequently.

LANDSCAPE USE: Coarse plants for the herbaceous border or, more usefully, the sunny wild or native plant garden.

PROPAGATION: Take stem cuttings in midsummer or sow seeds.

A. cana. Arizona, Mexico. Height 2 ft; spread 1 in. (60 × 30 cm). An almost woody herb with branching, hairy stems and coarse-toothed, lance-shaped leaves. The pink flowers, which appear in summer, are borne in dense spires up to 8 in. (20 cm) in length. Zones 6–9.

A. foeniculum. Giant blue hyssop. Midwestern North America. Height 3 ft, spread 18 in. (90 × 45 cm). A native American prairie plant with 3-in.-(7.5-cm-) long, coarse, egg-shaped, and toothed leaves with fine white hairs underneath. Cylindrical spikes of blue flowers up to 4 in. (10 cm) long are produced in summer. Zones 6–9.

A. nepetoides. Giant yellow hyssop. Eastern North America. Height 4–6 ft; spread 2 ft (120–180 × 60 cm). A woodland plant with toothed and egg-shaped leaves up to 5 in. (12.5 cm) long and greenish yellow, tubular flowers in summer. Zones 4–9.

A. urticifolia. Nettleleaf horsemint. Western North America. Height 4–6 ft; spread 2 ft (120–180 × 60 cm). A native of moist, open woodland with smooth stems, toothed, egg-shaped leaves, and dense spikes of pink to violet flowers in summer. Zones 6–9.

AGAVE

(Century Plant)

FAMILY: Agavaceae

A large genus of succulent plants with sword-shaped leaves native to North and South America. The species listed below is a hardy, sun-loving plant native to southwestern states and Mexico. The name century plant refers to its habit of taking many years to flower and then dying afterward.

CULTIVATION: Grow in a dry, sunny, sheltered location in sandy soil. Hardy to Zone 8 if grown in an area with good drainage and protection from winter wet. In areas of poor drainage the plant is likely to suffer from rot.

LANDSCAPE USE: A plant of great architectural presence. Plant in dry gardens, wild gardens, or a sunny corner of a herbaceous border. Particularly effective in coastal gardens, where it is tolerant of salt spray.

PROPAGATION: Remove suckers from the base of the old plant and pot.

A. americana. Century plant. Southwestern North America, Mexico. Height 6 ft; spread 8 ft (180 × 240 cm). Huge basal rosettes of succulent, sharply pointed, sword-shaped, gray-green leaves up to 6 ft (180 cm) long with a spike of fragrant greenish yellow flowers often 15 to 20 ft (4.5 to 6 m) high. There are a number of highly ornamental forms with variegated foliage, including 'Marginata' with yellow leaf edges and 'Medio-picta' with yellow-striped green leaves. Zones 8–10.

AJUGA

(Bugleweed)

FAMILY: Labiatae

Ajuga genevensis

Vigorous, groundcovering plants with creeping stems and mostly evergreen, opposite, deep-green or multicolored rounded leaves, with leafy spikes of two-lipped, mostly blue flowers in late spring.

CULTIVATION: Grow in any ordinary, moist but well-drained soil that does not get too dry in summer. Species listed do best in a partly shaded location as they are apt to show signs of stress during periods of high summer temperature. Remove faded flower spikes. Crown rot can be a serious problem.

LANDSCAPE USE: Excellent groundcovers and edging plants for a variety of situations. ***Ajuga*** can be invasive and care should be taken not to plant too close to less robust plants.

PROPAGATION: Division is easy at any time during the growing season.

A. genevensis. Geneva bugle. Europe, Asia. Height 12 in.; spread 18 in. (30 × 45 cm). A more upright plant than other cultivated species with clumps of rounded, spoon-shaped, and toothed leaves about 4 in. (10 cm) long and 2 in. (5 cm) wide. Blue, pink, or white flowers are borne in whorled spikes in summer. It is a robust species that is not invasive. 'Brockbankii' is a hybrid between this species and ***A. pyramidalis.*** An attractive plant with bright-blue flowers, it reaches a height of about 8 in. (20 cm); 'Pink Beauty' has whorls of light-pink flowers and grows to 8 in. (20 cm). Zones 2–9.

A. pyramidalis. Europe. Height 8 in.; spread 12 in. (20 × 30 cm). A creeping, semievergreen, nonspreading species with dark-green, spoon-shaped, toothed, and hairy leaves up to 4 in. (10 cm) long and pyramidal spikes of whorled, blue flowers in early summer. 'Metallica Crispa' has metallic, dark-red, glossy, and curled foliage and dark-blue flowers. Zones 2–9.

A. reptans. Bugle. Europe. Height 4–8 in.; spread 18 in. (10–20 × 45 cm). A vigorous, sometimes invasive groundcover with 4-in.- (10-cm-) long, semievergreen, egg-shaped basal leaves on winged stalks and upright, whorled spikes of violet-blue, purple, and white flowers produced in late spring. 'Atropurpurea' is a purple-leaved form with blue flowers that colors best in sun; 'Burgundy Glow' has white-, pink-, and green-splashed leaves with blue flowers; 'Gaiety' has dark-bronze leaves and blue flowers; 'Multicolor' (Rainbow) is splashed with pink and white; 'Variegata' has silver and green variegation, coloring best in shade. The variegated cultivars often revert to the green-leaved form. To maintain the variegation, remove green leaves and shoots as soon as they appear. Over time seedlings may take over from cultivated varieties. These should be removed if a unified planting is desired. Zones 3–8.

ALCHEMILLA

(Lady's Mantle)

FAMILY: Rosaceae

A genus of over 200 species native to north temperate regions. They are low-growing plants with decorative, scalloped foliage and masses of petalless, greenish yellow flowers. Widely grown in gardens in Europe, they deserve more attention in the United States. The origin of the common name, lady's mantle, is obscure; it is described as being the Latinized version of an arabic name.

CULTIVATION: Grow in a sunny to partly shaded site in moist but well-drained soil. In areas with high summer temperatures, grow in a shady location, as lady's mantle often reacts to the heat with leaf scorching and thin flowering. Cut back hard in midsummer for fresh foliage. Often spreads by seed. If it needs to be contained, deadhead the faded flowers.

Alchemilla erythropoda

LANDSCAPE USE: Excellent informal edging plants for the herbaceous border or rock garden or as a groundcover. Particularly effective in association with roses and other strongly colored shrubs. Associates well with ***Geranium*** 'Johnson's Blue.'

PROPAGATION: Divide clumps in early fall or early spring. Easily grown from fresh seed.

A. alpina. Alpine lady's mantle. Europe. Height 6 in.; spread 12 in. (15 × 30 cm). Tufts of 2-in.- (5-cm-) wide, deeply cut, rounded, and lobed green leaves with a glistening margin caused by silvery hairs on the underside of the leaf. Sprays of greenish yellow flowers are produced in summer. Zones 3–8.

A. conjuncta. Europe, Scandinavia. Height 8 in.; spread 12 in. (20 × 30 cm). A more robust species than the above with bright-green rounded leaves only partially cut to the base. The silvery underside creates a shining edge above. Chartreuse flowers appear in summer. Zones 3–7.

A. erythropoda. Europe. Height 6 in.; spread 12 in. (15 × 30 cm). A clump-forming plant with bluish green, divided foliage with sprays of sulfur-yellow flowers in midsummer. Zones 3–7.

A. mollis. Lady's mantle. Asia Minor. Height 12–18 in.; spread 2 ft (30–45 × 60 cm). An excellent groundcover with 6-in.- (15-cm-) wide densely hairy, scalloped leaves of light green and sprays of tiny lime-green flowers held above the foliage in summer. Zones 3–7.

A.* x *splendens. Height 10 in.; spread 18 in. (25 × 45 cm). A hybrid between ***A. alpina*** and ***A. mollis.*** A worthy plant with leaves silvery underneath and loose sprays of apple-green flowers in early summer. Zones 3–7.

ALOPECURUS

(Foxtail Grass)

FAMILY: Graminae

About 30 species of grasses with flat blades and flower spikes of tan or yellow green. One species is grown for its colorful foliage.

CULTIVATION: Grow in a rich, well-drained but moist soil in full sun. Does best in areas with cool summers of low humidity and may take two or three years to establish.

LANDSCAPE USE: Grow as a specimen in the herbaceous border or pool edge or in a mass planting. Works well with other grasses of strong color. Attractive in combination with ***Imperata cylindrica*** 'Red Baron.'

PROPAGATION: Divide in early spring or autumn.

A. pratensis* 'Variegatus.'** (A. pratensis*** 'Aureus'). Golden foxtail grass. Europe, Asia. Height 2 ft; spread 1 ft (60 × 30 cm). A handsome grass for spring and autumn display, with upright clumps of green-and-yellow, longitudinally striped, ¼-in.- (0.6-cm-) wide leaves. Branched heads of light-tan flowers appear in spring and early summer and are borne on erect stems about 6–8 in. (15–20 cm) above the 16–18-in.- (40–45-cm-) high foliage. This grass looks best in spring and very early summer. In areas with hot and humid summers, it should be cut down to within 6 in. (15 cm) of the ground in midsummer and allowed to produce new foliage for autumn. Zones 4–8.

ALSTROEMERIA

(Peruvian Lily)

FAMILY: Amaryllidaceae

Alstroemeria psittacina

A genus of about 50 species native to South America. Despite the common name, Peruvian lily, they are neither lilies nor, except for a few obscure species, native to Peru. They are fleshy-rooted plants with twisted, lance-shaped leaves often covered with a waxy patina. The trumpet-shaped flowers are produced in summer in clusters on erect stems. They make excellent long-lasting cut flowers and are a major part of the cut flower industry. Named after Baron Alstroemer (1736–94).

CULTIVATION: Plant in deep, well-drained soil with an initial addition of organic matter. Once established, ***Alstroemeria*** need little or no fertilizing. Although they do not like excessive heat, they are great sun lovers and do best at the foot of south- or west-facing wall. Mulch for winter protection. While most species are tender, those listed below can be grown in protected sites in Zone 6 or 7.

LANDSCAPE USE: Wonderful plants for the sunny border. They have a tendency, however, to be invasive and do best when planted in a bed or border to themselves. They die down by late summer, leaving the ground bare.

PROPAGATION: ***A. aurea*** is best propagated by division in early spring by breaking up the large clumps of fleshy roots and replanting. The ***Ligtu Hybrids*** should be propagated by seed sown as soon as possible after ripening, in pots in a cold frame or cool greenhouse where they will germinate in early spring. Once the seedlings enter their summer dormancy, plant the seedlings, without disturbing their roots, 6–7 in. (15–17.5 cm) deep in a permanent location.

A. aurea (A. aurantiaca). South America. Height 3 ft; spread 12 in. (90 × 30 cm). Where established, this species can be invasive. The leaves are narrowly lance-shaped and twisted, the stems are wiry, bearing long-lasting tubular flowers of orange and yellow, spotted brown with green tips. A number of named varieties are bred for their stronger color, usually within the orange range. Zones 7–10.

A. 'Ligtu Hybrids.' Height 3–4 ft; spread 18 in. (90–120 × 45 cm). An excellent group of hybrids raised in England in the 1920s. These colorful lilylike flowers in shades of pink, flame, tangerine, and white are, at this time, the most rewarding of the hardier ***Alstroemerias*** to grow. Hybrids of ***A. ligtu*** and ***A. haemantha.*** Zones 7–10.

A. psittacina (A. pulchella). Parrot lily. Brazil. Height 3 ft; spread 12 in. (90 × 30 cm). A delicate-looking but tough, clump-forming species with lance-shaped leaves and dramatical dark-red flowers tipped green. Hardier than first thought, this is a wonderful summer border plant. Zones 7–10.

ALYSSUM

(Madwort)

Family: Cruciferae

One hundred or more species of annual and perennial herbs belonging to the mustard family. The common name refers to its traditional ability to cure rabies. The leaves are alternate and hairy, in tight rosettes, with cross-shaped flowers of yellow or white. Taxonomists have been playing around with this genus and have now moved the well-known basket of gold, ***Alyssum saxatile,*** to the genus ***Aurinia.***

Cultivation: Grow in a sunny site in ordinary, even lean soil with good drainage. Shear after flowering to help keep compact.

Landscape Use: Excellent low-growing plants for the sunny rock garden, dry wall, or border edge.

Propagation: Take 2-in. (5 cm) stem cuttings in early summer. When rooted, pot on and plant out the following spring. Sow seeds in early spring, planting out when large enough, in early autumn.

A. alpestre. Europe. Height 4 in.; spread 8 in. (10 × 20 cm). An attractive, trailing, woody-stemmed species with oblong to linear gray leaves about ¼ in. (0.6 cm) long and a profusion of pale-yellow flowers in spring and early summer. A good rock-garden plant. Zones 3–9.

A. idaeum. Crete. Height 6 in.; spread 8 in. (15 × 20 cm). A prostrate plant with woody stems and egg-shaped oblong, silvery-green leaves and creamy white to soft-yellow flowers in spring. Grows well in gravelly soil. Zones 4–9.

A. moellendorfianum. Yugoslavia. Height 6 in.; spread 8 in. (15 × 20 cm). A prostrate woody plant with spoon-shaped gray leaves up to ½ in. (1.2 cm) long and tight clusters of yellow flowers on upright stems in spring. Zones 4–9.

A. montanum. Mountain alyssum. Eastern Europe. Height 6 in.; spread 8 in. (15 × 20 cm). A dense, mat-forming plant with spreading stems and oval, hairy, gray, evergreen leaves. The fragrant, soft-yellow flowers are produced throughout the spring and summer. Zones 4–9.

AMSONIA

(Blue Stars)

Family: Apocynaceae

Amsonia ciliata

A genus of about 20 species native to North America and eastern Asia. They are clump-forming plants with alternate or whorled linear leaves on stems with a milky sap and heads of star-shaped, blue to pale-blue flowers. The species frequently hybridize with each other, making identification difficult. Named after Charles Amson, an 18th-century physician.

CULTIVATION: Prefers light shade but will grow in full sun if planted in moist soil.

LANDSCAPE USE: Handsome plants for the woodland edge, streamside, wild garden, or herbaceous border, where their light foliage and pleasing blue flowers makes a good backdrop for smaller plants.

PROPAGATION: Divide in early spring or early autumn. Sow seeds in autumn.

A. ciliata. Blue star. North America. Height 2 ft; spread 12 in. (60 × 30 cm). A native of the southern states, sometimes called the feather amsonia because of its hairy, tapering leaves and numerous pale-blue, star-shaped flowers in clusters at the end of thin stems. Blooms during late spring to early summer and grows well in dry soil. Autumn color is a light, golden yellow. Zones 6–8.

A. tabernaemontana. Willow blue star. North America. Height 3 ft; spread 18 in. (90 × 45 cm). A tough plant with small and numerous star-shaped, light-blue flowers in late spring and early summer on upright stems with thin, mostly lance-shaped, thinly hairy leaves up to 6 in. (15 cm) long. The seed pods are soft and hairy. Deserves to be more widely grown. ***A. tabernaemontana*** var. ***salicifolia*** has narrower tapering and pointed leaves much like a willow. Zones 4–8.

ANACYCLUS

(Mount Atlas Daisy)

FAMILY: Compositae

A genus of about 25 species of daisy native to the mountains of Morocco. They are low-growing plants with ferny foliage and flower stems that are mostly prostrate until they turn up at the ends. The flowers are white or yellow with the underside of the ray petals rust red. This is a conspicuous ornamental feature when the flowers are closed at night, in the early morning, and in cloudy weather.

CULTIVATION: Plant in well-drained ordinary soil in full sun. They will rot over winter if planted in a site that remains wet.

LANDSCAPE USE: Grow in the rock garden, dry stone wall, or alpine border.

PROGAGATION: Sow fresh seed in early autumn or take tip cuttings throughout the summer.

A. depressus. Mount Atlas daisy. North Africa. Height 2 in.; spread 12 in. (5 × 30 cm). A mat-forming plant with gray-green, finely cut, fernlike leaves about 1½ in. (3.8 cm) long and prostrate stems. The white, up to 2-in.- (5-cm-) wide, daisylike flowers with a central disk of yellow appear in summer. The underside of the flowers are crimson. Other species grown in gardens, notably ***A. atlanticus*** and ***A. maroccanus,*** are similar. Zones 6–8.

ANAGALLIS

(Pimpernel)

FAMILY: Primulaceae

Anagallis monelli 'Pacific Blue'

A genus of mostly tropical annuals and perennials. Those species growing in temperate regions are mostly annuals, such as the scarlet pimpernel (*A. arvensis*), or short-lived perennials as mentioned below. They are known for their profusion of deep-blue or red flowers during the summer. The generic name is derived from the Greek, meaning "to delight or make happy," a reference to the scarlet pimpernel's supposed efficacy in treating liver diseases.

CULTIVATION: Grow ***A. monelli*** in well-drained, ordinary soil in full sun. ***A. tenella*** needs moist soil.

LANDSCAPE USE: Excellent plants for the rock garden or sunny border edge. ***A. monelli*** makes a good container plant for the alpine house.

PROPAGATION: Sow seeds in spring or take cuttings in summer. As the perennial species, especially ***A. monelli,*** are short-lived, it is a good idea to propagate annually.

A. monelli. Pimpernel. Spain. Height 12 in.; spread 18 in. (30 × 45 cm). A mound-forming perennial with 1-in.- (2.5-cm-) long, lance-shaped leaves and masses of starry, blue flowers in summer. Can be grown as an annual in climates colder than Zone 8. ***A. monelli*** 'Pacific Blue,' an introduction from the University of British Columbia, Vancouver, Canada, has gentian-blue flowers. ***A. monelli*** var. ***collina*** has red flowers. Zones 8–9.

A. tenella. Bog pimpernel. Western Europe. Height 1 in.; spread 12 in. (2.5 × 30 cm). A native of cool, boggy soils, this mat-forming plant has bright-green leaves and masses of small, pale-pink, star-shaped flowers in early summer. 'Studland' has flowers of a deeper, brighter pink. Zones 5–7.

ANAPHALIS

(Pearly Everlasting)

FAMILY: Compositae

A small genus of perennials native to mountainous areas of Europe, North America, and Asia, with white woolly stems and alternate leaves, topped with white flowers with yellow eyes.

CULTIVATION: Plant in the spring in well-drained soil in a sunny location. Unlike many other silver-leaved plants, ***Anaphalis*** will tolerate moist soil. In hot, humid summers they may develop stem rot and leaf fungus diseases. Caterpillar damage in early summer is also possible. They benefit from midsummer pruning if their growth becomes too lax.

LANDSCAPE USE: Silver-leaved plants for the herbaceous border; good for creating patches of light in dark designs. Can be cut and dried, hence the common name pearly everlasting.

PROPAGATION: Divide in spring. Take tip cuttings in late spring.

A. cinnamomea (A. yedoensis). Asia. Height 2 ft; spread 2 ft (60 × 60 cm). Silvery, hairy, erect stems with 2–4-in.- (5–10-cm-) long, lance-shaped leaves, green above, white beneath. Flat clusters of white flowers are produced from mid- to late summer. Can be invasive. Zones 6–8.

A. margaritacea. Pearly everlasting. North America. Height 12–24 in.; spread 2 ft (30 × 60 cm). Common to much of North America, it is particularly prominent in the mountains of the Pacific Northwest. This is an excellent plant for a cool, dry border. It is a bushy plant with up to 4-in.- (10-cm-) long, tapering, lance-shaped, white-edged, gray-green leaves with white felt beneath and masses of pearly white flowers in flattish clusters in late summer. It is more tolerant of drought than other species. Zones 4–8.

Anaphalis margaritacea

A. triplinervis. Asia. Height 18 in.; spread 2 ft (45 × 60 cm). A bushy species with gray-green, lance-shaped leaves on compact, silvery stems with tight masses of yellow-centered, white, starry flowers in mid- to late summer. Does not enjoy excessively dry soil. 'Summer Snow' is a dwarf cultivar, reading up to 8 in. (20 cm) in height. Zones 3–9.

ANCHUSA

(Italian Bugloss)

FAMILY: Boraginaceae

Anchusa azurea

This genus is known for its rich blue flowers resembling large forget-me-nots, blooming in early summer. The plants are generally short-lived, alternate and coarse-leaved, with hairy and erect, stalked, spirally arranged flower heads. The name ***Anchusa*** comes from the Greek for "to paint," referring to the use of the root as a dye. The curious common name is derived from the Greek for "ox tongue," a reference to the roughness and shape of the leaves.

CULTIVATION: Plant in spring in deep, well-drained, fertile soil in full sun. The leaves are susceptible to leaf scorch in hot summers. They are generally coarse plants, and the larger species need ample room and staking. Cut back and fertilize after flowering to stimulate a second flush of flowers.

LANDSCAPE USE: As the growth habit is somewhat ungainly, plant at the back of a border where the beautiful blue flowers can be enjoyed without the disappointment of the poor foliage.

PROPAGATION: Divide clumps, take root cuttings, or sow seed in spring. Divide every three years for young, vigorous plants.

A. angustissima. Europe. Height 12 in.; spread 12 in. (30 × 30 cm). A long-flowering but coarse rock-garden plant with hairy green rosettes covered with gentian-blue flowers in summer. Needs good drainage. Zones 3–8.

A. azurea (A. italica). Caucasus. Height 4 ft; spread 2 ft (120 × 60 cm). The most commonly grown species with a number of forms. The basal leaves are coarse and hairy, oblong to lance-shaped, and up to 8 in. (20 cm) long, on tough, bristly stems bearing large panicles of saucer-shaped, deep-blue flowers in early summer. 'Dropmore': height 3 ft (90 cm), blue flowers; 'Little John': height 18 in. (45 cm), dark-blue flowers; 'Loddon Royalist': height 3–4 ft (90–120 cm), rich blue flowers, 'Opal': height 4 ft (120 cm), pale-blue flowers that need staking. Zones 3–8.

A. caespitosa. Mediterranean. Height 3 in.; spread 9 in. (7.5 × 22.5 cm). An evergreen prostrate plant with rosettes of bristly, linear 4-in.- (10-cm) long leaves and almost stemless white-eyed, deep-blue flowers in midsummer. Prefers deep, rocky soil in full sun. Zones 5–7.

ANDROPOGON

(Bluestem, Beard Grass, Broom-Sedge)

FAMILY: Graminae

A large genus of about 200 species of widely distributed grasses, a number of which are native to the prairies and other open spaces of North America. Many species are subtle in their ornamental features, a polite way of saying they are rather dull. Their redeeming feature is that they are often highly attractive in autumn when many species turn a rich orange-wheat color.

CULTIVATION: Grow in full sun in well-drained soil. Cut down old foliage in early spring.

LANDSCAPE USE: Drought-resistant grasses for the dry, wild, or prairie garden, where they can be planted singly or in masses.

PROPAGATION: Divide in early spring or sow seed.

A. gerardii. Big bluestem. North America. Height 5–6 ft; spread 2–3 ft (150–180 × 60–90 cm). A clump-forming grass with blue-green stems and gray-green leaves about ½ in. (1.2 cm) wide. The foliage forms a clump 12–18 in. (30–45 cm) high, while

Andropogon gerardii

the light and airy purplish flowers tower over the foliage in early autumn. The leaves turn bronze-red in autumn. Zones 3–9.

A. virginicus. Broomsedge bluestem. North America. Height 3–4 ft; spread 1 ft (90–120 × 30 cm). A highly drought-resistant grass with little ornamental merit in spring and summer but with great charm in autumn. It is an upright and clump-forming plant with green leaves and often blue stem bases. The clustered spikelets are produced on 3-4-ft (90–120-cm) stems above the 1-ft- (30-cm-) high foliage in early autumn. The foliage turns bright orange in autumn and is a wonderful sight in open fields and meadows. It is particularly striking after a light snowfall. Zones 4–9.

ANDROSACE

(Rock Jasmine)

FAMILY: Primulaceae

Androsace lanuginosa

About 125 species of annual and perennial herbs native to the mountains of the northern hemisphere. Those widely grown are rock-garden plants forming tight mats or prostrate clumps. Many species grow in tufted domes with masses of tiny, primrose-like flowers in early summer.

CULTIVATION: Many of the species do best when grown in an alpine house. Those that can be grown outside require a sunny or lightly shaded location with well-drained soil that does not dry out, amended with limestone grit or coarse sand. In areas of hot summers, they require shade during the hottest part of the day. They have a reputation for being difficult to grow. Those few listed below are considered some of the easiest to cultivate in the garden.

LANDSCAPE USE: Gems for the rock garden.

PROPAGATION: Detach single rosettes in early summer and root in sand. Sow seeds in pans in winter after allowing them to freeze for 14 days. Seed may not germinate until the second year after sowing.

A. carnea. Europe. Height 3 in.; spread 9 in. (7.5 × 22.5 cm). Cushions of narrow pointed leaves with finely hairy edges and pink or white cup-shaped flowers on 3-in. (7.5-cm) stems. The subspecies ***laggeri*** from the Pyrenees is a mossy plant with deep-pink flowers with a yellow eye, ssp. ***brigantiaca*** has white flowers, and ssp. ***rosea*** has pink flowers. Zones 4–7.

A. lanuginosa. Himalayas. Height 1 in.; spread 18 in. (2.5 × 45 cm). A mat-forming plant with hairy, trailing stems and silvery white, round leaves with pink or red flowers with darker eyes in summer.

'Leitchlinii' has white flowers with a pink eye. Zones 4–6.

A. primuloides. Himalayas. Height 4 in.; spread 24 in. (10 × 60 cm). A spreading plant with hairy, green rosettes and rose-pink flowers borne in umbels on stems 2–4 in. (5–10 cm) long. 'Chumbyi' is a more robust plant hardy to Zones 4–7. There are a number of other varieties; all appreciate protection from winter rain.

A. sempervivoides. Himalayas. Height 2 in.; spread 12 in. (5 × 30 cm). A mound-forming species with smooth, green rosettes of leathery oblong leaves and pink flowers with yellow-and-red centers in early summer. Prefers some shade. Zones 5–7.

ANEMONE

(Windflower)

FAMILY: Ranunculaceae

Anemone apennina

Anemone x *hybrida* 'Margarete'

A large genus of notable garden plants ranging from delicate woodland spring flowers to robust autumn-flowering border plants. The flowers are generally bowl-shaped on branching, wiry stems. The foliage is divided or dissected. Many species are normally easy to grow and have a pleasing tendency toward invasiveness. They are native to wide areas of the northern hemisphere and range from high alpine meadows to lowland pastures. The name ***Anemone*** is supposed to derive from the Greek *anemos,* "wind." However, other sources say that the name refers to the slain Adonis, whose blood produced the red flowers of ***Anemone coronaria.*** Some species have tuberous rhizomes and are among the finest of spring flowers.

CULTIVATION: Plant in spring in fertile, moist but well-drained soil in sun to partial shade. They are best left undisturbed for several years. They do not need staking.

LANDSCAPE USE: The Japanese anemones are outstanding plants when used en masse, as can be seen at Van Dusen Botanical Gardens in Vancouver, Canada, or at the Berkeley Botanical Gardens in California. They also have a quiet elegance as single specimens or large background plantings in herbaceous borders.

PROPAGATION: Divide the summer- and autumn-flowering species in spring. Sow seeds of spring-flowering species as soon as they are ripe.

A. apennina. Southern Europe. Height 8 in.; spread 6 in. (20 × 15 cm). A spring-flowering, tuberous-rooted species with softly hairy, deeply cut leaves 3–4 in. (7.5–10 cm) wide and single, sky-blue flowers about 1½ in. (3.8 cm) across. 'Alba' has white flowers. Zones 5–8.

A. blanda. Windflower. Greece. Height 8 in.; spread 8 in. (20 × 20 cm). A rapidly spreading tuberous-rooted species with deeply cut, ferny leaves up to 3 in. (7.5 cm) wide and 2-in.- (5-cm-) wide, dark-blue flowers in early spring. 'Blue Star' has dark-blue flowers a little larger than the species; 'White Splendour' has white flowers; 'Radar' has mauve flowers. Purchased tubers may be shriveled and dry; there is some evidence that soaking them in water overnight is beneficial. Windflower takes at least two springs to establish, but once it does it will seed itself merrily. Zones 4–8.

A. canadensis. Meadow anemone. Eastern North America. Height 2 ft; spread 12 in. (60 × 30 cm). An excellent white-flowered ***Anemone*** for full sun or partial shade, with light-green, long-stalked, sharply toothed, five- to seven-parted leaves. The 2-in.- (5-cm-) wide, upward-facing, yellow-centered, buttercuplike flowers are produced in late spring or early summer on 2-ft (60-cm) stems. While this plant can be invasive in good soil, this is an advantage rather than an alarming attribute. Zones 3–8.

A. caroliniana. North America. Height 12 in.; spread 8 in. (30 × 20 cm). A tuberous-rooted, spring-flowering plant with three-parted, lobed leaves and solitary flowers in shades of cream, pink, and purple. Native to open prairies and chalky soils. Zones 5–8.

A. deltoidea. Western North America. Height 6–8 in.; spread 6 in. (15–20 × 15 cm). A beautiful woodland carpeter native from British Columbia to California. White blossoms up to 1 in. (2.5 cm) wide are produced in spring, above glossy, dark-green leaves that are divided into three egg-shaped leaflets. Zones 6–8.

A. hupehensis. Japan, China. Height 2 ft; spread 18 in. (60 × 45 cm). A clump-forming plant with lobed and deeply toothed, dark-green leaves, wiry stems, and saucer-shaped flowers of soft pink in late summer and early autumn. ***A. hupehensis japonica,*** a rare, semidouble form, has flowers with narrow petals of rose-pink. 'September Charm,' according to some sources, is a hybrid more closely connected with ***A. hupehensis*** than ***A. × hybrida.*** It has numerous saucer-shaped flowers of rose-pink with golden centers on 30-in. (75-cm) stems in early autumn. Zones 5–8.

A. × hybrida. Japanese anemone. Height 3–4 ft; spread 2 ft (90–120 × 60 cm). A hybrid of ***A. hupehensis japonica*** and ***A. tomentosa*** often called ***A. japonica*** in gardens, this is the common pink ***Anemone*** in cultivation. The dark-green leaves have long stalks and three serrated leaflets. The flowers are 2–3 in. (5–7.5 cm) across and are borne on branching stems. There are a number of forms, many of which are very desirable garden plants. All do best in full sun but flower in partial shade. 'Bressingham Glow': height 18 in. (45 cm), semidouble, rose-red flowers; 'Honorine Jobert'; height 3 ft (90 cm); single white flower; 'Lady Gilmour': height 2 ft (60 cm); almost double, pure pink flower; 'Margarete': height 3 ft (90 cm); almost double, deep-pink flower; 'Prince Henry': height 18 in. (45 cm); single rose-pink flower; 'Queen Charlotte': height 3 ft (90 cm); semidouble, pink flower; 'Whirlwind': height 3 ft (90 cm), semidouble, white flower; 'White Queen': height 2 ft (60 cm), large-flowered white flower. Zones 5–8.

A. narcissiflora. Europe, North America. Height 1–2 ft; spread 18 in. (30–60 × 45 cm). A white- or cream-flowered species with a pink to mauve flush on the outside of the petals and dark-green, deeply divided leaves. Flowers 1 in. (2.5 cm) wide appear in spring. Zones 4–8.

A. nemerosa. Wood anemone. Europe. Height 6–8 in.; spread 12 in. (15–20 × 30 cm). Woodland carpeters with white, sometimes blue, star-shaped flowers with a central boss of yellow stamens in spring. The deeply cut foliage dies down by summer. 'Allenii' has pale-lavender flowers; 'Lismore Blue,' flowers of lavender-blue; 'Lismore Pink,' pale-pink flowers; 'Robinsoniana,' lavender-pink flowers; 'Vestal,' double white flowers. Zones 4–8.

A. pulsatilla. See ***Pulsatilla.***

A. sylvestris. Snowdrop anemone. Europe. Height 1 ft; spread 8 in. (30 × 20 cm). Carpets of hairy, toothed, five-parted leaves and 2-in.- (5-cm-) wide, slightly drooping and fragrant, white, yellow-centered flowers are produced on wiry stems in late spring and early summer. Spreads freely by underground runners. 'Spring Beauty' has larger flowers. Zones 3–8.

A. tomentosa (A. vitifolia). Asia. Height 2–3 ft; spread 18 in. (60–90 × 45 cm). Similar to ***A. × hybrida*** but with lobed rather than divided leaves. It also flowers a few weeks before the autumn-flowering varieties and has pink-flushed white flowers above vinelike leaves. 'Robustissima' is slightly taller, reaching up to about 4 ft (120 cm), with pale-pink, saucer-shaped flowers. It is reputed to be slightly hardier than the species. Zones 4–8.

ANEMONOPSIS

(False Anemone)

Family: Ranunculaceae

A rare plant native to the mountains of Japan, it is similar to the Japanese anemone with more finely cut foliage.

Cultivation: Grow in lightly shaded location in good soil amended with leaf mold. Grows well in climates with cool summers.

Landscape Use: Woodland garden or shady herbaceous border.

Propagation: Divide mature plants in spring.

A. macrophylla. False anemone. Japan. Height 2 ft; spread 18 in. (60 × 45 cm). Long-stalked, finely divided fernlike leaves with nodding light-purple flowers up to 1½ in. (3.8 cm) long on branching stems in mid- to late summer. Zones 5–8.

ANGELICA

(Archangel)

Family: Umbelliferae

Angelica archangelica

About 50 species of herbs with white or greenish, round flower heads, rigid stems, and large dissected, aromatic leaves. One species is used in confectionery to make candied flower stems.

Cultivation: Grow in rich, moist soil in full sun to partial shade. As they tend to be short-lived if allowed to flower, remove the flower heads as they appear.

Landscape Use: Dramatic plants for the back of the border or as a focus in the large herb garden. Effective as stream- or pondside plants.

Propagation: Sow seeds in late summer or autumn.

A. archangelica. Syria. Height 6 ft; spread 3 ft (180 × 90 cm). A vigorous, coarse, short-lived plant with ridged stems and bright-green, divided and aromatic leaves up to 2 ft (60 cm) long. Numerous greenish white flowers in round heads in summer. The name ***archangelica*** may refer to the belief that this species kept away evil. Zones 4–9.

A. atropurpurea. Great angelica. North America. Height 6 ft; spread 3 ft (180 × 90 cm). A short-lived perennial or possibly a biennial with dark-purple stems and large white flower heads in summer. A native of swamplands. Zones 4–9.

ANTENNARIA

(Pussy-Toes)

FAMILY: Compositae

Many species of mostly evergreen, mat-forming plants native to North and South America, Europe and Asia. The leaves are often silvery gray and hairy, in basal rosettes. The tubular flowers are undistinguished except in certain species where the tufted, soft flowers are quietly ornamental.

CULTIVATION: Grow in dry, rocky soils in full sun. Spreads rapidly, which may be an advantage.

LANDSCAPE USE: Good groundcovers for the edge of a sunny border, dry bank, between paving stones, or in the rock garden.

PROPAGATION: Divide and plant in spring or take cuttings in summer.

A. dioica. Pussy-toes. Europe, Asia, North America. Height 10 in.; spread 18 in. (25 × 45 cm). A mat-forming plant with evergreen, spoon-shaped, woolly-gray leaves about 1 in. (2.5 cm) long and 10-in. (25-cm) stems bearing terminal clusters of fluffy white flowers in early summer. 'Minima' is a smaller version of the type; 'Nyewoods' has deep-pink flowers; 'Rosea,' flowers of light pink; 'Rubra,' flowers of deep rose-red. Zones 4–7.

A. plantaginifolia. Ladies tobacco. North America. Height 9 in.; spread 12 in. (22.5 × 30 cm). Spreading mats of round, hairy, gray-green leaves up to 3 in. (7.5 cm) long. White to cream-colored flowers on stems 6 to 9 in. (15–22.5 cm) long appear in early summer. Zones 5–8.

ANTHEMIS

(Chamomile)

FAMILY: Compositae

A genus of sun-loving plants widely distributed in Asia, Europe, and North Africa. The leaves are finely incised, dissected, often aromatic with leafy stems bearing solitary heads of mostly white or yellow daisylike flowers.

CULTIVATION: Grow in a sunny, well-drained site in ordinary or poor soil. Taller varieties may need staking.

LANDSCAPE USE: Many are tall plants for the herbaceous border and dry garden. A few make excellent cut flowers.

PROPAGATION: Divide or take cuttings of basal shoots in the spring.

A. cupaniana. Europe. Height 12 in.; spread 3 ft (30 × 90 cm). An evergreen plant forming broadly spreading mounds of finely cut gray, aromatic foliage and white, yellow-centered daisylike flowers throughout the summer. Zones 5–9.

Anthemis tinctoria 'Grallach Gold'

A. nobilis. Chamomile. See ***Chamaemelum nobile.***

A. marschalliana (A. biebersteinii). Caucasus. Height 6 in.; spread 12 in. (15 × 30 cm). A delicate ferny plant forming soft mounds of finely divided, silvery leaves with 1-in.- (2.5-cm-) wide, rich golden daisies on short stems in summer. Zones 4–8.

A. sancti-johannis. St. John's chamomile. Bulgaria. Height 2 ft; spread 18 in. (60 × 45 cm). A spreading plant with deeply cut, mid-green foliage with 2-in.- (5-cm-) wide orange daisies on 2-ft (60-cm) stems in mid- to late summer. Hybridizes freely with ***A. tinctoria*** to produce some excellent cultivars mentioned below. Zones 4–9.

A. tinctoria. Golden chamomile. Height 3 ft; spread 2 ft (90 × 60 cm). Finely cut, parsleylike foliage with robust stems on which golden yellow daisies are produced in summer. Often needs staking. A number of forms with larger flowers are fine ornamental plants: 'Beauty of Grallach': height 2 ft (60 cm), golden orange flowers; 'E. C. Buxton': height 12 in. (30 cm), almost-white petals around a central gold disc, very drought tolerant; 'Grallach Gold': height 3 ft (90 cm), bright-yellow blossoms; 'Kelwayi': height 3 ft (90 cm), golden yellow flowers; 'Moonlight': height 12 in. (30 cm), pale-yellow daisies; 'Pale Moon': height 30 in. (75 cm), canary-yellow flowers changing to white. Cut back hard to within 12 in. (30 cm) of the ground to stimulate fresh growth and secondary flowering. Zones 4–8.

AQUILEGIA

(Columbine)

Family: Ranunculaceae

Aquilegia canadensis

About 100 species of erect, branching plants with divided leaves, native to north temperate zones. The variably colored, funnel-shaped flowers have backward-pointing spurs that resemble birds, either a dove (*columba*) or an eagle (*aquila*). Columbines hybridize freely, resulting in many garden forms.

CULTIVATION: Most are easy to grow; however, a small number of the alpine and subalpine species are notoriously difficult and may be best grown in an alpine house. The border varieties should be planted in well-drained leafy soil in sun or partial shade. Deadhead after flowering. Leaf miner, aphids, and borer damage can be a great problem in midsummer.

LANDSCAPE USE: Rock garden or herbaceous border. Mass plantings of ***Aquilegia*** in wild gardens are highly recommended.

PROPAGATION: Species are "thoroughly amoral" and hybridize readily, so sowing from seed from mixed plantings is an adventure. Seed should be sown in early spring or, when ripe, in summer. Divide *young* plants in spring or late summer.

A. alpina. Switzerland. Height 12 in.; spread 8 in. (30×20 cm). A charming species with finely divided leaves and blue or white spurred flowers in late spring and early summer. 'Alba' flowers white; 'Hensoll Harebell,' a hybrid, grows to 30 in. (75 cm) and has deep-blue flowers with in-curved spurs. Zones 3–8.

A. caerulea. Colorado columbine. Rocky Mountains. Height 2 ft; spread 18 in. (60×45 cm). A highly variable species and an important contributor to many hybrids, this state flower of Colorado has two-parted leaves and sky-blue flowers with spurs straight or curved outward. Blooms in late spring and early summer. There are a number of forms, including 'Crimson Star' with red petals with a white center. Zones 3–8.

A. canadensis. Northeastern North America. Height 2 ft; spread 12 in. (60×30 cm). Native to lightly wooded or open slopes, the American columbine is a delicate-looking plant with mid- to dark-green leaves and nodding flowers with petals of red on the outside, yellow on the inside. Self-sows freely. An excellent and sadly underused plant for the wild garden or border. Blooms in early summer. Zones 3–9.

A. chrysantha. Golden columbine. Rocky Mountains, Texas. Height 2–3 ft; spread 18 in. (60–90×45 cm). Masses of yellow, long-spurred flowers are held above divided, bushy foliage in early summer. Along with ***A. caerulea,*** this is the parent of the long-spurred hybrids. 'Yellow Queen': height 3 ft (90 cm), golden yellow flowers 3 in. (7.5 cm) across; 'Silver Queen': long-blooming, pure-white flowers. Zones 3–9.

A. discolor. Spain. Height 4–12 in.; spread 6 in. (10–30×15 cm). Bright blue-and-white flowers with in-curved spurs held above finely cut foliage. Zones 4–9.

A. flabellata. Fan columbine. Japan. Height 18 in.; spread 8 in. (45×20 cm). A short, stocky species with a handsome basal rosette of blue-green foliage and short-spurred waxy flowers of light blue. 'Nana Alba' is a dwarf, white-flowering form reaching a height of about 8 in. (20 cm). Zones 3–9.

A. formosa. Western North America. Height 3 ft; spread 18 in. (90×45 cm). A taller version of its eastern cousin ***A. canadensis,*** with bright-yellow flowers with red spurs in early summer. Zones 3–9.

A. longissima. Southern United States, Mexico. Height 3 ft; spread 18 in. (90×45 cm). Native to streamsides, this early-summer-flowering plant with yellow flowers has the longest spurs of all the species, reaching 3 in. (7.5 cm) or more. 'Maxistar' is a vigorous plant with clear yellow flowers. Zones 4–9.

A. vulgaris. Europe. Height 3 ft; spread 18 in. (90×45 cm). The common columbine of Britain with gray-green, finely divided leaves and short-spurred flowers in a variety of colors, including white, violet, pink, and crimson. A large number of early-summer-flowering hybrids can be grouped under this parent. 'Biedermeier': height 12 in. (30 cm), upward-facing blooms, often two-toned, in pastel shades; 'McKana Hybrids': height 30 in. (75 cm), pastel flowers with flared spurs; 'Munstead': height 30 in. (75 cm), creamy-white flowers, comes true from seed; 'Nora Barlow': height 30 in. (75 cm), a curious flower with many-petaled, spurless, double, mixed pink, red, and green blooms; 'Langdon's Rainbow Hybrids': height 30 in. (75 cm), a bright-colored strain with long spurs. Zones 5–9.

ARABIS

(Rock Cress)

FAMILY: Cruciferae

The best of the species are cushion-forming plants with round or spoon-shaped leaves and small, terminal spikes of white or pink flowers in spring and summer. The name is derived from *Arabia*, a reference to the dry habitats preferred by many species.

CULTIVATION: Plant in a sunny position in lean and lime-rich soil.

LANDSCAPE USE: Sweetly fragrant plants for the rock garden, wall, alpine house, or border edging.

PROPAGATION: Easily propagated by division in early autumn or by cuttings in summer.

*A. **aubretioides.*** Turkey. Height 6 in.; spread 12 in. (15 × 30 cm). Compact cushions of silvery, hairy, egg-shaped, and toothed leaves with purplish pink flower spikes in summer. Zones 6–8.

*A. **blepharophylla.*** California. Height 6 in.; spread 12 in. (15 × 30 cm). A spring-flowering species with deep-pink flowers above a cusion of green, spoon-shaped leaves edged by fine hairs. Zones 7–8.

*A. **caucasica (A. albida).*** Europe. Height 10 in.; spread 18 in. (25 × 45 cm). A mat-forming species with gray, toothed, spoon-shaped leaves in rosettes with numerous and showy, sweetly fragrant white flowers in loose, unbranched heads in spring. 'Flore Pleno' has double white flowers; 'Monte Rosa' has deep-rose flowers; 'Variegata' has variegated foliage. Deadhead and trim back after flowering for compact plants. Zones 3–8.

Arabis caucasica

*A. **ferdinandi-coburgii.*** Greece. Height 6 in.; spread 12 in. (15 × 30 cm). Mats of gray-green, oval leaves becoming green in winter with small white flowers in early spring. A more attractive form 'Variegata,' has green-and-creamy-white foliage but often reverts to type. Zones 5–8.

*A. **procurrens.*** Europe. Height 12 in.; spread 18 in. (30 × 45 cm). A rapidly spreading carpeter with shiny green oblong leaves and leafy stems with sprays of single white flowers in spring. Tolerates light shade. Zones 5–8.

ARACHNIODES

(Shield Fern)

FAMILY: Aspleniaceae

Thirty species of fern native to temperate and subtropical regions with the majority concentrated in eastern Asia. The fronds have downward-pointing leaf segments (pinnae).

CULTIVATION: Plant in well-drained loam fortified with leaf mold in a semishady location. All species of Arachniode benefit from applications of slow-release fertilizers.

LANDSCAPE USE: Grow in a shady border or woodland garden. Members of this genus can be very effective when grown in containers.

PROPAGATION: Sow spores in late summer or increase by division in late spring or early summer.

A. aristata. Prickly shield fern. East Asia, Australia. Height 2–3 ft; spread 18 in. (60–90 × 45 cm). A coarse fern with triangular, leathery fronds up to 20 in. (50 cm) long, with the frond segments ending in spiky points. Requires moist soil but will tolerate some dryness. Zones 7–9.

A. simplicior. Variegated shield fern. China. Height 2 ft; spread 18 in. (60 × 45 cm). A slow-growing fern with glossy green fronds and yellowish bands of variegation on each side of the midrib. Often listed as ***A. aristata 'Variegata.'*** Zones 7–9.

A. standishii. Upside-down fern. Japan. Height 2 ft; spread 18 in. (60 × 45 cm). A truly delightful fern with delicate, thin fronds of lacy quality. The thinness of the fronds allows the black spore cases on the underside to be seen from above, hence the common name. Zones 6–9.

Arachniodes standishii

ARENARIA

(Sandwort)

FAMILY: Caryophyllaceae

A genus of about 150 annual and perennial plants. Those useful in the garden are mostly evergreen, subshrubby, cushion-forming species flowering in spring and summer. The name comes from the Latin *arena,* "sand," in reference to the fact that many species inhabit sandy sites.

CULTIVATION: Grow in well-drained, gritty soil. Most species prefer areas where the summers are mild and are best grown in full sun except for those noted below.

LANDSCAPE USE: Rock gardens, dry stone walls,. paving stones, dry banks.

PROPAGATION: Divide in spring or take cuttings of nonflowering shoots in summer.

A. balearica. Corsican sandwort. Corsica. Height 1 in.; spread 18 in. (2.5 × 45 cm). Tiny green, round leaves form a cushion above which appear white star-shaped flowers in spring and early summer. Requires a cool, shady location. Zones 6–7.

A. grandiflora. Large-flowered sandwort. Europe. Height 5 in.; spread 12 in. (12.5 × 30 cm). A mound-forming variety with ½ in.- (1.2-cm-) long linear leaves and upward-facing, bell-shaped white flowers in early summer. Zones 4–7.

A. ledebouriana. Turkey. Height 3 in.; spread 12 in. (7.5 × 30 cm). Spiny cushions of tiny, soft-green leaves above which small white flowers appear in spring. Zones 5–7.

A. montana. Europe. Height 4 in.; spread 12 in. (10 × 30 cm). A carpeting plant with trailing stems of grassy, dark-green, oblong to linear leaves up to 1 in. (2.5 cm) long and masses of white flowers with yellow eyes in spring. Grows well in light shade. Zones 4–7.

A. tetraquetra. Spain. Height 2 in.; spread 12 in. (5 × 30 cm). Flat cushions of egg-shaped, gray-green leaves with tiny, stemless, white flowers in spring. An attractive sun-loving plant for the rock garden or alpine house. Zones 4–6.

ARISAEMA

(Jack-in-the-Pulpit)

FAMILY: Araceae

Arisaema triphyllum

A large genus of tuberous-rooted, stemless plants with dramatic hooded cups (spathes) surrounding the flower spikes (spadix), followed by colorful berries in fall.

CULTIVATION: Plant the tubers in autumn 6 in. (15 cm) deep in leafy, moist soil in partial shade.

LANDSCAPE USE: Dramatic woodland plants for the shady garden. Their curious flowers make a strangely primal effect.

PROPAGATION: Sow seed in autumn or dig up and replant offsets in spring.

A. candidissimum. China. Height 12 in.; spread 18 in. (30×45 cm). An extraordinarily beautiful plant with large white-striped, pink-hooded spathes appearing in summer. The broad, lobed leaves appear after the flower. A magnificent woodland plant. Zones 7–9.

A. dracontium. Dragonroot. Eastern North America. Height 3 ft; spread 2 ft (90×60 cm). A green hoodlike spathe with a taillike flower spike is produced in spring followed by orange-red berries in late summer. A solitary, segmented leaf almost 1 ft (30 cm) long appears after the flower. Zones 3–9.

A. sikokianum. Asia. Height 18 in.; spread 18 in. (45×45 cm). A beautiful species with green or silver-green leaves and a dark-purple hooded spathe striped white. A desirable plant just coming into cultivation in the West. Zones 5–9.

A. triphyllum. Jack-in-the-pulpit. Eastern North America. Height 2–3 ft; spread 18 in. (60–90×45 cm). Common in woodlands of eastern North America with large, lobed leaves and a hooded spathe striped green and purple followed by scarlet berries in autumn. Variety ***stewardsonii*** has striping of green and white; 'Zebrinus' has a purple spathe striped with white. Zones 4–9.

ARMERIA

(Thrift)

Family: Plumbaginaceae

Dwarf evergreen perennials with linear leaves in dense rosettes and globular flower heads. Native to alpine meadows and maritime shores of temperate countries.

Cultivation: Grow in well-drained sandy soil in full sun. In highly fertile soil or in climates with hot and humid summers, the plants will often rot out in the center. If this happens, cut back hard to the ground to stimulate fresh growth. Remove the faded flower heads.

Landscape Use: Plant along a sunny border edge, rock garden, or seaside garden. Tolerant of sea salt spray.

Armeria maritima

Propagation: Divide and replant in spring or sow seeds in autumn.

A. juniperifolia (A. caespitosa). Spain. Height 2 in.; spread 12 in. (5×30 cm). A mound-forming plant with prickly, awl-shaped leaves about ½ in. (1.2 cm) long. Almost stalkless pink flowers appear in late spring and early summer. 'Alba' is a white cultivar, 'Rubra' is a cultivar with deeper-pink flowers. Zones 4–7.

A. maritima. Sea thrift. Europe. Height 6–12 in.; spread 12 in. (15–30×30 cm). A cushion plant with dark-green, glossy, and grassy leaves and round-headed pink or white flowers on 6-in. (15-cm) stems in late spring to early summer. There are a number of cultivars: 'Alba' has white flowers; 'Bloodstone,' blood-red flowers; 'Dusseldorf Pride,' rose-pink flowers; 'Laucheana,' deep rose-pink flowers; 'Vindictive,' dark almost purple-pink flowers. Zones 4–8.

A. pseudarmaria. Portugal. Height 1 ft; spread 1 ft (30×30 cm). Lance-shaped leaves 10 in. (25 cm) long appear in clumps with round flower heads of pink to white on stout stems in late spring to summer. 'Bees Ruby,' Height 18 in. (45 cm), has rose-carmine flowers; 'Royal Rose' has rose-pink flowers. Zones 4–8.

ARRHENATHERUM

(Striped Oat Grass)

Family: Graminae

A genus of six species native to the Mediterranean area. The plant is used for its foliage, and flowers are insignificant or nonexistent. The bases of the leaf stems are often swollen.

Cultivation: Grow in full sun to partial shade in average, well-drained soil. In areas of hot and humid summers this grass is susceptible to rust diseases and may turn unsightly; however, cutting to the ground in midsummer will produce good-looking foliage in autumn.

Landscape Use: Use as an edging plant or as a foliage foil against dark-green plants in the herbaceous border in spring and early summer.

Propagation: Divide in early spring.

A. elatius ssp. ***bulbosum*** 'Variegatum.' Striped oat grass. Europe. Height 12 in.; spread 8 in. (30×20 cm). A slow-growing, mound-forming grass with blue-green leaves and white stripes of variegation giving the overall effect of almost complete white foliage. It is at its best in spring, early summer, and autumn. In areas with hot summers it generally dies back and reappears in late summer when the night temperatures cool off. In mild areas the foliage remains semievergreen. Zones 4–8.

ARTEMISIA

(Wormwood, Sagebrush)

Family: Compositae

Artemisia 'Powis Castle'

Artemisia lactiflora

A large genus of annuals, herbaceous perennials, and shrubs, mostly aromatic and sun-loving. They are native to much of Europe, America, and Asia. The sagebrush of the American West is ***A. tridentata*** and ***A. arbuscula.*** In the garden representatives of this genus have been grown since Roman times. They are now used extensively as foliage plants, their gray or silver deeply cut, feathery leaves providing great textural quality to the border. The flowers, which are daisylike and tiny, are insignificant, except for one species. The name is derived from the goddess Artemis. The common name, wormwood, refers to herbalists' use of the plant to kill parasitic worms. Members of this genus have been used as herbs in medicine and magic for thousands of years.

Cultivation: Plant in well-drained to dry, light soil in full sun. Some varieties can be invasive, such as ***A. vulgaris,*** the chrysanthemum weed or mugwort, while others develop leaf and stem rot in hot and humid weather. If there are signs of rot, cut back hard in midsummer to produce good foliage for autumn.

Landscape Use: This genus contains some of the best of the silver foliage plants. Use in borders, rock gardens, and any sunny place as a foil for cool or bright colors or as a splash of brightness in a darker border.

Propagation: Divide and replant in spring. Take stem cuttings throughout the summer.

A. abrotanum. Southernwood. Europe. Height 3 ft; spread 18 in. (90×45 cm). A woody, bushy plant with feathery, threadlike, dark-green foliage and small heads of dull yellow flowers in summer. It is intoxicatingly aromatic, with a fruity, nose-wrinkling scent. Grow in poor soil and prune hard annually in spring. Zones 6–9.

A. absinthium. Wormwood. Europe. Height 3–4 ft; spread 2 ft (90–120×60). A coarse, shrubby plant with aromatic, hairy, silver-gray, deeply divided leaves with tiny gray flowers in summer. Used in making the liqueur absinthe. 'Huntington Gardens,' height 4 ft (120 cm), is a form with finely divided silver leaves persisting well into the winter; 'Lambrook Silver,' height 3 ft (90 cm), is an excellent variety with glossy, finely divided silver foliage. Hybrid 'Powis Castle,' height 3 ft; spread 2 ft (90×60 cm), is perhaps the best of the garden forms with feathery, sparkling silver foliage on woolly stems.

A. lactiflora. White mugwort. Asia. Height 4–6 ft; spread 2 ft (120–180×60 cm). Unlike the rest of the genus, this species is grown for its sprays of creamy white fragrant flowers, which appear in late summer. A strong-growing plant with lobed, dark-green, deeply cut leaves, it needs richer soil than most and will tolerate partial shade. Needs protection in areas where deer are a problem. Zones 3–9.

A. ludoviciana. White sagebrush. Western North America. Height 3 ft; spread 2 ft (90×60 cm). An attractive plant with aromatic, silver-gray, jagged-edged, lance-shaped leaves about 4 in. (10 cm) long on white, woolly stems; insignificant white flowers in summer. Often invasive, it spreads by underground rhizomes and may appear among neighboring plants in spring. Reacts poorly both to overly rich and moist soil and to hot and humid summers, when it may develop leaf rust and root rot. Responds well to a midsummer haircut. 'Silver Frost': height 18 in. (45 cm), gray-green foliage with a silvery underside; 'Silver King': height 2 ft (60 cm), silvery white foliage; 'Silver Queen': height 2 ft (60 cm), broader and more hairy leaves than its royal companion. Zones 4–8.

A. pontica. Roman wormwood. Europe. Height 2 ft; spread 18 in. (60×45 cm). Rapidly spreading by creeping rhizomes, this aromatic plant has white, deeply cut, lacy leaves and spikes of whitish yellow flowers in summer. Used in making vermouth, which derives its name from the German *Wermuth,* "preserver of the mind," for its supposed virtues as a mental restorative. This species is highly invasive in ordinary soil. Zones 4–9.

A. schmidtiana. Height 1 ft; spread 18 in. (30×45 cm). An edging plant or groundcover for poor, dry soil. Notable for its hummocks of silky, filigreed silver foliage, it frequently develops an ugly bald spot in the center when grown in anything but lean soil. Cut back hard for late summer refoliation. 'Silver Mound' (Nana) is a widely grown, low-growing cultivar reaching a height of about 4 in. (10 cm). Zones 5–8.

A. stelleriana. Beach wormwood, dusty miller. Eastern North America, Asia. Height 2 ft; spread 3 ft (60×90 cm). A front-of-the-border, spreading, carpeting plant with nonaromatic, lobed, white-felted leaves up to 4 in. (10 cm) long and tiny, dingy yellow flowers on gray stems in summer. Suffers more from "summer humidity rot" than many other species; it is not a good plant for hot and humid climates. Zones 3–8.

ARUNCUS

(Goatsbeard)

FAMILY: Rosaceae

A small genus of about 12 species notable for their feathery flowers in early summer. The long-stalked leaves are alternate and divided into many-toothed, egg-shaped to oblong, lance-shaped leaflets looking very much like ***Astilbe.***

CULTIVATION: Plant in partial shade in moist, rich soil. Remove the faded flower heads.

LANDSCAPE USE: Excellent, easily cultivated border plants. The larger species should be planted at the back of a border, along streams, or as a pondside plant. As the roots run deep, plant in a suitable site and leave alone for many years.

PROPAGATION: Divide and replant in autumn or spring.

A. aethusifolius. Korea. Height 12 in.; spread 12 in. (30 × 30 cm). A charming dwarf ***Astilbe***-like plant with deeply divided, olive-green ferny foliage and small, creamy white spires standing 6 in. (15 cm) above the foliage in summer. Grows well in full sun or shade. Useful as a groundcover or in the front of a shrub border. Hybrids between this species and ***A. dioicus*** are now coming into cultivation. They have the same creamy white flowers but grow to a height of 2–4 ft (60–120 cm). Zones 5–9.

A. dioicus (A. sylvester). Goatsbeard. Height 6 ft; spread 4 ft (180 × 120 cm). The dark-green leaves are divided two to three times into toothed leaflets, giving this large plant a deceptively delicate appearance. The stems are almost woody. Plumes of fine, creamy white flowers are borne in panicles that can be 1 ft (30 cm) long. ***Aruncus*** has male and female flowers on separate plants. Although it is almost impossible to buy identified plants, the males are usually more feathery in appearance. Variety ***astilbioides*** is a dwarf growing to 2 ft (60 cm); 'Child of Two Worlds' ('Zweiweltkind') has drooping, pendulous white flowers. 'Kneiffii,' height 3 ft, is a more dainty form with leaves more finely divided. Zones 3–9.

ARUNDINARIA

(Bamboo)

FAMILY: Gramineae

Arundinaria viridi-strata

A large genus of rhizomatous, semievergreen, grasslike plants with cylindrical woody canes and sharp-pointed lanceolate leaves. Flowering is infrequent and, in certain species, is followed by the death of the whole plant. The bamboos are constantly undergoing revision by taxonomists, and even just a mention of the group is likely to cause fierce argument. Most species are too woody to qualify for this book; the two species described are just herbaceous enough.

CULTIVATION: Plant in spring in sun or partial shade in moist but well-drained soil. They are fairly invasive and should be contained.

LANDSCAPE USE: The smaller bamboos create a tropical and exotic effect when used either as specimen clumps or en masse. They are particularly effective near water.

PROPAGATION: Divide and replant the clumps in spring. Root cuttings taken in early spring will produce good-size plants in two years.

A. variegata (Pleioblastus variegatus). White-stripe bamboo. Japan. Height 2–3 ft, spread 2 ft (60–90 × 60 cm). A charming, spreading bamboo with slender, pale-green canes and 6-in.- (15-cm-) long leaves striped with white variegation. Zones 6–9.

A. viridi-striata (Pleioblastus auricoma). Japan. Height 2 ft; spread 2 ft or more (60 × 60 cm). Dark purplish green stems with leaves that are variably sized, up to 8 in. (20 cm) long, strikingly striped green and yellow. Strongly invasive in light soils. Mulch for winter protection in cold areas. Afternoon shade is necessary in climates with hot summers. Zones 5–9.

ARUNDO

(Giant Reed)

FAMILY: Graminae

About six species of tall, upright, coarse reeds native to the tropics and subtropics as well as the temperate regions of the world. The blue-gray leaf blades are broad and linear on thick, woody stems that are topped by large plumes of bronze flowers. Known since ancient times, this grass grows along the banks of the Nile and the Dead Sea.

CULTIVATION: Grow in full sun in ordinary soil. Not generally invasive. Cut down to the ground in early winter.

LANDSCAPE USE: Dramatic plants either as single specimens or in small groups. Very effective reflected in water. Excellent autumn and winter effects from the straw-colored foliage. Good cut flower.

PROPAGATION: Divide in spring, or in autumn in areas of mild winters. A stem placed in water will produce shoots and roots that can be potted on.

Arundo donax

A. donax. Giant reed. Southern Europe. Height 14–18 ft; spread 6 ft (4.2–5.4 × 1.8 m). A dramatic, warm-season grass with blue-to-gray-green leaves 1–2 ft (30–60 cm) long on thick, bamboolike, woody stems that tend to lean outward. The stems, which can reach 16 ft (4.8 m), are topped by 2-ft (60-cm) bronze plumes that fade to silver in autumn, when the foliage turns a warm straw color. In subtropical areas the foliage is evergreen, but in northern parts the plant dies to the ground and may suffer winter damage at the limits of Zone 6. It grows to a much smaller height and rarely flowers in the cooler summers of Europe. 'Variegata' ('Versicolor'), height 8–10 ft (2.4–3.0 m), is a much less vigorous and less cold-tolerant variegated form, with creamy white striping, reliably hardy to Zones 7–9.

ASARUM

(Wild Ginger)

FAMILY: Aristolochiaceae

Asarum caudatum

Asarum hartwegii

A small genus of low-growing, rhizomatous, stemless plants with inconspicuous purple or brown pitcher-shaped flowers in mid- to late spring and attractive heart- or kidney-shaped leaves, some of which are evergreen. Native to woodland of North America and Asia. Some species formerly in the genus ***Asarum*** are not to be found under ***Hexastylis.*** The crushed rhizomes and leaves emit a gingerlike scent, hence the common name, although true ginger is a member of the tropical genus ***Zingiberaceae.***

CULTIVATION: Grow in acid, moist but well-drained soil, rich in organic matter in a shaded site. It will quickly die out in soil that is too dry.

LANDSCAPE USE: European ginger makes a good, spreading evergreen groundcover, while other species are of value as edging plants for shady areas or for textural interest in the woodland garden.

PROPAGATION: Divide in spring. Sow seeds in autumn and keep cold over winter. Grow seedlings for two years before planting in a permanent location.

A. canadense. Canadian snakeroot. Eastern North America. Height 8 in.; spread 12 in. (20×30 cm). A deciduous groundcover native to woodland from New Brunswick to North Carolina, with low tufts of dull green, hairy, heart-shaped leaves 2–7 in. (5–17.5 cm) across. The inconspicuous flowers are brown, bell-shaped, and hidden beneath the leaves. Zones 3–8.

A. caudatum. Western North America. Height 7 in.; spread 12 in. (17.5×30 cm). Dark-green and glossy, evergreen, heart-shaped leaves 2–6 in. (5–15 cm) across with hidden, reddish brown flowers in spring. Zones 4–8.

A. europaeum. European wild ginger. Europe. Height 6–10 in.; spread 12 in. (15–25×30 cm). An evergreen plant with dark-green, highly glossy, leathery, heart-shaped leaves 2–3 in. (5–7.5 cm) across with faintly marked veins. The pitcherlike brown flowers are borne beneath the foliage in spring. A valuable groundcover for shade. Zones 4–8.

A. hartwegii. Oregon and California. Height 8 in.; spread 12 in. (20×30 cm). An evergreen plant similar to ***A. caudatum*** except for the beautiful silvery-white mottling in the center of the heart-shaped, 4-in.- (10-cm-) wide leaves. Zones 6–8.

A. superbum. Asia. hybrid 12–18 in.; spread 18 in. (30–45×45 cm). A relatively recent introduction, this wonderful plant should rapidly become a favorite. It is an evergreen, mound-forming species with dark-green, heart-shaped leaves about 6 in. (15 cm) long and 4 in. (10 cm) wide. The leaves are irregularly mottled with silver-green. The insignificant brown flowers are produced beneath the foliage in spring. It is very similar to another Asian species, ***A. magnificum.*** Zones 6–8.

ASCLEPIAS

(Milkweed, Silkweed)

FAMILY: Asclepiadaceae

Asclepias tuberosa

A large genus of almost 200 species widely distributed over the northern hemisphere but concentrated in North America and Africa. The common name milkweed refers to the milky sap, while silkweed describes the soft white hairs attached to the seeds found in the spindle-shaped fruits. Most have deep, fleshy roots, mostly opposite lance-shaped leaves, and terminal umbels of crownlike flowers.

CULTIVATION: Grow in ordinary soil in full sun for best results. They are generally slow to come to life in spring, thus care should be taken to mark their position lest overzealous cultivation damage the crowns. Attractive to butterflies and good for long-lasting cut flowers.

LANDSCAPE USE: Effective plants for dry, sunny banks, hot herbaceous borders, or meadows.

PROPAGATION: As many species have deep taproots, deep digging is required during spring division to avoid damaging the roots. Sow seed in spring.

A. incarnata. Swamp milkweed. Eastern North America. Height 5 ft; spread 2 ft (150 × 60 cm). Commonly found growing in wet soils, this is a stout-stemmed perennial with alternate, linear, midgreen, pointed leaves 2–6 in. (5–15 cm) long and numerous crownlike pink flowers in late summer. Zones 2–9.

A. speciosa. Western North America. Height 3 ft; spread 18 in. (90 × 45 cm). Erect, woolly stems with oval leaves up to 8 in. (20 cm) long, green above and softly hairy underneath, and crowns of reddish purple flowers in summer. Zones 6–9.

A. syriaca. Common milkweed. North America. Height 3–5 ft; spread 3 ft (90–150 × 90 cm). An upright, clump-forming plant with egg-shaped leaves 8 in. (20 cm) long and drooping flower stalks bearing clusters of pink-purple flowers in summer. A favorite food source for a number of butterflies. Zones 4–9.

A. tuberosa. Butterfly weed. North America. Height 3 ft; spread 18 in. (90 × 45 cm). An attractive wildflower with spirals of lance-shaped leaves that are 2–6 in. (5–15) cm long, covered in short, stiff hairs. Tight clusters of showy, waxy, yellow to orange flowers are borne on downy stems in summer. The seed pods are long, pointed, and filled with silky white hairs. Best grown in dry sandy soils, this species is particularly attractive to butterflies. Zones 4–9.

ASPERULA

(Woodruff)

FAMILY: Rubiaceae

A genus of up to 200 species native to Europe, Asia, and Australia, some of which are suitable for rock gardens. They are spreading, mat-forming plants with square stems; whorled, divided leaves; and small, flat-topped flower heads in spring and summer. The white-flowering sweet woodruff is now listed under ***Galium.***

CULTIVATION: Grow in sun or partial shade in light, moist but well-drained soil. They generally need protection from winter wet and are uncomfortable in hot, humid climates.

Asperula tinctoria

LANDSCAPE USE: Pleasing rock-garden plants that are also useful as groundcovers under shrubs.

PROPAGATION: Divide in spring. Take cuttings of nonflowering shoots in spring.

A. gussonii. Greece. Height 6 in.; spread 12 in. (15 × 30 cm). Mats of slender stems with hairy gray leaves and clusters of salmon-pink, tubular flowers in spring. Should be protected from winter wet. Zones 5–8.

A. hirta. Pyrenees. Height 4 in.; spread 12 in. (10 × 30 cm). Spreading by underground runners, this species forms loose green cushions of whorled, narrow, pointed green leaves on square stems with masses of pink, starry flowers in summer. Zones 4–8.

A. lilaciflora. Mediterranean. Height 8 in.; spread 18 in. (20 × 45 cm). A dwarf, cushion-forming plant with dark-green, needlelike leaves and clusters of pink flowers. Zones 6–8.

A. tinctoria. Dyers woodruff. Height 12–20 in.; spread 18 in. (30–50 × 45 cm). A wiry-stemmed plant with reddish roots, hairless leaves in whorls of four to six, and clusters of white flowers in early summer. Zones 7–8.

ASPHODELINE

(Jacob's Rod)

FAMILY: Liliaceae

A small genus of plants native to the Mediterranean and Asia with linear leaves and candles of white or yellow flowers in early summer.

CULTIVATION: Grow in full sun in fertile well drained soil. It is usually best to plant Jacob's Rod in the fall.

LANDSCAPE USE: The tall yellow candles of the species described below are prominent in the herbaceous border but are also effective if grown in a group in the rock garden or above a dry wall.

PROPAGATION: Divide in early autumn or sow seed.

A. lutea. Jacob's Rod. Mediterranean. Height 3 ft; spread 1 ft (90 × 30 cm). A striking plant with gray-green linear leaves up to 10 in. (25 cm) long. The fragrant yellow flowers are starlike and appear in early to midsummer. 'Flore Pleno' has double flowers. Zones 6–8.

ASPHODELUS

(Asphodel)

FAMILY: Liliaceae

A small genus of about six species with basal triangular or linear leaves and dense cylindrical candles of white flowers in early summer. The name is derived from a Greek word meaning "scepter," a reference to the flowers.

CULTIVATION: Grow in well-drained fertile soil in full sun.

LANDSCAPE USE: With their stiff leaves and flower stems, ***Asphodels*** are perfect foils for the flat flowers of many of the taller daisies. Suitable for the wild garden or the border.

PROPAGATION: Sow seed or divide in early autumn.

A. albus. Southern Europe. Height 3–4 ft; spread 18 in. (90–120 × 45 cm). A clump-forming plant with linear leaves up to 2 ft (60 cm) long and stiff flower stems bearing white funnel-shaped flowers in early summer. Zones 5–8.

A. ramosus (A. cerasiferus) Europe, North Africa. Height 5 ft; spread 2 ft (150 × 60 cm). A vigorous plant for a warm site with stiff linear leaves and tall spikes of white or rarely pink flowers in early summer. Zones 7–9.

ASPLENIUM

(Spleenwort)

FAMILY: Polypodiaceae

A genus of about 600 species of ferns widely distributed throughout the world, many growing in tropical rain forests. Most cultivated kinds are tropical and in temperate regions are grown in containers or greenhouses; however, a number of hardy species are worthy plants for the garden. The leaves are usually evergreen, undivided, deeply cut or compound, with spore clusters arranged on each side of the midvein. The name spleenwort refers to its supposed properties of curing diseases of the spleen.

CULTIVATION: Plant between spring and autumn in partial shade in well-drained soil fortified with organic matter. Most species require acid soil, but some need neutral to alkaline conditions. They require plenty of water during the growing season but should be kept dry during the winter.

Landscape Use: Use as woodland foliage plants or in limestone pockets in the rock garden.

Propagation: Easily raised from fresh spores that ripen in mid- to late summer or by potting the small plantlets produced on the fronds of many species. Clump division in spring is also productive.

A. platyneuron. Ebony spleenwort. North America, South Africa. Height 6–12 in.; spread 8 in. (15–30 × 20 cm). An evergreen fern with creeping rhizomes. The deep-green, glossy fronds are 6-20 in. (15–50 cm) long and 1–2 in. (2.5–5 cm) wide, with dark midribs and 1-in.- (2.5-cm-) long leaflets forming a herringbone pattern. Zones 3–9.

A. ruta-muraria. Wall-rue spleenwort. North America, Europe. Height 6 in.; spread 3 in. (15 × 7.5 cm). Evergreen, bluish green, rounded-triangular leaves growing from mats of old leaf stalks. Needs lime. Zones 3–9.

A. trichomanes. Maidenhair spleenwort. North America, Europe, Asia. Height 6 in.; spread 3 in. (15 × 7.5 cm). A small, semievergreen fern with tapering, slender, dark-green leaves 8 in. (20 cm) long and ¾ in. (2 cm) wide, with ribbons of oval leaf segments on wiry, purple-brown stems. Found growing in limestone rocks. Zones 3–9.

Asplenium trichomanes

ASTER

(Michaelmas Daisy)

Family: Compositae

Aster nova-angliae 'Purple Dome'

A large genus of about 600 species predominantly native to the Americas. They range greatly in size and color but are generally sun-loving plants with daisylike flowers and slender and alternate leaves. They are strangely underused in the United States, whereas they are extremely popular in Europe in gardens. The name aster, Latin for "star," refers to the shape of the flower, which is composed of a central hub of disk flowers surrounded by colorful ray flowers.

Cultivation: Grow the garden forms in a sunny or lightly shaded location in well-drained fertile soil that does not dry out in late summer or remain too wet over winter. ***Asters*** do best in climates where the summers are cool and moist. Unless indicated by zone numbers, in areas colder than Zone 5, mulching for winter protection is advisable. Many of the taller ***Asters*** will need staking or pinching back in early summer to encourage branching and more compact growth. Many forms are susceptible to mildew and rust diseases, and a number are bred for resistance. Frequent, in some cases annual, division helps keep the plants healthy. Division is also needed when plants show obvious decline in vigor.

Landscape Use: The taller varieties are excellent late-summer-flowering plants for the herbaceous border. The smaller forms are used in the front of the border and for smaller gardens or in the rock garden. A number of species make fine woodland or meadow plants.

Propagation: Divide in spring. Many cultivars are very vigorous and require frequent division and replanting of small, healthy pieces from the outside of the clump.

A.* × *alpellus. Height 18 in.; spread 12 in. (45×30 cm). A hybrid between ***A. alpinus*** and ***A. amellus,*** the cultivar 'Triumph' is a tough, long-lasting plant with violet-blue flowers with a central yellow disk. Blooms from midsummer to frost. A rapid grower but not invasive. Zones 4–8.

A. alpinus. Europe, Asia. Height 10 in.; spread 18 in. (25×45 cm). A tufted plant with narrow, gray-green, spoon-shaped leaves and 1-in.- (2.5-cm-) wide blue to purple flowers with gold centers, carried singly on each stem in early summer. 'Albus' has white flowers and is less vigorous; 'Beechwood' has purple flowers; 'Goliath' has dark lavender flowers 3 in. (7.5 cm) wide. Good rock-garden plants. Zones 4–8.

A. amellus. Europe. Height 1–2 ft; spread 18 in. (30–60×45 cm). Grown in gardens since Roman times, this is a drought-tolerant species with rough gray-green leaves, 2 in. (5 cm) wide, on hairy, woody stems bearing clusters of 2-in.- (5-cm-) wide bluish lilac flowers with yellow centers in late summer. 'Brilliant' has bright-pink flowers; 'King George,' bright violet-blue flowers; 'Lady Hindlip,'

Aster praealtus

deep rose-pink blooms; 'Rudolph Goethe,' pale violet-blue blossoms; 'Sonia,' pink flowers; 'Violet Queen,' a dwarf form growing up to 18 in. (45 cm), has violet flowers. Zones 4–8.

A. divaricatus. White wood aster. North America. Height 3 ft; spread 2 ft (90×60 cm). Native to deciduous woodlands of eastern North America, this fall flowering wood aster has 7-in.- (17.50-cm-) long, variably shaped serrated leaves on wiry black stems and heads of 1-in. (2.5-cm) white daisies with brown centers. A common sight in the woodlands of Pennsylvania, it is a good plant for dry, light shade. Zones 4–8.

A. dumosus. North America. Height 4 ft; spread 18 in. (120×45 cm). A many-branched, late-flowering plant with narrow linear leaves about 4 in. (10 cm) long and clouds of tiny, yellow-centered white daisies in late summer and early autumn. Zones 3–8.

A. ericoides. Heath aster. North America. Height 3 ft; spread 1 ft (90×30 cm). Native to dry, open areas, this aster has sprawling, wiry stems with linear spear-shaped leaves and clouds of ½-in. (1.2-cm) white flowers in autumn. 'Blue Star' has white flowers tinged with blue; 'Ringdove' has white flowers tinged rose; 'White Heather' has white, yellow-centered daisies. Zones 5–8.

A.* × *frikartii. Height 2 ft; spread 12 in. (60×30 cm). A valuable hybrid between ***A. amellus*** and ***A. thompsonii*** with branching stems, dark-green, oblong leaves, and blue, yellow-eyed, 2-in.- (5-cm-) wide flowers in summer to autumn. There is considerable debate as to the difference between cultivars of ***A.*×*frikartii;*** in fact, it is almost impossible to tell which is which. It is highly questionable whether plants grown in the United States are the true cultivars originally introduced. Three, 'Wunder von Stafa,' 'Monch,' and 'Jungfrau,' are long-blooming cultivars with yellow-centered blue flowers growing to a height of 2–3 ft (60–90 cm) with a spread of 3 ft (90 cm). They are excellent perennials that deserve a bright spot in the garden. Another hybrid, 'Flora's Delight,' is a dwarf plant, height 18 in.; spread 12 in. (45 × 30 cm), with gray leaves and masses of light blue-lilac flowers in late summer. Zones 5–8.

A. laevis. Smooth aster. North America. Height 3 ft; spread 18 in. (90 × 45 cm). Unbranched stems, alternate, heart-shaped basal leaves turning to narrow, tapering leaves farther up the stem. The 1-in. (2.5-cm), mostly blue to pink or purple flowers are borne in open clusters over the upper third of the plant in midautumn. Native to dry, open woodland. Zones 4–8.

A. lateriflorus. North America. Height 4 ft; spread 2 ft (120 × 60 cm). A branching species with round basal leaves up to 6 in. (15 cm) long changing to narrow lance-shaped farther up the stem. The flowers, borne in clusters on one side of the stem, are clouds of half-in.- (1.2-cm-) wide white or pale-lilac daisies with deep-rose centers. 'Horizontalis' is a form with whitish flowers lying horizontally along the stem. Zones 4–8.

A. linariifolius. Bristly aster. North America. Height 2 ft; spread 12 in. (60 × 30 cm). A clump-forming plant with wiry, hairy stems with linear leaves 1½ in. (4 cm) long and loose clusters of 1-in. (2.5-cm) violet flowers in autumn. 'Purpureus' has dark-purple flowers. Zones 3–8.

A. linosyris. Goldilocks. Europe. Height 2 ft; spread 12 in. (60 × 30 cm). Dull gray-green, narrowly lance-shaped leaves, slender, hairless stems, and compact clusters of tiny, rayless yellow flowers in late summer. While a rather undistinguished plant, it does have value in areas with hot, dry summers. Zones 3–8.

A. novae-angliae. New England aster. North America. Height 5 ft; spread 2 ft (150 × 60 cm). A tough plant decorating much of the eastern half of North America; has upright, hairy stems, lance-shaped leaves, and variably colored but mostly purple flowers 1–2 in. (2.5–5 cm) wide in autumn. The range of flower color has given rise to some notable varieties for the garden. Most are prolifically flowering, tall growing, gangly plants that need either staking or pinching back early in the growing season. They are valuable late-flowering plants for the back of the herbaceous border. 'Alma Potschke': height 3½ ft (105 cm), vivid hot-pink blooms; 'Barr's Pink': height 3½ ft (105 cm); semi-double rose-pink flowers; 'Harrington's Pink': height 4 ft (120 cm), a well-known selection from Millard Harrington of Williamsburg, Iowa, is an excellent clear-pink flower; 'Honeysong Pink': height 3½ ft (105 cm), rich pink flowers with a lemon center; 'September Beauty': height 40 in. (100 cm), flowers of deep crimson; 'Treasurer': height 4 ft (120 cm), has masses of violet-blue flowers. Zones 5–8.

A. novi-belgi. New York aster. Eastern North America. Height 3–4 ft; spread 18 in. (90–120 × 45 cm). Named ***novi-belgi*** after "New Belgium," an early name for New York, this species is native not just to New York State but to much of eastern North America. Erect stems, mostly hairless with mid- to deep green, narrowly pointed leaves to 7 in. (17.5 cm) long, and clusters of blue-violet, sometimes pink or white flowers with yellow centers in autumn. There are many cultivated forms as well as the results of crossing the New York aster with smaller species to produce more compact plants. Many of them were bred in England, particularly by Ernest Ballard in the early part of the 20th century.

'Ada Ballard': height 3 ft (90 cm), mauve-blue flowers
'Alert': height 12 in. (30 cm), semidouble ruby-red flowers
'Alice Haslam': height 10 in. (25 cm), deep double-pink flowers
'Audrey': height 15 in. (37.5 cm), lavender-blue flowers
'Bonnie Blue': height 8 in. (20 cm), wisteria-blue flowers
'Bonningale White': height 3½ ft (105 cm), double white flowers
'Carnival': height 2 ft (60 cm), semidouble flowers of vivid cherry red
'Chequers': height 2 ft (60 cm), violet-purple flowers
'Coombe Margaret': height 3 ft (90 cm), semidouble, reddish pink flowers
'Crimson Brocade': height 3 ft (90 cm), crimson-red, semidouble flowers
'Eventide': height 3 ft (90 cm), semidouble purple flowers
'Little Pink Beauty': height 16 in. (40 cm), bright-pink blossoms
'Marie Ballard': height 30 in. (75 cm), large double flowers of powder blue

'Patricia Ballard': height 30 in. (75 cm), double rich pink flowers
'Peter Harrison': height 16 in. (40 cm), pink flowers
'Professor Kippenburg': height 12 in. (30 cm), masses of lavender-blue flowers
'Romany': height 8 in. (20 cm), rose-violet flowers
'Royal Opal': height 15 in. (37.5 cm), large light-blue flowers
'Royal Velvet': height 2 ft (60 cm), almost double violet-blue flowers
'Snowball': height 10 in. (25 cm), a mound-forming plant with small white flowers with yellow centers
'White Ladies': height 4 ft (120 cm), white flowers and dark-green foliage
'Winston Churchill': height 2½ ft (75 cm), ruby-red flowers.
Zones 4–8.

A. praealtus. North America. Height 5 ft; spread 2 ft (150 × 60 cm). A clump-forming plant with wiry, branching stems with narrow leaves to 5 in. (12.5 cm) long and dense sprays of 1-in.- (2.5-cm-) wide white daisies with yellow centers in autumn. Flowers well in dry conditions. Zones 4–8.

A. puniceus. Swamp aster. North America. Height 8 ft; spread 2 ft (270 cm × 60 cm). A robust plant native to swamps and wet fields. Tall red stems, narrowly oblong leaves, and an abundance of pale-lavender flowers in fall. A plant for the back of the border. Zones 2–8.

A. spathulifolius. Korea. Height 6–12 in.; spread 18 in. (15–30 × 45 cm). A low-growing, carpeting species with midgreen, spoon-shaped leaves and 2-in.- (5-cm-) wide, yellow-centered, pinkish white flowers in late summer. A relatively recent introduction from Korea, this species requires well-drained soil and is an excellent plant for the rock garden or dry stone wall. Zones 5–8.

A. spectabilis. Seaside aster. North America. Height 2 ft; spread 18 in. (60 × 45 cm). A spreading plant with elliptic leaves and violet, yellow-centered flowers 1½ in. (4 cm) wide on almost leafless stems. Not found in seaside areas but common in inland sandy, acid soils such as the Pine Barrens of New Jersey. Zones 4–8.

A. tartaricus. Asia. Height 6 ft; spread 2 ft (180 × 60 cm). The spoon-shaped basal leaves of this species can be up to 2 ft (60 cm) long, the upper leaves becoming increasingly smaller. Loose sprays of pinkish blue daisies are borne on sturdy stems in autumn. Zones 2–8.

A. thompsonii. Himalayas. Height 3 ft; spread 2 ft (90 × 60 cm). A long-blooming parent of *A.* × ***frikartii,*** with coarsely toothed, gray-green leaves and 2-in.- (5-cm-) wide, lilac-blue, long-petaled daisies in autumn. 'Nanus' grows to a height of about 18 in. (45 cm). Zones 5–8.

A. tongolensis. China. Height 15 in.; spread 12 in. (37.5 × 30 cm). A spreading plant with round, spatula-shaped, hairy, dark-green leaves up to 5 in. (12.5 cm) long and 3 in. (7.5 cm) wide. Mauve-blue, 2-in.- (5-cm-) wide flowers appear in summer. 'Bergarten' has lavender-blue, orange-centered flowers; 'Napsbury' has deep-blue flowers. Zones 5–8.

ASTILBE

(False Goat's Beard)

FAMILY: Saxifragaceae

A genus of about 25 species of attractive summer-flowering plants sometimes confused with ***Filipendula.*** The leaves are mostly divided into toothed or lobed leaflets often rich green or bronze in color. The small flowers are arranged in large feathery panicles borne above the foliage. The name comes from the Greek *a,* "without," and *stilbe,* "brightness," and refers to the dullness of the leaves of some species.

CULTIVATION: ***Astilbes*** prefer a rich, cool, moist even boggy soil in partial shade. They can be grown in areas of full sun, but without sufficient moisture will suffer from leaf scorch and decreased vigor.

LANDSCAPE USE: Most ***Astilbes*** are excellent border plants; however, they look at their best in large masses in woodland or waterside gardens.

Propagation: Divide and replant in spring or autumn.

A.* × *arendsii. Height 2–4 ft; spread 2–3 ft (60–120 × 60–90 cm). A group of hybrids, raised in Germany, between ***A. davidii, A. astilboides, A. japonica,*** and ***A. thunbergii.*** This group contains plants with a great variety of sizes, colors, and flowering times. The following is only a partial list of varieties available to the gardener. (Early, mid, and late refer to their approximate flowering times in summer.)

'America': height 3 ft (90 cm), early-mid, light-pink flowers
'Amethyst': height 40 in. (100 cm), mid, lilac-violet flowers
'Anita Pfeifer': height 30 in. (75 cm), mid-late, light-pink flowers
'Avalanche': height 3 ft (90 cm), late, white flowers on arching stems
'Bonn': height 2 ft (60 cm), early, compact medium-pink flowers
'Bremen': height 2 ft (60 cm), early-mid, carmine-rose flowers
'Bressingham Beauty': height 3 ft (90 cm), mid, rich pink spires
'Bridal Veil': height 3 ft (90 cm), mid, excellent open sprays of white
'Cattleya': height 40 in. (100 cm), late, rose-pink flowers
'Cologne': height 30 in. (75 cm), early, bright-pink flowers
'Deutschland': height 20 in. (50 cm), early, intense white flowers
'Diamond': height 3 ft (90 cm), mid, dense white panicles

Astilboides Cattleya

'Erica': height 3 ft (90 cm), mid, long panicles of heather pink
'Etna': height 30 in. (75 cm), early-mid, deep-red flowers
'Europa': height 18 in. (45 cm), early, pale-pink plumes
'Fanal': height 30 in. (75 cm), early-mid, dark-crimson flowers
'Federsee': height 30 in. (75 cm), early-mid, rosy red plumes
'Fire': height 3 ft (90 cm), late, salmon-red flowers
'Glow' (Glut): height 3 ft (90 cm), late, deep ruby-red flowers
'Hyacinth': height 3 ft (90 cm), mid, lilac-pink flowers
'Irrlicht': height 30 in. (75 cm), mid, white flowers with a pale-pink blush
'Mainz': height 30 in. (75 cm), early-mid, lilac-lavender-pink flowers
'Peach Blossom': height 2 ft (60 cm), early-mid, large salmon-pink flowers
'Red Sentinel': height 30 in. (75 cm), mid, deep-red plumes
'Rheinland': height 30 in. (75 cm), early, bright clear pink
'Snowdrift': height 2 ft (60 cm), mid-late, pure-white flowers
'Spinell': height 3 ft (90 cm), mid, carmine-red flowers
'Venus': height 3 ft (90 cm), early-mid, narrow plumes of pale pink
'Vesuvius': height 3 ft (90 cm), early-mid, salmon-red flowers
'White Gloria': height 2 ft (60 cm), mid, dense creamy white flowers

Zones 5–8.

A. biternata. False goat's beard. Eastern North America. Height 5 ft; spread 3–4 ft (150 × 90–120 cm). The only ***Astilbe*** native to North America, this is a sadly neglected plant. It is similar to ***Aruncus dioicus*** but has 2-ft- (60-cm-) wide leaves divided into egg-shaped leaflets with the terminal leaflet three-lobed. Large panicles of white flowers appear in early summer. Zones 5–8.

A. chinensis. China. Height 2 ft; spread 18 in. (60 × 45 cm). Toothed, dark-green leaves deeply divided and hairy, with dense, woolly, narrow-branching plumes of white, pink, or purplish flowers in late summer. This plant is more widely available in its dwarf form 'Pumila,' which grows from 8–18 in. (20–45 cm) and has stiff, upright flowers of mauve-pink blooming in late summer. The variety 'Davidii' grows from 2–4 ft (60–120 cm) and has rose-purple flowers in midsummer.

'Finale' has looser panicles of pink flowers than the type and grows to a height of about 18 in. (45 cm). Zones 4–8.

A. glaberrima var. ***saxatalis.*** Asia. Height 6 in.; spread 4 in. (15 × 10 cm). A dwarf plant with divided, ferny foliage and 3-in.- (7.5-cm-) long spikes of cream or pink flowers in mid- to late summer. Zones 4–8.

A. rivularis. Nepal, China. Height 6 ft; spread 4 ft (180 × 120 cm). A plant more interesting for its foliage than for its flowers. It is a creeping plant with 3-in.- (7.5-cm-) long, deeply divided leaves growing up on the stem and large panicles of greenish white flowers in summer. Zones 6–8.

A. simplicifolia. Japan. Height 6–8 in.; spread 8 in. (15–20 × 20 cm). Midgreen, often tinged bronze, deeply divided, egg-shaped leaves up to 3 in. (7.5 cm) long. Tiny pink or white flowers are borne in tight 4-in. (10-cm) arching panicles in late summer. A number of crosses with ***A.* × *arendsii*** or ***A* × *rosea*** have given rise to a group of hybrids represented by the following: 'Atrorosea': height 18 in. (45 cm), deep pink arching plumes; 'Gnome': height 6 in. (15 cm), dense spikes of pink flowers; 'Serenade': height 18 in. (45 cm), clear-pink feathery spikes; 'Sprite': height 12 in. (30 cm), shell-pink flowers with bronze foliage; 'William Buchanan': height 18 in. (45 cm), light-pink flowers and glossy, bronze foliage. Zones 4–8.

A. taquetii. China. Height 4 ft; spread 3 ft (120 × 90 cm). A late-summer-flowering plant with strong stems, rounded, crinkled leaves, and spikes of rosy purple flowers. 'Superba' is a commonly available cultivar with mahogany-red stems and bright rosy purple flowers. Zones 4–8.

A. thunbergii. Japan. Height 2 ft; spread 18 in. (60 × 45 cm). Rounded, hairy leaves 3 in. (7.5 cm) long and arching, open panicles of white flowers that become pink in midsummer. A hybrid, 'Ostrich Plume,' height 3 ft (90 cm), has drooping flowers of coral pink. Zones 4–8.

ASTILBOIDES

FAMILY: Saxifragaceae

One species formerly listed as ***Rodgersia tabularis,*** a name with which it is still associated. It differs from ***Rodgersia*** in having undivided, round leaves and ***Astilbe***-like panicles of white flowers.

CULTIVATION: Grow in a mild climate in moist soil in full sun or partial shade. Not a plant for areas with hot summers.

LANDSCAPE USE: A dramatic foliage plant for the bog garden or herbaceous border.

PROPAGATION: Divide in spring.

A. tabularis. China, Korea. Height 3 ft; spread 3 ft (90 × 90 cm). A clump-forming plant with bright-green, round, umbrellalike, shallow-lobbed leaves up to 2 ft (60 cm) across. In summer 9-in.- (22.5-cm-) long panicles of creamy white flowers are produced. Zones 5–7.

Astilbe biternata

ASTRANTIA

(Masterwort)

Family: Umbelliferae

Astrantia major

A genus of about nine species of hardy perennials with flowers of subtle beauty. In general, the leaves are hand-shaped with toothed margins, the stems are wiry and branching, and the flowers are delicate and starlike, surrounded by collars of thistle-like leaves (bracts) in summer. The generic name is an allusion to the star-shaped flowers.

Cultivation: Plant in humus-rich, moist but well-drained soil in sun to partial shade. They can be grown in full sun if the soil remains moist. More vigorous in climates with cooler summers, they are not plants for hot climates. The taller species may need staking.

Landscape Use: Wonderful additions to the herbaceous border and streamside garden; also good for cutting. The individual flowers have a lacy beauty that is seen to best effect if the plants are placed close to a path.

Propagation: Divide and replant in spring or fall. Sow seeds in autumn, plant in a nursery bed the following summer.

A. carniolica. Lesser masterwort. Europe. Height 1 ft; spread 6 in. (30× 15 cm). A clump-forming plant with basal leaves divided into five-toothed segments. The flowers are white-centered and surrounded by short green-and-pink bracts. 'Rubra' has maroon flower heads. Similar to ***A. major*** but smaller. Zones 5–7.

A. major. Great nasterwort. Europe. Height 2 ft; spread 18 in. (60 × 45 cm). Clumps of palm-shaped, toothed, five-lobed basal leaves and wiry stems ending in clusters of whitish flowers tinged pink and green. Blooms in early summer, stops in the heat of midsummer, and resumes blooming in autumn. Variety ***involucrata*** is a form with a larger collar of greenish bracts around the flower cluster and is often listed as either 'Shaggy' or 'Margery Fish.' 'Moira Reid' has larger, starry bracts. 'Rubra' or 'Rosea' has rosy pink flowers. 'Sunningdale Variegated' has leaves striped cream and yellow. Zones 5–7.

A. maxima. Europe. Height 2 ft; spread 1 ft (60 × 30 cm). Noticeably different from ***A. major*** in that the leaves are divided into three rather than five lobes. The starry flowers are dull pink with pale green on the outside, blooming once in summer. Zones 5–7.

A. minor. Europe. Height 6–9 in.; spread 4 in. (15–22.5 × 10 cm). Sharply toothed leaves divided into seven to nine segments. The small flowers are white with a white collar. Zones 5–7.

ATHYRIUM

(Lady Fern)

Family: Polypodiaceae

A large genus of mostly deciduous, shade-loving ferns that contain some very alluring species for the garden. They are similar to ***Asplenium*** and are sometimes incorrectly placed in the genus ***Polypodium.*** However, they are not evergreen and have distinctive new shoots (croziers) that are rounded to oblong and covered with dark-brown scales.

Cultivation: Grow in shade in humus-rich, neutral to acid soil that does not dry out. Apply compost or well-rotted manure in spring or summer.

Landscape Use: Grow in wild gardens with other ferns or in shady parts of the herbaceous border. Their delicate foliage is an attractive contrast to large-leaved perennials such as ***Hosta.***

Propagation: Divide clumps in spring or autumn or sow spores in late summer.

A. filix-femina. Lady fern. Asia, North America, Europe. Height 3 ft; spread 2 ft (90 × 60 cm). A very attractive, delicate fern with fresh green, lance-shaped deeply divided fronds 6–9 in. (15–22.5 cm) wide, giving a wonderfully lacy effect in spring and summer. The fronds continue to appear through the summer although they become tattered in early autumn. The variation in the fronds is considerable, and over 300 cultivars have been named. A few are 'Congestum Cristatum,' a dwarf form with crowded leaflets and a crest at the end of the frond; 'Glomeratum,' slender fronds with large crests at the end; 'Plumosum,' light-green fronds, deeply divided and feathery. Zones 4–9.

A. niponicum var. ***pictum.*** Japanese painted fern. China, Korea, Japan. Height 20 in.; spread 18 in. (50 × 45 cm). An unusual fern with multicolored, triangular fronds. They can reach a height of 20 in. (50cm) but are generally a little less. The fronds are about 8 in. (20 cm) in length, usually arching and divided, and are gray-green with a pink or wine-red blush in the center of the leaves. The color is stronger in light shade but may become washed out with too much sun. Zones 3–9.

A. pycnocarpon. Glade fern. North America. Height 30–48 in.; spread 2 ft (75–120 × 60 cm). A slowly spreading fern, native of moist woodland, with lance-shaped fronds of light green turning to dark green, with 20 to 40 pairs of leaflets arranged regularly on either side of the leaf axis. Needs lime. Zones 5–9.

AUBRIETA

(Rock Cress)

Family: Cruciferae

A genus of about 12 species of mat-forming alpine plants with soft, hairy leaves and masses of cross-shaped flowers mostly in shades of blue. Named after the French botanical artist Claude Aubriet (1668–1743).

Cultivation: Grow in a sunny site in well-drained, lime-rich, gravelly or rocky soil. Cut back hard after flowering to keep compact and encourage secondary bloom. They do best in cooler climates and perform poorly in warmer areas.

Landscape Use: Grow in crevices, rock walls, or as edging in a sunny border.

Propagation: Take cuttings in summer. Seed should be sown in late winter and plants put out in autumn. Self-collected seed will not come true to form.

Aubreita deltoidea

A. deltoidea. Europe, Asia Minor. Height 6–8 in.; spread 18 in. (15–20 × 45 cm). A mat-forming plant with gray-green, diamond- to spoon-shaped, hairy, toothed leaves and four-petaled flowers to ¾ in. (2 cm) wide in spring and again in late summer. 'Bob Sanders': height 10 in. (20 cm); large, double red-purple flowers; 'Dr. Mules': height 6 in. (15 cm), deep violet purple flowers; 'Purple Cascade': height 4 in. (10 cm), purple flowers; 'Red Carpet': height 4 in (10 cm), deep-red flowers; 'Variegata': height 4 in. (10 cm), golden green leaves and blue flowers; 'Whitewell Gem': height 8 in. (20 cm), violet-purple blooms. Zones 5–7.

AURINIA

(Basket of Gold)

FAMILY: Cruciferae

Aurinia saxatilis 'citrinum'

Aurinia saxatilis subsp. *orientale*

About seven species of yellow-flowered, sun-loving plants closely related to, and formerly in, the genus ***Alyssum.***

CULTIVATION: Grow in a sunny well-drained site. Prune back hard after flowering.

LANDSCAPE USE: Excellent rock-garden or edging plant. Looks best when allowed to hang over a rock edge.

PROPAGATION: Take stem cuttings in midsummer. Sow seed in spring, plant in autumn.

A. saxatilis. Basket of gold. Europe. Height 8–12 in.; spread 12 in. (20–30 × 30 cm). A mat-forming plant with long, gray, spoon-shaped basal leaves with smaller, lance-shaped leaves higher up the stem. The four-petaled flowers are borne in tight clusters in spring. 'Citrina': height 10 in. (25 cm), lemon-yellow flowers; 'Compactum': height 6 in. (15 cm), golden-yellow flowers; 'Dudley Neville': height 10 in. (25 cm), buff-colored flowers; 'Gold Dust': height 8 in (20 cm), bright yellow blossoms. Zones 4–7.

BALLOTA

Family: Labiatae

Ballota pseudo-dictamnus

About 35 species of woody-stemmed, sometimes aromatic, softly hairy perennials from the Mediterranean and Asia grown for their suedelike foliage rather than for flowers. The generic name comes form the Greek *ballo,* "to reject," and refers to cattle rejecting the black horehound. (***B. nigra***) because of its strong odor.

Cultivation: Grow in full sun in well-drained, poor soil. They are very susceptible to rotting from excess winter wet and may need the protection of a well-drained slope. In areas colder than Zone 7 they are generally not hardy and will need to be treated as annuals.

Landscape Use: Use as foliage plants in a sunny border, or rock garden or as a foil for brighter colors in containers. As they are not very hardy they should be grown against the shelter of a wall. The backdrop of a dark stone wall also accentuates their gray-green color.

Propagation: Take stem cuttings in mid- to late summer and plant the following spring.

B. acetabulosa. Greece. height 2 ft; spread 1 ft (60 × 30 cm). A woody, sprawling perennial with square stems; opposite, rounded, gray-green, woolly leaves up to 1½ in. (3.7 cm) wide; and minute mauve flowers borne in whorls in mid- to late summer. Zones 7–9.

B. pseudodictamnus. Crete. Height 12 in.; spread 18 in. (30 × 45 cm). Round, felt-covered leaves up to 1 in. (2.5 cm) wide slightly crinkled along the edges on felted, woody, square stems with insignificant pale-mauve flowers in late summer. This species differs from the above in having smaller, markedly whiter leaves. Zones 7–9.

BAPTISIA

(False Indigo)

Family: Leguminosae

Twenty-five species of magnificent, erect, branching perennials native to North America, with alternate leaves divided into three egg-shaped or oblong leaflets. Yellow, white, or blue pealike flowers are produced sometime between late spring and early summer. The common name refers to a dye extracted from ***B. tinctoria,*** while the generic name comes from the Greek for "to dye."

Baptisia australis

Cultivation: Plant in spring in full sun in a well-drained but not overly fertile soil. Taller plants may need staking. To encourage flowering, deadhead faded flowers before they set seed. This will remove the seed pods, which turn black in autumn and are quite ornamental.

Landscape Use: Good background plants for the herbaceous border.

Propagation: Sow seeds in spring and plant two years later.

B. alba. North America. Height 3 ft; spread 2 ft (90 × 60 cm). A wide-branching plant with smooth stems, stalked light-green leaves divided into three oblong leaflets, and spikes of white pealike flowers in early summer. Zones 5–9.

B. australis. North America. Height 3–4 ft; spread 2 ft (90–120 × 60 cm). A sturdy upright plant with gray-green stems and blue-green leaves divided into egg-shaped leaflets. Indigo-blue pealike flowers bloom for over a month in late spring. The flowers are followed by black, pendulous seed pods useful in flower arrangements. If there is such a thing as a low-maintenance perennial, this may be it; however, it may need staking. Zones 4–9.

B. leucophaea. North America. Height 16 in.; spread 18 in. (40 × 45 cm). A low-branching plant with spoon-shaped leaflets and creamy white flowers in early summer. Zones 5–9.

B. pendula. North America. Height 40 in.; spread 30 in. (75 × 50 cm). A white-flowering plant similar to ***B. australis.*** Gray-green stems and blue-gray leaves with spikes of white pealike flowers in late spring. Zones 5–9.

B. perfoliata. North America. Height 2 ft; spread 4 ft (60 × 120 cm). A low-growing, wide-branching, drought-resistant plant with the stem growing through the rounded gray-green, leathery leaves. Small yellow flowers are borne in the leaf axils in early summer. Zones 6–9.

B. tinctoria. False indigo. North America. Height 2 ft; spread 3 ft (60 × 90 cm). Another drought-resistant plant common in the eastern states. Bright-green, cloverlike leaves up to 1 in. (2.5 cm) long and small clusters of bright-yellow flowers in early summer. Zones 5–9.

BEGONIA

(Hardy Begonia)

Family: Begoniaceae

A genus of over 1,000 species of tropical plants used in temperate regions as bedding, container, and houseplants. The one species described below is hardy to Zone 6.

Cultivation: Grow in humus-rich, moist soil in partial shade. Provide a protective mulch over winter in Zone 6.

Landscape Use: A good border plant. An unusual addition to the dappled shade of a woodland or shady hill garden.

Propagation: Small bulbs formed in the leaf axils

Begonia grandis 'Alba'

should be stored in peat over winter and potted up and planted out to flower in autumn. Alternatively, transplant the self-sown seedlings in spring.

B. grandis. Hardy begonia. Asia. Height 2 ft; spread 1 ft (60 × 30 cm). Thick, glossy, large heart-shaped leaves, red underneath, mid-green above, with 1-in.- (2.5-cm-) wide, drooping pink flowers from reddish buds in late summer into autumn. The pink, three-winged ovary remains attractive into late autumn. 'Alba' has dull-white flowers. Zones 6–9.

BELLIS

(English Daisy)

Family: Compositae

A small genus of low-growing plants native to Europe. The common English daisy is a frequent weed in lawns, and much effort is spent in trying to eradicate it. The cultivated forms, although perennial, are often grown as biennials and are of some interest in the garden.

Cultivation: Plant in fertile soil in sun or partial shade. Daisies do not perform well in areas with hot and humid summers, preferring the cool climates of the British Isles and the Pacific Northwest. They may need the protection of a winter mulch in northern areas.

Landscape Use: Good plants for border edging, rock gardens or as formal bedding plants for spring display.

Propagation: Grow from seed sown in summer, planting in spring. Divide clumps in spring.

B. perennis. English daisy. Europe. Height 6 in.; spread 8 in. (15 × 20 cm). A clump-forming plant with spoon-shaped leaves up to 2 in. (5 cm) long with toothed edges. The flowers are borne on single stems and have a yellow disk surrounded by white, pink, or red ray flowers in spring. 'Dresden China' has light-pink double flowers; 'Monstrosa' has double dark-red flowers; 'White Pearl' has double white flowers. Zones 4–9.

B. rotundifolia. Europe. Height 6 in.; spread 8 in. (15 × 20 cm). Similar to ***B. perennis*** but with leaves more rounded and white flowers. 'Caerulescens' is a charming form with broad ray florets of a soft blue color. Zones 6–9.

BERGENIA

Family: Saxifragaceae

Named for Karl August von Bergen (1704–1760), a German professor of botany. An Asian genus of about 12 species mainly used for their effective evergreen foliage, with thick rhizomes, large shiny fleshy leaves, and bell- or cup-shaped pink or white flowers in spring.

Cultivation: Grow in any ordinary soil in sun or partial shade. Water during periods of drought. Remove the flower stems after blooming.

Landscape Use: Excellent groundcovers in the herbaceous border, as a large edging plant by a pathway or en masse under trees and shrubs. Many species have bronze-burnished leaves in late summer and autumn.

Propagation: Divide in spring by cutting into the fleshy rhizomes and planting deep.

B. ciliata. Pakistan. Height 12 in.; spread 18 in. (30 × 45 cm). Thick rhizomes and large rounded leaves up to 14 in. (35 cm) long, hairy on both sides, with clusters of white flowers turning to

Bergenia crassifolia

pink on 1-ft- (30-cm-) long stems in spring. ***B. ciliata*** var. ***ligulata*** is hairy on the leaf margins only and has white-tinged pink flowers in spring. The rhizomes of this species are hardy to Zone 5, but the foliage will be damaged and usually be deciduous in Zone 7 and colder. Zones 5–8.

B. cordifolia. Siberia. Height 18 in.; spread 2 ft (45 × 60 cm). Leaves up to 12 in. (30 cm) long that are evergreen, dark green, bronze tinged, round to heart-shaped with undulating saw-toothed edges. Pink or white flowers are borne on stems rising just above the foliage in spring with secondary flowering in late autumn. 'Purpurea' has large purplish leaves with magenta flowers on red stems 2 ft (60 cm) tall. Zones 4–8.

B. crassifolia. Siberia. Height 12 in.; spread 18 in. (30 × 45 cm). Rounded, spoon-shaped, hairless leaves up to 8 in. (20 cm) long and light-pink, saucer-shaped flowers in spring and autumn. Zones 2–8.

B. purpurascens. Asia. height 12 in.; spread 12 in. (30 × 30 cm). Elliptical, 10-in.- (25-cm-) long, dark-green leaves in summer that turn red in winter. Cup-shaped bright-pink flowers on red stems appear in spring. Zones 5–8.

B. stracheyi. Asia. Height 9 in.; spread 12 in. (22.5 × 30 cm). Rosettes of small, rounded leaves to 8 in. (20 cm) long with minute saw-toothed edges and numerous nodding pink flowers in spring. 'Alba' has white flowers. Zones 4–8.

A large number of hybrids, mostly bred in Germany, are crosses between the species mentioned above. A few of the finest are 'Bressingham White': height 12 in. (30 cm), pure white flowers; 'Evening Glow': height 10 in. (25 cm), semidouble deep magenta-crimson flowers; 'Morning Red': height 14 in. (35 cm), carmine-red flowers; 'Red Bloom': height 12 in. (30 cm), deep rose-red flowers; 'Silver Light': height 12 in. (30 cm), pure-white flowers developing a pink tinge; 'Sunningdale': height 18 in. (45 cm), deep reddish pink flowers. Zones 4–8.

BLECHNUM

(Water Fern)

FAMILY: Polypodiaceae

A large genus of over 200 species of mostly tropical evergreen and semievergreen ferns with young reddish fronds with leaf segments equally divided on either side of the midrib.

CULTIVATION: Grow in acid, humus-rich soil in dappled shade.

LANDSCAPE USE: Use under trees and shrubs in the wild or woodland garden.

PROPAGATION: Divide in spring or sow spores.

B. penna-marina. Australia, South America. Alpine water fern. Height 12 in.; spread 18 in. (30×45 cm). A fast-growing, creeping fern with divided and linear, dark-green fronds, the spore-bearing fronds upright, the sterile fronds lying prone. Zones 6–9.

B. spicant. Deer fern. North America, Europe. Height 2 ft; spread 12 in. (60×30 cm). An evergreen, creeping fern with sterile, leathery, and dark-green, glossy fronds about 30 in. (75 cm) long and 1–3 in. (2.5–7.5 cm) wide. Taller, more slender, spore-bearing fronds grow erect. Plant in light shade. Performs poorly in deep shade. Zones 4–8.

BOLTONIA

FAMILY: Compositae

About 10 species of hairless, leafy-stemmed, asterlike plants native to the central United States and eastern Asia. The leaves are alternate and narrow; the flower heads are small, daisylike, and usually borne in great profusion.

CULTIVATION: Grow in ordinary, well-drained soil in full sun. The taller species will need staking.

LANDSCAPE USE: Excellent flowering plants for the autumn border. One of the bets late-flowering plants for climates with hot summers.

PROPAGATION: Divide in spring or early autumn.

B. asteroides. North America. Height 7 ft; spread 4 ft (210×120 cm). A clump-forming plant with narrow, lance-shaped, and pointed gray-green leaves 5 in. (12.5 cm) long. Open panicles of starrywhite, lilac, or purple daisies appear in great profusion in autumn. Variety ***latisquama*** has denser flower clusters. 'Snowbank' is a great improvement on the species; it is only 4 ft (120 cm) tall and has masses of white flowers in late summer until hard frost. 'Pink Beauty,' a particularly good cultivar for the southern United States, is similar to 'Snowbank' but with light-pink flowers. The only disadvantage to these two cultivars is that they form rather stiff clumps with the lower stems bare. They should be grown behind a more leafy perennial that will hide the bare stems. Zones 3–8.

BOTRYCHIUM

(Rattlesnake Fern)

FAMILY: Ophioglossaceae

A genus of about 40 species of primitive, deciduous, leathery ferns many of which are native to North America.

CULTIVATION: Many members of this genus are difficult to grow because of their essential relationship with important fungi in the soil. The one species described below requires moist, slightly acid, woodland soil in open shade. Protect against slugs.

LANDSCAPE USE: A curious and attractive fern for the woodland.

Botrychium virginianum

Propagation: Divide in early spring or sow spores when ripe in mid- to late summer.

B. virginianum. Rattlesnake fern. North America. Height 6–30 in.; spread 12 in. (15–75 × 30 cm). A spreading fern with fleshy roots and triangular, deeply dissected, lacy fronds with an erect fertile stalk arising from the base of the sterile frond (an often large, finely divided leaf) like a flag on a pole. Rattlesnake fern forms its leaves underground in winter. In the spring the folded leaves push out of the soil and open when completely aboveground. One of the earliest of ferns to appear in spring. Zones 4–8.

BOYKINIA

Family: Saxifragaceae

About eight species of mound-forming plants native to mountains and woodlands of North America and Japan, with basal or alternate, round, lobed, or cleft leaves, and small, terminal clusters of white flowers in summer. Some species have been split into ***Telesonix*** and ***Peltoboykinia***. Named after Dr. Samuel Boykin of Georgia (1786–1846).

Cultivation: Grow in moist, acid soil in partial shade.

Landscape Use: Interesting but not greatly ornamental foliage plants for the woodland and wild garden or shady border.

Propagation: Divide in spring or sow seed in autumn.

B. aconitifolia. Eastern United States. Height 3 ft; spread 1 ft (90 × 30 cm). Mounds of nearly round or kidney-shaped leaves 2–6 in. (5–15 cm) wide are deeply cut into five to seven lobes. Stiff-branching stalks carry bell-shaped, yellow-eyed, creamy white flowers in summer. Zones 5–9.

BRIZA

(Quaking Grass)

Family: Graminae

Briza media

About 20 species of annual and perennial grasses with open panicles of attractive oatlike flower clusters. The species described below is a hardy perennial plant. Two other species, ***B. maxima*** and ***B. minor,*** are widely grown as ornamentals but are annuals.

CULTIVATION: Grow in well-drained, preferably poor soil in full sun. Tolerates drought.

LANDSCAPE USE: Plant en masse, on a rocky slope or in the cutting garden; the dried flowers are useful in arrangements.

PROPAGATION: Divide in spring or autumn or sow seed in spring.

B. media. Quaking grass. Europe, Asia. Height 2½ ft; spread 1 ft (75 × 30 cm). A tufted grass forming a clump about 16 in. (40 cm) high, with mid-green, slender leaf blades up to 4 in. (10 cm) long, green at first turning straw-colored by midsummer. The erect, 2-ft- (60-cm-) long flowering stems carry open panicles of heart-shaped spikelets up to ½ in. (1.2 cm) long in late spring and early summer. The flowers shake in the slightest breeze; hence the common name. This grass tends to look very tatty by summer and is best cut down at about 1 ft (30 cm) from the ground in midsummer. Tolerant of poorly drained, infertile soil. Zones 4–8.

BRUNNERA

(Siberian Bugloss)

FAMILY: Boraginaceae

Brunnera macrophylla

Three species of perennial plants native to western Siberia and the eastern Mediterranean, only one of which is important in the garden. The leaves are rounded, simple, and alternate on hairy stems carrying sprays of blue flowers in spring.

CULTIVATION: Grow in ordinary garden soil that does not dry out in summer. They do well in sun if the soil remains moist, but light shade is preferable.

LANDSCAPE USE: Excellent true-blue flowers and attractive foliage for the shady border or woodland walk. A good groundcover if not allowed to dry out in summer.

PROPAGATION: Easily divided in spring and autumn.

B. macrophylla. Siberia. Height 18 in.; spread 2 ft (45 × 60 cm). Clumps of heart-shaped, strongly veined, dull-green leaves 8 in. (20 cm) across with branched flower clusters of blue, forget-me-not-type flowers produced in spring. 'Dawson's White' ('Variegata') has green leaves variegated creamy white. It is more susceptible to drought than other forms. 'Hadspen Cream' has light-green leaves with cream-colored borders; 'Langtrees' has metallic silver spots on large leaves. Zones 3–9.

BUPHTHALMUM

(Oxeye)

FAMILY: Compositae

A small genus of vigorous, hardy plants native to Europe and Asia Minor. The name comes from the Greek *bous*, "ox," and *opthalmos*, "eye," referring to the appearance of the daisylike flower.

CULTIVATION: Easy to grow in moist but well-drained soil in full sun.

LANDSCAPE USE: Sun-loving daisies for the herbaceous border.

PROPAGATION: Divide in spring or autumn.

B. salicifolium. Willow-leaved oxeye. Europe. height 2 ft; spread 2 ft (60 × 60 cm). A clump-forming plant with lance-shaped leaves, smooth or slightly hairy to 7 in. (17.5 cm) long. The yellow daisies are 2 in. (5 cm) wide, one to each stem, blooming in summer. 'Golden Beauty' is a long-blooming cultivar flowering from mid- to late summer. Needs staking and may spread in good soil. Zones 6–9.

Buphthalmum salicifolium

BUPLEURUM

(Thoroughwax)

FAMILY: Umbelliferae

A large genus of about 100 species of weedy shrubs and herbaceous perennials from Europe and Asia. Those grown in gardens are not spectacular plants, but their Queen Anne's lace like flowers are useful foils for brighter plants.

CULTIVATION: Grow in any fertile soil in full sun.

LANDSCAPE USE: Restful plants for the border or, with the smaller species, the rock garden.

PROPAGATION: Divide in spring.

B. angulosum. Pyrenees. Height 12 in.; spread 8 in. (30 × 20 cm). A tufted plant with long, lance-shaped leaves and summer-blooming, sea-green, pincushion flowers surrounded by yellow bracts. Zones 5–9.

B. falcatum. Pyrenees. Height 3 ft; spread 2 ft (90 × 60 cm). Stiff, woody stems with linear to spoon-shaped leaves 8 in. (20 cm) long and tight heads of yellow flowers in summer. Zones 5–9.

B. ranunculoides. European Alps. Height 6–18 in.; spread 12 in. (15–45 × 30 cm). Narrow, linear leaves to 1½ in. (3.7 cm) long and umbels of yellow-green flowers in midsummer. Zones 5–9.

BUTOMUS

(Flowering Rush)

FAMILY: Butomaceae

A single species of aquatic plant native to Europe and Asia but naturalized in parts of eastern North America. The name comes from the Greek *bous,* "ox," and *temno,* "to cut," referring to the leaves being too sharp for cattle.

CULTIVATION: Grow in water 2–4 in. (5–10 cm) deep in a sunny location.

LANDSCAPE USE: A good water plant with strong architectural presence.

PROPAGATION: Divide and replant in spring.

B. umbellatus. Flowering rush, water gladiolus. Europe, Asia. Height 2–4 ft, spread 1 ft (60–120 × 30 cm). Swordlike leaves 2–3 ft (60–90 cm) long beginning bronze-purple, turning green in early summer. The rose-pink flowers are 1 in. (2.5 cm) across and are produced in summer. Zones 4–9.

CALAMAGROSTIS

(Reed Grass)

FAMILY: Graminae

A genus of about 120 tall ornamental reedlike perennials common to swampy soils. The generic name is derived from the Greek *calamos,* "reed," and *agrostis,* "grass." Those grown in gardens are elegant grasses with considerable architectural quality and flowering interest.

CULTIVATION: Grow in full sun in ordinary, well-drained soil. Although tolerant of partial shade, flowering decreases and the stems may not remain perfectly upright, Sometimes susceptible to foliage rust diseases. Cut down in early spring.

LANDSCAPE USE: Highly desirable vertical accent plants for use as single specimens or in a tightly planted mass.

PROPAGATION: Divide in spring or autumn.

Calamagrostis x *acutiflora* 'Stricta'

C.* × *acutiflora 'Stricta' (***C.* × *acutiflora*** 'Karl Foerster'). Feather reed grass. Europe. Height 6 ft; spread 2 ft (180 × 60 cm). A sterile hybrid between ***C. epigeios*** and ***C. arundinacea.*** It is the most upright of all the ornamental grasses, with finely pointed, dull, mid- to dark-green leaf blades up to 3 ft (90 cm) long and ½ in. (1.2 cm) wide. It is quick to leaf out in the spring, producing an erect clump of foliage up to 2½ ft (75 cm) high by mid- to late spring. In early summer the open, feathery inflorescence is purplish bronze; by mid- to late summer the inflorescence has tightened and the color has faded to light straw, remaining that way until midwinter. A cultivar under the name 'Karl Foerster' is widely sold in Europe and North America. It seems indistinguishable from ***C.* x *acutiflora*** 'Stricta.' Zones 5–9.

*C. **arundinacea*** var. ***brachytricha.*** Korean feather reed grass, foxtail grass. Korea. Height 4 ft; spread 18 in. (120×45 cm). A spreading, clump-forming grass collected in Korea and introduced into cultivation in the United States by Dr. R. W. Lighty of the Mount Cuba Center in Delaware. The upright, pointed, and narrow foliage reaches a height of 18–24 in. (45–60 cm) and angles away from the basal clump. This grass tolerates some shade and still flowers well starting in late summer to early autumn with a feathery, pinkish purple flower that quickly turns to a bright buff color in autumn. The flowers remain attractive until the New Year. Zones 5–9.

*C. **epigeios.*** Europe. Height 5 ft; spread 2 ft (150×60 cm). A tall, upright, clump-forming grass with narrow leaves and arching flower stems with feathery flowers starting purple-pink but quickly fading to buff. It is a rapidly spreading species notable for being one of the parents of *C.* x ***acutiflora*** 'Stricta.' Zones 5–9.

CALAMINTHA

(Calamint)

Family: Labiatae

Calamintha nepeta

A small genus of herbs natives to Europe and Asia. The name comes from the Greek *kalos,* "beautiful," and *minthe,* "mint." They are mostly aromatic plants with square stems, opposite leaves, and small, lipped flowers in summer.

Cultivation: Easy to grow in well-drained soil in full sun or light shade.

Landscape Use: Long-flowering plants for the border or sunny wild garden. Excellent foils for pink- or white-flowering plants.

Propagation: Sow seeds in early spring, take stem cuttings in summer, or divide in spring.

*C. **grandiflora.*** Europe. Height 9 in.; spread 18 in. (22.5×45 cm). A dense, bushy plant with light-green, toothed, hairy, egg-shaped, leaves about 2 in. (5 cm) long and pink, sagelike flowers in early summer. Zones 6–8.

*C. **nepeta.*** Europe. Height 1½ ft; spread 1 ft (45×30 cm). A charming plant with aromatic, grayish, and hairy, saw-toothed and egg-shaped leaves to ¾ in. (2 cm) long and masses of tiny light-blue flowers from late summer to midautumn. Subspecies ***nepeta*** is a more robust plant with mid-blue flowers. Zones 6–8.

CALANDRINIA

(Rock Purslane)

FAMILY: *Portulaceae*

A genus of about 150 species of mostly low-growing, spreading or trailing plants native to western North America and South America. They are short-lived, prolifically flowering plants that although strictly perennial are mostly cultivated as annuals. Named after a Swiss botanist, Jean Louis Calandrini (1703–1758).

CULTIVATION: Grow in well-drained, sandy soil in full sun. They are short-lived perennials often grown as annuals and biennials.

LANDSCAPE USE: Suitable for border edging or rock gardens.

PROPAGATION: Sow seeds in early spring. Seeds are produced very freely, and self-sown seedlings may be a welcome sight among older plants.

C. discolor. Chile. Height 18 in.; spread 1 ft (45 × 30 cm). A short-lived perennial with gray-green, spoon-shaped, fleshy leaves and 2-in.- (5-cm-) wide, bowl-shaped, light-purple flowers with yellow stamens in late summer. Zones 7–9.

C. umbellata. Peru. Height 6 in.; spread 12 in. (15 × 30 cm). Linear, softly hairy leaves on semi-trailing stems producing masses of ¾-in.- (2-cm-) wide, bowl-shaped, crimson-magenta flowers from midsummer to late autumn. Zones 7–9.

CALCEOLARIA

(Slipper Flower)

FAMILY: Scrophulariaceae.

Calceolaria darwinii

A large genus of over 500 species of annuals, biennials, perennials, and subshrubs almost exclusively native to South America. The name comes from the Latin *calceolus*, "slipper," a reference to the pouched flowers. Half-hardy annual ***Calceolaria*** were widely grown as bedding plants during the Victorian craze for formal gardening, but their popularity has since waned. Those few hardy or half-hardy perennials available are grown rarely except by enthusiasts.

CULTIVATION: Grow in a sheltered site in partial shade or full sun in a well-drained but moisture-retentive soil. Remove faded flower stems after flowering. They should be protected from winter damp. Most species are not hardy in temperate regions; those that can be grown are marginally hardy in Zones 8–9 except where indicated.

LANDSCAPE USE: Interesting rock-garden or border plants, they should be grown where the curiously shaped flowers can be seen to best advantage.

PROPAGATION: Sow the tiny seeds in early spring and plant in spring of the following year.

C. biflora. Chile. Height 12 in.; spread 18 in. (30×45 cm). Evergreen in mild areas with basal rosettes of rounded or spoon-shaped, pale-green leaves. Yellow flowers 1 in. (2.5 cm) long with the lower lip protruding and the underneath dotted red bloom in summer. Zones 8–10. *C.* x 'John Innes,' a hybrid between *C. **biflora*** and *C. **polyrrhiza,*** has 1½-in.- (3.7-cm-) wide, bright-yellow flowers, spotted reddish brown in late spring; grows to a height of 8 in. (20 cm); and is hardy in Zones 7–9.

C. darwinii. Magellan Straits. height 4 in.; spread 9 in. (10×22.5 cm). A short-lived, temperamental plant with extraordinary banded flowers. The dark-green leaves are egg-shaped to 3 in. (7.5 cm) long, toothed and wavy. The flowers, which open in early summer, are 1 in. (2.5 cm) long, chestnut brown with a pure-white horizontal band across the flower pouch. Zones 6–9.

C. polyrrhiza. Patagonia. Height 4 in.; spread 12 in. (10×30 cm). A dwarf, tufted perennial with crowded, basal, lance-shaped leaves and short, hairy stems with yellow flowers spotted purple, 1 in. (2.5 cm) long and blooming in summer. One of the hardiest species, grown with protection in Zones 6–9.

C. tenella. Chile. Height 4 in.; spread 12 in. (10×30 cm). A mat-forming, spreading species with egg-shaped, glossy leaves and bright-yellow flowers spotted orange inside, usually two or three to a stem, blooming sporadically throughout the summer. Zones 6–9.

CALLA

(Water-arum)

FAMILY: Araceae

One species of hardy plant common to bogs in the northern parts of North America. Not to be confused with the florist's calla lily, a species of ***Zantedeschia.***

CULTIVATION: Grow in constantly wet soil but not in deep or running water.

LANDSCAPE USE: An excellent plant for the bog garden and pond edge.

PROPAGATION: Divide in spring, root sections of the stem in mud in summer, or sow seeds in mud in autumn.

C. palustris. Water-arum. North America, Europe, Asia. Height 12 in.; spread 8 in. (30×20 cm). Fleshy stems and arrow-shaped leaves up to 6 in. (15 cm) long with a showy spathe, white on the inside, green on the outside, surrounding the yellow spadix, blooming in early summer and followed by bright-red berries in autumn. Zones 3–8.

CALLIRHOE

(Poppy-mallow)

FAMILY: Malvaceae

About eight species of annual and perennial herbaceous plants, one of which is a tough, long-blooming perennial for hot, dry sites. The leaves are alternate, hairy, hand-shaped and deeply divided into five to seven lobes. The brightly colored flowers bloom in summer.

CULTIVATION: Grow in hot, dry soil in full sun. It sounds too good to be true, but it is not. Evergreen in Zones 8–9.

LANDSCAPE USE: Excellent, bright plants for the hot rock garden, border front, or rock wall.

PROPAGATION: Sow seeds in spring, transplant before they get too large. Division is not easy because of the long taproot. Divide and plant young plants only. Take stem cuttings in early summer.

*C. **involucrata.*** Poppy mallow. Western United States, Mexico. Height 6–12 in.; spread 1–3 ft (15–30 × 30–90 cm). Hairy, divided foliage on prostrate stems with solitary, cup-shaped, red-purple flowers 2½ in. (6.2 cm) wide, blooming all summer. Zones 3–9.

Callirhoe involucrata

*C. **triangulata.*** Western United States. Height 2–3 ft; spread 2 ft (60–90 × 60 cm). A coarse, hairy perennial with triangular, unlobed, basal leaves and deep-purple, 2-in.- (5-cm-) wide flowers in summer. Zones 5–9.

CALTHA

(Marsh Marigold)

FAMILY: Ranunculaceae

Caltha palustris 'Flore Pleno'

A small genus of about 20 species of fleshy, water-loving plants in the buttercup family. Usually low-growing, they have alternate, hairless, rounded leaves and open-faced flowers of yellow, white, or pink.

Cultivation: Grow in sun or partial shade in neutral to acid soil in ground that is constantly moist. Species that grow in water should be planted 6 in. (15 cm) deep.

Landscape Use: Good, bright spring flowers for bog-, pond- or waterside. If kept moist they are also suitable for the herbaceous border.

Propagation: Divide and replant after flowering in early summer. Sow seeds in summer.

C. ***biflora.*** Northwestern North America. Height 10 in.; spread 12 in. (25 × 30 cm). A dwarf, tufted plant with heart-shaped leaves 2–3 in. (5–7.5 cm) wide and spring-blooming white flowers with a flush of blue on the petals. Zones 4–9.

C. ***leptosepala.*** Northwestern North America. Height 1 ft; spread 1 ft (30 × 30 cm). Heart-shaped, coarsely toothed leaves. Starlike white flowers with yellow centers appear in spring. Zones 4–8.

C. ***palustris.*** Marsh marigold. Europe. North America. Height 1 ft; spread 18 in. (30 × 45 cm). A wonderful wildflower with hollow stems and rounded, dark-green and shiny, heart-shaped leaves 3 to 4 in. (7.5–10 cm) wide. The 2-in.- (5-cm-) wide buttercuplike flowers are bright yellow, blooming in spring. Plant this species in water up to 6 in. (15 cm) deep or in constantly moist, boggy soil. 'Alba' is a less vigorous white-flowered form. 'Flore Pleno,' cultivated since the 17th century, has fully double, golden yellow flowers. Also sold under the name 'Multiplex' or 'Monstrosa.' Zones 3–9.

C. ***polypetala.*** Turkey. Height 2 ft; spread 3 ft (60 × 90 cm). A large, spreading plant with rounded leaves 10 in. (25 cm) across and 3-in. (7.5-cm) yellow flowers in early spring. Plant in water up to 6 in. (15 cm) in depth. Zones 5–9.

CAMPANULA

(Bellflower)

Family: Campanulaceae

A large, versatile genus of over 300 species of annuals, biennials, and herbaceous perennials. The name comes from the Latin *campana,* "bell," and refers to the predominantly bell-shaped flowers. ***Campanula*** is a genus with a great diversity of species, from 6-in. (15-cm), mat-forming rock-garden plants to 6-ft- (180-cm-) tall, erect border plants. Although the flowers are mostly bell-shaped, some species have open, starry flowers, while others are so pendulous as to make much of the flower hidden. The prevailing flower color is blue, although there are many forms with white, pink, or violet flowers. Except for a few alpine species they are easy to grow, attractive in leaf, and beautiful in flower.

Cultivation: Most members of this genus do well in any fertile, well-drained soil in sun or partial shade. In areas with hot summers partial shading, particularly in the afternoon, is important. Taller species may need staking and deadheading to encourage secondary flowering. Slugs and snails may be a problem.

Landscape Use: The range is so large that there probably is not anywhere, except deep shade, that bellflowers won't grow. The smaller species are excellent rock, wall, or paving plants, while the medium and taller forms are crucial to any herbaceous border. Every gardener should have ***Campanula*** growing somewhere.

Propagation: The seeds, which need light to germinate, should be sown in autumn or spring. Divide those species with more than a single crown in spring or take cuttings of nonflowering basal shoots in spring or summer. Divide every third or fourth year to keep under control.

C. ***alliariifolia.*** Asia Minor. Height 2–3 ft; spread 18 in. (60–90 × 45 cm). A clump-forming plant with erect, hairy stems branching at the top with heart-shaped, gray-green basal leaves about 10 in. (25 cm) long becoming smaller and narrower farther up the stem. The flowers are nodding white bells up to 2 in. (5 cm) long blooming the entire length of the stem in summer. 'Ivory Bells' has 20-in.- (50-cm-) long, arching stems with long-blooming, creamy white flowers. Grows best in average, well-drained soil in light shade. Zones 4–8.

C. barbata. Bearded bellflower. Europe. Height 18 in.; spread 12 in. (45 × 30 cm). A short-lived, tufted perennial with lance-shaped, roughly hairy leaves, and leafless stems carrying several nodding, bell-shaped blue to white flowers with long silky "beards" around the edge of the petals. Blooms in early summer. Requires a deep, rocky, acid soil. Zones 6–8.

Campanula lactiflora 'Prichard's Variety'

C. betulifolia. Armenia. Height 8 in.; spread 12 in. (20 × 30 cm). A low, tufted plant with toothed, glossy, wedge-shaped (birch leaf-shaped) leaves up to 1½ in. (4 cm) long; trailing stems radiating from the center of the plant bear small white or pinkish white flowers in summer. Zones 4–8.

C. bononiensis. Russian bellflower. Middle East. Height 3 ft; spread 1 ft (90 × 30 cm). Minutely saw-toothed, oval, pointed gray-green leaves 2–3 in. (5–7.5 cm) long becoming progressively smaller up on the stem with long spires of 60–100 pale blue starry bells in summer. Zones 3–8.

C. caespitosa. Europe. Height 8 in.; spread 12 in. (20 × 30 cm). A low, tufted plant with a deep taproot and serrated, egg-shaped leaves up to 1½ in. (4 cm) long. Loose clusters of nodding, blue bells are held above the leaves in summer. Zones 4–8.

C. carpatica. Carpathian bellflower. Carpathian Mountains. Height 9 in.; spread 1 ft (22.5 × 30 cm). A spreading plant with deeply toothed, triangular to egg-shaped, bright-green leaves up to 2 in. (5 cm) long. The bowl-shaped, upward-facing flowers are held erect on slender stems and are blue-lilac, 1–2 in. (2.5–6 cm) across, blooming in early to midsummer and intermittently throughout the summer. The type is not commonly seen; however, there are a number of named forms and hybrids that are excellent plants for edging or for the rock garden. 'Alba': height 9 in. (22.5 cm), white flowers; 'Blue Carpet,' deep blue flowers; 'Blue Clips,' height 6–8 in. (15–20 cm), blue flowers; 'Bressingham White': height 6 in. (15 cm), clear, white flowers; 'Jewel': height 9 in. (22.5 cm), dark-violet flowers; 'Wedgewood Blue': height 6 in. (15 cm), sky-blue flowers; 'Wedgewood White': height to 6 in. (15 cm), a white dwarf form; 'White Clips': height 6–8 in. (15–20 cm), a compact variety with white flowers. Prefers well-drained average soil in sun or partial shade. Quick to die out in soils that are too wet or are prone to drought. Divide annually in late summer to help it maintain its domed shape. Zones 3–8.

C. cochlearifolia. Fairy's thimble. Europe. Height 6 in.; spread 12 in. (15 × 30 cm). An easily grown, almost indestructible plant for the rockery, often confused with ***C. caespitosa*** and possibly a hybrid. It is a spreading plant with tiny, almost heart-shaped leaves and a profusion of small, ½-in- (1.2-cm-) long, dangling blooms on 4-in. (10-cm) stems held above the foliage, ranging in color from white to lavender and blue, flowering in mid- to late summer. 'R. B. Loder' is a form with semidouble pale-blue flowers. Grow in well-drained, gravelly soil. Zones 4–8.

C. garganica. Europe. Height 6 in.; spread 12 in. (15 × 30 cm). An aggressively spreading, mat-forming plant with thick rootstocks and rayed rosettes of pointed, ivy-shaped leaves with round-toothed edges. The trailing flower stems bear a profusion of white-eyed, pale-blue, or violet flowers from early to midsummer. 'W. H. Paine' has lavender-blue flowers. Zones 4–8.

C. glomerata. Clustered bellflower, twelve apostles. Europe. Height 1–3 ft; spread 2 ft (30–90 × 60 cm). An invasive, coarse, but useful plant that grows in almost any soil including one that remains wet. The rounded heart-shaped, alternate leaves are 4–5 in. (10–12.5 cm) long, becoming progressively oblong up on the stem. The bell-shaped, upward-facing blossoms are borne in tight clusters of up to a dozen violet flowers in early summer. The structure of the flower has given rise to its old common name of twelve apostles. 'Acaulis': height 6 in. (15 cm), a dwarf form, blue-violet flower clusters; 'Crown of Snow': height 2 ft (60 cm), white flowers; 'Dahurica': height 2 ft (60 cm), dark purple flowers; 'Joan Elliott': height 18 in. (45 cm), deep-violet flowers on a compact plant, flowers earlier than other varieties; 'Purple Pixie': height 1 ft (30 cm), violet purple flowers in late summer; 'Superba': height 2–3 ft (60–90 cm), rounded heads of deep violet-purple flowers, perhaps the best cultivar, although hot summer sun will often scorch the leaves. The cultivar 'Joan Elliott' seems particularly sensitive to hot weather. Frequent division keeps the plants from becoming weak. Zones 3–8.

C. lactiflora. Milky bellflower. Caucasus. Height 4–6 ft; spread 2 ft (120–180 × 60 cm). An outstanding border plant with strong stems; light-green, oval, and pointed leaves 5 in. (12.5 cm) long becoming smaller up on the stem, ending in masses of 1-in.- (2.5-cm-) wide, pale lavender-blue flowers throughout the summer. Likely to need staking. Flower color and height can be quite variable. The flowers can be of the palest blue to quite strong sky-blue. I have seen ***C. lactiflora*** reach heights of 6–8 ft (180–240 cm) in Ireland and barely 4 ft (120 cm) in Pennsylvania. 'Loddon Anna' has soft-pink flowers; 'Pouffe' is a dwarf, mounding form reaching 10 in. (25 cm) with lavender-blue flowers; 'Prichard's Variety' grows to a height of 3 ft (90 cm) and has violet-blue flowers; 'White Pouffe' is a dwarf form, height 10 in. (25 cm), with white flowers. Flowers best in full sun but can take light shade. Does not appear to suffer from sun scorch. Propagate by sowing seeds in situ or dividing in spring or autumn. Widely grown in Europe, ***C. lactiflora*** deserves to be more popular in North America. Zones 4–8.

C. latifolia. Giant bellflower. Europe, Asia. Height 4 ft; spread 2 ft (120 × 60 cm). A coarse perennial with hairy, heart-shaped basal leaves up to 6 in. (15 cm) long with saw-toothed margins. The large, tubular purple or dark-blue flowers, about 2 in. (5 cm) long and 1 in. (2.5 cm) wide, are borne on loose spikes 8 in. (20 cm) long in mid- to late summer. Variety ***macrantha*** has violet-purple flowers slightly larger than the species. 'Alba' is a good white-flowered form; 'Brantwood' has purple-violet flowers; 'Gloaming' has pale-mauve flowers. A fine plant for moist soil in light shade. Does not usually need staking. Zones 4–8.

C. latiloba (***C. persicifolia*** ssp. ***sessiliflora***). Europe, Africa, Asia. Height 3 ft; spread 18 in. (90 × 45 cm). A clump-forming plant with oval leaves and 3-ft- (90-cm-) long stems along which are produced stalkless, cup-shaped lavender flowers. 'Percy Piper' has deep-blue flowers. Zones 4–8.

C. persicifolia. Peach-leaf bellflower. Europe, Africa, Asia. Height 3 ft; spread 1 ft (90 × 30 cm). Probably the most widely grown bellflower. Vigorous, spreading mats with oblong, lance-shaped, mid-green and leathery leaves up to 8 in. (20 cm) in length with unbranched, wiry stems and stalked, nodding, outward-facing, saucer-shaped flowers up to 1 in. (2.5 cm) wide in shades of blue in early summer. Evergreen in mild areas. Although tolerant of a sunny position, ***C. persicifolia*** grows well in quite a bit of shade. 'Alba' is a pure-white form; 'Caerulea' has single blue flowers; 'Gardenia' is a double-flowered form with silvery blue flowers. Remove the spent flowers to stimulate repeat bloom later in the summer. Zones 3–8.

Campanula persicifolia

C. portenschlagiana. Dalmation bellflower. Europe. Height 6 in.; spread 2 ft (15 × 60 cm). An excellent mat-forming, early-summer- to early-autumn-blooming perennial with smooth, kidney-shaped, sharply toothed 1-in.- (2.5-cm-) wide, mid-green leaves and funnel-shaped lilac-blue flowers that almost obscure the foliage in summer. Pleasingly rampant in sun or, preferably, partial shade, its former name was *C. muralis,* referring to its preference for walls and rocks. Zones 4–8.

C. poscharskyana. Eastern Europe. Height 1 ft; spread 3 ft (30×90 cm). Another good plant for dry walls or rock gardens, this is an invasive perennial with rounded, sharply toothed leaves on long trailing stems covered in masses of starry lavender-blue flowers in midsummer. 'Alba' has pure-white flowers. Not to be confused with ***C. portenschlagiana,*** which is a more compact, less vigorous plant. Zones 3–8.

C. pyramidalis. Chimney bellflower. Europe. Height 5 ft; spread 2 ft (150×60 cm). Heart-shaped, rich-green basal leaves, erect stems with many side branches, and masses of blue or white bell-shaped flowers in pyramidal spikes throughout the summer. A short-lived species often grown as a biennial. Zones 7–8.

C. rapunculoides. Creeping bellflower. Europe. Height 3 ft; spread 2 ft (90×60 cm). A highly invasive plant for the large wild garden only. The leaves are narrow, lance-shaped to heart-shaped, on hairless stems. Single blue-violet bells are produced throughout the summer. Zones 3–8.

C. rotundifolia. Harebell. Europe, North America. Height 1–2 ft; spread 18 in. (30–60×45 cm). A deceptively delicate and graceful plant with a great deal of variation. It is a mat-forming plant with mid-green, heart-shaped basal leaves and narrower, linear leaves on the branched stems. The 1-in.- (2.5-cm-) long, pendulous blue bells appear from early to late summer. A more compact form, 'Olympica,' comes from the Olympic Mountains of Washington State. Self-sown seedlings may become a nuisance. Zones 3–8.

C. sarmatica. Caucasus. Height 18 in.; spread 12 in. (45×30 cm). A mounded species with gray-green, hairy leaves to 3 in. (7.5 cm) long and velvety lavender-blue blossoms in midsummer. Prefers full sun. Zones 3–8.

C. takesimana. Korea. height 2 ft; spread 18 in. (60×45 cm). Basal rosettes of roundly triangular toothed leaves 3 in. (7.5 cm) long and 3 in. (7.5 cm) wide at the base. Pale-lilac nodding bells with beautiful maroon spots inside the bell appear in summer. This floral attribute can be seen only if one lies on one's back and looks up into the flower. An enthusiastically invasive plant. Zone 6.

CAREX

(Sedge)

Family: Cyperaceae

A large genus of about 2,000 species of grasslike plants grown for their foliage rather than for their flowers. A few species are of ornamental value in the garden. The majority grow in dry soil, but the largest species grow in boggy ground, substantially contributing to the creation of peat moss and marsh hay. The stems are unjointed and triangular, with male and female flowers within the same flower spike.

Cultivation: Grow the ornamental species in a cool location in moist to well-drained soil in sun or partial shade.

Landscape Use: The smaller species are excellent edging plants, while the larger plants are worthwhile growing en masse or as specimens. Some species' ability to grow well in shade provides ornamental grasslike textures for the edge of the deciduous woodland.

Carex buchanii

Propagation: Divide in spring.

C. buchananii. Leather leaf sedge. New Zealand. Height 2 ft; spread 1 ft (60 × 30 cm). Stiff, narrow, and leathery triangular leaves of an attractive reddish bronze color, tapering into thin tips often curling at the ends. A good plant for contrasting with variegated ornamental grasses or large-leaved plants such as ***Hosta.*** Tolerates shade. Zones 6–8.

C. conica. Asia. Height 8–20 in.; spread 12 in. (20–50 × 30 cm). A tufted grasslike, semievergreen plant with flat, dark-green leaves up to 1½ in. (4 cm) wide. Several interesting dwarf forms are available: 'Hino-Kan-sugi': height 3–6 in. (7.5–15 cm), has white variegation along the narrow leaf margins; 'Marginata': height 2–4 in. (5–10 cm), has creamy yellow variegation along the leaf margins. Grow in shade in moist soil. Zones 5–8.

C. elata. Europe. Height 30 in.; spread 24 in. (75 × 60 cm). A tufted plant with arching, mid-green foliage common to wetlands of eastern England and central Ireland. Notable for its golden form, 'Aurea' ('Bowles' Golden'), which has narrow, drooping leaves that are a bright golden yellow with thin green edges. 'Knightshayes' is completely golden. Zones 6–8.

C. morrowi. Japanese sedge. Japan. Height 1–2 ft; spread 18 in. (30–60 × 45 cm). An evergreen, tufted plant with stiff, deep-green leaves ⅓ in. (0.8 cm) wide with a reddish basal sheaf forming a dense grasslike plant. 'Aureo-Variegata' grows to 18 in. (45 cm) tall and has a golden yellow stripe down the center of each leaf blade; 'Variegata' grows to 12 in. (30 cm) tall with a white stripe running down the leaf blade. All are good groundcovers for moist soil in partial shade. Zones 5–8.

C. nigra. Black sedge. Height 6–9 in.; spread 12 in. (15–22.5 × 30 cm). A tufted, spreading sedge with blue-green leaf blades and black flower stems and seed heads in late summer. Shade tolerant. Zones 4–8.

C. pendula. Drooping sedge. Europe, Asia. Height 2–4 ft; spread 2 ft (60–120 × 60 cm). A semievergreen, coarse plant with 18-in.- (45-cm-) long, arching, and leathery yellow-green leaves ½ in. (1.2 cm) wide, and delicate drooping stems of green flowers in late spring and throughout the summer. Native to damp woodlands. Zones 5–8.

CATANANCHE

(Cupid's Dart)

FAMILY: Compositae

Catananche caerulea

A small species of biennial or perennial plants native to the Mediterranean region. One species is commonly cultivated in the garden for its blue cornflowerlike flowers.

Cultivation: Grow in full sun in ordinary, well-drained soil.

Landscape Use: A good border plant when used en masse. Useful as a dried or cut flower.

Propagation: Divide in spring annually or sow seed in late winter.

C. caerulea. Cupid's dart. Southern Europe. Height 18 in.; spread 12 in. (45 × 30 cm). A drought-resistant plant with clumps of gray-green linear leaves up to 12 in. (30 cm) long and wiry flower stems bearing lavender-blue daisylike flowers 2 in. (5 cm) across enclosed in a papery sheath. 'Blue Giant' is a cultivar with pale-blue flowers. Variety ***alba*** has silvery-white flowers; var. ***major*** has lavender-blue flowers and grows to a height of 2 ft (60 cm). Zones 4–8.

CAULOPHYLLUM

(Blue Cohosh)

Family: Berberidaceae

Erect perennials with spreading rhizomes, one species native to North America, the other to east Asia. The North American species is a common native of deciduous woodlands from New Brunswick south to South Carolina and west to Missouri.

Cultivation: Grow in semishade in well-drained, woodland soil.

Landscape Use: An unusual plant for the shaded wild garden.

Propagation: Divide in spring or autumn.

C. thalictroides. Blue cohosh. North America. Height 2½ ft; spread 12 in. (75 × 30 cm). Upright, smooth bluish stems with one leaf toward the top of the stem, divided into three oval, toothed leaflets. The leaf color begins dark purple as it unfolds in spring, gradually turning to dark green in the summer. The yellow-green starry flowers are of little consequence except that deep-blue berries remain on the plant into late autumn. Zones 4–7.

CENTAUREA

(Knapweed)

Family: Compositae

A genus of about 500 species of annual, biennial, and perennial plants. The annual cornflower, or bachelor's buttons (***Centaurea cyanus***), is a member of this genus. The perennial species more commonly grown in gardens are noted for their long-blooming, thistlelike flowers. The name is derived from the centaur Chiron, who taught mankind the healing value of herbs.

Cultivation: Grow knapweeds in fertile, well-drained soil in a sunny site. Deadhead after flowering for secondary bloom. Stake the taller species.

Centaurea hypoleuca 'John Coutts'

Landscape Use: Useful long-flowering plants for the herbaceous border. Good cut flowers.

Propagation: Divide in spring or autumn. Sow seeds in early spring, planting out the following year.

C. cineraria. Dusty miller. Southern Europe. Height 3 ft; spread 2 ft (90 × 60 cm). Widely used in annual bedding schemes, the stems and leaves of this perennial plant are covered in tiny white hairs, giving the whole plant a white, felted appearance. The stems are erect and the leaves are deeply lobed, blunt at the ends. The purple flowers appear in summer but should be removed before the buds open to preserve the effect of the white foliage. Zones 6–8.

C. dealbata. Persian knapweed. Asia Minor. Height 3 ft; spread 2 ft (90 × 60 cm). Finely cut, light-green, stalked basal leaves up to 1½ in. (4 cm) long with leaves higher up the stem being more deeply cut and stalkless; both are covered in fine white hairs underneath. The pink-purple flowers are solitary, on stiff stems, and 2 to 3 in. (5–7.5 cm) across. Often needs staking. 'Steenbergii' is a cultivar with deep-rose flowers. Zones 4–8.

C. hypoleuca. Asia Minor. Height 2 ft; spread 18 in. (60 × 45 cm). The dark-green lower leaves are deeply divided and lobed while the upper leaves are oblong with round-toothed margins. The undersurface of the leaves is covered in white hairs. The flowers, which are 2–3 in. (5–7.5 cm) across, have white centers surrounded by rose-purple to pink ray flowers. 'John Coutts' is a superior plant often available commercially, with deep-rose flowers. Long lasting in bloom from late spring to midsummer with possible reblooming in autumn. Rarely needs staking. Zones 3–8.

C. macrocephala. Globe knapweed. Caucasus. Height 4 ft; spread 2 ft (120 × 60 cm). Hollow, hairy stems and 1-ft- (30-cm-) long leaves with undulating edges, elliptic and coarse to the touch. Large yellow flowers, 3–4 in. (7.5–10 cm) across, enclosed by rusty-colored bracts bloom in midsummer. A good cut or dried flower. Zones 4–8.

C. montana. Mountain knapweed. Europe. Height 18 in.; spread 2 ft (45 × 60 cm). An invasive plant with narrow, silvery leaves, the lower ones reaching 7 in. (17.5 cm) in length. Deep-blue star-shaped flowers with reddish thistlelike centers appear in early to midsummer. 'Alba' has white flowers; 'Carnea' has pink flowers. Requires division every two to three years. A good plant for areas with hot summers. Zones 4–8.

C. ruthenica. Europe. Height 3 ft; spread 18 in. (90 × 45 cm). Smooth, erect, branching stems and ferny, toothed, dark-green leaves, grayish underneath. Heads of lemon-yellow flowers with thistlelike centers appear in midsummer, making this an unusually attractive border plant. Zones 6–9.

C. simplicaulis. Armenia. Height 9 in.; spread 8 in. (22.5 × 20 cm). A good groundcover for the rock garden; dark-green, 5-in.- (12.5-cm-) long, thistlelike leaves with white underneath. Mauve flowers on 6-in. (15-cm) stems appear in early summer. Zones 7–9.

CENTRANTHUS

(Valerian)

Family: Valerianaceae

About 12 species of annual and perennial plants native to Europe. One species is widely grown in areas with cool summers, where it will often seed itself in walls and borders. The name comes from the Greek *kentron,* "spur," and *anthos,* "flower," in reference to the corolla having a spur at the base, distinguishing it from members of the genus ***Valeriana.***

Cultivation: Grow in well-drained, preferably poor soil that is neutral or alkaline, in full sun. Remove spent flowers to promote reblooming.

Landscape Use: Long-flowering plants for the sunny border or rock wall.

Propagation: Sow seeds in spring. Take cuttings of basal growth in early summer.

C. ruber. Red valerian. Europe. Height 2–3 ft; spread 18 in. (60–90 × 45 cm). A fleshy plant with oppo-

Centranthus ruber 'Coccineus'

site, bluish green, lance- to egg-shaped leaves about 4 in. (10 cm) long; almost woody stems; and 3-in. (7.5-cm) domed heads of fragrant starry, pink flowers in summer. Variety ***albus*** is a white-flowered form; var. ***coccineus*** has deep-red flowers; var. ***roseus*** has pink flowers. Zones 4–9.

CEPHALARIA

Family: Dipsacaceae

Coarse annual and perennial plants with round pincushionlike flower heads similar to that of ***Scabiosa***. The name refers to the Greek for "head." One species, ***C. gigantea,*** is often grown in gardens in Europe for its large flower heads of primrose yellow.

Cultivation: Grow in ordinary, well-drained soil in full sun to partial shade. Plant vigor is greatly reduced in areas with hot summers.

Landscape Use: The species more commonly grown are large plants for the back of the border. The pale-yellow flowers are of great interest in early summer.

Propagation: All species of Cephalaria divide in the spring.

C. alpina. Alps. Height 5 ft; spread 3 ft (150 × 90 cm). A coarse plant with ribbed stems, opposite, irregularly toothed leaves divided down to the midrib, with sulfur-yellow flowers 1¼ in. (3 cm) across in early summer. Zones 4–8.

C. gigantea. Caucasus. Height 6 ft; spread 4 ft (180 × 120 cm). Ribbed stems, hairy in the lower part, and dark-green leaves divided into oblong spear-shaped leaflets. Creamy-white, flat flower heads 2 in. (5 cm) across appear in early summer. Zones 3–8.

CERASTIUM

(Snow-in-Summer)

Family: Caryophyllaceae

Mat-forming or tufted plants with opposite leaves usually gray-white or gray-green. The name alludes to the shape of the seed pod and comes from the Greek *keras,* "horn." The common name is an indication of the value of its silvery foliage and starry white flowers.

CULTIVATION: Grow in well-drained, infertile soils in full sun. Shear hard after flowering.

LANDSCAPE USE: Good groundcovers for a sunny location. They tend to be invasive and should be kept away from more delicate rock garden plants.

PROPAGATION: Divide in spring or autumn; take cuttings in early summer.

C. ***alpinum.*** Europe. Height 4 in.; spread 10 in. (10 × 25 cm). A prostrate, spreading plant with trailing stems with ½-in- (1.2-cm-) long, gray-green oval leaves and white star-shaped flowers with deeply cut petals flowering sporadically from late spring to late summer. Zones 4–8.

C. ***biebersteinii.*** Crimea. Height 6 in.; spread 24 in. (15 × 60 cm). A spreading, mat-forming, and invasive species with linear, white, woolly leaves up to 2 in. (5 cm) long and white, cup-shaped flowers 1 in. (2.5 cm) across in late spring to early summer. Zones 3–8.

C. ***tomentosum.*** Snow-in-summer. Italy. Height 6 in.; spread 24 in. (15 × 60 cm). A mat-forming plant with 12-in.- (30-cm-) long trailing stems and silvery, linear to lance-shaped leaves up to 1 in. (2.5 cm) long. The starry flowers are no more than ¾ in. (2 cm) across and appear in mid- to late spring. Variety ***columnae*** grows to a height of 8 in. (20 cm) and is less rampant than the species; 'Yoyo' is a more compact form. This species is similar to ***C. biebersteinii*** except that the leaves are smaller and less silvery. Zones 3–8.

Cerastium tomentosum

CERATOSTIGMA

(Plumbago, Leadwort)

FAMILY: Plumbaginaceae

Eight species of perennials and shrubs native to India and China. Strictly speaking, those commonly grown in gardens are shrubs and subshrubs, but in climates of Zone 8 and colder they die down in winter, qualifying them, at least in this book, as honorary herbaceous perennials.

CULTIVATION: Grow in full sun or partial shade in ordinary, well-drained soil.

LANDSCAPE USE: The smaller species is a good groundcover for a large area, although it comes into leaf late in the spring. The larger species is a good small shrub for use as a specimen or en masse in a shrub border.

PROPAGATION: Divide in spring. Take stem cuttings in midsummer.

C. ***plumbaginoides.*** Leadwort. China. Height 12

in.; spread 18 in. (30 × 45 cm). A spreading, often invasive plant with woody stems and alternate, mid-green, hairless, strongly egg-shaped leaves up to 3½ in. (8.7 cm) long. The intense, dark-blue flowers are borne in small groups at the ends of the stems in summer to late autumn. Autumn color is often a wonderful bronze-red. Divide every few years if the clumps begin to thin out. *C. **plumbaginoides*** makes an excellent groundcover for areas planted with ***Crocus*** bulbs, coming into leaf as the bulbs fade. Zones 5–8.

*C. **willmottianum.*** China. Height 3 ft; spread 3 ft (90 × 90 cm). A half-hardy shrub often treated as a herbaceous plant. The stems are woody with dark-green, diamond-shaped leaves with bristly hair on both surfaces and rich-blue flowers in terminal clusters in midsummer. Often turns a good autumn color. Zones 7–8.

Ceratostigma plumbaginoides

CHAMAEMELUM

(Chamomile)

FAMILY: Compositae

Formerly placed in the genus ***Anthemis***, chamomile has been grown since ancient times. In the 13th century it was used both as a medicinal plant and as a lawnlike groundcover, reaching great popularity in the 17th century. The origin of the name chamomile is its distinct apple scent. The Greeks called the plant ground apple: *kamai,* "on the ground," and *melon,* "apple."

CULTIVATION: Grow in a sunny position in ordinary, well-drained soil.

LANDSCAPE USE: Chamomile makes an excellent edging plant for the border or for planting in paving. Chamomile lawns are interesting and aromatic alternatives to turf grass lawns.

PROPAGATION: Divide in spring. Take cuttings between late spring and late summer.

*C. **nobile.*** Chamomile. Europe. Height 9 in.; spread 24 in. (22.5 × 60 cm). An aromatic, mat-forming plant with downy, finely divided leaves up to 2 in. (5 cm) long. Tiny white daisies are borne on thin stems in summer. 'Flore Pleno' is a more ornamental form with double flowers. 'Treneague' is a dwarf, nonflowering form growing to 2 in. (5 cm) high and used in the making of chamomile lawns. To create a lawn, plant *C. **nobile*** 'Treneague' 6–9 in. (15–22.5 cm) apart in sandy soil in early spring. Zones 6–9.

CHASMANTHIUM

(Wild Oats)

FAMILY: Graminae

A small genus of grasses native to the eastern and southeastern United States. The leaf blades are flat, the flowers are drooping oatlike spikelets. Sometimes called sea oats, but this name belongs to a

Chasmanthium latifolium

related genus ***Uniola.*** One species of ***Chasmanthium*** is grown as an ornamental grass in gardens, useful for its tolerance of shade.

CULTIVATION: Grow in shade or full sun in rich, well-drained soil.

LANDSCAPE USE: Wild oats is an adaptable grass for use in shady as well as sunny areas. It is particularly effective near water, in naturalized areas, or as a spot plant in borders. The flowers are attractive in dried arrangements. Both the flowers and the foliage remain handsome in autumn and winter.

PROPAGATION: Divide in spring or autumn.

C. latifolium (Uniola latifolia). Wild oats. North America. Height 3–4 ft; spread 18 in. (90–120 × 45 cm). A woodland native of eastern North America with broad, flat leaf blades 1 in. (2.5 cm) wide and 9 in. (22.5 cm) long. Tall flower stems produce beautiful green, drooping spikelets in midsummer. The spikelets turn a bronze color in autumn and will remain on the plant throughout the winter until spring. The foliage also turns an attractive bronze color in autumn and becomes straw yellow in winter.

When grown in shade, ***C. latifolium*** foliage is dark green and the flowering stems will reach a height of 3–4 ft (90–120 cm). When grown in sun, the height is reduced to 2½ ft (75 cm) but the foliage is light green. Zones 5–8.

CHELONE

(Turtle-head)

FAMILY: Scrophulariaceae

About five species of perennial plants native to North America. The leaves are hairless, opposite, and serrated. The snapdragonlike flowers are pink, red, or white and resemble the head of a turtle with its mouth open.

CULTIVATION: Grow in partial shade to full sun in boggy soil.

LANDSCAPE USE: Useful summer-flowering plants for the semishaded border, bog garden, or waterside.

PROPAGATION: Divide in spring or autumn.

C. glabra. North America. Height 6 ft; spread 2 ft (180 × 60 cm). A clump-forming plant with lance-shaped leaves up to 6 in. (15 cm) long on sturdy stems with 1-in.- (2.5-cm-) long white or rose-tinted flowers in late summer. Zones 5–9.

C. lyonii. North America. Height 3 ft; spread 18 in. (90 × 45 cm). Dark-green, lance-shaped, serrated leaves up to 6 in. (15 cm) long and tight clusters of hooded rose-purple flowers in late summer to early autumn. Zones 4–9.

C. obliqua. North America. Height 3 ft; spread 18 in. (90 × 45 cm). A similar species to ***C. lyonii***, with deeper-pink flowers. Blooms in late summer. 'Alba' has white flowers; 'Praecox Nana,' height 12 in. (30 cm), has deep-pink flowers. Variety ***speciosa*** has larger, bright rose-pink flowers. Zones 3–9.

Chelone lyonii

CHRYSANTHEMUM

FAMILY: Compositae

Chrysanthemum pacificum

The genus ***Chrysanthemum*** has been largely dismantled and scattered into different genera. Perhaps only four or five species are still valid under the name; however, in this book the smaller genera are still listed under ***Chrysanthemum***, with their correct name in parentheses. For further information see ***Leucanthemum*** or ***Tanacetum***. The florist's chrysanthemum ***C. × morifolium*** is now listed under ***Dendranthema***. Although hardy, they are used essentially as annuals and are not included in this encyclopedia of perennials.

C. alpinum (Leucanthemopsis alpina). Europe. Height 6 in.; spread 12 in. (15 × 30 cm). A tufted plant with 2-in.- (5-cm-) long, deeply cut, white, woolly leaves and white, golden-eyed flowers up to 1½ in. (4 cm) long blooming in summer. A short-lived plant that requires full sun and well-drained soil. Zones 5–9.

C. frutescens (Argyranthemum frutescens). Marguerite. Canary Islands. Height 3 ft; spread 3 ft (90 × 90 cm). Often grown from cuttings as an annual, this is a shrubby plant hardy only in Zones 9–10. The deeply divided, pale-green, ferny leaves are 2–4 in. (5–10 cm) long. The solitary white flowers are borne in great profusion throughout the summer. There are pink and yellow forms. 'Chrysaster,' the Boston yellow-daisy, is a cultivar with yellow flowers. Grow in full sun in moist but well-drained soil. Zones 9–10.

C. nipponicum. (Nipponanthemum nipponicum). Japan. Height 2 ft; spread 2 ft (60 × 60 cm). A plant useful for its late-flowering habit, this daisy has thick, almost succulent, oblong to spoon-shaped, dark-green leaves 2 to 3 in. (5–7.5 cm) long. The single flower heads of up to 3½-in.- (8.7-cm-) wide white daisies with yellow centers appear in mid- to late autumn. This species can quickly become overly woody, and propagation by taking stem cuttings every spring is advisable. Zones 5–9.

***C. pacificum* (*Leucanthemum pacificum*).** Japan. Height 2 ft; spread 18 in. (60×45 cm). A very attractive plant more useful for the ornamental qualities of its foliage than for the display of its flowers. The leaves are spoon-shaped, roundly lobed, mid-green above, white woolly underneath, with the white underside creating an elegant silvery edge to the leaf margin. The small, rayless yellow flowers are borne on branched flower heads in mid- to late autumn. Zones 6–9.

***C. serotinum* (*Leucanthemella serotina*).** Hungary. Height 6 ft; spread 2 ft (180×60 cm). An erect, bushy plant for the back of the border. The leaves are dark green, spear-shaped, coarsely toothed, up to 4 in. (10 cm) long. The large white daisies with yellow eyes appear in autumn. Zones 2–9.

***C. weyrichii* (*Dendranthema Weyrichii*).** Asia. Height 12 in; spread 12 in. (30×30 cm). A creeping plant with deep-green foliage, lower leaves with rounded blades, upper leaves pinately lobed. White, yellow-eyed daisies almost 2 in. (5 cm) wide appear in autumn. 'Pink Bomb' has pink flowers and grows to 10 in. (25 cm). 'White Bomb' grows to 12 in. (30 cm) and has white flowers faintly tinged pink. Zones 3–9.

C. rubellum* (*Dendranthema rubella*).** Asia. Height 18 in.; spread 18 in. (45×45 cm). Confusingly described as ***C. zawadskii var. ***latilobum***, it is more commonly found in the cultivar 'Clara Curtis,' which is a pleasing, pink-flowered form with deeply cut, lobed foliage. It is a pretty pink chrysanthemum that blooms in mid- to late summer. Zones 5–9.

CHRYSOGONUM

(Goldenstar)

FAMILY: Compositae

An excellent native American groundcover indigenous from Pennsylvania south to Florida. It inhabits sandy banks and deciduous woodland edges and is a useful plant for the edge of a woodland garden.

CULTIVATION: Grow in well-drained, fertile soil that does not become too dry or too wet, in partial shade to full sun. Occasionally suffers from mildew when grown in shade.

LANDSCAPE USE: A good long-flowering groundcover for the wild garden or sunny bank, its golden yellow flowers are sometimes hard to use in association with other colors except the various shades of green.

PROPAGATION: Divide in spring or autumn.

***C. virginianum*.** Goldenstar. Eastern United States. Height 6–10 in.; spread 12 in. (15–25×30 cm). A low-growing groundcover with dark-green, opposite, rounded triangular leaves with serrated edges.

Chrysogonum virginianum

Yellow five-rayed flowers 1 in. (2.5 cm) wide appear in spring with sporadic flowering reaching into late summer. The variety ***australe*** is more compact, growing to a height of 6 in. (15 cm). A number of cultivars have become available; at the time of writing, none appear sufficiently distinctive to merit attention. Zones 5–8.

CHRYSOPSIS

(Golden Aster)

FAMILY: Compositae

Approximately 30 species of spreading, late-summer-flowering annuals and perennials native to North America. The flowers are generally yellow and similar to ***Aster.*** While many of them are coarse plants, a few are of ornamental value for their tolerance of hot summers and their late-flowering brightness.

CULTIVATION: Grow in full sun in well-drained soil. The taller species will need staking or pinching back to avoid flopping.

LANDSCAPE USE: Coarse-textured yellow daisies for the summer border or dry meadow.

PROPAGATION: Easily divided in spring or autumn.

C. bakeri. North America. Height 12 in.; spread 18 in. (30 × 45 cm). A many-branched perennial with hairy stems and pointed, dark-green leaves to 2 in. (5 cm) long, and masses of golden ray flowers in mid- to late summer. Native from the Great Lakes, west to Idaho, and south to New Mexico. Zones 4–9.

C. mariana. Maryland golden aster. North America. Height 3 ft; spread 18 in. (90 × 45 cm). A semievergreen plant native to woodland clearings, with hairy stems and twisted, lance-shaped leaves; the lower ones are up to 9 in. (22.5 cm) long. Masses of bright-yellow flowers appear in late summer and continue into autumn. A good plant for hot, dry sites. Zones 4–9.

C. villosa. Hairy golden aster. North America. Height 3–6 ft; spread 2 ft (90–180 × 60 cm). A variable plant with coarse, woody, branched stems and lance-shaped leaves. Yellow daisylike flowers 1–1½ in. (2.5–4 cm) wide appear through late summer to autumn. 'Golden Sunshine' is a cultivar growing to a height of 6 ft (180 cm) with sprays of golden yellow flowers. Needs staking. Zones 4–9.

CIMICIFUGA

(Bugbane, Snakeroot)

FAMILY: Ranunculaceae

Cimicifuga simplex 'White Pearl'

Fifteen species of woodland plants with ferny leaves with three-toothed leaflets and spires of white bottlebrushlike flowers in summer and autumn. The generic name, from *cimex*, "bug," and *fugere*, "to repel," refers to the scented leaves of some species, which have been used as insect repellents.

Cultivation: Grow in woodland soil in partial shade. If grown in full sun, provide constantly moist soil. The tall flower stems may need staking.

Landscape Use: The tall white flowers are wonderful additions to the herbaceous border or woodland garden, particularly effective in combination with blue-leaved hostas, rodgersias, and other coarse-leaved plants.

Propagation: Divide in spring or autumn.

C. ***americana.*** American bugbane. North America. Height 2–4 ft; spread 2 ft (60–120 × 60 cm). A slender, branched plant with dark-green ferny leaves with pale undersides and 1–2-ft- (30–60-cm-) long spikes of creamy white flowers in late summer. Zones 3–8.

C. ***japonica.*** Japan. Height 3 ft; spread 18 in. (90 × 45 cm). An elegant plant with long-stemmed, shiny, lobed leaves and branched spikes of soft-white flowers in summer. The variety ***acerina*** has maple-like leaves that do not develop until the plant has been established for at least three years. Zones 5–8.

C. ***racemosa.*** Black cohosh. North America. Height 6–8 ft; spread 2 ft (180–240 × 60 cm). A clump-forming plant with toothed leaves, two to three times divided and 1–4 in. (2.5–10 cm) long, with fluffy white flower spikes on 3-ft (90-cm) stems in midsummer. A wonderful woodland plant. The variety ***cordifolia*** grows to 4–5 ft (120–150 cm) tall and has heart-shaped terminal leaflets. Zones 3–8.

C. ***ramosa.*** Japan. Height 5–6 ft; spread 2 ft (150–180 × 60 cm). Vigorous clumps of ferny foliage and stout stems with tapering spikes of feathery ivory-white flowers in early autumn. 'Atropurpurea' is a striking plant with purplish stems and leaves and white flower spikes. 'Brunette' has dark-purple leaves and pinkish white flowers. Zones 4–8.

C. ***simplex.*** Siberia, Japan. Height 3–4 ft; spread 2 ft (90–120 × 60 cm). The last of the bugbanes to flower with purplish stems, smooth, divided foliage, and white, slightly fragrant, bottlebrushlike flowers in late summer to midautumn. 'White Pearl' is an excellent form, with masses of bright-white flowers. One of the best plants for late display. It is an extraordinary sight when grown in large groups. Zones 3–8.

CLEMATIS

Family: Ranunculaceae

Clematis heracleifolia 'Wyevale'

Clematis recta

A large genus of about 200 species, the majority of which are woody climbing vines not included in this encyclopedia. There are a small number of nonclimbing herbaceous perennials that are of great value as ornamental plants for the garden.

CULTIVATION: Grow in a sunny position in fertile soil. The addition of lime to an acid soil may be beneficial. Mulch annually. Provide support for those species that are weak-stemmed.

LANDSCAPE USE: Because they are nonclimbing, these ***Clematis*** are fine plants for the herbaceous border.

PROPAGATION: Take basal cuttings in late spring. Carefully divide in spring.

C. heracleifolia. China. Height 3 ft; spread 4 ft (90 × 120 cm). A broadly growing plant with a woody base and dark-green, slightly hairy leaves divided into three leaflets. Scented blue-purple, tubular flowers up to 1 in. (2.5 cm) long are borne in axillary clusters in late summer. May need staking. The variety ***davidiana*** grows to 3½ ft (105 cm) and has violet-blue flowers slightly larger than the species. 'Crepescule' grows to 3 ft (90 cm) and has azure-blue flowers; 'Wyevale' is 3–4 ft (90–120 cm) high and has dark-blue flowers. Zones 4–9.

C. integrifolia. Europe. Height 2–5 ft; spread 4 ft (60–150 × 120 cm). A spreading rather than climbing ***Clematis*** that can be grown over the ground or with the support of sticks or another plant. The leaves are heavily veined, egg-shaped, up to 4 in. (10 cm) long, and widely spaced upon the stem. The solitary, nodding, bell-shaped flowers are borne at the end of the stems and are blue-purple, 1½ in. (4 cm) long, appearing in midsummer. The variety ***alba*** has white flowers. 'Hendersonii' has deep-blue flowers and grows to about 18 in. (45 cm) in height. Zones 3–9.

C. recta. Europe. Height 4 ft; spread 2 ft (120 × 60 cm). Almost a climber, this species has thin, wiry stems and leaves divided into five to nine leaflets. Clouds of white, scented, starry flowers appear in midsummer. A wonderful, foamy plant for the herbaceous border. Needs support. 'Purpurea' has white flowers but the foliage is reddish purple. Zones 3–9.

CLINTONIA

(Bride's Bonnet, Bead Lily)

FAMILY: Liliaceae

Clintonia borealis

A small genus of woodland plants native to North America and Asia. Named for De Witt Clinton (1769–1828), a former governor of the State of New York. They are low-growing plants with tufted, broad, shining leaves a little like lily-of-the-valley, with greenish white or rose flowers.

CULTIVATION: Grow in light, lime-free woodland soil in partial shade.

LANDSCAPE USE: Interesting spring-flowering plants for the woodland garden.

PROPAGATION: Divide the rhizomes in the spring or sow seed in autumn.

C. andrewsiana. California. Height 18 in.; spread 12 in. (45×30 cm). The most ornamental of the genus, with five to six broadly elliptic, glossy leaves 6–10 in. (15–25 cm) long and small, bell-like, rose-colored flowers clustered on the end of the stems in early summer. Deep-blue berries follow in autumn. Zones 4–9.

C. borealis. Blue bead lily. North America. Height 1 ft; spread 1 ft (30×30 cm). A plant more interesting than ornamental, with large dark-green, shining leaves up to 12 in. (30 cm) long and small clusters of greenish yellow flowers in early summer followed by blue berries in autumn. Zones 3–9.

C. umbellulata. Speckled wood lily. North America. Height 18 in.; spread 12 in. (45×30 cm). A spreading plant with two to five rounded, dark-green leaves up to 10 in. (25 cm) long and small clusters of fragrant white flowers in early summer. Zones 4–9.

CODONOPSIS

FAMILY: Campanulaceae

A small genus with fleshy roots native to the Himalayas and Japan. They are twining or reclining perennials with bell-shaped flowers. The name comes from the Greek *kodon,* "bell."

CULTIVATION: Grow in a sunny or lightly shaded position in well-drained soil in climates with cool summers. Plant next to a supporting shrub or provide a framework on which to climb. Do not disturb once the plants are established.

LANDSCAPE USE: Loose-growing plants with nodding flowers to be grown over shrubs or along the ground. Grow at the top of a bank or rock garden.

PROPAGATION: Take cuttings of basal shoots in spring, plant rooted plants in autumn. Sow seed in spring or autumn.

C. clematidea. Asia. Height 2 ft; spread 18 in. (60×45 cm). A climbing plant with rounded, pointed, light-green leaves about 1 in. (2.5 cm) long on trailing, sprawling stems. The nodding, bell-shaped flowers are light blue with striking orange and black markings inside the bell. The blooms appear in late summer. Zones 6–9.

C. ovata. Himalayas. Height 12 in.; spread 12 in. (30×30 cm). A low, spreading plant with light-green, hairy, egg-shaped leaves and pale-blue, bell-shaped flowers with orange-and-purple inner markings, flowering in mid- to late summer. Zones 6–9.

CONVALLARIA

(Lily-of-the-Valley)

FAMILY: Liliaceae

A good groundcover for a shady site, lily-of-the-valley is an easy plant to grow, quickly spreading. Native to much of the northern hemisphere, the generic name comes from the Latin *convallis,* "valley." One species, famous for its sweetly scented flowers, is widely available.

Cultivation: Grow in partial shade or full sun, in soil containing leaf mold or other organic matter. Old beds of lily-of-the-valley may exhaust themselves in time and need to be replaced, but generally this plant is happy to be left alone. May suffer from stem rot and anthracnose, particularly in areas with hot summers.

Landscape Use: An excellent plant for growing under deciduous trees or as a groundcover for a shrub border. The pips can also be forced for pot culture.

Propagation: Divide the rhizomes in autumn or spring, planting the individual crowns just below the surface.

C. majalis. Lily-of-the-valley. Europe, Asia, North America. Height 8 in.; spread 12 in. (20 × 30 cm). A rampant groundcover with spreading rhizomes producing upright shoots or "pips" from which appear two or three broad, elliptic, mid-green leaves 8 in. (20 cm) long and 3 in. (7.5 cm) wide. Arching stems produce scented, waxy, bell-shaped white flowers in spring. 'Flore Pleno' has double white flowers and less invasive habits; 'Fortin's Giant,' a form with broader foliage and slightly larger flowers on 10 in. (25 cm) stems, blooms a little later than the type; 'Rosea' has pretty pink flowers. Zones 2–9.

CONVOLVULUS

(Bindweed)

Family: Convolvulaceae

Convolvulus sabiatus

A large genus of twining annuals, herbaceous perennials, and deciduous subshrubs and shrubs. The name comes from the Latin *convolvo,* "to entwine." The funnel-shaped flowers bloom in a day, generally fading by late afternoon. The stems are either twining up or trailing along the ground, with opposite leaves. ***C. arvensis,*** the European bindweed, is a highly invasive plant almost impossible to eradicate.

Cultivation: Grow in full sun in ordinary, well-drained soil in a sheltered position.

Landscape Use: Those species suitable for the garden are attractive in sunny borders or rocky banks.

Propagation: Take basal cuttings in mid- to late summer. Sow seed in spring.

C. althaeoides. Europe. Height 2–3 in.; spread 3 ft (5–7.5 × 90 cm). An invasive trailing or climbing plant with rounded triangular, gray-green foliage becoming deeply dissected toward the upper half of the stem. Strong pink flowers 1 in. (2.5 cm) wide appear in late summer. Zones 6–8.

C. ***cneorum.*** Europe. Height 3 ft; spread 3 ft (90×90 cm). An evergreen shrub that can be used as a herbaceous perennial in cool climates. The leaves are narrow, spoon-shaped, and silky gray. The blossoms appear from late spring to early autumn with pink buds opening to yellow-eyed, white flowers. Zones 8–10.

C. ***sabatius (C. mauritanicus).*** Europe. Height 1 ft; spread 3 ft (30×90 cm). A loosely trailing species with gray-green, egg-shaped leaves and open-facing, lavender-blue flowers from early summer to autumn. An excellent plant for dry soils and a sheltered site. Zone 8–9.

COREOPSIS

(Tickseed)

Family: Compositae

Coreopsis 'Moonbeam'

The common name comes from the Greek *koris,* "bug," and *opsis,* "like." The seeds are thought to resemble a bug or tick. Despite this less than glamorous name, ***Coreopsis*** is a large and important genus of over 100 annual and perennial plants with daisylike flowers blooming in the summer and autumn. A number of species and cultivars are valuable long-blooming plants for the garden.

Cultivation: Grow in full sun in a dry, light soil. Remove faded flowers to encourage further flowering.

Landscape Use: The smaller species are excellent plants for the sunny rock garden, while the larger species are long-flowering border plants for use either as specimens or in large masses.

Propagation: Divide in spring or early autumn. Sow seeds in spring.

C. ***auriculata.*** North America. Height 2 ft; spread 18 in. (60×45 cm). A spreading plant with rounded, triangular leaves up to 5 in. (12.5 cm) long with two basal earlike lobes to each leaf. The orange-yellow, daisylike flowers appear in late spring and early summer. 'Nana,' a dwarf form more widely represented in the trade, grows to a height of 6 in. (15 cm) and is an excellent rock plant; 'Superba' has warm orange-yellow flowers and grows to a height of 14 in. (35 cm). Zones 4–9.

C. ***grandiflora.*** North America. Height 2 ft; spread 18 in. (60×45 cm). A common flowering weed of grassland in Missouri, Kansas, south to Florida, and west to New Mexico. There is considerable confusion between this species and *C. lanceolata.* The same cultivars are attributed under both species in many listings. ***C. grandiflora*** has divided, opposite leaves borne almost to the top of the stems and yellow daisylike flowers to 2½ in. (6.2 cm) across, notched at the tip, with yellow centers, blooming through much of the summer. 'Badengold' height 2½ ft (75 cm), buttercup-yellow flowers; 'Goldfink': height 10–12 in. (25–30 cm), a dwarf, spreading plant; 'Mayfield Giant': height 2½ ft (75 cm); 'Sunray' height 2 ft (60 cm), double yellow flowers up to 4 in. (10 cm) across.

C. ***lanceolata.*** Lance-leaved tickseed. North America. Height 2 ft; spread 18 in. (60 × 45 cm). Similar to the above species but differing most obviously in that the leaves are basal and are not borne high up on the stem. Yellow flowers appear throughout the summer. 'Double Sunburst' has double, golden yellow flowers; 'Sunburst' has semidouble yellow flowers. Zones 5–9.

C. ***rosea.*** Pink tickseed. North America. Height 2 ft; spread 2 ft (60 × 60 cm). Similar to *C.* 'Moonbeam' but with pink flowers. The leaves are linear, the flowers about 1 inch (2.5 cm) wide and light pink. Relatively rare in cultivation until 1990, it is now commonly available. Zones 4–9.

C. ***tripteris.*** Atlantic coreopsis. North America. Height 4–8 ft; spread 2 ft (120–240 × 60 cm). A stout, erect plant with 8-in. (20-cm) leaves divided into three, lobed leaflets, and flower heads of pale yellow in late summer. Common to wood margins of New England and the central states. Zones 4–9.

C. ***verticillata.*** Threadleaf coreopsis. North America. Height 2–3 ft; spread 3 ft (60–90 × 90 cm). A clump-forming, spreading plant with erect stems and bright-green, threadlike, finely divided foliage. The yellow daisylike flowers are borne in late spring through to early autumn. A number of outstanding cultivars and hybrids provide some of the best long-season flowering plants for the garden. 'Golden Showers' grows to a height of 2–3 ft (60–90 cm) and has bright-yellow, starry flowers throughout the summer. Perhaps the longest flowering, 'Moonbeam,' is a hybrid of complex parentage that reaches 18 in. (45 cm) in height and has lemon-yellow flowers that bloom from late spring to early autumn. It is able to flower in light shade and is best deadheaded by shearing halfway back in late summer. It performs best when divided every three to four years. 'Zagreb' is a dwarf form reaching 15 in. (37.5 cm) with golden yellow flowers. All three are superb garden plants that need warm summers to flower well. After a number of years large areas of thread-leaf coreopsis may become less vigorous, indicating the need for rigorous division and replanting. Zones 3–9.

CORIARIA

Family: Coriariaceae

A small genus of subshrubs, shrubs, and trees native to South America, Europe, Asia, and New Zealand. The one species mentioned is a subshrub that frequently dies to the ground during winter. Used in tanning leather since ancient times, the plant is named for *corium,* Latin for "skin" or "leather."

Cultivation: Grow in full sun to partial shade in well-drained soil.

Landscape Use: With its arching stems, ***Coriaria*** is an attractive plant for the top of a rock wall or the edge of the border.

Propagation: Take stem cuttings in midsummer.

Coriaria terminalis

*C. **terminalis.*** China. Height 3 ft; spread 3 ft (90 × 90 cm). A spreading plant with arching stems, egg-shaped leaves up to 3 in. (7.5 cm) long, and insignificant flowers that produce striking black fruits in late summer and autumn. The variety ***xanthocarpa*** has yellow fruits. Zone 7.

CORNUS

(Dogwood, Bunchberry, Crackerberry)

Family: Cornaceae

Cornus canadensis

About 44 species of trees and shrubs with one significant herbaceous perennial.

Cultivation: Grow bunchberry in moist woodland soil in shade. Requires a climate of cool summer nights.

Landscape Use: A good evergreen groundcover for the woodland garden.

Propagation: Divide the woody rhizomes and plant in spring.

*C. **canadensis.*** Bunchberry, crackerberry. North America. Height 9 in.; spread 24 in. (22.5 × 60 cm). An evergreen woodland plant with a creeping rootstock and mid-green, whorled, stalkless, egg-shaped leaves to 3 in. (7.5 cm) long. The white flowers, which are made up of central, yellow flowers, are surrounded by four large white bracts and appear in late spring to early summer. The flowers are followed by bright-red edible berries in late summer. Zones 2–7.

CORONILLA

(Crown Vetch)

Family: Leguminosae

A genus of hardy herbaceous perennials and shrubs. The one herbaceous species more commonly grown is widely used in the United States as a deciduous groundcover and erosion-control plant for the dry banks of highways. It has spread throughout the roadside verges of northeastern North America, often suppressing or eradicating native flora.

Cultivation: If you must, grow in full sun in well-drained soil.

Landscape Use: A vigorous groundcover for large areas. Do not plant in the small garden or near small shrubs or other plants that can be overwhelmed by this hungry spreader.

Propagation: Divide the roots in autumn or spring. Sow seed in spring.

C. varia. Crown vetch. Europe. Height 1–2 ft; spread 4 ft (30–60 × 120 cm). Widely naturalized in the northeastern United States, this enthusiastic groundcover has alternate leaves with a dozen or more oblong leaflets and numerous heads of lilac-pink flowers in late spring to midsummer. 'Penngift' has pink-and-white flowers that bloom throughout the growing season. Zones 3–9.

CORTADERIA

(Pampas Grass)

Family: Graminae

About 20 species of large, ornamental grasses native to South America and New Zealand. The commonly grown pampas grass is native to temperate South America and is evergreen in mild climates. The name comes from the Spanish *cortdero* "to cut" referring to the sharp, cutting edges of the grass.

Cultivation: Grow pampas grass in full sun or partial shade in moist but well-drained soil. Hardy to Zone 8 but will occasionally survive the winter in Zone 7. Plant in spring.

Landscape Use: Commonly used as a solitary specimen plant. It looks best when planted in groups or at the back of a large herbaceous border. A good plant for cut flowers.

Propagation: Divide and replant in spring.

C. jubata. South America. Height 8–12 ft; spread 6 ft (240–360 × 180 cm). Similar to the species described below but with looser pinkish purple panicles and smaller spikelets. This species is most noticeable along the coast of California from San Francisco to Santa Barbara, where it is rapidly invading the cliffsides and roadside verges. It is another example of an exotic species dominating the indigenous flora.

C. selloana. Pampas grass. South America. Height 8–12 ft; spread 6 ft (240–360 × 180 cm). An elegant, upright, clump-forming grass with gray-green, narrow, arching foliage with serrated edges. The clump of foliage reaches a height of 4–8 ft (120–240 ft). The feathery plumes, which are borne on stiff stems that can reach 12 ft (360 cm), open greenish white and turn to silver-white when fully open in the autumn. 'Argenteum' is a form with silver flowers; 'Gold Band,' also sold as 'Aureo-variegata,' has variegated leaves of gold and green and silvery plumes reaching a height of 5–6 ft (150–160 cm); 'Monstrosa' has creamy white flowers larger than the type; 'Pumila,' a compact plant with a mound of foliage up to 3 ft (90 cm) high and flower stems of 6 ft (180 cm) in flower, seems hardier than other cultivars and can be grown in the warmer parts of Zone 7. 'Rendatleri' is a tall cultivar, up to 10 ft (300 cm) high, with rosy pink plumes; 'Silver Comet' is a dwarf pampas grass reaching a height of 4 ft (120 cm) with snowy white flowers; 'Sunningdale Silver' grows to about 7 ft (210 cm) and has feathery white open plumes. Zones 8–10.

Cortaderia selloana

CORYDALIS

Family: Fumariaceae

Corydalis lutea

Corydalis wilsonii

A large genus of generally prostrate plants with finely dissected, lobed leaves and yellow, blue, and rose-purple tubular, spurred flowers. Many are very desirable garden plants. ***Corydalis*** is a Greek word meaning "lark," referring to the flowers having spurs like those of the lark.

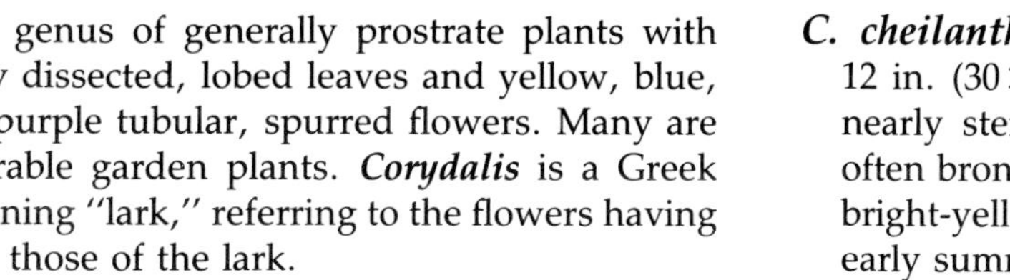

Cultivation: Grow in partial shade or full sun in fertile, well-drained soil.

Landscape Use: Good plants for lightly shaded borders or for under shrubs. Some are happy in rock walls or as deciduous woodland groundcovers.

Propagation: Divide clump-forming plants in spring or early autumn. Sow seeds in spring or autumn.

C. ***bulbosa.*** Europe. Height 8 in.; spread 12 in. (20 × 30 cm). A tuberous-rooted perennial with blue-green, finely divided leaves with rounded lobes and clusters of rosy lilac tubular flowers beginning in early spring and continuing to late spring. The whole plant dies down by midsummer. Zones 6–8.

C. ***cashmeriana.*** Kashmir. Height 6 in.; spread 9 in. (15 × 22.5 cm). A very beautiful plant with a delicate filigree of blue-green leaves and clusters of 1-in.- (2.5-cm-) long, clear-blue flowers throughout the summer. A difficult but desirable species to grow, best cultivated in an alpine house or in a climate with cool summer nights. Zones 5–6.

C. ***cheilanthifolia.*** China. Height 12 in.; spread 12 in. (30 × 30 cm). A tuberous-rooted plant with nearly stemless, deeply divided, fernlike leaves, often bronze-tinged, about 8 in. (20 cm) long, and bright-yellow, spurred flowers in late spring to early summer. Zones 5–8.

C. ***lutea.*** Europe. Height 12 in.; spread 12 in. (30 × 30 cm). A useful and easily cultivated plant with ferny, gray-green leaves and bright-yellow flowers ½ in. (1.2 cm) long, blooming from late spring to early autumn. A wonderful and robust species that self-seeds freely, is easily divided, and blooms throughout the growing season. One of the best small plants for spot planting or planting en masse as a groundcover. Zones 5–8.

C. ***nobilis.*** Siberia. Height 18 in.; spread 12 in. (45 × 30 cm). Green, deeply divided, fernlike leaves and long-spurred flowers that are cream colored, edged with purple, blooming in late spring. Zones 3–8.

C. ***ochroleuca.*** Europe. Height 12 in.; spread 12 in. (30 × 30 cm). Very similar to *C.* ***lutea*** but with creamy white flowers. Zones 6–8.

C. ***scouleri.*** Northwestern North America. Height 2 ft; spread 18 in. (60 × 45 cm). A many-stemmed plant with finely divided, lacy leaves and spikes of purple-rose or white tubular flowers with long spurs. Zones 6–8.

C. wilsonii. China. Height 6–10 in.; spread 10 in. (15–25 × 25 cm). An evergreen or semievergreen species with blue-green, lobed, and divided leaves and green-tipped, yellow flowers about ¾ in. (1.8 cm) long, appearing in spring. A finely textured plant for the rock garden. Zones 6–7.

CRAMBE

FAMILY: Cruciferae

About 20 species of annual and perennial herbs, two of which are grown in gardens. The stems are often woody, the leaves large and thick, and the flowers in clouds of white stars in early summer.

CULTIVATION: Grow in full sun in well-drained soil. Cut back faded flower heads. Susceptible to damage from cabbage-loving insects.

LANDSCAPE USE: The larger species is an excellent plant for the back of the herbaceous border or wild garden, while the smaller is a good seaside border plant.

PROPAGATION: Take root cuttings in spring. Transplant self-sown seedlings.

C. cordifolia. Caucasus. Height 6 ft; spread 4 ft (180 × 120 cm). A large plant with mounds of hairy, crinkled, coarsely toothed, dark-green basal leaves 2 ft (60 cm) wide or more, and branched stalks bearing clouds of sweetly fragrant, starry flowers in early summer. A magnificent plant for the large garden. Zones 6–9.

Crambe cordifolia

C. maritima. Sea kale. Europe. Height 2 ft; spread 2 ft (60 × 60 cm). Large, lobed, undulating silvery green, waxed, edible leaves up to 2 ft (60 cm) long and just as wide with handsome heads of sweetly scented white flowers in early summer. A better plant for the border than the vegetable garden. Zones 6–9.

CREPIS

(Hawk's Beard)

FAMILY: Compositae

A large genus of annuals and perennials somewhat weedy and inelegant. There are three species, two of which are perennial and are sometimes grown in gardens. They have dandelion-like leaves and rayed flowers of copper red or pink.

CULTIVATION: Grow *Crepis* in full sun in ordinary, even poor, soil.

LANDSCAPE USE: Small plants for the front of the border or top of a rock wall.

PROPAGATION: Divide and replant in spring. Sow seed in spring.

C. aurea. Alps. Height 6 in.; spread 9 in. (15 × 22.5 cm). A tufted plant with light-green, dandelionlike

Crepis incana

leaves and orange or red 1-in.- (2.5-cm-) wide flowers with blunt petals in mid- to late summer. Zones 4–7.

C. ***incana.*** Greece. Height 9 in.; spread 12 in. (22.5 × 30 cm). A charming plant with rosettes of gray-green, jagged leaves 4–5 in. (10–12.5 cm) long and stiff, branching stems of pink dandelionlike flowers with deep-rose centers. A long-blooming plant for late summer. Zones 5–7.

CYANANTHUS

(Trailing Bell Flower)

FAMILY: Campanulaceae

A small genus of rock-garden plants from central and eastern Asia. They are mat-forming perennials that like an open, sunny site. Although not widely grown, they are valuable for their rich-blue, gentianlike flowers in late summer and early autumn. The name comes from the Greek *kyanos,* "blue," and *anthos,* "flower."

CULTIVATION: Grow in full sun, in well-drained but constantly moist, lime-free soil.

LANDSCAPE USE: Plant in the rock garden or wall or border edge.

PROPAGATION: Take cuttings in spring or early summer.

C. ***lobatus.*** Himalayas. Height 4 in.; spread 12 in. (10 × 30 cm). A prostrate plant with rounded pale-green leaves to 1 in. (2.5 cm) long and upturned, rich-blue, round-petaled starry flowers in late summer. Forma ***albus*** has white flowers. Zones 6–7.

C. ***microphyllus.*** India. Height 3 in.; spread 12 in. (7.5 × 30 cm). A trailing plant with red stems and tiny, elliptic leaves, hairy-white underneath. Purple-blue, funnel-shaped flowers 1 in. (2.5 cm) across appear in early autumn. Zones 6–7.

CYNARA

(Cardoon)

FAMILY: Compositae

Eleven species of perennial plants, two of which are grown for the table and for their ornamental value. *C.* ***scolymus*** is that prince of vegetables, the artichoke; the cardoon has thickened leaf stalks that are blanched for eating.

CULTIVATION: Grow in a warm, sunny site in well-drained soil.

LANDSCAPE USE: A silvery thistle for architectural presence in the garden.

PROPAGATION: Sow seed in late winter or early spring, planting in early summer.

C. cardunculus. Cardoon. Europe. Height 6 ft; spread 3 ft (180×90 cm). An elegant plant with gray-green, divided, thistlelike leaves, silvery white underneath with the lower leaves growing up to 3 ft (90 cm) in length. Large, solitary, purple heads of thistle flowers appear in summer. Zones 6–8.

CYPRIPEDIUM

(Lady's-slipper)

FAMILY: Orchidaceae

Cypripedium reginae

Thirty to 50 species of orchids native to North America, Europe, and Asia. They are deciduous plants with finely hairy, pleated leaves and curiously beautiful flowers with two lower sepals often fused to form a pouch or slipper. Many species have become rare in the wild due to the depradations caused by zealous plant-hunters. They are notoriously difficult to grow, requiring highly specific climates and soils.

CULTIVATION: Grow in a cool climate in neutral to acid, well-drained but moist soil in full to partial shade.

LANDSCAPE USE: Wonderful specimens for the

shade garden, border, or woodland garden. The pink lady's slipper is one of the few flowering plants able to grow under conifers.

PROPAGATION: Divide in spring. Do not purchase plants taken from the wild.

C. acaule. Pink lady's slipper. Northeastern North America. Height 12 –16 in.; spread 12 in. (30–40 × 30 cm). A clump-forming orchid with a pair of oval to broadly lance-shaped, petaled leaves up to 10 in. (25 cm) long and 3 in. (7.5 cm) wide. A single flower is produced on a stem about 12 in. (30 cm) tall in late spring and early summer. The flower is generally reddish brown with a prominently veined, deep-pink pouch. This species is native to woodlands with acid soil; therefore, cultivation requires as close approximation as possible to these conditions. Zones 4–8.

C. calceolus. Yellow lady's slipper. North America, Europe, Asia. Height 12–18 in.; spread 12 in. (30–45 × 30 cm). A highly variable species that causes much debate among taxonomists. In general, it is a clump-forming orchid with broadly lance-shaped, slightly hairy leaves up to 8 in. (20 cm) long, organized in a spiral up on the stem. One to three maroon-purple flowers with a yellow pouch are produced on 12-in. (30-cm) stems in late spring and early summer. The variety ***pubescens*** is a hairier, larger plant, growing up to 2–2½ ft (60–75 cm) with a purple-veined, yellow pouch. Requires rich neutral to slightly acid soil in partial shade. Zones 4–8.

C. reginae. Showy lady's slipper. North America. Height 2–3 ft; spread 1 ft (60–90 × 30 cm). A highly desirable plant for the shade garden, with pleated, egg-shaped, stem-clasping, and hairy leaves up to 8 in. (20 cm) long. The 3–4-in.- (7.5–10-cm-) wide flowers are produced in late spring and early summer and are white with a rose-pink, striped white, pouch. Grow in constantly moist but not boggy soil in partial shade. Zones 5–8.

CYSTOPTERIS

(Bladder-fern)

FAMILY: Polypodiaceae

A small genus of ferns native to North and South America. Two species are cultivated in northern gardens.

CULTIVATION: Grow in neutral to alkaline soil in moist soil that does not dry out. A cool climate and open shade are essential.

LANDSCAPE USE: Bladder-fern is a delicate-looking fern for rock crevices or rock walls where the graceful foliage is allowed to arch downward.

PROPAGATION: Sow spores when ripe in midsummer, divide in spring, or sow the bulblets of ***C. bulbifera*** in summer.

C. bulbifera. Bulblet bladder-fern. North America. Height 2–3 ft; spread 18 in. (60–90 × 45 cm). A delicate-looking fern with tapering, yellow-green leaves divided into 20 or more gracefully cut leaf segments. Small bulblets can be found along the base of the leaflets. The variety ***crispa*** has curled, parsleylike foliage. Zones 3–7.

C. fragilis. Fragile bladder-fern. North America. Height 12 in.; spread 9 in. (30 × 22.5 cm). Despite its name, this is a tough fern with lance-shaped leaves about 10 in. (25 cm) long, divided into eight to 12 opposite-leaf segments. The lower leaflets are widely spaced. Plant in neutral to slightly acid soil. Zones 2–7.

Cystopteris bulbifera

DARMERA

See PELTIPHYLLUM.

DEINANTHE

FAMILY: Saxifragaceae

Two species of coarse perennials with unusual flowers. The name is derived from the Greek *deinos,* "wonderful," and *anthe,* "flower." They are woodland plants from China and Japan that flower in late summer.

CULTIVATION: Grow in lime-free, peaty soil in a protected site.

LANDSCAPE USE: Late-flowering plants for the shady border or woodland garden.

PROPAGATION: Divide in spring.

D. bifida. Japan. Height 2 ft; spread 18 in. (60 × 45 cm). A mound-forming species with creeping rhizomes and opposite, hairy, egg-shaped leaves with divided and lobed tips. The small, star-shaped, pinkish white flowers are borne in terminal clusters among the foliage in summer. Zones 5–9.

D. caerulea. China. Height 18 in.; spread 18 in. (45 × 45 cm). A slow-growing species with unbranched stems with toothed and rounded, hairy leaves to 10 in. (25 cm) long and cup-shaped, pale-violet flowers on reddish stalks. Zones 5–9.

DELPHINIUM

(Larkspur)

FAMILY: Ranunculaceae

A genus of more than 300 species native to the northern hemisphere. Most are stately plants with hand-shaped foliage and showy, spurred flowers borne in shades of blue but sometimes white, yellow, or red. The name comes from the Greek *delphinion,* derived from *delphis,* "dolphin," referring to the shape of the flowers of some species. The most popular garden varieties are hybrid strains that are showstoppers in the perennial border in mild climates. First bred in Europe in the 1800s, hybrid ***Delphiniums*** that are more suited to North American climates have been bred in the United States since the early 1900s. The annual larkspurs are now placed in the genus ***Consolida.***

CULTIVATION: Grow in a sunny location, protected from wind, in a well-drained, slightly alkaline, rich soil that does not dry out in summer or remain wet in winter. ***Delphiniums*** do best and grow to their full potential in climates where summers are cool and moist. Heavy feeders, they need regular fertilization. Flower stems are hollow and brittle and need staking. To encourage rebloom, deadhead after flowering, leaving leafy stems to turn yellow before cutting back to the base. ***Delphiniums*** are susceptible to slug damage, powdery mildew, and a number of other fungal diseases, notably root rot and crown rot. Infected plants should be discarded. To avoid crown rot, plant crowns at, not below, soil level. As a rule they are short-lived plants and will need replacing every two to three years.

LANDSCAPE USE: Glamorous staples of the perennial border, the taller varieties best at the back of the border. Good cut flowers.

PROPAGATION: Easily raised from seed. Sow seeds indoors in late winter for flowering the first year. Plants grown from seed sown outdoors in spring or summer will flower the next year. Take cuttings of basal growth or carefully divide the crowns in spring.

D. x ***belladona.*** Height 3–5 ft; spread 2 ft (90–150 × 60 cm). A hybrid strain with heat-tolerant properties, first developed in 1900. They are large, many-branched plants with many stems of airy, blue flowers in midsummer. Cultivars include 'Belladona,' with light-blue flowers; 'Bellamosa,' with deep-blue flowers; 'Casa Blanca,' with pure-white flowers; 'Cliveden Beauty,' with azure-blue flowers; 'Lamartine,' with deep violet-blue flowers. Zones 3–9.

D. cardinale. Scarlet larkspur. North America. Height 2 ft; spread 1 ft (60 × 30 cm). A native of dry, warm areas of California, this is a short-lived species with thick, woody roots, deeply divided palm-shaped leaves, and spikes of cardinal-red, cup-shaped flowers with yellow centers in mid- to late summer. Most important for its use as a parent for red-flowered hybrids. Zones 8–9.

D. elatum. Siberia. Height 4–6 ft; spread 2 ft (120–180 × 60 cm). A species with large palmate leaves, rigidly upright stems, and 1–2-in.- (2.5–5-cm-) wide blue flowers. Zones 3–9. This species is the main parent of many important hybrid strains characterized by large, showy, flat florets often with a cluster of short central petals called a bee. These include:

Blackmore and Langdon Hybrids: Developed in England in 1905, now mostly sold as seedling mixes. Flower colors range from white, cream, blue, and mauve, to purple. They are borne on 5–6-ft (150–180-cm) stems in early summer. A so-called dwarf strain reaches a height of 3–4 ft (90–120 cm). Hardy to Zone 3 but intolerant of hot and humid summers.

Fantasia Hybrids: Developed by W. Atlee Burpee, these semidrawf plants are 24–30 in. (60–75 cm) tall with sturdy stems. Flowers in early summer are white, lavender, and blue with white bees. 'Snow White' is a white cultivar. Zones 3–9.

Giant Pacific Hybrids: Spectacular 5–6-ft (150–180-cm) spikes of large double flowers in blue, violet, purple, pink, and white in early summer. Bred by Frank Reinett of California, these are better suited to North American climates. Mixes are sometimes listed as Round Table series or Blue Bird series. Individual cultivars include 'Astolat,' with pink flowers with black or gold bee; 'Black Knight,' with dark-violet flowers with a black bee; 'Blue Bird' with medium-blue flowers with a white bee; 'Galahad,' pure white, beeless flowers that bloom in midsummer; 'Guinevere,' with lavender-pink flowers with a white bee; 'King Arthur, with dark royal violet flowers with a white bee; 'Summer Skies,' with sky-blue flowers with a white bee. Zones 3–9.

Delphinium hybrid

Dwarf Pacific Hybrids: Flowers similar to the Giant series but on 2-ft (60-cm) plants. Often treated as annuals. 'Blue Fountains' are shades of blue; 'Blue Heaven' is a medium blue with a white bee.

D. grandiflorum. Chinese larkspur. Asia. Height 2 ft; spread 1 ft (60 × 30 cm). Freely branched, bushy plants with finely cut foliage. Flowers are in loose, airy blue sprays, blooming over a long period in summer. Native to dry meadows in Siberia and China. 'Album' has white flowers; 'Blue Butterfly' has deep-blue flowers; 'Blue Mirror' has gentian blue flowers. Zones 3–9.

D. x ***ruysii.*** Height 3–4 ft; spread 2 ft (90–120 × 60 cm). A pink hybrid between ***D. elatum*** and ***D. nudicaule*** with a similar habit to the *D.* x ***belladona*** hybrids. 'Pink Sensation,' a rose-pink variety, is the most widely grown. It is short-lived in the garden and does not perform well in areas with hot summers. Zones 7–9.

D. zalil. Iran. Height 2 ft; spread 1 ft (60 × 30 cm). A yellow-flowering plant with deeply cut leaves and spurred blossoms appearing in early summer. Requires a warm and well-drained location. Zones 8–9.

DENNSTAEDTIA

(Hay-scented Fern)

FAMILY: Polypodiaceae

A genus of about 70 species of tropical and subtropical ferns with one species native to eastern North America. The common name refers to the scent of fresh hay that comes from the silvery white glands on the leaf stem and midrib.

CULTIVATION: Grow in moist well-drained soil in partial shade. Hay-scented fern is very adaptable and will grow in almost any garden soil in varying degrees of sunlight.

LANDSCAPE USE: A good fern for deciduous woodland groundcover, for sunny woodland glades and moist banks.

PROPAGATION: Divide the rhizomes in the spring. Propagate from spores collected in late summer.

D. punctilobula. Hay-scented fern. Eastern North America. Height 2–3 ft; spread 1 ft (60–90 × 30 cm). A spreading, easily grown fern with pale-green, lacy, lance-shaped fronds up to 3 ft (90 cm) tall and 6 in. (15 cm) wide. It is a clump-forming plant with arching fronds and a tendency to spread vigorously, making it a fine fern for colonizing a bank or other difficult site. Zones 3–8.

DENTARIA

(Toothwort)

FAMILY: Cruciferae

Dentaria laciniata

Woodland plants found throughout the northern hemisphere. The two or three leaves are opposite, toothed, and generally divided into three parts, while the flowers are white or pale purple in spring. They are not greatly ornamental but do have value, particularly in a collection of American native plants. The name comes from the Latin *dens*, "tooth," a reference to the toothlike root scales.

CULTIVATION: Grow toothwort in well-drained woodland soil in partial shade.

LANDSCAPE USE: Best grown in the wild or in woodland gardens.

PROPAGATION: Divide the fleshy root stocks in spring or autumn.

D. diphylla. Crinkleroot toothwort. Eastern North America. Height 12 in.; spread 8 in. (30×20 cm). A delicate-looking woodland plant with long, toothed roots, two leaves divided into three toothed segments, and an open cluster of four-petaled flowers that are white on the inside, pale pink or purple on the outside. Zones 5–8.

D. laciniata. Cutleaf toothwort. Eastern North America. Height 12 in.; spread 8 in. (30×20 cm). A tuberous-rooted plant with slightly hairy stems and three leaves divided into narrow segments. The terminal clusters of pale-purple to white flowers are borne in spring. Zones 5–8.

DESCHAMPSIA

(Tufted Hair Grass)

FAMILY: Graminae

A genus of hardy tufted grasses named after the French botanist Deslongchamps. One species, described below, is becoming increasingly popular as a sturdy but beautiful, easy-to-grow, cool-climate ornamental grass noted for its rich green foliage and its tolerance of shady conditions.

CULTIVATION: For optimum growth, plant in a well-drained soil in full sun. Will also tolerate partial to fully shaded locations.

LANDSCAPE USE: A handsome grass for the border, rock or shade garden, or pondside. The inflorescence is valuable as a cut or dried flower.

PROPAGATION: Divide in spring or autumn. Sow seed in spring.

Deschampsia caespitosa 'Goldstaub'

D. caespitosa. Tufted hair grass. Europe, Asia, North America. Height 2–3 ft; spread 2 ft (60–90×60 cm). A tufted, evergreen, mound-forming grass with arching, dark-green, ribbed leaves up to 2 ft (60 cm) long. The flowers are borne in a delicate-looking branched flower head about 2 ft (60 cm) long and 8 in. (20 cm) wide, beginning yellow-green in early summer and fading to light buff by mid- to late summer. The flowers are very delicate in appearance and need a dark-green background to stand out. 'Bronzeschleier' has bronze-yellow flower spikes; 'Goldgehaenge' has a golden yellow inforescence; 'Goldschleier' has bright-yellow flowers; 'Goldstaub' has yellow flowers; 'Schottland' is a vigorous cultivar growing up to 4 ft (120 cm). In areas with hot summers, cutting back hard in midsummer will produce an attractive clump of basal foliage for autumn and winter. Zones 4–9.

D. flexuosa. Crinkled hair grass. Eurasia, North America. Height 20 in.; spread 12 in. (50×30 cm). Similar to ***D. caespitosa*** but reaching a maximum of 20 in. (50 cm), often growing smaller. The inforescence also differs in being purplish or bronze fading to buff. Tolerates dense shade. Zones 3–9.

DIANTHUS

(Carnation, Pink)

FAMILY: Caryophyllaceae

Dianthus x *allwoodii* 'Beatrix'

Dianthus deltoides 'Brilliant'

Three hundred fifty species and many hybrids of important and mostly desirable garden plants, including such stalwarts as the garden pinks, carnations, sweet william, and alpine pinks. Sweet william, which is a biennial, and the carnations, which are primarily a greenhouse crop, will not be included here. The hardy perennial members of the genus are generally low, mounded, evergreen plants with pairs of opposite, linear to lance-shaped leaves often blue-green in color. The five-petaled flowers are frequently fringed and come in a large range of colors, notably white, pink, and red. The species are quite promiscuous and hybridize freely, giving taxonomists considerable trouble and the rest of us great pleasure. They are often short-lived and may need propagating frequently. The name comes from the Greek *dios,* "divine," and *anthos,* "flower," in reference to the beauty of the flowers.

CULTIVATION: Relatively easy to grow when cultivated in a sunny site, in well-drained, sandy soil that is neutral to alkaline. Wet soil, particularly over the winter, will kill many of the mound- and mat-forming kind. Those grown in rock gardens require minimal feeding, while those grown in borders need fertilizing in the spring. Mulching will cause the crowns to rot. Old flower stalks should be removed once the flowers have faded, after which a light trim will keep the plants compact. Many species and hybrids have a tendency to be weak and short-lived; propagation every two to three years helps ensure plant health.

LANDSCAPE USE: ***Dianthus*** species are an essential element of any good rock garden, stone wall, or herbaceous border. It is hard to imagine a garden without them. They are particularly useful as edging plants in a sunny garden.

PROPAGATION: The species are easily grown from seed sown in spring. Taking cuttings and layering stems is the most reliable method of propagation. Nonflowering shoots root readily when cut just below a node and placed in a well-drained propagation medium. Layering is successful for those types with long stems.

D.* × *allwoodii. Height 12–18 in.; spread 12 in. (30–45 × 30 cm). A group of hybrids produced from the crossing of ***D. caryophyllus,*** the carnation, with ***D. plumarius,*** the cottage pink. The flowers are fragrant, single, semidouble, or double, often fringed or patterned, and appear in summer. The leaves are bluish gray. Deadhead often to ensure greater length of bloom. Increase by layering every three to four years. Notable cultivars are: 'Aqua' with double white flowers; 'Daphne,' with single, pale pink flowers with a darker eye; 'Doris,' with semidouble, pale salmon-pink flowers; 'Essex Witch,' with semidouble, finely fringed pink flowers; 'Helen,' with double-flowering salmon-pink flowers; 'Ian,' with double red flowers; 'Lillian,' with pearly white, fringed flowers; 'Robin,' with scarlet to orange flowers; 'Timothy,' with silvery pink flowers flecked vivid red. Zones 4–8.

D. alpinus. European Alps. Height 4 in.; spread 6 in. (10×15 cm). A mat-forming, evergreen plant with narrow, dark-green leaves and 1½-in.- (3.8-cm-) wide rose to crimson flowers with overlapping petals and a white eye, blooming in late spring and throughout the summer. 'Albus' has white flowers. A short-lived variable species requiring propagation from cuttings every two to three years. Zones 4–8.

D. arenarius. Sand pink. Europe. Height 12 in.; spread 6–8 in. (30×15–20 cm). A mat-forming species with gray-green or green leaves up to 2 in. (5 cm) long and slightly fragrant white flowers with notched petals and a green eye. Blooms in early summer. Zones 2–8.

D. × arvernensis. France. Height 6 in.; spread 6 in. (15×15 cm). Possibly a hybrid, perhaps a form of ***D. gratianopolitanus.*** It is a handsome plant with mats of gray foliage and numerous pink, fragrant flowers on short stems from late spring through summer. Zones 3–8.

D. deltoides. Maiden pink. Europe. Height 6–18 in.; spread 12 in. (15–45×30 cm). A highly variable, mat-forming plant with bright-green, linear leaves often with hairy margins and a red or purple flush. They are excellent plants for the rock garden or for planting in crevices. The flowers, up to ¾ in. (1.8 cm) across, range from purple through red to pink and white. They are long-blooming and are tolerant of very light shade. 'Albus' has white flowers; 'Brighteyes' has red-centered, white flowers; 'Brilliant' has bright, deep-rose, double flowers; 'Flashing Light' has salmon-scarlet flowers; 'Hansen's Red' has crimson flowers; 'Samos' has carmine red flowers; 'Wisley Variety' has dark-green foliage flushed purple with dark-red flowers. Zones 3–8.

D. gratianopolitanus. Cheddar pink. Europe. Height 12 in.; spread 24 in. (30×60 cm). A long-lived, densely mat-forming plant with evergreen, blue-gray, linear leaves. The pink flowers are solitary, strongly fragrant, and fringed, appearing in spring and early summer. 'Flore-Pleno' has double pink flowers; 'Petite' grows to a height of 3 in. (7.5 cm) and has masses of bright-pink flowers; 'Splendens' is a compact plant with red flowers; 'Tiny Rubies' has double, rich-pink flowers. Zones 5–8.

D. knappii. Eastern Europe. Height 16 in.; spread 12 in. (40×30 cm). An unusual yellow-flowered species with an untidy, awkward habit. The long stems often need staking. The spring flowers are bright yellow and are borne in clusters at the end of the stems. The foliage is pale green. This species often dies after flowering and is best treated as a biennial. Comes true from seed. Zones 3–8.

D. petraeus. Balkans. Height 10 in.; spread 12 in. (25×30 cm). A variable plant with cushions of densely tufted, evergreen, needlelike leaves and leafless stems bearing small white flowers with notched petals.

D. plumarius. Cottage pink. Height 6–12 in.; spread 8 in. (15–30×20 cm). This species is notable for its role in the development of the garden pinks so widely grown today. The species itself is a mound-forming plant with gray, veined, narrowly lance-shaped leaves up to 4 in. (10 cm) long. The sharply fragrant pink flowers, up to 1½ in. (3.8 cm) wide, are single, semidouble, or double, with deeply fringed petals. Blooms for a long period if constantly deadheaded. 'Agatha' has deep-pink semi-double flowers with a crimson eye; 'Excelsior' has carmine flowers with a dark eye; 'Inchmery' has pale-pink flowers; 'Mrs. Sinkins' has double white, fragrant flowers; 'Musgrave's Pink' has single white flowers with a pale-green eye; 'White Ladies' has double white flowers. Zones 4–8.

DIASCIA

(Twinspur)

FAMILY: Scrophulariaceae

A genus of about 50 species of annual and perennial summer-flowering plants native to South Africa. They are generally low-growing, sprawling plants with square stems, opposite leaves broad at the base, and terminal spikes of pink flowers. They are not widely cultivated outside of their native habitat and have only recently become available to the gardening public. One species, ***D. rigescens,*** is now increasingly available in Canada and the northwest United States due to the University of British Columbia Botanical Garden's Plant Introduction Scheme.

Cultivation: Grow in well-drained soil in an open, sunny location that is not prone to drought. In areas with hot summers, particularly those of the midatlantic, southern, and midwestern United States, ***Diascia*** may well cease flowering and, in the hottest summers, may need the protection of light shade. Except where indicated, most species in cultivation will overwinter in Zones 7–8.

Landscape Use: Plant in the front of the herbaceous border or rock garden or use as an annual bedding or container plant.

Propagation: Take stem cuttings in summer and autumn.

D. barberae. South Africa. Height 12 in.; spread 18 in. (30 × 45 cm). A short-lived species often grown as an annual. It is a mat-forming plant with serrated, hairless, egg-shaped leaves and loose terminal spikes of rose-pink flowers in summer. The flowers are distinguished by having two small black glands on the outer face of the flower throat. Hardy to Zones 8–9. ***D.*** x 'Ruby Field' is a hybrid between ***D. barberae*** and ***D. cordifolia,*** has smaller, deeper-pink flowers than ***D. barberae,*** and is hardy in protected areas in Zones 6–8. Although it is a straggling plant, it makes an excellent container plant and withstands the ravages of hot and humid summers better than other species.

D. fetcaniensis. South Africa. Height 20 in.; spread 18 in. (50 × 45 cm). A floriferous, branching, hairy plant with oval, serrated leaves clothed in glandular-tipped hairs. The 9-in. (22.5-cm) flowering spikes are covered in rose-pink flowers from early summer until frost. Flowers best in areas with gentle summers. Zones 8–9.

D. integerrima. South Africa. Height 18 in.; spread 20 in. (45 × 50 cm). A spreading, wiry plant with hairless, grayish, narrow leaves and delicate, erect racemes of rose-pink flowers in summer. More tolerant of dry sites than other species. Zones 8–9.

D. lilacina. South Africa. Height 12 in.; spread 18 in. (30 × 45 cm). The smallest-flowered ***Diascia*** is a sprawling, mat-forming species with bright-green, veined leaves and solitary lilac-pink flowers appearing from the axils of the leaflike bracts in early summer. Zones 8–9.

D. rigescens. South Africa. Height 2 ft; spread 18 in. (60 × 45 cm). A robust plant noted for its habit of flowering from late spring until autumn. Unfortunately, it performs poorly in areas where summer temperatures reach 90° F or more. In areas with cool summers it is a wonderful perennial with thick, stalkless, sharply toothed leaves and crowded 6-in. (15-cm) spikes of strong pink flowers. It is quickly becoming an indispensable part of the herbaceous border in Europe and the Pacific Northwest and deserves to be tested to the limits of its hardiness and heat-tolerance zones. Zones 8–9.

D. vigilis. South Africa. height 12–18 in.; spread 18 in. (30–45 × 45 cm). A bushy species with toothed, egg-shaped leaves up to 2 in. (5 cm) long and spikes of pale-pink lipped flowers produced in summer. This species appears to be just a little more hardy and a little less susceptible to the ravages of summer heat than others. Zones 7–9.

Diascia rigescens

DICENTRA

(Bleeding Heart, Dutchman's Breeches)

FAMILY: Fumariaceae

Dicentra eximia 'Alba'

A genus of about 20 graceful plants mostly native to North America. The leaves are often finely divided and blue-green. The flowers range in color from creamy yellow, pink and white, to hot pink. They often flower as they unfold in spring, continuing to late autumn, making them valuable long-flowering plants for the lightly shaded border. The common names refer to the unusual shape of the flowers. The Latin name is derived from the Greek, *dis kentron,* "two-spurred," referring to the flower spurs.

CULTIVATION: Grow bleeding hearts in well-drained soil enriched with compost or peat moss in a cool, partly shaded location.

LANDSCAPE USE: Valuable plants for the border or woodland garden, providing long-season flowering with attractive foliage. ***D. spectabilis*** and ***D. cucullaria*** die down in midsummer and need to be associated with other plants that will cover the subsequent bare area.

PROPAGATION: Carefully divide in spring. Sow seeds in late summer. Take stem cuttings after flowering.

D. canadensis. Squirrel-corn. North America. Height 12 in.; spread 8 in. (30 × 20 cm). A tuberous-rooted plant called squirrel-corn because its underground tubers resemble yellow kernels of corn. The basal leaves are stemless, blue-green, and finely cut. The fragrant, nodding, white-tipped pink flowers are ⅔ in. (1.6 cm) long, have rounded spurs, are bunched in clusters, and appear in spring. They are particularly impressive when seen in the thousands in an eastern North American woodland. Zones 4–8.

D. cucullaria. Dutchman's breeches. North America. Height 10 in.; spread 8 in. (25 × 20 cm). Clusters of small underground tubers form a delicate-looking plant with finely cut pale to mid-green foliage and arching stems bearing white, heart-shaped flowers with yellow tips. The rounded basal flower spurs resemble "pantaloons" or "dutchman's breeches" when held upside down. The plant becomes dormant after the flowering season. Zones 3–8.

D. eximia. Turkey corn. North America. Height 18–24 in.; spread 18 in. (45–60 × 45 cm). An exceptionally long-flowering plant blooming from spring until autumn. The three-times-divided basal leaves are blue-gray in color with leaves farther up the stem becoming more finely divided. The pink to purple, heart-shaped, nodding flowers are borne in drooping clusters throughout the growing season. There are a number of cultivars listed; however, many of these are undoubtedly hybrids with ***D. formosa.*** 'Alba' has pure-white flowers; 'Adrian Bloom' has blue-green foliage and deep-red flowers; 'Bountiful' is a prolifically flowering plant with pale-pink flowers, synonymous with 'Zestful'; 'Luxuriant' is more tolerant of dry soils and summer heat than others, has pinkish stems, and produces masses of deep-pink flowers throughout the growing season. 'Stuart Boothman' has gray-green foliage and flesh-pink flowers. Zones 3–8.

D. formosa. North America. Height 18 in.; spread 2 ft (45 × 60 cm). A species similar to ***D. eximia,*** with ferny, bright-green, long-stalked, and divided leaves and terminal clusters of deep-pink flowers. Native from British Columbia to California. Zones 3–8.

D. spectabilis. Bleeding heart. China, Japan. Height 2 ft; spread 18 in. (60 × 45 cm). A popular cottage-garden plant grown for its beautiful arching stems of heart-shaped rose-red flowers with white protruding inner petals. The gray-green foliage is divided into rounded, wedge-shaped segments. The flowers are borne in late spring to early summer, after which the foliage may die down. Despite this characteristic, bleeding heart should be a required plant for every garden. 'Alba' has white flowers. 'Pantaloons' is listed as being a white form of ***D. spectabilis*** and appears to be indistinguishable from 'Alba.' Zones 3–8.

Dicentra spectabilis 'Alba'

D. uniflora. Steer's-head. North America. Height 3 in.; spread 6 in. (7.5 × 15 cm). Native to the western United States with basal, divided leaves and solitary white, sometimes pink flowers with the two outer petals curving back to resemble the horns of a steer. Zones 3–8.

DICTAMNUS

(Gas Plant)

Family: Rutaceae

A small genus with one species widely grown in gardens. The gas plant has aromatic leaves and flowering spikes covered with tiny glands that exude a volatile oil in hot weather. A lighted match placed at the base of the flower spike will ignite the oil and send a flame shooting through the spike without harming the flowers. This fact is often quoted in garden books, and it is true; try it and see.

Cultivation: Grow in well-drained soil in full sun. One should not disturb once the plants are established. ***Dictamnus*** is slow to appear in the spring, and existing clumps should be clearly marked.

Landscape Use: A useful plant for the sunny border.

Propagation: Sow seed in the autumn, plant young plants in the spring. Division is not recommended, as plants resent disturbance.

D. albus. Gas plant, dittany. Europe, Asia. Height 3 ft; spread 2 ft (90 × 60 cm). An erect plant developing woody stems. The leaves are alternate, divided into odd-numbered leaflets up to 3 in. (7.5 cm) long, glossy, dark green, and aromatic. The fragrant white flowers are borne in terminal spikes and are star-shaped, having five petals and ten showy stamens. The variety ***purpureus*** has purplish pink flowers with red veins. Zones 2–8.

DIGITALIS

(Foxglove)

FAMILY: Scrophulariaceae

Digitalis purpurea 'Alba'

A small genus of summer-flowering biennials and perennials bearing tubular flowers with attractively speckled throats. The common name is derived from the shape of the flowers, resembling the finger of a glove. Foxglove was originally Folks-glove, the glove of the good folk, or fairies, who inhabited the woodland where foxglove naturally grows. The drug digitalin is obtained from strains of ***D. purpurea.***

CULTIVATION: Grow in moist but well-drained soil in partial shade. Remove the central spike after flowering to encourage flowering side shoots.

LANDSCAPE USE: Erect, elegant plants for the herbaceous border, shade garden, or woodland garden.

PROPAGATION: Sow seeds in early summer, planting in early autumn. Divide in spring or autumn.

D. ferruginea. Rusty foxglove. Europe, Asia. Height 6 ft; spread 2 ft (180 × 60 cm). A short-lived perennial with basal rosettes of rough, oval leaves and leafy spikes of mid-green, lance-shaped, smooth or fringed leaves. In midsummer 2-ft (60-cm) spikes of rusty-red-and-white flowers, covered in soft hairs, appear. Zones 4–8.

D. grandiflora (D. ambigua). Yellow foxglove. Greece. Height 3 ft; spread 1 ft (90 × 30 cm). A clump-forming plant with mid-green, hairy, alternate, oblong, and toothed leaves up to 8 in. (20 cm) long becoming smaller and stalkless farther up the stem. In late spring to early summer 12-in (30-cm) spikes of pendant, tubular yellow flowers with brown-speckled throats appear. Will often rebloom if the faded flower heads are removed. 'Temple Bells' is a dwarf form growing to a height of 18 in. (45 cm). Zones 3–8.

D. lanata. Grecian foxglove. Europe. Height 2–3 ft; spread 1 ft (60–90 × 30 cm). A clump-forming plant with rosettes of hairless, oblong or spear-shaped leaves and spikes of 1-in.- (2.5-cm-) long creamy yellow, sometimes gray-purple flowers with a large white lower lip appearing in mid- to late summer. Zones 4–8.

D. lutea. Europe, North Africa. Height 2 ft; spread 1 ft (60 × 30 cm). Rosettes of glossy, green, oblong leaves with finely toothed margins and slender spikes of pale-yellow, narrow flowers with the upper lip parted in two, blooming in early summer. Zones 3–8.

D.* x *mertonensis. Height 3 ft; spread 18 in. (90 × 45 cm). A hybrid between ***D. purpurea*** and ***D. grandiflora*** with large basal rosettes of mid-green oval leaves and lipstick-pink tubular flowers on 2-ft (60-cm) flower spikes. A short-lived plant that will prosper if divided after flowering. Zones 5–8.

D. purpurea. Foxglove. Europe, North America. Height 3–5 ft; spread 2 ft (90–150×60 cm). Not strictly perennial, the biennial foxglove may persist for more than two years under good conditions. It frequently self-sows and when in flower in early to midsummer is one of the most delightful of woodland plants. The wrinkled, frequently downy leaves are oblong and long-stalked, becoming smaller and stalkless up on the stem. The tall, elegant spikes bear drooping tubular flowers with speckled throats in purple, pink, white, red or maroon. The 'Excelsior' hybrids have flowers around the spike in shades of pink, mauve, and white; 'Foxy' is a strain with mixed colors growing to a height of 2½ ft (75 cm); 'Shirley Hybrids' grow to a height of 5 ft (150 cm), have white to purple flowers borne on one side of the spike only; 'Sutton's Apricot' grows to 5 ft (150 cm) and has pale-apricot flowers. Hybrid strains will decrease in vigor in time. Zones 4–8.

DIPHYLLEIA

(Umbrella-leaf)

FAMILY: Berberidaceae

A small genus of plants native to eastern North America and Japan. One species is grown in wild gardens and is native to wet areas in the mountains of Virginia to Georgia.

CULTIVATION: Grow umbrella-leaf in moist woodland soil in shade.

LANDSCAPE USE: A bold plant for the woodland garden or shade border.

PROPAGATION: Divide the creeping rootstock in spring.

D. cymosa. Umbrella-leaf. North America. Height 3 ft; spread 2 ft (90×60 cm). An elegant plant with one lobed, umbrellalike leaf up to 2 ft across and a flowering stem bearing two smaller, cleft, alternate leaves. The heads of white flowers appear in summer, followed by stalks of bright-blue berries in the autumn. Zones 6–8.

DISPORUM

(Fairy-bells)

FAMILY: Liliaceae

A small species of woodland perennials with leafy stems and usually nodding flowers in spring and early summer. They are native to North America and Asia, related to Solomon's-seal, and useful for their ability to grow in dry shade.

CULTIVATION: Grow in partial shade to full shade in well-drained soil.

LANDSCAPE USE: Particularly good plants for dry shade. Use in the shady border, under trees and shrubs, and in the woodland garden.

PROPAGATION: Divide in spring.

D. flavum. North America. Height 2–3 ft; spread 12 in. (60–90×30 cm). Bamboolike stems and oblong to egg-shaped, alternate, leathery, stalkless leaves with marked parallel veins and downy undersides. The nodding, bell-shaped, lemon-yellow flowers are borne on the ends of the branching tips in spring. Zones 4–8.

D. hookeri. North America. Height 2½ ft; spread 12 in. (75×30 cm). Oblong to egg-shaped leaves up to 4 in. (10 cm) long and greenish white nodding, bell-like flowers in spring. The variety ***oreganum*** has sharply pointed leaves. Zones 4–8.

Disporum sessile 'Variegatum'

D. lanuginosum. Yellow mandarin. North America. Height 2½ ft; spread 12 in. (75 × 30 cm). Hairy stems and oblong to spear-shaped leaves, downy beneath and pointed at the tips. The bell-shaped flowers are yellowish green and appear in spring. Zones 4–8.

D. maculatum. Nodding mandarin. North America. Height 2 ft; spread 12 in. (60 × 30 cm). Oblong or oblong to egg-shaped leaves with stiff hairs underneath. The bell-like flowers are white spotted with purple in spring. Zones 4–8.

D. pullum. Asia. Height 3 ft; spread 12 in. (90 × 30 cm). Pointed egg-shaped leaves on blackish stems and nodding, tubular purplish green flowers in late spring. Zones 5–8.

D. sessile. Asia. Height 2 ft; spread 2 ft (60 × 60 cm). A spreading plant more interesting for its variegated form. The type has oblong or oblong to spear-shaped green leaves up to 4 in. (10 cm) long on bamboolike zigzagging stems. The flowers, which are usually solitary or in small bunches, are greenish white and appear in spring. 'Variegatum' has green-and-white striped foliage and is a handsome and unusual plant for dry shade. Zones 4–8.

DODECATHEON

(Shooting-star)

FAMILY: Primulaceae

A small genus of woodland plants with cyclamen-like flowers on leafless stems. They are native to North America, with one species native to Siberia. The name shooting-star is an allusion to the backward sweep of the petals. The botanical name comes from the Greek *dodeka,* "twelve," and *theos,* "god," a name given by Pliny to a plant under the care of the twelve gods.

Dodecatheon clevelandii

CULTIVATION: Plant in moist, woodland soil in partial shade. Leave undisturbed until the plants have established themselves in large clumps. Tolerant of summer drought.

Landscape Use: Bright early-summer-blooming flowers for the woodland garden or the shady rock garden. The plants die down in midsummer leaving a bare spot to be filled.

Propagation: Sow seeds in autumn or spring. Divide large clumps in autumn.

D. alpinum. Alpine shooting-star. North America. Height 6 in.; spread 8 in. (15 × 20 cm). Native to the mountains of California, Oregon, and Nevada with narrow, linear leaves to 2½ in. (6.2 cm) long and magenta flowers with a yellow tube and purple-ringed throat. Zones 4–8.

D. clevelandii. North America. Height 8 in.; spread 8 in. (20 × 20 cm). Pale-green, spoon-shaped leaves to 4½ in. (11.2 cm) long with toothed margins and umbels of yellow-based purple flowers. Native to southern California and hardy to Zone 9.

D. cusickii. North America. Height 9 in.; spread 6 in. (22.5 × 15 cm). A tufted plant from the Rocky Mountains with hairy, egg-shaped leaves up to 6½ in. (16.2 cm) long and rich purple, yellow-throated flowers. Zones 5–8.

D. jeffreyi. North America. Height 12 in.; spread 20 in. (30 × 50 cm). Distinguished by its light-green, erect, spoon-shaped leaves up to 20 in. (50 cm) long. The many-flowered umbels of reddish purple flowers with dark-purple stamens appear in early summer. Zones 5–8.

D. meadia. Common shooting-star. North America. Height 18 in.; spread 12 in. (45 × 30 cm). Rosettes of pale-green egg-shaped leaves with toothed margins. Rose-purple flowers with white bases and bright-yellow anthers appear in late spring to early summer. Forma ***alba*** has white flowers. Zones 4–8.

D. pulchellum. North America. Height 12 in.; spread 10 in. (30 × 20 cm). Basal tufts of mid-green, spoon-shaped leaves up to 10 in. (20 cm) long. In spring 12-in. (30-cm) stems bear loose umbels of lilac-purple flowers. 'Red Wings' has crimson flowers. Zones 3–8.

DORONICUM

(Leopard's-bane)

Family: Compositae

Doronicum columnae 'Spring Beauty'

About 35 species of hardy plants with alternate, mostly heart-shaped leaves and bright, open daisylike flowers in spring and early summer. They grow well in sun in climates with cool summers but have difficulty in hot and humid summers, when they are best grown in partial shade. They are shallow-rooted plants that go dormant in summer and return in the cooler weather of autumn. The common name apparently comes from the practice of hunting leopards with arrows dipped in the juice of one species. (This may account for the sparsity of leopards in the garden.)

Cultivation: Grow in sun or partial shade in moist but not boggy soil. ***Doronicum*** responds poorly to drought and must be watered during the summer. Deadhead the faded flowers for secondary flowering and clean up the leaves once summer dormancy begins. Zones 4–8.

Landscape Use: Good plants for the cut-flower garden or spring borders, flowering as daffodils pass. Summer dormancy leaves bare patches that may be filled with annual flowers, although care should be taken not to disturb the shallow roots.

Propagation: Divide in late summer.

D. austriacum. Europe. Height 2 ft; spread 1 ft (60×30 cm). Stem-clasping, bright-green, heart-shaped leaves with undulating, toothed margins. The single yellow daisies about 2 in. (5 cm) across appear in spring. Zones 5–8.

D. columnae (D. cordatum). Leopards-bane. Europe. Height 18 in.; spread 2 ft (45×60 cm). A widely grown species with fibrous roots and heart-shaped, basal, coarsely toothed leaves. Rounded, stem-clasping leaves appear farther up the stem. The single yellow daisies 2 in. (5 cm) wide are borne on stout stems in early to midspring. 'Finesse' has bright-yellow blooms 3 in. (7.5 cm) across; 'Spring Beauty' has double yellow flowers. 'Miss Mason' is a hybrid between this species and ***D. austriacum,*** with compact growth up to 18 in. (45 cm) and single yellow daisies. Zones 4–8.

D. orientale (D. caucasicum). Europe, Asia. Height 1–2 ft; spread 2 ft (30–60×60 cm). Very similar to ***D. columnae,*** with bright-green, deeply toothed leaves and single yellow daisies. Variety ***magnificum*** grows to 2 ft (60 cm) and has yellow daisies 2½ in. (6.2 cm) wide. Zones 4–8.

D. plantagineum. Europe. Height 2 ft; spread 1 ft (60×30 cm). Hairy, slightly toothed, heart-shaped leaves and masses of 2½-in. (6.2-cm), golden yellow daisies in spring to early summer. The cultivar 'Excelsum'; ('Harpur Crewe') has 3-in.- (7.5-cm-) wide flowers. Zones 4–8.

DORYCNIUM

(Canary-clover)

Family: Leguminosae

A small genus of shrubby herbs native to the Mediterranean and the Canary Isles. The leaves are cloverlike with five leaflets and the flowers are pealike, white with purple-tipped keels.

Cultivation: Grow in well-drained soil in a sunny location. Shear back the foliage after flowering for compact growth.

Landscape Use: A good groundcover for a sunny site.

Propagation: Take cuttings in summer. Divide in spring and autumn.

D. hirsutum (Lotus hirsutus). Canary-clover. Europe. Height 2 ft; spread 3 ft (60×30 cm) A lax, cloverlike, spreading subshrub covered with downy white hairs. The pale-green, hairy, compound leaves have three to five, rounded, wedge-shaped leaflets up to ½ in. (1.2 cm) long. The white pealike flowers with purple keels are borne in late summer to early autumn. Zones 5–9.

DRABA

(Whitlow Grass)

FAMILY: Cruciferae

A large genus of about 250 species of rock garden or alpine-house plants. They are generally mound-forming, with deep taproots, basal rosettes, and wiry stems holding small, mostly yellow, four-petaled flowers blooming in spring and early summer.

CULTIVATION: Plant in a sunny site in well-drained, lime-rich soil that does not dry out during the growing season. Protect the foliage from winter rains.

LANDSCAPE USE: Diminutive plants for the rock garden.

PROPAGATION: Take cuttings of nonflowering rosettes in summer. Sow seed in spring, plant the following year.

D. aizoides. Whitlowgrass. Europe. Height 4 in.; spread 6 in. (10×15 cm). A tiny, tufted perennial with narrow, lance-shaped, gray-green leaves ½ in. (1.2 cm) long and clusters of lemon-yellow flowers ¼ in. (0.6 cm) wide in spring. Zones 5–8.

D. bryoides (D. rigida* var. *bryoides). Caucasus. Height 2 in.; spread 3 in. (5×7.5 cm). A minute cushion of green oblong leaves and golden flowers on 1-in. (2.5-cm), wiry stems blooming in spring. Zones 6–8.

D. lasiocarpa. Europe. Height 8 in.; spread 12 in. (20×30 cm). A densely tufted, robust plant with gray-green, linear leaves and many-flowered spikes of yellow flowers in spring. Zones 4–8.

D. sibirica. Siberia. Height 1 in.; spread 12 in. (2.5×30 cm). A prostrate plant forming hairy rosettes of oblong, spear-shaped leaves and drooping stems bearing clusters of yellow flowers in spring. Perhaps the easiest species to cultivate. Zones 3–8.

DRACOCEPHALUM

(Dragonhead)

FAMILY: Labiatae

Dracocephalum ruyschianum

A genus of annual and perennial plants with square stems, opposite leaves, and flowers in terminal spikes often in shades of blue. They are similar to the genus ***Nepeta*** but differ in having a slightly different-shaped flower with a two-lipped calyx. They are not widely grown, which is a pity, as their loose habit and blue flowers make them useful additions to the cottage garden. The name alludes to the shape of the flowers.

Cultivation: Grow in good, moist but well-drained soil in full sun to partial shade. Remove the faded flower heads.

Landscape Use: Summer-flowering plants for the herbaceous border. A few of the smaller growing species can be grown in the rock garden.

Propagation: Divide or sow seed in spring.

D. austriacum. Europe. Height 2 ft; spread 1 ft (60 × 30 cm). An erect plant with square stems and hairless leaves divided into three to seven linear segments. The blue-violet funnel-shaped flowers are borne in whorls along the flower spike in mid- to late summer. Zones 4–8.

D. nutans. Europe. Height 18 in.; spread 12 in. (45 × 30 cm). Coarsely toothed, egg-shaped to oblong leaves up to 2 in. (5 cm) long on square stems and whorled spikes of blue flowers throughout the summer. With diligent deadheading, this species will flower for three months. Zones 3–8.

D. ruyschianum. Europe. Height 2 ft; spread 1 ft (60 × 30 cm). Hairy stems and linear to lance-shaped leaves up to 3 in. (7.5 cm) long with dense, whorled spikes of 1-in.- (2.5-cm-) long violet-blue flowers throughout the summer. Zones 3–8.

DRYOPTERIS

(Wood Fern, Buckler Fern)

Family: Polypodiaceae

A genus of about 150 deciduous or semievergreen ferns with handsome, dissected foliage, native to temperate and tropical areas of the world. Many are native to the woodlands of North America and are attractive plants for the shade garden. The common name buckler fern refers to the shape of the scales that protect the spore capsules—they resemble belt buckles.

Cultivation: Grow in moist, woodland soil in shade. Clean up the faded fronds in spring as the new growth appears.

Landscape Use: Excellent, easily cultivated ferns for the woodland garden or shade border. Particularly effective when grown in large groups.

Propagation: Sow spores when they ripen in mid- to late summer, or divide the crowns in midspring.

D. aemula. Hay-scented buckler fern. Europe. Height 2 ft; spread 1 ft (60 × 30 cm). An upright fern with yellow-green, dissected, triangular fronds smelling of new-mown hay. Zones 4–8.

D. cristata. Crested shield fern. Europe, Asia, North America. Height 3 ft; spread 2 ft (90 × 60 cm). A swamp-inhabiting semievergreen fern with open rosettes of linear, spear-shaped, dark-green fronds with the fertile frond erect and the sterile frond spreading. Grow in wet areas. Zones 4–8.

Dryopteris marginalis

D. dilatata. Broad buckler fern. Europe, Asia, North America. Height 3–4 ft; spread 2 ft (90–120 × 60 cm). A vigorous, semievergreen fern with broad, triangular, arching, dark-green fronds with oval leaf segments and deep-brown stems. Zones 4–8.

D. erythrosora. Autumn fern, Japanese red shield fern. Asia. Height 18 in.; spread 12 in. (45 × 30 cm). An unusually beautiful fern with coppery red young fronds that turn glossy green when mature. Requires well-drained soil that does not dry out. Zones 5–8.

D. filix-mas. Male fern. Europe, Asia, North America. Height 2–4 ft; spread 3 ft (60–120 × 90 cm). A common wild fern in Europe but rare in the United States, where overcollecting has endangered wild populations. Except in mild areas, this is a deciduous fern with leathery oblong, spear-shaped fronds beginning yellow-green and maturing to deep green. It is an adaptable fern growing in almost any soil except very boggy. There are a number of cultivars including: 'Crispa,' a dwarf form with crested fronds; 'Cristata,' known as the king of the male ferns, whose frond divisions terminate in divided, crested tips; 'Grandiceps,' with arching, tasseled fronds; 'Linearis,' with fronds with slender, linear divisions. Zones 4–8.

D. goldieana. Goldie's fern. North America. Height 4 ft; spread 2 ft (120 × 60 cm). A large, coarse fern with leathery, deep-green oblong, egg-shaped fronds up to 14 in. (35 cm) wide. A large, deciduous fern for the woodland garden. Zones 3–8.

D. intermedia. Intermediate shield fern. North America. Height 3 ft; spread 2 ft (90 × 60 cm). Native to eastern North American deciduous woodland, this is an evergreen or semievergreen, crown-forming fern with oblong, spear-shaped, divided fronds 30 in. (75 cm) long and 10 in. (25 cm) wide. It is a tough fern that requires neutral to acid, constantly moist soil and open shade. Zones 4–8.

D. marginalis. Marginal shield fern. Height 2 ft; spread 2 ft (60 × 60 cm). An evergreen fern with spear-shaped, blue-green, leathery fronds up to 20 in. (50 cm) long and 8 in. (20 cm) wide. The crowns are partially exposed above the soil. Grows well in full to open shade in neutral soil. Zones 4–8.

ECHINACEA

(Coneflower)

FAMILY: Compositae

Echinacea purpurea 'White Swan'

Echinacea purpurea 'Magnus'

A small genus of summer-flowering perennials native to North America. They are coarse plants with erect stems and daisylike rose, purple, and crimson flowers with cone-shaped centers. The flowers appear in summer and continue blooming for two months or more. The name comes from the Greek *echinos,* "hedgehog," a reference to the sharp, pointed bracts of the flower.

Cultivation: Plant in a sunny site in well-drained, fertile soil. Remove faded flower heads for extended flowering.

Landscape Use: Long-flowering daisies for the sunny border, prairie garden, or wildflower meadow.

Propagation: The easiest method is to divide the clumps in spring or early autumn.

E. ***angustifolia.*** North America. Height 2 ft; spread 12 in. (60 × 30 cm). Native to the prairies from Saskatchewan to Texas, this is a coarse, bristly plant with alternate, narrowly spear-shaped leaves and rose-purple, cone-centered flowers. Increasingly used in medicine as an immune-system stimulant. Zones 3–9.

E. ***pallida.*** North America. Height 3 ft; spread 18 in. (90 × 45 cm). Native to the midwestern and southern United States, similar to *E.* ***angustifolia*** but stouter and taller with rose-purple flowers. Zones 3–9.

E. ***purpurea.*** Purple cone-flower. North America. Height 2–4 ft; spread 18 in. (60–120 × 45 cm). A coarse perennial with mid-green, broadly lance-shaped, toothed leaves and daisylike flowers made up of drooping purple ray-flowers and cone-shaped orange-brown centers. 'Alba' has creamy white flowers with coppery cones; 'Bright Star' has rose-red flowers with petals extending more horizontally than the species; 'Magnus' has broad, flaring pink petals around a dark cone; 'Robert Bloom' has red-purple flowers with purple-brown center; 'The King' has deep-pink flowers around a brown cone; 'White Lustre' has reflexed white petals around an orange cone; 'White Swan' has bright-white flowers with a deep-orange center. Zones 3–9.

E. ***tennesseensis.*** Tennessee coneflower. Southeastern United States. Height 2–3 ft; spread 18 in. (60–90 × 45 cm). An endangered species now propagated by a handful of nurseries. It is not a very vigorous plant, but it does have a certain charm. The leaves are narrowly lance-shaped, mid to dark green. The flowers are produced in summer and are deep pink with pinkish green centers and upturned petals. Zones 3–9.

ECHINOPS

(Globe-thistle)

Family: Compositae

Echinops ritro 'Taplow Blue'

Echinops humilis

A genus of about 100 species of erect plants with round, spiny heads of white, blue, or steel-blue flowers. The leaves are alternate, coarse, and thistle-like with varying degrees of spinyness. The name

Echinops means 'Hedgehoglike," referring to the spiny flowers.

CULTIVATION: Grow in well-drained soil in a sunny location. Tolerant of dry, poor soils and hot climates.

LANDSCAPE USE: Bold plants good for creating striking effects in the large herbaecous border, where they should be planted in clumps. For flower arrangements, cut just as the flower is opening.

PROPAGATION: Divide in the spring or autumn.

E. exaltatus. Siberia. Height 5 ft; spread 2 ft (150 × 60 cm). Distinguished by its tall, erect, downy-white stem. The thistlelike deep-green, rough leaves have spiny-toothed margins. The round blue flowers appear in mid- to late summer. Zones 3–9.

E. humilis. Asia. Height 3–4 ft; spread 2 ft (90–120 × 60 cm). Dark-green, thistlelike leaves with wavy leaf margins and little or no spines. The leaves are downy-white underneath and cobwebby above. The steel-blue flowers appear in late summer. Zones 3–9.

E. ritro. Europe, Asia. Height 4 ft; spread 2 ft (120 × 60 cm). A thistlelike plant having green leaves with downy-gray undersides. The margins are spineless. The steel-blue flowers appear in mid- to late summer. 'Taplow Blue,' which is often confusingly listed under a number of species is a vigorous cultivar growing up to 5 ft (150 cm) with soft-blue flowers; 'Veitch's Blue' has smaller but more abundant flowers than 'Taplow Blue.' Zones 3–9.

E. ruthenicus. Europe, Asia. Height 4 ft; spread 2 ft (120 × 60 cm). Possibly a subspecies of ***E. ritro,*** this is a handsome plant with silvery white stems, prickly, shiny green leaves with downy-white undersides, and bright-blue globe flowers in midsummer. Zones 3–9.

EDRAIANTHUS

(Grassy-bells)

FAMILY: Campanulaceae

A small genus of short-lived rock-garden plants closely related to ***Campanula.*** They are clump- or mat-forming plants with stalkless, upturned, bell-shaped purplish or violet flowers in spring and summer. The name comes from the Greek *hedraios,* "sitting," and *anthos,* "flower," referring to the cluster of flowers at the growing tips of the plant.

CULTIVATION: Grow in a sunny position in deep, well-drained, gritty soil.

LANDSCAPE USE: Rock-garden, scree, or trough plants.

PROPAGATION: Take cuttings of nonflowering basal shoots in summer. Sow seed in early spring.

E. graminifolius. Mediterranean. Height 3 in.; spread 9 in. (7.5 × 22.5 cm). A tufted, bristly plant with rosettes of needle-shaped, gray-green leaves up to 2 in. (5 cm) long and upward-facing, bell-shaped purple flowers in late spring to midsummer. Zones 5–7.

E. pumilio. Yugoslavia. Height 2 in.; spread 9 in. (5 × 22.5 cm). A clump-forming plant with linear gray-green leaves about 1 in. (2.5 cm) long. Violet-blue funnel-shaped flowers are borne among the leaves and appear sometime between late spring to midsummer. Needs protection from winter rains. Zones 5–7.

ELYMUS

(Wild Rye, Lyme Grass)

FAMILY: Graminae

About 50 species of annual and perennial grasses with flat leaf blades and bristly flowers. Many of those grown for ornamental value are native to seashores and are rampant colonizers; steps should be taken to see that they do not take over the garden.

CULTIVATION: Grow in full sun in a moist but well-drained soil. Will tolerate dry conditions. Cut back faded foliage in winter or spring.

LANDSCAPE USE: Coarse and invasive grasses valuable for their blue leaves that contrast handsomely with silver foliage plants. To keep contained, plant in a bottomless pot in the ground.

PROPAGATION: Divide in the spring or autumn.

E. arenarius. European dune grass. Europe, Asia. Height 3–4 ft; spread 3 ft (90–120×90 cm). A vigorously invasive, spreading grass with blue-gray, flat leaves and 1-ft (30-cm) spikes of wheat-like gray flowers in summer. Frequently used to control sand dune erosion, the good blue forms of this species are often erroneously sold as the more desirable ***E. racemosus*** 'Glaucus.' Zones 4–8.

E. glaucus. Blue wild rye. North America. Height 3 ft; spread 2 ft (90×60 cm). Probably the bluest of all ornamental grasses, this is a vigorous warm-season plant with clustered stems and light-glaucous-blue, arching foliage with narrow, gray flower spikes in midsummer. It frequently does not flower. Its tufts and the fact that it does not spread by means of stolons distinguish it from ***E. arenarius.*** Drought resistant. Zones 4–8.

E. racemosus (E. giganteus). Volga wild rye. Siberia. Height 4–6 ft; spread 2–3 ft (120–180×60–90 cm). A robust and vigorous species that spreads by means of rhizomes and is also used for erosion control. The leaf bladesa are clustered and flat, the flowers are bristly and appear in midsummer but are of little consequence and should be removed. 'Glaucus' is a cultivar with attractive light-blue foliage that looks good from late spring until early winter. Zones 3–8.

Elymus arenarius

EOMECON

(Dawn Poppy)

FAMILY: Papaveraceae

A single species native to eastern China. It is a spreading plant with heart-shaped, gray-green leaves and panicles of four-petaled white flowers in late spring. The name is from the Greek *eos,* "dawn," and *mekon,* "poppy."

CULTIVATION: Grow in moist but not wet soil in shade.

Landscape Use: A spring-flowering plant for the woodland garden or shady border edge.

Propagation: Divide in spring or early autumn.

E. ***chionanthum.*** Dawn poppy. Height 18 in.; spread 18 in. (45 × 45 cm). A spreading, rhizomatous plant with reddish orange sap. The stems are branched, the leaves are basal, gray-green, heart-shaped with long leaf stalks. The pendulous white flowers are borne in panicles in late spring or early summer. Zones 6–9.

EPILOBIUM

(Willow Herb)

Family: Onagraceae

A large genus of about 200 species of annual and perennial plants spread throughout the northern hemisphere. Some are weedy invaders of disturbed sites while others are good garden plants. The leaves are opposite or alternate, the flowers are often held in tall spikes. They are sun-loving plants that bloom in summer.

Cultivation: Plant in well-drained soil in a sunny location.

Landscape Use: The taller species are useful for the herbaceous border, while some smaller species make good rock-garden plants. Those species that spread widely by means of seed can be controlled by timely deadheading. The late-summer-blooming fuchsialike species are outstanding plants for the dry garden.

Propagation: Sow seeds in early spring. Take cuttings of basal shoots in spring.

E. ***angustifolium.*** Fireweed. Northern hemisphere. Height 5–6 ft; spread 2 ft (150–180 × 60 cm). A very invasive but beautiful weed that has a place in the wild garden. The stems are leafy up to 6 ft (180 cm) tall, the leaves are dark green, 2–6 in. (5–15 cm) long, alternate, and tapering to a point. The bright, showy, pink flowers are borne in loose spikes about 12 in. (30 cm) long in late summer. It is called fireweed because of its habit of colonizing areas damaged by fire. Many areas of post-blitz London were softened by the profusion of fireweed growing amid the rubble. A white variety, 'Alba,' has spikes of white flowers, with both an invasive and a noninvasive form. It is very desirable as an accent plant. Zones 3–8.

E. ***canum (Zauschneria californica).*** California.

Epilobium canum ssp. *etteri*

Height 1–2 ft; spread 2 ft (30–60 × 60 cm). A spreading, woody plant with ½-in.- (1.2-cm-) long, gray-green linear to lance-shaped, stemless, opposite leaves becoming alternate at the top of the stem. Bright-scarlet, 1–2-in.- (2.5–5-cm-) long, tubular, fuchsialike flowers are produced in late summer to early autumn. 'Album' has white flowers; 'Glasnevin' has even brighter scarlet flowers and darker foliage; 'Solidarity Pink' has rosy pink flowers. Subspecies ***canum*** (***Zauschneria cana***) grows to about 1 ft (30 cm), has linear, gray leaves and scarlet flowers. 'Hurricane Point' reaches a height of about 6 in. (15 cm) and a spread of 12 in. (30 cm). Ssp. ***latifolia*** (***Zauschneria californica*** ssp. ***latifolia***) has egg-shaped, gray-green leaves and shorter stems and forms a mat 3–6 in. (7.5–15 cm) high. Grow in well-drained soil in full sun to light shade. This species is hardier than first thought and can take quite cold winter temperatures if protected from winter wet. It does best in Zones 7–10 but is hardy with some protection in Zones 4–10.

E. dodonaei. Europe. Height 3 ft; spread 2 ft (90×60 cm). A clump-forming plant with alternate, softly hairy, linear leaves up to 2½ in. (6 cm) long and purplish red flowers on long spires appearing in summer. Zones 3–8.

E. glabellum. New Zealand. Height 12 in.; spread 8 in. (30×20 cm). A long-flowering plant with outward-facing, creamy white, funnel-shaped flowers on leafy stems from mid- to late summer. The leaves are mid-green, glossy, often with a slight bronze tint. A hybrid with ***E. glabellum*** as one of its parents is × 'Broadwell Hybrid,' an attractive plant growing to a height of 9 in. (22.5 cm) with funnel-shaped white, flushed-pink flowers. Zones 8–9.

E. latifolium. Red willow-weed. North America, Europe, Asia. Height 18 in.; spread 18 in. (45×45 cm). Native to moist meadows in northwestern North America with glaucous, lance-shaped leaves up to 2 in. (5 cm) long and 2-in.- (5-cm-) wide magenta-red flowers in summer. Zones 2–8.

EPIMEDIUM

(Barrenwort)

FAMILY: Berberidaceae

Epimedium grandiflorum 'Rose Queen'

Approximately 25 species of low-growing, spreading perennials with divided leaves with heart-shaped, toothed leaflets. In areas with mild winters, many species will retain their leaves. In spring the leaves of many species are attractively tinged with red tones. The flowers, which appear early in the growing season, are borne on delicate, wiry stems and are sometimes spurred and saucer-shaped. They are invaluable plants as groundcovers for light shade. The common name barrenwort refers to the ability the plant was once thought to have to prevent conception.

CULTIVATION: Grow in moist, well-drained soil in light shade. It can be grown in full sun if given adequate water. Cut down the foliage of deciduous species in late winter so that the spring flowers can be seen more easily.

LANDSCAPE USE: Excellent groundcovers for shade. Also effective as rock-garden and border plants.

PROPAGATION: Divide in spring or autumn.

E. acuminatum. China. Height 18 in.; spread 12 in. (45×30 cm). A rare plant just becoming available from specialized growers. It it a clump-forming plant with shiny, dark-green, lance-shaped leaflets, blue-green beneath, tapering to a slender point. The flowers, which have dramatic curving spurs, appear in midspring, are borne on wiry stems clear of the leaves, and are an unusual contrast of purple and white. They continue into early summer. Zones 5–9.

E. alpinum. Europe. Height 18 in.; spread 12 in. (45 × 30 cm). Heart-shaped leaves up to 5 in. (12.5 cm) long with a reddish margin in spring. The blossoms are held in lose panicles of 15 to 20 flowers and are red and yellow with short spurs. Plants sold under this name are usually ***E. × rubrum.*** Zones 3–9.

E. diphyllum. Japan. Height 6 in.; spread 12 in. (15 × 30 cm). An unusual dwarf species from Japan with heart-shaped, toothed leaves up to 2 in. (5 cm) long and drooping, white, nonspurred flowers partly hidden by the foliage in spring. Zones 6–9.

E. grandiflorum. Asia. Height 12 in.; spread 12 in. (30 × 30 cm). Clumps of dense foliage, reddish in spring turning to dark green in summer. The leaves are divided into sharply toothed, pointed, and heart-shaped leaflets on wiry stems. The spidery flowers are purplish pink with white spurs. 'Rose Queen' has compact strawberry-pink flowers with long, white-tipped spurs; 'White Queen' has large white, spurred flowers; 'Violaceum; has deep-violet flowers. Zones 4–9.

E. perralderianum. Algeria. Height 12 in.; spread 18 in. (30 × 45 cm). Heart-shaped, sharply toothed, glossy leaves with leaflets divided into threes. The leaves are bronze when young, turning fresh green in summer and copper-bronze in winter. The pale-yellow flowers appear in early spring. Zones 6–9.

E. pinnatum. Caucasus. Height 12 in.; spread 18 in. (30 × 45 cm). One of the best ***Epimediums*** for groundcover, it is similar to ***E. perralderianum*** although with conspicuously less-toothed, divided leaves. The leaves are glossy and almost evergreen on wiry stems. The flowers are borne on leafless stems and are yellow with tiny brown spurs. The subspecies ***colchicum*** has strong yellow flowers with longer spurs and almost spineless foliage. 'Frohnleiten,' a cultivar of the cross between ***E. perralderianum*** and this species, has yellow flowers and prickly leaves that turn red in autumn. Zones 4–9.

Epimedium pinnatum var colchicum

E. × rubrum. Height 12 in.; spread 12 in. (30 × 30 cm). A hybrid between ***E. alpinum*** and ***E. grandiflorum.*** It resembles a larger ***E. alpinum*** with mid-green, heart-shaped leaves tinged red when young, turning pale green in summer and coppery red and yellow in autumn. The abundant flowers are rose-red with white, slightly up-curved spurs. Notable for its excellent foliage color. Zones 4–9.

E. sagittatum. China. Height 10 in,; spread 12 in. (25 × 30 cm). Rarely cultivated in the West, which is unfortunate because it is an unusual plant for the connoisseur. Evergreen, light-green leaflets up to 6 in. (15 cm) long are edged with numerous spiny teeth that look as if they bite. Tiny greenish flowers are produced in spring. Zones 5–9.

E. × versicolor. Height 12 in.; spread 12 in. (30 × 30 cm). A vigorously spreading hybrid between ***E. grandiflorum*** and ***E. pinnatum colchicum*** with sharply pointed, heart-shaped, spiny-toothed, mid-green leaves, marked red in spring. Drooping yellow, pink, or red flowers in early spring. The cultivar 'Sulphureum' has flowers of pale yellow on the inside, darker yellow on the outside. 'Versicolor' has flowers of rose and pale yellow. Zones 5–9.

E. × warleyense. Height 12 in.; spread 12 in. (30 × 30 cm). A hybrid with mid-green, heart-shaped leaves with prickly margins and a reddish color when young. The flowers are unusual for the genus in that they are bright orange with bright-yellow spurs. Zones 4–9.

E. × youngianum. Height 8 in.; spread 12 in. (20 × 30 cm). A series of clones between ***E. diphyllum*** and ***E. grandiflorum*** that is smaller in habit than other cultivated species. A compact plant with the young foliage beginning reddish and turning mid-green in summer. The leaflets are prickly toothed and the flowers are pink and appear in early spring. 'Niveum' is a commonly grown form, with white flowers that bloom in late spring and early summer; 'Roseum' has rose-pink flowers that appear slightly earlier than those of 'Niveum.' Zones 4–9.

EQUISETUM

(Horsetail)

Family: Equisataceae

A genus of evergreen, flowerless plants widely distributed throughout the world. They are common to wet places and are allied to club mosses and ferns. The leaves are inconspicuous and scalelike, being wrapped around the evergreen, hollow stems. The name comes from the Latin *equus,* "horse," and *seta,* "bristle." While not widely grown as ornamental plants, they are of interest to the curious and are attractive garden plants.

Cultivation: Grow in moist to wet soil in sun or partial shade.

Landscape Use: Rarely grown as ornamentals except in Japan, where they are cultivated for their architectural qualities. They are elegant plants for the pondside or wild garden. Care should be taken not to plant in areas where their invasive qualities will dominate other plants. ***E. arvense,*** the field horsetail, is a serious weed once it has invaded the herbaceous border.

Propagation: Easily divided in spring or autumn.

E. hyemale. Common horsetail. Height 4 ft; spread 5 in. (120 cm). An apparently leafless plant with light-green, evergreen stems furrowed with ridges. Occasionally used as an ornamental in wet places. Zones 1–9.

E. scirpoides. Dwarf horsetail. Scandinavia. Height 8 in. (20 cm). Spreading mats of leafless evergreen stems for use as a groundcover in wet places. Zones 1–9.

ERAGROSTIS

(Love Grass)

Family: Graminae

Eragrostis curvula

A large genus of about 250 species of annual and perennial grasses. The few perennial species grown as ornamentals are valued for their delicate-looking, arching inflorescences. They are pleasing grasses flowering in midsummer, with the leaves and inflorescence remaining attractive into autumn and early winter.

Cultivation: Grow in full sun in ordinary soil. Weeping love grass will tolerate considerable drought.

Landscape Use: For use as a specimen plant or in groups.

Propagation: Divide in the spring or sow seed.

E. curvula. Weeping love grass. North America. Height 3 ft; spread 2 ft (90 × 60 cm). A tufted grass with an upright habit and arching leaves. The gracefully arching inflorescence begins dark green in early summer and fades to a straw color by late summer. The foliage turns a buff color and remains attractive into early winter. Used for erosion control in parts of the southern United States. Zones 5–9.

E. trichodes. Sand love grass. North America. Height 4 ft; spread 2 ft (120 × 60 cm). A clump-forming, erect grass with dark-green foliage reaching a height of 2 ft (60 cm) and upright-arching flowers beginning bronze but fading to a light-straw color in late summer. A cultivar 'Bend' is slightly taller at 5 ft (150 cm). Zones 4–9.

ERANTHIS

(Winter Aconite)

Family: Ranunculaceae

A small genus of low-growing plants flowering in late winter and early spring. The dissected, basal, hand-shaped leaves spring from small tubers along with bright-yellow, upward-facing, buttercuplike flowers. The entire plant dies down by early summer. The name is derived from the Greek *er*, "spring," and *anthos*, "flower."

Cultivation: Grow winter aconites in a cool, shaded site in leafy soil. They can be grown successfully in full sun but will require moist soil.

Landscape Use: Wonderful early-flowering plants for massing in deciduous woodland, under shrubs, or in the herbaceous border. Their brightly glowing flowers are a welcome sight after a long winter.

Propagation: Divide the tuberous roots after flowering. Sow seed in early summer to germinate the following spring. Seedlings will take about four years to flower. Purchased tubers have varying degrees of success but should be planted 2 in. (5 cm) deep in late summer.

E. cilicicus. Greece. Height 3 in.; spread 4 in. (7.5 × 10 cm). A slightly smaller, less robust version of ***E. hyemalis*** with purple-pink stems and a more finely dissected collar of involucral bracts beneath the flower. Zones 4–9.

E. hyemalis. Winter aconite. Greece. Height 6 in.; spread 4 in. (15 × 10 cm). A widely grown harbinger of spring, with long-stemmed, deeply dissected, hand-shaped, pale-green leaves and lemon-yellow buttercuplike flowers up to 1 in. (2.5 cm) across in late winter. The collar beneath the flower consists of 12 to 15 green, lobed, involucral bracts. Zones 5–9.

E. × tubergenii. Height 6 in.; spread 4 in. (15 × 10 cm). A hybrid between the above species sharing the characteristics of both but being slightly more vigorous and having bright-yellow flowers blooming a little later than the species. 'Guinea Gold' has golden yellow flowers surrounded by a collar of green-bronze bracts. Zones 5–9.

ERIANTHUS

(Plume Grass)

Family: Graminae

A genus of about 20 species of grasses, one of which is grown as an ornamental grass particularly in areas where pampas grass is not hardy. Plume grass is a coarse, reedlike grass with a silvery inflorescence that is useful in dried arrangements.

Erianthus ravennae

The name comes from the Greek *erion,* "wool," and *anthos,* "flower," and refers to the silky nature of the flower.

Cultivation: Grow in full sun in well-drained soil.

Landscape Use: An excellent grass for use as a specimen or in small groups.

Propagation: Divide in spring.

E. ravennae. Plume grass. Europe. Height 12 ft; spread 4 ft (360 × 120 cm). A large, rapidly growing, clump-forming grass with gray-green, coarsely hairy leaf blades up to 30 in. (75 cm) long, on reddish stems. The foliage grows to a height of 4–6 ft (120–180 cm) and often turns orange in autumn. The plumes of silver-bronze flowers, which are borne on as many as 40 flower stalks, open in late summer and quickly turn to silver in early autumn. They remain attractive into midwinter. Staking is often necessary, although planting in less than fertile soil helps keep this species from opening up. Zones 6–9.

ERIGERON

(Fleabane)

Family: Compositae

A genus of annual biennial, and perennial summer-flowering daisies mostly native to North America. They are similar to but much smaller than ***Aster,*** generally flowering much earlier. They are strangely neglected in gardens, suffering from changes in fashion that make them "old-fashioned" plants. Easy to grow, they flower well in mild climates and are stalwart additions to any border. The name comes from the Greek *er,* "spring," and *geron,* "old man," referring to the old and tired appearance of some species. According to the British herbalist Culpepper, fleabane was so called because the seeds resemble fleas.

Cultivation: Fleabane requires an open, sunny site in well-drained, fertile soil. In hot climates shade from afternoon sun is advisable.

Landscape Use: Excellent open-faced daisies for the herbaceous border. Many are low-growing and are good edging plants for a sunny site. They also make fine cut flowers.

Propagation: Divide in spring or autumn. Sow seeds in early spring and plant young plants in late summer.

Erigeron 'Dimity'

E. aurantiacus. Turkestan. Height 12 in.; spread 10 in. (30 × 20 cm). A velvety plant with spoon-shaped basal leaves covered in fine hairs and yellow-orange daisies on leafy stems throughout the summer. 'Sulphureus' has pale-yellow flowers. Zones 4–8.

E. aureus (Haplopappus grandegeei). North America. Height 4 in.; spread 9 in. (15 × 22.5 cm). A dense, mat-forming plant with round, spoon-shaped leaves covered in gray hairs. The rich-yellow, daisylike flowers appear from early to midsummer. Zones 3–8.

E. compositus. Fernleaf fleabane. North America. Height 6 in.; spread 12 in. (15 × 30 cm). A low-growing, mat-forming plant with finely dissected, woolly leaves and pale-blue to white, daisylike flowers in summer. Native to the Rocky Mountains and a useful plant for hot, dry, gravelly sites. Zones 2–8.

E. glaucus. North America. Height 12 in.; spread 18 in. (30 × 45 cm). A sprawling perennial with evergreen, waxy, oval leaves up to 6 in. (15 cm) long. The mauve flowers have yellow centers and appear throughout the summer. Native to the Pacific Coast, making it a useful plant for coastal gardens. 'Elstead' has lilac-pink flowers. Zones 3–8.

E. karvinskianus (E. mucronatus). Mexico. Height 6 in.; spread 9 in. (15 × 22.5 cm). A dwarf, trailing plant with branching stems, lobed green leaves, and masses of ¾-in. (1.8-cm-) wide, white to pink daisy flowers throughout the summer. Seeds itself freely. Zones 8–9.

E. philadelphicus. North America. Height 3 ft; spread 1ft (90 × 30 cm). Widely distributed throughout North America, it is a clump-forming plant with unbranched stems and round, toothed, basal leaves. The stem leaves are untoothed and hairy. Loose clusters of yellow-centered pink or white flowers appear throughout the summer. Self-seeds freely. Zones 2–9.

E. pulchellus. Poor Robin's plantain. Height 2 ft; spread 1 ft (60 × 30 cm). A short-lived, weedy perennial with rounded basal leaves up to 5 in. (12.5 cm) long and stem leaves up to 2 in. (5 cm) long. Numerous heads of yellow-centered bluish white or pink flowers are borne in summer. Zones 3–9.

E. speciosus. Oregon fleabane. Height 2 ft; spread 2 ft (60 × 60 cm). A dense, clump-forming plant with hairless, spoon-shaped leaves with hairy leaf edges and lilac flowers with yellow centers. The species has been surpassed by a number of hybrids and cultivars:

'Adria': height 30 in (75 cm), lavender-blue flowers
'Charity': height 2 ft (60 cm), light-pink flowers
'Darkest of All': height 2 ft (60 cm), deep-violet-blue flowers
'Dimity': height 12 in. (30 cm), a dwarf pink
'Double Beauty': height 18 in. (45 cm), double violet-blue flowers
'Foerster's Leibling': height 16 in. (40 cm), semidouble deep-pink flowers
'Pink Jewel': height 2 ft (60 cm), single pink flowers
'Prosperity': height 18 in. (45 cm), semidouble light-blue flowers
'Rose Jewel': height 18 in. (45 cm), lilac-rose flowers
'Quakeress': height 2 ft (60 cm), lilac-pink flowers
'White Quakeress': height 2 ft (60 cm), white flowers.
Zones 2–9.

ERINUS

(Liver Balsam)

Family: Scrophulariaceae

A genus of two species native to Europe and Africa, with one species grown as a rock-garden plant. It has become naturalized in Western Europe.

Cultivation: Grow in well-drained soil in a sunny or partly shaded location.

Landscape Use: A short-lived but freely seeding plant for a dry stone wall, rock garden, or scree planting.

Propagation: Sow seed in spring.

E. ***alpinus.*** Europe. Height 3 in.; spread 6 in. (7.5×15 cm). A tufted, evergreen plant with spoon-shaped, coarsely toothed mid-green leaves up to ½ in. (1.2 cm) long and masses of starry, lavender-pink, white, or red flowers during late spring and early summer. 'Albus' is a white-flowered form; 'Dr. Haenele' has rosy red flowers. Zones 4–7.

ERIOGONUM

(Wild Buckwheat, Sulfur Flower)

Family: Polygonaceae

A large genus of generally drought-resistant plants native to North America. The opposite or alternate leaves are often woolly, the stems usually woody. Those species cultivated in gardens have either yellow or white flowers in summer.

Cultivation: Grow in well-drained soil in full sun. Protect those species with white woolly leaves from winter wet. Apart from ***E. allenii,*** species are more susceptible to damage from winter wet than cold temperatures. Desert or semidesert conditions are ideal.

Landscape: Long-blooming plants for the rock garden.

Propagation: Take cuttings in early summer or sow seed.

E. ***allenii.*** Eastern North America. Height 1 ft; spread 1 ft (30×30 cm). The only species native east of the Mississippi, this plant produces basal clumps of leaves up to 8 in. (20 cm) long and up to 3 in. (7.5 cm) wide. The golden yellow flowers are borne in flat-headed clusters from midsummer until early autumn. Zones 5–8.

E. ***crocatum.*** Saffron buckwheat. Southwestern North America. Height 1 ft; spread 1 ft (30×30 cm). A shrubby species with white wooly stems and egg-shaped leaves. The tiny sulfur-yellow flowers are borne in flat clusters in spring and early summer. Zones 9–10.

E. ***umbellatum.*** Sulfur flower. Western North America. Height 8–12 in.; spread 18 in. (20–30×45 cm). A shrubby plant with silver-gray spoon-shaped leaves and bright-yellow flowers in flat clusters in summer.

ERODIUM

(Heron's-bill)

Family: Geraniaceae

A genus of about 60 species related to ***Geranium.*** They are mostly low-growing, easily cultivated plants with finely cut foliage and saucer-shaped, pink, purple, or white, veined flowers. They are often woody stemmed with opposite or alternate, strongly scented leaves. Not widely grown in North America, they are better known in Europe. The name is from the Greek, meaning "heron," and refers to the beaked fruit.

Cultivation: Grow in a sunny site in well-drained, lime-rich soil.

Landscape Use: Good plants for the front of the herbaecous border or for the rock garden.

Propagation: Take cuttings of old basal wood in spring. Divide and sow seed in spring.

E. chrysanthum. Greece. Height 6 in.; spread 10 in. (15 × 25 cm). A densely tufted plant with delicate, finely cut silvery leaves and branching stems carrying heads of sulfur-yellow flowers throughout the summer. Zones 7–8.

E. glandulosum. Pyrenees. height 6 in.; spread 12 in. (15 × 30 cm). A mat-forming plant with basal, fernlike, mid-green leaves and pale-lilac flowers with deep-purple spots on the two upper petals. Blooms from early to late summer. 'Roseum' has rose-pink flowers. Zones 7–8.

Erodium petraeum ssp. *crispum*

E. petraeum. Spain, North Africa. Height 4 in.; spread 9 in. (10 × 22.5 cm). A tufted plant with gray-green, deeply cut leaves and pale-pink flowers with strong pink viens, blooming in late spring and early summer. Subspecies ***crispum*** (***E. cheilanthifolium***) has deeply cut and crinkled leaves. Zones 7–8.

E. reichardii (E. chamaedryoides). Majorca. Height 3 in.; spread 9 in. (7.5 × 22.5 cm). A mat-forming plant with dark-green, scalloped, toothed leaves and white, pink-veined flowers throughout the summer. 'Roseum' is a pink-flowering variety. Zones 8–9.

ERYNGIUM

(Sea Holly)

Family: Umbelliferae

About 230 species of spiny-leaved, thistle-headed perennial plants with long taproots and blue or white flowers with collars of narrow, spiny bracts. They are mostly mid- to late-summer-flowering plants that deserve to be more widely grown in American gardens.

Cultivation: Grow in light, well-drained, moderately fertile soil in full sun.

Landscape Use: Good plants for the herbaceous border, where their shimmering silvery blue flowers contrast well with ornamental grasses and other

Eryngium x oliveranum

delicately textured plants. Many are suitable for dried arrangements.

Propagation: Because of their long taproots, division is not recommended. Easily grown from seed sown in spring or root cuttings taken in late winter.

E. alpinum. Europe. Height 2½ ft; spread 18 in. (75 × 45 cm). Heart-shaped, glossy, blue-green, and spiny basal leaves becoming lobed or hand-shaped farther up the bluish stem. The flowers, which are the largest of the genus, are steel-blue cones surrounded by a ruff of frilly bracts in late summer. 'Amethyst' has 2-in.- (5-cm-), bright-blue flower heads on 2½-ft (75-cm) stems; 'Opal' is similar to 'Amethyst' but grows to a height of 18–24 in. (45–60 cm); 'Superbum' is a slightly more vigorous variety than the species. Zones 5–8.

E. bourgatii. Pyrennees. Height 2 ft; spread 1 ft (60 × 30 cm). Deeply cut, alternate, gray-green, and curly, palm-shaped leaves with white veins and stiff stems of silver-blue flowers surrounded by collars of silvery bracts held high above the foliage in mid- to late summer. Zones 5–8.

E. giganteum. Iran. Height 3–4 ft; spread 2 ft (90–120 × 60 cm). A short-lived perennial or biennial member of the genus with toothed, spiny green, rounded triangular leaves and strong silvery blue stems bearing silver-blue flower heads up to 2 in. (5 cm) long in late summer. Zones 5–8.

E. maritimum. Sea holly. Europe. Height 1 ft; spread 1 ft (30 × 30 cm). Native to coastal areas of Britain and naturalized in some areas along the Atlantic coast of the United States. The basal foliage is bright silver-green, three-lobed, fleshy, and roundly hand-shaped, while the stem leaves are more deeply cut. The flowers appear from mid- to late summer and are pale-blue, 1-in. (2.5-cm) cones surrounded by a collar of coarse, spiny bracts. Zones 5–8.

E. × oliverianum. Height 2–3 ft; spread 18 in. (60–90 × 45 cm). A hybrid, possibly between ***E. alpinum*** and ***E. planum,*** with round, blue-green basal leaves and deeply cut stem leaves. Steel-blue stems support masses of blue flowers surrounded by spiky bract collars. Zones 5–8.

E. planum. Europe. Height 3 ft; spread 18 in. (90 × 45 cm). Dark-green, heart-shaped basal leaves, stem leaves three to five times lobed. The flowers are light-blue globes surrounded by a collar of blue-green spiky bracts. 'Blue Dwarf' is a form reaching about 2 ft (60 cm) in height. Zones 3–8.

E. × tripartitum. Height 3 ft; spread 2 ft (90 × 60 cm). Probably a hybrid and one of the best of the genus with dark-green, wedge-shaped basal leaves less spiny than those of many other species. Masses of ½-in.- (1.2-cm-) wide blue flowers with a ruff of dark-blue bracts are borne on branching, wiry stems in summer. Zones 5–8.

E. variifolium. North Africa. Height 18 in.; spread 12 in. (45 × 30 cm). More interesting for its foliage than flowers. The rosette of evergreen, glossy, dark-green, rounded leaves is marbled with white veins. The round, blue flowers are sparsely produced in summer. Zones 7–8.

E. yuccifolium. Rattlesnake master. North America. Height 3–4 ft; spread 2 ft (90–120 × 60 cm). Possibly the least attractive of the sea hollies grown in gardens, this species has swordlike, spiny blue-gray leaves and green-white flower cones with a tiny collar of gray-green bracts. Blooms in mid- to late summer. Zones 3–8.

E.* × *zabelli. Height 2 ft; spread 18 in. (60 × 45 cm). A hybrid probably between ***E. bourgatii*** and ***E. alpinum*** with green, spiny, lobed foliage and blue cone-shaped flower heads with finely cut collars of bracts around the flower. Cultivars are 'Jewel,' 'James Ivory,' and 'Slieve Donard,' the latter having upward-curving, finely cut, toothed bracts. Zones 5–8.

EUPATORIUM

(Joe-pye Weed, Boneset, Mist-flower)

FAMILY: Compositae

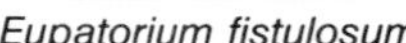

Eupatorium fistulosum

Eupatorium rugosum

A large genus of herbaceous perennials and shrubs. Most are native to tropical America, while many of the hardy herbaceous species grown in gardens are native to North America and Europe. The leaves are opposite or whorled, mostly lance-shaped. The flowers are generally held in flat-topped or rounded clusters and appear in late summer and early autumn. A number of species were grown for medicinal purposes, in fact, the name ***Eupatorium*** commemorates Mithridates Eupator, physician and king of Pontus.

CULTIVATION: Tolerant of a great variety of soil conditions, but in general, plant in moist, well-drained soil in sun to partial shade.

LANDSCAPE USE: Late-season flowers for the herbaceous border, meadow garden, or wild garden. Attractive to butterflies and good for cutting.

PROPAGATION: Divide in spring.

E. cannabinum. Hemp agrimony. Europe, Asia. Height 4 ft; spread 2 ft (120 × 60 cm). A rangy weed with opposite, mid-green, broadly lance-shaped, coarsely toothed leaves three to five times parted into segments. Terminal clusters of purplish flowers appear in summer. A double form 'Plenum' is more ornamental and has the advantage of being sterile and not self-seeding. An ancient herb much used in medicine. The name agrimony comes from the Greek *argemone,* referring to a plant that heals the eyes. It was prized by Native Americans to cool fevers. Zones 5–8.

E. coelestinum. Mist flower, hardy ageratum. Eastern North America. Height 2 ft; spread 2 ft (60 × 60 cm). Opposite, roundly triangular, coarsely toothed leaves up to 3 in. (7.5 cm) long. Bluish violet flowers are borne in compact clusters from midsummer to midautumn. The flowers resemble the annual ***Ageratum houstonianum.*** 'Album' has white flowers; 'Wayside Variety' is a dwarf form growing to a height of 15 in. (37.5 cm) with crinkled leaves. An invasive plant requiring well-drained soil. Useful for its colonizing habits in poor soil in full sun or light shade. Zones 6–8.

E. fistulosum. Joe-pye-weed. Eastern North America. Height 6–10 ft; spread 3–4 ft (180–300 × 90–120 cm). Considerable confusion exists concerning the identification of Joe-pye weed. The species are very similar and are highly promiscuous. For many years Joe-pye-weed was listed under ***E. purpureum.*** This has now been found to be incorrect, as ***E. purpureum*** is a shade-loving species with domed clusters of light-pink, almost white flowers and thin, narrowly lance-shaped, dark-green leaves. It is fairly safe to say that the Joe-pye weed found in open meadows and grown in gardens is ***E. fistulosum,*** a clump-forming plant with stout stems that are variably speckled and unspeckled. The lance-shaped leaves are up to 12 in. (30 cm) long and are arranged in whorls of three to six. Domed heads of tubular, reddish purple flowers are borne in late summer and early autumn. ***E. maculatum*** is virtually indistinguishable from ***E. fistulosum*** and often interbreeds with it. ***E. maculatum*** has more densely clustered flower heads that are flat rather than domed. 'Atropurpureum' has purplish foliage and rosy lilac flowers. 'Future Music' is a relatively new plant with large clusters of white flowers borne on stout stems up to 6 ft (180 cm) high; 'Gateway' has dark-pink flowers and grows to a height of 4½ ft (135 cm) the first year and up to 8 ft (240 cm) in the following years. Both cultivars are probably hybrids. Joe-pye weeds are found in great abundance in roadside ditches and marshy land from New England to North Carolina. Zones 2–4.

E. hyssopifolium. North America. Height 2 ft; spread 1 ft (60 × 30 cm). A variable plant with unbranched stems and opposite, linear leaves arranged in whorls of four and held at a 45-degree angle. Platelike cluster of off-white flowers appear in late summer and autumn. Native to dry wood edges, pine barrens, and sand dunes. Zones 5–8.

E. perfoliatum. Boneset. Eastern North America. Height 5 ft; spread 2 ft (150 × 60 cm). Common to wet areas of eastern North America, with hairy stems and opposite lance-shaped, gray-green leaves up to 8 in. (20 cm) long, tapering to a sharp point and with a broad base that surrounds the stem. Large, flat heads of greenish white flowers appear from late summer to midautumn. Once widely used as a medicinal herb by Native Americans, the name boneset is derived from the value of this herb in treating a type of influenza that was so painful it was called break-bone fever. Zones 4–8.

E. purpureum. Bluestem Joe-pye weed. Eastern North America. Height 10 ft; spread 3 ft (300 × 90 cm). The fourth of the Joe-pye weeds with stout, greenish blue stems without spots. Whorled, oval to lance-shaped, mid-green leaves grow up to 12 in. (30 cm) long, are sharply serrated, and smell of vanilla when bruised. Flat heads of tubular pinkish purple flowers are less striking than those of the other species. The name Joe-pye weed derives from the story that a Native American medicine man by this name used the plants for healing. Zones 3–8.

E. rugosum. White snakeroot. Eastern North America.. Height 4 ft; spread 2 ft (120 × 60 cm). Common to dry woodland margins of eastern North America with stiff stems and oval, bright-green, toothed leaves up to 7 in. (17.5 cm) long. Open clusters of pure-white flowers similar to those of large white annual ***Ageratum*** appear in autumn. Zones 3–8.

EUPHORBIA

(Spurge)

FAMILY: Euphorbiaceae

Over 1,800 species of diverse plants, from prostrate weeds to tall cactuslike trees. Crown of thorns, ***E. milii splendens,*** is a common greenhouse plant in temperate areas as is the poinsettia, ***E. pulcherrima.*** The hardy herbaceous species worthy of garden use are robust, easily cultivated plants with undivided, usually untoothed, mostly spear-shaped leaves. The flowers are rather insignificant although surrounded by large and attractive, mostly yellow cup-shaped and petallike bracts. A caustic, milky sap is produced from cut stems, and care should be taken to keep this sap away from eyes, mouth, and skin. The genus is supposedly named after Euphorbus, physician to the king of Mauretania in ancient times.

Euphorbia griffithii

Euphorbia polychroma

Cultivation: Grow in ordinary, well-drained soil in full sun. Light shade may be needed in areas with hot summers.

Landscape Use: A broad range of uses, from rock gardens to large borders.

Propagation: Sow seeds in early spring. Division in spring is possible if care is taken not to damage the fleshy roots.

E. amygdaloides. Wood spurge. Europe, Asia. Height 18 in.; spread 12 in. (45 × 30 cm). An erect species, branching from the base, with downy, often orange-tinted, narrowly lance-shaped leaves. Columnar-shaped, lime-green flower heads are borne in spring. A woodland plant for shade. The variety ***robbiae*** is more robust than the type with a rosette of broader, dark-green, glossy leaves and pale-green petallike bracts. Useful for dry shade, var. ***rubra*** has reddish purple foliage. 'Variegata' has leaves with cream margins. Zones 7–9.

E. characias. Europe. Height 3 ft; spread 3 ft (90 × 90 cm). A woody-based, shrubby perennial hardy to Zone 8. Evergreen, blue-gray, oblong, spear-shaped leaves up to 4 in. (10 cm) long arranged in close spirals. The flowers, borne in large terminal heads, are yellowish green surrounded by papery bracts. The subspecies ***wulfenii*** grows to a height of 4–6 ft (120–180 cm) and has broader flower spikes. 'Lambrook Gold' has yellow flowers. Zones 8–9.

E. corollata. North America. Height 3 ft; spread 18 in. (90 × 45 cm). Native to fields and open woods of eastern North America, this little-used plant has an open, loose habit and jade-green, narrowly elliptical leaves on wiry stems. Delicate white flowers reminiscent of baby's-breath (***Gypsophila***) appear in summer. It is a good plant for cut flowers and, unlike many other spurges, propagates well from cuttings. Zones 3–9.

E. griffithii. Asia. Height 3 ft; spread 2 ft (90 × 60 cm). A spreading plant with thick, pithy stems and spear-shaped, mid-green leaves with pink midribs. The flower cluster ranges through a number of different tones from coppery red to dark orange, depending on environmental conditions. A good plant for the sunny, sheltered border. 'Dixter,' a selection from the famous British gardener Christopher Lloyd, has dark-green foliage with a reddish tinge and orange bracts; 'Fireglow' has bright-red flowerlike bracts. Zones 5–9.

E. myrsinites. Europe. Height 6 in.; spread 12 in. (15 × 30 cm). A trailing, evergreen spurge with spirals of pointed, blue-green leaves on woody stems. Sulfur-yellow flowers appear in spring and early summer. Requires good drainage and full sun. Cut back faded flower stems. Suffers from wilt in areas with hot and humid summers. 'Washfield' is a form with a red tinge to the flower cluster. Zones 5–9.

E. palustris. Eurasia. Height 3 ft; spread 3 ft (90 × 90 cm). A bushy plant with yellow-green, oblong, spear-shaped leaves and bright-yellow domed flower heads in late spring. A plant for wet sites although it is often listed as being recommended for dry shade. Zones 7–9.

E. polychroma. Europe. Height 18 in.; spread 18 in. (45 × 45 cm). Often listed as ***E. epithymoides,*** this is one of the most valuable spurges for garden use. It is a clump-forming plant that bursts into a mound of chartreuse in spring. The leaves are bright green and egg-shaped. The 3-in.- (7.5-cm-)

wide, flowerlike bracts are bright, bright yellow in spring. Easily cultivated except in wet soil, where it will rot, and in hot and humid areas, where it will often suffer from wilt diseases. Zones 3–9.

E. wallichii. Himalayas. Height 18 in.; spread 2 ft (45 × 60 cm). One of the best of the spurges, unfortunately not widely available in the United States. A large, clump-forming plant with a rounded habit and tapering, dark-green leaves with a white central vein. The flowerlike bracts are a bright greeny yellow, almost starlike in appearance. Zones 7–9.

FESTUCA

(Fescue)

FAMILY: Graminae

A large genus of annual and perennial grasses. Those perennial species of value in the garden are cool-season, tufted, mound-forming species, many of which have blue or blue-green foliage.

CULTIVATION: Grow in full sun or light shade in ordinary, well-drained soil. Good drainage is essential. Remove spent flower heads in late summer. Many species are often susceptible to rust diseases, which cause the plants to rot from the center. In general, ornamental fescues do not perform well in the heat of midsummer. Hot and humid summers will often contribute to the complete failure of the plant.

LANDSCAPE USE: Attractive blue foliage grasses for edging or planting en masse on a bank. The tufts remain distinct and do not grow together to form matted masses; however, the individual clumps planted closely together create an effective blue carpet.

PROPAGATION: Divide in spring or early autumn every two or three years.

F. amethystina. Europe. Height 2 ft; spread 1 ft (60 × 30 cm). A blue-green grass with foliage reaching a height of 8–12 in. (20–30 cm) and 4-in. (10-cm) flower spikes on strong stems up to 2 ft (60 cm) tall in early summer. Cultivars include: 'April Green': green foliage and gray-green flowers; 'Bronzeglanz': greenish white flowers maturing to bronze; 'Klose': olive-green leaves; 'Superba': blue foliage with highly attractive amethyst-blue flower stems in early summer. Zones 4–9.

F. cinerea. Europe. Height 14 in.; spread 8 in. (35 × 20 cm). A low-growing, tufted grass with blue foliage. There are many cultivars, most with tufts of leaves up to 8 in. (20 cm) in height and flowers on stems up to 14 in (35 cm). 'Blue Finch': height 12 in. (30 cm), blue foliage; 'Blauglut': height 14 in. (35 cm), silver-blue foliage; 'Harz': height 12 in. (30 cm), blue-green leaves with an olive-green tint; 'Sea-blue': height 12 in. (30 cm), blue-green foliage; 'Silver-blue': height 14 in. (35 cm), silver-blue leaves; 'Soehrenwald': height 14 in. (35 cm), olive-green foliage; 'Solling': height 8 in. (20 cm), a blue fescue that normally does not flower; 'Tom Thumb': height 6 in. (15 cm), blue foliage. Zones 4–9.

F. ovina var. ***glauca.*** Sheep's fescue. Europe, Asia, North America, North Africa. Height 14–16 in.; spread 9 in. (35–40 × 22.5 cm). The most commonly grown blue fescue, it is a variable plant with differing foliage shades, habits, and heights. In general, it is a clump-forming plant with blue-green leaves forming a tuft about 8 in. (20 cm) high and spikes of gray-green flowers reaching a height of about 14–16 in. (35–40 cm). This plant has been superseded by the cultivars of ***F. cinerea.*** Zones 4–9.

FIBIGIA

Family: Cruciferae

Fibigia clypeolata

A small species of perennials native to the Mediterranean. The leaves are linear to spoon-shaped. The yellow or violet flowers are produced in spring, followed by rounded seed heads like small paddles.

Cultivation: Grow the one species available in well-drained, gravelly soil in full sun.

Landscape Use: While not greatly ornamental, *Fibigia* is an interesting plant for the rock garden.

Propagation: Sow seed in late summer.

F. clypeata. Mediterranean. Height 8 in.; spread 6 in. (20 × 15 cm). An erect plant with oval-oblong leaves either green or gray green. The small yellow flowers are produced in spring followed by elliptic seed heads. Zones 5–9.

FILIPENDULA

(Meadow-sweet, Dropwort)

Family: Rosaceae

A small genus of attractive spiraealike plants with alternate, usually divided, and serrated leaves and fluffed heads of white, pink, or red flowers in summer. They are native to swamps, marshes, and riverbanks and grow best in moist soils in climates where the summer does not get too hot and dry. They are closely related to ***Spiraea*** and ***Astilbe*** and are sometimes confused with those two genera. The generic name comes from the Latin for "hanging thread," a reference to the thin, threadlike tubers that are attached to the fleshy roots of some species.

Cultivation: Plant in moist, rich soil in sun or partial shade. The hotter the summers, the greater the shade required. Prone to mildew and leaf scorch if grown in full sun in dry soil.

Landscape Use: Wonderful border plants also used by streamsides, wet meadows, bog gardens, and among shrubs. A number of species are particularly effective in combination with moisture-loving, large-leaved plants such as ***Ligularia*** and ***Hosta*** species.

Propagation: Division in spring is the easiest method.

F. camtschatica. Manchuria. Height 6–8 ft; spread 3 ft (180–240 × 90 cm). A vigorous and coarse meadow plant with mid-green, doubly saw-toothed, hand-shaped leaves and white to pale-pink flowers in fluffy plumes up to 8 in. (20 cm) across in midsummer. Zones 3–8.

F. palmata. Siberia. Height 3–4 ft; spread 2 ft (90–120 × 60 cm). A clump-forming plant with up to 8-in.- (20-cm-) wide, dark-green, five-lobed leaves often with two-paired lateral leaflets, all densely covered with white hairs underneath. In midsummer appear 6-in.- (15-cm-) wide, flat plumes of pale-pink flowers that turn white as they age. 'Nana' is a dwarf form growing to a height of 10 in. (25 cm); 'Rosea' has deeper pink flowers. Zones 3–8.

F. purpurea. Japan. Height 4 ft; spread 2 ft (120 × 60 cm). Similar to ***F. palmata*** but with five- to seven-lobed terminal leaflets with the lateral leaflets often missing and no undercovering of white hairs. Flat terminal heads of carmine to pink flowers are borne on red stems and appear in early to midsummer. 'Alba' has white flowers; 'Rubra' has rosy red blossoms. An outstanding plant in combination with blue-leaved hostas or in a mass planting near water. Zones 4–9.

Filipendula rubra

F. rubra. Queen of the prairie. Eastern United States. Height 6–8 ft; spread 4 ft (180–240 × 120 cm). An erect, clump-forming plant with mid-green, jagged leaves divided into seven to nine incised leaflets with a large terminal leaflet. Up to 9-in.- (22.5-cm-) wide clusters of soft-pink flowers are borne on branching stems in midsummer. Sometimes flowers are also produced in autumn. 'Venusta' ('Magnifica') has deep-pink flowers and is more vigorous. It is not a plant for areas with very hot and humid summers. This species is an outstanding border or meadow plant, particularly useful for its tall habit and good pink flowers. Zones 3–8.

F. ulmaria. Meadow sweet. Europe, Asia. Height 3–6 ft; spread 1–2 ft (90–180 × 30–60 cm). A spreading species native to wet meadows and ditches. It has coarsely saw-toothed, long-stalked, dark-green leaves covered with white hairs underneath and divided into three to five egg-shaped leaflets. Creamy-white, sweetly fragrant flowers are borne in flat clusters in midsummer. It is not an individually showy plant, but is very pretty when planted in masses in a boggy site. 'Aurea' has golden yellow foliage in spring, turning pale green in summer. 'Flore Pleno' has double white flowers and green foliage. Susceptible to drought. Zones 3–9.

F. vulgaris (F. hexapetala). Dropwort. Europe, Asia. Height 2 ft; spread 18 in. (60 × 45 cm). Called dropwort from the drooping tuberous rootstock. A delicate-looking plant of great beauty with deeply cut, mid-green, fernlike foliage and flat, branched heads up to 6 in. (15 cm) across of creamy-white flowers in summer. Unlike the rest of the genus grown in gardens, this species can take poor, dry soil, although it does best in fertile soil. 'Flore Pleno,' an excellent double form, has masses of white flowers and is an excellent plant for the front of the border. Zones 3–8.

FOENICULUM

(Fennel)

Family: Umbelliferae

About three species of fragrant-leaved plants grown for culinary flavoring as well as ornamental foliage. The one species commonly grown has soft, finely divided leaves that provide a smoky presence in the herbaceous border. Flat-topped clusters of yellow flowers are produced in summer.

Cultivation: Grow in full sun in ordinary soil. Remove flower heads before they ripen to prevent self-seeding. In some areas swallowtail butterfly larvae are partial to fennel and can be quite damaging; carefully remove the black-and-yellow striped caterpillars.

Landscape Use: A culinary herb for the kitchen garden as well as a foliage foil for the herbeceous border. It is particularly good as a contrast to some of the coarse-leaved, yellow-blooming daisies or, in a cooler design, a wonderful accompaniment to ***Campanula lactiflora.***

Propagation: Separate the long, fleshy roots in spring. Take root cuttings in early spring. Sow seeds in autumn, plant young plants in spring.

F. vulgare. Europe. Height 4–6 ft; spread 2 ft (120–180 × 60 cm). An erect perennial with stiff, branching stems and finely divided, threadlike, dark-green and glossy foliage. Flat heads of dull yellow flowers are produced in summer. A better form is ***F. vulgare*** var. ***purpureum,*** with dark purple-bronze foliage that gives a smoky effect. It is a very useful plant as a background for stronger colors, particularly red or yellow flowers. It remains purple-bronze throughout the summer if grown in full sun. 'Giant Bronze' has bronze-purple foliage and grows to a height of 6 ft (180 cm). Zones 4–9.

FRANCOA

(Bridal-wreath)

Family: Saxifragaceae

A small genus of similar species native to Chile. They require a cool, moist, and mild climate and grow well in southwestern England, much of Ireland, and coastal western North America. Where they do grow well, bridal-wreaths are long-flowering, "old-fashioned" plants with great charm. The leaves are hairy, lobed, and wavy-edged and largely evergreen. The long wands of pink or white flowers bloom throughout the summer and into early autumn.

Cultivation: Grow in full sun to light shade in moist but well-drained, fertile soil. Although they are cold hardy to Zone 7, they do not like hot summers and quickly perish in the hot climates of much of North America. However, they can be overwintered in a greenhouse and forced for winter and spring flowering.

Propagation: Divide the clumps in spring or sow seed in spring or autumn.

Landscape Use: Long-flowering plants for the border. They make wonderful container plants.

F. ramosa. Chile. Height 3 ft; spread 18 in. (90 × 45 cm). Similar to the species mentioned below but taller and with flowers on branched stems. Zones 7–8.

Francoa appendiculata

F. sonchifolia. Chile. Height 2½ ft; spread 18 in. (75 × 45 cm). A clump-forming plant with hairy leaves of mid- to dark green, lobed and wavy-edged, up to 12 in. (30 cm) long. Pale-pink, bell-shaped flowers with darker centers are produced on unbranched stems in summer. Zones 7–9.

GAILLARDIA

(Blanket Flower)

Family: Compositae

Gaillardia 'Goblin'

A genus of widely grown annuals and perennials suitable for the sunny border and meadow garden. The leaves are alternate and often toothed. The daisylike flowers are produced one to a stem and are brightly colorful. The commonly grown blanket flower ***G.* × *grandiflora*** is a hybrid between the annual ***G. pulchella*** and the perennial ***G. aristata.*** Named after M. Gaillard, a French botanist.

Cultivation: Grow in full sun in a light, sandy soil. Tolerant of dry soils. Deadhead frequently for continuous bloom.

Landscape Use: Long-blooming but short-lived plants of great value in the cut-flower garden, herbaceous border, or meadow. For a bright display, try mixing in blanket flower with black-eyed susan (***Rudbeckia***) or some of the perennial sunflowers.

Propagation: Divide, sow seed, or take root cuttings in spring. Named cultivars should be propagated by cuttings or division only.

G.* × *grandiflora. Blanket flower. Height 2–3 ft; spread 18 in. (60–90 × 45 cm). A sprawling, summer-flowering hybrid with gray-green, hairy leaves that are 4–6 in. (10–15 cm) long and brightly colored, daisylike flowers ranging from deep red to golden yellow with maroon centers. Cultivars include 'Baby Cole': height 8 in. (20 cm), red with yellow edges; 'Burgundy': height 30 in. (75 cm), burgundy-red flowers, 'Dazzler': height 3 ft (90 cm), golden yellow flowers with dark-red centers; 'Goblin': height 12 in. (30 cm), dark-red flowers; 'Monarch Strain': height 30 in. (75 cm), a mixture of red and yellow flowers; 'Yellow Queen': height 2 ft (60 cm), yellow flowers. The taller cultivars will need staking. Seeds sown in late winter will often flower in the first year. Zones 3–9.

G. pulchella. Western United States. Height 18 in.; spread 12 in. (45 × 30 cm). A short-lived perennial or annual with hairy, gray-green, spoon-shaped leaves up to 5 in. (12.5 cm) long and pom-pom heads of red and yellow double flowers in summer. Zones 3–9.

GALAX

(Wandflower, Galaxy)

Family: Diaspensiaceae

One species of evergreen plant native from Virginia to Georgia, with creeping rhizomes and almost round, shiny leaves up to 5 in. (12.5 cm) across. Small spikes of white flowers appear in late spring to early summer.

Cultivation: Grow in a shaded, moist site in acid soil.

Landscape Use: A useful groundcover in woodland gardens and shrub borders. The leaves are used extensively in flower arrangements.

Propagation: Divide the scaly rhizomes in spring or early autumn. Sow seed in autumn.

G. urceolata (G. aphylla). Wandflower. Eastern North America. Height 1 ft; spread 1 ft (30×30 cm). An evergreen woodland plant with bright, shiny green, nearly circular leaves up to 5 in. (12.5 cm) across that often turn bronze as frost develops in the winter. In early summer 6–12-in. (15–30-cm) spikes carry wands of small white flowers. Zones 3–8.

GALEGA

(Goat's Rue)

Family: Leguminosae

A small genus of erect, perennial plants not commonly grown in North America. They have limited popularity in Europe. The leaves are light green, alternate, and divided into pairs of egg-shaped leaflets. The lupinlike flowers, which range from pale blue to cream, are borne in summer. The origin of the common name is unclear. While the plant has no scent, the leaves emit an unpleasant odor when bruised, perhaps similar to the smell of a goat. It is described as being a good herb for fevers and like so many plants, is described as "curing the bite of serpents."

Cultivation: Grow in full sun in moist but well-drained soil. Staking is usually necessary. Goat's rue is intolerant of hot and humid climates.

Landscape Use: Because of their size and tendency to ranginess, these plants are best suited to the back of the border. They are, however, good summer-blooming perennials that deserve to come back into fashion.

Propagation: Divide in spring or autumn or sow seed in late winter.

Galega officinalis

G. × hartlandii. Southern Europe, Asia Minor. Height 4–5 ft; spread 3 ft (120–150×90 cm). A cross between ***G. officianalis*** and ***G. patula,*** this hybrid has dark-green leaves divided into five to eight pairs of oblong leaflets and creamy-white and pale-lilac, coconut-scented flowers in summer. 'His

Majesty' has lilac-mauve and white flowers, 'Lady Wilson' has pale-pink and blue flowers. Zones 3–9.

G. officinalis. Goat's rue. Southern Europe, Asia Minor. Height 4 ft; spread 3 ft (120 × 90 cm). An upright perennial with light-green leaves consisting of up to 17 leaflets. White to pale-lilac, lupinlike flowers are borne in long spikes in midsummer. 'Alba' is a pure-white form. Cut back after flowering. Zones 3–7.

G. orientalis. Caucasus. Height 3 ft; spread 2 ft (90 × 60 cm). An upright plant with violet, lupinlike flowers in summer, above light-green leaves divided into pairs of oval leaflets. This species can be invasive in good soil. Zones 3–9.

GALIUM

(Sweet Woodruff)

FAMILY: Rubiaceae

A large family of mostly weedy plants for the garden except for one species, the sweet woodruff. Formerly placed in the genus ***Asperula,*** this plant is a woodland groundcover for partial shade, with fresh green leaves and masses of tiny white flowers in spring. Another common name is bedstraw, a reference to the sweet, haylike scent produced when the plant is crushed. The name woodruff is said to have been derived from the French *rovelle,* "wheel," an allusion to the whorled leaves.

CULTIVATION: Grow in partial shade in moist woodland soil.

LANDSCAPE USE: A softly invasive groundcover in the shady border or woodland garden. It is tolerant of acid soils and performs quite well in the shade of rhododendrons and other acid loving plants.

PROPAGATION: Divide in spring or autumn.

G. odorata. Sweet woodruff, bedstraw. Europe. Height 6–9 in.; spread 12 in. (15–22.5 × 30 cm). A spreading, sprawling plant with whorls of six to eight linear leaves about 1 in. (2.5 cm) long. The white flowers are tiny, up to ¼ in. (0.6 cm) long, and fragrant. It is an exceedingly pretty plant when planted in large numbers. In the middle of a hot and humid summer it can often die back, but it will produce fresh new growth when the weather cools. Zones 3–8.

GAURA

FAMILY: Onagraceae

About 18 species of perennial and annual plants native to North and South America, with one species coming to the fore in the southern United States as a valuable plant for hot, dry gardens. The generic name comes from the Greek for "superb."

CULTIVATION: Grow in ordinary, well-drained soil in full sun. The one species now widley grown in gardens takes two to three years to become fully established and look its ornamental best.

LANDSCAPE USE: A long-flowering plant for the sunny border. Useful for hot, dry slopes or for gardens under water restriction. Once established, its pinkish white flowers are of great value as a softening agent for brighter colors.

PROPAGATION: Sow seed. Because of a long taproot, division in spring, although possible, is not recommended.

G. lindheimeri. Southern United States. Height 4

Gaura lindheimeri

ft; spread 2–3 ft (120×60–90 cm). A bushy plant native to Louisiana and Texas with lance-shaped, stalkless leaves up to 3 in. (7.5 cm) long and thin flower spikes up to 4 ft (120 cm) long with 1-in.-(2.5-cm-) long, four-petaled white flowers fading to pink. Only a few flowers are in bloom at the same time, but this thin flowering habit is compensated for by the long blooming time throughout the summer until frost. Deadhead to promote further flowering. Zones 6–9.

GENTIANA

(Gentian)

FAMILY: Gentianaceae

A large genus of about 400 species of perennials and annuals, the majority of which are low-growing alpine plants. They are notable for the color of their flowers, which is often strong blue, although flower color ranges from forget-me-not blue to deep cobalt blue to white, yellow, pink, and purple. They have a reputation, quite correctly, for being difficult to grow, especially in climates that are not cool and moist. A few species do grow well under average conditions. They are listed below. In general, gentians have stalkless, untoothed, opposite leaves that clasp the stem. Most flowers are trumpet-shaped with five petals, often with fringes, notches, or folds between the petals. Some species are clump-forming, others are mat-forming, and some are erect. The name comes from King Gentius of Illyria, c. 500 B.C., who reportedly discovered the medicinal properties of the yellow gentian as a tonic.

CULTIVATION: With such a large genus, it is almost impossible to give general guidelines to cultivation. Specific information is included under each species; however, as a general rule, gentians prefer well-drained, humus-rich soil and cool growing conditions. They are best planted in spring.

LANDSCAPE USE: Those listed below are gentians for the herbaceous border, woodland border, or rock garden. Their astonishing blue flowers capture the eye and are a strong feature in any planting.

PROPAGATION: Sow seed in autumn, take stem cuttings of nonflowering material in summer, or divide in spring.

G. ***andrewsii.*** Bottle gentian. North America. Height 15–24 in.; spread 12 in. (37.5–60×30 cm). Often called the closed gentian because the club-shaped flowers do not open. The dark-green leaves are lance-shaped to egg-shaped, about 6 in. (15 cm) long. The dark-blue, white-tipped flowers are borne in the leaf axils and in clusters at the top of the stem in late summer and early autumn. The form ***albiflora*** has white flowers. Easily cultivated in humus-enriched moist soil in light shade. Propagate by seed. Zones 3–9.

G. asclepiadea. Willow gentian. Europe. Height 3 ft; spread 2 ft (90 × 60 cm). A relatively easy plant to grow in a damp, shady site in humus-rich, lime-rich to acid soil. It has a graceful, arching habit with leafy stems of willowlike, 3-in.- (7.5-cm-) long, mid-green leaves. The bell-shaped, deep-blue flowers are spotted inside with purple and are borne in the upper leaf axils in summer and early autumn. Var. *alba* has white flowers and a green throat. 'Knightshayes' is an erect plant with rich-blue, white-throated flowers. Propagate by stem cuttings or careful division in spring. Zones 5–9.

G. lutea. Yellow gentian. Europe. Height 4 ft; spread 2 ft (120 × 60 cm). A coarse and erect species with unbranched stems and egg-shaped, stalked and veined basal leaves up to 12 in. (30 cm) long, becoming smaller and stalkless farther up the stem. Dense whorls of starry golden yellow flowers are formed at the end of the stem and in the leaf axils in summer. Grow in moist, well-drained soil in full sun. Propagate from seed. Zones 6–9.

G. scabra. Rough gentian. Northern Asia. Height 12 in.; spread 12 in. (30 × 30 cm). A variable species with pairs of 1½-in.- (3.8-cm-) long, lance-shaped to egg-shaped, three-veined leaves, pale green underneath. Deep-blue bell-shaped flowers are borne in terminal clusters of four or five or in pairs in the leaf axils. Grow in a moist, well-drained soil in a shady site. Propagate by seed. There are a number of varieties; var. *buergeri* has larger flowers of deep blue and grows to a height of 3 ft (90 cm); var. *saxatalis* has semitrailing stems with upward-facing, sapphire-blue flowers appearing from the leaf axils and stem tip in autumn. Zones 5–9.

G. septemfida. Asia Minor. Height 12 in.; spread 12 in. (30 × 30 cm). An extremely variable species but probably the easiest to cultivate. Low, evergreen domes of mid-green, egg-shaped, 1½-in.- (3.8-cm-) long leaves in pairs along the many stems, with terminal clusters of narrow bell-shaped, dark-blue flowers with purple-speckled white throats in late summer. A conspicuously fringed membrane connects the flower lobes. Increase by seed, stem cuttings, or careful division. Grow in sun or partial shade in rich, moist, but well-drained soil. Zones 3–9.

G. sino-ornata. Western China. Height 6–8 in.; spread 12–15 in. (15–20 × 30–37.5 cm). An evergreen species with a central rosette of linear to lance-shaped mid-green leaves and brilliant-blue funnel-shaped flowers striped with deep-blue bands. The flowers are produced in the autumn through to a heavy frost. In cool climates this is not a difficult gentian to grow. It requires lime-free, rich soil in partial shade, and division every three years. 'Marianne Lyle' has dark-green foliage and ultramarine flowers with the ends of the petals rolled back. Zones 5–9.

G. verna. Spring gentian. Europe, Asia. Height 3 in.; spread 6 in. (7.5 × 15 cm). Not an easy species to grow but well worth the enthusiast's effort. It is a short-lived tufted plant with rosettes of mid-green, lance- to egg-shaped leaves up to ¾-in. (1.8-cm) long, and saucer-shaped 1-in. (2.5-cm) long azure-blue flowers in late spring and summer. Grow in lime-rich, rich, well-drained, gritty soil in full sun. It should be propagated by seed. Zones 6–9.

Gentiana asclepidea 'Alba'

GERANIUM

(Cranesbill)

Family: Geraniaceae

Geraniums have long been essential elements in herbaceous perennial plantings. They are important for their value as groundcovers, midborder plants, and accent plants. The variety of different

Geranium x *magnificum*

Geranium x *oxonianum* 'A. T. Johnson'

growth habits and flowering periods ensure their continued cultivation as indispensable ornamental plants. They are not to be confused with those popular bedding and pot plants that are members of the genus ***Pelargonium. Geranium*** is a large genus, with 400 species being widely distributed over the temperate regions of the world. The many-lobed leaves are alternate or opposite, often coarsely toothed and hairy. In mild climates the foliage is often evergreen. The saucer-shaped, veined flowers have five petals and are produced from the leaf axils or clustered at the stem tip. Flower colors range from white, pink, blue, to purple. The common name cranesbill, comes from the Greek *geranos,* "crane," referring to the beaklike fruits.

CULTIVATION: Cranesbills are relatively easy to grow, requiring ordinary, well-drained soil. Most grow in full sun except in the hottest climates. A number are useful flowering plants for partial to deep shade. In climates with hot summers partial shade and moist soils are essential. In hot summers most species will stop flowering and become weak. Cutting hard back after flowering will promote new basal growth and, often, reblooming. Many species need dividing every three or four years. The taller species will need staking. They are generally free of pests and diseases, but some species are particularly tasty to Japanese beetles.

LANDSCAPE USE: There is not one area of a garden that cannot support cranesbills. Flowering in late spring, summer, and autumn, some species are suitable for rock gardens and dry walls; others are fine plants for shade, while still others are integral to the herbaceous border. Many are effective groundcovers as well as plants for troughs and pots. Grow as many as you can!

PROPAGATION: Division in spring or early autumn is by far the best method. Seeds can be sown in the winter, grown during the spring and summer, and planted in the autumn. Stem and root cuttings are also largely successful.

G. argenteum. Silver-leaved geranium. Europe. Height 4 in.; spread 8 in. (10 × 20 cm). A branching plant with tufts of silvery, hairy, deeply cut leaves divided into seven three-lobed segments. The 1-in.- (2.5-cm-) wide, flesh-pink flowers with notched petals and dark-pink veins appear in summer. 'Apple Blossom' and 'Lissadell' are cultivars of the cross between this species and ***G. cinereum*** and are correctly listed under ***G × lindavicum.*** 'Apple Blossom' has very pale-pink flowers and light veins while 'Lissadell' has wine-purple flowers. All need gritty, lime-rich soil in full sun, and are perfect candidates for the rock garden. Zones 4–9.

G. cinereum. Balkans. Height 6 in.; spread 12 in. (15 × 30 cm). Similar to the above species and an easy-to-grow alpine requiring well-drained, gritty soil in full sun. It is a mound-forming plant with deeply cut, gray-green leaves divided into five to seven lobed segments. Pale-pink cup-shaped, dark-veined flowers about 1 in. (2.5 cm) across are borne on thin stems throughout the growing season. The subspecies ***subcaulescens*** has crimson-magenta flowers with dark-purple centers. ***G. cinereum*** ssp. ***subcaulescens*** 'Guiseppii' has crimson-purple flowers, while 'Splendens' has long-blooming salmon-pink flowers with a dark-red center. 'Ballerina' has lilac-pink flowers with dark-red veins and a red center. A hybrid between ***G. cinereum*** 'Ballerina' and ***G. cinereum*** subsp. ***subcaulescens*** is 'Lawrence Flatman,' which is similar to 'Ballerina' with blotched, pink flowers and crimson veins. Zones 4–9.

G. clarkei. Kashmir. Height 18–20 in.; spread 18 in. (45–50 × 45 cm). A handsome species with a loose, sometimes straggling habit with 2–6 in.- (5–15-cm-) wide basal leaves deeply divided into seven segments, each finely cut into feathery lobes. In early summer 1½-in.- (3.8-cm-) wide, upward-facing blue flowers with pink veins appear. 'Kashmir Purple' has violet-purple flowers and comes true from seed; 'Kashmir White' has lilac-veined white flowers and is less vigorous than the purple form. Zones 4–8.

G. dalmaticum. Yugoslavia and Albania. Height 6 in.; spread 12 in. (15 × 30 cm). A fragrant, easily cultivated rock-garden plant forming dense cushions of glossy, rounded, leaves about 1½ in. (3.8 cm) long that turn red and orange in autumn. The clear-pink, 1-in.- (2.5-cm-) wide flowers appear in spring and sporadically into summer. 'Album' has white flowers faintly flushed pink. A hybrid between this species and the similar but larger ***G. macrorrhizum*** is ***G. × cantabrigiense,*** a trailing plant with a height of 12 in. (30 cm) and a spread of 18 in. (45 cm), with aromatic light-green leaves and bright-pink or white flowers in summer. Zones 4–8.

G. endressii. Western Pyrenees. Height 12–18 in.; spread 18 in. (30–45 × 45 cm). A mound-forming, evergreen plant with mid-green, hand-shaped leaves deeply divided into five pointed segments. Bright-pink, funnel-shaped flowers with dark-pink veins bloom in early summer and occasionally into autumn. Requires light shade. 'Wargrave Pink' is a more vigorous plant up to 2 ft (60 cm) high with clear, almost salmon-pink flowers. Despite the claims of imaginative nurserymen, it does not flower throughout the summer in hot climates of much of the United States; in fact, it looks awful when temperatures get into the 90s. However, cutting it back after flowering and watering it in dry periods will help it to survive the summer and rebloom in late summer to early autumn. A fertile hybrid with ***G. versicolor, G. × oxonianum*** has funnel-shaped veined flowers. There are a number of cultivars; 'A. T. Johnson' grows up to 12 in. (30 cm) tall and has silvery pink flowers. The similar if not synonymous 'Rose Clair' grows to 18 in. (45 cm) and has rose-colored flowers with purple veining. The more commonly grown cultivar is 'Claridge Druce,' a vigorous and spreading, hairy plant with a loose, straggling habit, rose-pink 1½-in.- (3.8-cm-) wide flowers with darker veining. 'Claridge Druce' flowers intermittently throughout the summer and performs quite well in shade. Zones 4–9.

G. himalayense (G. grandiflorum). Central Asia. Height 12 in.; spread 18–24 in. (30 × 30–45 cm). A spreading, mound-forming plant with mid-green, long stalked leaves up to 8 in. (20 cm) wide and cut into seven lobed segments. Deep-blue saucer-shaped flowers up to 2 in. (5 cm) wide are beautifully veined dark purple and are borne on flower stalks 2–7 in. (5–17.5 cm) long in early summer and sporadically into autumn. 'Gravetye' (var. ***alpinum***) has blue flowers with a purple-red center and grows to 12 in. (30 cm) high; 'Plenum' (Birch Double) has double, purplish pink flowers. Zones 4–9. A popular hybrid between ***G. himalayense*** and ***G. pratense*** (see below) is 'Johnson's Blue.' The dark-green, finely toothed and lobed leaves are divided into seven segments. The lavender-blue flowers bloom in late spring to midsummer. Cut back hard after flowering to produce mounds of new, handsome foliage. Grow in full sun to partial shade. Zones 5–8.

G. macrorrhizum. Southern Europe. Height 12–15 in.; spread 18 in. (30–37.5 × 45 cm). An excellent groundcover with an almost woody stem and mid-green, palm-shaped leaves deeply cut almost to the leaf base. The leaves are divided into seven and are sharply aromatic. The terminal clusters of magenta-pink flowers appear in late spring to early summer and periodically until frost. 'Album' has white flowers; 'Bevan's Variety' has deep-magenta flowers; 'Ingwersen's Variety' has pale-pink flowers; 'Variegatum' has magenta-pink flowers and a leaf variegation of cream, yellow, and green. Semi-evergreen in mild areas, the leaves turn an attractive yellow-orange in autumn. Grows best in partial shade and fertile soil in hot summer climates. A useful species for dry shade. Zones 5–9.

G. maculatum. Spotted cranesbill. North America. Height 2 ft; spread 18 in. (60 × 45 cm). A common plant of sunny moist sites, the spotted cranesbill has leaves deeply divided into five to seven acutely lobed segments, and 1½-in.- (3.8-cm-) wide, pale-to deep-pink flowers in spring and early summer. In the wild it is often seen growing with hay-scented fern, ***Dennstaedtia punctilobula.*** It is particularly good in lightly shaded woodland where the clear-colored flowers are counterpoints for ***Phlox divaricata.*** An excellent plant for the wild garden. The variety ***album*** has white flowers. Zones 4–8.

G × magnificum. Height 2 ft; spread 2–3 ft (60 × 60–90 cm). A sterile hybrid between ***G. ibericum*** and ***G. platypetalum,*** this plant rightly deserves its specific epithet. It is a magnificent cranesbill with a rounded, mound-forming habit and hairy, mid-green leaves often cut into seven to nine overlapping lobed divisions. The basal leaves can reach up to 6 in. (15 cm) wide. The strongly veined, saucer-shaped, rich violet-blue flowers appear in late spring to early summer. It does not flower a second time. Although the intensity of the flower color may sometimes make it difficult to use with other plants, this is one of the best border cranesbills for late spring/early summer color. Japanese beetles like it, too. Zones 4–8.

G. phaeum. Mourning widow. Europe. Height 2 ft; spread 18 in. (60 × 45 cm). A splendid and still underused plant for half to full shade. Growth habit and flower color are variable, but the usual form has an upright, branching stem and lightly divided leaves with five to seven toothed and lobed segments. The almost circular, ¾-in.- (1.8-cm-) wide flowers are generally maroon to dark purple; however, they can range from black through pink to white. They appear in late spring and last through to midsummer. ***G. phaeum*** var. ***album*** has white flowers; ***G. phaeum*** var. ***lividum*** has slate-blue flowers. 'Lily Lovell' is slightly larger than the species and has deep-mauve flowers. The type self-sows freely particularly in moist soil and blooms even under the shade of beech trees. Zones 4–9.

G. pratense. Meadow cranesbill. Europe, Asia. Height 2 ft; spread 2 ft (60 × 60 cm). A clump-forming plant with long-stalked, mid-green leaves finely cut into seven to nine lobed divisions. Saucer-shaped, ½-in.- (1.2-cm-) wide, violet-blue to white flowers appear in early summer. 'Plenum Album' has dingy-white double flowers; 'Plenum Caeruleum' has double flowers of lavender-blue, tinged lilac. 'Plenum Violaceum' is an excellent plant with double flowers of rich violet-blue tinged with purple. 'Mrs. Kendall Clark' has single pinkish gray flowers although it is also described as having pale-blue flowers. All tend to be weak-stemmed and need staking. Partial shade is advisable in hot climates. Zones 4–8.

G. psilostemon. Armenia. Height 4 ft; spread 3–4 ft (120 × 90–120 cm). A tall, upright plant with 8-in.- (20-cm-) wide, palm-shaped, lobed, and toothed mid-green leaves divided into seven segments. The flowers are a bright magenta with black veins and black centers and appear in midsummer. 'Ann Folkard,' a hybrid between ***G. psilostemon*** and ***G. procurrens,*** has light-green leaves and black-centered, purplish magenta flowers and grows to a height of 18 in. (45 cm). Neither the species nor the hybrid grows particularly well in areas with hot and humid summers. Zones 4–8.

G. renardii. Caucasus. Height 1 ft; spread 1 ft (30 × 30 cm). A beautiful species with softly hairy, rounded, and veined gray-green leaves up to 4 in. (10 cm) wide and lavender-white flowers with violet veins in early summer. A fine rock-garden plant, it requires good drainage and cool summers. Zones 6–8.

G. × riversleaianum. Height 9 in.; spread 2–3 ft; (22.5 × 60–90 cm). A hybrid between ***G. endressii*** and ***G. traversii*** with hairy, dull gray-green leaves coarsely dissected into seven tapering segments. The trailing stems bear funnel-shaped, pink to magenta flowers in late spring through to early autumn. Noted for the cultivars 'Mavis Simpson,' with shell-pink flowers with purple veins, and 'Russell Prichard' with bright-magenta flowers. Both are excellent long-blooming groundcovers for mild areas. Zones 7–9.

G. sanguineum. Bloody cranesbill. Europe, Asia. Height 12 in.; spread 18 in. (30 × 45 cm). A low, mound-forming plant with deeply cut leaves with mostly seven segments, usually three lobed. The 1½-in.- (3.8-cm-) wide, dark-veined flowers range from pink to white, often purple-red. The variety ***striatum*** is often incorrectly named 'Lancastriense' or 'Prostratum.' It reaches a height of about 8 in. (20 cm) and has pale-pink flowers with red veins. 'Album' has white flowers and a vigorous loose habit; 'Alpenglow' reaches 8 in. (20 cm) in height and has rose-red flowers; 'Glenluce' has 2-in.- (5-cm-) wide deep-rose flowers; 'Shepherd's Warning' is a less-than-robust plant that grows to about 6 in. (15 cm) tall and has bright rose-pink flowers. All flower in summer. Zones 4–10.

G. sylvaticum. Wood cranesbill. Europe, Asia Minor. Height 2 ft; spread 2 ft (60 × 60 cm). An upright plant with light-green, toothed and lobed leaves deeply divided into seven to nine segments and 1-in.- (2.5-cm-) wide, violet-blue, white-eyed flowers for many weeks in spring. 'Album' has white flowers from pinkish buds; 'Mayflower' has violet-blue flowers with a white eye. Variety ***wannerii*** has light-pink flowers. Requires a shady site and moist soil. Zones 4–8.

G. wallichianum. Himalayas. Height 12 in.; spread 2 ft (30 × 60 cm). A low-growing trailing plant with marbled, coarsely lobed leaves divided into five segments. The flowers are purplish pink or blue with a white eye and dark veins, blooming from midsummer to autumn. 'Buxton's Variety' ('Buxton's Blue') is a more compact plant with blue flowers with well-defined white central eyes. It is a prolifically flowering plant in well-drained soil in full sun to light shade. Zones 4–8.

GEUM

(Avens)

FAMILY: Rosaceae

Geum quellyon 'Red Wings'

Geum rivale 'Leonard's Variety'

A genus of 40 to 50 species of clump-forming plants with twice-divided, lyre-shaped, hairy, mostly basal leaves with a large terminal lobe and saucer-shaped, mostly red or yellow flowers in late spring and early summer.

CULTIVATION: Grow in humus-rich, moist but well-drained soil in full sun or partial shade. A wet site in winter often causes plants to die. Frequent division—annually or biannually—keeps the plants healthy. The taller cultivars require support.

LANDSCAPE USE: Pleasing if not overwhelming plants for the front of the border or the rock garden. Flower color is quite strong, and ***Geums*** look their best in association with equally strong shades, particularly dark-blue and purple. They are poor plants for hot and humid climates.

PROPAGATION: Divide after flowering in late summer.

G. × borisii. Height 10 in.; spread 12 in. (25 × 30 cm). A dense, hummock-forming plant with hairy, rounded leaves divided into three and bright orange flowers up to 1 in. (2.5 cm) wide borne above the basal foliage on wiry stems in early summer. Zones 4–8.

G. montanum. Europe. Height 6–12 in.; spread 12 in. (15–30 × 30 cm). A slowly spreading alpine plant with densely hairy leaves up to 4 in. (10 cm) long with 1-in.- (2.5-cm-) wide, golden yellow flowers in summer followed by silver-gray seed heads. Zones 4–8.

G. quellyon Chile. Height 2 ft; spread 18 in. (60 × 45 cm). Listed under ***G. chiloense*** as well as ***G. coccineum,*** this species is more widely known for its cultivated varieties. The species has large, hairy leaves with large terminal leaflets. It is very short-lived, as are the cultivars, and requires frequent division. Notable cultivars, many of which are hybrids, are: 'Fire Opal,' with semidouble red flowers; 'Lady Stratheden,' with double yellow flowers on 2-ft (60-cm) stems; 'Mrs. Bradshaw,' a popular cultivar up to 18 in. (45 cm) in height, with semidouble orange-red flowers; 'Princess Juliana,' with semidouble bronze flowers; 'Red Wings,' with semidouble orange-scarlet flowers; 'Starkers Magnificent,' with double apricot flowers on 15-in. (37.5-cm) stems. Zones 5–8.

G. reptans. Europe. Height 9 in.; spread 12 in. (22.5 × 30 cm). Similar to ***G. montanum*** but with loose rosettes of leaves producing long red shoots that root at the tips, effectively spreading the plant. Single, golden yellow flowers about 1 in. (2.5 cm) across appear in early summer followed by attractive silvery seed heads. Requires a well-drained, gravelly soil. Zones 4–8.

G. rivale. Water avens. Northern hemisphere. Height 2–3 ft; spread 18 in. (60–90 × 45 cm). A water-loving plant with hairy, toothed, and divided, lyre-shaped leaves with a large terminal lobe. The flowers are nodding, bell-shaped, and soft pink, flushed purple. Prefers cool summer temperatures. 'Album' is a white form, 'Leonard's Variety' has coppery red flowers, and 'Lionel Cox' has pale-yellow flowers. Zones 3–8.

G. rossii. Alaska. Height 9–12 in.; spread 12 in. (22.5–30 × 30 cm). A very hardy spreading species with hairy, toothed leaves and deep-yellow, saucer-shaped flowers in summer. Zones 2–9.

GILLENIA

See PORTERANTHUS.

GLAUCIDIUM

Family: Ranunculaceae

Two species of perennial plants native to Japan and China. One species is regarded as a great treasure in occidental gardens but is unfortunately not widely available except from specialist nurseries.

Cultivation: Grow in a sheltered woodland site in moist, well-drained fertile soil. Often slow to establish but well worth the wait.

Landscape Use: A gem for the woodland garden or sheltered border.

Propagation: Seed or division.

G. palmatum. Japan. Height 2–3 ft; spread 2 ft (60–90 × 60 cm). A clump-forming perennial with fresh green, mostly two-lobed, kidney-shaped leaves up to 12 in. (30 cm) across and masses of 3–4-in.- (7.5–10-cm-) wide lavender-pink to white, four-petaled, poppylike flowers with a central crown of yellow stamens in late spring and early summer. Seed is occasionally listed in alpine or rock-garden society seed lists. Zones 6–9.

GLAUCIUM

(Horned Poppy)

Family: Papaveraceae

A small genus of short-lived perennials, biennials, and annuals with poppylike flowers, gray-green leaves, and orange sap. One species, described below, is a short-lived plant grown for its golden yellow flowers.

Cultivation: Grow in full sun in lean, well-drained soil.

Landscape Use: A coarse-leaved plant with papery yellow flowers. Although biennial rather than perennial, it is a useful plant for hot, dry sites, particularly the top of a rock wall.

Propagation: Sow seed in early spring.

G. flavum. Horned poppy. Southern Europe, North

Africa. Height 12–18 in.; spread 18 in. (30–45×45 cm). A short-lived plant with an untidy, flopping habit. The lobed and cut leaves are blue-green while the 3-in.- (7.5-cm-) wide, poppylike, golden yellow or orange flowers are produced on long stalks in mid- to late summer. Zones 5–9.

GLOBULARIA

(Globe Daisy)

Family: Globulariaceae

Globularia trichosantha

A small genus of mostly evergreen plants from the Mediterranean, central Europe, and Asia often with woody stems, hairless leaves alternate or in basal rosettes, and small round stalkless flower heads of pink or blue flowers in summer. The name comes from the Latin *globulus,* "ball," and refers to the shape of the flowers.

Cultivation: Grow in a dry, sunny location in ordinary, lime-rich to neutral soil.

Landscape Use: Tough, undemanding rock-garden plants valued for their show of pink or lavender-blue flowers in summer.

Propagation: Seed or division in spring or early autumn.

G. cordifolia. Heartleaf globularia. South and Central Europe. Height 4 in.; spread 6 in. (10×15 cm). An evergreen subshrub with woody stems and dark-green and glossy, alternate, spoon-shaped leaves up to 1 in. (2.5 cm) long. Stalkless, ½-in.- (1.2-cm-) wide, round-headed lavender-blue flowers are produced in late spring and early summer. Zones 5–8.

G. meridonalis (G. cordifolia **var.** ***bellidifolia).*** Europe, Western Asia. Height 4 in.; spread 8 in. (10×20 cm). An evergreen, mound-forming species with woody stems and mats of tiny, leathery, broadly lance-shaped leaves about 3 in. (7.5 cm) long. Lavender-purple flowers are borne just above the foliage in early summer. Zones 6–9.

G. repens. Southern Europe. Height 1–2 in.; spread 6 in. (2.5–5×15 cm). Similar to ***G. cordifolia*** but smaller, forming a dense mat of narrow lance-shaped, leathery leaves on woody stems. In early summer ½-in.- (1.2-cm-) wide, pinkish blue flowers appear. Zones 6–9.

G. trichosantha. Balkans. Height 9 in.; spread 12 in. (22.5×30 cm). A bushy species with dull-green, spoon-shaped leaves that are usually three-toothed at the tips. Masses of bright-blue flowers appear in summer. Zones 6–9.

GLYCERIA

(Manna Grass)

Family: Graminae

A small genus of marsh-loving grasses with one species and its variegated form being an attractive addition to the water garden.

Cultivation: Grow in standing water or wet soil for best effect. Although this grass tolerates average soil, the foliage color is at its brightest in wet soil in full sun.

Landscape Use: Streamsides, bog gardens, and pond edges.

Propagation: Division in spring and autumn.

G. maxima 'Variegata' (***G. aquatica*** 'Variegata'). Variegated manna grass. Europe, Asia. Height 18–24 in.; spread 2 ft (45–60 × 60 cm). An invasive, water-loving grass with clumps of 2-ft- (60-cm-) long leaves striped yellow-green to creamy yellow. Greenish cream flowers are rarely produced. A fine grass for bank control and water edging. Cut back in early winter. Zones 5–9.

GUNNERA

Family: Gunneraceae

Gunnera manicata

About 35 species of tropical or warm temperate-region plants. Two species are widely grown for their large leaves and exotic flowers. Beloved by Victorian gardeners for its evocation of the jungle landscape, ***Gunnera*** continues to be popular for large-scale waterside planting. Basal, leathery leaves are borne on strong, prickly stems from large, sensuous crowns. Large panicles of green flowers appear in late spring and develop with the plant throughout the summer.

Cultivation: Plant in a sheltered site in deep, rich, moist soil in sun or partial shade. Protect the crowns by mulching in winter. Best grown in Zones

8–10 but root-hardy by the skin of its teeth in Zone 7.

Landscape Use: Large-leaved plants for the romantic wild garden.

Propagation: Sow seed in spring or divide the small crowns that form around the old plant in spring.

G. tinctoria (G. chilensis). Chile. Height 6 ft; spread 5 ft (180 × 150 cm). A large, clump-forming plant with prickly palm-shaped, lobed, and toothed dark-green leaves up to 5 ft (150 cm) across on erect prickly stems. Dense panicles of reddish flowers are hidden among the foliage in summer. Zones 8–10.

G. manicata. Brazil. Height 6–10 ft; spread 10 ft (180–300 × 300 cm). A larger, more open species than the above. Huge, prickly, coarsely toothed, lobed and leathery leaves form a massive presence in the garden. Cones of light-green flowers are produced amid the foliage in summer. Zones 8–10.

GYMNOCARPIUM

(Oak Fern)

Family: Polypodiaceae

Four species and several hybrids of delicate ferns, one of which is abundant in rocky woodland and swamps from Labrador to Alaska, south to Arizona and North Carolina.

Cultivation: Easy to grow in damp, neutral to slightly acid, stony soil in light shade.

Landscape Use: Handsome ferns for the woodland garden or pot culture.

Propagation: Sow spores when they ripen in midsummer, or divide the rootstalk in spring.

G. dryopteris. Oak fern. North America, Europe, Asia. Height 10 in.; spread 18 in. (25 × 45 cm). A delicate-looking fern with long, creeping rhizomes and leaves up to 16 in. (40 cm) long with triangular blades with leaflets in threes. Easily grown in damp woodland. Zones 3–8.

Gymnocarpium dryopteris

GYPSOPHILA

(Baby's Breath)

Family: Caryophyllaceae

A large genus of over 100 annual, biennial, and perennial species with just a few species and hybrids in general cultivation. They are noted for their light masses of airy flowers that are a boon to the florist and gardener alike. They have small, opposite leaves on branched, wiry stems and clouds of tiny white or pink flowers in the summer. The name comes from the Greek *gypos,* "gypsum," and *philos,*

Gypsophila repens

"friend," referring to the plant's love of alkaline soil.

Cultivation: Plant in a well-drained, lime-rich soil in full sun. ***G. paniculata*** and its cultivars need staking. Deadhead after flowering to promote secondary bloom. Many double-flowered cultivars are still grafted onto single-flowered cultivars and should be planted so that the graft union is below the soil surface.

Landscape Use: Excellent border or rock-garden plants. Baby's breath is an important commercial cut flower and is also useful for its wispy contrast to many of the summer-flowering daisies, such as ***Rudbeckia.***

Propagation: Sow seeds in spring or take cuttings of basal shoots in spring or lateral shoots in summer. Divide ***G. repens*** in late spring.

G. cerastioides. Himalayas. Height 3 in.; spread 18 in. (7.5 × 45 cm). A tufted, spreading plant with spoon-shaped and hairy green leaves ½–2 in. (1.2–5 cm) long and ½-in.-(1.2-cm-) wide, cup-shaped white flowers with purple veins. Blooms in summer and requires good drainage in sun or partial shade. Zones 6–9.

G. oldhamiana. Korea. Height 3 ft; spread 3 ft (80 × 90 cm). A tangled many-branched plant with linear, lance-shaped leaves up to 2½ in. (6.2 cm) long and masses of tiny pale-pink flowers in late summer. Zones 5–9.

G. paniculata. Baby's breath. Europe. Height 2–3 ft; spread 3 ft (60–90 × 90 cm). This, the most important species of the genus, produces masses of tiny white flowers borne on branched stems with narrowly spear-shaped, 4-in (10-cm-) long, gray-green leaves. Flowring is generally so heavy that staking is necessary. Remove faded flowers for continuous bloom and mulch in cold winter areas. There are many cultivars; 'Bristol Fairy' is a popular cultivar with double white flowers on 30-in. (75 cm) stems; 'Compacta Plena' is a double white form growing to a height of 18 in. (45 cm); 'Flamingo' is a vigorous plant growing to 3 ft (90 cm) with double pale-pink flowers; 'Perfecta' is an improved form of 'Bristol Fairy' and grows to 4 ft (120 cm) in height; 'Pink Fairy' has double light-pink flowers and grows to 18 in. (45 cm); 'Pink Star' has double pink flowers and grows to 2 ft (60 cm); 'Red Sea' has double rose-pink flowers and grows to 4 ft (120 cm); 'Rosy Veil' has semidouble pale-pink flowers and grows to 18 in. (45 cm); 'Viette's Dwarf Form' grows to 15 in. (37.5 cm) and has white-tinged pink flowers. Zones 4–8.

G. repens. Creeping baby's breath. Europe. Height 8 in.; spread 12–18 in. (20 × 30–45 cm). A vigorous mat-forming plant with light gray-green leaves up to 1 in. (2.5 cm) long and masses of lilac-tinged white flowers throughout the summer. An easy-to-grow rock plant particularly effective tumbling over walls. Not as sensitive to soil acidity as the above species. 'Bodgeri' has double light-pink flowers; 'Dorothy Teacher' has white flowers aging to strong pink; 'Fratensis' is a compact plant with strong pink flowers; 'Rosea' has pale-pink flowers. Cut back hard after flowering for compact growth and secondary bloom. Zones 3–8.

HAKONECHLOA

(Hakone Grass)

Family: Graminae

A beautiful, arching grass for sun or shade. Insignificant yellow-green flowers appear in summer, but it is the bamboolike foliage that is effective. This is a comparatively recent introduction from Japan destined to be come a widely appreciated and cultivated ornamental grass.

Cultivation: Grow in moist, well-drained soil in sun or partial to full shade. The variegated form requires more light to produce strong variegation.

Landscape Use: An elegant grass for use as a groundcover or as a single specimen. It is stunning when planted in contrast to large-leaved hostas. A masture specimen is a very desirable container plant.

Propagation: Divide in spring.

Hakenochloa macra

H. macra. Hakone grass. Japan. Height 1–2 ft; spread 3 ft (30–60 × 90 cm). A slow-growing but beautiful ornamental grass with an upright, arching habit and glossy mid-green leaves that turn a light bronze color in autumn. A useful grass for fertile, moist soil in shade. Zones 6–9 (Zone 5 with winter protection). The cultivar 'Aureola' is a very desirable plant, smaller than the species, with leaves growing to about 12 in. (30 cm) long and with an overall height of 12–18 in. (30–45 cm). It is variegated with creamy-white-and-yellow-green stripes. When grown in a sunny site the variegation is sometimes near white. If grown in sun the leaves often become tinged with pink toward autumn, making the grass doubly attractive. Requires additional watering and protection from leaf scorch in a sunny location. Zones 7–9.

HEDYOTIS

(Bluets, Quaker Ladies)

Family: Rubiaceae

A large genus of tropical and subtropical shrubs, subshrubs, and perennials. Those of relevance to the perennial gardener are small, tufted perennials with white, purple, or blue flowers and opposite leaves. They were formerly classified under the genus ***Houstonia.***

Cultivation: Grow bluets in moist well-drained soil in light shade.

Landscape Use: Delicate-looking plants for the moist shaded bank, woodland border, or meadow. Bluets are beautiful when allowed to seed themselves in moss.

Propagation: Divide in spring or sow seed in summer.

H. caerulea. Bluets, quaker ladies. North America. Height 6 in.; spread 2 in. (15 × 5 cm). A dainty tufted plant with tiny, glossy, broadly lance-shaped leaves and masses of soft-blue to white four-pet-

Hedyotis caerulea

aled flowers with a yellow eye in spring and summer. Often flowers throughout the summer. Zones 4–9.

H. michauxii. Creeping bluets. Northeastern United States. Height 4 in.; spread 12 in. (10 × 30 cm). A spreading plant rooting at the stems, with mats of egg-shaped leaves and masses of yellow-centered violet-blue flowers in spring and summer. Zones 5–8.

HELENIUM

(Sneezeweed)

FAMILY: Compositae

Helenium autumnale 'Butterpat'

About 40 species of annual or perennial plants, most of which are native to North America. They are essential elements in late summer and early autumn displays with their long-lasting yellow, orange, or red flowers preempting the flaming colors of autumn foliage. The stems are erect and generally strong, with alternate, stalkless, toothed leaves and daisylike flowers. The flowers were reputed to spring from the ground watered by Helen of Troy's tears. The common name refers to the dried leaves' use as a substitute for snuff.

CULTIVATION: Plant in ordinary soil in a sunny location. Water well in hot summers. Tolerant of poor soils, they need minimal fertilizer. The taller cultivars will need staking. Pinch back taller plants to reduce height and to promote branching. Divide every three years.

LANDSCAPE USE: Wonderful warm-colored plants for the back of the herbaceous border and meadow. The yellow cultivars associate particularly well with the bright reds of ***Crocosmia*** cultivars or the purple-blue of ***Buddleia.*** They make excellent and long-lasting cut flowers.

PROPAGATION: Divide in spring or autumn.

H. autumnale. Common sneezeweed. Eastern North America. Height 3–5 ft; spread 2 ft (90–150 × 60 cm). A fibrous-rooted, clump-forming plant with stiff, branched stems and serrated, lance-shaped leaves up to 6 in. (15 cm) long, with the base of each leaf extending down and along the stem, making the stem appear winged (decurrent). The drooping yellow ray flowers are 2-in. (5 cm) wide with notched petals and a pronounced central disk. The flowers are produced in late summer and autumn. There are many cultivars, which are probably hybrids between ***H. autumnale, H, bigelovii,*** and ***H. hoopesii.***

'Brilliant': height 3 ft (60 cm), masses of bronze flowers in late summer.
'Bruno': height 4 ft (120 cm), mahogany-red flowers in autumn
'Butterpat': height 4 ft (120 cm), deep-yellow flowers in late summer and autumn
'Coppelia': height 3 ft (90 cm), orange and copper-red flowers
'Gartensonne': height 5 ft (150 cm), yellow flowers with brown centers
'July Sun': height 3 ft (90 cm), golden orange flowers
'Moerheim Beauty': height 3 ft (90 cm), orange-red flowers with brown centers
'Peregrina': height 3 ft (90 cm), dark-mahogany flowers
'Red-Gold Hybrid': height 4 ft (120 cm), red-and-gold flowers
'Riverton Beauty': height 4 ft (120 cm), golden yellow flowers with bronze centers
'The Bishop': height 2½ ft (75 cm), yellow flowers
'Wyndley': height 3 ft (90 cm), large copper-brown flowers in late summer. Zones 3–8.

H. bigelovii. Western North America. Height 3 ft; spread 18 in. (90 × 45 cm). Largely unbranched stems with shining green leaves up to 10 in. (25 cm) long, also making the stems appear winged. The usually solitary flower heads are made up of 2½-in.- (6.8-cm-) wide yellow flowers with dark-brown centers. Zones 7–9.

H. flexuosum. Purple-headed sneezewood. North America. Height 2–3 ft; spread 18 in. (60–90 × 45 cm). An erect plant with a single, many-branched, winged stem with narrow lance-shaped leaves to 8 in. (20 cm) long and dark-centered, yellow daisylike flowers with drooping, notched petals in late summer. Zones 5–9.

H. hoopesii. Orange sneezewood. Rocky Mountains. Height 2–3 ft; spread 18 in. (60–90 × 45 cm). A clump-forming plant with wineglass stems and blunt, lance-shaped, gray-green leaves up to 1 ft (30 cm) long. Yellow-orange flowers are borne in clusters of 3–8 in. in early summer. Not tolerant of hot summers. Zones 3–8.

HELIANTHUS

(Sunflower)

FAMILY: Compositae

About 150 species of tall annual and perennial plants mostly native to North America, with large daisylike flowers generally with brown or purple disc flowers and yellow ray flowers. The annual sunflower, ***H. annuus,*** is widely grown for its seed, oil, and beauty. They are coarse plants with toothed, rough leaves, often with the lower leaves opposite and the upper leaves alternate. The name is derived from the Greek *helios,* "sun," and *anthos,* "flower." The annual sunflower was revered by the Aztecs and is often represented in their sculpture and mosiac work.

CULTIVATION: Grow in a well-drained, ordinary soil in full sun. Stake the taller species.

LANDSCAPE USE: Bright, long-blooming but coarse plants for the back of the border or meadow garden. Good plants for areas with hot summers.

PROPAGATION: Sow seeds in spring. Divide in autumn or spring.

H. angustifolius. Swamp sunflower. Eastern United States. Height 5–7 ft; spread 4 ft (150–210 × 120 cm). A spectacular late-flowering sunflower with alternate, untoothed, narrowly lance-shaped leaves up to 8 in. (20 cm) long on rough, hairy stems. Clusters of 3-in.- (7.5-cm-) wide yellow flowers with dark-brown centers appear in late autumn, often surviving periods of light frost. Grow in rich, moist soil in full sun. Stake to prevent breaking. The late-flowering habit of this plant makes it especially useful in combination with large ornamental grasses such as ***Miscanthus*** species. Zones 6–9.

H. decapetalus. Thin-leaf sunflower. United States. Height 4–5 ft; spread 2 ft (120–150 × 60 cm). A coarse plant with mid-green, broadly egg-shaped, sharply toothed leaves up to 8 in. (20 cm) long and all-yellow flowers in summer and late summer. Zones 5–9.

H. maximilliani. Maximillian sunflower. North America. Height 10 ft; spread 3 ft (300 × 90 cm). A desirable sunflower with alternately lance-shaped leaves up to 1 ft (30 cm) long and 3-in. (7.5-cm) bright-yellow flowers in late summer and autumn. Zones 4–9.

Helianthus angustifolius

H. × multiflorus. Height 4–6 ft; spread 2 ft (120–180 × 60 cm). A hybrid between the annual sunflower ***H. annuus*** and the perennial ***H. decapetalus,*** with hairy, alternate, egg-shaped leaves up to 10 in. (25 cm) long and 6 in. (15 cm) wide and single or double yellow flowers in late summer and autumn. There are a number of cultivars. 'Capenoch Star': height 3½ ft (105 cm), single lemon-yellow flowers; 'Flore Pleno': height 3 ft (90 cm), golden yellow double flowers; 'Loddon Gold': height 6 ft (180 cm), double, bright-yellow flowers. Zones 3–10.

H. salicifolius. Willowleaf sunflower. United States. Height 5–7 ft; spread 4 ft (150–210 × 120 cm). So similar to ***H. angustifolius*** that plants sold under this name may be one or the other. However, this species prefers dry soil. The willowleaf sunflower has drooping linear to narrowly lance-shaped leaves up to 8 in. (20 cm) long on smooth, hairless stems and yellow daisylike flowers with purple-brown centers in late autumn. Zones 4–9.

HELICHRYSUM

(Everlasting)

FAMILY: Compositae

A large genus of shrubs, perennials, and annuals, with the most interesting and ornamental species being native to Australia and New Zealand. Only a few are gardenworthy herbaceous plants for temperate climates, with one hybrid, described below, being especially desirable. Those more commonly grown are shrubs or subshrubs such as the curry plant ***H. italicum (H. angustifolium),*** the popular

Helichrysum 'Sulfur Light'

container plant ***H. petiolare,*** or the short-lived perennial strawflower ***H. bracteatum.***

Cultivation: Grow in full sun in well-drained soil.

Landscape Use: The sulfur-yellow flowers are particularly strong in contrast to the many shades of blue of ***Campanula*** species. As a specimen or planted in groups, this is a wonderful plant for the rock garden or sunny border.

Propagation: Take stem cuttings in midsummer or divide in spring.

H. 'Sulfur Light.' Height 18–24 in.; spread 18 in. (45–60 × 45 cm). A hybrid of complex parentage, this is a clump-forming plant with white, woolly stems and narrowly lance-shaped, silver-gray leaves. Fluffy clusters up to 2 in. (5 cm) across of sulfur-yellow flowers are produced in mid- to late summer. Zone 5.

HELICTOTRICHON

(Blue Oat Grass)

Family: Graminae

About 40 species of cool-season, tufted grasses native to central Europe. One species is becoming widely appreciated for its blue foliage and stiff, architectural habit.

Cultivation: Grow in full sun in light, well-drained soil. Often develops foliage rust diseases in climates with hot and humid summers. Spraying with a fungicide helps.

Landscape Use: An excellent grass for massing or as a single specimen in combination with silver-gray plants or deep-green foliage in the rock garden or herbaceous border.

Propagation: Divide in spring.

Helictotrichon sempervirens

H. sempervirens. Blue oat grass. Central Europe. Height 3–4 ft; spread 1 ft (90–120 × 30 cm). A tufted, hummock,-forming grass with stiff, blue or gray-green, slightly arching leaf blades up to 16 in. (40 cm) long and ½ in. (1.2 cm) wide. Although primarily grown for its foliage, the inflorescence is an arching, beige panicle appearing from early summer. It is sometimes slow to recover from spring division. Evergreen in mild climates with a tendency to go into semidormancy in summer in hot climates. Zones 4–9.

HELIOPSIS

(False Sunflower)

Family: Compositae

Heliopsis helianthoides ssp. *scabra*

Yellow daisies closely related to the sunflower. They are invaluable for their long blooming period and their ability to grow in hot, dry climates. Their form is generally smaller than the true sunflowers, while some of the cultivars are less coarse than the species. The leaves are opposite or whorled, roundly lance-shaped to egg-shaped, and coarsely toothed. The flowers are yellow daisies surrounded by a leafy involucral collar. The species are apt to be weedy, but a number of worthy garden forms are available.

Cultivation: Grow in full sun in ordinary but well-drained soil. Overly fertile soil will produce long, leggy plants. Divide every two to three years and deadhead often.

Landscape Use: Strong, expectionally long-blooming, brightly colored plants for the herbaceous border or meadow garden. They are not subtle plants, and the bright yellows often overwhelm more delicate shades, but they are invaluable as brassy additions to the summer display.

Propagation: Divide in spring and autumn or sow seed. Some cultivars come true from seed.

H. helianthoides. False sunflower. North America. Height 5 ft; spread 2–3 (150 × 60–90 cm). A vigorous and erect, branching plant with opposite, 5-in.- (12.5-cm-) long, coarsely toothed, narrowly egg-shaped mid-green leaves and 3-in.- (7.5-cm-) wide, yellow daisylike flowers with brownish centers appearing in large quantity for most of the summer and part of the autumn. The subspecies ***scabra*** has leaves and stem that are rough to the touch. There are many fine cultivars. 'Gigantea': height 5 ft (90 cm), semidouble golden yellow flowers; 'Golden Greenheart': height 3 ft (90 cm), double yellow flowers with a green center; 'Golden Plume': height about 4 ft (120 cm), double deep-yellow flowers; 'Incomparabilis': height 2–3 ft (60–90 cm), semi-double orange-yellow flowers; 'Karat': height 3–4 ft (90–120 cm), bright-yellow flowers; 'Patula': height 3 ft (90 cm), semidouble yellow-orange flowers; 'Summer Sun': height 3–4 ft (90–120 cm) 4-in- (10-cm-) wide yellow flowers (a popular cultivar). Zones 4–9.

HELLEBORUS

(Christmas Rose, Lenten Rose)

FAMILY: Ranunculaceae

A genus of about 20 species of flowering plants that are essential elements in the spring garden. They are often one of the first of the nonbulbous plants to appear in spring, a characteristic that makes up for their frequently ragged appearance in summer. The flowers are mostly nodding and cup-shaped in many subtle hues of green, white, pink, and purple. The species can be divided into two groups: those with leafy stems and flowers carried at the apex, and those without stems with both leaves and flowers carried at the base. The leaves are generally leathery, pale to dark green, palm-shaped, and deeply divided. The name comes from the Greek *elein*, "to injure," and *bora*, "food," referring to the poisonous leaves and roots.

CULTIVATION: Most require some shade and moist soil. All benefit from snow cover or mulch in areas with cold winters. Remove the old and tattered leaves before flowering. In mild climates they are evergreen and flower from late winter to early spring. In general, they should be planted in sheltered areas and left undisturbed.

LANDSCAPE USE: Grow in light woodland or shaded borders under trees and shrubs or among other large-leaved herbaceous perennials.

PROPAGATION: Careful division in spring is more successful than sowing the fresh seed, which is difficult because of the need for warm and cool stratification periods. However, most species self-sow, and seedlings can be carefully transplanted in spring.

H. argutifolius (H. corsicus, H. lividus corsicus). Corsican hellebore. Corsica. Height 2 ft; spread 18 in. (60 × 45 cm). This handsome plant has gray-green, veined, and three-parted, spiny-toothed leaves on several stems and 15 to 30 pale-green, cupped flowers about 1 in. (2.5 cm) wide in terminal clusters in early spring. Best grown in light shade away from afternoon sun. Tolerates dry soil and in mild climates may bloom in late winter. Mulch in winter. Not suitable for climates with hot and humid summers. Zones 6–8.

H. atrorubens. Europe. Height 12 in.; spread 18 in. (30 × 45 cm). Similar to and possibly a variety of ***H. orientalis*** described below but with deep-purple cup-shaped flowers in late winter and early spring. Zones 4–9.

H. foetidus. Stinking hellebore. Western Europe. Height 18 in.; spread 18 in. (45 × 45 cm). An evergreen plant forming vigorous clumps of dark-green leaves that are deeply divided into four to nine leaflets. Unpleasant-smelling, pale-green, 1-in.- (2.5-cm-) wide, cup-shaped flowers appear in late winter to early spring. Prefers neutral to alkaline, moist but well-drained soil. Often self-sows, and seedlings should be transplanted as a means of propagation rather than dividing the parent plant. Zones 3–9.

H. lividus. Balearic Islands. Height 18 in.; spread 12 in. (45 × 30 cm). Similar to ***H. argutifolius*** but smaller, less hardy, and difficult to establish. Smooth-edged, dark-green leaves are divided into threes and are marbled with white veins. The cup-shaped flowers are green suffused with dark pink. A parent, along with ***H. argutifolius*** of the still largely unavailable hybrids grouped under ***H. × sternii.*** Zones 7–9.

H. niger. Christmas rose. Southern Europe. Height 12 in.; spread 18 in. (30 × 45 cm). A low-growing species, evergreen in mild areas, with dark-green, sometimes spiny basal leaves divided into seven to nine egg-shaped leaflets. In late winter and early spring 2–4-in.- (5–7.5-cm-) wide, white, golden-centered, cup-shaped flowers appear on short, red-spotted stems. There is great variability in this species, and flowering time is often capricious. Not the easiest plants to grow, they should be left alone to establish themselves. They benefit from moist but well-drained neutral to alkaline soil in partial shade. There are a number of subspecies, varieties, and cultivars. The subspecies ***macranthus*** has narrower, shinier leaves and white flowers tinged pink on unspotted stems. 'Potter's Wheel' has large rounded flowers with a green eye. Crosses between this species and ***H. argutifolius*** are listed as ***H. × nigericors.*** 'Alabaster,' one of the few cultivars of this hybrid commercially available, is a vigorous plant with white flowers. Zones 3–9.

H. orientalis. Lenten rose. Height 18 in.; spread 2 ft (45 × 60 cm). Glossy, long-stemmed, leathery leaves 12–16 in. (30–40 cm) across divided into seven to nine finely toothed leaflets. The 2–4-in.- (5–10-cm) wide, cup-shaped nodding flowers appear in late winter to early spring and range in color from pure white to deep purple and are often blotched or speckled with dark spots. They are exquisite flowers for the garden or for the house, where they can be floated in bowls of water. The Lenten rose requires average soil augmented by fertilizer in spring. There are almost 60 cultivars listed, many of which may be varieties or hybrids. This species is in desperate need of taxonomic revision. Zones 5–9.

H. viridis. Green hellebore. Europe. Height 12 in.; spread 18 in. (30 × 45 cm). A little-grown deciduous species with light-green leaves divided into seven to 11 leaflets and 1-in.- (2.5-cm-) wide, pure-green flowers. It is a desirable plant with subtle grace. Zones 6–8.

HELONIAS

(Swamp Pink)

Family: Liliaceae

One species of spring-blooming perennial native to sphagnum bogs ranging from New Jersey to North Carolina.

Cultivation: Grow in boggy soil in sun or partial shade.

Landscape Use: Plant either singly or in masses on the edges of bogs and ponds.

Propagation: Divide in spring or sow seed in summer.

H. bullata. Swamp pink. Eastern United States. Height 2 ft; spread 1 ft (60 × 30 cm). Large basal rosettes of narrowly oblong, spoon-shaped leaves up to 15 in. (37.5 cm) long and 2 in. (5 cm) wide, arising from a tuberous rhizome. In spring 3-in.- (7.5-cm-) long dense spikes of fragrant purple-pink flowers are borne at the top of hollow, fleshy stalks. An underused, easily cultivated bog plant. Zones 6–9.

Helonias bullata

HEMEROCALLIS

(Daylily)

Family: Liliaceae

Few perennials are as popular and easy to grow as daylilies. We enjoy their exotic flower forms, their tremendous range of color, and the seemingly effortless methods of propagation it takes to produce them. The growing and hybridizing of daylilies has reached fever pitch in North America, less so in

Hemerocallis 'Catherine Woodbury'

Europe. Since the first daylily cultivar, 'Apricot,' was developed by hybridist George Yeld in 1890, daylily breeding has been a fast and furious enterprise for many prominent hotriculturists. Almost 900 new cultivars were registered with the American Hemerocallis Society in 1987, making a total of 28,000 cultivars listed. Life (and this book) is too short to go into details about every one. Many fine plants are being produced. Many awful plants are being produced. The commercial success of daylily production has not necessarily paralleled an aesthetic success. In the mind of this writer, too many cultivars are too large and too coarse, making them difficult to use in the garden. However, in general they are appealing plants with flowers in an incredible variety of colors. They are clump-forming plants with deciduous or every-green straplike, arching leaves grooved in the center. The funnel- or trumpet-shaped flowers are borne on branched stems from spring until late autumn. In subtropical regions it is possible to have a display of daylilies year round. The individual flowers bloom for just a day. The genus name comes from the Greek *hemero,* "day," and *kallos,* "beauty."

CULTIVATION: Daylilies are easy to grow in any well-drained, fertile soil in full sun or partial shade. They do best in full sun, but many cultivars benefit from afternoon shading in hot climates. The gorgeous flowers mostly last for a day only, which means that daily deadheading is the only way to keep the plants looking neat. For those gardeners less obsessed by neatness, twice-weekly deadheading is probably enough. Water in periods of drought. Cut down the old flower stems when the flowers are finished.

LANDSCAPE USE: Daylilies do best in the mixed herbaceous border, where careful selection of contrasting and complimentary colors can make them a summer star. They are also outstanding plants for mass planting and for container growing.

PROPAGATION: Easily divided in spring or early autumn. While they will falter temporarily, dividing them while they are in flower is an excellent way for the gardener to increase desirable plants. Be sure to water well and often after this somewhat brutal exercise.

Cultivars. Cultivars come in an almost infinite variety of colors and forms. Almost all colors are represented, from near white to near black. The form of the flowers is extensive, too. The American Hemerocallis Society recognizes a number of forms including trumpet, cockerel, spider, star, pinwheel, orchid, triangular, and recurved.

The following is a list of a very few of the daylilies available. Height denotes the height of the flowering scape (stem). Early, mid and late describe their approximate blooming period in summer. All have foliage that dies down in winter unless otherwise noted and are suitable for Zones 3–9. For further information consult specialist nurseries or relevant plant societies.

'Apricot Angel': height 18 in. (45 cm), early-mid, melon pink flowers with a light-orange throat, slightly ruffled, semievergreen

'Autumn Daffodil': height 30 in. (75 cm), late, bright-yellow trumpets

'Autumn Minaret': height 5½ ft (165 cm), late, light yellow-orange flowers with a gold throat, foliage to 30 in. (75 cm)

'Autumn Prince': height 42 in. (105 cm), late, light-yellow, very fragrant flowers

'Autumn Red': height 38 in. (95 cm), mid, red flowers with a gold throat

'Ava Michelle': height 18 in. (45 cm), mid-late, ruffled yellow flowers with a green throat, semi-evergreen

'Beau Brummel': height 38 in. (95 cm), mid-late, velvety red flowers with a green-gold throat

'Bengal Tiger': height 40 in. (75 cm), mid-late, bright-orange flowers flushed copper

'Betty Woods': height 26 in. (65 cm), early-mid, a double-flowered apricot with a green throat, very fragrant, evergreen

'Bitsy': height 18 in. (45 cm), early, small, slightly ruffled bright-yellow flowers with a green throat, semievergreen, night-blooming

'Cartwheels': height 30 in. (75 cm), mid, orange-gold flowers with white midribs, round and flat form

'Catherine Woodbery': height 30 in. (75 cm), mid-late, orchid and lavender off-white flowers with a chartreuse throat, slightly ruffled

'Cherry Cheeks': height 28 in. (70 cm), mid-late, cherry-pink flowers with a yellow-green throat

'Chosen Love': height 26 in. (65 cm), early, pale-lavender flowers with a yellow-green throat semievergreen, fragrant

'Corky': height 34 in. (85 cm), mid, pale yellow, a good cut flower

'Dauntless': height 36 in. (90 cm), early-mid, creamy yellow and light buff flowers with a pale-green throat, semievergreen, fragrant

'Earlianna': height 32 in. (80 cm), very early, yellow-orange, fragrant flowers

'Eenie Weenie': height 10 in. (25 cm), early-mid, yellow flowers with a green throat

'Eleanor Apps': height 30 in. (75 cm), mid, light purple and deep violet, fragrant flowers

'Elijah': height 24 in. (60 cm), mid-late, tomato red flowers with an olive throat

'Elizabeth': height 32 in. (80 cm), very early, bright-yellow, fragrant flowers

'Emily Brown': height 36 in. (90 cm), mid, orange, slightly fragrant flowers

'Flame of Hades': height 62 in. (155 cm), mid-late, orange-red flowers with darker veins and a gold throat

'Frances Fay': height 28 in. (70 cm), mid, melon pink flowers with a tiny green throat, slightly ruffled

'Gentle Shepherd': height 29 in. (72.5 cm), early-mid, ruffled and overlapped nearly white flowers with a chartreuse throat, semievergreen

'Golden Yellow': height 36 in. (90 cm), early-mid, slightly ruffled petals, golden yellow flowers

'Golden Scroll': height 18 in. (45 cm), early, tangerine and gold flowers, ruffled and overlapping, green throat

'Golden Triangle': height 36 in. (90 cm), mid, buttercup-yellow, fragrant flowers with a triangular form

Hemerocallis 'Joan Senior'

'Green Flutter': height 24 in. (60 cm), mid-late, rich yellow flowers with chartreuse tones, light-green throat, semievergreen

'Guardian Angel': height 26 in. (65 cm), early-mid, triangular nearly white flowers with a light-green throat, semievergreen

'Hyperion': height 40 in. (100 cm), mid, lemon-yellow flowers, an old performer

'Irish August': height 38 in. (95 cm), very late, greenish yellow flowers with a green throat

'Jack Frost': height 36 in. (90 cm), mid-late, pale greenish yellow flowers, a good plant for partial shade

'Jake Russell': height 36 in. (90 cm), mid-late, recurved and ruffled, golden yellow, velvety flowers

'Joan Senior': height 24 in. (60 cm), early-mid, nearly white, deeply veined and textured flowers with a lime-green throat, evergreen

'Kindly Light': height 28 in. (70 cm), mid, glowing yellow, flowers in a spider form with twisted petals

'Korean Silk': height 26 in. (65 cm), mid pink-and-cream flowers wth a lime-green throat

'Lady Neva': height 42 in. (105 cm), early-mid, soft-yellow flowers with rose and green, semievergreen

'Lemon Balm': height 36 in. (90 cm), mid-late, sulfur yellow, flaring flowers, fragrant

'Lilting Lavender': height 30 in. (75 cm), mid-late, clear lavender flowers with a spider form

'Little Grapette': height 12 in. (30 cm), early, grape-purple flowers, semievergreen

'Little Rainbow': height 24 in. (60 cm), early-mid, pale pink, cream, yellow, and orchid flowers with an orange throat

'Little Red Hen': height 30 in. (75 cm), mid, red flowers with a yellow throat

'Mary Todd': height 26 in. (65 cm) early to early-mid, light yellow, lighter midribs, a heavy flower with recurved, crimped petals, semievergreen
'Midnight Magic': height 28 in. (70 cm), early-mid, black-red flowers with a green throat, evergreen
'Miss Jessie': height 40 in. (100 cm), mid, orchid-mauve and light-yellow, fragrant flowers
'Oriental Ruby': height 34 in. (85 cm), mid-late, carmine red flowers with a green throat
'Persian Princess': height 40 in (100 cm), early-mid, velvety deep-red flowers with a deep-purple sheen
'Pinwheel': height 33 in. (82.5 cm), early-mid, bright-red flowers with creamy edging, a yellow throat, raised midribs
'Prester John': height 26 in. (65 cm), early-mid, double orange, very fragrant flowers
'Prince Hal': height 34 in. (85 cm), mid, light-yellow flowers with a green throat
'Ruffled Apricot': height 28 in. (70 cm), early-mid, ruffled deep-apricot flowers with pink midribs and an apricot throat, fragrant
'Shooting Star': height 38 in. (95 cm), mid-late, pale creamy-yellow flowers
'So Sweet': height 22 in. (55 cm), early, soft-yellow flowers with a green throat, very fragrant
'Spring Fantasy': height 36 in. (90 cm), very early, lilac and pale-yellow flowers
'Stella de Oro': height 18 in. (45 cm), early, orange-yellow flowers, lightly ruffled and curled; a deservedly popular daylily that needs constant deadheading for continued repeat bloom
'Swamp Yankee': height 34 in. (85 cm), late, orange-and-gold flowers, triangular, ruffled
'Swirling Water': height 24 in. (60 cm), mid-late, bluish purple flowers splashed yellow and green
'Tender Love': height 22 in. (55 cm), late, pastel pink flowers
'Yazoo Green Octopus': height 28 in. (70 cm), mid, double greenish-yellow flowers, semievergreen, wonderful just for its name.

H. citrina. China. Height 40–45 in.; spread 24 in. (100–112.5 × 60 cm). A semievergreen daylily forming a large clump of coarse, dark-green leaves 40 in. (100 cm) long. Fragrant pale-yellow, narrow-petaled, trumpet-shaped, 6-in.-(15-cm-) wide flowers open just before sunset and close before noon the next day. Zones 3–9.

H. dumortieri. Japan. Height 2 ft; spread 18 in. (60 × 45 cm). Mounds of arching leaves 18 in. (45 cm) long and ½ in. (1.2 cm) wide, with spreading rather than erect flower stems shorter than the leaves. The brownish red flower buds are enclosed by two overlapping bracts. The flowers are light golden orange, two to four per stem in spring and early summer. Zones 3–9.

H. fulva. 'Europa.' Tawny daylily. Asia. Height 4–5 ft; spread 3 ft (120–150 × 90 cm). This is the common roadside daylily that has naturalized throughout a large part of the world. It is a sterile plant that does not set seed but does have fertile pollen; thus it is an essential contributor to the modern hybrids. It spreads by means of underground rhizomes, covering the ground with its bright-green, 2-ft- (60-cm-) long, arching leaves and its erect stems bearing in summer, up to 12 tawny orange flowers that are 7 in. (17.5 cm) wide. The variety ***rosea*** has pinkish red flowers with a prominent midrib, a darker eye, and a yellow throat. 'Flore Pleno' has double flowers with eight to 14 petals and bluish green foliage; 'Kwanso' is similar but has double flowers comprising nine petals; 'Maculata' has golden yellow flowers with a red-purple eye and a yellow throat. Zones 3–9.

H. lilio-asphodelus. Lemon daylily. Siberia, China, Japan. Height 30–36 in.; spread 18 in. (75–90 × 45 cm). Arching clumps of 2-ft- (60-cm-) long and ¾-in.- (1.8-cm-) wide dark-green leaves and branched, curving stems of five to nine delightfully fragrant, slightly reflexed lemon-yellow flowers in early summer. Although surpassed by modern hybrids, this is still a very desirable daylily. It is slow to respond to division but, within a year or two, rewards the diligent gardener with a mass of flowers. A good daylily for planting on steep banks. Zones 3–9.

H. middendorfii. Siberia, Japan. Height 2–3 ft; spread 2 ft (60–90 × 60 cm). Very similar to ***H. dumortieri*** with fragrant yellow-orange flowers 2–3 in. (5–7.5 cm) long, held above the foliage in spring and early summer. Zones 3–9.

H. minor. Siberia, Japan. Height 18–24 in.; spread 18 in. (45–60 × 45 cm). Grassy, arching leaves to 18

Hemerocallis minor

in. (45 cm) long and bell-shaped, light-yellow, fragrant flowers opening in the afternoon and lasting two days. Zones 3–9.

H. multiflora. China. Height 2–4 ft; spread 2 ft (60–120 × 60 cm). Clumps of dark-green leaves and many-branched stems bearing as many as 100 buds opening to light-orange flowers in late summer and autumn. So numerous and full are the flowers that the stems often bend over from the weight. Zones 5–9.

H. thunbergii. China, Korea. Height 2–4 ft; spread 2 ft (60–120 × 60 cm). A variable species with dark-green foliage and night-blooming, fragrant, lemon-yellow flowers with a green throat. Zones 3–9.

HEPATICA

(Liverleaf)

FAMILY: Ranunculaceae

A small genus of spring-flowering plants for shady positions. The genus name comes from the Greek *hepar,* "liver," and is a reference to the shape and color of the leaves. The flowers are produced before or just as the leaves unfold in spring.

CULTIVATION: Grow in a woodland soil that is neutral or only slightly acid, in partial shade.

LANDSCAPE USE: Diminutive plants for the woodland or shaded rock garden.

PROPAGATION: Divide after flowering or sow fresh seed in summer. Leave undisturbed as much as possible.

H. nobilis. Liverleaf. Northern hemisphere. Height 6–9 in.; spread 6 in. (15–22.5 × 15 cm). Heart-shaped, silky leaves with three rounded lobes and blue, petalless, anemonelike flowers up to 1 in. (2.5 cm) across in spring. The variety ***acuta (H. acutiloba)*** has less rounded, more pointed leaves, while the variety ***obtusa (H. americana)*** grows to 6 in. (15 cm) and has spherical, kidney-shaped leaves and lavender-blue to white flowers. Zones 4–8.

H. transsilvanica. Eastern Europe. Height 6 in.; spread 12 in. (15 × 30 cm). Similar to the above species, with scalloped leaves and 1-in.- (2.5-cm-) wide, pale mauve-blue, saucer-shaped flowers in spring. A hybrid between this and selected forms of ***H. nobilis*** named ***H. × media*** 'Ballardii' has flowers of intense blue. Zones 5–8.

HERACLEUM

(Hogweed)

FAMILY: Umbelliferae

Sixty species of coarse perennial and biennial herbs with large white flower clusters and deeply cut leaves. The two species listed below are beautiful plants for the water garden or woodland garden. The sap sometimes causes dermatitis in susceptible persons.

CULTIVATION: Grow in rich, moist soil in sun or shade. Remove faded flower heads to prevent overwhelming self-seeding.

LANDSCAPE USE: Wonderfully exotic-looking plants for the bog garden or waterside. The giant hogweed creates an exciting primeval effect. Not for the small garden.

PROPAGATION: Sow seeds in spring.

Heracleum mantegazzianum

H. mantegazzianum. Giant hogweed. Caucasus. Height 8–10 ft; spread 3 ft (240–300 × 90 cm). A giant, coarse biennial or short-lived perennial with red-spotted stems and 3-ft- (90-cm-) long, three-lobed, and toothed mid-green leaves. Enormous round heads of tiny white flowers appear in summer. Zones 3–9.

H. lanatum ***(H. sphondylium montanum).*** American cow parsley. North America, Europe, Asia. Height 8–10 ft; spread 3 ft (240–300 × 90 cm). A plant with 1-ft- (30-cm-) long lower leaves, divided into three-lobed toothed leaflets, hairy underneath. The upper leaves are smaller. Large unbels of white flowers appear in summer. Zones 3–9.

HESPERIS

(Dame's Rocket)

Family: Cruciferae

A little-grown genus of 24 species of annuals and perennials native from southern Europe to central Asia. One species is a short-lived perennial or biennial that is widely naturalized in deciduous woodland. The name Hesperis refers to the generic habit of perfuming the evening air when Hesperus, the evening star, is in the sky.

Cultivation: Grow in sun to partial shade in moist, rich soil. Deadhead after flowering.

Landscape Use: Delicately shaded plants for the woodland edge, where dappled sunlight exaggerates the flower color. Grow in large masses for dramatic effect.

Propagation: Sow seed in spring.

Hesperis matronalis

H. matronalis. Dame's rocket. Europe, Asia. Height 2–3 ft; spread 18 in. (60–90 × 45 cm). A coarse, many-branched plant with lance-shaped, toothed leaves up to 4 in. (10 cm) long. White, lilac, or purple ½-in.- (1.2-cm-) wide, four-petaled, cross-shaped flowers appear in late spring to early summer. Variety ***alba*** has bright-white flowers and comes true from seed most of the time. A double form elicits much excitement in some circles; it should be propagated from cuttings. Zones 4–9.

HEUCHERA

(Alumroot)

FAMILY: Saxifragaceae

Heuchera micrantha 'Palace Purple'

Almost 70 species of generally low-growing herbaceous perennials native to mountains and deciduous woodlands of North America, grown for their delicate flowers and largely evergreen marbled foliage. The leaves are lobed and often toothed, rounded to heart-shaped, long-stemmed and basal. The flower stalks are often long and arching, carrying sprays of tiny flowers from late spring to late summer and, in some species, into late autumn. Named after the distinguished German botanist Johann Heinrich von Heucher (1677–1747).

CULTIVATION: Grow in the open, in full sun or light shade. Shade becomes more important the higher the summer temperatures. Well-drained neutral to slightly lime-rich soil with average fertility but good organic content suits them well.

LANDSCAPE USE: Heucheras are invaluable plants for the front of the herbaceous border or as a groundcover under deciduous trees and shrubs, where their marbled foliage and delicate flower sprays create a delicate touch among heavy shrubs.

PROPAGATION: Sow seed in spring for planting in the early autumn. Divide in spring or autumn when the roots become overly woody and flowering begins to diminish. There is some dispute whether spring is better than autumn to divide the plants. To this gardner, there seems to be little or no difference.

H. americana. Alumroot. Eastern North America. Height 2–3 ft; spread 18 in. (60–90 × 45 cm). A clump-forming plant with 6-in.- (15-cm-) long basal, rounded, heart-shaped and veined evergreen leaves, hairy underneath. The young foliage is a wonderfully marbled purple color. The delicate greenish white flowers appear in early summer. A fine plant for areas with hot summers, where it should be grown in partial shade. In cooler climates it does particularly well growing at the sunnier margins of woodland plantings. There are a number of cultivars with pronounced purple foliage; 'Sunset' has strong purple veins. Zones 4–9.

H. bracteata. Rocky Mountains. Height 6 in.; spread 6 in. (15 × 15 cm). A densely tufted species with kidney-shaped, lobed and toothed leaves, and spikes of creamy white flowers in summer. An alpine plant enthusiasts appreciate. Zones 4–9.

H. × brizoides. Height 1–2½ ft; spread 12–18 in. (30–75 × 30–45 cm). Hybrids of ***H. micrantha, H. americana,*** and ***H. sanguinea*** have largely supplanted the species. They are mounded plants with dark-green, rounded, scallop-edged leaves and sprays of red, pink, or white flowers in late spring and early summer. Cultivars are often listed under the species; they include 'Bressingham Hybrids,' height 2 ft (60 cm), with mixed flower color; 'Chatterbox,' with long-lasting pink flowers; 'Coral Cloud,' with coral salmon-pink flowers; 'Fire Bird,' with scarlet flowers; 'June Bride,' with creamy white flowers; 'Mt. St. Helens,' height 18 in. (45 cm), with red flowers on erect stems; 'Oakington Jewel,' with marbled foliage and coral-red flowers; 'Pluie de Feu,' with scarlet flowers; 'Splendour,' with pink-scarlet flowers; 'Red Spangles,' height 20 in. (50 cm), with crimson-scarlet flowers; 'Scintillation,' with pink-red tipped flowers; 'Snowflake,' with white blooms; 'Sparkler,' with deep-red flowers; 'Tattletale' with clear-pink flowers; 'White Cloud,' with masses of tiny white flowers. Zones 4–8.

H. cylindrica. Northwestern North America. Height 2 ft; spread 1 ft (60 × 30 cm). Deeply lobed and dark-green leaves 2–3 in. (5–7.5 cm) wide with the creamy green flowers borne in slender panicles on hairy stems in early summer. The variety ***glabella*** has hairless flower stems. 'Greenfinch' grows to 2½ ft (75 cm) and has greenish white flowers; 'Green Ivory' has white flowers with a green throat. Zones 3–9.

H. micrantha. Western North America. Height 2 ft; spread 18 in. (60 × 45 cm). A mounded species with heart-shaped, rounded, gray-green leaves up to 4 in. (10 cm) long and wiry sprays of whitish flowers in summer. The cultivar 'Palace Purple' is now widely grown. The wrinkled leaves are dark purple above and wine red beneath, providing a dramatic display of dark foliage. The greenish white flowers, although sparse, are a delicate addition to the broad foliage. Populations of 'Palace Purple' are increasingly becoming seed-propagated, which not only renders the name meaningless but produces weaker and less purple forms. Strongly purple forms should be selected and propagated vegetatively. Zones 4–9.

H. sanguinea. Coral bells. Southwestern North America. Height 12–18 in.; spread 12 in. (30–45 × 30 cm). Has 1–2-in.- (2.5–5-cm-) wide, rounded to heart-shaped basal leaves and slender panicles of bright-red, bell-shaped flowers produced in late spring. The only red-flowered species and a parent of most of the hybrids listed under ***H. brizoides.*** Needs good drainage and full sun to light shade in neutral to lime-rich soil. Zones 4–9.

H. villosa. Hairy alumroot. Southeastern United States. Height 2–3 ft; spread 18 in. (60–90 × 45 cm). A magnificent species with softly hairy stems and rounded lobed leaves 4–6 in. (10–15 cm) wide, light green with slightly darker green mottling. Large panicles of creamy white flowers appear in late summer and last into autumn, making this the last ***Heuchera*** to flower. Although not widely grown, it deserves greater cultivation for its long-lasting, softly delicate flowers and its ability to grow in climates with hot summers. Zones 4–9.

Heuchera villosa

HEUCHERELLA

FAMILY: Saxifragaceae

Two intergeneric hybrids produced from ***Heuchera × brizoides, Tiarella cordifolia,*** and ***Tiarella cordifolia*** var. ***collina.*** Culture and landscape use are the same as ***Heuchera.*** Propagate by division only.

H. alba. 'Bridget Bloom.' Height 18 in.; spread 12 in. (45 × 30 cm). A clump-forming plant with wiry stems and delicate spikes of long-lasting, pale-pink flowers in late spring and early summer. Zones 4–8.

H. tiarelloides. Height 2 ft; spread 18 in. (60 × 45 cm). A slowly spreading, plant with evergreen, heart-shaped mottled leaves up to 4 in. (10 cm) long, lobed and toothed. Sprays of pale-pink flowers are borne on wiry stems in spring and early summer, often reblooming in autumn. Zones 4–8.

HEXASTYLIS

FAMILY: Aristolochiaceae

Hexastylis shuttleworthii 'Callaway'

Formerly placed in the genus ***Asarum,*** this is a genus of nine species of low-growing woodland plants almost indistinguishable from ***Asarum*** species. They are rhizomatous, slowly spreading, stemless plants with kidney-shaped leaves and small brown or purple flowers that are hidden under the leaves in spring.

CULTIVATION: Grow in well-drained but moist, acid soil in woodland shade.

LANDSCAPE USE: Subtle groundcovers for the shady border, woodland collection, or American native plant collection.

PROPAGATION: Divide in spring.

H. arifolia. Virginia to Florida. Height 8 in.; spread 12 in. (20 × 30 cm). Clumps of arrow-shaped, faintly blotched evergreen leaves up to 5 in. (12.5 cm) long with 1-in.- (2.5-cm-) long, brownish purple flowers in spring. Zones 6–9.

H. shuttleworthii. Virginia to Alabama. Height 8 in.; spread 12 in. (20 × 30 cm). Rounded heart-shaped leaves up to 3 in. (7.5 cm) across often mottled with gray or light green. The cultivar 'Callaway' has yellow marbled veining and is an especially handsome groundcover. Zones 6–9.

H. virginicum. Virginia to Alabama. Height 8 in.; spread 12 in. (20 × 30 cm). Heart-shaped to arrow-shaped leaves up to 3 in. (7.5 cm) across with 1-in.- (2.5-cm-) long purple flowers hidden under the evergreen leaves in spring. Zones 6–9.

HIERACIUM

(Hawkweed)

Family: Compositae

A genus of almost 1,000 species, few of which are of ornamental value. They are widely spread throughout the world, native to sites of steep drainage and poor soil. The majority are rampant weeds with a milky sap and basal leaves. The flowers, which bloom in the summer and autumn, are similar to dandelions. The common name comes from the Greek *hierakion,* "falcon," a reference to the belief that hawks eat the plants to sharpen their eyesight.

Cultivation: Grow in well-drained, gravelly soil in full sun. Plant away from more precious plants as many members of this genus are highly invasive.

Landscape Use: Coarse plants for the rock garden or sunny bank.

Propagation: Divide in spring or sow seed in autumn.

H. aurantiacum. Devil's paintbrush, grim-the-collier. Europe, North America. Height 1–2 ft; spread 1 ft (30–60 × 30 cm). An invasive weed that may be of value in a dry, rocky garden. Hairy lance-shaped basal leaves up to 8 in. (20 cm) long and hairy stems carrying orange-red flowers 1 in. (2.5 cm) wide from early summer to autumn. The curious name grim-the-collier comes from the black hairs that clothe the flower stem. Zones 3–9.

H. lanatum. Europe. Height 2 ft; spread 1 ft (60 × 30 cm). A clump-forming plant with silver-gray rosettes of downy, egg-shaped leaves up to 12 in. (30 cm) long and branching stems of 1-in.- (2.5-cm-) wide yellow daisies in summer. The faded flowers should be removed to prevent rampant self-seeding. Zones 4–9.

H. maculatum. Europe. Height 1–2 ft; spread 1 ft (30–60 × 30 cm). A clump-forming species with hairy, lance-shaped green leaves blotched chocolate brown. Reddish stalks bear yellow daisies in early summer. The foliage has some ornamental value and the flowers are best removed before turning to seed. Zones 3–9.

H. venosum. Rattlesnake weed. North America. Height 2–3 ft; spread 1 ft (60–90 × 30 cm). Basal rosettes of mostly hairless green leaves dramatically veined deep red. Branching stems of yellow flowers are produced in summer. Commonly found on rocky slopes of deciduous woodland from Vermont to Georgia. Zones 3–9.

H. villosum. Shaggy hawkweed. Europe. Height 1–2 ft; spread 1 ft (30–60 × 30 cm). A mat-forming plant with finely toothed woolly, gray-green foilage and fragrant yellow flowers up to 2 in. (5 cm) wide in summer. Zones 3–9.

HOSTA

(Plantain-lily)

Family: Liliaceae

Undoubtedly *the* foliage plant for the shade garden, hostas are now so widely grown as to be almost commonplace. The reason for their widespread cultivation is not just fashion. They are long-lived reliable plants that are easily grown for their fresh and often dramatic foliage as well as their attractive and sometimes sweet-smelling flowers. Many thrive in deep shade, while others will tolerate considerable sun. Although there are hundreds of varieties of hybrids and cultivars, there are only approxomately 15 to 20 species. All are native to the Far East. Two species are indigenous to China; the

Hosta 'Piedmont Gold'

rest belong to Japan and Korea. The nomenclature of the genus is highly confused, beginning with the naming of the wild species and continuing into the maze of cultivars. Breeders have been particularly enthusiastic about hostas, partly because there is so much variability in seed-grown plants and partly because growers can make considerable amounts of money from new introductions. The market may well be glutted at this time, with many new cultivars becoming increasingly indistinguishable from each other.

The range of hostas is enormous, from 3-ft- (90-cm-) high clumps of beefy foliage to tiny, dew-dropped tufts 6 in. (15 cm) high. The leaves range in color from dark green, blue, yellow- and cream-variegated, some with wavy edges, puckered spots, distinct veins, or shiny surfaces. The flowers can be small, funnel-shaped, and lavender or large, waxy, and white. They are largely pest-free, although slugs and snails clearly regard them as a delicacy.

Describing hostas is fraught with peril, as many with Latin names are not species and many hybrids and cultivars have such an extensive lineage that establishing parentage is very confusing. In the descriptions below, the species are described along with their varieties and cultivars, then the cultivars that are not clearly attributable to one or more species.

Cultivation: Easily grown, long-lived plants for a wide range of environments although they grow best in rich, moist but well-drained soil in light shade. A number of hostas can take bright sun in climates with cool summers, but in general they are shade-loving perennials. Many hostas produce wonderful flowers, while others, particularly the more violently variegated, display pale-violet flowers that contrast in far too alarming a manner with the foliage. It does not harm the plants to remove these flowers before they open. If the plants are grown in dry soil, repeated irrigation and yearly mulching will help. Hostas should be left alone to develop into large clumps. Constant division, while not weakening the plant substantially, will keep it small and mean.

Landscape Use: Stalwart but exciting plants for the shade garden or border as groundcovers and edging, foliage and flowering contrasts, container plants and cut plants for flowers and foliage. There are few shady places that hostas won't brighten.

Propagation: Division is by far the best method, although hostas do best when left alone for many years. Seed propagation is useful for developing new forms.

H. capitata. Korea, Japan. Height 12 in.; spread 18 in. (30 × 45 cm). Dark-green, 5-in.- (12.5-cm-) long and 3-in.- (7.5-cm-) wide, heart-shaped, glossy leaves with fluted margins. The 12-in.- (30-cm-) high flower stem is rigid and carries up to 20 purple flowers in summer. Zones 3–9.

H. crispula. Japan. Height 3 ft; spread 2 ft (90 × 60 cm). White-edged, very dark-green, wavy, almost twisted, egg-shaped leaves up to 4 in. (10 cm) wide and 8 in. (20 cm) long with drooping tips. The large number of pale-lavender flowers are held well above the mound of foliage. This is the earliest white-edged hosta to bloom, doing so in early summer. Grow in full to half shade and protect from strong wind. Zones 3–9.

H. elata. Japan. Height 30 in.; spread 30 in. (75 × 75 cm). Eight-in.- (20-cm-) wide, dull medium-green, slightly gray leaves with distinct undulating margins. One of the earliest to bloom, the pale-purple to whitish flowers are funnel-shaped up to 2⅓ in. (6 cm) long. Zones 3–9.

H. decorata. Japan. Height 2 ft; spread 2 ft (60 × 60 cm). A flat, mounded plant with broadly oval, 3-in.- (7.5-cm-) wide, 4-in.- (10-cm-) long, dull green leaves with white slightly wavy edges. In summer 2-ft- (60-cm-) high flower stems bear dark-violet, urn-shaped flowers. The cultivar 'Thomas Hogg' is a good example of the confusion in naming hostas. In England ***H.*** 'Thomas Hogg' is described as being synonymous with ***H. undulata*** 'Albo-marginata,' while in the United States it is listed is being synonymous with ***H. decorata.*** Zones 3–9.

H. fortunei. Japan. Height 2 ft; spread 2–2½ ft (60 × 60–75 cm). Probably a group of garden hybrids or perhaps a variety of ***H. sieboldinana;*** the details are inconclusive. The true form has pointed, egg-shaped, slightly gray-green leaves up to 12 in. (30 cm) long and 4–8 in. (10–20 cm) wide. Funnel-shaped, pale-lilac flowers with one or more bracts beneath appear in summer. The variety ***obscura*** has exceptionally dark-green leaves 8 in. (20 cm) long, 5½ in. (14 cm) wide. 'Albo-marginata' has medium-green leaves with wide, white margins, 'Albo-picta' has irregular edges of dark green on a bright-yellow leaf that becomes completely dark green by summer's end, 'Aurea' has completely yellow leaves that unfold in late spring, gradually turning pale green by summer. 'Aureo-marginata' has dark-green leaves with deep-yellow margins fading to pale yellow or white as summer progresses. 'Gloriosa' has furrowed, spear-shaped, white-edged leaves. 'Golden Haze' is very similar to 'Aurea' but retains its yellow leaf color throughout the season. 'Gold Standard' is a vigorous plant with yellow leaves irregularly edged deep green. 'Hyacinthina' has greenish gray leaves edged with a thin white line. 'Francee' is a fine cultivar with 5-in.- (12.5-cm-) wide, 6-in.- (15-cm-) long, deep-green leaves with bright-white margins. Zones 3–9.

H. lancifolia. Japan. Height 2 ft; spread 18 in. (60 × 45 cm). Known since 1690, this is a parent of many hybrids. Lance-shaped to oblong leaves 7 in. (17.5 cm) long, 1 in. (2.5 cm), wide that are green and glossy with sharply pointed tips. Long-lasting, trumpet-shaped, lilac-purple flowers are held almost horizontally on stiff, green stems in late summer. 'Louisa' has white-variegated spear-shaped leaves. Zones 3–9.

H. minor. Korea. Height 18–24 in.; spread 12 in. (45–60 × 30 cm). A slowly spreading species with slightly wavy, widely egg-shaped mid-green leaves and funnel-shaped mauve flowers on 2-ft (60-cm) stems in summer. The variety ***alba*** has white flowers. Zones 3–9.

H. nigrescens. Japan. Height 3 ft; spread 2 ft (90 × 60 cm). The dusty gray-green leaves are 7 in. (17.5 cm) wide, slightly wavy, roundly egg-shaped, with the leaf base rolled into a funnel onto the stem. Thick erect or arching stems carry pale-violet flowers in late summer. Variety ***elatior*** is a larger plant with shiny leaves dusted gray. Zones 3–9.

H. plantaginea. China. Height 30 in.; spread 3 ft (75 × 90 cm). Cultivated since the late 1800s, the species and its hybrids are among the most popular of hostas. Long-stemmed, heart-shaped, medium-green leaves up to 10 in (25 cm) long form large mounds with sweet-smelling white and waxy trumpet-shaped flowers up to 4 in. (10 cm) long, held almost horizontally on the stem. Some hybrids are more tolerant of sun and heat than many others; 'Honeybells' (***H. plantaginea*** × ***H. lancifolia***) has light-green leaves with wavy margins and fragrant, pale-violet flowers in late summer; 'Royal Standard' has medium to light-green slightly puckered glossy leaves 8 in. (20 cm) long with stiff flower stems and near-white fragrant flowers in late summer. Tolerant of strong sunshine in cool climates. Zones 3–9.

H. sieboldiana. Japan. Height 2½–3 ft; spread 4 ft (75–90 × 120 cm). Almost round greenish blue, puckered leaves over 12 in. (30 cm) long and 9 in. (22.5 cm) wide, covered in a waxy glaucous dust, on 1-ft- (30-cm-) long leaf stalks. Grayish white to pale-lilac flowers are borne on erect flower stems seldom rising above the mound of foliage in early to midsummer. The variety ***elegans*** has pale-lavender flowers and blue-gray leaves; 'Aureo-marginata' is very similar to the more popular 'Frances Williams' but with narrower more even gold mar-

Hosta fortunei 'Albo-Marginata'

gins; 'Frances Williams' has blue-green leaves unevenly edged with yellow variegation and is one of the most popular hostas available. 'Ryan's Big One' has large rounded and crinkled, powdery blue leaves. Zones 3–9.

H. sieboldii. Japan. Height 18 in.; spread 20 in. (45 × 50 cm). Formerly known as ***H. albomarginata,*** with lance-shaped, undulating, 5-in.- (12.5-cm-) long, dark-green leaves with thin white margins, glossy underneath, dull above. Bell-shaped purple flowers with violet veins appear in late summer. 'Alba' has green leaves and white flowers; 'Kabitan' has pale-yellow lance-shaped leaves with undulating thin green margins; 'Subcrocea' is similar to 'Kabitan' but without the green margins. Zones 3–9.

H. tardiflora. Japan. Height 1 ft; spread 18 in. (30 × 45 cm). A small, clump-forming species with lance-shaped and shiny, dark-green, 6-in.- (15-cm-) long leaves with a broad base and tapering tip. Dense spikes of mauve flowers appear in autumn. ***H.*** × ***tardiana*** is probably an invalid but published name for the cross between ***H. tardiflora*** and ***H. sieboldiana*** var. ***elegans.*** Cultivars include: 'Blue Moon,' blue leaves 3 in. (7.5 cm) long, 2 in. (5 cm) wide with white flowers in late summer; 'Blue Wedgewood,' blue leaves 7 in. (17.5 cm) long, 3 in. (7.5 cm) wide with pale-lavender flowers in early summer; 'Buckshaw Blue,' cupped and boat-shaped blue leaves and light-mauve flowers in midsummer; 'Hadspen Blue,' strong blue leaves and lavender flowers; 'Hadspen Heron,' narrow blue leaves and lavender flowers; 'Halcyon,' spear-shaped, ribbed, light-blue leaves with pale-lilac flowers. Zones 3–9.

H. tokudama. Japan. Height 1 ft; spread 18 in. (30 × 45 cm). Resembling ***H. sieboldiana*** but slower growing and smaller in stature. Rounded puckered, and cup-shaped blue-gray leaves to 8 in. (20 cm) long. Whitish gray flowers appear in midsummer. 'Aurea-nebulosa' has blue-green margins and yellow-cream centers; 'Flavo-circinalis' has blue-green leaves with yellow margins; 'Flavo-planata' has narrow, dark blue-green margins and yellow centers; 'Variegata' has blue-green leaves striped pale creamy green. Zones 3–9.

H. undulata. Japan. Height 18 in.; spread 18 in. (45 × 45 cm). The specific name is pleasingly descriptive as this hosta has strongly undulating, shiny dark-green leaves marked creamy white. The often spirally twisted leaves are elliptical to egg-shaped and up to 6 in. (15 cm) long. Pale-lilac flowers are borne on leafy stems in early summer. It may well be a sterile hybrid of ***H. crispula*** or ***H. decorata.*** 'Albo-marginata' (Thomas Hogg?) has white-margined, spear-shaped to egg-shaped leaves that are the opposite of the species; 'Erromena' is a green-leaved variety with broadly egg-shaped leaves up to 9 in. (22.5 cm) long and almost 4-ft- (120-cm) tall flower stems bearing pale-lilac flowers in summer; 'Univittata' has leaves less wavy than the species with a white central stripe. Zone 3–9.

H. ventricosa. China. Height 2–3 ft; spread 3 ft (60–90 × 90 cm). Tapering, heart-shaped, dark-green glossy leaves 6–7 in. (15–17.5 cm) long and 5 in. (12.5 cm) wide. In summer 3-ft (90-cm) flower stems carry urn-shaped deep violet-blue flowers. It is a magnificently sturdy plant. 'Aureo-maculata' has green margins on yellow leaves that turn almost fully green in summer; 'Aureo-marginata' (Variegata) has green leaves with yellow to cream edges. Zones 3–9.

H. venusta. Japan. Height 4 in.; spread 12 in. (10 × 30 cm). Perhaps the smallest hosta with a spreading rootstock and green elliptical to egg-shaped abruptly pointed leaves 1½ in. (3.8 cm) long and ½ in. (1.2 cm) wide. Funnel-shaped lilac flowers appear in early summer. 'Variegata' has creamy white leaves with green edges. Zones 3–9.

Hybrids and Cultivars Literally hundreds of hybrids and cultivars are available, with new ones coming out every year. The following is a list of a few of the more interesting. 'Antioch': a medium size plant with large, medium-green leaves, mottled light green with wide white edges and lavender flowers; 'August Moon': puckered golden green leaves and white flowers on a 20-in. (50-cm) flower stem; 'Betsy King': a medium-size plant with small, shiny, deep-green foliage, early deep-purple flowers; 'Big Mama': large mounds of cupped and crinkled blue leaves, off-white flowers; 'Citation': small mounds of twisted greenish yellow foliage with white margins, pale-lavender flowers in midsummer; 'Ginko Craig': spear-shaped dark-green leaves edged white, long-lasting deep-lilac flowers on 1-ft (30-cm) stems; 'Ground Master': a low-growing, spreading plant with undulating white edges and a green center; 'Invincible': small mounds of brightly shiny, wavy and pointed leaves and long-lasting blue flowers in summer, tolerates full sun; 'Krossa Regal': leathery, pointed, frosty blue leaves and 5-ft- (150-cm-) tall flower stems bearing soft-lavender flowers in summer; 'North Hills': medium-size shiny green leaves, narrow white margins turning to yellow and pale green; 'Pearl Lake':

blue-green heart-shaped leaves and masses of pale-lavender flowers in midsummer; 'Piedmont Gold': a large plant with golden yellow puckered leaves and white flowers; 'Sea Drift': a large plant with oval green leaves with ruffled edges and lavender-pink flowers; 'Shade Master': a medium-size, mound-forming plant with early golden leaves turning green and lavender flowers in midsummer; 'Sun Power': a large plant with large, twisted, gold foliage and soft-orchid flowers in midsummer; 'Wide Brim': blue-green leaves and wide, irregular edges of creamy white, flushed yellow, many pale-lavender flowers in summer. Zones 3–9.

HOUTTUYNIA

Family: Saururaceae

Houttuynia cordata 'Chamaeleon'

One species of a spreading and invasive nature with evil-smelling, heart-shaped, alternate leaves and spikes of white flowers in summer. Named after M. Houttuyn, a Dutch writer on natural history.

Cultivation: Grow in damp soil in full sun to partial shade. Highly invasive when growing well. Best grown in cool conditions far from civilization. Fortunately, it tends to deteriorate by midsummer, particularly in areas of high temperatures.

Landscape Use: An effective but sometimes ugly groundcover for wet sites, where it can become almost impossible to eradicate. Be warned!

Propagation: Division or cuttings in spring or summer.

H. cordata. Asia. Height 6–24 in.; spread 18 in. (15–60 × 45 cm). A rampant groundcover with dark-green, red-edged, heart-shaped leaves up to 3 in. (7.5 cm) long with 2-in. (5-cm) spikes of tiny flowers ringed by four white bracts. 'Chameleon,' also known as 'Variegata,' has highly variegated leaves blotched green, white (or cream), and red, 'Flore Pleno' has green leaves tinged purple and double white flowers with enlarged petal-like bracts. Zones 6–9.

HYSSOPUS

(Hyssop)

Family: Labiatae

Five species of aromatic herbs and subshrubs native from southern Europe to central Asia. One species is widely grown as an ornamental and medicinal herb. The name hyssop comes from the Arabic *azob*, "holy herb," from its use for cleaning sacred places.

Cultivation: Grow in full sun in well-drained, sandy soil.

Landscape Use: Use as a low hedge or single specimen in the sunny border or herb garden.

Propagation: Sow seeds in spring. Carefully divide the woody roots in spring or take cuttings in summer.

H. officinalis. Hyssop. Southern Europe. Height 2 ft; spread 18 in. (60 × 45 cm). An erect, bushy plant with square stems and linear leaves up to 1½ in. (3.8 cm) long in whorled opposite pairs. Whorls of blue, tubular flowers appear in summer. Variety ***albus*** has white flowers; var. ***purpurascens*** has purple flowers; and var. ***roseus*** has pale-pink flowers. Zones 3–10.

IBERIS

(Candytufts)

Family: Cruciferae

Thirty to 40 species of annual and perennial plants, many of which are woody and are subshrubs. The popular candytufts are generally evergreen with alternate, dark-green leaves and cross-shaped white or pink flowers. ***Iberis*** refers to the fact that many of the species are native to Spain (Iberia). The common name also denotes native origin. Candie was an old English name for the island of Crete, where many early forms were first observed.

Cultivation: Easily grown in light, lime-rich, well-drained soil in full sun or very light shade. Shear back hard after flowering to encourage bushy growth. In cold, snowless areas mulch to protect against winter damage.

Landscape Use: Use sturdy spring-flowering plants for the rock garden or the front of the border.

Propagation: Sow seed in autumn or spring. Take cuttings in midsummer.

I. gibraltarica. Gibraltar candytuft. Gibraltar. Height 12 in.; spread 12–18 in. (30 × 30–45 cm). A clump-forming plant with basal rosettes of toothed evergreen leaves up to 1 in. (2.5 cm) long and flat clusters of lilac to light-purple flowers in late spring and early summer. Protect from winter cold. Zones 7–9.

Iberis sempervirens

I. saxatilis. Southern Europe. Height 3 in.; spread 12 in. (7.5 × 30 cm). A low-growing, tufted evergreen subshrub with dark-green, ¾-in.- (1.8- cm-) long linear leaves and masses of white flowers in flat-topped terminal clusters in spring. Zones 4–8.

I. sempervirens. Candytuft. Mediterranean. Height 1 ft; spread 3 ft (30 × 90 cm). A popular evergreen tufted plant forming an irregular circle of woody stems and dark-green, linear to narrowly oblong leaves up to 2 in. (5 cm) long. The pure-white flower heads are produced from the sides of the stems in spring and early summer. 'Alexander's White' has brilliant white flowers; 'Autumn Snow' has white flowers that rebloom in the autumn; 'Kingwood Compact,' height 8 in. (20 cm), has fine leaves and white flowers; 'Litttle Gem' is a dwarf compact form growing to a height of 8 in. (20 cm); 'Purity' has long-blooming white flowers; 'Pygmaea' reaches a height of 4 in. (10 cm); 'Snowflake' is 10 in. (25 cm) tall with bright-white flowers. Zones 3–9.

IMPERATA

(Japanese Blood Grass)

FAMILY: Graminae

Imperata cylindrica 'Red Baron'

A genus primarily known for one cultivar, ***I. cylindrica*** 'Red Baron.' Long cultivated in Japan, it has only recently begun to be grown in the West, where it has caused great excitement among fans of ornamental grasses for its blood-red color from early summer until early autumn.

CULTIVATION: Grow in moist but well-drained soil in full sun or light shade. Leaf color is stronger when grown in full sun. Water well in periods of drought. Although it spreads by means of rhizomes just below the soil surface, it is not an invasive grass.

LANDSCAPE USE: A dramatic plant for containers, mass plantings, and lightly shaded woodland areas. Combines well with yellow variegated grasses or silver- or gray-leaf plants. This grass becomes especially fiery if backlit by the setting summer sun.

PROPAGATION: Divide in spring.

I. cylindrica 'Red Baron.' Japanese blood grass. Japan. Height 18–20 in.; spread 12 in. (45–50 × 30 cm). A nonflowering, shallow-rooted, brightly ornamental grass with an upright habit and brilliant red leaves with green bases. The leaves are green with red tips in spring but by early summer are bright, fiery red. The color intensifies in autumn. Flowers are rarely produced. Zones 5–9.

INCARVILLEA

(Hardy Gloxinia)

FAMILY: Bignoniaceae

A small genus of annual, biennial, and perennial plants not widely cultivated in gardens. Those grown are exotic-looking plants with fleshy pink flowers like large foxgloves. They have fleshy tuberous roots and leaves divided into leaflets. They grow well in mild climates but have trouble surviving in areas with cold winters or hot summers. Named after Incarville, an 18th-century Jesuit missionary to China.

CULTIVATION: Grow in a deep, sandy but fertile soil in full sun to light shade. Protect from full sun in hot climates. Mulch for winter protection. Hardy gloxinias are generally late to break growth in spring and their location should be marked to prevent damaging them when cultivating the ground.

LANDSCAPE USE: Exotic-looking plants for the sunny border.

PROPAGATION: Sow seeds in spring and transplant to their permanent position the following spring. Division is difficult because of their woody taproots. Carefully divide in late spring.

I. ***delavayi.*** Hardy gloxinia. Western China. Height 2 ft; spread 1 ft (60 × 30 cm). Large basal clumps of deep-green leaves up to 1 ft (30 cm) long, divided into pairs of toothed leaflets appearing with or after the 2-in.- (5-cm-) wide, yellow-throated, rich-pink flowers in late spring and early summer. The flowers begin a few inches above the ground but as the season develops, the flower stalks reach a height of 2 ft (60 cm). Deadhead the faded flowers for extended bloom. Zones 5–8.

I. ***mairei.*** China. Height 1 ft; spread 1 ft (30 × 30 cm). Similar to the above species but a smaller plant with shorter leaves and fewer and more rounded leaflets. The variety ***grandiflora*** has cerise-pink flowers reaching up to 4 in. (10 cm) in diameter appearing in late spring and blooming into summer. Zones 5–8.

INULA

(Elecampane)

FAMILY: Compositae

Inula royleana

A large genus of daisies, most of which are native to Europe, Asia, and Africa although some are native and naturalized in North America. They are hairy plants with alternate leaves and large yellow flowers held either singly or in clusters. Leafy bracts collar the flower. The common name of this medicinal herb, elecampane, is a corruption of the name of another daisy, Helenium, and refers to the plant being found growing wild in the fields of Campania in Italy.

Cultivation: Easily cultivated in fertile, moisture-retentive soil in full sun.

Landscape Use: Coarse plants for the sunny garden or, for the taller species, the wild garden or meadow.

Propagation: Divide in spring or autumn.

I. acaulis. Asia. Height 2–4 in.; spread 12 in. (5–10 × 30 cm). A stemless perennial with oblong, spoon-shaped, mid-green leaves and golden yellow daisies 2 in. (5 cm) wide, blooming in summer. A curious plant for the rock garden. Zones 4–8.

I. ensifolia. Swordleaf inula. Europe, Asia. Height 1–2 ft; spread 2 ft (30–60 × 60 cm). Narrow, stalkless, swordlike leaves up to 4 in. (10 cm) long on branching stems with solitary yellow daisies 2 in. (5 cm) wide in summer. If seeds are sown in spring, the plants will flower in summer. 'Compacta' grows to a height of 10 in. (25 cm); 'Gold Star' is a bushy plant that reaches a height of 2 ft (60 cm) and is covered in golden yellow flowers. Deadhead for consistent flowering into autumn. Zones 3–9.

I. helenium. Elecampane. Eurasia. Height 4–6 ft; spread 4 ft (120–180 × 120 cm). A coarse, erect plant with hairy leaves, velvety underneath, bristly above. The lower leaves are oblong to elliptical and up to 2 ft (60 cm) long; they become smaller and stalkless farther up the furrowed and hairy stem. The 4-in.- (10-cm-) wide yellow flowers appear in summer and autumn, are either solitary or in a cluster of two to three, and are surrounded by a collar of leafy bracts. Naturalized in eastern North America. Zones 3–9.

I. hookeri. Himalaya. Height 2½ ft; spread 2 ft (75 × 60 cm). A many-branched plant with softly hairy, oblong to lance-shaped leaves up to 4 in. (10 cm) long with small-toothed edges. The pale-yellow flowers are up to 3 in. (7.5 cm) wide and appear in late summer and early autumn. Zones 4–8.

I. magnifica. Caucasus. Height 6 ft; spread 3 ft (180 × 90 cm). A larger-flowered version of ***I. helenium*** with thick, erect brownish stems and round to elliptical hairy leaves becoming smaller farther up the stem. In late summer 6-in.- (15-cm-) wide yellow flowers appear. Zones 5–8.

I. orientalis. Caucasus. Height 2 ft; spread 18 in. (60 × 45 cm). Oblong, hairy basal leaves up to 6 in. (15 cm) long clasping the stem base. In late summer 3-in.- (7.5-cm-) wide orange-yellow flowers appear. Zones 4–8.

I. royleana. Himalayan elecampane. Himalayas. Height 2 ft; spread 18 in. (60 × 45 cm). Strong, unbranched stems with clasping, egg-shaped, 10-in.- (25-cm-) long mid-green leaves that are hairy underneath. Single 4-in.- (10-cm-) wide orange-yellow flowers are produced in summer. Less tolerant of heat than other species. Zones 3–7.

IRIS

Family: Iridaceae

A large genus of about 300 species with many subspecies and varieties, hybrids and cultivars. In general, they are widely distributed throughout the northern hemisphere, inhabiting a diverse range of environments from boggy swamps to dry uplands.

They have geen grown for centuries, often for their medicinal properties or for their contribution to the perfume industry. They are now extremely popular as garden plants for display in herbaceous borders, for focal points in bog gardens and naturalistic gardens, and as specimens in rock gardens.

Irises are divided into many groups. Some are bulbs while others have rhizomes and rhizomatous roots. Some have flowers with "beards" while others are "beardless" or have crests. Most have swordlike leaves in clumps or fans. The often exquisite flowers

Iris 'Banbury Beauty'

Iris confusa

Iris laevigata 'Albo-violacea'

have a deliciously intricate structure. The flower buds are often sheathed in papery bracts. The inner, mostly vertical segments of the flower are called the "standards." The horizontal flower segments are called the "falls," and these narrow at the base to form the "haft." The falls are often adorned with a crest, ridge, or beard. The genus is named for Iris, the goddess of the rainbow.

The following descriptions are of nonbulbous irises.

Cultivation: Information on cultivation is included in the individual species descpritions. The bearded irises are particularly susceptible to the iris borer, an insect that lays eggs in the rhizomes. The eggs hatch into voracious larvae that rapidly destroy the rhizome, reducing it to a soggy mush. Systemic insecticides plus a wetting agent will control the insect, as does removing and destroying the affected part. Irises, particularly the Japanese irises, are also prone to aphid and thrip damage. In North America bacterial wet rot is a serious problem, as is leaf spot. In general, the water-loving species appear to be more disease and insect resistant than the garden hybrids.

Landscape Use: Irises of one kind or another should be grown in every garden. Whether they are grown as bog plants or border plants, they are exquisite. The swordlike leaves and large, multicolored flowers are perfect in the herbaceous border, as a contrast to the larger leaves of many bog-garden plants, or as spears of leaf and flower in the naturalistic garden.

Propagation: Division is generally the best method, although sowing seed is often easy. See under the individual listings for further information.

I. aphylla. Europe. Height 1 ft; spread 2–3 ft (30 × 60–90 cm). A bearded iris with curved outer leaves about ¾ in. (1.8 cm) wide and branched flower stalks bearing masses of white-bearded, dark-purple or violet-blue flowers up to 3 in. (7.5 cm) across in late spring and occasionally in autumn. Grow in well-drained average soil in full sun. Easily raised from seed. Zones 5–8.

I. brevicaulis. South and central United States. Height 12–20 in.; spread 2–3 ft (30–50 × 60–90 cm). A moisture-loving beardless iris blooming in spring, native to the Mississippi River basin and the central United States. It is a leafy plant with zigzagging flower stalks and terminal and axillary blue-violet flowers with whitish yellow, egg-shaped falls. It is easily grown in moisture-retentive soil in full sun or partial shade. Divide in spring or autumn. Zones 5–9.

I. chrysographes. Goldvein iris. China, Burma. Height 18 in; spread 2 ft (45 × 60 cm). A beautiful beardless iris with ½-in.- (1.2-cm-) wide gray-green leaves and hollow, unbranched flower stalks bearing usually two fragrant, dark-violet, velvety flowers wth drooping gold-veined falls in summer. Variety ***rubellum*** has red-violet flowers, var. ***nigra*** has very dark-red almost black flowers. Forms with almost-black flowers are particularly desirable. 'Holden Clough' is a notable hybrid with brownish yellow flowers with marked purple veining and golden yellow-tinged falls. It is probably a hybrid with ***I. foetidissima.*** Grow in a slightly acid, moisture-retentive soil in full sun. Divide in early autumn. Zones 7–9.

I. confusa. China. Height 30 in.; spread 3 ft (75 × 90 cm). A spreading, crested iris with broad, mid-green leaves up to 2 in. (5 cm) wide and 15 in.

(37.5 cm) long. The 2-in.- (5-cm-) wide, short-lived white flowers have a heavily fringed yellow crest and are produced in long succession in early to midsummer. This species is evergreen and performs best in mild and subtropical climates. It prefers moisture-retentive soil and partial shade. Divide in late summer. Zones 8–10.

I. cristata. Dwarf crested iris. Eastern North America. Height 6 in.; spread 12 in. (15 × 30 cm). A spring-blooming woodland native, this delightful crested iris has fans of light-green, 1-in.- (2.5-cm-) wide ribbed leaves up to 9 in. (22.5 cm) long. The fragrant flowers are almost stalkless and range in color from lilac to purple. The flowers have a yellow crest and a white center that is spotted dark violet. Variety ***alba*** has white flowers; 'Shenandoah Sky' has light-blue flowers. Grow in full sun to partial shade in leafy, woodland soil. Irrigate in dry soil. Divide after flowering every few years. Protect from slugs. Zones 4–8.

I. douglasiana. Pacific Coast iris. Oregon, California. Height 1–2 ft; spread 2 ft (30–60 × 60 cm). A tough, variable species native to the cliffs of the Pacific Coast. It is a beardless iris with arching evergreen, 1-in.- (2.5-cm-) wide, deep-green leaves with a red base. The branched stalks bear many flowers in a range of colors from purple-red to pale blue, with dark-blue veins and a yellow center, blooming in spring and early summer. This species has been crossed with others particularly ***I. innominata,*** to produce the 'Pacific Coast Hybrids.' These are generally superior to the parents. A notable few of the many hybrids are 'Banbury Beauty,' with 6-in.- (15-cm-) wide lavender flowers with purple-tinged falls; 'Cabrillo,' with light-purple-and-lavender flowers; 'Canyon Snow,' with white flowers with dark veins and yellow centers; 'Harland Hand,' with dark-purple flowers with a heavily veined lavender central zone. Grow in sun to partial shade in ordinary soil that does not dry out. Divide in spring. Zones 8–10.

I. ensata (I. kaempferi). Japanese iris. Eastern Asia. Height 2–3 ft; spread 18 in. (60–90 × 45 cm). A beardless iris with hundreds of exquisite garden forms. The species has 1-in.- (2.5-cm-) wide, stiffly arching bright-green leaves with a prominent midrib. The flower stalks are taller than the leaves and bear three to four flowers up to 6 in. (15 cm) in diameter in early and midsummer. The flower color ranges from white, blue, to deep violet, many with yellow-tinged falls. The Japanese have been perfecting this species for over 500 years. A number of cultivars and hybrids are available to the gardener, but the Japanese irises are still rather neglected in the West. A few notable forms are 'Cry of Rejoice,' with deep-purple flowers with a yellow center; 'Eleanor Perry,' with dark-lilac flowers and purple veins; 'Festive Greeting,' with red, white-veined flowers; 'Hidden Treasure,' with wine-red flowers with silver veins; 'Moonlight Waves,' with white flowers; 'Pinstripe,' with pale-lavender, dark-veined flowers with a purple center; 'Summer Storm,' with deep-violet flowers. Plant the crowns 2–3 in. (5–7.5 cm) below the soil surface in autumn. Grow in full sun to light shade in rich, acid, moisture-retentive but not necessarily boggy soil. The Japanese iris is strongly sensitive to lime and will quickly show signs of stress if the soil is not acid. Divide every three or four years, preferably in autumn. zones 5–9.

I. foetidissima. Stinking iris, gladywn iris. Europe, North Africa. Height 2–3 ft; spread 2 ft (60–90 × 60 cm). The name stinking iris refers to the odor of the crushed leaves, while the name gladywn iris is probably derived from the Latin *gladiolus,* meaning a "sword," a reference to the leaves. It is a beardless iris with evergreen, dark-green leaves about 1 in. (2.5 cm) wide and 2 ft (30 cm) long. The flattened, branching stalk bears one to three flowers of gray-lilac with dark-violet veins and a tinge of dull yellow in late spring and summer. The flowers are less ornamental than the seeds, which are bright red and remain on the plant for a long time in winter. They are useful in flower arrangements. Variety ***citrina*** has pale-yellow flowers with purple viens; var. ***lutescens*** has clear-yellow-veined flowers. 'Variegata' has green-and-golden yellow foliage. Grow in part shade in moist but well-drained rich soil. Divide in spring or autumn. Zones 7–9.

Iris ensata 'Eleanor Perry'

I. fulva. Copper iris. Southern and central United States. Height 2–3 ft; spread 2 ft (60–90 × 60 cm). A common plant of the marshes of the Mississippi Valley, this beardless iris has 1-in.- (2.5-cm-) wide leaves with drooping tips. The drooping flowers are coppery red to orange-pink in spring. It is an excellent plant for the bog garden, where it should be grown in full sun to partial shade. Divide immediately after flowering. Zones 7–9. The species has hybridized with ***I. brevicaulis*** to produce ***I. × fulvala,*** which has purple-red flowers. Since the 1920s these species and others native to the Mississippi have been offered to growers under the banner of the 'Louisiana Hybrids.' Many fine plants in a wide range of colors have been produced and are now available. They are best grown in moist soil in sun or light shade and should be divided every three or four years in autumn or spring. Zones 7–10.

I. × germanica. German iris. Widely distributed. Height 2–4 ft; spread 2 ft (60–120 × 60 cm). A widely grown hybrid of unknown origin more noted for its contribution to the hundreds of hybrids and cultivars that make up the commercially available bearded iris. The species itself is highly variable with gray-green leaves about 3½ ft (40 cm) long and yellow-bearded flowers in shades of violet blue in late spring and early summer. It is not the best of the bearded irises, but it is a tough and persistent species that is interesting for its historical value rather than its aesthetic presence. 'Florentina,' the orris root, is grown for its contribution to the perfume industry. It has bluish white flowers. Zones 4–9.

I. hexagona. Dixie iris. Southeastern United States. Height 2–3 ft; spread 2 ft (60–90 × 60 cm). A spring-blooming, swamp-inhabiting beardless iris with branching flower stalks and 4–5-in.- (10–12.5-cm-) wide, bluish purple to lavender flowers with a yellow zone on the falls. Native from South Carolina to Florida, west to Louisiana. Zones 7–10.

I. laevigata. Eastern Russia, Asia. Height 30 in.; spread 24 in. (75 × 60 cm). Similar to ***I. ensata*** but without the prominent midrib on the leaf. The flower color is variable, ranging from purple-blue to white. The blooms are 4–6 in. (10–15 cm) in diameter, appearing in early to midsummer. There are a number of garden forms. 'Alba' has white blossoms; 'Albopurpurea' has white blooms speckled purple; 'Alboviolacea' is an exquisite form with white-centered violet flowers; 'Colchesterensis' has double white flowers dotted with blue; 'Rose Queen' has pink flowers. Plant 2–3 in. (5–7.5 cm) deep in moist, fertile soil in full sun. More tolerant of wet soil and lime than is ***I. ensata.*** Divide in autumn. Zones 4–9.

I. missouriensis. Rocky Mountain iris. Western North America. Height 2 ft; spread 2 ft (60 × 60 cm). A highly variable beardless iris native from British Columbia to Mexico and east into Arizona. The leaves are narrow, reaching ⅜ in. (1 cm) wide, often growing higher than the veined flowers, which are pale to deep blue with a white central zone, blooming in late spring and early summer. This species requires a sunny site in soil that is moist in spring but dries out in the summer. Variety ***arizonica*** grows to about 2½ ft (75 cm) and has smaller, paler flowers; var. ***pelogonus*** is an almost dwarf variety growing to about 12 in. (30 cm) with veined, pale-lavender flowers with a yellow spot. Divide in spring or early autumn. Zones 3–8.

I. pallida. Dalmatian iris. Southern Europe. Height 3–4 ft; spread 2 ft (90–120 × 60 cm). A highly attractive bearded iris with silvery gray-green leaves up to 1½ in. (3.8 cm) wide and about 2 ft (60 cm) long. The branched stalks bear wonderfully scented lilac-blue flowers with a yellow beard, surrounded by papery bracts. 'Argentea Variegata,' with gray-green-and-white variegated leaves, is a highly desirable plant; 'Variegata' has variegated leaves of gray-green and yellowish white. The species and its cultivars are fine garden plants requiring well-drained soil and full sun. Divide in spring or autumn. Zones 6–9.

I. pseudacorus. Yellow flag. Europe, North Africa. Height 3–6 ft; spread 2 ft (90–180 × 60 cm). A widely naturalized beardless iris for wet sites. The specific name means *false acorus,* the foliage resembling that of the sweet flag, ***Acorus calamus.*** The deep-green leaves are about 1 in. (2.5 cm) wide and stiffly upright. The yellow flowers are borne on branched stalks and are bright yellow with brown-violet veins. They appear in late spring and early summer. 'Flore Pleno' has double flowers; 'Variegata' has leaves variegated greenish yellow. It is tolerant of dry soils, although it is a water-loving species that grows best in wet areas and requires full sun. Deadhead after flowering to prevent a mass of self-sown seedlings. Divide in spring and autumn. It is susceptible to iris borer in dry soil but not in wet soil. Zones 5–9.

I. pumila. Dwarf bearded iris. Europe, Asia. Height 4–5 in.; spread 12 in. (10–12.5 × 30 cm). A highly variable species with great differences in flower color and size. It is notable for being one of the parents of the popular dwarf bearded irises. In general, it is a dwarf plant with gray-green erect leaves and unbranched flower stalks bearing a fragrant single flower of yellow, purple, or blue with a yellow beard in spring. It requires full sun and well-drained soil. It is a fine iris for the rock garden. Divide after flowering or in autumn. Zones 4–9.

I. setosa. Siberia, Asia, North America. Height 6 in.–3 ft; spread 1–2 ft (15–90 × 30–60 cm). A highly variable beardless iris blooming in late spring to early summer with purple flowers veined violet with a white-spotted base. The stalks are many-branched while the leaves are ribbed and often red at the base. Subspecies ***canadensis*** grows to about 18 in. (45 cm) and generally has lavender-blue flowers. It is native to eastern North America. 'Tricuspis' grows to about 30 in. (75 cm) and has purple flowers. This iris is one of if not the hardiest of the species and requires moist, acid soil in full sun. Divide in spring or autumn. Zones 2–8.

I. sibirica. Siberian iris. Europe. Height 2–4 ft; spread 3 ft (60–120 × 90 cm). Perhaps the loveliest of the more popular species, this long-lived and tough beardless iris is an elegant plant with narrow, erect but slightly arching bright-green leaves up to ¾ in. (1.8 cm) wide. Above the leaves, the flowers, usually one or two per stalk, are violet-blue with a violet-veined central white blotch. They appear in late spring and early summer before the Japanese irises. There are many outstanding hybrids, with ***I. sibirica*** being crossed with ***I. sanguinea*** and others. 'Caesar' is still one of the best cultivars with violet purple flowers on 40 in. (100 cm) flower stalks. Others include: 'Caesar's Brother,' height 3 ft (90 cm), with deep-purple flowers; 'Eric the Red,' height 3 ft (90 cm), with wine-red flowers; 'Sky Wings,' height 30 in. (75 cm) with pale-blue flowers; 'White Swirl,' height 40 in. (100 cm), with white flowers. Grow in full sun or light shade in moisture-retentive, fertile soil. Divide in early autumn. Zones 4–9.

I. tectorum. Roof iris. China. Height 1–1½ ft; spread 1 ft (30–45 × 30 cm). Called the roof iris because it is grown on thatched roofs in Japan, this is a crested iris with thick rhizomes and fans of light-green, ribbed leaves up to 2 in. (5 cm) wide. The flattish flowers, appearing in early summer, are borne on branched stalks and are lilac with darker veins and a frilly white crest. Plant in moist but well-drained soil in full sun. Often subject to the ravages of slugs. Divide after flowering. Variety ***alba*** has white flowers with a few yellow veins. Zones 5–9.

I. versicolor. Blue flag. Northeastern North America. Height 1–3 ft; spread 2 ft (30–90 × 60 cm). A robust, clump-forming beardless iris with erect or arching leaves almost 1 in. (2.5 cm) wide and branching flower stalks bearing lavender-blue, violet, or purple flowers with a greenish yellow blotch and purple veins. Variety ***kermesina*** has purple-red flowers. Although this iris is tolerant of dry soils, it grows best in wet ground in full sun. Divide in spring or autumn. Zones 3–9.

The bearded iris. This group consists of an enormous range of forms divided into subgroups defined by height. They are one of the most popular of garden plants, widely grown for their spectacular flowers. So many new ones are produced each year that it is pointless to list them. They require well-drained, fertile soil in full sun. Plant the fleshy rhizomes with about half the rhizome in the soil. They need dividing every three or four years for best performance. They are highly susceptible to the insect and disease problems described in "Cultivation," above.

JEFFERSONIA

(Twinleaf)

Family: Berberidaceae

Two species of charming woodland plants, one native to North America, the other to northeastern Asia. They are rhizomatous plants with basal, veined leaves divided into two lobes. Named in honor of Thomas Jefferson.

Cultivation: Grow in woodland soil in partial shade.

Landscape Use: Woodland plants for the shady border.

Jeffersonia diphylla

PROPAGATION: Divide in spring or autumn. Sow seeds in summer. May take 18 months to germinate and three years to reach flowering size.

J. diphylla. Twinleaf. Eastern North America. Height 12 in.; spread 6 in. (30 × 15 cm). Wiry stems support light-green leaves 3–6 in. (7.5–15 cm) long and 2–4 in. (5–10 cm) wide. The leaves are deeply divided into two kidney-shaped divisions, hence the common name. Solitary, 1-in.- (2.5-cm-) wide, cup-shaped, yellow-centered white flowers appear for a brief few days in early spring. Not an especially stunning plant but one with some charm. Zones 5–8.

J. dubia. Manchuria. Height 12 in.; spread 6 in. (30 × 15 cm). Almost circular, 4-in.- (10-cm-) wide, mid-green, violet-tinted leaves deeply divided at the base into two distinct lobes. The cup-shaped lavender-blue flowers appear in spring. Zones 5–8.

JUNCUS

(Rush)

FAMILY: Juncaceae

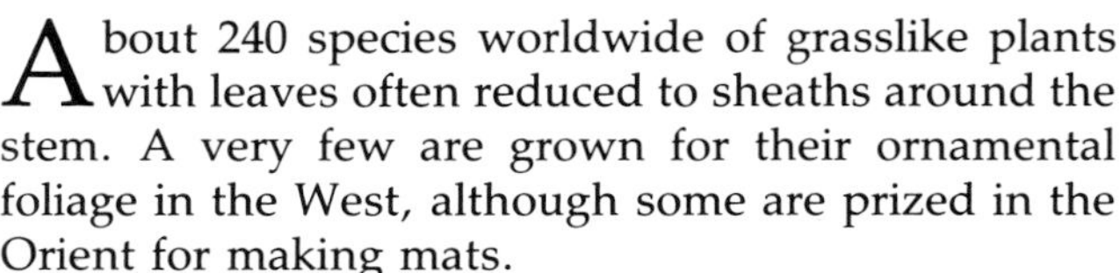

About 240 species worldwide of grasslike plants with leaves often reduced to sheaths around the stem. A very few are grown for their ornamental foliage in the West, although some are prized in the Orient for making mats.

CULTIVATION: Grow in soil covered with up to 3 in. (7.5 cm) of water in sun or partial shade.

LANDSCAPE USE: Arresting aquatic plants for pool margins.

PROPAGATION: Divide in spring or early autumn.

J. effusus. Bog rush. Japan. Height 1–4 ft; spread 18 in. (30–120 × 45 cm). A clump-forming plant with dark, evergreen, cylindrical stems in erect tussocks. Insignificant yellowish green flowers appear in summer. A more curious form is the cultivar 'Spiralis,' the corkscrew rush, which has twisting and curling stems. Zones 3–9.

J. glaucus. Europe. Height 3 ft; spread 2 ft (90 × 60 cm). An erect but arching plant with evergreen stems and gray-blue needlelike leaves. Greenish tufts of flowers appear in late summer and early autumn. Zones 3–9.

KALIMERIS

FAMILY: Compositae

An asterlike genus with one species related to ***Boltonia.*** Taxonomists are still arguing over the correct name. For the moment gardeners should enjoy growing this wonderful plant and leave the debate to those with a passion for nomenclature.

CULTIVATION: Grow in moist soil in sun to light shade.

LANDSCAPE USE: Plant in a sunny herbaceous border, edge of a bog garden, or pondside.

PROPAGATION: Divide and replant in spring.

K. pinnatifida var. ***hortensis.*** Asia. Height 2 ft; spread 2 ft (60 × 60 cm). An upright bushy plant with light-green, lance-shaped leaves ¼ in. (0.6 cm) wide with semidouble white flowers with yellow centers, blooming from midsummer to early autumn. Zones 6–8.

KIRENGESHOMA

FAMILY: Hydrangeaceae

Two species of shrubby acid-loving perennials with arching purple stems; large maplelike, lobed and hairy leaves; and funnel-shaped, waxy, pale-yellow flowers in summer to early autumn. They are plants for foliage rather than flowers but both attributes create an exotic effect in the shady garden.

CULTIVATION: Grow in a cool, sheltered site in moist but well-drained rich soil in partial shade. Leave undisturbed for three to five years before attempting to propagate. Plants perform poorly in areas with hot and humid summers.

LANDSCAPE USE: Handsome plants for the shady border or woodland walk. Useful as a large specimen plant for a foil against the finer foliage of ferns.

PROPAGATION: Divide in spring or autumn.

K. koreana. Korea. Height 4–4 ½ ft; spread 3 ft (120–135 × 90 cm). Very similar to the species described below but slightly taller and with flowers that open a little wider. In fact, this species is so similar to ***K. palmata*** that it may not be a distinct species but rather a subspecies. Zones 5–8.

K. palmata. Japan. Height 4 ft; spread 3 ft (120 × 90 cm). An erect plant with upright purplish stems arching toward the top, with 6–7-in.- (15–17.5-cm-) wide, maplelike, lobed and hairy leaves becoming smaller and stalkless toward the top of the stem. Waxy, 1½-in.- (3.8-cm-) long, pale-yellow nodding funnel-shaped flowers are borne at the top of the stem or from the leaf axils. They appear in late summer and early autumn and are followed by horned brownish green seed capsules. Zones 5–8.

Kirengeshoma palmata

KNAUTIA

Family: Dipsacaceae

Knautia macedonica

Forty species of rarely cultivated plants native to Europe, North Africa, and Asia with opposite oblong-linear or lyre-shaped leaves. Some have been placed in the genus ***Scabiosa,*** which they closely resemble. For the time being the two species described below remain as ***Knautia.***

Cultivation: Grow in full sun in ordinary, well-drained soil. Staking is often necessary.

Landscape Use: The unusual color of the flowers adds a strong spot in a pale border, particularly against ornamental grasses, silver foliage plants, or the softer blue shades of ***Geranium*** species.

Propagation: Divide in spring or early autumn or sow seed in spring.

K. arvensis. Blue buttons. Europe, North Africa. Height 4 ft; spread 2 ft (120 × 60 cm). An upright, bushy plant with highly variable lyre-shaped to oval, deeply divided and hairy leaves. Tight, rounded heads of lilac-blue flowers are produced on tall stems in summer. Zones 5–9.

K. macedonica. Europe. Height 2 ft; spread 2 ft (60 × 60 cm). An erect, many-branched plant with lyre-shaped basal leaves and stem leaves becoming divided and featherlike. Masses of 2-in.- (5-cm-) wide, globular, crimson flowers are produced in summer. Deadhead for further bloom. It usually needs staking, although it looks particularly good leaning against more erect plants. Zones 6–9.

KNIPHOFIA

(Red Hot Poker, Torch Lily)

Family: Liliaceae

A genus of about 70 species of flowering plants native to Africa with swordlike leaves and cylindrical flower spikes made up of tight clusters of drooping, tubular flowers. Most plants available are hybrids and cultivars, although a few species are cultivated. The lower flowers tend to open first, the upper ones following in a long succession. They are valuable for their stiff architectural presence and their

Kniphofia caulescens

long blooming season from summer until autumn. Named after Johann Hieronymus Kniphof (1704–1765).

Cultivation: Plant in spring only, in well-drained soil in full sun. In cold areas tie in the foliage over the crowns and mulch with salt hay to help prevent winter rot. Remove the faded flower spikes close to the basal foliage to encourage further flowering. In very cold areas lift the plants, store over the winter, and plant in the spring. Unless you are particularly passionate about red hot pokers, in cold climates I recommend you grow something else.

Landscape Use: Stately plants for the sunny border, where their grassy foliage and stiff 'pokers' create a dramatic effect. Fortunately, newer cultivars are being developed that are shorter and are not such a screaming orange.

Propagation: Divide in spring. Sow seed in spring. Plants flower the second year.

K. caulescens. South Africa. Height 4 ft; spread 2 ft (120 × 60 cm). Large tufts of woody often recumbent stems with rosettes of bluish green evergreen leaves 3 ft (90 cm) long by 3 in. (7.5 cm) wide. In late summer and autumn appear 6-in. (15-cm) spikes of coral-red flowers quickly turning to pale yellow. Protect from winter cold. Zones 7–9.

K. uvaria. Red hot poker. South Africa. Height 4 ft; spread 3 ft (120 × 90 cm). Perhaps the major contributor to the numerous group of hybrids and cultivars grown. The species itself has been superseded by superior forms. The loose clumps of gray-green foliage consist of swordlike leaves 3 ft (90 cm) long and 1 in. (2.5 cm) wide with abrasive edges. Tall spikes of red "pokers" turning to orange bloom in summer through autumn. Zones 5–9.

Hybrids. There are numerous hybrids, with flowers of bright red to palest yellow. They are tall and short, blooming in early, mid-, and late summer and autumn. A few of the most notable are:

- 'Ada': height 3½ ft (105 cm), deep orange-yellow spikes in midsummer
- 'Alcazar': height 3 ft (90 cm), orange flowers in early summer
- 'Atlanta': height 3 ft (90 cm), orange-yellow flowers in midsummer
- 'Bee's Lemon': height 3 ft (90 cm), greenish lemon-yellow spikes in late summer and autumn
- 'Bressingham Torch': height 3 ft (90 cm), orange-yellow flowers in early summer
- 'Earliest of All': height 2½ ft (75 cm), coral-red flowers in early summer
- 'Fiery Fred': height 4 ft (120 cm), strong-orange flowers in late summer
- 'Firefly': height 3 ft (90 cm), orange-red spikes in midsummer
- 'Gold Mine': height 3 ft (90 cm), deep-yellow flowers in late summer
- 'Jenny Bloom': height 3 ft (90 cm), yellow tinged orange spikes in midsummer
- 'John Benary': height 3 ft (90 cm), orange-red flowers in late summer
- 'Little Maid': height 2 ft (60 cm), delicate creamy spikes in late summer
- 'Primrose Beauty': height 3 ft (90 cm), primrose-yellow flowers in early summer to autumn
- 'Rosea Superba': height 3 ft (90 cm), rose-red flowers in late summer
- 'Royal Castle': height 3 ft (90 cm), yellow-orange flowers in late summer

'Royal Standard': height 3 ft (90 cm), brilliant red-and-yellow flowers in midsummer
'Samuel's Sensation': height 4 ft (120 cm), scarlet-red spikes in late summer
'Shenandoah': height 3½ ft (105 cm), orange-and-yellow flowers
'Springtime': height 3 ft (90 cm), coral red-and-yellow flowers in midsummer
'Sulphur Gem': height 3 ft (90 cm), sulfur-yellow spikes in midsummer
'Underway': height 3 ft (90 cm), light-orange flowers in late summer and autumn
'Vanilla': height 2 ft (60 cm), pale-yellow flowers in early summer
'Wayside Flame': height 3 ft (90 cm), bright orange-red flowers in late summer and autumn

Zones 8–9.

LAMIUM

(Dead Nettle, White Archangel)

Family: Labiatae

Lamium maculatum

About 40 species of largely weedy plants with a few good species being grown in gardens. The stems are square, the leaves are opposite and mostly toothed. The flowers are lipped and hooded and bloom in spring to late summer. Members of this genus strongly resemble the stinging nettle, ***Urtica dioica,*** but lack the stinging hairs, hence one common name, dead nettle. The other common name white archangel, probably refers to the flowering time beginning in late April, on or near the day dedicated to the Archangel Michael.

Cultivation: Grow in moist but well-drained soil in partial shade. Trim back after flowering to keep plants orderly. Sometimes prone to rust diseases. The yellow archangel, ***Lamium galeobdolon,*** is often highly invasive.

Landscape Use: Valuable flowering and foliage plants for the shady garden as a groundcover under trees and shrubs.

Propagation: Divide in spring or autumn. Take cuttings in late spring.

L. album. White dead nettle. Europe, Asia. Height 1–2; spread 1 ft (30–60 × 30 cm). A trailing, sprawling plant with unbranched, square stems and pointed, egg-shaped, round-toothed, and hairy leaves to 3 in. (7.5 cm) long. Hairy, white flowers are borne in the upper leaf axils in late spring to late summer. Zones 3–9.

L. galeobdolon. Yellow archangel. Europe. Height 1–2 ft; spread 2 ft (30–60 × 60 cm). A rapidly spreading, sprawling plant with square stems and

3-in.- (7.5-cm-) long, pointed, egg-shaped, coarsely toothed leaves. Whorls of yellow, lipped flowers appear in late spring and summer. Tolerates full shade in hot summer areas and less shade in cooler areas. 'Florentinum' ('Variegatum') is silver variegated but with the midrib and the margins green; 'Herman's Pride' is a little less invasive than the species and has striking silver-flecked leaves that are a more attractive attribute than the yellow flowers. Zones 3–9. The species goes backward and forward between being listed as ***Lamiastrum, Galeobdolon,*** and ***Lamium.*** The specific epithet ***galeobdolon*** comes from the Greek, *gale,* "weasel," and *obdolos,* "disagreeable odor," a reference to the smell of the plant when crushed.

L. maculatum. Spotted dead nettle. Europe, Asia. Height 12 in.; spread 18 in. (30 × 45 cm). A widely grown perennial for the partly shady garden, with opposite, mid-green leaves with a central greenish white stripe. Whorls of purple-pink, 1-in.- (2.5-cm-) long flowers are in bloom from late spring to late summer. The variety ***roseum*** ('Shell Pink') has soft-pink flowers. The species is invasive and straggling and has been successfully superseded by the following cultivars. 'Album' has white flowers and pale-green-and-greenish white leaves; 'Aureum,' with pink flowers and soft yellow-and-white foliage, is a slow-growing cultivar requiring full shade; 'Beacon Silver,' with rose-pink flowers and silver leaves with green edges, is a shade-loving cultivar; 'Chequers' is a vigorous form of the species with a silver stripe down the center of the leaf. It is often confused with 'Beacon Silver.' 'White Nancy' is an outstanding plant with white flowers and silver leaves edged in green. Zones 4–8.

LATHYRUS

(Sweet Pea)

Family: Leguminosae

Known and grown for the beloved sweet pea, an annual vine, this genus also includes a few non-climbing perennials with alternate leaves divided into featherlike segments and colorful pealike flowers in summer.

Cultivation: Grow in well-drained, ordinary soil in full sun.

Landscape Use: Loose, sprawling plants for dry banks and gravelly soils.

Propagation: Sow seeds in spring. Division is possible but difficult in spring.

L. luteus. Turkey. Height 2 ft; spread 1 ft (60 × 30 cm). An erect, mound-forming plant with five pairs of oval leaflets with a bluish cast beneath. In late spring and early summer appear 1-in.- (2.5-cm-) long, unbranched clusters of yellow flowers. The variety ***aureus*** has yellowish-brown flowers. Zones 3–8.

Lathyrus vernus

L. vernus. Spring vetchling. Europe. Height 1 ft; spread 1 ft (30 × 30 cm). A clump-forming plant with deep roots and finely divided pale-green leaves with two to three pairs of 2-in.- (7.5-cm-) long, egg-shaped leaflets. In spring 2-in.- (5-cm-) long, unbranched clusters of purple-blue flowers are produced. The plant dies down after flowering. The variety ***alboroseus*** has pink-and-white flowers; var. ***cyaneus*** has light-blue flowers; var. ***roseus*** has pink flowers. The cultivar 'Spring Delight' grows to 15 in. (37.5 cm) tall and has light-pink flowers; 'Spring Melody' has violet-blue flowers. Zones 5–9.

LEONOTIS

(Lion's-ear)

Family: Labiatae

About 30 species of annual and perennial tropical plants with one species squeaking in under the temperate banner. The genus has square stems typical of the family and opposite, toothed leaves. The flowers range in color from white, yellow, to orange and scarlet and are said resemble the shape of a lion's ear.

Cultivation: Grow in well-drained, fertile soil in full sun. In cooler areas plant in a protected site, cut down in autumn, and mulch the crown for winter protection.

Landscape Use: A shrubby plant for the sunny border. The bright-orange flowers are shown to greater effect against a dark-green background.

Propagation: Take cuttings in late spring to midsummer.

L. leonurus. Lion's ear. South Africa. Height 3–6 ft; spread 3 ft (90–180 × 90 cm). A branching, shrubby plant with hairy, square stems and 2-in.-(5-cm-) long, hairy, coarsely toothed, oblong, lance-shaped leaves. Whorls of bright-orange tubular flowers are carried in the leaf axils from summer to autumn. Stem hardy in Zones 8–10, although it is just root hardy with protection during winters in Zone 7.

LEONTOPODIUM

(Edelweiss)

Family: Compositae

Leontopodium alpinum

Thirty species of little-grown plants except for two or three species, one of which is the well-known edelweiss of Switzerland and *The Sound of Music.* They are difficult to distinguish from each other, which means the gardener can safely forget about many of them.

Cultivation: Grow edelweiss in an open, sunny position in well-drained, lime-rich soil. They are alpine plants and need as alpine an environment as possible. Be sure to divide and replant every two years.

Landscape Use: Easily grown in the sunny rock garden.

Propagation: Sow seed in early spring, planting the following year. Carefully divide in spring.

L. alpinum. Edelweiss. European Alps. Height 6–12 in.; spread 12 in. (15–30 × 30 cm). A short-lived species with a variety of forms, edelweiss is a tufted plant with woolly gray, lance-shaped leaves 3–4 in. (7.5–10 cm) long. Unbranched, hairy stems bear ¼-in. (0.6-cm) wide white flowers surrounded by star-shaped, woolly bracts. The flowers appear in late spring to early summer. It is best enjoyed in the wild; in cultivation it is a generally drab plant. Zones 4–7.

LESPEDEZA

(Bush Clover)

Family: Leguminosae

Lespedeza thunbergii

One hundred twenty species of shrubs and shrubby herbaceous perennials native to North America, Asia, and Australia. The leaves are alternate and divided into three leaflets. Large numbers of pealike flowers are produced in late summer and early autumn. A number of species are native to dry areas and are generally not grown in the garden. As water conservation becomes more important, it is to be hoped that dry-soil plants such as many in this genus will be more widely cultivated. Named after D. Lespedez, a Spanish governor of Florida.

Cultivation: Grow in well-drained soil in full sun. Thrips can be a troublesome pest in some areas. Cut down the woody stems in winter.

Landscape Use: Dramatic late-flowering shrubby perennials for the sunny border or sunny bank. The many flowers often bend the stems into a graceful arch. This attribute is particularly attractive if seen from below.

Propagation: Divide the woody clumps in spring. Take cuttings in midsummer.

L. buergii. Japan. Height 6 ft; spread 4 ft (180 × 120 cm). Similar to the species described below but with hairier leaves and with ascending, unbranched clusters of purple to white flowers. Zones 6–9.

L. thunbergii. Japan, China. Height 6 ft; spread 4 ft (180 × 120 cm). A shrubby perennial with woody stems arching at the tips and silky leaves divided into three elliptical leaflets up to 2 in. (5 cm) long.

The mauve-purple pealike flowers are borne in large numbers in unbranched clusters in late summer. A magnificent plant for autumn flower color. 'Albiflora' has soft white flowers; 'Gibraltar' has deep mauve-purple flowers and is more floriferous than the species. Zones 6–9.

LEUCANTHEMUM

(Ox-eye Daisy)

FAMILY: Compositae

Formerly in the genus ***Chrysanthemum***, the ox-eye daisies are widely distributed throughout the temperate world. The stems are often branching, the leaves alternate as well as in basal rosettes. The daisy flowers with a central boss of largely yellow disks surrounded by white rays are either single or borne in branched clusters at the end of the stems.

Leucanthemum x *superbum* 'Alaska'

CULTIVATION: Grow in full sun in well-drained soil. Remove the faded flowers.

LANDSCAPE USE: Many of these daisies are wonderful border plants as well as fine additions to the meadow garden. Although the Shasta daisies are relatively short-lived, they make superb cut flowers.

PROPAGATION: Divide in spring or autumn. Take stem cuttings in early summer, or sow seed.

***L.* × *superbum* (*Chrysanthemum* × *superbum*).** Shasta daisy. Height 1–4 ft; spread 18 in. (30–120 × 45 cm). A widely grown, tough perennial with summer-blooming white flowers with yellow centers. The common name Shasta daisy is frequently connected with the late Luther Burbank, whose experimental horticultural test plots were near Mt. Shasta in California. The lower leaves are thinly lance-shaped, up to 12 in. (30 cm) long and coarsely toothed; the upper leaves become narrow. The white flowers are 2–3 in. (5–7.5 cm) across and bloom from early summer to frost. There are a number of excellent cultivars. 'Aglaya' has double white flowers; 'Alaska' has single flowers 3 in. (7.5 cm) across; 'Antwerp Star' grows up to 4 ft (120 cm) and has single flowers; 'Beaute Nivelloise' grows to 4 ft (120 cm) and has flowers with shaggy petals; 'Little Princess' grows to 1 ft (30 cm) and has single flowers; 'Marconi' has large double flowers up to 6 in. (15 cm) across; 'Snow Lady' grows to about 12 in. (30 cm) and has 3-in.- (7.5-cm-) wide single flowers; 'Wirral Pride' is a profuse bloomer with 4-in.- (10-cm-) wide flowers with a shaggy central crest. Hardiness varies with cultivars; Zone 5 appears to be the cold limit, but individuals may exceed this limitation. In climates with hot summers, grow in partial shade. Divide every two or three years. Zones 5–8.

L. vulgare. Ox-eye daisy. Europe. Asia. Height 2 ft; spread 1 ft (60 × 30 cm). Widely naturalized in North America, this is a common flower of open grassland. The basal leaves are hairy, coarsely toothed, and spoon-shaped up to 6 in. (15 cm) long, while the stem leaves are shorter and narrower. The single flowers are borne at the end of the stems and are white with a yellow center. They appear in early summer. 'May Queen' is an early-blooming cultivar, beginning in late spring and flowering into early summer. Zones 3–9.

LEWISIA

(Bitter Root)

Family: Portulacaceae

Lewisia cotyledon

Approximately 20 species of alpine plants native to mountain meadows and cliffs of western North America. They are deciduous or evergreen stemless plants with fleshy roots or corms and basal rosettes of fleshy leaves. White, rose, or red cup-shaped flowers are produced in spring and early summer. They are a rock gardener's delight: sometimes difficult to grow but rewarding the diligent enthusiast with beautiful displays of flowers. Named after Captain Meriwether Lewis of the Lewis and Clark expedition.

Cultivation: Good drainage is the key to growing *Lewisia.* A rock wall or crevice in full sun is the best environment. Although reputed to be lime-haters, they can take some degree of lime; however, the best soil is a fertile, gritty loam supplemented with a little bonemeal. Most of the species need a dry period after flowering, something that, in wet climates, can be provided by suspending sheets of glass as a canopy 12 in. (30 cm) above the plant. Like so many rock-garden plants, they thrive with less rather than more attention.

Landscape Use: Perfect rock-garden plants for a dry wall or trough.

Propagation: Detach offsets after flowering and pot. After rooting, plant the following spring. Sow seeds in spring for planting the following year.

L. columbiana. Washington and Oregon. Height 6–12 in.; spread 6 in. (15–30 × 15 cm). An evergreen, tufted plant with rosettes of spoon-shaped, glossy green leaves up to 3 in. (7.5 cm) long. In late spring 1½-in.- (3.8-cm-) wide sprays of white or magenta, pink-veined flowers are produced. 'Rosea,' possibly a hybrid, has purple-red flowers. Plant in a site shaded from midday or afternoon sun. Zones 6–8.

L. cotyledon. Western United States. Height 12 in.; spread 8 in. (30 × 20 cm). A widely grown and variable species with evergreen, spoon-shaped to egg-shaped, 3-in.- (7.5-cm-) long leaves often with undulating edges. Many-flowered clusters of pink, white-veined, 1-in.- (2.5-cm-) wide blossoms appear in spring. The variety ***heckneri*** has toothed leaves and pink to rose flowers striped dark pink. Var. ***howellii*** has in-curved, crinkly leaves and rose-pink flowers. 'Alba' has white flowers; 'Carroll Watson' has pure yellow flowers; 'Rose Splendour' has clear-rose flowers. 'Sunset Strain' comes in a range of colors from pink to orange. Zones 6–7.

L. tweedyi. Washington. Height 6 in.; spread 9 in. (15 × 22.5 cm). Erect rosettes of 2–4 in.- (5–10-cm-) wide, fleshy, evergreen leaves and 2-in.- (5-cm-) wide light-pink, yellow to apricot flowers in spring. Zones 6–7.

LIATRIS

(Blazing Star, Gayfeather)

FAMILY: Compositae

Forty species of rhizomatous perennials native to North America with alternate, grassy, linear leaves and stiff, erect flower spikes of crowded, generally purple flowers that open from the top of the flower spike and continue downward.

Liatris spicata

CULTIVATION: Plant in moist but well-drained soil in full sun.

LANDSCAPE USE: Excellent wildflowers for the sunny border or wildflower meadow where they are enjoyed by bees and butterflies as well as gardeners. They are good cut flowers.

PROPAGATION: Divide and replant the fleshy, tuberous roots in spring every three to four years. Sow seed in spring and plant in autumn of the following year.

L. aspera. Rough gayfeather. North America. Height 6 ft; spread 18 in. (180 × 45 cm). A large, clump-forming plant with linear, grassy leaves up to 16 in. (40 cm) long. Spiky heads of 1 in. (2.5 cm) wide lavender-purple flowers are surrounded by round papery bracts. The flowers open on the spike at the same time in late summer and early autumn. 'September Glory' grows to 4 ft (120 cm) and has rosy purple flowers; 'White Spire' has white flowers. Zones 4–9.

L. gramnifolia. Eastern North America. Height 4 ft; spread 18 in. (120 × 45 cm). Clumps of striped stems of linear leaves up to 1 ft (30 cm) long and spikes of purple flowers blooming in late summer. Requires well-drained soil. Zones 4–9.

L. pycnostachya. Kansas gayfeather. Central United States. Height 5 ft; spread 2 ft (150 × 60 cm). A vigorous, clump-forming plant with erect, leafy stems with linear, lance-shaped leaves ½ in. (1.2 cm) wide with the lower leaves up to 16 in. (40 cm) long. In summer to early autumn 18-in.-(45-cm-) long spikes of mauve-purple flowers appear. 'Alba' is a white-flowered form. It is a rather coarse plant that often needs staking. Requires moisture-retentive but not boggy soil. Zones 3–9.

L. spicata. Spike gayfeather. Eastern and central United States. Height 3 ft; spread 2 ft (90 × 60 cm). The most desirable species for garden use with basal, linear leaves to 12 in. (30 cm) long and ½ in. (0.8 cm) wide reduced progressively toward the top of the stem. The tall flower spikes bear mauve-purple flowers in summer to early autumn. There are a number of fine cultivars. 'Alba' has off-white flowers; 'August Glory' grows to 4 ft (120 cm) and has bluish purple flowers; 'Floristan White' grows to a height of about 3 ft (90 cm) and has creamy white flowers; 'Kobold' grows from 18 in. (45 cm) to 2 ft (60 cm) and has mauve-pink spikes; 'Silver Tip' grows 3 ft (90 cm) tall and has lavender flowers. Staking may be necessary. ***L. spicata*** can be grown successfully in moist soils.

LIGULARIA

(Golden Ray)

FAMILY: Compositae

Ligularia stenocephala 'The Rocket'

About 80 species of generally large and coarse yellow-flowering, moisture-loving plants with basal, long-stemmed leaves and tall spikes of daisy-like flowers in summer. They differ from the closely related *Senecio* by having the leaf stalk encircling the stem.

Cultivation: Grow in a cool site shaded from afternoon sun in moisture-retentive if not down-right wet soil. If exposed to hot afternoon sun, the large leaves will droop but will recover when the sun sets. All members of this genus seem to be great favorites of slugs and snails.

Landscape Use: Dramatic plants for the bog garden, streamside, or shady border where their large leaves and tall flower spikes effectively contrast with ferns and other fine-textured plants.

Propagation: Divide in spring. Sow seed when ripe and plant the following year.

L. dentata (L. clivorum) China, Japan. Height 4 ft; spread 3 ft (120 × 90 cm). A clump-forming plant with kidney-shaped, coarsely toothed, leathery leaves on 1-ft- (30-cm-) long stalks. Stout stems bear braching heads of orange daisies up to 5 in. (12.5 cm) wide in summer. The flowers attract large numbers of butterflies. 'Desdemona' has purple leaves in spring turning to green in summer but remaining mahogany-purple underneath; 'Othello' is almost identical to 'Desdemona.' Zones 4–8.

L. × hessei. Height 6 ft; spread 3 ft (180 × 90 cm). A hybrid between ***L. dentata, L. veitchiana,*** and ***L. wilsoniana*** with toothed, kidney-shaped leaves and orange-yellow flowers. 'Gregynog Gold' has heart-shaped, sharply toothed, deep-green leaves and stout stems with conical spikes or orange-yellow flowers in midsummer. Zones 4–8.

L. hodgsonii. Japan. Height 2–3 ft; spread 2 ft (60–90 × 60 cm). Similar to ***L. dentata*** but smaller with orange-yellow flowers in summer. Zones 4–8.

L. macrophylla. Asia. Height 4–6 ft; spread 2 ft (120–180 × 60 cm). A handsome species with elliptical to oblong toothed leaves up to 2 ft (60 cm) long and erect stems bearing conical spikes of canary-yellow flowers in summer and late summer. A dramatically elephantine plant. Zones 4–8.

L. przewalskii. Northern China. Height 4–5 ft; spread 3 ft (120–150 × 90 cm). This is similar to the species described below, with deeply cut triangular, 1-ft- (30-cm-) long leaves with toothed lobes. Spikes of small yellow flowers are produced in summer and late summer. The flowers of this species differ from that of ***L. stenocephala*** in having five ray florets instead of three. Zones 4–8.

L. stenocephala. Japan, northern China. Height 4–5 ft; spread 3 ft (120–150 × 90 cm). The stems are dark purple and the leaves light green, heart-shaped to triangular, up to 1 ft (30 cm) long with coarse teeth. In early summer 12–18-in.- (30–45-cm-) long spikes of bright-yellow flowers are produced. The leaves of this species are heart shaped and less coarsely divided than those of ***L. przewalskii.*** 'The Rocket' is an excellent form that grows 3–4 ft (90–120 cm) tall with golden yellow flowers. Often listed under ***L. przewalskii*** although it may be a hybrid between the two. Zones 4–8.

L. veitchiana. China. Height 5–6 ft; spread 3 ft (150–180 × 90 cm). Heart-shaped, rounded to triangular leaves up to 12 in. (30 cm) across and stiff spikes of golden yellow daisies up to 2½ in. (6.8 cm) across appearing in summer. Zones 4–8.

LIMONIUM

(Sea Lavender)

Family: Plumbaginaceae

A large genus of annual, herbaceous perennial, and shrubby plants with alternate or basal leaves. A number of annual species are widely grown for cut flowers, either fresh or dried. The common name refers to the perennial species and its ability to tolerate the salty sprays of the seaside.

Cultivation: Grow in well-drained neutral soil in full sun. The sea lavender blooms thinly the first year but produces clouds of flowers from the second year on. It may be necessary to shade sea-lavender from afternoon sun in climates with hot summers.

Landscape Use: The species described below are outstanding plants for the front of the border, where their masses of flowers are an excellent foil for silver-foliage plants.

Propagation: Carefully divide the long roots in spring or early autumn. Sow seeds in spring.

L. latifolium. Sea lavender, statice. Europe. Height 2 ft; spread 18 in. (60 × 45 cm). A clump-forming plant with leathery, evergreen, basal rosettes of 10-in.- (25-cm-) long, spoon-shaped leaves with many-branched wiry stems bearing masses of lavender-blue flowers in 2-ft- (60-cm-) wide clouds. A beautifully delicate flower. 'Blue Cloud' has light-blue flowers; 'Collier's Pink' has pink flowers; 'Robert Butler' has violet-blue flowers on a compact plant 16 in. (40 cm) tall; 'Violetta' is a gorgeous plant with dark violet flowers. The leaves can be scorched by hot afternoon sun. Zones 4–9.

Limonium latifolium 'Violetta'

L. tataricum (Goniolimon tataricum). Europe. Height 10–15 in.; spread 15 in. (25–37.5 × 37.5 cm). A beautifully delicate plant when in flower with clouds of tiny pale-blue to white flowers in mid- to late summer. The rosettes of leathery, spear-shaped, tapering leaves grow to 6 in. (15 cm) long. The variety ***angustifolium*** has narrower leaves and silvery flowers. Var. ***nanum*** grows to 9 in. (22.5 cm) tall and has pinkish flowers. Zones 4–9.

LINARIA

(Toadflax)

Family: Scrophulariaceae

One hundred species of annual and perennial plants with opposite whorled leaves, the upper leaves being alternate and often toothed or lobed. Yellow, white, blue, or purple snapdragonlike flowers with asymmertrical, two-lipped blossoms are borne in terminal spikes throughout the summer. The generic name comes from the Greek *linon,* "flax," a reference to the leaves resembling flax.

Cultivation: Grow in ordinary, well-drained soil in a sunny location.

Landscape Use: Good long-blooming border plants

Linaria purpurea

or rock-garden specimens. ***Linaria purpurea*** is effective growing out of the clouds of the yellow-flowered ***Coreopsis*** 'Moonbeam.'

PROPAGATION: Sow seeds in early spring, planting in late spring. Divide in spring or take cuttings in early summer.

L. alpina. European Alps. Height 6 in.; spread 9 in. (15 × 22.5 cm). A mat-forming plant with whorls of blue-gray linear to lance-shaped leaves and violet-orange lipped, snapdragonlike flowers blooming in summer. A short-lived plant that needs propagating annually. Zones 4–9.

L. dalmatica. Europe. Height 3 ft; spread 1 ft (90 × 30 cm). An erect plant with branched stems with stalkless, gray-green, linear to egg-shaped leaves up to 1½ in. (3.8 cm) long. Orange-throated yellow flowers bloom throughout the summer. Enjoys poor soil and full sun. Zones 4–9.

L. purpurea. Purple toadflax. Europe. Height 3 ft; spread 1 ft (90 × 30 cm). An erect plant with narrow gray-green, lance-shaped to linear leaves whorled at the base, the upper leaves alternate, on slender stems. Spires of lilac-purple flowers with a white-dotted lower lip bloom in early summer. Self-seeds freely. 'Canon Went' has light-pink flowers, which are balanced with gray-green foliage. Zones 4–9.

L. triornithophora. Three-birds-flying. Europe. Height 3–4 ft; spread 18 in. (90–120 × 45 cm). Tall, erect stems with whorls of egg-shaped to lance-shaped gray-green leaves and lilac-purple flowers marked orange or yellow on the lower lip. Mulch for winter protection. Zones 7–9.

L. vulgaris. Butter and eggs. Eurasia. Height 2 ft; spread 1 ft (60 × 30 cm). A charming wayside weed with linear grayish leaves and scrambled-egg-yellow snapdragonlike flowers in summer. 'Flore Pleno' has double yellow flowers. Zones 3–9.

LINUM

(Flax)

FAMILY: Linaceae

About 200 or so species of annual and perennial plants widely distributed throughout the temperate world. ***L. usitatissimum*** is the plant that provides flax fiber and linseed oil. The leaves are generally narrow and alternate. The five-petaled flowers are funnel- or cup-shaped and come in red, yellow, blue, or white. They are short-lived plants that "pay their rent" by being prolific in flower throughout late spring and summer.

CULTIVATION: Sun-loving perennials of easy culture in well-drained soil. They are intolerant of poorly drained sites.

Landscape Use: Valuable long-blooming plants for dry, sunny sites. Effective in association with gray- and silver-foliage plants.

Propagation: Divide in spring or early autumn. Sow seed or take stem cuttings. Often flowers from seed the first year.

L. flavum. Golden flax. Europe. Height 18 in.; spread 12 in. (45 × 30 cm). A busy plant with erect, woody stems with spoon-shaped, dark bluish green leaves. Masses of 1-in.- (2.5-cm-) wide, bright-yellow, funnel-shaped flowers appear in spring and summer. 'Compactum' grows to 6 in. (15 cm) and is covered with yellow flowers; 'Gemmel's Hybrid' grows to about 1 ft (30 cm) and has golden yellow flowers. Zones 5–9.

L. narbonense. Narbonne flax. Mediterranean. Height 1–2 ft; spread 18 in. (30–60 × 45 cm). The best of the cultivated species with gray-green and stiff, narrowly lance-shaped leaves ¾ in. (1.8 cm) long on erect stems. The 2-in.- (5-cm-) wide flowers are blue with a white eye, blooming in late spring and early summer. Often requires staking. Cut hard back after flowering. 'Album' has white flowers; 'Heavenly Blue' has dark-blue flowers on 12–18-in. (30–45-cm) stems. Zones 5–8.

L. perenne. Blue flax. Europe. Height 18 in.; spread 12 in. (45 × 30 cm). A short-lived plant with blue-green, grassy leaves 1 in. (2.5 cm) long. The nearly leafless arching stems bear branched clusters of blue, 1-in.- (2.5-cm-) wide, upward flowers without a white eye in late spring to midsummer. Tolerant of heat. Prune hard after flowering. Variety ***album*** has white flowers; var. ***alpinum*** has finer foliage and slightly smaller clear-blue flowers. 'Blue Sapphire' grows to about 12 in. (30 cm) tall and has sapphire-blue flowers. Zones 5–9.

LIRIOPE

(Lilyturf)

Family: Liliaceae

Liriope muscari 'Lilac Beauty'

Five species of stemless, evergreen, grasslike plants native to Japan, China, and Southeast Asia. Two species and their cultivars are now widely grown as heat-tolerant, easily cultivated groundcovers. They are valuable both for their foliage and for their flowers, which are deep lavender in one species and almost white in another. Named after the nymph Liriope.

Cultivation: Grow in well-drained, ordinary soil in full sun to shade. Although flowering best in sun, they grow well in almost any situation except in poorly drained soil. If necessary, cut down the foliage in late winter or early spring. This is often done for reasons of tidiness, although the plants look bristly coarse for several weeks in spring. If tidiness is not required, merely rake the dead leaves in spring.

Landscape Use: Invaluable groundcovers for hot and humid areas, for sun or shade, as path edging or grassy plants in the herbaceous border.

Propagation: Divide the plants at any time throughout the growing season; spring and autumn are best. In summer provide plenty of irrigation.

L. muscari. Blue lilyturf. China, Japan. Height 18 in.; spread 18 in. (45 × 45 cm). A clump-forming plant with arching evergreen straplike leaves ¾–1 in. (1.8–2.5 cm) wide. Lilac-purple spikes up to 5 in. (12.5 cm) long appear in late summer and autumn followed by black fruits. An excellent plant for dry soils in sun or shade. 'Christmas Tree' has tapering lilac flowers and deep-green foliage; 'Densiflora' forms tight clumps of green erect leaves with lilac-purple flowers; 'Gold Banded' has lavender flowers and green foliage with a central gold band; 'John Burch' has yellow variegated foliage and crested lavender flowers; 'Lilac Beauty' has stiff lilac flowers held high above the green foliage; 'Majestic' has large spikes of deep-lilac flowers and dark-green foliage, one of the best cultivars for flower display; 'Monroe's White' has white flowers and dark-green foliage; 'Silver Dragon,' a handsome cultivar that requires shade, has variegated leaves of pale green and silvery white; 'Silvery Midget' is a dwarf plant growing to 8 in. (20 cm) with pale-yellow variegation and violet flowers; 'Silvery Sunproof' is a sun-tolerant cultivar with pale yellow to white variegation and lilac-purple flowers, similar to 'Variegata' with striped cream-and-green leaves and lilac flowers; 'Webster's Wideleaf' has broad arching leaves and lilac-purple leaves. Zones 5–9.

L. spicata. Creeping lilyturf. Height 12 in.; spread 18 in. (30 × 45 cm). A vigorous, spreading, grassy plant with invasive rhizomatous roots and narrow, dark-green leaves ¼ in. (0.6 cm) wide. In late summer and early autumn 3-in.- (7.5-cm-) tall spikes of pale-lavender to white flowers appear just above the foliage. 'Alba' has white flowers; 'Franklin Mint,' possibly a hybrid between the two species, is a robust, creeping form with erect pale-lavender flower spikes. Zones 4–9.

LOBELIA

(Cardinal Flower)

Family: Campanulaceae

A genus of over 250 species of herbaceous plants, shrubs, and trees. Those commonly grown are the annual ***L. erinus*** and the cardinal flower, ***L. cardinalis.*** Lobelias have alternate lance-shaped leaves and asymmetrical tubular or starry, lipped and lobed red, yellow, or blue flowers. Named after Mathias de L'Obel, (1538–1616) a Flemish botanist. Cardinal flower refers to the red, hoodlike flowers described below.

Cultivation: Plant in rich, moist soil in sun to partial shade in cool areas. Grow in partial to full shade in climates with hot summers.

Landscape Use: Effective plants for the bog, streamside, or woodland garden. The dark-purple-leaved forms are dramatic punctuations in the border.

Propagation: Divide in spring. Sow seeds in spring, planting the following year. Leave seed heads on the mature plant to allow self-seeding. Easily propagated from divisions or stem cuttings taken in midsummer.

L. cardinalis. Cardinal flower. Eastern and central United States. Height 3–4 ft; spread 1 ft (90–120 × 30 cm). From a basal rosette rise stout, reddish purple stems with narrow, tapering, mid-green, oblong to lance-shaped, toothed leaves up to 4 in. (10 cm) long. Scarlet spikes, up to 2 ft (60 cm) long, bearing masses of downward bending, three-lobed and lipped flowers, appear in late summer. The flower color is extraordinarily strong, particularly when placed against white and yellow companions. 'Alba'

Lobelia splendens 'Queen Victoria'

has pinkish white flowers; 'Angel Song' has salmon-and-cream flowers; 'Arabella's Vision' has brilliant red blossoms; 'Rosea' has pink flowers; 'Twilight Zone' has soft-pink flowers. The species has an unfounded reputation for being difficult to grow. It is a short-lived, moisture-loving species that requires propagation every three or four years. Zones 2–9.

L.* x *gerardii* (*L.* x *vedrariensis*).** Height 3 ft; spread 1 ft (90 × 30 cm). A hybrid, possibly between *L.* 'Queen Victoria' and ***L. siphilitica, with dark-green, 6-in.- (15-cm-) long, lance-shaped leaves and spikes of two-lipped purple flowers in summer. It is tolerant of drier soil and greater sunlight than the cardinal flower. Mulch for winter protection. Zones 5–8.

L. siphilitica. Great blue lobelia. Eastern United States. Height 3 ft; spread 1 ft (90 × 30 cm). The specific name refers to the plant's supposed power to cure syphilis. (This remedy is not to be relied on.) It is a short-lived, clump-forming plant with unbranched, stiff stems and egg-shaped to lance-shaped light-green leaves up to 6 in. (15 cm) long, with toothed edges. Spikes of light-blue flowers are produced in late summer, beginning after ***L. cardinalis.*** Variety ***alba*** is a bluish white-flowered form. Zones 4–8.

L.* × *speciosa. Height 2–5 ft; spread 2 ft (60–150 × 60 cm). Hybrids of complex parentage containing ***L. siphilitica*** var. ***siphilitica*** and ***L. cardinalis*** var. ***cardinalis.*** They are vigorous plants that require a sheltered location and a winter mulch. 'Brightness' grows to a height of 4 ft (120 cm) and has cherry-red flowers and bronze foliage; 'Oakes Ames' reaches a height of 3 ft (90 cm) and has dark-green leaves and scarlet flowers; 'Wisley' grows 2½ ft (75 cm) tall and has mid-green leaves and red flowers. Zones 3–9.

L. splendens. Mexican lobelia. Mexico. Height 3 ft; spread 1 ft (90 × 30 cm). Differs from ***L. cardinalis*** in having lance-shaped to linear leaves up to 7 in. (17.5 cm) long and slightly larger flowers. More interesting are the cultivars 'Bee's Flame,' with bright-red flowers and dark-red foliage, and 'Queen Victoria,' with brilliant-red flowers and maroon foliage. In mild climates these two cultivars can reach a height of 5 ft (150 cm) when in flower. They are magnificent garden plants that require constantly moist soil and partial shade. Zones 7–9.

LUNARIA

(Honesty)

Family: Cruciferae

Two or three species of erect herbaceous plants, only one of which is perennial. The more commonly known honesty (***L. annua***) is a biennial that sows itself in gardens. It is called honesty for its nearly transparent, round, papery fruit pods, which also gives it its Latin name, from *luna,* the silvery moon. The perennial species has elliptical seed pods that are also useful for indoor flower arrangements.

Cultivation: Grow in well-drained soil in sun to partial shade.

Landscape Use: Midsize plants for the middle of the border, where their lavender-white, fragrant flowers and glistening seed pods can be seen to best effect.

Propagation: Divide or sow seed in spring.

L. rediviva. Perennial honesty. Europe. Height 2–3 ft; spread 18 in. (60–90 × 45 cm). A bushy, hairy-stemmed plant with deep-green, finely toothed, egg-shaped leaves up to 5 in. (12.5 cm) long and terminal clusters of fragrant lavender to white four-petaled flowers in late spring and early summer. Elliptical, papery seed pods are held on the stems into the winter. A perennial that only lives for a short period of time, it needs dividing every few years. Zones 6–9.

LUPINUS

(Lupine)

Family: Fabaceae

Lupinus perennis

A large genus of 200 species, very few of which are cultivated in gardens. They are annual, perennial, and shrubby plants with fanlike leaves with three or more leaflets and slender spires of pealike flowers. The name is derived from the Latin *lupus* "wolf," from the erroneous belief that the deep-rooted plant ravaged the soil, making it infertile. In fact, because they are able to fertilize the soil by means of nitrogen-fixing nodules, lupines are often used to restore fertility in soil. Perhaps one of the most wonderful sights in the world is the mass of Texas bluebonnets (***L. subcarnosus*** and ***L. texensis***) carpeting the Texas grassland in spring.

Cultivation: Grow in light, neutral soil in full sun to partial shade. Deadhead faded flowers to encourage further blooming. Slugs and snails are a problem. In general, they are not plants for hot and humid climates, but they are still worth growing as annuals. Plant in autumn, so they flower in early summer before the onset of very hot weather.

Landscape Use: Where they do grow well they are a tremendous addition to the summer garden, being an integral part of the cottage garden. They look particularly splendid grown in large masses.

Propagation: Take basal cuttings of named hybrids in early spring. Seed should be sown in spring after soaking in water overnight and given a month of 30° to 40°F temperatures either by overwintering outdoors or in a refrigerator.

L. latifolius. Washington to California. Height 4 ft; spread 2 ft (120 × 60 cm). A bushy, erect plant with mid-green, fanlike leaves divided into five to nine pointed leaflets up to 4 in. (10 cm) long. In early summer 18-in. (45-cm) spikes of blue to purple flowers appear. Zones 4–8.

L. perennis. Wild lupine. Maine to Florida. Height 2 ft; spread 18 in. (60 × 45 cm). An erect, softly hairy plant with fanlike leaves divided into seven to 11 leaflets, each one 1–2 in. (2.5–5 cm) long.

Mostly blue but occasionally pink or white flowers appear on 1-ft- (30-cm-) long spikes in early summer. An excellent plant for the wild garden. Zones 4–9.

L. polyphyllus. British Columbia to California. Height 2–5 ft; spread 2 ft (60–150 × 60 cm). Tall tufts of stout stems with long-stemmed, fanlike leaves with 12 to 18 lance-shaped leaflets 2–6 in. (5–15 cm) long, hairless above, silkily hairy beneath. Deep-blue flowers are borne on 2-ft (60-cm) spikes through the summer. Zones 4–9.

Hybrids and Cultivars. Hybrid lupines are such a prominent part of the garden that is odd to think that before people such as Kelway, Downer, Harkness, and especially Russell began working on hybridizing lupines in the early part of this century, the hybrids were largely nonexistent. Now we can choose lupines with single colors and bicolors in shades of purple, blue, red, to pink, orange, yellow, and white. Their average height is 3 ft (90 cm) and spread, 2 ft (60 cm). A few of the many cultivars: 'Blue Jacket,' with deep blue-and-white flowers; 'Blushing Bride,' with ivory-white flowers; 'Chandelier,' with shades of yellow flowers; 'Cherry Pie,' with cherry red-and-pink flowers flushed yellow; 'Freedom,' with sky-blue-and-white flowers; 'Gallery Hybrids,' with mixed colors of blue, pink, white, and red on 18-in.- (45-cm-) tall plants; 'Lilac Time,' with lilac-and-white blossoms flushed pink; 'My Castle,' with brick-red shades; 'Noble Maiden,' with white flowers; 'Serenade,' with orange-red and crimson-and-gold flowers; 'The Chatelaine,' with flowers of pink and white; 'The Governor,' with blue-and-white flowers; 'Wheatsheaf,' with golden yellow flowers. Zones 4–8.

LUZULA

(Wood Rush)

FAMILY: Juncaceae

About 80 species of widely distributed, cool-season, coarse, grasslike tufted plants with green or white flowers and flat, often arching green leaves.

CULTIVATION: Grow in moist but well-drained, acid soil in a shady site.

LANDSCAPE USE: Useful plants for dry woodland shade.

PROPAGATION: Divide in spring or autumn. Sow seed in autumn.

L. nivea. Snowy wood rush. Europe. Height 1–2 ft; spread 1 ft (30–60 × 30 cm). An evergreen, tufted, spreading plant with linear leaves with hairy edges and panicles of white grassy flowers in late spring and early summer. Grows well in acid soil and tolerates dry shade. Zones 4–9.

L. pilosa. Hairy wood rush. Europe, Asia, North America. Height 8–12 in.; spread 12 in. (20–30 × 30 cm). A dense, evergreen, tufted rush with hairy-edged pale-green leaves about ½ in. (1.2 cm) wide and tan flowers in spring. It spreads rapidly but is not invasive. Zones 3–7.

Luzula sylvatica

L. sylvatica. Greater wood rush. Europe, Asia. Height 3 ft; spread 18 in. (90 × 45 cm). A robust plant with bright-green, evergreen foliage 1 ft (30 cm) long and ¾ in. (1.8 cm) wide. Chestnut-brown flowers are borne in loose terminal clusters in spring. It requires fertile, moist soil in shade. 'Marginata' has white-striped edges. Zones 5–9.

LYCHNIS

(Campion, Catchfly)

Family: Caryophyllaceae

Lychnis chalcedonica

Ten to 12 species of generally short-lived, variable, annual and perennial plants with opposite leaves and white, pink, scarlet, and orange salver-shaped flowers in summer. ***Lychnis*** comes from the Greek *lychnos,* "lamp," a reference to the bright colors of some species. "Catch-fly" is applied to ***L. viscaria*** for its sticky flower stalks.

Cultivation: Grow in well-drained soil in full sun or light shade. Deadhead regularly and support the taller species.

Landscape Use: 'Old-fashioned' plants for the flower garden.

Propagation: Take basal cuttings in spring, divide in spring or autumn, or sow seed in late spring.

L. alpina. Europe, North America. Height 4 in.; spread 4 in. (10 × 10 cm). Tufts of basal, dark-green linear leaves and heads of pink-purple flowers in spring to summer. 'Alba' has white flowers; 'Rosea' has rich pink flowers.

L. × arkwrightii. Height 12–18 in.; spread 12 in. (30–45 × 30 cm). A hybrid between ***L. chalcedonica*** and ***L. × haageana*** with 1½- in.- (3.8-cm-) wide, orange-scarlet flowers with notched petals and oblong, spear-shaped, mid-green leaves. Grow in light shade in climates with hot summers. 'Vesuvius' has bright orange-red flowers. It is an eye-opener. Zones 6–8.

L. chalcedonica. Maltese cross. Eastern Russia. Height 3–4 ft; spread 1 ft (90–120 × 30 cm). A clump-forming species with flat clusters of brilliant-red flowers on upright, hairy stems with egg-shaped, dark-green leaves 2–4 in. (5–10 cm) long. The individual flowers are cross-shaped; hence the common name. An outstanding plant for the back of the border, it often needs staking. The variety ***alba*** has white flowers; ***rosea*** has pale-pink flowers. 'Plena' is a double red form. Zones 4–8.

L. cognata. East Asia, Japan. Height 6 in.; spread 12 in. (15 × 30 cm). A trailing plant with egg-shaped leaves and orange flowers with lobed petals blooming in summer. While orange is a difficult color to use successfully in gardens, the orange of this species is soft and pleasing. Zones 6–9.

L. coronaria. Rose campion. Southern Europe. Height 2–3 ft; spread 18 in. (60–90 × 45 cm). A short-lived plant with basal rosettes of woolly, gray, egg-shaped leaves up to 4 in. (10 cm) long. Branched, woolly stems bear 1-in.- (2.5-cm-) wide, shocking crimson-pink flowers in mid- to late summer. Grows well in dry, poor soils. The variety ***alba*** has white flowers that wonderfully compliment the silvery foliage; ***atrosanguinea*** has carmine-red flowers; var. ***oculata*** has white flowers with a cherry-red eye. Zones 4–8.

L. flos-cuculi. Ragged robin. Europe, naturalized in North America. Height 3 ft; spread 18 in. (90 × 45 cm). Gray-green oblong, spear-shaped leaves in a basal rosette with branched, leafy stems bearing rose-red flowers with deeply cut or "ragged" petals. The variety ***albiflora*** has white flowers. Zones 3–8.

L. flos-jovis. Flower-of-Jove. Europe. Height 18 in.; spread 18 in. (45 × 45 cm). Similar to ***L. coronaria*** in that it has silver, woolly foliage but with lance-shaped leaves and deep rose-pink flowers ½ in. (1.2 cm) across in mid- to late summer. 'Hort's Variety,' an introduction from the English nursery Blooms of Bressingham, grows to about 10 in. (25 cm) and has clear-pink flowers in summer. Zones 4–8.

L. × haageana. Height 18 in.; spread 12 in. (45 × 30 cm). A hybrid between ***L. coronaria*** var. ***sieboldii*** and ***L. fulgens*** to be grown in moist soil in full sun to partial shade. Two-in.- (5-cm-) wide orange-scarlet flowers are borne on weak stems from basal clumps with dark-green, 4-in. (10-cm-) long, lance-shaped leaves. Zones 4–8.

L. viscaria. Catchfly. Eurasia. Height 18 in.; spread 12 in. (45 × 30 cm). A clump-forming plant with tufts of basal oblong, dark-green leaves up to 5 in. (12.5 cm) long. Strong, sticky stems bear clusters of 1-in.- (2.5-cm-) wide, purplish pink flowers in early summer. The variety ***alba*** has white flowers. The cultivar 'Splendens' has bright-magenta flowers; 'Splendens Plena' has double magenta flowers; and 'Splendens Rosea' has double rose-pink flowers. Zone 3–9.

L. × walkeri. Height 12 in.; spread 12 in. (30 × 30 cm). A hybrid between ***L. coronaria*** and ***L. flos-jovis*** with silvery, hairy stems and leaves and carmine-red flowers in late spring to early summer. 'Abbotswood Rose' has rose-pink flowers. Zones 4–8.

LYSICHITON

(Skunk Cabbage)

Family: Araceae

Two species of stemless plants with yellow or white flowerlike bracts (spathe) surrounding green flowers (spadix).

Cultivation: Grow in constantly wet soil in sun or partial shade.

Landscape Use: Dramatic plants for the bog or woodland stream garden.

Propagation: Divide in spring or sow seeds in late summer, plant in two to three years.

L. americanus. Western skunk cabbage. Western North America. Height 2–4 ft; spread 2 ft (60–120 × 60 cm). A fleshy, vigorous plant with golden yellow spathes surrounding a green spadix in spring followed by glossy, leathery leaves 4 ft (120 cm) long by 1 ft (30 cm) wide. Although the flowers are foul smelling, it is an excellent plant for the bog gardens. Zones 7–9.

Lysichiton camtschatcensis

L. camtschatcensis. Asia. Height 2–3 ft; spread 2 ft (60–90 × 60 cm). Similar to the western skunk cabbage but possibly more attractive, with its smaller, blue-green leaves and sweet-smelling flowers with a broad white spathe like a nun's wimple surrounding a green spadix. Zone 6–9.

LYSIMACHIA

(Loosestrife)

Family: Primulaceae

About 165 species of annual and perennial plants with opposite or whorled leaves and summer-blooming, mostly white or yellow flowers in open spikes or dense spires. The name comes from the Greek *lusis*, "concluding," and *mache*, "strife," and refers to the supposed soothing qualities for pacifying angry oxen.

Cultivation: Easily grown in moist soil in sun or partial shade. Deadhead faded flowers and guard against invasion.

Landscape Use: Useful if invasive border plants for moist soils. Their great attraction counteracts their invasiveness. The cultivated species are essential elements of the summer bog garden.

Propagation: Divide in spring or autumn; take stem cuttings or sow seed.

Lysimachia ephemerum

L. ciliata. Northeastern United States. Height 3½ ft; spread 2 ft (105 × 60 cm). A clump-forming plant with erect stems and wine-red, narrowly egg-shaped, pointed leaves 4–6 in. (10–15 cm) long with the leaf stems covered in fine hairs. Light-yellow flowers are borne in the upper leaf axils in summer. The wine-red foliage fades to green as summer gets into its stride. Cutting the plant down to the ground in midsummer produces fresh, red foliage. Zones 3–9.

L. clethroides. Gooseneck loosestrife. China, Japan. Height 3 ft; spread 3 ft (90 × 90 cm). For once a common name that immediately makes sense. Dense curved spikes of white flowers borne at the end of the flower stalk really do resemble a goose's neck. The opposite leaves are about 3–6 in. (7.5–15 cm) long and taper at both ends. In some soils this is a highly invasive plant; be careful. Zones 3–8.

L. ephemerum. Europe. Height 3 ft; spread 1 ft (90 × 30 cm). A noninvasive, upright plant with stiff, pale-green stems and leathery gray-green, stemless, lance-shaped leaves 4–6 in. (10–15 cm) long. Spires of small white flowers are produced in late summer. Fortunately, this excellent plant is now widely available. It is not suitable for persistently hot and humid climates, although it can take considerable summer heat if planted in constantly moist soil. Zones 6–9.

L. nummularia. Creeping jenny, moneywort. Europe. Height 4–8 in.; spread 2 ft (10–20 × 60 cm). This plant has a wonderful list of common names: twopenny grass, meadow runagates, strings of sovereigns, wandering tailor, and so on. The names are allusions to its rapid trailing nature and the coinlike roundness of its leaves. It is a prostrate species with long, frequently rooting stems bearing 1-in.- (2.5-cm-) long, mid-green leaves and fragrant yellow flowers ½ in. (1.2 cm) across. 'Aurea' has bright-yellowish green leaves that really brighten up a shady spot. Zones 3–9.

L. punctata. Yellow loosestrife. Europe. Height 2 ft; spread 1 ft (60 × 30 cm). Another often invasive species with mid-green, whorled or opposite, spear-shaped leaves to 4 in. (10 cm) long and whorls of brown-throated, bright-yellow, 1-in.- (2.5-cm-) wide starry flowers in summer. The flowers' yellow is of a particularly good tone. It performs best in mild climates. Although it is commonly cultivated, snobbery should not prevent us from using this plant. Zones 4–9.

LYTHRUM

(Purple Loosestrife)

Family: Lythraceae

Thirty or so species of annual and perennial herbs with angled or winged stems, mostly opposite leaves, and purple to white flowers. Two species and their cultivars are widely grown in gardens for their long-blooming late-summer to autumn flowers. Gardeners should have considerable misgivings about growing ***Lythrum.*** In much of the northern half of the United States, purple loosestrife has become an extremely dominant weed, spreading widely through wetlands and overwhelming indigenous plants. Reportedly 25,000 acres of Minnesota's wetlands are infested with this pretty but noxious weed. At the time of this writing, Minnesota and Wisconsin have banned the sale and distribution of all varieties of loosestrife. While this measure has been taken too late, gardeners should be aware that even a small contribution to the population may cause problems. Many cultivars of loosestrife are listed as being sterile and therefore not invasive; however, there is much dispute about the seed viability of certain cultivars, including information that so-called sterile cultivars do self-seed in large numbers. It is also increasingly difficult to distinguish the wild purple loosestrife, ***L. salicaria,*** from the supposedly sterile varieties of ***L. virgatum.*** This does not appear to be a great problem in the southern United States or Europe; however, *caveat emptor*.

Lythrum salicaria 'Lady Sackville'

Cultivation: Grows far too well in average to wet soil in full sun or partial shade.

Landscape Use: Dangerous plants for the sunny border or bog garden. See above.

Propagation: Far too easily.

L. salicaria. Purple loosestrife. Europe, Asia. Height 2–5 ft; spread 2 ft (60–150 × 60 cm). An upright plant with branching stems and slightly hairy, lance-shaped, willowlike leaves up to 4–6 in. (10–15 cm) long. Terminal spikes up to 1-ft (30-cm) long carry whorls of ¾-in.- (1.8-cm-) long, purple-pink flowers in summer and early autumn. Cultivars (which may be hybrids) include: 'Firecandle,' with intense violet-red flowers; 'Happy,' a dwarf cultivar growing to 18 in. (45 cm) with dark-pink flowers; 'Lady Sackville,' with rose-pink flowers; 'Morden's Gleam,' with rose flowers; 'Morden's Pink,' with bright-pink flowers; 'Pink Spires,' with deep-pink flowers; 'Purple Spires,' with purple-rose flowers; 'Robert' height 2 ft (60 cm), with deep-pink flowers. 'The Beacon,' height 3 ft (90 cm), with rose-red flowers; 'The Rocket,' height 3 ft (90 cm), with deep-pink flowers. Zones 3–9.

L. virgatum. Europe, Asia. Height 2–3 ft; spread 2 ft (60–90 × 60 cm). Very similar to the species described above but with a more slender habit and slightly smaller, stalked flowers. Purple-pink flowers appear in summer. 'Rose Queen' grows 18 in. (45 cm) tall and has clear-pink flowers. Zones 3–9.

MACLEYA

(Plume Poppy)

Family: Papaveraceae

Two species of robust perennials with light-green leaves with the undersides covered in bright white, soft hairs. Tall plumes of white, pink, or buff petalless flowers are borne on stout stems in summer.

Cultivation: Grow in deep, fertile soil in a sunny, sheltered site. Stake when necessary.

Landscape Use: Tall, stately plants for the back of the border or in large beds where their adventurous habits will not overwhelm other plants. They are effective foils for ***Delphiniums, Verbascums,*** and other plants with candlelike flowers.

Propagation: Easily divided in spring or autumn. Take cuttings of basal shoots in spring.

M. cordata. Plume poppy. China, Japan. Height 8 ft; spread 3 ft (240 × 90 cm). A spreading plant with stout, unbranched, leafy stems with heart-shaped, lobed, 8-in- (20-cm-) wide leaves with undersides covered in white felt. Throughout the summer 1-ft- (30-cm-) long plumes of creamy white, petalless flowers are produced. There are two forms. The most widely grown is often highly invasive by means of underground suckers. The other form, unnamed and less available, grows in large clumps and does not spread. 'Flamingo,' a cultivar uncommon in North America, has pink flowers. Zones 4–9.

M. microcarpa. China. Height 8 ft; spread 3 ft (240 × 90 cm). Very similar to the above species but with smaller, buff-colored flowers on branched spikes. It is a highly invasive plant in most soils except the very wet. 'Coral Plume' has feathery pink flowers. Zones 4–9.

MAIANTHEMUM

(False Lily-of-the-Valley)

Family: Liliaceae

Three species of creeping woodland plants native to Europe, Asia, and North America closely related to ***Smilacina*** and ***Convallaria.*** They are not the most ornamental of woodland plants, but one species is widely distributed in North America and is of interest to gardeners who appreciate wildflowers.

Cultivation: Grow in a cool, moist but well-drained, shady location.

Landscape Use: Attractive groundcovers for woodland conditions.

Propagation: Divide in spring or sow seed in autumn.

Maianthemum canadense

M. canadense. North America. Height 8 in.; spread 6 in. (20 × 15 cm). A low-growing woodland species with one to three oblong to egg-shaped, stemless, glossy leaves up to 4 in. (10 cm) long. In spring and early summer (5-cm) spikes of small, fragrant white flowers appear, followed by red berries in autumn. Zones 3–8.

M. dilatatum (M. bifolium). Europe, Asia. Height 9 in.; spread 6 in. (22.5 × 15 cm). An often invasive species with the upper stem white and hairy and the lower stem hairless, with two triangular to egg-shaped, glossy dark-green leaves with 1-in.- (2.5 -cm.-) long leaf stems. In spring 1-in.- (2.5-cm.-) high spikes of small white flowers are produced. Zones 4–7.

MALVA

(Mallow)

FAMILY: Malvaceae

About 40 species of short-lived but long-blooming annuals and perennials closely related to ***Lavatera*** and ***Sidalcea,*** with alternate, dissected, or lobed, toothed leaves and long spikes of purple, pink, to white notched and lobed flowers in summer and early autumn. The Latin name is derived from the Greek *malake,* "soft," a reference to mallows' reputation for healing and softening.

CULTIVATION: Plant in ordinary, well-drained soil in full sun to light shade.

LANDSCAPE USE: Long-blooming, generally drought-tolerant plants for summer and early autumn display. The spikes of pink, saucer-shaped flowers are particularly prominent in a mixed herbaceous border.

PROPAGATION: Divide in autumn or spring or take basal cuttings in spring.

M. alcea. Hollyhock mallow. Europe. Height 3–4 ft; spread 18 in. (90–120 × 45 cm). An erect, many-branched plant with alternate, slightly hairy, five-lobed, toothed leaves. Pink to light-purple flowers with notched petals are borne in large numbers from the leaf axils and in terminal spikes throughout the summer and into autumn. Self-seeds freely. Variety ***fastigiata*** has rose-pink flowers and a more upright habit. Zones 4–8.

M. moschata. Musk mallow. Europe, naturalized in the northeastern United States. Height 2–3 ft; spread 2 ft (60–90 × 60 cm). A hairy, many-branched, bushy plant with mid-green, three-lobed lower leaves with stem leaves deeply divided into five to seven segments, giving off a musky odor when crushed. Rose-pink flowers 2 in. (5 cm) across bloom in early summer occasionally into early autumn. The variety ***alba*** has white flowers; var. ***rosea,*** rose-pink flowers. Zones 3–9.

MARRUBIUM

(Horehound)

FAMILY: Labiatae

About 30 species of woolly-leaved, branching plants native to the Mediterranean, much of Europe, and Asia. All have square stems typical of the family; opposite, round-toothed, wrinkled, felted leaves; and lipped and lobed flowers. The Latin name is possibly derived from the Hebrew *marrob,* "bitter juice," a reference to the herb's taste. Horehound has been widely used for its medicinal properties since ancient times. The common name may be derived from "Seed of Horus," used by Egyptian apothecaries.

Marrubium cylleneum

CULTIVATION: Grow in well-drained but poor soil in full sun.

LANDSCAPE USE: Valuable silver-leaved plants for the hot, dry garden in full sun. Attractive container plants. Excellent in contrast with lavender, rue, and other colorful, sun-loving herbs.

PROPAGATION: Take stem cuttings in midsummer. Sow seed in spring.

M. cylleneum. Europe, Asia. Height 12 in.; spread 18 in. (30 × 45 cm). Soft gray-green, round-toothed, egg-shaped leaves 1 in. (2.5 cm) long with leaves and stems covered in white, woolly hairs. Grayish pink flowers are produced in whorled clusters on short terminal spikes in summer. This is a particularly attractive species, useful for its soft-toned gray-green leaves. Zones 6–9.

M. incanum. Southeastern Europe. Height 2–3 ft; spread 2 ft (60–90 × 60 cm). A shrubby plant with a woody base and egg-shaped, gray-green leaves up to 2 in. (5 cm) long on square stems. The entire plant is covered in grayish white hairs, with whorls of white flowers set in a woolly collar of sepals. Zones 3–9.

M. vulgare. Horehound. Europe. Height 1 ft; spread 18 in. (30 × 45 cm). A bushy, many-branched plant with wrinkled, egg-shaped, 1-in.- (2.5-cm.-) long, felted, strongly aromatic leaves and whitish flowers borne in crowded whorls in summer. Used in the past for treating lung troubles. Zones 3–9.

MARSHALLIA

FAMILY: Compositae

A small genus of perennials native to the southeastern United States with basal or alternate leaves and disc-shaped heads of tubular flowers. Named after Humphrey Marshall, an 18th-century American botanist.

CULTIVATION: Grow in moist soil in sun to partial shade.

LANDSCAPE USE: Little-known American native plants for use in the sunny or shady border or wild garden.

PROPAGATION: Divide in spring or autumn or sow seed in spring.

M. grandiflora. Southeastern United States. Height 2 ft; spread 1 ft (60 × 30 cm). Basal rosettes of deep-green, ribbed, elliptical to spoon-shaped leaves 4–8 in. (10–20 cm) long with thinner, narrower leaves farther up the stem. Solitary flower heads 1¼ in. (3.2 cm) across are surrounded by a papery collar and are made up of ¾-in. (1.8-cm), pinkish blue florets. Blooms in summer. Zones 5–9.

MATTEUCIA

(Ostrich Fern)

Family: Aspleniaceae

Three species of ferns native to North America, Europe, and Asia. Spreading underground runners produce an almost stemlike crown from which are produced large feathery lance-shaped leaves.

Cultivation: Plant in fertile, moisture-retentive soil in partial shade.

Landscape Use: Tall, elegant ferns for the woodland garden, streamside, or shady border.

Propagation: Dig up and remove offsets in spring or sow spores in early summer.

Matteucia struthiopteris

M. struthiopteris. Ostrich fern. North America. Europe, Asia. Height 3–5 ft; spread 2–3 ft (90–150 × 60–90 cm). Tall, shiny, dark-green, feathery fronds are produced from a stemlike crown in midspring after many other ferns have already appeared. The overall form is vaselike, with the individual leaves being elliptical to lance-shaped. The leaves are of two different types; the larger, feathery leaves are sterile while the later-emerging, greeny bronze fronds are fertile and half the height of the sterile ones. The fertile fronds turn dark brown and are ornamental throughout the winter. Zones 2–9.

MAZUS

Family: Scrophulariaceae

Mazus miguelli 'Albus'

About 30 species of low-growing carpeting plants native to Asia, New Zealand, and Australia, with opposite basal leaves and alternate upper leaves. Tiny blue, purple, and white snapdragonlike flowers appear in spring and summer. ***Mazus*** comes from the Greek, *mazos,* "teat," referring to the small, rounded projections in the mouth of the corolla.

Cultivation: Plant in moist but well-drained soil in partial shade to full sun; protect from afternoon sun in hot climates.

Landscape Use: Mat-forming groundcovers particularly useful for rock gardens, between paving stones, and within shaded woodland walks.

Propagation: Divide in spring or autumn.

M. miguelli (M. reptans). Asia. Height 2 in.; spread 12 in. (5 × 30 cm). A spreading, mat-forming plant with lance-shaped to elliptical 1-in.- (2.5-cm.-) long, coarsely toothed leaves. In spring ¾-in.- (1.8-cm-) long, purplish-blue flowers with the lower lip spotted white, yellow, and purple bloom. 'Albus' has white flowers. Divide every three to five years to keep the plant vigorous. This species can successfully compete with lawn grasses and can be quite invasive. It is, however, a very pretty plant that is worth growing despite its brazen habit. Zones 3–9.

M. pumilus. New Zealand, Australia. Height 2 in.; spread 12 in. (5 × 30 cm). Slowly spreading mats of rounded, egg-shaped, 3-in.- (7.5-cm.-) long, dark-green leaves with blue-and-white-lipped flowers in summer. Zones 7–9.

MECONOPSIS

(Blue Poppy)

Family: Papaveraceae

Meconopsis grandis 'Branklyn'

About 45 species of short-lived perennials, most native to the alpine meadows and screes of the Himalayas. They bloom in late spring to early summer, with a few species producing flowers in late summer. The blooms are large, some almost to 12 in. (30 cm) across, ranging from the most gorgeous blue to the sunniest yellow. The leaves are often borne in basal rosettes and are of various shapes, from hearts to spoons, often lobed or dissected. Some species are monocarpic—they die after flowering, although it may take some species two to four years to bloom. Most produce abundant seed and are easily propagated. They are not commonly cultivated in the gardens of North America except in the Pacific Northwest, where the mild climate suits them. While not a genus for much of North America, experimental gardeners should take their chances and try as many species in as many different habitats as possible.

CULTIVATION: ***Meconopsis*** prefer a partly sheltered site in rich, acid to neutral soil that is moist in summer but dry in winter. They are subject to mildew in climates that are too dry. Applications of organic matter and liquid fertilizer prove highly beneficial.

LANDSCAPE USE: There is nothing so beautiful as a stand of blue poppies in full flower. As lovers of acid soils and shaded sites, ***Meconopsis*** cohabit with rhododendrons and other acid-loving plants to form a delightfully vibrant understory. They are also a magnificent addition to the bog garden or wild garden where they can be grown in association with ferns, primulas, rodgersias, and others.

PROPAGATION: Sow freshly ripe seed in late summer or ripe seed in spring. Grow the young plants and plant the following autumn. Divide in spring.

M. betonicifolia. Himalayan blue poppy. Asia. Height 4 ft; spread 18 in. (120 × 45 cm). A variable species with basal rosettes of oblong, often hairy leaves with a heart-shaped base. They become stemless on the flower. The poppylike flowers are borne in late spring and early summer in outward-facing clusters and range in color from sky-blue, 3-in.- (8-cm.-) wide blooms (the best form) through muddy purple and pink forms. There is a short-lived white form variety ***alba.*** This species often produces strains that die after flowering. This habit can be delayed by removing the young flower stems before blooming or by selecting truly perennial strains from known sources. Zones 6–8.

M. cambrica. Welsh poppy. Western Europe. Height 12 in.; spread 12 in. (30 × 30 cm). The only non-Asian species with delicate yellow or orange 2-in.- (5-cm.-) wide poppies in summer. The leaves are softly hairy, deeply dissected with stemmed basal leaves and stalkless stem leaves. This species is the easiest of the genus to grow, often seeding in cracks and crevices. Seeds are best sown where the plants are to flower. Variety ***aurantiaca*** has orange flowers; var. ***flore-pleno*** has double flowers. 'Frances Perry' has deep-orange flowers. Zones 6–8.

M. grandis. Asia. Height 2–4 ft; spread 2 ft (60–120 × 60 cm). One of the best of the blue poppies, although flowers come in colors ranging from purple to white. It is a clump-forming species with upward-pointing, slightly sharply toothed and hairy oblong to lance-shaped leaves. The 4–5-in.- (10–12-cm.-) wide, upward-facing, purple to sky-blue flowers are produced in early summer. 'Branklyn' is an excellent cultivar with strong-blue flowers; 'Miss Jebbs' is a compact form with deep-blue poppies, flowering at about 3 ft (90 cm). Often confused with ***M. betonicifolia,*** although the latter has more roundly toothed leaves and outward- rather than upward-facing flowers. There are a number of hybrids between the two species, particularly ***M. × sheldonii,*** with large, cup-shaped, deep-blue flowers produced in early summer. 'Slieve Donard' has smaller flowers. Zones 6–8.

M. integrifolia. Lampshade poppy. Asia. Height 2 ft; spread 18 in. (60 × 45 cm). A short-lived perennial often dying after flowering. The basal, pale-green leaves are oblong, lance-shaped, and hairy, often up to 15 in. (37.5 cm) in length. The 9-in.- (23-cm.-) wide yellow flowers are produced in late spring and are borne singly on the flower stem. A cross between this species and ***M. betonicifolia, M. × sarsonii,*** produces pale-yellow or cream flowers in late spring. Zones 6–8.

MEDEOLA

(Indian Cucumber-root)

FAMILY: Liliaceae

One species native to North America and allied to ***Trillium,*** with whorled leaves and greenish yellow flowers. Named after the sorceress Medea because of its supposed medicinal power.

CULTIVATION: Grow in rich, moist soil in partial shade.

LANDSCAPE USE: Hardly an overwhelmingly ornamental plant, but it is useful as an addition to the woodland garden or shady border.

PROPAGATION: Sow seed in autumn or carefully divide in spring.

M. virginiana. Indian cucumber-root. Height 3 ft;

spread 1 ft (90 × 30 cm). From short rootstocks that taste of cucumber rise stiff stems with two whorls of leaves, the lower composed of five to nine pointed, rounded, lance-shaped, and ribbed leaves 5 in. (12.5 cm) long. The upper whorl (a circular arrangement of leaves) has between three to five egg-shaped leaves up to 2 in. (5 cm) long with a stemless cluster of greenish yellow flowers in early summer. Dark-purple berries follow in autumn. Zones 2–8.

MELIANTHUS

(Honeybush)

Family: Melianthaceae

Six species of tender, shrubby plants native to South Africa and India. One species is grown in warmer temperate gardens for its magnificent foliage.

Cultivation: Grow in fertile, well-drained soil in full sun or light shade in a protected site.

Landscape Use: A dramatic textural plant for foliage contrast. Its arching blue-gray leaves are a magnificently art-deco presence in the border.

Propagation: Sow seed in spring, plant the following year. Take stem cuttings in midsummer.

M. major. Honeybush. South Africa, India. Height 6 ft; spread 4 ft (180 × 120 cm). Huge expanses of beautiful blue-green, deeply divided, coarsely toothed, and ruffled leaves to 18 in. (45 cm) long are borne on woody, hollow stems. The flowers, which are rarely produced in temperate climates, are brownish red and appear in summer. Highly desirable for its magnificent foliage, this species is difficult to grow in much of North America except the Pacific states. Zones 8–10.

Melianthus major

M. minor. Southern Africa. Height 4–5 ft; spread 3 ft (120–150 × 90 cm). Similar to the above species but smaller in stature with leaves to 7 in. (17.5 cm) long and leaflets 2 in. (5 cm) long. Zones 8–10.

MELICA

(Melic Grass)

Family: Graminae

About 60 species of grasses with flat leaf blades, slender stems swollen at the base, and narrow panicles of attractive flowers with two or more spikelets generally appearing in summer.

Cultivation: Grow in full sun or light shade in moist, well-drained soil.

Landscape Use: Underused grasses for edging or in small groups in the sunny border. Melic grass

Melica ciliata

fades by late summer and should be planted among other plants that screen this shortfall.

Propagation: Divide in spring or autumn, or sow seed in spring.

M. altissima. Europe. Height 2 ft; spread 1 ft (60 × 30 cm). An evergreen species forming bright-green tufts of broad leaves and arching panicles of buff-colored flowers in summer. 'Atropurpurea' has purple-red flowers. Zones 5–8.

M. ciliata. Hairy melic grass. Europe, Asia, North Africa. Height 1–2 ft; spread 1 ft (30–60 × 30 cm). A tufted, cool-season species with blue-green, flat or rolled leaves forming clumps about 10 in. (25 cm) high. Silky panicles of white flowers appear in early to midsummer. In hot climates grow in light shade. Zones 5–8.

MELISSA

(Balm)

Family: Labiatae

A small genus of herbs with square stems and opposite, toothed leaves. One species is cultivated for its lemon-scented leaves. The genus name is derived from the Greek word for "bee," since the flowers are attractive to bees. Balm is an abbreviation of balsam, the sweet-scented oil.

Cultivation: Plant in well-drained soil in full sun. Beware of its spreading nature.

Landscape Use: A sweet-smelling plant for the herb garden or sunny border. Harvest the stems and leaves throughout the summer for culinary use. Pick before flowering for drying.

Propagation: Divide in spring of early autumn.

M. officinalis. Balm. Europe. Height 2 ft; spread 18 in. (60 × 45 cm). A clump-forming, bushy plant with hairy stems and broadly egg-shaped to heart-shaped, toothed, and lemon-scented leaves 1–3 in.

Melissa officianalis 'Aurea'

(2.5–7.5 cm) long. Very small white tubular flowers are borne on leafy spikes in summer. 'All Gold' has bright-golden foliage; 'Aurea' (Variegata) has variegated leaves of green and gold. Both cultivars often revert to the green form, and these green shoots should be removed. Zones 4–9.

MENTHA

(Mint)

Family: Labiatae

Mentha suaveolens 'Variegata'

About 25 species of well-known aromatic plants frequently used in the herb garden for their culinary and medicinal value. They are invasive plants with spreading roots, square stems, mostly opposite leaves, and whorls of dense mauve-lavender flowers. This is a promiscuous genus with much interbreeding, and many natural hybrids have been produced. Those listed below are mints of ornamental value in the garden. Highly esteemed for centuries, the herbal mints were introduced to Britain by the Romans and thence to the New World. The name Mentha comes from the mythological nymph Menthe, who, loved by Pluto, was turned into the herb by the jealous Prosperine.

Cultivation: Grow in ordinary soil that does not dry out in full sun or partial shade. Many species and hybrids are highly invasive and should be contained by being planted in a large pot that is sunk into the ground. Even then the adventurous runners will spread and root.

Landscape Use: The variegated forms are useful for foliage contrast, while most are wonderful additions to the fragrant garden.

Propagation: Divide in spring or autumn.

M.* × *gentilis. Height 18 in.; spread 2 ft (45 × 60 cm). A natural hybrid between ***M. arvensis,*** the field mint, and ***M. spicata,*** spearmint. Hairless, square stems often tinged red with egg-shaped, toothed, dark-green leaves to 2 in. (5 cm) long. In mid- to late summer 5-in. (12.5-cm) spikes of tiny, tubular, pale-purple flowers appear. 'Variegata' has bright-green leaves splashed with yellow. Zones 5–9.

M. requenii. Corsica. Height 1 in.; spread 12 in. (2.5 cm × 30 cm). A creeping, carpeting semievergreen species with tiny, round leaves ⅜ in. (1 cm) long, smelling of peppermint. In late summer ½-in.- (1.2-cm.-) long spikes of pale-purple flowers appear. This is a strongly aromatic plant that is best in partial shade and is useful for growing in the cracks between paving stones. Zones 7–9.

M. suaveolens. Apple mint. Europe. Height 3 ft; spread 18 in. (90 × 45 cm). An ornamental but invasive mint with hairy stems and pale-green, rounded, toothed, and wrinkled leaves often heavily hairy underneath. Crowded spikes of mauve flowers are borne on square stems in summer. 'Variegata' is a desirable but invasive plant with softly woolly, cream-and-white variegated leaves and few flowers. It is effective with lavender, thyme, and other ornamental herbs. Zones 5–9.

MERTENSIA

(Bluebells)

Family: Boraginaceae

Mertensia virginica

Approximately 50 species of spring- and summer-blooming wildflowers native to Europe, Asia, and North America. They are not widely grown in gardens and deserve greater attention. From fleshy rootstocks rise leafy stems with bluish green alternate leaves and blue, purple, or white, often nodding, tubular flowers. Named after a German botanist Franz Carl Mertens (1764–1831).

Cultivation: Grow in moist, rich soil in a partly shaded site.

Landscape Use: Wonderful woodland spring wildflowers or delicate pastel flowers for the border or bog garden. Most species that are cultivated in gardens become dormant by midsummer.

Propagation: Sow fresh seed in early summer or divide in spring.

M. ciliata. Mountain bluebell. Rocky Mountains. Height 2 ft; spread 18 in. (60 × 45 cm). Blue-green, hairy-edged, lance-shaped to egg-shaped leaves 6 in. (15 cm) long on arching stems. Strong-blue, ¾-in.- (1.8-cm.-) long, tubular flowers open from pinkish purple buds in spring and last into summer. Tolerates less shade than other species. Zones 4–8.

M. paniculata. North America. Height 2–3 ft; spread 2 ft (60–90 × 60 cm). A bushy, sprawling plant with egg-shaped to lance-shaped, hairy leaves and cool blue, ½-in.- (1.2-cm.-) long flowers in great profusion in spring. Zones 3–8.

M. virginica. (M. pulmanarioides). Virginia bluebells. Eastern United States. Height 2 ft; spread 18 in. (60 × 45 cm). Blue-gray, hairless, roundly egg-shaped leaves to 4 in. (10 cm) long on upright, ridged stems bearing nodding clusters of 1-in.- (2.5-cm.-) long, sky-blue flowers in spring. What would spring in Pennsylvania be without this wonderful plant? It seeds itself widely in moist soil, combines marvelously with other spring-flowering plants, and has the good grace to disappear in midsummer before it becomes tatty. 'Alba' has white flowers; 'Rubra' has pink flowers. Zones 5–9.

M. viridis. Western United States. Height 15 in.; spread 12 in. (37.5 × 30 cm). Blue-green leaves, hairy above, hairless underneath, with ¾-in. (1.8-cm) blue flowers in spring and early summer. Grows in sun to light shade in moist soils. Zones 3–8.

MILLIUM

(Wood Millet)

Family: Graminae

A small genus of annual and perennial grasses native to North America, Europe, and Asia with flat leaf blades and open panicles of one-flowered spikelets. The one species worth cultivating is interesting for its yellow-green form.

Cultivation: Grow in moist soil in full sun to partial shade for the greatest leaf coloration. This grass dislikes hot climates and should be grown in full shade if you insist on struggling with it in the heat.

Landscape Use: The yellow leaves of this grass are superb in spring when combined with deep-green foliage and bright-blue flowers.

Propagation: Divide in spring or autumn. Comes true from seed.

M. effusum var. ***aureum.*** Bowles golden grass. North America, Europe. Height 18 in.; spread 12 in. (45 × 30 cm). A tough but delicate-looking grass with bright-golden to greenish yellow leaves becoming greener as the summer commences. Drooping panicles of feathery, light-brown flowers appear in midsummer. Leaf color is best before it flowers. In hot climates this grass will often die out by midsummer. Zones 6–9.

MIMULUS

(Monkey Flower)

Family: Scrophulariaceae

Over 100 species of annual, perennial, and shrubby plants native throughout the world. The leaves are opposite and sometimes sticky. The flowers are lipped, lobed, and toothed in a range of colors from orange and yellow to violet and purple. Many hybrids are used for annual bedding and container displays. The Latin name means "little mimic," from the grinning, open-mouthed flowers.

Cultivation: Grow in full sun or partial shade in soil that does not dry out during the summer months. Cut back bushy varieties to encourage further bloom and good shape.

Landscape Use: Colorful flowers for a damp, sunny spot.

Propagation: Divide and replant in spring. Take cuttings in spring. Sow seed in late winter.

M. cardinalis. Scarlet monkey flower. Western and southwestern United States. Height 3–4 ft; spread 2 ft (90–120 × 60 cm). Sticky and hairy, roundly egg-shaped, stemless mid-green leaves to 4½ in. (11.2 cm) long on branched stems. Scarlet, yellow-tinted, snapdragonlike flowers bloom from early summer to autumn. Zones 7–9.

M. guttatus. Monkey flower. Height 2 ft; spread 2 ft (60 × 60 cm). A lush and loose-formed plant either erect or sprawling with toothed, egg-shaped, mid-green leaves up to 6 in. (15 cm) long and bright-yellow flowers with reddish brown dappled throats blooming throughout the summer. Grows well in wet soil. A number of hybrids are the result of crosses with this species and ***M. luteus,*** including 'A. T. Johnson': height 16 in. (40 cm); with deep-yellow flowers with a red throat; 'Calypso': height 14 in. (35 cm), with mixed colors of yellows and reds.

M. luteus. Golden monkey flower. North and South America. Height 1 ft; spread 1 ft (30 × 30 cm). Possibly a form of ***M. guttatus*** rather than a species. It is a spreading, carpeting plant with conspicuously veined, toothed oval leaves to 1 in. (2.5 cm) long. Bright-yellow, snapdragonlike flowers bloom throughout the summer. Zones 6–9.

M. ringens. Allegheny monkey flower. Eastern United States. Height 3 ft; spread 1 ft (90 × 30 cm). A spreading plant with erect stems and stemless, toothed, oblong to elliptical dark-green leaves to 4 in. (10 cm) long. Mauve-purple flowers are borne in the axils of the leaves throughout the summer. Grow in water up to 6 in. (15 cm) deep or in constantly wet, boggy soil. Zones 3–9.

Mimulus guttatus

MISCANTHUS

(Eulalia)

Family: Graminae

Miscanthus sinensis 'Cabaret'

Miscanthus sinensis 'Purpurascens'

If there is one grass that has benefited from the current passion for ornamental grass gardening, it is ***Miscanthus sinensis.*** Largely uncultivated in Western gardens until the 1970s, the species and its increasing number of cultivars are now so widespread as to almost overwhelm other grasses. A number of species and cultivars grown in Japan deserve wider attention in the West. In general, the representatives of this genus that are currently cultivated are tall, robust grasses with long, flat leaf blades and feathery panicles of bronze to silver flowers in late summer and autumn. They are splendid, graceful plants. The name comes from the Greek *miskos,* "stem," and *anthos,* "flower."

CULTIVATION: Grow in full sun to light shade in ordinary soil. Cut back faded foliage in spring. Many cultivars of ***M. sinensis*** need annual staking and tying and are prone to dying out in the center after a few years. Dividing the plants every three to five years will help keep them young and vigorous. Choose cultivars that do not need staking over those that do. If you thought all ornamental grasses were maintenance free, think again.

LANDSCAPE USE: Excellent although often invasive grasses for specimen planting or mixing with other perennials in borders. Although they are extensively planted with other grasses, their linear leaves are far more attractive when contrasted with coarse-leaved perennials. Their flowers also make them outstanding autumn-flowering perennials.

PROPAGATION: Best divided in spring, although early autumn division is possible in warm climates. Dividing large plants requires considerable energy and a large ax. Often self-sows.

M. sacchariflorus. Silver banner grass. Eastern Asia. Height 5 ft; spread 3 ft (150 × 90 cm). An upright grass that spreads rapidly by means of long rhizomes. The leaves are 3 ft (90 cm) long and ¾ in. (1.8 cm) wide, and the flowers, which first appear in late summer, are bronze upon opening, swiftly turning silver. They are narrow and silky and lack the bristlelike appendages (awn) of the flowers of other species. Tolerates wet soil but has an invasive nature. 'Robustus' grows to 7 ft (210 cm) and is a more robust plant. Zones 4–9.

M. sinensis. Eulalia grass, Japanese silver grass. Eastern Asia. Height 8 ft; spread 3 ft (240 × 90 cm). A clump-forming, upright plant with gracefully arching and tapering, mid-green leaves ⅜ in. (1 cm) wide with a thin white central stripe and rough, sharp edges. Panicles of feathery copper-bronze flowers turning silver in autumn are borne on stiff stems from late summer/early autumn onward. The foliage fades to a light straw color by winter, but both the foliage and the faded flowers remain attractive to early spring. Zones 4–9.

The species is rarely grown and has largely been surpassed by a number of selected forms. There are many of them, with many more expected. Hardy in Zones 4–9 except where otherwise indicated.

'Autumn Light': height 8 ft (240 cm), a narrow-leaved grass with green leaves with a thin white central stripe. Similar to ***M. sinensis*** 'Gracillimus' but blooms in late summer.

'Cabaret': height 8 ft (240 cm), wide leaves with an attractive broad central stripe of creamy white edged by thin, dark-green margins. The coppery purple flowers appear in very early autumn. A handsome and desirable cultivar that does not require staking. Zones 6–9.

'Goldfeder' (goldfeather): height 7 ft (210 cm), dark-green leaves edged golden yellow. The flowers are silvery and appear in early autumn. A slow-growing grass that requires soil that does not dry out in summer. Zones 7–9.

'Gracillimus': height 8 ft (240 cm), light-green narrow leaves ⅓ in. (0.8 cm) wide with a prominent white central stripe. An arching plant with bronze flowers turning silver. A mid-autumn-blooming, graceful grass with copper-colored flowers. It tends to open up in midautumn and frequently requires staking.

'Graziella': Similar to 'Gracillimus' but is more upright in habit and flowers a few weeks earlier. It does not need staking.

'Malepartus': height up to 8 ft (240 cm), with arching leaves forming a clump almost 5 ft (150 cm) wide. The coppery flowers become white and feathery while the foliage often turns burgundy red in autumn. Does not require staking.

'Morning Light': height 5 ft (150 cm), a delicately variegated plant with light-green leaves with a white central stripe and thin creamy white margins. One of the best of the recent cultivars, it does not need staking. Zones 6–9.

'Purpurascens': height 5 ft (150 cm), deep-green leaves changing to a wonderful array of purple-bronze tones in autumn. It is a narrowly upright plant that does not need staking. The best cultivar for autumn color, it must have adequate water during the growing season to color well. Zones 6–9.

'Silberfeder' (silver feather): height 9 ft (270 cm), mid-green leaves with a white central stripe. The flowers are the prominent feature of this grass. They open in late summer, standing 3 ft (90 cm) above the foliage, and open silver with a slight touch of bronze that quickly disappears to become completely silver. Needs staking. Zones 6–9.

'Strictus': height 8 ft (240 cm), an upright, clump-forming grass with mid-green leaves with horizontal bands of yellow variegation. Similar to ***M. sinensis*** 'Zebrinus,' but it remains upright and does not require staking. Zones 6–9.

'Variegatus': height 7 ft (210 cm), dark-green leaves with prominent creamy white to white stripes creating a very bright, white effect. Somewhat drought tolerant but tends to flop all over the place after just a couple of years and always needs staking. Zones 6–9.

'Yaku Jima': a dwarf cultivar with foliage and flowers much like those of 'Gracillimus' but the leaves form a clump about 3 ft (90 cm) high with the flowers just 1 ft (30 cm) higher.

'Zebrinus': height 8 ft (240 cm), mid-green arching leaves with horizontal stripes of yellow variegation. Tends to be laxly formed and often requires staking. Zones 6–9.

M. transmorrisonensis. Taiwan. Height 5 ft; spread 3 ft (150 × 90 cm). Flat, green leaves and a white central stripe form a clump about 2½ ft (75 cm) tall. Feathery panicles of bronze flowers that become silver stand high above the 3-ft (90-cm) foliage and begin blooming in the early part of late summer. The leaves hold their color well into the winter, becoming blue-green to the end of the year. Divide in spring only. Zones 7–9.

MITELLA

(Bishop's Cap)

Family: Saxifragaceae

Mitella diphylla

Approximately 12 species of woodland groundcovers native to North America and northeast Asia with heart-shaped, basal, or alternate leaves and tiny, delicate flowers in spring. The name refers to the cap-shaped flower.

Cultivation: Grown in leafy, acid soil in partial shade.

Landscape Use: Charming groundcovers for a woodland site.

Propagation: Divide in spring or sow seeds in summer.

M. breweri. British Columbia to California. Height 12 in.; spread 12 in. (30 × 30 cm). A clump-forming species with mottled, kidney-shaped basal leaves and thin, erect, hairy flower stems with tiny greenish white, drooping flowers in early summer. Zones 5–7.

M. diphylla. Bishop's cap. Eastern North America. Height 12 in.; spread 12 in. (30 × 30 cm). A delicate woodland plant with heart-shaped, toothed, and lobed leaves and 8-in.- (20-cm.-) long flower spikes with terminal clusters of finely fringed flowers ¼ in. (0.6 cm) across. Not a greatly ornamental plant, it does have a pleasing delicacy in the shade garden. Zones 3–8.

MOLINIA

(Moor Grass)

Family: Graminae

A small genus of hardy grasses with flat leaf blades and panicles of purplish brown flowers with two to four flowered spikelets. Named after Juan Molina (1740–1829), an expert on Chilean plants.

Cultivation: Grow in moist, acid soil in full sun or light shade.

Landscape Use: Delicate, almost transparent grasses, particularly effective as single specimens. The flowers are so delicate that they are almost invisible unless grown against a dark background.

Propagation: Divide in spring or early autumn. Slow to establish after division.

Molinia caerulea ssp. *arundinacea* 'Variegata'

M. caerulea. Moor grass. Europe, Asia. Height 3 ft; spread 2 ft (90 × 60 cm). An upright, arching, tufted plant with pointed, dark blue-green leaves forming a mound 1½ ft (45 cm) high with panicles of delicately textured purplish flowers in summer. The foliage turns golden yellow in autumn. ***M. caerulea*** ssp. ***arundinacea*** is a larger plant with foliage reaching a height of 3 ft (90 cm) and tall stems of delicate purple flowers reaching a height of 8 ft (240 cm) in midsummer. There are a number of cultivars, including 'Transparent,' with finer foliage and a maximum height of about 6 ft (180 cm), and 'Windspiel,' reaching a height of about 8 ft (240 cm). ***M. caerulea*** ssp. ***caerulea*** 'Variegata,' the variegated moor grass, is a slow-growing grass that is best divided in autumn. It forms a 1-ft (30-cm) mound of white-striped, variegated leaves and delicate flowers on yellow stems about 2 ft (60 cm) tall. Zones 4–8.

MONARDA

(Horse-mint)

Family: Labiatae

About 12 species of annual and perennial plants with running rootstocks; erect, square stems; opposite, mostly toothed, aromatic leaves; and dense heads of tubular curved flowers in shades of white, red, mauve, or purple. Named after Nicholas Monardes, a Spanish botanist. Commonly used as an herbal tea in colonial times, Oswego tea (***M. didyma***) was first collected by the 17th century botanist John Bartram in Oswego, New York. The plant is also called bee-balm, for its attractiveness to bees.

Cultivation: Plant in moisture-retentive soil in full sun to partial shade. Dry soil and hot climates do not make members of this genus happy. They are predisposed to mildew, and dry conditions exaggerate that inclination. Applications of fungicide or an antidesiccant spray from summer to autumn help control the disease. Bee-balm is also susceptible to caterpillar damage to the flowers, particularly when in full bloom in summer. Deadhead frequently, divided every two to three years, and be careful of their invasive nature.

Landscape Use: Summer-blooming plants for the

Monarda fistulosa

sunny border, bright streamside, or bog garden. They are attractive to bees, butterflies, and hummingbirds.

PROPAGATION: Divide in spring only or sow fresh seed.

M. didyma. Oswego tea, bee-balm. Eastern United States. Height 2–3 ft; spread 18 in. (60–90 × 45 cm). A spreading species with erect stems, and leaves that are mid- to dark green, hairy, toothed, aromatic, egg-shaped, and pointed, to 6 in. (15 cm) long. Dense whorled clusters of tubular red flowers surrounded by reddish bracts appear in summer. Deadhead to encourage further bloom. Zones 4–9. There are a number of cultivars, many of which may be hybrids. 'Adam' has bright red flowers; 'Blue Stocking' has violet-purple flowers; 'Cambridge Scarlet' has shocking scarlet flowers; 'Croftway Pink' has soft-pink flowers; 'Mahogany' has deep dark-red flowers; 'Panorama' has mixed colors; 'Prairie Night' has rich deep-purple flowers; 'Snow White' has creamy white blossoms; 'Souris' has bright fuchsia-colored flowers; 'Violet Queen' has rich-lilac flowers and is less susceptible to mildew. Zones 4–9.

M. fistulosa. Wild bergamot. North America. Height 4 ft; spread 2 ft (120 × 60 cm). Leaves are 4-in.- (10-cm.-) long, hairy and only slightly toothed, egg-shaped to lance-shaped, and pointed. Dense whorled clusters of lavender to pale-pink flowers are surrounded by whitish bracts. Prefers drier soil than the above species and is less susceptible to mildew. Zones 3–9.

MONARDELLA

FAMILY: Labiatae

A small genus of aromatic plants native to western North America, with square stems, opposite leaves, and whorled clusters of purple and pink flowers. The name is a diminutive of ***Monarda,*** which this genus resembles.

CULTIVATION: Grow in well-drained soil in full sun to very light shade.

LANDSCAPE USE: Good rock-garden plants with colorful flowers.

PROPAGATION: Divide in spring.

M. macrantha. California. Height 12 in.; spread 12 in. (30 × 30 cm). A creeping, tufted plant with egg-shaped, leathery leaves to 1½ in. (3.8 cm) long and whorled clusters of tubular scarlet flowers in early summer. Zones 8–9.

M. villosa. California, Oregon. Height 18 in.; spread 12 in. (45 × 30 cm). A woody stemmed plant with gray-green, hairy, rounded lance-shaped leaves to 1¼ in. (3.2 cm) long and 1 1/2-in.- (3.8-cm.-) diameter heads of pale purple, red, to white flowers in summer. Zones 8–9.

MORINA

(Whorlflower)

Family: Dipsacaceae

A genus of thistlelike evergreen perennials with opposite or whorled spiny leaves and whorls of white, pink, or purple tubular flowers with spiny bracts. The one species generally available for growing in gardens can be difficult to cultivate. Named after the French botanist Louis Morin.

Cultivation: Grow in moist, well-drained soil in full sun or partial shade in a cool but protected site. Mulch for protection in winter.

Landscape Use: A good border plant with unusual flowers and foliage.

Propagation: Sow seeds in spring and plant the following year.

M. longifolia. Whorlflower. Asia. Height 2–3 ft; spread 18 in. (60–90 × 45 cm). Basal linear to oblong spiny leaves up to 12 in. (30 cm) long with stem leaves similar but smaller. Whorls of tubular and hooded flowers of white turning pink-purple with spiny bracts are borne on brownish red stems in summer. It is still an uncommon plant in North America and deserves greater cultivation. Zones 6–9.

Morina longifolia

MYOSOTIS

(Forget-me-not)

Family: Boraginaceae

Myosotis palustris

A genus of about 50 species of annual, biennial, and perennial species with a small number of species suitable for the rock garden and bog garden. The leaves are borne in basal clumps and are usually oblong to spoon-shaped. The flowers grow in great numbers and are funnel-shaped and largely sky-blue with a small yellow eye. Forget-me-not is widely grown as a biennial for formal bedding schemes.

CULTIVATION: Grow the perennial species in partial shade in a moisture-retentive but well-drained soil rich in organic matter. The water forget-me-not ***(M. palustris)*** requires planting in wet soil in full sun or partial shade.

LANDSCAPE USE: "Old-fashioned" plants for the shaded garden, woodland stream, or sheltered rock garden. The water forget-me-not is particularly effective when allowed to colonize small, soft-flowing streams.

PROPAGATION: Sow seed in spring, plant in early autumn.

M. alpestris. Europe. Height 8 in.; spread 8 in. (20 × 20 cm). A compact, clump-forming perennial with strong green, oval to oblong leaves and dense clusters of yellow-eyed, bright-blue flowers sometime between spring and early summer. There are a number of hybrids. Although a short-lived perennial, it is a particularly good plant for the rock garden. Zones 5–8.

M. palustris (M. scorpioides). Water forget-me-not. Europe. Height 6 in.; spread 12 in. (15 × 30 cm). A water-loving plant that can be grown in shallow water. Spoon-shaped, roughly hairy leaves are produced in open mounds with flowering stems above the foliage bearing pale-blue, yellow-eyed flowers from spring to midsummer. A wonderful water plant. Zones 4–9.

MYRRHIS

(Sweet Cicely, Anise)

FAMILY: Umbelliferae

A European herb with lacy heads of tiny white flowers and filigree foliage. It is grown for its floral and foliage display as well as its sweetly scented foliage seeds and roots, which are used in medicine as well as for seasoning food. Not to be confused with ***Osmorrhiza,*** which is also called sweet cicely in the United States.

Myrrhis odorata

CULTIVATION: Grow in moist, well-drained soil in sun to partial shade.

LANDSCAPE USE: The delicate foliage and white flowers are a wonderful contrast to heavier shrubs or large-leaved perennials.

PROPAGATION: Sow seed in autumn and plant the following spring.

M. odorata. Sweet cicely. Europe. Height 5 ft; spread 2 ft (150 × 60 cm). A sweetly scented bushy plant with delicate, ferny foliage consisting of 1-ft-(30-cm)- long leaves that are two to three times divided. Flat-topped clusters of tiny white flowers are produced in early summer followed by dark-brown seeds. Deadhead to prevent self-seeding. Zones 4–9.

NEPETA

(Catmint, Catnip)

Family: Labiatae

One species of this large genus ***N. cataria*** is catmint, an herb famous for driving cats crazy. However, other species have greater value in the garden. In general, they have opposite, toothed or deeply cut leaves, white, yellow, and blue flowers, and the square stems common to ***Labiatae.*** Supposedly named after Nepet, a town in Tuscany.

Nepeta sibirica

Cultivation: Easily cultivated plants when grown in well-drained soil in full sun to light shade. Partial shade is more necessary in hot climates. Cut the mound-forming varieties down to the ground after the first flush of flowers to encourage bushy new growth and subsequent flowering in late summer and autumn.

Landscape Use: Good edging plants for the border or path. Their blue-green foliage and blue flowers create a pleasingly smoky effect. Often useful in softening the hard lines of daylily flower and foliage.

Propagation: Divide in spring or take cuttings in summer.

N. × faassenii. Height 18–24 in.; spread 18 in. (45–60 × 45 cm). A vigorous clump-forming, sterile hybrid between ***N. mussinii*** and ***N. nepetella*** with branching stems and gray-green, oblong, egg-shaped, softly toothed 1½-in.- (3.8-cm.-) long leaves with a triangular base. In early summer 6-in. (15-cm) spikes of lavender-blue flowers are produced, with a secondary flush in late summer. Often erroneously identified as ***N. mussinii.*** 'Dropmore' grows to 2 ft (60 cm) and has lavender-blue flowers and gray-green, finely toothed foliage. 'Six Hills Giant' grows to a height and spread of 3 ft (90 cm) and has 9–12-in. (22.5–30-cm) spikes of deep lavender-blue flowers. A very desirable and widely available plant that performs well in warmer climates if cut back hard immediately after flowering. Zones 4–9.

N. govaniana. Kashmir. Height 3 ft; spread 2 ft (90 × 60 cm). A bushy upright plant with toothed and hairy, egg-shaped and pointed pale-green leaves and open spikes of pale-yellow tubular flowers in summer. Uncommon in North American gardens although it requires a cool summer climate. Zones 4–8.

N. mussinii. Caucasus. Height 1 ft; spread 1 ft (30 × 30 cm). Hairy, softly toothed, gray-green, roundly heart-shaped leaves to 1 in. (2.5 cm) long on sprawling stems. Lavender-blue flowers are borne on terminal spikes for a short time in summer. Inferior to ***M. × faassenii*** and self-seeds far too freely. 'Blue Wonder' is a rounded, compact form with grayish pale-green leaves and blue flowers; 'White Wonder' has white flowers and looks even more washed out than the blue form. Cut back after flowering for a further flush of flowers. Zones 3–8.

N. sibirica. Far East. Height 2–3 ft; spread 18 in. (60–90 × 45 cm). An upright, bushy plant with square, leafy stems with light-green leaves that are toothed and lance-shaped, hairless on top, softly hairy underneath, and about 3 in. (7.5 cm) long. Unbranched spikes of bright-blue flowers bloom for about a month in midsummer. Although it tends to look rather ragged by late summer, this excellent plant for a dry sunny border deserves to be more widely grown. 'Blue Beauty' grows to 18 in. (45 cm) tall. Zones 3–9.

OENOTHERA

(Evening Primrose, Sundrops)

Family: Onagraceae

Oenothera speciosa

About 80 species of annual, biennial, and perennial plants chiefly native to North America; most have alternate leaves and cup-shaped flowers of yellow, pink, or white. Some have flowers that open in the evening and are called, not surprisingly, evening primroses, while most open in daylight and are called sundrops. The name ***Oenothera*** is derived from the Greek *oinos,* "wine," and *thera,* "hunt," in reference to the ancient practice of eating the roots to stimulate a thirst for wine.

Cultivation: Grow in well-drained soil that is not overly fertile, in full sun. Many are good plants for hot climates, although they will require water during dry summers. Remove the flowering stems after blooming.

Landscape Use: Summer-blooming plants of great floral charm but with a lax, inelegant form. Many are good for the front or middle of the border growing amid other plants that have more gracious foliage.

Propagation: Divide or sow seed in spring or autumn.

O. missouriensis. Ozark sundrop. South and central United States. Height 1 ft; spread 18 in. (30 × 45 cm). A sprawling, spreading plant with reddish stems and mid-green lance-shaped leaves up to 6 in. (15 cm) in length, and red-spotted flower buds opening on a summer afternoon to yellow cup-shaped flowers up to 5 in. (12.5 cm) across. 'Greencourt Lemon' has lemon-yellow flowers. Divide after flowering or sow seed in autumn. Zones 4–8.

O. odorata. South America. Height 2–3 ft; spread 2 ft (60–90 × 60 cm). An evening primrose with a woody base and basal rosettes of mid-green leaves. The leafy stem has 6-in.- (15-cm-) long stalkless, lance-shaped leaves with wavy edges. Red buds open to fragrant, single pale-yellow flowers up to 3 in. (7.5 cm) across. Variety ***sulphurea*** has deeper yellow flowers. Because the flowers open only sporadically during daytime and fully at night, this species is best grown among more attractive perennials. Zones 5–8.

O. perennis. Eastern North America. Height 18 in.; spread 12 in. (45 × 30 cm). An invasive species with lance-shaped to spoon-shaped leaves forming a basal clump. Leafy flower stems bear masses of small yellow flowers in summer. Zones 4–9.

O. pilosella. Central United States. Height 1–2 ft; spread 18 in. (30–60 × 45 cm). A spreading, erect plant with hairy stems and rounded, lance-shaped lower leaves to 4 in. (10 cm) long, becoming thinner and pointed higher up the stem. Pale-yellow day-blooming flowers with veined petals are borne in the leaf axils in early summer. Zones 4–8.

O. speciosa. Southern North America. Height 12–18 in.; spread 24 in. (30–45 × 60 cm). An aggressively spreading plant with linear lance-shaped, lobed leaves to 3 in. (7.5 cm) long. In early summer 2-in.- (5-cm.-) wide, cup-shaped, pale-pink flowers are borne in the leaf axils. The delicate pink tones of the flowers are wonderful with the deep-blue spikes of ***Salvia × superba,*** but don't be too easily seduced; this is a very assertive plant. 'Rosea' has more consistently pink flowers. Zones 5–8.

O. tetragona. Sundrops. Eastern North America. Height 2 ft; spread 18 in. (60 × 45 cm). Often listed as synonymous with ***O. fruticosa,*** this prolifically flowering species has red, hairy stems with egg-shaped to lance-shaped, dark-green stalkless leaves to 3 in. (7.5 cm) in length. Terminal clusters of bright-yellow, cup-shaped, day-blooming flowers are produced in summer. 'Fireworks,' height 18 in. (45 cm), has red stems and buds and bright-yellow flowers; 'Yellow River,' height 18 in. (45 cm), has 2-in.- (5-cm.-) wide canary-yellow flowers. Zones 4–8.

OMPHALODES

(Navelwort)

FAMILY: Boraginaceae

A small genus of annual and perennial plants native to the Mediterranean, East Asia, and Mexico. The seed, which is hollowed on one side, looks like the human navel. They have basal or alternate leaves and white or blue flowers similar to large forget-me-nots.

CULTIVATION: Plant in a cool site in leafy soil in partial shade. Remove the faded flowers to prolong the blooming period.

LANDSCAPE USE: Charming and underused plants for edging in the shady garden or rock garden.

PROPAGATION: Divide in spring. Sow seeds in summer.

O. cappadocica. Asia Minor. Height 6–9 in; spread 12 in. (15–22.5 × 30 cm). A spreading species with egg-shaped, hairy, long-stemmed, bright-green leaves up to 4 in. (10 cm) long and sprays of bright sky-blue flowers in early spring. Variety ***alba*** has white flowers. 'Anthea Bloom' has clear-blue flowers that are darker than the species. Zones 6–9.

O. luciliae. Greece, Asia Minor. Height 4–6 in.; spread 12 in. (10–15 × 30 cm). A lime-loving rock-garden plant that forms tufts of egg-shaped to oblong gray-green leaves and sprays of pale-blue flowers from pink buds in spring. Needs more sun than other cultivated species. Protect from winter wet. Zones 4–9.

O. verna. Blue-eyed Mary. Southern Europe. Height 6–8 in.; spread 12 in. (15–20 × 30 cm). A spreading, trailing plant with egg-shaped, long-stemmed, noticeably veined basal leaves. They remain evergreen in mild climates. White-eyed deep-blue flowers are produced in spring and early summer. Variety ***alba*** has white flowers. Favored by slugs. Zones 6–9.

ONOCLEA

(Sensitive Fern)

FAMILY: Aspleniaceae

One species of hardy deciduous fern native to North America, Europe, and northern Asia. It is named sensitive fern because of its sensitivity to cold, which causes it to turn brown after cool spring

Onoclea sensibilis

nights or early-autumn frosts. The name Onoclea, from the Greek "closed vessel," refers to the tightly rolled capsules covering the spores.

Cultivation: Plant in moist soil in sun or shade. The brighter the light, the wetter the soil should be.

Landscape Use: A robust groundcover for shady streambanks or woodland gardens.

Propagation: Divide in spring or autumn, sow spores in early autumn.

O. sensibilis. Sensitive fern. North America, Nothern Europe, and Asia. Height 1–2 ft; spread 2 ft (30–60 × 60 cm). A long-stemmed fern with two types of leaves (dimorphic). The broader "ferny" leaves are sterile. They are pale green, roundly triangular in outline, and coarsely segmented. They appear in spring, followed by the fertile fronds in midsummer. The fertile fronds are upright and dark brown, composed of beadlike segments that are a protective covering for the spores. Zones 3–8.

OPHIOPOGON

(Mondo Grass)

Family: Liliaceae

A small genus of about ten species similar to ***Liriope,*** with which it is often confused. The differences are fairly clear, as mondo grass is less hardy, has narrower leaves, and metallic blue fruits. The name is from the Greek for "snake's beard," a translation of the Japanese name.

Ophiopogon planiscapus var nigrescens

Cultivation: Grow in moist but well-drained soil in partial shade. Full sun is tolerated, but some shade is preferred.

Landscape Use: Slow to establish, but after two years they make good groundcovers and edging plants. Black mondo grass is particularly effective between paving stones or as an edging plant. Dramatic in combination with Japanese blood grass, ***Imperata cylindrica*** 'Red Baron.'

Propagation: Divide in spring and early autumn. Sow seed in spring.

O. japonicus. Mondo grass. Japan. Height 12 in.; spread 9–12 in. (30 × 22.5–30 cm). A spreading, clump-forming plant with dark-green, grassy leaves about ¼ in. (0.6 cm) wide and 12 in. (30 cm) long. Pale-lilac flowers appearing in summer are often hidden by the leaves. The variety ***variegatus*** has white-edged leaves. 'Nana' (Kyoto) grows to a height of 4 in. (10 cm) and has very pale flowers; 'Shiroshima Ryu' grows to 6 in. (15 cm) tall and has white-striped leaves. Zones 7–9.

O. planiscapus var. ***nigrescens.*** Black mondo grass. Height 6 in.; spread 12 in. (15 × 30 cm). Slowly spreading clumps of dark-purple, almost black leaves, with white flowers that are tinted pale pink in summer followed by black berries in autumn. Contrasts beautifully with light-green, large-leaved plants or blue grasses. Zones 6–9.

ORIGANUM

(Marjoram)

Family: Libiatae

Origanum rotundifolium

Twenty or so species of aromatic plants native to the Mediterranean, southeastern Europe, and parts of Asia. The stems are square, the leaves are opposite, and the lipped and lobed flowers are often surrounded by overlapping bracts. Some are grown for their culinary contributions, others for their charming summer-blooming tubular flowers. The name is from the Greek and is said to mean "delight of the mountains."

Cultivation: Grow in well-drained soil in a sunny, sheltered location. They are hardier than often thought, but they do suffer from rot brought on by winter wet and should be grown in as well-drained a site as possible.

Landscape Use: Underused rock-garden plants for a warm and sunny corner.

Propagation: Take cuttings in summer or divide in spring.

O. amanum. Turkey. Height 6–8 in.; spread 8 in. (15–20 × 20 cm). A deciduous subshrub with pale-green, heart-shaped leaves and pale-pink tubular flowers with purple-pink bracts produced throughout the summer. Very susceptible to damage from wet conditions. Zones 5–8.

O. dictamnus. Greece. Height 1 ft; spread 1 ft (30 × 30 cm). A wiry plant with arching stems and rounded grayish white leaves 1 in. (2.5 cm) long.

Nodding heads of purplish pink flowers with leafy bracts are produced in open panicles in mid- to late summer. Zones 7–9.

O. laevigatum. Turkey. Height 12 in.; spread 8 in. (30 × 20 cm). A spreading subshrub with dark-green, lance-shaped aromatic leaves and branching red stems with masses of tubular purple-pink flowers surrounded by purple-red bracts in summer. 'Hopley's' has purple-pink flowers blooming in late summer to late autumn. Zones 5–8.

O. libanoticum. Turkey. Height 12 in.; spread 8 in. (30 × 20 cm). This species has the longest clusters of bracts of the genus. The leaves are mid-green and roundly lance-shaped. The flowers are pink but are covered by 4-in.- (10-cm.-) long, apple-green bracts flushed pink held on arching stems. A very desirable plant. Zones 6–9.

O. pulchellum. Southeastern Europe. Height 8 in.; spread 8 in. (20 × 20 cm). A wiry plant with egg-shaped leaves ¾ in. (1.8 cm) long and nodding heads of tubular pink flowers surrounded by large yellow-green, papery bracts. Zones 5–8.

O. rotundifolium. Turkey. Height 9–12 in.; spread 12 in. (22.5–30 × 30 cm). A clump-forming plant with wiry stems and rounded, heart-shaped leaves in stem-clasping pairs. Whorls of large yellow-green bracts and small pink flowers are borne in drooping spikes at the end of the stems throughout the summer. 'Kent Beauty,' a hybrid, has rounded leaves and spikes of pale-pink flowers with dark-pink bracts. Zones 4–8.

OSMUNDA

(Royal Fern, Cinnamon Fern)

Family: Osmundaceae

About ten species of large, deciduous, slow-growing ferns with sterile and fertile leaves produced from substantial crowns. Three species are widely grown for their unfolding croziers in spring, their attractive fertile fronds, and their large, coarse, sterile leaves. The Royal Fern, *Osmunda regalis,* is called Osmund the Waterman from a legend that the wife and daughter of a Scots waterman took refuge among the ferns during an invasion by the Danes. There have been a number of attempts at determining the derivation of the Latin name; one is that it comes from the Saxon name for the god Thor (Osmunda); another is that it is derived from the Latin *os,* for "bone," and *mundare,* "to cleanse," a reference to its medicinal value.

Cultivation: Grow in moist, acid soil in partial shade.

Landscape Use: Handsome ferns for streamside, bog garden, or damp woodland.

Propagation: Divide the crowns in spring. Sow spores when ripe in late spring and early summer.

O. cinnamomea. Cinnamon fern. Transglobal. Height 3 ft; spread 18 in. (90 × 45 cm). Groups of three and four fertile croziers first unfold in spring. These are erect fronds with cinnamon-brown spore capsules resembling cinnamon sticks. The large and coarse sterile fronds unfold after the fertile ones. They are light to deep green, lance-shaped in outline, with divided leaf segments (pinnae). The sterile, ferny fronds surround the fertile stick until midsummer, when the fertile fronds whither and drop to the ground. Zones 4–9.

O. claytoniana. Interrrupted fern. Height 3 ft; spread 18 in. (90 × 45 cm). Two or more pairs of fertile fronds first unfold in spring to be followed by large, coarse, and leathery sterile fronds forming the outer circle of the plant. They are oblong to lance-shaped in outline, yellow-green to dark green in color. The brown fertile fronds have erect stems. The bottom half has fertile leaf segments growing thinly and sporadically until they fill out to form a brown "feather" at the top. Zones 4–9.

O. regalis. Royal fern. Height 3–4 ft; spread 18 in. (90–120 × 45 cm). A slowly spreading fern that is best grown in wet soil in full sun to partial shade. The light-green fronds are sterile, divided, and lance-shaped in outline with the leaf segments resembling the leaves of the ash tree. The brown flowerlike fertile top unfolds in summer. A large mass of royal ferns with their feet at the edge of a pond is a magnificent sight. Zones 4–9.

OURISIA

Family: Scrophulariaceae

A genus of about 25 low-growing evergreen perennials native to the mountains of South America, New Zealand, and Tasmania. The leaves are mostly basal, sometimes opposite and toothed. The flowers are mostly white but also come in purple and scarlet. They bloom in the spring and summer in cool climates. Named for Governor Ouris of the Malvinas.

Cultivation: Grow in acid, fertile, moist but well-drained soil in partial shade.

Landscape Use: Floriferous plants for the sheltered and shaded rock garden.

Propagation: Divide or sow seed in spring.

O. caespitosa. New Zealand. Height 1 in.; spread 4 in. (2.5 × 10 cm). A prostrate, mat-forming plant with oval leaves and cup-shaped, lobed, and outward-facing white flowers in spring. Zones 6–7.

O. macrocarpa. New Zealand. Height 2 ft; spread 8 in. (60 × 20 cm). A thick-stemmed plant with rosettes of dark-green, 8-in.- (20-cm.-) long, leathery leaves and spikes of cup-shaped, white, yellow-eyed flowers in spring. Zones 7–8.

OXALIS

(Wood Sorrel)

Family: Oxalidaceae

Oxalis adenophylla

An enormous genus of about 850 species native to much of the world but concentrated in South Africa and South America. A number are monstrous weeds, but some are exquisite rock-garden plants.

They come in all shapes and sizes, ranging from tiny groundcovers to shrubs. They are bulbous, rhizomatous, or tuberous, with alternate or basal leaves often divided into cloverlike leaflets. The flowers come in a great range of colors and bloom in spring and summer. The name comes from the Greek *oxys,* meaning "sour" or "sharp," a reference to the rhubarblike taste of the leaves.

Cultivation: Grow in well-drained soil enriched with organic matter, in sun or partial shade.

Landscape Use: A few are fine woodland plants while others can be grown in the rock garden or alpine house to show off their delicate cup-shaped flowers and angular foliage.

Propagation: Divide and replant in spring.

O. acetosella. Wood sorrel. Northern hemisphere. Height 3 in.; spread 12–18 in. (7.5×30–45 cm). A creeping, delicate plant with red-scaled rhizomatous rootstocks and thin, dainty leaves divided into three bright-green, heart-shaped leaflets, purplish blue underneath. The leaflets are particularly sensitive and fold up in strong sunlight, at night, and during storms. The white flowers, borne on long stems in spring, are cup-shaped, ½ in. (1.2 cm) across, and five-petaled, veined with purple. 'Rosea' has soft-pink flowers with darker veins. Zones 5–8.

O. adenopylla. Chile. Height 2 in.; spread 4 in. (5×10 cm). A tufted perennial with a bulblike, tuberous rootstock and gray-green, crinkled leaves divided into many narrow leaflets ½ in. (1.2 cm) long. In spring are produced flowers 1 in. (2.5 cm) across, cup-shaped, veined, and purple-pink with a dark-purple eye. Zones 7–9.

O. laciniata. Patagonia. Height 2 in.; spread 3 in. (5×7.5 cm). A tufted plant with blue-green leaves divided into nine to 12 crinkled leaflets. The 1-in.- (2.5-cm.-) wide fragrant flowers are trumpet-shaped, lavender-blue with darker veins, and produced in summer. Zones 7–9.

O. tetraphylla (O. deppei). Mexico. Height 8 in.; spread 6 in. (20×15 cm). A tuft-forming, tuberous plant with basal leaves divided into four rounded leaflets 1½ in. (3.8 cm) long marked with purple bands. Funnel-shaped purple-pink flowers are produced in late spring and early summer. Requires a warm, sheltered site. Zones 7–9.

PACHYSANDRA

(Spurge)

Family: Buxaceae

Six species of herbaceous or subshrubby plants. One is native to North America, the others are indigenous to northeastern Asia. One species, the Japanese spurge, is extensively planted as a groundcover for shaded areas. Although it is an easy plant to cultivate and admirably fulfills its purpose, it is so widely planted that it has become boring. The name ***Pachysandra*** comes from the Greek *pachys,* "thick," and *andros,* "man," referring to the thick stamens of the male flowers. The leaves are alternate, usually whorled. The flowers are petalless and creamy white, appearing in spring.

Cultivation: Grow in fertile, well-drained soil in partial to full shade. Susceptible to various fungus diseases and the ravages of Euonymus scale.

Landscape Use: The term groundcover may well have been invented for the Japanese spurge. The North American Allegheny spurge is a more subtle plant useful in conjunction with spring wildflowers.

Propagation: Divide in spring.

P. axillaris. Asia. Height 8 in.; spread 12 in. (20×30 cm). A mat-forming, evergreen species with whorls of three to six dark-green, leathery and toothed leaves with the erect spikes of white flowers produced from the leaf axils in late spring. Zones 5–9.

P. procumbens. Allegheny spurge. Southeastern United States. Height 12 in.; spread 12 in. (30×30 cm). A little-known plant that deserves greater fame. The 2–4-in.- (5–10-cm.-) long green leaves mottled purple appear like wind-blown umbrellas on stems 4 in. (10 cm) long. The whitish flowers are produced at ground level in spring. The flowers are a curious and interesting sight if the partly evergreen leaves are removed before the flowers bloom. While not as effective as its Asian counterparts, Allegheny spurge can become a substantial groundcover if divided every two or three years. Zones 5–9.

P. terminalis. Japanese spurge. Height 12 in.; spread 18 in. (30 × 45 cm). The ubiquitous pachysandra. I hesitate to write too much about it. The alternate but whorled leaves are dark green, 2–3 in. (5–7.5 cm) long, and toothed. Attractive creamy white flowers are produced from the top of the stem in late spring. 'Green Carpet' is a more compact form growing to a height of 8 in. (20 cm); 'Variegata,' with creamy white variegated leaves, is a handsome plant that suffers from leaf scorch in strong sunlight. Zones 4–9.

PAEONIA

(Peony)

Family: Ranunculaceae

Paeonia peregrina 'Sunbeam'

Paeonia veitchii

A small genus of about 33 species of shrubs and herbaceous perennials native from Europe to eastern Asia. They are popular for their large bowl-shaped flowers in spring and their alternate leaves, which remain handsome until the hard frosts of late autumn. Most peonies grown are hybrids and cultivars. There are a great many to choose from, and interested gardeners should consult nurseries specializing in peonies.

Cultivation: Peonies require a well-prepared site with moist but well-drained soil enriched with compost, in full sun. The fleshy roots and the crown where the buds are found should be planted with the buds no deeper than 2 in. (5 cm). A balanced fertilizer, not too high in nitrogen, should be added to the soil in spring and after blooming in early summer. Beware of overfertilizing. Botrytis and leaf spot diseases can be a problem, particularly if the plants are given too much nitrogen. They are not good plants for climates with hot summers, performing spectacularly badly in the southern United States.

Landscape Use: The most boring thing to do with peonies is to grow them all together in a peony garden. They are excellent border plants. Combining them with other perennials often compensates for the short blooming period that many peony cultivars suffer from.

Propagation: Divide the tuberous root, making sure that each piece has two to three buds, and plant in good soil in autumn. Protect the crowns from winter heaving by mulching in early winter.

***P. daurica* (*P. mascula* var. *triternata*).** Yugoslavia to Asia Minor. Height 2 ft; spread 2 ft (60 × 60 cm). This clump-forming plant has stout stems often tinged red and leathery oblong or oval leaves twice divided into threes, with the leaf edges undulating. The single rose-red flowers reach up to 5 in. (12.5 cm) wide and appear in mid- to late spring. Zones 5–9.

P. emodii. Himalayas. Height 2½ ft; spread 2 ft (75 × 60 cm). A mountain peony with several white, nodding flowers up to 5 in. (12.5 cm) wide and lower leaves twice divided into threes, upper leaves three times divided into threes. The leaflets are generally elliptic. The flowers appear in late spring. Mulch for winter protection. Zones 6–8.

P. lactiflora. Chinese peony. Height 18 in.–3½ ft; spread 2–3 ft (45–105 × 60–90 cm). A handsome species notable as the most important source for the thousands of hybrids and cultivars produced since the early 19th century. The species itself has red-brown stems, leaves usually twice divided into threes, and elliptical to lance-shaped leaflets. The white or pink flowers are up to 4 in. (10 cm) wide with a central crown of yellow stamens. Zones 4–8. There are several flower types among the hybrids, including single, semidouble, and anemone-flowered. Pages and pages could be written describing these hybrids and cultivars. I will refrain from doing so, but urge the reader to visit gardens, talk to peony growers, and join peony societies for further information.

P. mlokosewitschii. Central Caucasus. Height 3 ft; spread 2 ft (90 × 60 cm). An excellent peony with bluish green leaves twice divided into threes with the veins and leaf edges often outlined in red. The single lemon-yellow flowers reach up to 5 in. (12.5 cm) wide and are produced in mid-spring. Zones 5–8.

P. peregrina. Southeastern Europe. Height 3 ft; spread 2 ft (90 × 60 cm). A handsome species with glossy green leaves twice divided into threes with the leaflets toothed. Deep-red flowers about 4 in. (10 cm) wide are produced in late spring. 'Sunbeam' has purplish blood-red flowers. Zones 6–8.

P. tenuifolia. Southeastern Europe to Asia Minor. Height 2½ ft; spread 1½ ft (75 × 45 cm). A very different species from the commonly grown peonies, this plant has dark-green, finely divided, ferny foliage and deep-red to purple-red flowers in spring. 'Latifolia' has carmine-red flowers and coarse leaf divisions; 'Plena' has dark-red, double flowers. Zones 5–8.

P. veitchii. China. Height 2½ ft; spread 2 ft (75 × 60 cm). Vigorous clumps of stout stems bearing light-green, glossy leaves divided into oblong leaflets and several 4-in.- (10-cm.-) wide, purple-red flowers in midspring. Zones 6–8.

PANICUM

(Switch-grass)

Family: Graminae

A large genus of annual and perennial grasses with flat leaf blades. Most species are tropical while a few temperate species are used for forage and as ornamental grasses in the garden. Not at the same time, however.

Cultivation: Grow in ordinary soil in full sun.

Landscape Use: Switch-grass is a handsome grass for the midborder or as a low, finely textured screen.

Propagation: Divide in spring or autumn.

P. virgatum. Switch-grass. North to Central America. Height 4–8 ft; spread 2 ft (120–240 × 60 cm).

Panicum virgatum

An upright, clump-forming grass with bluish green to mid-green leaves ½ in. (1.2 cm) wide and feathery masses of green to pink flowers in late summer. Switch-grass is an excellent grass for autumn and winter display, with the autumn leaf color ranging from dusty yellow to purple-red, with the seedheads becoming beautifully straw-yellow. 'Haense Herms' (Rotstrahlbusch) grows to 4½ ft (135 cm), has maroon flowers and deep burgundy-red foliage by early autumn; 'Heavy Metal' grows just over 4 ft (120 cm) and has blue leaves that turn yellow in autumn. It is one of the best of the blue-leaved ornamental grasses. 'Rehbraun' grows to 4 ft (120 cm) and has purple-red autumn color; 'Strictum' grows to 6 ft (180 cm) and forms stiffly upright clumps of light-blue-green foliage that turns purple-red in autumn. Zones 5–9.

PAPAVER

(Poppy)

Family: Papaveraceae

Papaver orientale 'Beauty of Livermore'

Papaver orientale 'Black & White'

A large genus of about 100 species of annual, biennial, and perennial plants, with mostly basal-lobed or dissected leaves and solitary, papery flowers that are crumpled in bud, cup-shaped and four-petaled in flower. Many garden poppies are annuals, such as the corn poppy and opium poppy, or are short-lived perennials, such as the Iceland poppy. The perennial species of value to the gardener is the Oriental poppy and its cultivars. The common name is thought to come from the Saxon *popig,* meaning "sleep," a reference to the opium poppy.

Cultivation: Grow in well-drained soil in full sun. Stake tall cultivars and deadhead after flowering if you do not want them to self-seed. Perennial poppies do poorly in hot climates.

Landscape Use: Spectacular plants for early-summer display. They die down in midsummer, and the empty space should be occupied by summer-blooming perennials such as ***Gypsophila*** species and the many cultivars of ***Aster.***

Propagation: Divide in spring or when the plants are dormant in summer. Take root cuttings in the winter and spring and plant the following year.

P. burseri alpinum. Alps. Height 10 in.; spread 8 in. (25 × 20 cm). There is considerable confusion over the names of a number of species similar to this one; ***P. alpinum*** is often included either as a variety or a species in its own right. For the gardener the differences are too small to be worth the trouble. This species is a tufted plant with gray-green, 2-in.- (5-cm.-) long, finely segmented leaves. The fragrant, white or pink, papery, cup-shaped flowers are 1 in. (2.5 cm) wide and are borne on hairy stems in early summer. This is a short-lived species that self-seeds enthusiastically. Zones 4–7.

P. nudicaule. Iceland poppy. Asia, Arctic. Height 12 in.; spread 6 in. (30 × 15 cm). A short-lived perennial lasting two to three years at best. Gray-green, deeply lobed leaves grow up to 3 in. (7.5 cm) long. The leafless flower stem carries 6-in.- (15-cm.-) wide, fragrant flowers in a wide range of colors in summer. They make fine cut flowers. 'Champagne Bubbles,' height 18 in. (45 cm), is a strain with long-stemmed flowers in mixed pastel shades; 'Iceland Giant,' height 2 ft (60 cm), has 6-in.- (15-cm-) wide blooms in mixed colors; 'Wonderland,' height 16 in. (40 cm), has 3-in.- (7.5-cm.-) diameter flowers in mixed colors. Zones 2–8.

P. orientale. Oriental poppy. Asia. Height 2–4 ft; spread 2–3 ft (60–120 × 60–90 cm). By far the best poppy for the flower garden even though many of them flop all over the place and die down in midsummer. The stems are bristly-hairy and the leaves are lobed, toothed, and roughly hairy, mid- to deep green. The flowers reach up to 4 in. (10 cm) across and are papery and cup-shaped, often arrestingly scarlet in color, with a black eye. There are a number of cultivars, some of which are hybrids.

'Allegro': height 16 in. (40 cm), brilliant-scarlet flowers
'Barr's White': height 3 ft (90 cm), white flowers with a black eye
'Beauty of Livermore': height 3 ft (90 cm), stunningly bright blood-red flowers
'Beauty Queen': height 40 in. (100 cm), apricot-brown flowers
'Black and White': height 2 ft (60 cm), white flowers with six deep-red, almost black blotches
'Bonfire': height 3 ft (90 cm), brilliant-red, crinkled flowers
'Brilliant': height 3 ft (90 cm), fiery red flowers
'Carousel': height 3 ft (90 cm), snow-white flowers with red borders
'China Boy': height 42 in. (105 cm), orange flowers with a white center
'Curlilocks': height 30 in. (75 cm), ruffled orange-red flowers with a black throat
'Fireball': height 1 ft (30 cm), double orange-scarlet flowers
'Glowing Embers': height 30 in. (75 cm), crinkled crimson-red flowers
'Harvest Moon': height 40 in. (100 cm), golden orange, semidouble flowers
'Helen Elizabeth': height 30 in. (75 cm), long-lasting, crinkled salmon-pink flowers
'Lighthouse': height 3 ft (90 cm), light-pink flowers
'Mrs. Perry': height 30 in. (75 cm), salmon-pink flowers
'Perry's White'; 3 ft (90 cm), white flowers, maroon base
'Springtime': height 3 ft (90 cm), white flowers with a broad pink border
'Sultana': height 3 ft (90 cm), shiny pink flowers
'Warlord': height 40 in. (100 cm), deep-crimson flowers
Zones 3–8.

PARIS

(Herb Paris)

FAMILY: Liliaceae

Twenty species of curious rather than ornamental plants indigenous to woods and mountainous regions of Europe and Asia, closely related to ***Trillium*** but differing in having their floral parts in fours rather than threes. The name comes from the Latin *par,* meaning "equal," referring to the regularity of the leaves and flowers. More interestingly, the great American botanist Liberty Hyde Bailey suggests that the berries and leaves symbolize the apple of discord, with Paris and the goddesses Juno, Minerva, and Venus surrounding it.

CULTIVATION: Grow in damp, acid, leafy soil in partial to full shade.

LANDSCAPE USE: Rare and curiously formed, long-flowering plants for the woodland garden or shady border.

Propagation: Divide in spring or sow seed in autumn.

P. polyphylla. Himalayas. Height 2–3 ft; spread 18 in. (60–90×45 cm). Not a common plant but one worth growing if you can get hold of it. It is desirable for its long summer blooming period. The rootstock is rhizomatous, the stems are slender and bare and are topped with a whorl of dark-green, 6-in.- (15-cm-) long, pointed, egg-shaped, and veined leaves. Peculiar spidery flowers are borne just above the whorl of leaves and consist of a collar of leaflike sepals with a circle of yellow stringlike petals. It is weird but wonderful. Zones 5–8.

P. quadrifolia. Herb paris. Height 12 in.; spread 8 in. (30×20 cm). A smooth-stemmed plant crowned with a whorl of four-pointed, dark-green and veined leaves. Unpleasant-smelling four-parted, greenish white flowers appear in late spring and early summer followed by bluish black berries in autumn. Formerly widely used in medicine as a narcotic. Zones 4–8.

Paris polyphylla

PATRINIA

Family: Valerianaceae

Patrinia triloba

Fifteen species of Asian plants with clumps of opposite or basal leaves and clusters of yellow or white flowers in summer. Named after the French naturalist E. L. Patrin (1724–1815).

Cultivation: Grow in acid, moist but well-drained soil in light shade.

Landscape Use: Little-grown plants useful for their summer-blooming yellow flowers in the mixed border or rock garden.

Propagation: Divide in spring or sow seed in autumn.

P. gibbosa. Japan. Height 2 ft; spread 1 ft (60 × 30 cm). A clump-forming plant with erect stems and divided, coarsely toothed, 6-in.- (15-cm.-) long, broadly egg-shaped leaves. Branched clusters of lemon-yellow flowers are produced throughout the summer. Zones 4–8.

P. scabiosifolia. Eastern Asia. Height 3 ft; spread 18 in. (90 × 45 cm). Erect, leafy stems with divided and coarsely toothed hairy leaves 6 in. (15 cm) long; the basal leaves are egg-shaped to oblong, the stem leaves are divided into segments, with the terminal segment longer than the others. Open clusters of lemon-yellow flowers are produced in summer. Zones 5–8.

P. triloba. Japan. Height 2 ft; spread 1 ft (60 × 30 cm). Erect and wiry brown stems, with fan-shaped, three-lobed or divided, coarsely toothed leaves and clusters of golden yellow flowers borne from the leaf axils but held above the foliage in summer. The variety ***palmata*** has hand-shaped (palmate) leaves. Zones 5–8.

PELTIPHYLLUM (DARMERA)

(Umbrella Plant)

FAMILY: Saxifragaceae

One species native to wet soils of southwest Oregon and northern California with large umbrellalike leaves. The name is from the Greek *pelta,* "shield," and *phyllon,* "leaf," and is a reference to the shape of the leaf. Sometimes listed under the genus *Darmera.*

CULTIVATION: Grow in constantly moist soil in shade.

LANDSCAPE USE: A grand but coarse plant for the streamside or bog garden. Effective with primulas, ligularias, and other water-loving plants.

PROPAGATION: Divide in spring.

P. pelatatum (Darmera peltata). Umbrella plant. Western North America. Height 2–4 ft; spread 3 ft (60–120 × 90 cm). A large, clump-forming species with round, lobed, and toothed leaves up to 18 in. (45 cm) across, borne on thick and hairy leaf stems, with the stem attached to the center of the leaf like a handle on an umbrella (peltate). Short, broad clusters of pale-pink flowers appear in spring before the leaves develop. 'Nana' grows to 18 in. (45 cm) tall and is an excellent foliage plant for the small garden. Zones 6–8.

Peltiphyllum peltatum

PELTOBOYKINIA

FAMILY: Saxifragaceae

Two species of large and coarse water-loving plants with long-stemmed, round leaves.

CULTIVATION: Grow in moist soil in shade.

LANDSCAPE USE: Attractive foliage plants for the bog or stream garden.

PROPAGATION: Divide in spring.

P. tellimoides. Japan. Height 2 ft; spread 2 ft (60 × 60 cm). Similar to ***Peltiphyllum*** and ***Boykinia,*** hence the name. The basal leaves are rounded, lobed, and 6 in. (15 cm) across, with the leaf stems connected to the leaves in the center. The flowers are white and larger than ***Peltiphyllum pelatatum,*** and, like that plant, they bloom in spring before the leaves develop. Zones 5–8.

PENNISETUM

(Fountain Grass)

Family: Graminae

Pennisetum alopecuroides 'Hameln'

A large genus of annual and perennial grasses, the majority of which are native to the tropics. A few warm-season hardy species and their cultivars are quickly becoming popular ornamental grasses, useful for their arching foliage and attractive, bristly flowers in late summer and autumn. The name comes from the Latin *penna* "feather," and *seta,* "bristly," referring to the flower form.

Cultivation: Grow in full sun or light shade in well-drained soil. Tolerant of a wide range of soil types. Some are likely to self-seed and can be quite invasive in some areas.

Landscape Use: Generally fine-textured grasses for use in the border as contrasts for coarser plants. The flowers can be very fine either on a specimen plant or en masse and are particularly beautiful on dewy mornings. Fountain grass is useful when grown in combination with the coarser daisies or stronger-toned perennials.

Propagation: Divide in spring or sow seed in autumn.

P. alopecuroides. Fountain grass. Eastern Asia. Height 2–4 ft; spread 18–24 in. (60–120 × 45–60 cm). The hardy fountain grass is gaining increasing respect from gardeners for its ease of cultivation and for its ornamental grace. It is a mound-forming grass with shiny, arching, mid-green leaves and upright, 6-in.- (15-cm.-) long, green, white, or purple flower spikes. The earliest forms bloom in midsummer, the latest in midautumn. The flowers and foliage fade to tan in winter but often remain attractive for much of that season. Variety ***caudatum*** has gray-white flowers. Forma ***purpurascens*** has purplish flowers. 'Hameln' is an excellent dwarf cultivar, growing to a height of 3 ft (90 cm), with foliage producing a mound up to 20 in. (50 cm) tall. Arching sprays of near-white flowers in midsummer remain attractive until late autumn. The foliate turns golden yellow in autumn. 'Moudry' grows to 3 ft (90 cm), is far less graceful than 'Hameln,' and has stiff, bottlebrushlike, dark-purple flowers that are produced from the center of the mound of glossy foliage; 'Weserbergland' is very similar to 'Hameln' but grows to a height of about 3½ ft (105 cm). Zones 5–9.

P. incomptum. Eastern Asia. Height 4 ft; spread 2 ft (120 × 60 cm). A highly invasive, coarse-leaved grass for use as erosion control or in a garden site where its conquest can be restricted. It is an upright species with mounds of bluish green foliage up to 2½ ft (75 cm) in height. Slender spikes of 5-in.- (12.5-cm.-) long, off-white flowers are borne on stiff, 18-in.- (45-cm.-) long stems in midsummer to early autumn. Zones 6–9.

P. orientale. North Africa, Asia, India. Height 2 ft; spread 18 in. (60 × 45 cm). A clump-forming grass of great beauty. The light-green leaves form an attractive mound. Masses of white, flushed-pink flowers are produced in delicate spikes in midsummer to midautumn. Clean up the faded foliage by cutting back no lower than 6 in. (15 cm) in winter or early spring. Carefully divide in spring. Zones 7–9.

P. setaceum. Africa. Height 4 ft; spread 2 ft (120 × 60 cm). Although hardy only in Zones 8–10, this beautiful grass can be grown outside in temperate areas if it is overwintered inside. It should be brought inside and potted before the onset of frost. It is a clump-forming grass with narrow, green, arching leaves and nodding spikes of purplish pink flowers in summer to autumn. The cultivars 'Cupreum,' 'Rubrum,' and 'Atrosanguineum' are synonymous. The foliage is a striking reddish purple, while the flowers are a slightly darker red-purple. Propagate by division only. 'Burgundy Giant' is also fully hardy only in Zones 8–10, but farther north can be a plant for summer display if overwintered inside. It is a large grass with burgundy-red leaves over 1 in. (2.5 cm) wide, forming bold clumps up to 6 ft (180 cm) high. The burgundy flowers reach 7 ft (210 cm) high and begin to appear in midsummer continuing until frost. It can be propagated by stem cuttings or by division. Zones 8–10.

PENSTEMON

(Beard-Tongue)

Family: Scrophulariaceae

Penstemon digitalis

About 250 species of annual, perennial, and shrubby plants, many of which are difficult to cultivate outside of their natural habitats. One species is native to northeast Asia; the rest are indigenous to North America, many of them to the western United States, where many are outstanding garden plants. Those that can be grown successfully in gardens are generally short-lived but very beautiful plants, with opposite leaves, the lower leaves with stalks, the upper leaves without, and snapdragonlike flowers with five petals and five stamens. They come in a rich range of colors from white, pink, blue, purple, to scarlet. There are many cultivars. The genus comes from the Greek, meaning "five stamens."

CULTIVATION: Grow in well-drained, fertile soil in full sun.

LANDSCAPE USE: Brightly colored flowers for the rock garden or sunny border.

PROPAGATION: Sow seed or take cuttings of non-flowering shoots in midsummer.

P. alpinus. Rocky Mountains. Height 12 in.; spread 6 in. (30 × 15 cm). A tufted plant with lance-shaped leaves up to 4 in. (10 cm) long and spikes of clear-blue, white-throated flowers in early summer. Requires a sunny and well-drained site. Zones 4–7.

P. barbatus. Beard-tongue. Southwestern United States. Height 2–3 ft; spread 18 in. (60–90 × 45 cm). An erect plant with basal tufts of mid-green leaves that are oblong to egg-shaped, up to 6 in. (15 cm) long, becoming lance-shaped and smaller up on the stem. Spikes of slightly nodding, tubular, 1-in.- (2.5-cm.-) long scarlet flowers with a bearded lower lip are produced in late spring to midsummer. 'Bashful' grows to a height of 14 in. (35 cm) and has orange flowers; 'Crystal' grows to 14 in. (35 cm) and has white flowers; 'Praecox Nanus' grows to a height of 12 in (30 cm) and flowers in late spring with scarlet flowers; 'Prairie Dawn' grows to a height of 18 in. (45 cm) and has pale-pink flowers; 'Rose Elf' grows to a height of about 18 in. (45 cm) and has rose-pink flowers. Zones 3–8.

P. campanulatus. Central America. Height 2 ft; spread 18–24 in. (60 × 45–60 cm). A seldom-grown species with linear to lance-shaped, toothed and pointed leaves, and purple, violet, or white flowers. Zones 7–9. This species is crossed with ***P. barbatus, P. hartwegii,*** and others to produce a number of very good garden plants. 'Alice Hindley' has deep-pink flowers with a white throat, Zones 8–9; 'Apple Blossom' has pale-pink flowers, Zones 6–9; 'Evelyn' has rose-pink flowers, Zones 6–9; 'Garnet has burgundy-red flowers, Zones 7–9; 'Pennington Gem' flowers at a height of about 2 ft (60 cm), and has warm-pink flowers, Zones 6–9. Grow in well-drained soil and mulch for winter protection.

P. confertus. Northwestern North America. Height 18 in.; spread 12 in. (45 × 30 cm). A clump-forming species requiring a mild climate. The leaves are lance-shaped up to 2 in. (5 cm) long. The tubular flowers are pale yellow and are produced in early summer. Zones 7–9.

P. digitalis. Eastern United States. Height 3 ft; spread 2 ft (90 × 60 cm). An erect, clump-forming plant native to open meadows, with elliptic to broadly lance-shaped basal leaves becoming narrower and smaller up on the flower stem. Spikes of bell-shaped, white flowers sometimes flushed pink are produced in early summer. This is a variable species. 'Husker Red' has purple-red leaves, red stems, and white-flushed purple flowers and is a highly desirable cultivar. In general, this species and its cultivar are far easier to grow in hot and humid climates than their western relatives. Zones 3–9.

P. hartwegii. Mexico. Height 2 ft; spread 1 ft (60 × 30 cm). An upright species with mid-green, egg-shaped to lance-shaped leaves up to 4 in. (10 cm) long and drooping, bell-shaped scarlet flowers in summer. This species has been crossed with ***P. cobaea*** to produce a strain of tender cultivars sometimes referred to as ***P.* × *gloxinioides.*** These can be grown as annuals in Zones 4–7 or as perennials in Zones 8–9. 'Firebird' has deep-red flowers; 'King George' has crimson-scarlet flowers with a white throat; 'Sour Grapes' has purple flowers.

P. smallii. Southeastern United States. Height 3 ft; spread 1–2 ft (90 × 30–60 cm). A bushy, erect plant with serrated elliptic or egg-shaped basal leaves and lance-shaped stem leaves. Tubular, pinkish violet flowers with a white-striped throat are produced in early summer. Zones 4–8.

PEROVSKIA

(Russian Sage)

FAMILY: Labiatae

A small genus of aromatic subshrubs native from Iran to northwest India. The leaves are opposite, dissected, or toothed. The blue flowers are held in short panicles or spikes and are lipped and lobed.

They appear in late summer. The plant commonly grown in North America as Russian sage is a hybrid between ***P. atriplicifolia*** and ***P. abrotanoides.*** It is an extremely variable hybrid that produces seedlings with undissected to filigreed leaves and purple-blue flowers. Named after B. A. Perovski, a governor of the Russian province of Orenburg.

CULTIVATION: Grow in full sun in well-drained soil. Cut the plants back hard in early spring to produce a bushy, free-flowering plant.

LANDSCAPE USE: Late-flowering sprays of blue flowers are wonderful stalwarts for the sunny border or dry bank. The smoky blue flowers and fine foliage make ***Perovskia*** an excellent plant for the herbaceous border, particularly in association with daylilies and daisies of all kinds.

PROPAGATION: Take cuttings in summer.

P. abrotanoides. Height 3–4 ft; spread 2 ft (90–120 × 60 cm). A lax, flopping plant with branching stems and silvery, gray-green, finely divided, linear to oblong leaves to 2 in. (5 cm) long. Panicles of purplish blue flowers appear in late summer. Rare in cultivation but important for its contribution to ***P. × hybrida.*** Zones 5–9.

P. atriplicifolia. Russian sage. Height 3–4 ft; spread 2–3 ft (90–120 × 60–90 cm). Light-green, lance- to egg-shaped leaves up to 2 in. (5 cm) long, slightly toothed but not deeply cut on silvery, square, and stiffly erect stems. Spikes of long-lasting lavender-blue flowers appear in summer to late summer. Zones 5–9.

Perovskia x hybrida

P. × hybrida. Height 3–4 ft; spread 2–3 ft (90–120 × 60–90 cm). A widely grown summer-flowering subshrub with variably cut and toothed leaves that range from being barely dentated to finely divided. Purple-blue flowers are produced in summer. The range of form and foliage is extensive, some plants are lightly bushy with masses of flowers while others are rangy, poor things. Further selection and vegetative propagation is necessary. 'Blue Haze' has light-blue flowers and lightly toothed leaves; 'Blue Spire' has finely dissected leaves and an upright habit; 'Longen' has barely dissected foliage and purple-blue flowers. Zones 5–9.

PERSICARIA

(Knotweed, Fleeceflower)

FAMILY: Polygonaceae

Until recently fleeceflower was placed in the genus ***Polygonum.*** It has now been redirected to ***Persicaria*** and ***Fallopia,*** with most herbaceous perennials now grouped under this genus. It is also called knotweed because of its many joints or knots, which are swollen nodes. This is a large genus of annual and perennial plants, including a few woody-stemmed vines. The stems are jointed, with the Latin name referring to the joints in the stems. The leaves are alternate, the flowers petalless, held in cylindrical spikes or sometimes fleecy masses of white, pink, or red flowers in summer. They tend to be invasive, with a few species so rampant as to completely take over a garden. These will not be described in the following text; however, gardeners should be wary of ***P. cuspidatum*** and ***P. sachalinense,*** as they are almost impossible to eradicate once established.

CULTIVATION: Grow in rich, moist soil in sun or partial shade. They do best in climates with cool summers and are prone to scorching in the heat of the midday sun. Japanese beetles may develop an unseemly fondness for some of the species.

LANDSCAPE USE: Coarse-leaved plants for the sunny

Persicaria bistorta 'Superbum'

border, as groundcovers, or as contrast plants. Their unusual flowers and often deep-red coloring make them valuable additions to the herbaceous border.

Propagation: Divide in spring or autumn.

P. affinis (Polygonum affine). Himalayas. Height 12 in.; spread 12 in. (30 × 30 cm). A mat-forming, spreading plant with semiwoody stems. The leaves are dark green, glossy, lance-shaped, and up to 4 in. (10 cm) long, tapering toward the leaf stem. They turn bronze in the autumn and remain on the plant until fresh green leaves are produced in spring. The pinkish red flowers appear in summer to early autumn and are held in dense, 2–3-in.- (5–7-cm.-) tall, terminal spikes above the foliage. 'Border Jewel' grows to about 10 in. (25 cm) tall and has pale pink-and-white flowers; 'Darjeeling Red' has pink flowers turning to crimson; 'Donald Lowndes' grows to about 10 in. (25 cm) tall, with pinkish red flowers that darken with age; 'Superbum' has pale-pink flowers that age to crimson. Zones 3–8.

P. amplexicaulis (Polygonum amplexicaule). Himalayas. Height 4 ft; spread 4 ft (120 × 120 cm). A large, leafy plant with deep-green, egg-shaped to heart-shaped, pointed leaves up to 6 in. (15 cm) long and numerous thin, 6-in. (15-cm) spikes of rich-red flowers in late summer and autumn. The variety ***astrosanguineum*** has crimson flowers; var. ***oxyphyllum*** has pale-pink flowers; var. ***roseum*** has rosy pink flowers. There are some very fine cultivars: 'Album' grows to a height of 2–3 ft (60–90 cm) and has white flowers; 'Arun Gem' grows to 12 in. (30 cm) and has bright-pink flowers; 'Firetail' grows to 4 ft (120 cm) and has bright-scarlet flower spikes; 'Inverleith' grows to just 20 in. (50 cm) and has 4-in.- (10-cm.-) long, red flower spikes; 'Speciosum' reaches 4 ft (120 cm) and has pinkish-red flowers. Zones 5–9.

P. bistorta 'Superbum' ***(Polygonum bistorta).*** Europe, Asia. Height 2–3 ft; spread 2 ft (60–90 × 60 cm). A clump-forming, vigorous plant with 6–10-in.- (15–25-cm.-) long, light- to medium-green, wavy leaves with a prominent white midrib. In early summer 4-in. (10-cm) spikes of soft-pink flowers are held high above the foliage, often reblooming in late summer if grown in moist soil away from hot afternoon sun. The species is largely unknown in gardens, being supplanted by this fine cultivar. Zones 3–8.

P. campanulata (Polygonum campanulatum). Himalayas. Height 3 ft; spread 3 ft (90 × 90 cm). A stout, branching plant with shallow roots and a tendency to be invasive. The leaves are prominently veined, dark green, felted with brown hairs underneath, egg-shaped to elliptical, reaching a length of 5 in. (12.5 cm). Terminal panicles of beautiful, bell-shaped ½-in. (1.2-cm) pink flowers are produced in midsummer to early autumn. Variety ***album*** has white flowers. 'Southcombe White' has white flowers flushed pink. Zones 5–9.

P. macrophylla (Polygonum macrophyllum). Himalayas. Height 24 in.; spread 12 in. (60 × 30 cm). A bushy, branching plant with long-stemmed, narrow, and bright-green, lance-shaped leaves up to 9 in. (22.5 cm) long with 3-in. (7.5-cm) spikes of bright-pink flowers in late summer. Zones 4–9.

P. milletii (Polygonum milletii). Himalayas. Height 12–18 in.; spread 12 in. (30 × 45 cm). A slow-growing, moisture-loving plant with oblong lance-shaped, dark-green leaves and 2–3-in. (5–

7.5-cm) spikes of deep-red flowers from midsummer to early autumn. Zones 5–9.

P. vacciniifolia (Polygonum vacciniifolia). Himalayas. Height 4–6 in.; spread 1–3 ft (10–15 × 60–120 cm). A mat-forming evergreen with woody stems and egg-shaped to elliptical glossy leaves that are tinged red in autumn. The upright, 4-in.- (10-cm-) long dense spikes of rose-red flowers are produced in late summer and autumn. A fine trailing plant for a partly shaded rock wall. Zones 4–8.

P. virginiana (Polygonum virginianum, Tovara virginiana). Height 2–3 ft; spread 2 ft (60–90 × 60 cm). A spreading, mound-forming, leafy plant with inconspicuous flowers and elliptical mid-green leaves up to 8 in. (20 cm) long. The green-leaved form is seldom grown in gardens but variety ***variegata,*** with marbled green-and-cream leaves, and cultivar 'Painter's Palette,' with chocolate, creamy yellow, and pink variegation, are sometimes seen. The variegated forms require a lightly shaded site in moist but well-drained soil. Can be somewhat invasive. Zones 4–8.

PETASTIES

(Butterbur)

Family: Compositae

A small genus of invasive plants closely allied to coltsfoot and valuable for their ability to grow in poor, moist soils and produce handsome, rounded, heart-shaped leaves. The less-than-ornamental male and female flowers range from purple to white and are borne in clublike spikes in late winter and early spring. The name is from the Greek *petasos,* "broad hat," a reference to the shape and size of the leaves.

Cultivation: Grow in moist soil in sun to partial shade.

Landscape Use: Sturdy and invasive groundcovers for streambanks and difficult situations. Not recommended for inclusion with other plants because of their aggressively invasive habits.

Propagation: Divide in spring or autumn.

P. fragrans. Sweet coltsfoot. Europe. Height 12 in.; spread 3–4 ft (30 × 90–120 cm). Almost round to heart-shaped, toothed, light-green, and hairy leaves up to 8 in. (20 cm) wide and slightly fragrant pinkish flowers in a tight cluster appearing in late winter before the foliage. Zones 5–9.

P. hybridus. Butterbur. Europe, Asia. Height 1–2 ft; spread 3–4 ft (30–60 × 90–120 cm). In early spring 12-in.- (30-cm-) high stems bearing clustered spikes of purplish flowers are produced before the leaves. The leaves are coarse and long-stemmed, lightly toothed and felted underneath, heart-shaped or kidney-shaped, and up to 3 ft (90 cm) across. The name butterbur comes from their former use as a wrapping for blocks of butter. Zones 5–8.

P. japonicus. Japanese butterbur. Asia. Height 2–3 ft; spread 5 ft (60–90 × 150 cm). Round clusters of yellowish white flowers are surrounded by light-green bracts and appear in late winter and early spring before the leaves appear. The basal leaves are toothed and hairy underneath, kidney-shaped to round, and up to 18 in. (45 cm) across. An effective groundcover for a large, moist site. The variety ***giganteus*** has leaves 2–3 ft (60–90 cm) across. In Japan this species is widely cultivated for its edible leaf stem. Zones 5–9.

PETRORHAGIA

Family: Caryophyllacae

A small genus of about 25 species of annual and perennial plants native to dry, mountainous regions. One species, described below, is a long-flowering rock-garden plant native to southern and southeastern Europe and Asia Minor.

Cultivation: Grow in sandy, lime-rich soil in full sun.

Landscape Use: A sturdy and long-blooming plant for the rock garden.

Propagation: Sow seed in autumn.

Petrorhagia saxifraga

P. saxifraga (Tunica saxifraga). Europe, Asia. Height 4–6 in.; spread 6 in. (10–15 × 15 cm). A mat-forming species with woody-based stems and linear, lance-shaped leaves. Open clusters of bell-shaped white or rose-pink flowers are produced in summer. 'Alba' has while flowers; 'Alba Plena' has double white flowers and blooms for much of the summer; 'Rosette' has double pink flowers. Zones 5–7.

PHALARIS

(Ribbon Grass)

Family: Graminae

Phalaris arundinacea var. *picta*

A small genus of annual and perennial grasses. The only aspects of the Phalaris which have current importance to the gardener are its one species and its variegated form.

Cultivation: Grow in ordinary soil in full sun to partial shade. In climates with warm summers, cut down to the ground in midsummer for new growth in late summer and autumn.

LANDSCAPE USE: A brightly luminescent ornamental grass for groundcover planting rather than association with other plants. Can be very pleasing near the reflective surface of water.

PROPAGATION: Divide in spring or autumn.

P. arundinacea var. ***picta.*** Variegated ribbon grass, gardener's garters. North America, Europe, Asia. Height 3–4 ft; spread 3 ft and more (90–120 × 90 cm). A rapidly spreading, highly invasive grass with green longitudinally striped white leaves sometimes flushed pink. The insignificant flowers are produced sporadically in midsummer. This is a cool-season grass that is at its best in late spring to early summer. In a hot summer it is prone to leaf scorch and in general looks miserable. If you can put up with a few weeks of almost bare ground, cut it down in midsummer and it will reward you with fresh new growth that will quickly fill the site by late summer. Although despised by ornamental grass aficionados, variegated ribbon grass can be highly attractive, particularly in late-afternoon sun. 'Feesey' is a cultivar with good white variegation that is more toleratant of summer heat and does not need rejuvenation in midsummer. Zones 4–9.

PHLOMIS

(Jerusalem Sage)

FAMILY: Labiatae

About 100 species of subshrubs, shrubs, and herbaceous perennials native from the Mediterranean to China. The stems are square and usually hairy. The leaves are opposite and often woolly. The yellow, white, to purple hooded flowers are carried in whorls in summer. The Jerusalem sage, ***P. fruticosa,*** is a bushy shrub widely seen in gardens. Two species, described below, are herbaceous perennials that are becoming more commonly available.

CULTIVATION: Grow in full sun in well-drained soil.

LANDSCAPE USE: Useful for their large, almost coarse leaves and their attractive whorled flowers. ***P. russeliana*** is particularly worthwhile when used as a visual anchor for more delicate, feathery plants.

PROPAGATION: Divide in spring or early autumn. Sow seed in spring.

P. russeliana. Asia Minor. ***(P. viscosa, P. samia).*** Height 3–4 ft; spread 2 ft (90–120 × 60 cm). A large plant with square, woolly, upright stems and coarse, wrinkled, 8-in.- (20-cm-) long leaves that are broadly heart-shaped and woolly underneath, mid-green on the top surface. Butter-yellow, hooded flowers are produced in axillary whorls in summer. Zones 5–9.

Phlomis tuberosa

P. tuberosa. Europe, Asia. Height 4–6 ft; spread 3 ft (120–180 × 90 cm). A prolifically flowering, bushy plant with a tuberous rootstock and erect stems with wrinkled and hairy, 10-in.- (25-cm-) long leaves that are egg-shaped with a heart-shaped base. Whorls of lilac-purple flowers appear in summer. Zones 3–9.

PHLOX

Family: Polemoniaceae

Phlox paniculata 'Eva Cullum'

Phlox divaricata

Almost exclusively a North American genus with a broad variety of species, from mat-forming carpeting plants, to tall and erect species. A garden doesn't seem like a garden without at least a few phlox. Most have opposite leaves and lobed and notched flowers in terminal clusters in a broad range of colors from white, pink, red, purple, blue, yellow, to orange. The generic name comes from the Greek for "flame" and was applied to species of ***Lychnis.***

Cultivation: The range of site requirements is too large to be generalized here. Soil and light needs are discussed under each species. The taller garden varieties suffer greatly from powdery mildew and, to a lesser extent, the ravages of spider mites. Fungicides and insecticides are frequently suggested as controls. However, integrated pest-management methods, particularly using beneficial parasites for spider mites and a variety of cultural techniques for powdery mildew, may control the problems to some degree without harming the environment. In general, all species require fertile, moist but well-drained soil. The taller garden phlox will need thinning and staking.

Landscape Use: There are very few sites in the garden where phlox will not be a successful and worthwhile element. From woodland borders to dry rock gardens, from formal beds to meadows, try them all.

Propagation: Take cuttings of species and hybrids in midsummer. Sow seed in spring or autumn, or divide in spring or early autumn.

P. adsurgens. Periwinkle phlox. Western United States. Height 4 in.; spread 12 in. (10 × 30 cm). A trailing, evergreen plant with glossy mid-green, stemless, elliptical leaves and short stems bearing clusters of 1-in.- (2.5-cm-) wide, saucer-shaped, mostly pink flowers with a white eye in spring. The variety ***alba*** has white flowers. 'Red Buttes' has brick-red flowers; 'Wagon Wheels' has pink flowers with narrow petals like the spokes of a wheel. Grow in well-drained, acid soil in partial shade. Zones 5–9.

P. bifida. Sand phlox. United States. Height 6 in.; spread 12 in. (15 × 30 cm). An evergreen, mat-forming plant similar to ***P. subulata,*** with lance-shaped leaves 1–2 in. (2.5–5 cm) long and masses of starry, lilac to lavender flowers in early summer, with the petals noticeably notched to about ⅛ in. (0.3 cm). 'Colvin's White' has bright-white flowers. Grow in full sun in well-drained, sandy soil. Cut back after flowering to keep the plant compact. Often produces a few flowers in late summer. Zones 4–8.

P. carolina. Carolina phlox. Southern United States. Height 2–3 ft; spread 2 ft (60–90 × 60 cm). One of the taller species with erect stems and dark-green, lance-shaped leaves 4–5 in. (10–12.5 cm) long. Terminal clusters of ¾-in.- (1.8-cm-) wide pink or purple flowers are produced in early summer. It is resistant to mildew and spider mites and is one of the best species for hot climates. Grow in moist, rich soil in full sun to light shade. Zones 4–9.

P. divaricata. Wild blue phlox. United States. Height 1 ft; spread 1 ft (30 × 30 cm). Native to deciduous woodland from New England to the southern states, this semievergreen plant has creeping rhizomes and trailing shoots that root at the nodes. The leaves are dark green and oblong up to 2 in. (5 cm) long. The slightly fragrant light-blue flowers appear in spring and are five-petaled and somewhat lobed. An outstanding groundcover for woodland shade. Subspecies ***laphammii*** is native to the western United States and has dark-blue flowers without lobed petals. 'Dirigo Ice' has ice-blue flowers; 'Fuller's White' is a compact plant growing to about 8 in. (20 cm) tall with white flowers with conspicuously notched petals. 'Spring Delight' may be a hybrid of this species and ***P. ovata.*** It has rose-pink flowers and basal rosettes of deep-green, rounded leaves. Grow in moist but well-drained soil in partial shade. Mildew is a slight problem if the site is dry. Zones 4–9.

P. douglasii. Western United States. Height 2–4 in.; spread 12 in. (5–10 × 30 cm). A mound-forming plant with dense mats of evergreen, subshrubby growth. The leaves are mid-green, sharply pointed, linear to lance-shaped up to ½ in. (1.2 cm) long. Saucer-shaped, pale-lavender flowers are produced in large masses in early summer. 'Boothman's Variety' has lavender-blue flowers with violet-blue markings around the center; 'Crackerjack' has bright-magenta flowers; 'Daniel's Cushion' has rose-pink flowers; 'Eva' has mauve flowers; 'May Snow' has pure-white flowers; 'Red Admiral' has crimson flowers; 'Waterloo' has crimson-red flowers. Cut back after flowering. Grow in well-drained soil in full sun in a mild climate. Zones 5–7.

P. glaberrima. Smooth phlox. Southeastern United States. Height 2–3 ft; spread 18 in. (60–90 × 45 cm). A vigorous, clump-forming plant with a rosette of lance-shaped leaves up to 4 in. (10 cm) long and smaller, narrower, lance-shaped stem leaves with rolled margins. Purple-pink, saucer-shaped flowers are produced in great numbers in late spring and early summer. The variety ***triflora*** is a more compact plant, reaching a height of about 18 in. (45 cm) with purple-pink flowers in early summer, often coinciding with the first flush of roses. Grow in moist but well-drained soil in full sun to partial shade. Cut back hard after flowering. Zones 3–9.

P. × lilacina. Height 9 in.; spread 12 in. (22.5 × 30 cm). A hybrid between ***P. bifida*** and ***P. subulata*** with narrow, mid-green leaves and star-shaped, early-spring-blooming flowers. 'Mars' has red flowers with notched petals; 'Millstream Jupiter' has deep-blue, notched flowers; 'Venus' has pink, notched flowers. Zones 3–9.

P. maculata. Wild sweet william. United States. Height 2–3 ft; spread 2 ft (60–90 × 60 cm). An erect plant with hairy and often mottled red stems and 2–4-in.- (5–10-cm-) long, roundly lance-shaped, glossy, dark-green leaves. Cylindrical clusters of fragrant, mauve-pink flowers are produced in early summer. 'Alpha' has rose-pink flowers; 'Miss Lingard' is an outstanding cultivar with pure-white flowers. 'Omega' has near-white flowers with a violet eye; 'Reine du Jour' has clear white flowers with a red eye; 'Rosalinde' has deep rose-pink flowers. Grow in full sun in moist, well-drained soil. Somewhat mildew resistant. Zones 4–8.

P. nivalis. Trailing phlox. Southeastern United States. Height 9 in.; spread 12 in. (22.5 × 30 cm). Similar to ***P. subulata*** but with dark-green, ½-in.- (1.2-cm-) long, linear leaves on trailing stems forming a dense carpet. In spring 1-in.- (2.5-cm-) wide, purple-pink, saucer-shaped flowers with mostly unnotched petals are produced. 'Camla' has rich-pink flowers with slightly notched petals. 'Eco Brilliant' has pink flowers with a mauve eye; 'Eco Flirtie Eyes' has pink flowers with a white eye. Grow in full sun in well-drained soil. Zones 6–9.

P. ovata. Mountain phlox. Eastern United States. Height 18–24 in.; spread 12 in. (45–60 × 30 cm). A clump-forming, bushy plant with leafy stems and basal rosettes of egg-shaped leaves up to 6 in. (15 cm) long. The stem leaves are stalkless and narrower. Flat clusters of deep-pink flowers are produced in late spring and early summer. Grow in full sun to partial shade in well-drained soil. Zones 3–8.

P. paniculata. Garden phlox. United States. Height 3–4 ft; spread 2 ft (90–120 × 60 cm). The garden phlox come in an enormous range of colors, from purple, pink, red, to white. They are spectacular border plants for summer display. Unfortunately, in areas with hot and humid summers they have a number of problems that the smaller-growing species do not. Powdery mildew and spider mites are serious problems, with the less controllable powdery mildew disfiguring the plants to such a degree as to make them stunted and ugly. Spider mites can be dealt with by using mite parasites or miticides. Powdery mildew can be controlled to some degree by the use of fungicides, but this is not an ideal solution. Plants should be divided every two or three years, with only the strongest and freshest divisions replanted. They should be thinned to four to six stems to increase air circulation and to prevent the plants building up a heavy mass of stems. Irrigation should be applied to the roots only; watering the leaves helps distribute mildew spores.

P. paniculata and its cultivars require fertile, moist but well-drained soil in full sun. Deadhead to maintain vigor and prevent self-seeding. They are poor plants for hot climates and require afternoon sun in regions with hot summers. While they are beautiful garden plants, gardeners who do not want to fuss may well want explore other species that are less susceptible to pests and diseases.

The species is a clump-forming plant with stiff, erect, leafy stems. The leaves are 2–6 in. (5–15 cm) long, lance-shaped to egg-shaped, veined, pointed, and minutely toothed. Pyramidal panicles of purplish magenta, ¾-in.- (1.8-cm-) wide flowers are produced in midsummer to early autumn. There are many cultivars, a few of which are:

'Amethyst': violet flowers
'Ann': lavender flowers
'Blue Boy': clear-blue flowers
'Blue Ice': bluish white flowers with a pink eye
'Bright Eyes': soft-pink blooms with a red eye
'Cecil Hanbury': crimson eyes and salmon-orange flowers
'Cherry Pink': bright-pink flowers
'Dodo Hanbury Forbes': clear pink blossoms
'Dresden China': pale-pink flowers with a darker eye
'Eva Cullum': clear-pink flowers with a red eye
'Eventide': pale-lavender flowers flushed lilac
'Fairest One': salmon-pink flowers with a darker eye
'Fairy's Petticoat': light-pink flowers with a darker eye
'Harlequin': purple flowers and white variegated leaves
'Inspiration': light-red flowers with a darker eye
'Mother of Pearl': white flowers tinted pink
'Mt. Fuji': bright-white flowers
'Norah Leigh': lavender flowers and green-and-creamy white variegated leaves
'Orange Perfection': salmon-orange flowers
'Othello': deep-red blossoms
'Prime Minister': white flowers with a red eye
'San Antonio': dark purple-red flowers
'Sir John Falstaff': salmon-pink flowers
'Starfire': deep-red blossoms
'The King': deep-violet flowers
'Thunderbolt': bright-scarlet flowers
'White Admiral': pure-white flowers
'Windsor': carmine-rose flowers with a darker eye
Zones 4–8.

P. pilosa. United States. Height 12–18 in.; spread 18 in. (30–45 × 45 cm). A clump-forming, vigorously spreading species with softly hairy stems and leaves, the leaves are lance-shaped up to 3 in. (7.5 cm) long. Strong pink, ¾-in.- (1.8-cm-) wide, saucer-shaped flowers are produced in large numbers throughout late spring and early summer, often reblooming in late summer. Subspecies ***ozarkana*** has egg-shaped leaves. It is an excellent plant that is easily divided at almost any point in the growing season. Grow in moist but well-drained soil in full sun to partial shade. An outstanding if somewhat rampant groundcover under shrub roses. Zones 4–8. 'Moody Blue', height 6–8 in.; spread 8 in. (15–20 × 20 cm), is often listed as a hybrid under the name ***P.*** × 'Chattahootchee.' This is now thought to be a form of ***P. pilosa.*** It has dark-green, lance-shaped leaves and lavender-blue flowers with a purple eye. Grow in moist, well-drained soil in partial shade. The flowers are very attractive, but the plant tends to flower itself into a state of weakness and often death. It is susceptible to powdery mildew in dry soils. Zones 4–9.

P.* × *procumbens. Height 10 in; spread 12 in. (25 × 30 cm). A hybrid between ***P. stolonifera*** and ***P. subulata,*** with evergreen, elliptical, glossy, dark-green leaves up to 1 in. (2.5 cm) long and ¾-in.- (1.8-cm-) wide, saucer-shaped, purple flowers in early summer. 'Millstream' has mauve-pink flowers with a darker eye surrounded by a white circle. 'Folio-Variegata' has bright-pink flowers and dark-green leaves edged with white. Grow in well-drained soil in full sun to partial shade. Zones 5–8.

P. stolonifera. Creeping phlox. Eastern United States. Height 6–8 in.; spread 12 in. (15–20 × 30

Phlox stolonifera 'Sherwood Purple'

cm). An evergreen, mat-forming plant with spreading prostrate shoots that root at the nodes and spoon-shaped leaves 1–3 in. (2.5–7.5 cm) long. Short, flowering shoots with oval leaves up to 1 in. (2.5 cm) long bear ¾-in.- (1.8-cm-) wide, lavender-blue, unnotched flowers in spring. 'Alba' has white flowers; 'Blue Ridge' has pale-blue flowers; 'Bruce's White' has white flowers with a yellow eye; 'Home Fires' has deep-pink flowers; 'Pink Ridge' has bright-pink flowers; 'Sherwood Purple' is an exceptionally heavy flowering cultivar with purple-blue flowers on 6-in. (15-cm) stems. Excellent groundcovers for shade. Zones 3–8.

P. subulata. Moss pink. Eastern United States. Height 6–9 in.; spread 12 in. (15–22.5 × 30 cm). An evergreen, mound-forming plant with stiff, linear, mid-green leaves about ½ in. (1.2 cm) long. In early spring great numbers of ½–¾-in.- (1.2–1.8-cm-) wide, star-shaped purple, pink, or white flowers with and without notched petals are produced. The subspecies ***brittonii*** has pale-blue flowers with deeply notched petals. 'Alexander's Surprise' has salmon-pink flowers; 'Benita' has lavender flowers with a purple center; 'Bluets' has sky-blue flowers with a darker eye; 'Brightness' has pink flowers with a crimson eye; 'Emerald Cushion Pink' has soft-pink flowers; 'Oakington Blue' has clear-blue flowers; 'Marjory' has rose-pink flowers; 'Profusion' has white flowers with a red eye; 'Red Wings' has crimson flowers with a darker eye; 'Scarlet Flame' has scarlet-red flowers; 'Starglow' has dark-red flowers; 'White Delight' has snow-white flowers. Grow in full sun in well-drained soil. Some cultivars will produce a few flowers in autumn. Zones 3–9.

PHORMIUM

(New Zealand Flax)

Family: Agavaceae

Phormium tenax 'Maori Sunset'

Two species of evergreen plants with stiff, sword-shaped leaves in a great array of colors. Although known for more than 200 years, they are still relatively new to cultivation. Hybridizers are continuing to produce new forms with ever more multicolored leaves.

Cultivation: Grow in full sun in well-drained soil.

Landscape Use: Dramatically colored, architectural plants for specimen planting, container display, or mass planting.

Propagation: Divide named forms in spring. Sow seed in spring.

P. cookianum. New Zealand. Height 3–6 ft; spread 1–2 ft (90–180 × 30–60 cm). An evergreen, leafy plant with sword-shaped, dark-green leaves and tall panicles of tubular, 1½-in.- (3.8-cm-) long, pale greenish yellow flowers in summer. 'Cream Delight' has a broad creamy band in the center of the leaf and green margins; 'Tricolor' has red-, yellow-, and green-striped leaves. Zones 8–10.

P. tenax. New Zealand. Height 8–10 ft; spread 3–6 ft (240–300 × 90–180 cm). An erect plant with stiff, sword-shaped mid- to deep-green leaves and tall panicles of rust-red, tubular flowers up to 2 in. (5 cm) long in summer. There are a great many hybrid cultivars. 'Aurora' has red, yellow, pink, and bronze stripes; 'Maori Sunset' has pink, apricot, and bronze leaves; 'Purpureum' has dark-purple leaves; 'Sundowner' has purple-and-pink striped leaves. Zones 8–10.

PHRAGMITES

(Reed)

Family: Graminae

The common reed is used for thatching and basket-making as well soil conservation in flood areas. It is common in those parts of the temperate world that haven't destroyed their wetlands. It is not a good garden plant unless you have a large marsh in your backyard. However, if you do, the feathery flowers create a wonderfully silky effect in the landscape. The rootstock spreads rapidly, the leaf blades are flat and broad, and the flowers are held in terminal panicles in late summer. The name comes from the Greek and means "growing in hedges," a reference to its hedgelike appearance in ditches.

Cultivation: Grow, if you must, in marshy soil of either salt or fresh water in full sun.

Landscape Use: A large, coarse reed with delicate flowers for the wild garden.

Propagation: So invasive that it will do the job for you. Divide in spring or autumn.

P. australis. Common reed, thatch. Global distribution. Height 10–12 ft; spread 4 ft (300–360 × 120 cm). A tall and coarse reed with mid-green, flat leaf blades to 2 in. (5 cm) wide. Silky panicles of tawny purple flowers appear in late summer and autumn. 'Variegatus' is striped creamy yellow. Zones 5–9.

PHUOPSIS

Family: Rubiaceae

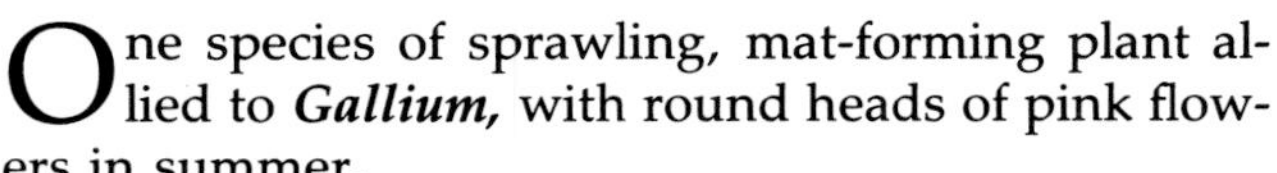

One species of sprawling, mat-forming plant allied to ***Gallium,*** with round heads of pink flowers in summer.

Cultivation: Grow in well-drained soil in full sun to partial shade.

Landscape Use: Plant as an edging plant or groundcover. Particularly effective growing under shrub roses or in the rock garden.

Propagation: Divide in spring or sow seed in autumn.

P. stylosa. Caucasus. Height 12 in.; spread 12 in. (30 × 30 cm). Although often grown as an annual, this fine perennial is easily cultivated. Whorls of pale-green, piquant, lance-shaped leaves to ¾ in. (1.8 cm) long are produced from square stems. Round heads up to 1½ in. (3.8 cm) across of tubular, pink, starry flowers appear in summer. The delicacy of the flowers contrasts with the sickly onion smell of the foliage. It is a wonderful plant despite that. 'Purpurea' has rich-purple flowers. Zones 5–8.

Phuopsis stylosa

PHYGELIUS

(Cape Fuchsia)

FAMILY: Scrophulariaceae

Two species of subshrubs native to South Africa, with woody bases; opposite, toothed leaves; and tubular, nodding, pink, red, yellow, or white flowers in summer and autumn. Evergreen or semievergreen in mild areas, they are cut to the ground by the frost of cold winters. Their winter hardiness in North America is still in question; the more we grow the more we will know.

CULTIVATION: Plant in a sunny, sheltered site in well-drained soil. Mulch for winter protection and provide afternoon shade in areas with hot and humid summers.

LANDSCAPE USE: Pleasantly attractive late-summer-flowering plants for a sheltered position in the garden.

PROPAGATION: Take stem cuttings in summer and autumn. Sow seed in spring or divide in spring or autumn.

P. aequalis. South Africa. Height 3 ft; spread 18 in. (90 × 45 cm). Slender stems with a woody base and dark-green, opposite, egg-shaped, and lightly toothed leaves 1–4 in. (2.5–10 cm) long. The flowers, which appear in late summer and autumn are borne in nodding clusters and are tubular, pinkish red with yellow throats. 'Yellow Trumpet' has pale-yellow flowers that contrast well with the dark-green leaves. This cultivar is also listed as 'Alba,' 'Aureus,' and 'Cream Trumpet.' Zones 6–9.

Phygelius aequalis 'Yellow Trumpet'

P. capensis. Cape Fuchsia. South Africa. Height 3–4 ft; spread 3 ft (90–120 × 90 cm). Similar to the above species but with triangular to egg-shaped, dark-green leaves and clusters of orange to red flowers with a yellow throat and red mouth. 'Coccineus' has orange-red flowers. Zones 7–9.

P. × rectus. Height 3–4 ft; spread 3 ft (90–120 × 90

cm). A hybrid between the two species, with triangular, slightly toothed dark-green leaves. 'African Queen' has pendulous red flowers; 'Pink Elf' is a dwarf form with pale-pink flowers; 'Winchester Fanfare' has pale-red flowers with scarlet trumpet and yellow throat. Zones 7–9.

PHYLLITIS

(Hart's-tongue Fern)

Family: Aspleniaceae

About eight species of ferns sometimes listed under ***Asplenium,*** native to temperate, subtropical, and tropical areas of the world with bright-green, tonguelike, strap-shaped leaves. One hardy species is rare in the wild in North America but common in Europe. It is a variable species, with over 180 variations in leaf structure having been recorded.

Cultivation: Grow in neutral to lime-rich soil in shade. Its native habitat is damp limestone rock near streams and rivers.

Landscape Use: An attractive fern for the shady border or wild garden.

Propagation: Sow spores or divide in spring.

P. scolopendrium (Asplenium scolopendrium). Hart's-tongue. Transglobal. Height 18 in.; spread 18 in. (45 × 45 cm). An evergreen fern with straplike, bright-green, and leathery leaves 6–18 in. (15–45 cm) long and 1–2 in. (2.5–5 cm) wide. The base of the leaf is heart-shaped, the tip pointed or blunt. There are many cultivars. 'Crispum' has upright leaves with wavy margins; 'Cristata' has branched and crested fronds. Zones 4–8.

PHYSOPLEXIS

Family: Campanulaceae

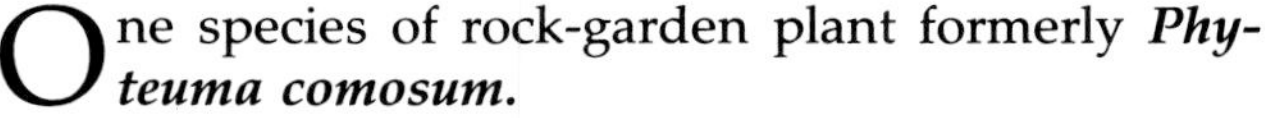

One species of rock-garden plant formerly ***Phyteuma comosum.***

Cultivation: Grow in well-drained, lime-rich soil in sun or partial shade. Protect from midday and afternoon sun and winter wet conditions.

Landscape Use: An odd but beautiful plant for the rock garden or alpine house.

Propagation: Take cuttings in summer or sow seed in autumn.

P. comosa. European Alps. Height 3 in.; spread 4 in. (7.5 × 10 cm). A tufted plant with serrated, kidney-shaped basal leaves and lance-shaped stem leaves. Round, spiky heads of tubular, claw-shaped, purple-lilac-blue flowers are produced in summer. Zones 5–7.

PHYSOSTEGIA

(Obedient Plant)

FAMILY: Labiatae

Twelve species of square-stemmed plants native to North America. One species is cultivated in the garden for its erect habit and white, pink, or mauve flower spikes. The Latin name is of Greek derivation and means "bladder covering", referring to the inflated calyx of the seed. It is called "obedient plant" because the snapdragonlike flowers remain at a new angle when twisted on the stem.

CULTIVATION: Grow in moist but well-drained soil in full sun or partial shade. They are spreading plants that need dividing every two to three years to control them.

LANDSCAPE USE: Their stiff stems and colorful flower spikes are useful in the summer border. The white forms are particularly eye-catching. Good cut flowers.

PROPAGATION: Divide in spring or autumn. Take cuttings in spring.

Physostegia virginiana 'Variegata'

P. virginiana. Obedient plant. Eastern United States. Height 3–4 ft; spread 2 ft (90–120 × 60 cm). A clump-forming plant with spreading roots. The stems are stiff and do not require staking; the mid-green leaves are 3–5 in. (7.5–12.5 cm) long, sharply toothed, and lance-shaped. In late summer and early autumn 12-in. (30-cm) long leafy spikes of tubular, lipped, and lobed, 1-in.- (2.5-cm-) long pale-pink to purple-pink flowers are produced. The variety ***alba*** has white flowers and is generally the first to flower in summer; var. ***grandiflora*** grows to a height of 4–5 ft (120–150 cm) and has bright-pink flowers; var. ***nana*** grows 12–18 in. (30 × 45 cm) tall and has pink flowers; 'Pink Bouquet' grows 3–4 ft (90–120 cm) tall, needs staking, and has bright-pink flowers; 'Rose Bouquet' reaches a height of 3–4 ft (90–120 cm) and has lilac-pink flowers; 'Summer Snow' has pure-white flowers that appear later than those of var. ***alba;*** 'Variegata' has gray-green leaves with white margins and lilac-pink flowers; 'Vivid' is precisely that, flowering in late summer with stiff, compact spikes of bright-pink blooms. Zones 3–9.

PHYTEUMA

(Horned Rampion)

FAMILY: Campanulaceae

A genus of about 40 alpine and subalpine plants native to Europe and Asia with leaves in basal rosettes and small, "horned" flowers in dense, terminal spikes in spring and summer. For ***P. comosum,*** see ***Physoplexis***.

CULTIVATION: Grow in well-drained soil in sun or partial shade. Protect from afternoon sun in hot climates and winter wet in cold climates.

LANDSCAPE USE: Little-grown rock-garden plants for a dry wall or scree bed.

Propagation: Divide in spring or autumn, or sow seed in autumn.

P. hemisphaericum. European Alps. Height 6 in.; spread 9 in. (15 × 22.5 cm). A tufted plant with linear, grasslike leaves 2–4 in. (5–10 cm) long and globular heads of spiky blue flowers 1 in. (2.5 cm) across in early summer. Zones 5–7.

P. orbiculare. Europe. Height 12 in.; spread 18 in. (30 × 45 cm). Basal rosettes of mid-green, egg-shaped to elliptical leaves with the stem leaves more narrow and pointed, with a heart-shaped base. Round heads of dark-blue flowers are produced in early summer. Zones 5–7.

P. ovatum. European Alps. Height 2 ft; spread 18 in. (60 × 45 cm). A robust, flopping plant with heart-shaped, pointed, and toothed leaves and cylindrical heads of dark-blue, spiky flowers. Zones 5–7.

P. scheuchzeri. European Alps. Height 12 in.; spread 8 in. (30 × 20 cm). A tufted perennial with toothed, egg-shaped to lance-shaped dark-green leaves and spherical heads of bright-blue flowers in late spring and early summer. Zones 5–7.

PHYTOLACCA

(Pokeweed)

Family: Phytolaccaceae

Twenty-six species of trees, shrubs, and herbaceous plants, with two hardy herbaceous perennials grown for their attractive candlelike flowers and shiny purple-black berries. They have semisucculent, hollow stems and alternate leaves. The berries are poisonous.

Cultivation: Plant in moist soil in sun or partial shade.

Landscape Use: Coarse plants for the back of the border or wild garden.

Propagation: Sow seeds in spring. Divide in spring or autumn.

P. americana. Pokeweed. North America. Height 4–6 ft; spread 3 ft (120–180 × 90 cm). A coarse, erect plant with egg-shaped, mid-green leaves that turn red and purple in autumn. In summer 8-in. (20-cm) spikes of petalless green-and-white, often pink-flushed flowers bloom, followed by shiny purple-black berries in autumn. Zones 3–9.

Phytolacca clavigera

P. clavigera. China. Height 4 ft; spread 3 ft (120 × 90 cm). Far more attractive than its American relative, with oval to lance-shaped leaves and dense spikes of pink flowers in summer, followed by purple-black berries in autumn. In autumn the stems turn red, while the leaves turn yellow. Zones 6–9.

PLATYCODON

(Balloonflower)

FAMILY: Campanulaceae

A genus of one species with a number of varieties and cultivated varieties, native to Eastern Asia and related to ***Campanula.*** It differs distinctly from that genus and others by its balloon-shaped flower bud. The name comes from the Greek *platys,* "broad," and *kodon,* "bell," from the shape of the open flower. It is a long-lived perennial with whorled leaves and solitary blue flowers.

CULTIVATION: Grow in ordinary, well-drained soil in full sun. Growth resumes in late spring, and plants should be marked to avoid damage in early spring.

LANDSCAPE USE: Slow-growing and long-lived plants for the herbaceous border.

PROPAGATION: Sow seeds in spring. Take basal cuttings in summer. Carefully divide older plants in spring. They are slow to establish after division.

Platycodon grandiflorus

P. grandiflorus. Balloonflower. China, Japan. Height 3 ft; spread 18 in. (90 × 45 cm). Has 3-in.- (7.5-cm-) long, bluish green, egg-shaped, and sharply serrated leaves in whorls along smooth green stems with single, terminal flowers that are balloon-shaped in bud and open to a five-lobed, pointed, bell-shaped blue blossom in summer.The flower is veined with purple and has yellowish white stamens. The variety ***albus*** has white flowers; var. ***apoyama*** grows to 18 in. (45 cm) and has violet-blue flowers; var. ***mariesii*** reaches a height of 2 ft (60 cm) and has 2-in.- (5-cm-) wide, purple-blue flowers; var. ***mariesii albus*** is a white form; var. ***plenus*** has double blue flowers; var. ***roseus*** has rosy pink flowers. 'Double Blue' has bright-blue double flowers on 2-ft- (60-cm-) tall plants; 'Komachi' has blue flowers that keep their balloon-shape longer than others; 'Mother of Pearl' has pale-pink flowers; 'Shell Pink' has pink flowers; 'Snowflake' has semidouble white flowers. Zones 3–9.

PODOPHYLLUM

(Mayapple)

FAMILY: Berberidaceae

A small genus of woodland plants native to North America and Asia with circular, lobed leaves and single, saucer-shaped flowers in spring. The mayapple is common in woodlands in the eastern United States, creating a carpet of light-green, umbrellalike leaves as most deciduous trees come into full leaf. The name is derived from *anapodophyllum,* duck's-foot leaf.

CULTIVATION: Plant in moist, leafy soil in a partly shaded site.

LANDSCAPE USE: Spring-flowering plants for the

woodland garden. Their invasive habits demand a large, shady garden in which to spread.

PROPAGATION: Divide in spring or sow seed in autumn.

P. hexandrum (P. emodii). Himalayan mayapple. India. Height 12 in.; spread 12 in. (30 × 30 cm). A rhizomatous perennial with pairs of nearly circular, three-lobed, sharply toothed leaves that are mottled purplish brown and up to 10 in. (25 cm) across. In spring 2-in.- (5-cm-) wide, upward-facing, saucer-shaped white flowers appear, followed by red berries in autumn. The variety ***chinense*** has pink flowers; var. ***majus*** grows to 18 in. (45 cm) in height. Zones 5–8.

P. peltatum. Mayapple. North America. Height 18 in.; spread 12 in. (45 × 30 cm). A vigorous, spreading plant with 12-in.- (30-cm-) wide, light-green, rounded, three to five lobed, sharply toothed leaves with the stem attached to the center of the leaf (peltate). Below the leaves is a single, nodding, saucer-shaped white flower that produces a yellow, round, applelike fruit that turns deep pink in autumn. Zones 3–9.

Podophyllum peltatum

POLEMONIUM

(Jacob's Ladder)

FAMILY: Polemoniaceae

Polemonium foliosissimum

About 30 species of annual and perennial plants native to North and South America, Europe, and Asia. Many are indigenous to western North America and do best in cool climates. The leaves are alternate, with leaflets arranged in pairs like the rungs of a ladder. Clusters of blue, pink, white, or yellow flowers appear in late spring and summer.

CULTIVATION: Grow in rich soil in a partly shaded site. Remove faded flower stems.

LANDSCAPE USE: The finely divided foliage and mostly blue flowers make many of the species pleasant additions to the early-summer border or woodland garden.

Propagation: Divide in spring or sow seed in autumn.

P. caeruleum. Jacob's ladder. Europe, Asia. Height 2 ft; spread 18 in. (60×45 cm). An upright plant with 3–5-in.- (7.5–12.5-cm-) long, arching leaves attached to the stem by 4–6-in.- (10–15-cm-) long stems. The leaves are divided into as many as 27 pairs of lance-shaped leaflets and are arranged like the rungs of a ladder. Nodding, terminal clusters of blue, 1-in.- (2.5-cm-) wide, cup-shaped flowers are produced in late spring and summer. The variety ***album*** has white flowers. 'Blue Bell' has light-blue flowers; 'Sapphire' is a compact plant growing to 14 in. (35 cm) with light-blue flowers. Zones 3–8.

P. carneum. Western United States. Height 18 in.; spread 12 in. (45×30 cm). A clump-forming plant with finely divided leaves up to 8 in. (20 cm) long, sectioned into 13 to 21 lance-shaped leaflets. Nodding pink flowers appear in early summer. Not an easy plant to grow except in well-drained sandy soil. Zones 5–8.

P. foliosissimum. Western United States. Height 30 in.; spread 24 in. (75×60 cm). An erect plant with up to 12 pairs of narrow, lance-shaped, dark-green leaves and dense clusters of lilac-blue, ½-in.- (1.2-cm-) wide, cup-shaped flowers with yellow to orange stamens. Blooms throughout the summer. Zones 4–8.

P. pulcherrimum. Skunkleaf Jacob's ladder. Height 1 ft; spread 1 ft (30×30 cm). A vigorous, tufted plant with 6-in.- (15-cm-) long, bright-green leaves divided into up to 11 pairs of egg-shaped leaflets. Dense clusters of tubular blue flowers with a yellow throat appear in summer. Zones 3–8.

P. reptans. Creeping Jacob's ladder. Eastern North America. Height 8–12 in.; spread 12 in. (20–30×30 cm). A weak-stemmed, sprawling plant with seven to 15 egg-shaped, 1-in.- (2.5-cm-) long, deep-green leaflets and terminal clusters of ½-in.- (1.2-cm-) long, bell-shaped blue flowers in spring. 'Blue Pearl' grows to 10 in. (25 cm) and has bright-blue flowers. Zones 3–8.

POLYGALA

(Milkwort)

Family: Polygalaceae

A large genus of between 500 to 600 species of trees, shrubs, herbaceous perennials and annuals widely distributed throughout the world. The herbaceous species are not widely grown in gardens, although one species is an attractive rock-garden plant. The name comes from the Greek *polys,* "much," and *gala,* "milk," and is a reference to the plant's traditional use to aid mothers in milk production.

Cultivation: Plant in full sun in rich, well-drained, lime-rich soil.

Landscape Use: Grow in alpine troughs or in the rock garden.

Propagation: Take basal cuttings in summer.

P. calcarea. Milkwort. Europe. Height 1 in.; spread 6 in. (2.5×15 cm). A short-lived, evergreen, mat-forming plant with dark-green oval to spoon-shaped leaves and unbranched, 2-in.- (5-cm-) long clusters of six to 12 small, bright-blue flowers in late spring and early summer. 'Bulley's Variety' has larger flowers of a deeper blue. Zones 5–7.

POLYGONATUM

(Solomon's Seal)

Family: Liliaceae

Polygonatum biflorum

A genus of mostly woodland plants grown for their architectural grace. ***Polygonatum*** means "many kneed," referring to the numerous knots or swellings of the rhizomatous roots. Solomon's seal is a name with many possible derivations; some say the flat, round scars on the root resemble the seals on ancient documents. The stems are long and unbranched, the leaves alternate and veined, while the flowers are white and often pendulous, blooming in late spring.

Cultivation: Plant in moist, leafy soil in partial to full shade.

Landscape Use: Graceful woodland plants for the shady border or woodland garden. Useful perennials for cultivation under trees and shrubs. Good cut flowers.

Propagation: Divide in spring and autumn. Sow seed in autumn.

P. biflorum. North America. Height 1–3 ft; spread 2 ft (30–90 × 60 cm). A variable plant with arching stems and alternate, nearly stemless, broadly elliptical, 4½-in.- (11.2-cm-) long leaves with noticeable veins. Pairs of ½-in.- (1.2-cm-) long, greenish white, bell-shaped flowers hang from the leaf axils in late spring. Dark-blue berries are produced in fall. Variety ***commutatum (P. commutatum, P. canaliculatum, P. giganteum)*** grows from 3–7 ft (90–210 cm) high, has 7-in.- (17.5-cm-) long leaves, and bears three to eight greenish white flowers in pendulous clusters from the leaf axil. Valued for their arching stems and decorative flowers. Zones 4–9.

P. falcatum. Japan, Korea. Height 8 in.; spread 12 in. (20 × 30 cm). A tufted, prostrate plant with narrowly oval, stemless leaves and greenish white pendant flowers produced from the leaf axils in spring. Zones 4–9.

P. hirtum. Europe. Height 3 ft; spread 1 ft (90 × 30 cm). Arching stems, oval to lance-shaped 6-in.- (15-cm-) long leaves, and clusters of drooping, bell-shaped, two to five greenish white flowers in late spring. The underside of the stem and leaves is hairy. Zones 4–9.

P. hookeri. Himalayas. Height 2–4 in.; spread 12 in. (5–10 × 30 cm). A low- and slow-growing species with ½-in.- (1.2-cm-) long, lance-shaped leaves and upward-facing, bell-shaped, lilac-pink, six-petaled flowers in spring and early summer. Zones 5–9.

P. × hybridum. Solomon's seal. Height 4 ft; spread 3 ft (120 × 90 cm). A hybrid between ***P. biflorum*** and ***P. multiflorum,*** with arching stems and elliptical 6-in.- (15-cm-) long, conspicuously veined leaves. Clusters of three to five greenish white flowers hang from the leaf axils in late spring.

'Flore Pleno' has double flowers; 'Nanum' grows to 18 in. (45 cm) tall; 'Variegatum' has creamy striped leaves. Zones 3–9.

P. odoratum. Fragrant Solomon's seal. Europe, Asia. Height 2 ft; spread 1 ft (60 × 30 cm). Angular or ridged arching stems with oval to lance-shaped, 4-in.- (10-cm-) long leaves and fragrant greenish white, bell-shaped flowers in pairs or singly hanging from the leaf axils in spring. 'Variegata' has green leaves edged and tipped creamy white. One of the most elegant variegated plants grown in gardens. Zones 4–9.

P. verticillatum. Europe, Asia. Height 4 ft; spread 18 in. (120 × 45 cm). Erect stems with linear, lance-shaped, 5-in.- (12.5-cm-) long leaves in whorls around the stem. Greenish white flowers are produced from the axils of each whorl in spring, to be followed by red berries in autumn. Zones 4–9.

POLYGONUM

See PERSICARIA.

POLYPODIUM

(Polypody)

Family: Polypodiaceae

A large genus of evergreen and deciduous ferns, most of which are tropical. The two species described below are evergreen with mid-green, lance-shaped fronds. The generic name means "many feet" and refers either to the footprintlike scar that remains on the rhizome when the dead leaves fall off or to the footlike rhizomes themselves.

Cultivation: Grow in rich, well-drained, leafy soil in partial shade. Sometimes difficult to establish.

Landscape Use: Handsome ferns for ground-cover use.

Propagation: Divide in spring or sow spores in late summer.

P. virginianum. Rock polypody. North America. Height 1 ft; spread 9 in. (30 × 22.5 cm). An evergreen, creeping fern with pale- to mid-green leaves, 10 in. (25 cm) long, 2 in. (5 cm) wide, oblong-to-lance-shaped in outline with alternate, blunt leaf segments. The rhizomes are partially visible and may form dense mats in rocky soil. Zones 5–9.

P. vulgare. Europe, Asia. Height 12–16 in.; spread 12 in. (30–40 × 30 cm). An evergreen fern with mid-green, deeply cut, leathery leaves egg-shaped to oblong in outline 12 in. (30 cm) long and 5 in. (12.5 cm) wide, with deeply cut, alternate leaf segments. There are many cultivated forms with finely cut or fringed leaf segments. 'Bifidum' has noticeably notched lower segments; 'Cornubiense' has lobed segments creating the appearance of lacy foliage; 'Cristatum' has crested segments and leaf tips; 'Ramosum' has distinctly forked fronds. Zones 5–8.

POLYSTICHUM

(Christmas Fern, Holy Fern, Shield Fern)

FAMILY: Aspleniaceae

Polystichum setiferum

A large genus of evergreen, semievergreen, and deciduous ferns mostly native to the temperate regions of the world. Clumps of ascending rhizomes bear clusters of green fronds, many with spiny margins. ***Polystichum*** means "many rows," and refers to the clusters of spore-bearing organs.

CULTIVATION: Grow in rich, neutral, moist but well-drained soil in partial shade.

LANDSCAPE USE: Beautiful ferns for the woodland garden or as groundcovers under deciduous trees and shrubs.

PROPAGATION: Divide in late spring or sow spores in summer.

P. acrostichoides. Christmas fern. North America. Height 2 ft; spread 2 ft in (60 × 60 cm). Called Christmas fern because of its evergreen nature. The fronds are generally dark green and lance-shaped up to 3 ft (90 cm) long and 5 in. (12.5 cm) wide, with spiny leaf segments. The new fronds emerge in early spring from tightly coiled, silvery croziers. The emerging leaves are fertile, with sterile leaves following. More sterile leaves are occasionally produced during the summer. There are many forms, including 'Crispum' with ruffled edges and 'Incisum' with deeply cut leaflets. Zones 3–9.

P. aculeatum. Hard shield fern. Europe, Asia. Height 3 ft; spread 2 ft (90 × 60 cm). A semievergreen, hardy fern with stiff, lance-shaped, and leathery fronds with spiny, hollylike leaflets, pale green in spring maturing to dark green. 'Acutilobum' has narrow, sharply pointed leaflets; 'Cambricum' has egg-shaped, coarsely toothed leaflets. 'Pulcherrimum' has finely cut, silky fronds. Zones 4–8.

P. setiferum. Soft shield fern. Europe. Height 4 ft; spread 3 ft (120 × 90 cm). Rosettes of spreading, soft green, and divided fronds, lance-shaped to oval in outline, with brown scaly bases. This fern is highly variable, with over 300 cultivars known. 'Acutilobum' has narrow, pointed fronds; 'Congestum' has upright fronds with overlapping leaflets; 'Plumoso-divisilobum' has fronds deeply divided into slender overlapping segments; 'Rotundatum' has almost circular leaflets; 'Tripinnatum' has delicate, finely divided fronds. Zones 5–8.

PONTEDERIA

(Pickerel-weed)

Family: Pontederiaceae

A small genus of about four species of aquatic plants native to North and South America, with heart-shaped leaves and spikes of blue or white flowers in summer.

Cultivation: Plant in 3–9 in. (7.5–22.5 cm) of water in full sun. Remove faded flowers.

Landscape Use: An attractive plant for the edges of ponds or lakes.

Propagation: Separate rooted lateral stems and replant in spring.

P. cordata. Pickerel weed. North America. Height 30 in.; spread 18 in. (75 × 45 cm). Stout green stems bear glossy green, lance-shaped leaves with heart-shaped bases, to 10 in. (25 cm) long and 6 in. (15 cm) wide. Clustered spikes of blue flowers are produced in late summer. Variety ***alba*** has white flowers. Zones 4–9.

PORTERANTHUS

(Bowman's-root)

Family: Rosaceae

Porteranthus trifoliata

Two species of woodland plants native to North America and formerly placed in the genus ***Gillenia.*** The stems are branched and wiry, the compound leaves have three leaflets, and the flowers are white or pinkish white, blooming in summer.

Cultivation: Easily cultivated plants in moist but well-drained, humus-rich soil, in sun or partial shade.

Landscape Use: Grow in a shady border or woodland garden where dappled sunlight can illuminate the starry flowers.

PROPAGATION: Divide in spring or sow seed in autumn.

P. stipulata. Eastern North America. Height 4 ft; spread 2 ft (120 × 60 cm). A clump-forming plant with dark-green, lance-shaped, deeply cut leaves with leaflike appendages (stipules) at the base of each leaf stem. Starry, white flowers appear in summer. Zones 4–8.

P. trifoliata. Bowman's-root. Eastern North America. Height 4 ft; spread 2 ft (120 × 60 cm). Similar to the above species but with more rounded leaflets and smaller, awl-shaped, leaflike appendages at the base of the leaf stem. Masses of starry, white flowers on reddish stems appear in summer. Zones 4–8.

POTENTILLA

(Cinquefoil)

FAMILY: Rosaceae

Potentilla alba

Potentilla nepalensis 'Miss Willmott'

About 500 species of herbaceous perennials and shrubs, most with toothed and veined, fan-shaped leaves similar to the leaves of the strawberry. The five-petaled flowers come in yellow, white, pink, or red in late spring or summer. The generic name, ***Potentilla,*** is derived from the Latin *potens,* "powerful," a reference to the medicinal properties of some of the species. The common name refers to the five-parted flowers.

CULTIVATION: Grow in well-drained soil that is not too rich, in full sun or light shade. In hot climates provide afternoon shade.

LANDSCAPE USE: Open-faced, long-blooming flowers for the rock garden or border.

PROPAGATION: Divide in spring or autumn. Take basal cuttings in late spring or sow seed in spring.

P. alba. Europe. Height 3 in.; spread 3 in. (7.5 × 7.5 cm). A mat-forming plant with fanlike leaves divided into five stemless oval to lance-shaped mid-green leaflets 1–2 in. (2.5–5 cm) long, silvery underneath. Heads of white, yellow-eyed flowers are produced on short stems in summer and occasionally in autumn. A fine, vigorous plant for the rock garden or path edging. Zones 4–7.

P. atrosanguinea. Himalayas. Height 2 ft; spread 2 ft (60 × 60 cm). A clump-forming, somewhat coarse perennial more important for its contribution to a number of hybrids and cultivars. The leaves are held on long stems and are mid-green, silky green above, white underneath, divided into three elliptical to egg-shaped toothed leaflets. Sprays of 1-in.- (2.5-cm-) wide, blood-red, cup-shaped flowers are produced in summer. This species has been crossed with ***P. argyrophylla,*** which is a similar species but with yellow flowers, to produce a range of plants that are sometimes listed ***P. × menziesii***

or ***P. atrosanguinea Argyrophylla*** group. Whatever they are named, they are superior to both parents. 'Blazeway': height about 16 in. (40 cm), orange-red flowers; 'Firedance': height 15 in. (37.5 cm) with red-centered orange flowers; 'Fireflame': height 14 in. (35 cm) with deep-red flowers; 'Gibson's Scarlet': height 12–18 in. (30–45 cm), brilliant scarlet flowers, a popular cultivar with an open, rather lax habit; 'Gloire de Nancy': height 18 in. (45 cm), semidouble orange-crimson flowers, 'Yellow Queen': height 12 in. (30 cm), red-eyed yellow flowers. Although drought tolerant; they do best in cooler climates shaded from the full heat of the sun. More compact forms are desirable as this group tend to open out, leaving a bald center. Zones 5–8.

***P* aurea.** Europe. Height 4 in.; spread 8–12 in. (10 × 20–30 cm). A clump-forming plant with woody stems and green, hand-shaped leaves divided into five oblong leaflets silky underneath. Sprays of flat, dark-eyed, golden-yellow, ½-in.- (1.2-cm-) wide flowers are produced in late summer. 'Plena' has semidouble flowers. Zones 5–8.

P. eriocarpa. Himalayas. Height 4 in.; spread 12 in. (10 × 30 cm). A spreading, clump-forming species with oval, dark-green leaves divided into three toothed, wedge-shaped leaflets. Pale-yellow flowers are borne singly throughout the summer. Zones 5–7.

P. nepalensis. Nepal. Height 18 in.; spread 2 ft (45 × 60 cm). A short-lived species with long-stemmed, fan-shaped, strawberrylike, toothed, and hairy leaves divided into five leaflets up to 2 in. (5 cm) long. Branching stems carry single pink to deep-pink flowers throughout the summer. 'Miss Willmott' has cherry-red flowers with a darker eye; 'Roxana' has pink, orange, and dark-red flowers. Zones 5–8.

P. nitida. Europe. Height 2 in.; spread 8 in. (5 × 20 cm). A mat-forming tufted plant with rounded leaves divided into three spoon-shaped, silky leaflets about ½ in. (1.2 cm) long. In early summer 1-in.- (2.5-cm-) wide, saucer-shaped rose-pink flowers with darker centers are sparingly produced. 'Rubra' has deep-pink flowers. Zones 5–8.

P. recta. Europe. Height 1–2 ft; spread 2 ft (30–60 × 60 cm). A weedy, clump-forming plant with dark-green, hairy, and toothed leaves divided into five to nine oblong, 2–4-in.- (5–10-cm-) long leaflets. Terminal clusters of bright-yellow flowers are produced throughout the summer. Variety ***sulphurea*** has sulfur-yellow flowers; 'Warrenii' is less weedy and has 1-in.- (2.5-cm-) wide golden yellow flowers. Zones 4–8.

P. tabernaemontana. Europe. Height 6 in.; spread 12 in. (15 × 30 cm). A mat-forming plant with semi-procumbent stems that root themselves into the soil and dark-green, hand-shaped leaves divided into five wedge-shaped, toothed leaflets ¾ in. (1.8 cm) long. Clusters of golden yellow flowers, ½ in. (1.2 cm) wide, are produced in spring. 'Nana' grows to about 3 in. (7.5 cm) high. Zones 4–8.

P. × tongueii. Height 6 in.; spread 1 ft (15 × 30 cm). A hybrid between ***P. anglica*** and ***P. nepalensis*** with trailing stems and evergreen leaves divided into five broadly egg-shaped, coarsely toothed leaflets. In early summer 1-in.- (2.5-cm-) wide, red-eyed apricot flowers are produced. Zones 5–8.

P. tridentata. North America. Height 6–12 in.; spread 12 in. (15–30 × 30 cm). It is an alarming thought that this tough but charming plant may now have the unwieldy name ***Sibbaldiopsis tridentata.*** It is an excellent plant for the rock garden, for rocky soil, or for dry banks that are too difficult for many other plants. The base is often woody, the fan-shaped leaves in basal tufts, divided into three wedge-shaped leaflets with three conspicuous teeth at the leaflet apex. Sprays of ¼-in.- (0.6-cm-) wide white flowers are produced in early summer. It spreads fairly rapidly. Zones 2–8.

PRIMULA

(Primrose)

Family: Primulaceae

Up to 550 mostly perennial species native to Europe, Asia, and North America with a few species scattered in South America, Africa, and the Middle East. With so many species, much taxonomic subdi-

Primula elatior

Primula vulgaris ssp. *sibthorpii*

vision has been attempted, dividing the genus into seven subgenera and 30 sections. Within a few of these sections are the primulas cultivated in North American, European, and Asian gardens.

The leaves are held in basal rosettes, sometimes with leaf stems, sometimes without. The tubular, funnel-shaped, bell-shaped, or flat flowers are borne in a variety of forms, including spikes, domed heads, whorls, or singly from the leaf axils. Many species have the leaves and flower stems covered in a mealy substance called "farina." Most species bloom in spring and early summer, in a wide range of colors from white, yellow, pink, red, purple, to blue. Many have been hybridized to create an extraordinary range of plants from the low-growing Elatior Hybrids to the wide range of candelabra primulas.

In general, they are plants for mild climates, being particularly susceptible to the heat of continental summers. In North America primulas are especially at home in the cool climates of the Pacific Northwest. North American gardeners have been singularly shy of experimenting with members of this genus. In fact, so little cultivation of primulas has taken place on the continent that it is hard to assess how many species can be cultivated well. It seems that most species native to mountainous regions do not do well in the subtropical summers of much of the United States. However, if we continue to experiment, I believe we will find that primulas are better garden plants for a wider area of the country than has first been supposed.

Cultivation: The wide range of requirements for primula cultivation make generalization difficult. Comments on cultivation are included under individual descriptions. Most garden primulas are susceptible to damage from slugs and snails, black vine weevil, and aphids. Rusts and leaf spot diseases are also common. Mulch for winter protection.

Landscape Use: There are primulas for almost every occasion. The tall candelabra primulas are exceptionally beautiful when grown in large numbers in the bog garden. The cowslips and oxlips are plants for the deciduous woodland and shrub border. Others are for rock gardens and screes. No garden, large or small, should be without primulas.

Propagation: Divide after flowering or in early autumn, or sow seeds as soon as ripe.

P. alpicola. Section Sikkimensis. Tibet. Height 6–20 in.; spread 12 in. (15–50 × 30 cm). The toothed basal leaves are elliptical to oblong-elliptical, up to 6 in. (15 cm) long, with the upper leaf surface wrinkled. The flower stem is farinose (covered in mealy farina). The funnel-shaped flowers are borne in drooping clusters and are light yellow. They are produced in midsummer. Variety ***alba*** has white flowers; var. ***luna*** has lemon-yellow flowers. Grow in full or partial shade in moist, peaty soil. Zones 6–8.

P. aurantiaca. Section Proliferae (Candelabra). China. Height 1–2 ft; spread 1 ft (30–60 × 30 cm). A vigorous primula with finely toothed, oval, blunt-tipped leaves up to 8 in. (20 cm) long and whorls of flat, red-tinged, orange-yellow flowers just over 1 in. (2.5 cm) wide in midsummer. Grow in constantly moist soil in sun to partial shade. Zones 6–8.

P. auricula. Section Auricula. Subsection Euauricula. European Alps. Height 6 in.; spread 6 in.

(15 × 15 cm). A variable plant with wavy-edged, roundly egg-shaped, leathery leaves up to 6 in. (15 cm) long often covered with farina. The fragrant, mostly yellow, flat flowers are produced in early spring. Subspecies ***ciliata*** has odorless flowers and green leaves not covered in farina. Grow in partial shade in alkaline and gritty soil. There are a number of cultivars. Zones 3–8.

P. beesiana. Section Proliferae (Candelabra). China. Height 2 ft; spread 1 ft (60 × 30 cm). A short-lived, clump-forming species with egg-shaped to lance-shaped, blunt-tipped and finely serrated leaves up to 20 in. (50 cm) long and rosy lilac, orange- or yellow-eyed flowers borne in whorled clusters in late spring and early summer. Variety ***leucantha*** has pure-white flowers. Requires constantly moist soil and partial shade. Zones 6–8.

P. bulleyana. Section Proliferae (Candelabra). China. Height 2 ft; spread 1 ft (60 × 30 cm). The leaves are thin and are egg-shaped to lance-shaped with a red midrib and irregularly toothed edges. The tubular, orange-yellow to deep orange flowers are borne in dense whorled clusters in early to midsummer. Grow in moist soil in full sun to partial shade. Zones 6–8. Hybrids between this species and ***P. bulleyana*** ae named ***P. × bullesiana*** and come in a range of colors, including yellow, orange, pink, and violet. Zones 6–8.

P. denticulata. Section Denticulata. Drumstick primula. Himalayas. Height 12 in.; spread 9 in. (30 × 22.5 cm). The spoon-shaped, finely toothed leaves appear with the flowers and are about 4 in. (10 cm) at that time, but grow to about 12 in. (30 cm) long after flowering. Flowering in early spring with drumstick heads of yellow-eyed lilac, white, or pink flowers, this is one of the easiest primulas to grow. Variety ***alba*** has white flowers; var. ***cashmeriana*** has purple flowers in the autumn. There are a number of cultivars. Grow in full sun to partial shade in moist but well-drained soil. Zones 5–8.

P. elatior. Section Primula. Oxlip. Europe, Asia. Height 12 in.; spread 6 in. (30 × 15 cm). A diminutive primula with fresh green, toothed, and wrinkled, rounded to egg-shaped leaves and tubular, light-yellow flowers in spring. It is a variable species with a number of subspecies. Hybrids between this species, ***P. vulgaris,*** the English primrose, and ***P. veris,*** the cowslip, are called the Elatior Hybrids or ***P. × polyantha.*** They are early-blooming plants forming low-growing clumps of wrinkled, strong green leaves with masses of both single and double (hose-in-hose) flowers in an enormous range of colors. Some are also edged with bicolored margins. There are a large number of cultivars. Both the species and the hybrids grow best in moist but well-drained soil in partial shade. Zones 4–8.

P. florindae. Section Sikkimensis. Tibetan primrose. Tibet. Height 2–3 ft; spread 1–2 ft (60–90 × 30–60 cm). One of the easiest of the Himalayan primulas to grow, although it does not grow well in climates with hot summers. The dark-green and glossy leaves are broadly egg-shaped to heart-shaped and up to 8 in. (20 cm) long. The flower cluster, which is borne on a reddish stem, is mealy and bears drooping, funnel-shaped, sulfur-yellow flowers in summer. Flower color is variable, and orange and red tones are common. It is an elegant plant, often seeding itself in streambeds and other wet places. Grow in constantly moist soil in partial shade. Zones 6–8.

P. frondosa. Section Aleuritia (Farinosa). Balkans. Height 6 in.; spread 6 in. (15 × 15 cm). A mealy primula covered in farina, this species has egg-shaped leaves about 3 in. (7.5 cm) long and lilac-rose flowers with a yellow eye, on 6-in. (15-cm) stems in spring. It is a delicate-looking plant best grown in partial shade in humus-rich, gritty soil. Zones 6–8.

P. japonica. Section Proliferae (Candelabra). Japanese primrose. Japan. Height 1–2 ft; spread 12–18 in. (30–60 × 30–45). By far the easiest primula to grow, this is a vigorous species quickly colonizing wet ground. The broadly spoon-shaped leaves are fine-toothed and irregularly lobed, reaching a length of about 12 in. (30 cm). The flower stem is thick and erect, bearing whorls of purple to magenta-red, pink, or white flowers in late spring. There are a number of cultivars, including 'Apple

Primula japonica

Blossom,' with pinkish white flowers; 'Miller's Crimson,' with red flowers; 'Postford White,' with pure-white flowers. Grow in full sun in wet soil, in partial to full shade in moist soil. Zones 6–8.

P. kisoana. Section Cortusoides. Japan. Height 8 in.; spread 12 in. (20 × 30 cm). Uncommon in cultivation, this primula grows well in shaded areas in climates with hot summers. The leaves are rounded with a heart-shaped base, lobed and toothed, up to 6 in. (15 cm) long. The attractive flowers are just over 1 in. (2.5 cm) wide borne on short stems and are soft pink in color. They appear in spring. 'Alba' has pure-white flowers. Grow in neutral, humus-rich soil in partial shade. Zones 6–8.

P. pulverulenta. Section Proliferae (Candelabra). China. Height 2–3 ft; spread 12–18 in. (60–90 × 30–45 cm). A vigorous candelabra primula with coarsely toothed, egg-shaped leaves up to 12 in. (30 cm) long and slender, mealy flower stems bearing many-flowered whorls of deep-red flowers with a darker eye. Blooms in early summer. Grow in moist soil in full sun to partial shade. Zones 6–8.

P. sieboldii. Section Cortusoides. East Asia. Height 12 in.; spread 12 in. (30 × 30 cm). An easily cultivated primula with wrinkled, egg-shaped to oblong downy leaves up to 8 in. (20 cm) long. The flower stem reaches up to 12 in. (30 cm) high and bears variably colored flowers in shades of pink, red, and white. The plants die down after flowering, making this a good selection for hot climates. There are a number of cultivars, including 'Alba,' with white flowers; 'Isotaka,' with purple flowers flushed white; 'Wine Lady,' with white flowers flushed purple-red. Grow in humus-rich, moist soil in partial to full shade. Zones 5–8.

P. veris. Section Vernales (Primula). Cowslip. Europe, west and central Asia. Height 6–8 in.; spread 8 in. (15–20 × 20 cm). A variable species with 4-in.-(10-cm-) long, egg-shaped to roundly lance-shaped, wrinkled leaves, hairy-white underneath. The downy flower stem bears a many-flowered, one-sided cluster of egg-yolk-yellow flowers in spring. There are many hybrids. Grow in a sunny site in moist but well-drained soil. Zones 5–9.

P. viallii. Section Muscarioides. China. Height 18 in.; spread 12 in. (45 × 30 cm). A short-lived species with hairy, broadly lance-shaped to oblong, irregularly toothed leaves up to 12 in. (30 cm) long. The flower stem is mealy toward the top and bears a conical spike of red-and-purple flowers in late spring and early summer. It performs poorly in areas with hot summers and should be grown in moist, humus-rich soil in partial shade. Zones 6–7.

P. vulgaris. Section Vernales. English primrose. West and southwest Europe. Height 6–8 in.; spread 8 in. (15–20 × 20 cm). Common to woodland and shaded meadows of Europe, this spring favorite has egg-shaped to roundly lance-shaped, toothed and wrinkled, bright-green leaves up to 6 in. (15 cm) long. The apparently stemless, unscented dark-eyed primrose-yellow flowers are produced in spring. Subspecies ***balearica*** has fragrant white flowers. Subspecies ***sibthorpii*** (***P. abchasica***) has red, purple, or pink flowers and blooms in early spring. Both subspecies and others are important in the breeding of multicolored strains. Grow in full sun to partial shade in moist soil. Zones 5–9.

PRUNELLA

(Self-heal)

FAMILY: Labiatae

Seven to 12 species of semievergreen, mat-forming plants with square stems, opposite leaves, and hooded and lobed flowers in summer. The common self-heal, ***P. vulgaris*** is native to Europe and Asia and was highly prized for its medicinal value. It is naturalized in North America, where it is a common lawn weed. The generic name comes from *brunellen,* the German word for an inflammation of the mouth supposedly cured by the plant. It was also favored for its putative ability to speed the healing of wounds.

CULTIVATION: Often invasive plants for cool climates, growing best in moist soil in full sun to partial shade. Remove the faded flower heads to avoid self-seeding.

Landscape Use: Spreading plants for the rock garden, border, or pondside.

Propagation: Divide in spring or autumn.

P. grandiflora. Europe. Height 6 in.; spread 18 in. (15 × 45 cm). A mat-forming plant with hairy and leafy stems and with egg-shaped to wedge-shaped dark-green leaves up to 2 in. (5 cm) long becoming smaller up on the stem. The violet-purple flowers are lipped and hooded and held in whorled clusters in summer. 'Alba' has white flowers; 'Rosea' has rosy red flowers. Zones 5–8.

P.* × *webbiana. Europe. Height 6–8 in.; spread 12–18 in. (15–20 × 30–45 cm). Possibly a hybrid or subspecies of ***P. grandiflora.*** Whatever it is, it is very similar but has smaller leaves in basal rosettes, more compact spikes of violet-purple flowers, and grows a little taller. 'Alba' has white flowers, 'Blue Loveliness' has purple-blue flowers; 'Pink Loveliness' has pink flowers; 'White Loveliness' has heavy clusters of white flowers. Zones 5–8.

Prunella x *webbiana* 'Lilac Loveliness'

PTERIDIUM

(Bracken)

Family: Dennstaedtiaceae

One species of hardy fern native to much of the temperate world. Strictly speaking, it is not commonly a garden plant, but it can be highly effective in large masses in deciduous woodland.

Cultivation: An invasive fern in damp or dry, leafy or sandy soil in sun and shade.

Landscape Use: A coarse fern useful as a backdrop for finer plants or as a mass planting in woodland. The yellow autumn color is particularly wonderful in conjunction with the reds and yellows of maples and other deciduous trees.

Propagation: Divide in spring or autumn.

P. aquilinum. Bracken. Transglobal. Height 4 ft; spread 2 ft (120 × 60 cm). A coarse, deciduous fern with deep-green, leathery, widely spaced fronds egg-shaped to triangular in outline, with the leaf segments finely divided with conspicuous veins on the undersides. Zones 3–9.

PULMONARIA

(Lungwort)

Family: Boraginaceae

Twelve species of low-growing, clump-forming, spring-flowering plants native to Europe and Asia, with blue, red, pink, or white five-lobed, funnel-shaped flowers that open before or just as the foliage appears in spring. They are often pink in bud but open to bright blue, sometimes fading back to pinkish blue. The leaves are mostly basal, sometimes dappled with greenish-white to silver, on long, often hairy

Pulmonaria longifolia

Pulmonaria rubra 'Bowles Red'

stems. The stem leaves are alternate. The generic and common names refer to the traditional use of the plant for treating lung ailments.

CULTIVATION: Grow in moist but well-drained soil in partial to full shade. Mulch and water well in dry areas.

LANDSCAPE USE: Champion groundcovers for shady areas, particularly under trees and shrubs. The spotted foliage makes an excellent foil for delicate flowers either as a specimen in the border or as a large, sweeping mass along a shady path.

PROPAGATION: Easily divided in spring or autumn. Seed-grown plants are often inferior.

P. angustifolia. Blue lungwort. Europe. Height 9–12 in.; spread 18 in. (22.5–30 × 45 cm). The dark-green, unspotted, lance-shaped and bristly basal leaves are 8–12 in. (20–30 cm) long. Funnel-shaped nodding flowers, pink in bud, open to deep blue in early spring, approximately at the same time that forsythia blooms. Variety ***azurea*** has rich-blue flowers; 'Mawson's Blue' has slightly narrower leaves and violet-blue flowers tinged red with age; 'Munstead Blue' has rich-blue flowers. All are fairly similar to each other. Zones 3–8.

P. longifolia. Long-leaf lungwort. Europe. Height 9–12 in.; spread 18 in. (22.5–30 × 45 cm). An underused lungwort with narrow, spotted, and pointed leaves up to 12–18 in. (30–45 cm) long. The stem leaves become smaller and more narrow toward the flower cluster. Dense sprays of vivid violet-blue, funnel-shaped flowers appear in spring. 'Bertram Anderson' has silvery green spots but doesn't differ greatly from the species. Zones 3–8.

P. mollis. Europe, Asia. Height 18 in.; spread 2 ft (45 × 60 cm). A large, clump-forming plant easily recognizable by its greater size. Long-stemmed deep-green leaves are covered in soft hairs. The flowers are deep blue, often fading to pinkish blue to red. Zones 4–8.

P. officinalis. Common lungwort. Europe. Height 1 ft; spread 1 ft (30 × 30 cm). Greenish white and spotted, bristly, heart-shaped basal leaves and funnel-shaped pinkish blue flowers that turn violet-blue in spring. Variety ***alba*** has white flowers; var. ***rubra*** has reddish purple flowers. 'Cambridge Blue' has light-blue flowers; 'Sissinghurst White' has white flowers and small silver spots. Zones 4–8.

P. rubra (P. montana). Red lungwort. Europe. Height 1 ft; spread 2 ft (30 × 60 cm). One of the earliest to flower with sprays of coral-red, tubular flowers appearing before the foliage in early spring. The pale-green leaves are almost stemless, unspotted, and elliptical to lance-shaped, evergreen in mild climates. 'Barfield Pink' has deep-pink flowers; 'Bowles Red' has reddish pink flowers slightly spotted with darker pink; 'Lewis Palmer' has pale-pink flowers; 'Redstart' has brick-red flowers; 'Salmon Glow' has salmon-pink flowers. Zones 4–8.

P. saccharata. Bethlehem sage. Europe. Height 1 ft; spread 2 ft (30 × 60 cm). Similar but superior to ***P. officianalis,*** with leaves more heavily spotted with silver and gray, sometimes consolidating to almost exclude any green. Pink buds open to blue funnel-shaped flowers in spring. The variety ***argentea*** has silvery green leaves. 'Highdown' grows to 12 in. (30 cm) high and has nodding blue flowers; 'Margery Fish' is a vigorous species (sometimes seen as ***P. vallarsae*** 'Margery Fish') with spotted leaves and pinkish blue flowers; 'Mrs. Moon' has silver-spotted leaves and pinkish blue flowers; 'Pink Dawn' has pink flowers. All are excellent groundcovers. Zones 3–8.

PULSATILLA

(Pasque Flower)

Family: Ranunculaceae

About 12 species of spring-flowering plants formerly placed in the genus ***Anemone.*** The leaves are feathery and often silky. The flowers, which appear before the foliage, are urn-shaped and petalless, the petallike segments being sepals. The foliage dies down in midsummer. The generic name comes from the Latin *pulsc,* "beat," supposedly from the silky seeds being beaten by the wind. The herbalist John Gerard (1545–1612) named the common species Pasque flower from its habit of flowering at Easter.

Cultivation: Grow in well-drained soil in full sun. In climates with hot summers, shade from afternoon sun.

Landscape Use: Silky plants for the rock garden or dry bank.

Propagation: Sow seed in summer. They do not take to division happily.

P. vulgaris. Pasque flower. Europe. Height 6–12 in.; spread 9 in. (15–30 × 22.5 cm). The most widely grown ***Pulsatilla*** with saucer-shaped flowers with pointed purple sepals and yellow centers. The flowers appear in spring before the finely hairy, light-green, dissected leaves have fully opened. After flowering, silky seed heads are produced on the elongating stems, which reach a height of about 12 in. (30 cm). The variety ***alba*** has white flowers; var. ***rubra*** has reddish purple flowers. 'Barton's Pink' has clear pink flowers; 'Burgundy' has ruby-red flowers 'Mrs. Van der Elst' has salmon-pink flowers; 'White Swan' has white flowers.

Pulsatilla vulgaris var. *rubra*

PYCNANTHEMUM

(Mountain Mint)

Family: Labiatae

Approximately 20 species of aromatic herbs with square stems, opposite leaves mostly untoothed, and short, dense flower heads surrounded by bracts. The generic name is from the Greek meaning "dense blossom." This is an underused genus of plants that are particularly attractive in late summer and autumn. They are native to North America, generally inhabiting prairie and meadowland.

Cultivation: Easily grown in full sun in ordinary soil.

Landscape Use: Excellent late-summer-flowering

plants for the back or midborder, meadow, or wildflower garden. They make an admirable display in combination with ***Eupatorium fistulosum.***

Propagation: Divide in spring or autumn.

P. flexuosum. United States. Height 1–3 ft; spread 18 in. (30–90 × 45 cm). An erect plant covered in minute, soft hairs, with slender stems and linear to oblong leaves up to 2 in. (5 cm) long. Heads of lipped and lobed mauve-pink flowers are produced in late summer. The whole plant has a minty aroma when crushed. Grow in dry soil in full sun. Zones 5–8.

P. pilosum. Eastern United States. Height 2–3 ft; spread 18 in. (60–90 × 45 cm). An erect plant with lance-shaped leaves with wedge-shaped leaf bases. The leaves are densely hairy underneath. Pinkish white flowers are produced in late summer. Zones 5–8.

P. tenuifolium. Slender mountain mint. Eastern United States. Height 2 ft; spread 18 in. (60 × 45 cm). An upright plant with branched, smooth stems and fragrant, linear, smooth or slightly hairy leaves. Purple-speckled white flowers are produced in dense terminal clusters throughout the summer. Zones 5–8.

P. virginianum. Eastern United States. Height 3 ft; spread 18 in. (90 × 45 cm). A stiff, upright species with stout, branched stems and lance-shaped leaves. The whitish purple flowers are surrounded by leafy bracts and bloom in late summer. Zones 5–8.

RAMONDA

Family: Gesneriaceae

Ramonda myconi var. *rosea*

A small genus of hairy, evergreen plants native to the mountains of southern and eastern Europe. They form dark-green rosettes of wrinkled and toothed leaves and produce flat, rounded flowers of purple-blue, pink, or white flowers that are reminiscent of African violets. Named after Louis Francis Ramond (1753–1827), traveler and botanist.

Cultivation: Grow in well-drained, peaty soil in a shaded rock wall or crevice, preferably facing north.

Landscape Use: Attractive and unusual alpines for the rock garden.

Propagation: Take leaf cuttings in early autumn or root offsets in summer.

R. myconi. Pyrennes. Height 3–4 in.; spread 4 in. (7.5–10 × 10 cm). Evergreen rosettes of crinkled and toothed, elliptical to egg-shaped leaves with red hairs covering both the base and underneath the leaf. Branching stems carry 1-in.- (2.5-cm-) wide, flat and rounded, purple-blue flowers with a yellow center in late spring and early summer. Variety ***alba*** has white flowers; var. ***rosea*** has rosy red flowers. Zones 6–7.

R. nathaliae. Bulgaria, Yugoslavia. Height 4 in.; spread 4 in. (10 × 10 cm). Similar to the above species but with pale-green, glossy leaves with dark hairs and lavender flowers in late spring and early summer. 'Alba' has white flowers. Zones 6–7.

RANUNCULUS

(Buttercup)

FAMILY: Ranunculaceae

A large genus of annual and perennial plants most of which are hardy though a few are tender. Most species are not garden-worthy plants, and a few are so invasive that they can quickly take over large areas. Both ***R. ficaria,*** the lesser celandine, and ***R. repens,*** the creeping buttercup, are highly invasive plants. The leaves are alternate, often fan-shaped and divided. The flowers are mostly cup-shaped with five petals and yellow, white, and red flowers. The generic name is derived from the Latin *rana,* "frog," an allusion to the wet sites many of the species inhabit.

CULTIVATION: Grow the cultivated species in moist, well-drained soil in sun or partial shade.

LANDSCAPE USE: A few species of good border or rock-garden plants.

PROPAGATION: Divide in spring or autumn or sow seed in spring.

R. aconitifolius. Europe. Height 3 ft; spread 3 ft (90 × 90 cm). A vigorous, clump-forming plant with leafy stems. The leaves are fan-shaped, glossy, and dark green; divided into three to five lobed and notched sections, they are similar to the leaves of many species of ***Aconitum.*** Single white, yellow-centered, 1-in.- (2.5-cm-) wide flowers are produced in spring and summer. Variety ***platanifolius*** has larger, maplelike leaves. 'Flore Pleno,' commonly called Fair-Maids-of-France, has much greater ornamental value. The pure-white, cushionlike flowers are produced in large masses on branched stems in spring and summer. Zones 5–9.

Ranunculus aconitifolius var. *platanifolius*

R. amplexicaulis. Pyrenees. Height 10 in.; spread 4 in. (25 × 10 cm). An upright plant with lance-shaped, gray-green leaves that clasp the stem. One-in.- (2.5-cm-) wide, cup-shaped white flowers with a yellow center are produced in early summer. Zones 4–8.

R. gramineus. Europe. Height 20 in.; spread 4 in. (50 × 10 cm). An upright plant with linear blue-green leaves and 1-in.- (2.5-cm-) wide, bright-yellow, cup-shaped flowers in late spring. Zones 6–8.

R. montanus. Europe. Height 6 in.; spread 4 in. (15 × 10 cm). A spreading, tufted plant with rounded leaves divided into three to five linear to oblong segments. Single buttercup flowers appear in early summer. 'Molten Gold' has larger golden yellow flowers. Zones 5–8.

RAOULIA

Family: Compositae

A genus of about 25 species of cushion-forming foliage plants mostly native to New Zealand. Those that are easy to cultivate, and that's not many, make fine rock-garden or alpine house plants. The leaves are alternate, crowded, and overlapping. The flowers are disc-shaped and largely insignificant. Named after Edouard Raoul, a 19th-century French traveler to New Zealand.

Cultivation: Grow in a mild climate in full sun and well-drained, gritty soil. Protect from wet winter weather.

Landscape Use: Charming cushion plants for the rock garden.

Propagation: Divide and replant in spring.

R. australis. Silvermat. New Zealand. Height ½ in.; spread 12 in. (1.2 × 30 cm). A carpeting plant with tiny rosettes of crowded silvery green, overlapping, and spoon-shaped leaves. Dense heads of minute, sulfur-yellow, starlike flowers appear in summer. Zones 8–9.

R. eximia. Vegetable sheep. New Zealand. Height 1 in.; spread 12 in. (2.5 × 30 cm). The wonderful common name more than adequately describes the appearance of this silvery white, hummock-forming plant. It has rosettes of woolly gray, crowded and overlapping, linear, spoon-shaped leaves to ⅛ in. (0.3 cm) long. Tiny heads of creamy white flowers are produced in early summer. A challenge to grow, perhaps best cultivated in an alpine house. Zones 7–8.

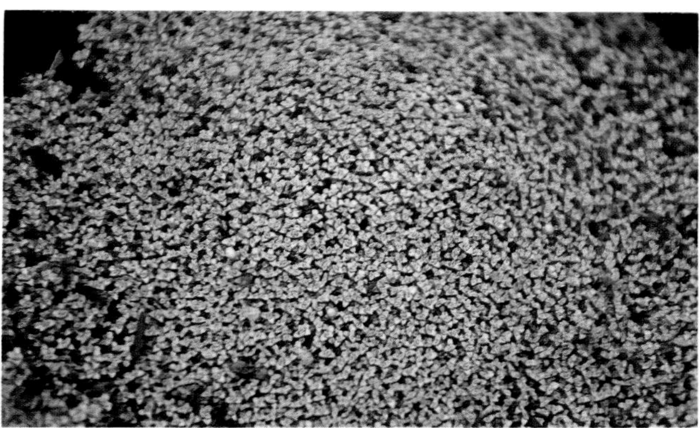

Raoulia australis

R. haastii. New Zealand. Height ½ in.; spread 12 in. (1.2 × 30 cm). A hummock-forming plant with tiny, overlapping, bright-green leaves that turn coppery brown in winter. Starry yellow flowers are produced somewhat randomly in summer. Zones 7–8.

RATIBIDA

(Coneflower)

Family: Compositae

A small genus of hairy perennials native to North America. They are coarse plants with alternate, divided leaves and daisylike flowers of yellow ray flowers and conical or oblong disk flowers a bit like the crown of a hat.

Cultivation: Grow in ordinary, well-drained soil in full sun.

Landscape Use: Underused plants for the sunny border, wild garden, or meadow.

Propagation: Sow seed in spring or divide in spring or autumn.

R. columnifera. Mexican hat, prairie coneflower. North America. Height 2–3 ft; spread 18 in. (60–90 × 45 cm). A coarse, hairy plant with stems branching from the base and leaves divided into seven to nine linear to narrow lance-shaped segments. The summer-blooming flowers are held singly on the flower stems and are made up of drooping, blunt-toothed, yellow ray flowers surrounding a prominent 1½-in.- (3.8-cm-) long cone of gray to tan disk flowers. Forma ***pulcherrima*** has mahogany-red, yellow-edged ray flowers. Zones 3–9.

R. pinnata. Yellow coneflower. North America. Height 4 ft; spread 18 in. (120 × 45 cm). Coarse and hairy, with branching stems and alternate leaves divided into three to five lance-shaped, serated leaflets. The flower is similar to the above species, but the ray flowers are golden yellow and the conelike disk flowers are not as prominent, only ¾ in. (1.8 cm) long. Zones 3–9.

REHMANNIA

Family: Gesneriaceae

Rehmannia elata

Eight to ten species of clump-forming plants with mostly basal, lobed leaves and luscious foxglovelike flowers in late spring and early summer. They are native to China and grow best in subtropical climates, although the one species described below may sneak in under the line.

Cultivation: Grow in a sunny sheltered site and protect from the ravages of winter cold and wet.

Landscape Use: Almost tender plants for the sheltered border, valuable for their exotic-looking, long-blooming pink or red flowers.

Propagation: Sow seeds in spring.

R. elata. Chinese foxglove. China. Height 3 ft; spread 18 in. (90 × 45 cm). A clump-forming plant with lax stems and basal, egg-shaped to elliptical, coarsely lobed leaves. Tubular rose-purple, foxglovelike flowers with red-spotted yellow throats are produced from early to midsummer. Zones 8–10.

RHAZYA

Family: Apocynaceae

Two species, one native to Greece, the other native to northwest India, with alternate mostly lance-shaped leaves and bright-blue flowers in summer.

Cultivation: Grow in moist but well-drained soil

in full sun or partial shade.

LANDSCAPE USE: Early summer blooms are always useful particularly if they are blue. The one species cultivated is an excellent front-of-border plant.

PROPAGATION: Divide in spring or early autumn, or sow seed in spring.

R. orientalis. Greece. Height 18 in.; spread 12 in. (45 × 30 cm). A clump-forming plant with stiff stems, lance-shaped leaves up to 2 inches (5 cm) long, and loose clusters of bright- to dark-blue, funnel-shaped flowers in early summer. The stiff leaves and flowers are reminiscent of ***Amsonia*** species. Zones 6–9.

Rhazya orientalis

RHEUM

(Rhubarb)

FAMILY: Polygonaceae

Rheum palmatum 'Bowles Crimson'

Fifty species of generally large, basal-leaved plants with small cream, white, or brick-red flowers in large hollow-stemmed spikes appearing in the summer. They are cool-climate plants and do not take kindly to much of North America's hot weather, preferring cool summers and mild winters. The edible rhubarb, ***R. × cultorum,*** is quite an ornamental plant, but it is better stewed. It is the main reason for the invention of custard.

CULTIVATION: Plant in rich, moist soil in full sun to partial shade. Cut the faded flower spikes down to the ground.

LANDSCAPE USE: Large and dramatic foliage plants for the side of a pond, stream, or bog garden. Very effective in the dappled shade of a deciduous woodland.

PROPAGATION: Divide in spring or sow seed in spring, plant the following year.

R. alexandrae. Himalayas. Height 3 ft; spread 2 ft (90 × 60 cm). Not widely cultivated because of its capricious nature but worth the effort for its long-stemmed, glossy, dark-green, egg-shaped, conspicuously veined leaves with a deep cleft at the base and its panicles of creamy white flowers covered by egg-shaped, greenish white bracts in early summer. The bracts turn red as they age. Zone 6–8.

R. palmatum. China. Height 6–8 ft; spread 4–6 ft (180–240 × 120–180 cm). The most widely grown of the ornamental rhubarbs, with leaves that are dark-green, up to 3 ft (90 cm) wide, rounded, fanlike, lobed and toothed with a heart-shaped base and 2-ft- (60-cm-) long branched spikes of white, pink, or red flowers in early summer. The variety ***tanguticum*** has less deeply cut leaves that are dark purple; 'Atrosanguineum' is a wonderful cultivar, with dark purple-red leaves when young that become green by the summer but retain their purple-red coloring on the underside. Tall panicles of red flowers appear in early summer; 'Bowles' Crimson' is very similar. It is unfortunate that this species does not flourish in warm climates; it is the consummate waterside plant. Although cold hardy within Zones 5–9, it grows best in climates without extremes of temperature. They can, however, survive in warmer zones that have cool summers, as in Northern California.

RODGERSIA

Family: Saxifragaceae

Rodgersia pinnata 'Superba'

A small genus of large-leaved perennials native to eastern Asia, named after Rear Admiral John Rodgers of the U.S. Navy. The alternate leaves are thick, dark green, fan-shaped, and divided into five to nine leaflets. The white or pink flowers, except for one species, are without petals and are held in large pyramidal panicles in summer.

Cultivation: Grow in a sheltered site in sun to partial shade in moist but well-drained or boggy soil. They are plants for mild climates and do not enjoy hot and humid summers. Once planted, leave for two or three years to establish before propagating. They are prone to leaf scorch when grown in too much sun or too dry a soil.

Landscape Use: Effective foliage and flowering plants for the bog garden, pondside, or herbaceous border. Great with large-leaved hostas or the palmate foliage of ***Filipendula*** species.

Propagation: Divide in spring. Sow seeds in spring, planting into a permanent position two years later.

R. aesculifolia. China. Height 3–5 ft; spread 3 ft (90–150 × 90 cm). A clump-forming plant with fan-shaped, bronze-tinged, veined, and toothed leaves divided into seven leaflets up to 10 in. (25 cm) long. The leaves resemble those of the horsechestnut; hence the specific name. Tall panicles, up to 2 ft (60 cm) high, of fragrant creamy white to pink flowers are produced in summer. Zones 5–6.

R. pinnata. China. Height 3–4 ft; spread 3 ft (90–120 × 90 cm). Basal clumps of bronze-tinged, deep-green compound leaves divided into five to nine toothed, inversely lance-shaped leaflets up to 8 in. (20 cm) long. Branched, red-stemmed panicles of rose-red flowers are produced in early to midsummer. Variety ***elegans*** has creamy white to pale-pink flowers. 'Alba' has creamy yellow flowers; 'Irish Bronze' has strongly bronze-tinged foliage. 'Superba' has bronze-tinged leaves and long-blooming bright-pink flowers. Zones 5–7.

R. podophylla. China, Japan. Height 4 ft; spread 3 ft (120 × 90 cm). Fan-shaped, bronze-tinged leaves divided into five coarsely lobed and toothed, broadly egg-shaped leaflets up to 10 in. (25 cm) long. The leaves emerge bronze in spring, quickly turn light green, and then develop a coppery bronze tint in summer. Panicles of creamy white flowers are produced in summer. 'Pagoda' has attractive white flowers. Zones 5–7.

R. sambucifolia. China. Height 3–4 ft; spread 3 ft (90–120 × 90 cm). A clump-forming plant with up to 11 bright-green leaflets and flat-topped panicles of feathery white flowers in summer. 'Rothaut' (Red Skin) has dark-red leaves. Zones 5–7.

ROMNEYA

(Matilija Poppy)

FAMILY: Papaveraceae

Two species of subshrubby, woody-based plants with blue-green leaves and poppylike flowers. Native to southern California and parts of Mexico, they are invasive plants that are often difficult to establish, but once they are established they are exquisite. There is much debate as to their hardiness. With a winter mulch they are root hardy to Zone 6, but generally they are hardy to Zones 8–10. Named after T. Romney Robinson who discovered them in the mid-19th century. The common name refers to Matilija Canyon in Ventura County, where it is found in large numbers.

CULTIVATION: Grow in full sun in well-drained and preferably poor soil. They are slow to establish and resent disturbance but spread rapidly once they are settled in the soil. Mulch for winter protection.

LANDSCAPE USE: Large, shrubby plants for the warm and sheltered site.

PROPAGATION: Sow seeds in spring. Take basal stem cuttings in spring.

R. coulteri. Southern California, Mexico. Height 6–8 ft; spread 6 ft (180–240 × 180 cm). A shrubby perennial with thick, running roots and erect, branching stems. The blue-green leaves are broadly egg-shaped, divided into two to three pairs of lance-shaped lobes. Papery, 6-in.- (15-cm-) wide white flowers with six crinkled petals and golden centers are borne in large numbers on the ends of the stems in summer. The flowers are fragrant with the smell of ripe apricots. 'White Cloud' has masses of cup-shaped white flowers with conspicuous golden yellow stamens. Zones 8–10.

R. trichocalyx. Southern California, Mexico. Height 6–8 ft; spread 6 ft (180–240 × 180 cm). Similar to ***R. coulteri*** but with leaves less lobed and leathery, flower buds bristly, and petals less crinkled. Zones 8–10.

ROSCOEA

FAMILY: Zingiberaceae

Seventeen hardy species of the ginger family native from the Himalayas to China. They are not widely grown in North America, growing best in climates with mild winters and cool summers. They have alternate leaves that sheath the stem and orchidlike purple, blue, or yellow flowers in summer and early

Roscoea cautleoides 'Kew Form'

autumn. Named after William Roscoe (1753–1831), one of the founders of the Liverpool Botanic Garden in Britain.

CULTIVATION: Plant the fleshy roots 3–5 in. (7.5–12.5 cm) below soil level and mark the spot, as the new growth does not appear before mid- to late-spring. Grow in full sun or partial shade in moist but well-drained soil.

LANDSCAPE USE: Plant in shaded borders or rock gardens in large drifts for maximum effect.

PROPAGATION: Divide in spring or sow seed in late summer.

R. auriculata. Himalayas. Height 18 in.; spread 6 in. (45 × 15 cm). A tuberous plant with erect stems and bright-green, lance-shaped leaves with earlike lobes at the base of the leaf. A succession of violet-purple orchidlike flowers are produced on fleshy stems with leaflike bracts periodically throughout the summer. Zones 8–9.

R. cautleoides. China. Height 10 in.; spread 6 in. (25 × 15 cm). An erect plant with mid-green, lance-shaped leaves and spikes of pale-yellow, hooded, lipped, and lobed flowers in summer. 'Kew Form' appears to be slightly taller and longer lasting in flower than the species. ***R.*** × 'Beesiana' is possibly a hybrid between this species and ***R. auriculata*** and has pale-yellow flowers with the lip streaked buff and lilac. Zones 8–9.

R. humeana. China. Height 6–10 in.; spread 6 in. (15–25 × 15 cm). A striking plant with lance-shaped, rich green leaves and tubular, bright-purple flowers with one upright hooded petal and two curling downward, blooming in summer. Zones 8–9.

RUDBECKIA

(Coneflower)

FAMILY: Compositae

Twenty-five to 30 species of North American annuals, biennials, and perennials with mostly alternate leaves and daisylike flowers consisting of yellow or orange-yellow ray flowers and black or purple-brown central disks. ***Rudbeckia fulgida*** var. ***sullivantii*** 'Goldsturm' is now widely planted in North America. Oddly enough, although this cultivar was developed in Germany, it is regarded as one of the mainstays of what is ambitiously called the 'New American Garden.' It is currently much in vogue, along with ***Miscanthus sinensis*** cultivars and ***Sedum*** × 'Autumn Joy.' While this is a heartening trend in the development of perennials for use in gardens, I believe we should be cautious about establishing such a limited orthodoxy in our plant palette. Named after Olaf Rudbeck, a Swedish botanist.

Cultivation: Grow in full sun to partial shade in ordinary soil. Deadhead to encourage secondary flowering. The taller varieties require staking.

Landscape Use: Bright and coarse summer-blooming plants for the sunny border or meadow. Particularly effective in large masses.

Propagation: Divide in spring or autumn. Sow seed in spring.

R. fulgida. Orange coneflower. United States. Height 2–3 ft; spread 18 in. (60–90 × 45 cm). An erect, hairy plant with dark-green, toothed, lance-shaped to egg-shaped, long-stemmed leaves up to 6 in. (15 cm) long at the base, becoming smaller and stemless up on the flower stem. The branching stems bear 2–3-in.- (5–7.5-cm-) wide flowers with orange-yellow ray flowers around a brownish black disk. The variety ***deamii*** has broader leaves and is more floriferous; var. ***sullivantii*** has stem leaves that are reduced to bracts toward the top of the stem; var. ***sullivantii*** 'Goldsturm' grows to about 2 ft (60 cm) and produces masses of up to 4-in.- (10-cm-) wide yellow flowers with black centers. If it still exits, 'Goldsturm' should be propagated vegatatively. Zones 3–9.

Rudbeckia fulgida var. *deamii*

R. laciniata. North America. Height 4–8 ft; spread 2–3 ft (120–240 × 60–90 cm). A vigorous, clump-forming plant with hairy stems and egg-shaped to lance-shaped, deeply cut, mid- to dark-green, toothed leaves. Branching stems carry 3–4-in.- (7.5–10-cm-) wide flowers consisting of a central, green, raised disk and drooping, yellow ray flowers. 'Golden Glow' has double golden yellow flowers with green centers and reaches a height of 5 ft (150 cm). Zones 3–9.

R. maxima. North America. Height 5–6 ft; spread 2 ft (150–180 × 60 cm). A coarse plant with elliptical to spoon-shaped gray-green leaves, the basal leaves up to 12 in. (30 cm) long, becoming smaller and clasping up on the stem. In late summer 3-in.- (7.5-cm-) wide drooping yellow flowers with a brown center are produced. This species can be extraordinarily effective when planted in large numbers. I find that the flowers detract from the magnificent foliage. Zones 4–9.

R. nitida. Southern United States. Height 3–4 ft; spread 2 ft (90–120 × 60 cm). Similar to ***R. laciniata*** but much smaller and with egg-shaped, lobeless leaves. Drooping yellow flowers surrounding a greenish central disk are produced in late summer. 'Goldquelle' has double, yellow, 4-in.- (10-cm-) wide flowers. 'Herbstonne' ('Autumn Sun') grows to a height of 6–8 ft (180–240 cm) and has numerous drooping yellow flowers with a green central disk. It is a magnificent cultivar that deserves its popularity. Zones 4–9.

RUMEX

(Sorrel)

Family: Polygonaceae

A large genus of largely invasive weeds sometimes used as leafy vegetables and herbs but not as ornamentals. One species has some ornamental value as a groundcover for shade.

Cultivation: Grow in partial to full shade in moist, well-drained soil.

Landscape Use: An invasive plant for use as a groundcover under shrubs and robust herbaceous plants.

Propagation: Divide in spring or early autumn.

R. scuttatus. French sorrel. Europe, Asia. Height

Rumex scuttatus 'Silver Shield'

12 in.; spread 18 in. (30 × 45 cm). A leafy perennial with branching, prostrate stems and rich green, heart-shaped or arrow-shaped leaves about 2 in. (5 cm) wide. 'Silver Shield' is considerably more ornamental than the species and has variegated leaves of pale-green and silver-green. Zones 6–9.

RUTA

(Rue, Herb of Grace)

FAMILY: Rutaceae

A genus of 40 species of aromatic herbs, with only one species widely cultivated in gardens. Native to southern Europe, it was introduced into Britain by the Romans and widely used as a medicine. It was regarded as a powerful weapon against witches and was used later as a brush to dispense holy water; hence its common name herb of grace. The generic name is said to be derived from the Greek *reuo,* "to set free," because of its efficacy in freeing the sick from illness.

CULTIVATION: Grow in ordinary, well-drained soil in full sun. Cut back to old wood in spring. The volatile oil produced by this plant in hot weather may cause blistering of the skin.

LANDSCAPE USE: A handsome blue-green foliage plant for the sunny border. One of the best foliage plants for edging formal borders, providing bolts of blue to cool hot colors or to bridge the gap between silver foliage and green leaves.

Ruta graveolens

PROPAGATION: Take cuttings in late summer and early autumn.

R. graveolens. Rue, herb of grace. Southern Europe. Height 2–3 ft; spread 18 in. (60–90 × 45 cm).

An aromatic subshrub with a pungent odor and bitter taste. The alternate blue-green leaves are deeply cut into spoon-shaped leaflets. Greenish yellow, four-petaled flowers are produced in summer. The black-and-yellow-striped larvae of the black swallowtail butterfly especially enjoy this plant. If prevented from defoliating the plant, they can be a wonderful accompaniment to the blue-green foliage. 'Jackman's Blue' has waxy, blue foliage. 'Variegata' has blue-green leaves dappled with creamy white that revert to blue-green as they age. Zones 4–9.

SAGINA

(Pearlwort)

Family: Caryophyllaceae

A small genus of tuft-forming plants mostly native to the mountains of Europe. One species is commonly grown for its mats of green foliage and white flowers in spring.

Cultivation: Grow in well-drained soil in light shade.

Landscape Use: A diminutive plant for the rock garden, stone trough, or path edge.

Propagation: Divide in spring.

S. ***subulata.*** Pearlwort. Europe. Height 6 in.; spread 8 in. (15 × 20 cm). A mat-forming plant with dull-green, threadlike leaves and masses of single white flowers in midsummer. 'Aurea' is a more interesting plant, producing white flowers but with golden green leaves. Zones 6–9.

SALVIA

(Sage)

Family: Labiatae

Salvia pratensis 'Rosea'

A large genus of over 700 species of annuals, biennials, herbaceous perennials, subshrubs, and shrubs. All have square stems and opposite, often roundly toothed and aromatic leaves. The flowers, frequently surrounded by attractive bracts, are arranged in whorls and are two-lipped, with the upper lip almost hoodlike and the lower lip often protruding. They come in a great range of color, from blue, violet, pink, red, white, and even pale yellow. Many of the most exotic-looking salvias are indigenous to tropical and subtropical parts of the world and, though perennial, must be grown as annuals in temperate climates. There are, however, many species and hybrids that are excellent perennials for the garden.

The generic name is derived from the Latin *salvere,* "to be saved," and refers to the healing properties of many members of the genus. Common sage, ***S. officianalis,*** has been highly prized since ancient times. The herbalist John Gerard (1545–1612) wrote, "Sage is singularly good for the head and brain; it quickeneth the senses and memory, stengtheneth the sinews and taketh away the shakey trembling of the members."

CULTIVATION: Grow in full sun in fertile, well-drained soil. Cut back the hardy perennial species after flowering to induce compact growth and further flowering.

LANDSCAPE USE: The summer-flowering species are integral parts of any border. They are useful for their stalwart flowers in midsummer and again in autumn. The less hardy summer- and- fall-blooming species create a dramatically tropical effect, which is particularly useful as other herbaceous plants cease flowering at the back end of the year.

PROPAGATION: Divide herbaceous perennials in spring. Take cuttings in midsummer. Sow seeds in early spring.

S. argentea. Silver sage. Europe. Height 3 ft; spread 2 ft (90 × 60 cm). Up to 8-in.- (10-cm-) long, silver and woolly, egg-shaped to wedge-shaped, wrinkled and toothed leaves in basal rosettes that make a bright splash in the garden. The white flowers, which appear in the second year after starting from seed, are borne on upright, branching stems in summer. To some eyes they detract from the glory of the foliage; they may be removed. Although grown as an annual or biennial, this species is a short-lived perennial, particularly if the flowers are removed. Zones 5–9.

S. azurea. Azure sage. Southeastern United States. Height 4–6 ft; spread 2–3 ft (120–180 × 60–90 cm). Erect branching and hairless stems with light-green basal leaves, lance-shaped to oblong up to 3 in. (7.5 cm) long, becoming narrower up on the stem. Spikes of azure-blue flowers are borne in whorled clusters in late summer to midautumn. Tolerant of high temperatures and valuable for its beautiful blue flowers. The variety ***grandiflora*** (***S. pitcheri***) has larger flowers of sky blue and hairy stems. Both are flopping plants that need staking or should be allowed to lie on the ground and flower through other plants. Zones 5–9.

S. farinacea. Mealy-cup sage. Southwestern United States. Height 2–3 ft; spread 18 in. (60–90 × 45 cm). A bushy perennial often grown as an annual with whitish stems and gray-green, minutely toothed, lance-shaped leaves up to 3 in. (7.5 cm) long. Spikes of felted, blue flowers are produced in early summer to frost. An excellent long-blooming bedding plant for hot climates. 'Blue Bedder' has violet-blue flowers; 'Silver White' has pearly white flowers; 'Victoria' grows to a height of about 18 in. (45 cm) and has violet-blue flowers; 'White Bedder' has white flowers. It squeaks through as a perennial only in the milder areas. Zones 8–9.

S. fulgens. Mexico. Height 3 ft; spread 2 ft (90 × 60 cm). An erect, evergreen plant with woody stems and pointed, egg-shaped, toothed leaves to 3 in. (7.5 cm) long. The leaves are covered in white felt underneath and are softly hairy above. Tubular and lipped, scarlet flowers are borne on slender stems in late summer. It is hardy in Zone 8 in a sheltered site, but reliable in Zones 9–10.

S. greggii. Autumn sage. Southwestern North America. Mexico. Height 2–3 ft; spread 18 in. (60–90 × 45 cm). A shrubby plant with woody stems and oblong to spoon-shaped deep-green leaves up to 1 in. (2.5 cm) long. Short spikes of crimson flowers are produced in summer. 'Cherry Queen' has cherry-red flowers; 'Raspberry Royal' has bright pinkish red flowers. This species is being found to be more variable than first thought, and hardier forms are beginning to appear. We can expect a number of new hardier cultivars in the coming years. Zones 7–9.

S. guaranitica. South America. Height 3–5 ft; spread 3 ft (90–150 × 90 cm). A shrubby plant with woody, branching stems and coarsely toothed, dark-green, egg-shaped, rough leaves up to 5 in. (12.5 cm) long, pale green underneath. Slender spikes of deep-blue flowers are produced from midsummer to midautumn. Although not a heavy bloomer, this plant provides a display for much of the growing season. It is an excellent plant for the back or midborder. 'Black and Blue' has deep-blue flowers with dark-blue, almost black bracts. The leaves of this cultivar are velvety and almost double the size of the species. Although both are hardy to Zone 7, semiripe cuttings taken in midsummer provide better specimens for the following year. Zones 7–9.

S. juriscii. Yugoslavia. Height 18 in.; spread 18 in. (45 × 45 cm). A branched plant with densely hairy stems but with hairless toothed oblong leaves. The stem leaves are deeply divided into linear leaflets. The deep-lilac flowers are produced in early summer on branching spikes and are upside down. A unique sage that is not widely cultivated. Zones 6–9.

S. leucantha. Mexico. Height 3–4 ft; spread 3 ft (90–120 × 90 cm). A branching subshrub with white-felted woody stems and deep-green, wrinkled, linear, lance-shaped, and acutely pointed, toothed leaves up to 6 in. (15 cm) long covered in white felt underneath. Long spikes of woolly, white-and-violet flowers are produced in summer and autumn. There are a few as yet unnamed forms with reddish violet to blue-violet flowers. Although they are frost tender, they are handsome plants for the late summer and autumn border. Zones 8–9.

S. patens. Gentian sage. Mexico. Height 2 ft; spread 18 in. (60 × 45 cm). An upright, branching, hairy plant with egg-shaped to triangular bright-green toothed leaves up to 5 in. (12.5 cm) long. Gentian-blue, hooded flowers are sparsely produced in spikes in summer and autumn. 'Cambridge Blue' has light-blue flowers; 'Royal Blue' has deep-blue flowers. Zones 8–9.

S. pratensis (S. haematodes). Meadow sage. Europe. Height 2–3 ft; spread 2 ft (60–90 × 60 cm). One of the finest salvias to associate with the first bloom of shrub roses. It has long-stemmed, basal, egg-shaped to oblong, wrinkled, toothed, and hairy leaves up to 6 in. (15 cm) long. Branching, flowering stems bear lavender-blue flowers in early summer and, if deadheaded, occasionally in late summer. Self-seeds vigorously. Whether this species is synonymous with ***S. haematodes*** is hotly debated. It appears that ***S. haematodes*** may be a variety or subspecies, but it is so similar to ***S. pratensis*** as to be dismissed by ordinary mortals. Let the taxonomists fight it out and the gardeners enjoy it. 'Atroviolacea' has violet flowers; 'Indigo' has rich-blue flowers. Zones 7–9.

Salvia x *superba* 'Lubeca'

S. × superba. Height 18–36 in.; spread 36 in. (45–90 × 90 cm). A hybrid between ***S. nemerosa, S. pratenis,*** and ***S. villicaulis*** often sold as ***S. nemerosa*** or ***S. sylvestris.*** The type is a woody-based, clump-forming plant with leafy stems of gray-green, toothed, and rough, egg-shaped to oblong leaves up to 3 in. (7.5 cm) long. Dense spikes of violet-blue flowers with purple bracts are produced in early to midsummer. It is a superb, long-flowering summer-blooming plant that often repeats in late summer. A number of cultivars are fairly similar to each other: 'Blue Queen': height about 2 ft (60 cm), deep blue-purple flowers; 'East Friesland': height 2½ ft (75 cm), deep-purple flowers; 'Lubeca': height about 18 in. (45 cm), violet-purple spikes; 'May Night': height 2–3 ft (60–90 cm), blooms in very early summer with dark violet-blue flowers; 'Rose Queen': height 30 in (75 cm), rose-pink flowers. Cut back hard to basal growth after the first flowering. Zones 5–9.

SANGUINARIA

(Bloodroot)

Family: Papaveraceae

A single genus native to North America with lobed leaves and clear-white flowers in early to midspring. The sap is orange-red and has long been used by Native Americans as a dye.

Sanguinaria canadensis 'Multiplex'

Cultivation: Grow in moist but well-drained, leafy soil in full sun to partial shade.

Landscape Use: One of the finest of wildflowers in the deciduous woodlands of North America, this plant makes a fine display under shrubs and trees, or as a specimen in the border.

Propagation: Divide the fleshy rootstocks just after flowering. Sow seed in spring. When buying bloodroot, please ensure that the nursery source does not take plants from the wild.

S. canadensis. Bloodroot. North America. Height 6–9 in.; spread 12 in. (15–22.5 × 30 cm). Gray-green, up to 12-in.- (30-cm-) wide, kidney-shaped and wavy leaves are deeply lobed and borne on 6-in. (15-cm) stems. The white flowers appear from a tightly coiled bud before the leaves are fully opened in early spring. The 3-in.- (7.5-cm-) wide flowers last for just a few days, but additional flowers are produced. The foliage is magnificent in spring but begins to look poor in summer and dies down in late summer. 'Multiplex' is a double-flowered cultivar that is in bloom much longer than the species. It is highly desirable for its waterlilylike flowers and broad, gray-green leaves. Zones 4–9.

SANGUISORBA

(Burnet)

Family: Rosaceae

A small genus of late-summer-flowering plants with dense, cylindrical spikes of petalless white, pink, or red flowers, and pale-green leaves divided into many leaflets. The generic name comes from the Latin *sanguis,* "blood," and *sorbeo,* "to staunch," a reference to its use as a blood-clotting agent.

Sanguisorba canadensis

Cultivation: Plant in moist, acid soil in full sun to partial shade.

Landscape Use: Elegant and underused late-flowering plants for the summer border or bog garden. Effective en masse by a pool or lake.

Propagation: Divide in spring or sow seed.

S. canadensis. American burnet. Eastern North America. Height 4–6 ft; spread 2 ft (120–180 × 60 cm). A vigorous clump-forming plant with pale-green, 12-in.- (30-cm-) long leaves divided into sharply toothed, oblong leaflets up to 3 in. (7.5 cm) long. Terminal 6-in.- (15-cm-) long, cylindrical spikes of white flowers are produced in late summer and early autumn. Zones 4–8.

S. obtusa. Japan. Height 4 ft; spread 2 ft (120 × 60 cm). Up to 18-in.- (45-cm-) long, pale-green leaves with blue-green undersides, divided into toothed, oval leaflets. Arching spikes 3–4 in. (7.5–10 cm) long bear bright reddish pink flowers in midsummer. Zones 5–8.

S. ***officinalis.*** Great burnet. Europe, Asia. Height 4 ft; spread 2 ft (120 × 60 cm). A clump-forming plant with branched stems and 12-in.- (30-cm-) long leaves divided into toothed oval leaflets. Spikes of deep purple-brown flowers are produced in late summer. It is not a greatly ornamental plant, but it is attractive when planted in large numbers in a bog garden or by a pond. 'Rubra' has reddish brown flowers. Zones 4–8.

S. ***tenuifolia.*** Northern Asia. Height 4 ft; spread 2 ft (120 × 60 cm). Pale-green leaves divided into linear to oblong leaflets up to 3 in. (7.5 cm) long and arching flower spikes bearing 2-in.- (5-cm-) long, cylindrical clusters of wine-red flowers in midsummer. Zones 4–8.

SAPONARIA

(Soapwort)

FAMILY: Caryophyllaceae

About 30 species of low-growing annual, biennial, and perennial plants with opposite leaves and salver-shaped flowers in late spring and summer. The generic and common name refers to the sap of ***S. officinalis,*** the root of which was once used to make soap.

CULTIVATION: Grow in well-drained, preferably poor soil in full sun. Cut back hard after flowering to induce new growth and subsequent blooms. Most species are not suitable for areas with hot and humid summers.

LANDSCAPE USE: The desirable species are rock-garden or dry-bank plants for mild climates. Their bright-pink flowers makes a great splash of color after most ***Aubretia*** have finished flowering and while the rock-garden ***Dianthus*** are still blooming.

PROPAGATION: Sow seed in spring or autumn or take cuttings in midsummer.

S. ***caespitosa.*** Pyrenees. Height 3 in.; spread 4 in. (7.5 × 10 cm). A mat-forming plant with linear, lance-shaped leaves up to 1 in. (2.5 cm) long and masses of single rosy purple and five-petaled flowers in summer. Zones 4–7.

S. × ***lempergii.*** Height 12 in.; spread 12–18 in. (30 × 30–45 cm). A hybrid between ***S. cypria*** and ***S. naussknechtii,*** notable for the cultivar 'Max Frei.' This cultivar has lance-shaped leaves and carmine-pink flowers in midsummer. It is an outstanding rock-garden plant rapidly becoming commercially available. Zones 6–8.

Saponaria ocymoides

S. ***ocymoides.*** Rock soapwort. Alps. Height 6 in; spread 12 in. (15 × 30 cm). A sprawling plant forming lax mats of many-branched stems with hairy, oval leaves ½–1 in. (1.2–2.5 cm) long. Terminal sprays of pink to crimson flowers are produced in early summer. Cut back hard for repeat bloom in late summmer. 'Rubra Compacta' has bright-red flowers and does not sprawl but rather forms a compact mound; 'Splendens' has rose-pink flowers. Zones 4–8.

S. ***officinalis.*** Southern Europe. Height 1–3 ft; spread 18 in. (30–90 × 45 cm). An erect plant with unbranched stems and veined, egg-shaped leaves up to 4 in. (10 cm) long. Pale-pink flowers with notched petals are borne from the upper leaf axils in summer. Requires staking or pinching back to control the straggling growth. The double flower forms are more ornamental. 'Alba Plena' has double white flowers; 'Rosea Plena' has double rose-pink flowers; 'Rubra Plena' has double crimson flowers. Zones 5–8.

S. × olivana. Height 3 in.; spread 4 in. (7.5×10 cm). A compact, cushion-forming plant with linear, lance-shaped leaves ½–1 in. (1.2–2.5 cm) long and flat, salver-shaped, pale-pink flowers produced from the outer edges of the plant in summer. It is a hybrid between ***S. caespitosa*** and ***S. ocymoides.*** Zones 4–7. 'Bressingham' is a hybrid between ***S. ocymoides*** and ***S. × olivana.*** It grows to a height of about 3 in. (7.5 cm) and a spread of 4 in. (10 cm) and has narrowly elliptical leaves and pink flowers in clusters in the summer. Zones 4–8.

SAXIFRAGA

(Saxifrage)

FAMILY: Saxifragaceae

Saxifraga x *urbium* 'Miss Chambers'

Approximately 370 species and hundreds of forms, hybrids, and cultivars, of mostly dwarf plants widely distributed throughout the northern hemisphere. There is such a great variety of saxifrages that a work such as this can only briefly touch on a few.

The majority grown in gardens are suitable for rock gardens and raised beds, although some are used as groundcovers or as edging plants for herbaceous borders. Those widely cultivated are rosette-forming and produce starry white, pink, red, and yellow flowers. Some of the most attractive have their leaves thickly encrusted with lime, giving the foliage a handsome silver rime. Many are difficult to grow, which makes them particularly beloved by the enthusiast.

The genus is divided into a number of sections and subsections, but most are uncommon in cultivation or are unavailable commercially. Those listed below are some of the easiest and most rewarding to grow. Many species have been neglected by all but the specialist and deserve a wider audience.

The name is derived from the Latin *saxum,* "rock," and *frangere,* "to break." This is a reference to some species supposedly being able to crack the rocks they inhabit.

CULTIVATION: In general, saxifrages require a well-drained neutral to lime-rich soil in partial shade to full sun. They are plants for cool climates and do not enjoy the subtropical summers of much of North America.

LANDSCAPE USE: Most are highly suitable for rock gardens, alpine houses, and trough gardens, although a few species are excellent groundcovers.

PROPAGATION: Divide in spring or sow seed when ripe.

S. aizoides. Section Xanthizoon. Yellow mountain saxifrage. Europe, Asia, North America. Height 6–8 in.; spread 8 in. (15–20 × 20 cm). An evergreen plant forming a loose carpet of thick, green, linear leaves. Branched stems bear flat-topped clusters of yellow flowers that are often speckled red, blooming in summer. Not particularly easy to cultivate, it requires moist, rocky soil in sun to partial shade. 'Atrorubens' has blood-red flowers; 'Aurantia' has orange flowers. Zones 2–6.

S. × apiculata. Height 3 in.; spread 6 in. (7.5 × 15 cm). One of the most easily cultivated saxifrages, this hybrid has rosettes of ½-in.- (1.2-cm-) long, bright-green, linear leaves and clusters of yellow flowers in early spring. 'Gregor Mendel' has pale-yellow flowers. 'Pungens' has fragrant pale-yellow flowers. Zones 6–7.

S. × arendsii. A group of saxifrage hybrids notable for their mossy evergreen leaves and colorful, starry flowers in spring. A few of the most notable: 'Bride's Maid,' height 6 in. (15 cm), white flowers; 'Dubarry,' height 8 in. (20 cm), red flowers; 'Purple Carpet,' height 6 in. (15 cm), purple-red flowers; 'Triumph,' height 6 in. (15 cm), dark-red flowers. Zones 6–7.

S. cochlearis. Section Euaizoonia. Alps. Height 8 in.; spread 10 in. (20 × 25 cm). A desirable saxifrage with spoon-shaped leaves up to 1½ in. (3.7 cm) long heavily encrusted with lime and one-sided clusters of starry, pure-white flowers in late spring and early summer. 'Major' has larger flowers; 'Minor' has smaller flowers and grows up to 4 in. (10 cm) high. Zones 7–8.

S. cortusifolia. Section Diptera. Asia. Height 12–18 in.; spread 12 in. (30–45 × 30 cm). A deciduous species with lobed, rounded leaves up to 3 in. (8 cm) long and pyramidal clusters of white, starry flowers in the fall. 'Rosea' is slightly smaller in height and has pink flowers. Variety ***fortunei*** (***S. fortunei***) has lobed, kidney-shaped leaves, brownish green on top, red underneath. The white flowers are produced in autumn. 'Rubrifolium' has rusty red leaves and flower stems. Zones 6–8.

S. oppositifolia. Section Porphyrion. Europe, North America, Himalayas. Height 2 in.; spread 6 in. (5 × 15 cm). A densely mat-forming species with ¼-in. (0.6-cm) elliptical leaves with hairy margins and solitary purple-red flowers produced at the end of the shoots in early spring. 'Wetterhorn' has rose-red flowers. Zones 2–7.

Saxifraga paniculata

S. paniculata (S. aizoon). Section Euaizoonia. Europe, Asia, North America. Height 6 in.–2 ft × 1 ft (15–60 × 30 cm). One of the most widely grown saxifrages, with a large number of varieties. This is a cushion-forming species with toothed, gray-green, narrowly spoon-shaped leaves up to 2 in. (5 cm) long; its branching flower clusters, usually white, bloom in summer. There are many forms. Variety ***balcana,*** has flat rosettes and rose-spotted white flowers; height 8 in. (20 cm), var. ***lutea*** has pale-yellow flowers; var. ***minutifolia*** is a densely cushion-forming plant with white flowers, cultivars of which include 'Rex,' with silver-gray leaves, red flower stems, and white flowers, and 'Rosea,' with soft-pink flowers. Subspecies ***brevifolia*** has leaves just under ½ in. (1.2 cm) long and creamy white flowers. Grow in partial shade. Zones 2–6.

S. pensylvanica. Section Boraphila. Eastern and central North America. Height 3 ft; spread 18 in. (90 × 45 cm). A shade-loving saxifrage with a thick rootstock; basal, leathery, spoon-shaped leaves up to 1 ft (30 cm) long; and pyramidal flower clusters made up of yellowish white flowers appearing in late spring to early summer. Zones 6–7.

S. stolonifera. Section Diptera. Mother-of-thousands. Asia. Height 12 in.; spread 8 in. (30 × 20 cm). It gets its common name from its habit of sending out long, threadlike shoots (stolons) that root in the soil to form new plants. The lobed and undulating leaves are roundly kidney-shaped up to 4 in. (10 cm) wide, deep green and silver-veined on top, hairy red underneath. Panicles of white flowers are produced in summer. This species is often grown as a houseplant, but it is tolerant of some cold and is probably the best saxifrage for warmer climates. Grow in partial shade in moist but well-drained soil. 'Tricolor' has gray-green, red-and-white variegated leaves and is reputed to be less hardy than the type. Zones 6–8.

S. × ***urbium.*** Section Robertsoniana. London pride. Height 12 in.; spread 18 in. (30 × 45 cm). Perhaps the easiest of the genus to grow, this plant is widely used as a groundcover, particularly in urban gardens; hence the common name. It is best grown in moist but well-drained soil in partial shade. Often listed as ***S. umbrosa,*** it is a hybrid between that species and ***S. spathularis.*** The dark-green rosettes consist of fleshy, spoon-shaped leaves about 2 in. (5 cm) long, and sticky flower stems bear loose clusters of starry, white flowers in early summer. It is a particularly good groundcover under roses. 'Aureopunctata' has gold-splashed leaves; 'Miss Chambers' ('Chamber's Pink Pride') has soft-pink flowers. Divide in early spring or after flowering. Zones 6–7.

SCABIOSA

(Scabious, Pincushion)

Family: Dipsacaceae

Scabiosa caucasica var. *perfecta* 'Alba'

About 80 species of annuals and perennials native to Europe, Asia, and Africa, with mostly basal, opposite leaves and long-stemmed, flat or pincushionlike domed flower heads in mid- to late summer. The generic name comes from the Latin *scabies,* "itch," a reference both to the roughness of the leaves and the ailment it was supposed to heal.

Cultivation: Grow in neutral, fertile, well-drained soil in full sun. Deadhead to stimulate repeat flowering.

Landscape Use: Grow in sunny borders or in the cutting garden.

Propagation: Divide in spring, take basal cuttings in midsummer, and sow seed in spring or autumn.

S. alpina. Alps. Height 6 in.; spread 12 in. (15 × 30 cm). A mat-forming evergreen plant with deeply cut gray-green leaves and bright-blue flower heads on 6-in. (15 cm) stems above the foliage. Variety ***nana*** grows to a height of 3 in. (7.5 cm). Zones 4–8.

S. caucasica. Caucasus. Height 2 ft; spread 18 in. (60 × 45 cm). Lance-shaped and long-stemmed mid-green basal leaves with the upper part cut into lobed segments. The stem's leaves are lobed and

Scabiosa 'Butterfly Blue'

divided into linear sections.The flat flower heads, up to 3 in (7.5 cm) across, are held on slender stems in summer. The flowers are pale blue, becoming increasingly pale to white in the center. Variety ***perfecta alba*** has white flowers with fringed petals. There are a number of cultivars including 'Bressingham White,' with clear white flowers; 'Butterfly Blue,' with pale-green leaves and pale-blue flowers that bloom from spring to autumn at a height of about 12 in. (30 cm); 'Clive Greaves,' with lavender-blue flowers with white centers; 'Fama,' with strong blue, silver-centered flowers; 'Floral Queen,' with violet-blue flowers; 'Miss Willmott,' with creamy white flowers. Not great performers in hot climates, as they tend to look ragged by midsummer. Plant in partial shade in areas with hot summers. Zones 4–9.

S. ***columbaria.*** Europe, Asia, Africa. Height 1 ft; spread 18 in. (60 × 45 cm) A short-lived perennial with roundly egg-shaped basal leaves sometimes lobed to look lyre shaped. The upper leaves are smaller and cut into linear segments. The 1½-in.- (3.8-cm-) wide domed flower heads are usually pale blue, sometimes pinkish blue, and held on slender stems throughout the summer. Zones 5–8.

S. ***graminifolia.*** Europe. Height 10–12 in.; spread 12 in. (25–30 × 30 cm). An evergreen plant with a woody base and mounds of silvery, grasslike leaves with stiff flower stems bearing 2-in.- (5-cm-) wide pincushions of lilac-blue to pale-pink blooms throughout the summer. Grow in well-drained soil. Zones 5–9.

S. ***ochroleuca.*** Europe. Height 2 ft; spread 2 ft (60 × 60 cm). A short-lived perennial with hairy stems and gray-green, egg-shaped basal leaves that are slightly lobed. Slender stems bear 1-in.- (2.5-cm-) wide, sulfur-yellow, rounded pincushionlike flowers in late summer. Zones 5–7.

SCIRPUS

(Club Rush)

Family: Cyperaceae

Scirpus lacustris var. tabernaemontani

A large genus of grasslike plants native to much of the planet. Those species of ornamental value in the garden are largely aquatic plants with erect, leafless stems and brown spikelets.

CULTIVATION: Grow in rich soil in 6 in. (15 cm) of water or in soil that is constantly wet. Remove the green stems of variegated forms.

LANDSCAPE USE: Coarse plants for the margins of ponds and lakes.

PROPAGATION: Divide in spring.

S. ***holoschoenus.*** Europe, Asia. Height 4 ft; spread 1 ft (120 × 30 cm). An upright, clump-forming plant with stiff cylindrical green stems with narrow erect leaves at the base of the stem. Spherical head of brown spikelets appear in summer. 'Variegatus' has stems horizontally striped creamy white. Zones 6–9.

S. ***lacustris var. tabernaemontani.*** Great bulrush. Europe, Asia, North America. Height 5 ft; spread 2 ft (150 × 60 cm). A vigorously spreading rush with stout, dark-green, almost leafless stems, the leaves being reduced to a few basal sheaths. Pale-brown, conical heads of brown spikelets are produced in summer. Not a greatly ornamental plant but useful, particularly in brackish water where little else will grow. Two more ornamental forms are 'Albescens,' with stems that are vertically striped green and white, and 'Zebrinus,' with stems that are horizontally striped green and white. Both variegated forms tend to produce unvariegated stems that take over if not removed. Zones 6–9.

SCROPHULARIA

(Figwort)

FAMILY: Scrophulariaceae

Scrophularia auriculata 'Variegata'

A large genus of annual and perennial plants native to much of the northern hemisphere. The stems are angled, the leaves are opposite, and the rather insignificant flowers are mostly maroon, red, or yellow. They are not particularly ornamental plants and would hardly be worth mentioning except for the variegated form of *S.* ***auriculata*** described below.

CULTIVATION: Plant in moist soil in partial shade. Remove the flowers as they appear.

LANDSCAPE USE: A charming plant for the pool margin or streambank.

PROPAGATION: Divide in the spring.

S. ***auriculata.*** 'Variegata' (*S.* ***aquatica*** 'Variegata'). Variegated figwort. Europe. Height 2 ft; spread 1 ft (60 × 30 cm). A clump-forming plant with erect, angled stems and up to 6-in.- (15-cm-) long, dark-green, egg-shaped, toothed, and wrinkled leaves edged creamy white. Spikes of maroon, two-lipped flowers are produced in summer but detract from the foliage and should be pinched off. Zones 6–9.

S. marilandica. Carpenter's-square. North America. Height 5 ft; spread 2 ft (150 × 60 cm). Not really a plant for the cultivated garden but a curious addition to the wild garden. The stems of this plant are angled and have sunken, grooved sides, thus giving rise to the common name. The leaves are egg-shaped with pointed tips, dark green, toothed and wrinkled, and up to 5 in. (12.5 cm) long. Rather boring greenish purple flowers apprear in late summer and autumn. Zones 4–8.

SCUTELLARIA

(Skullcap)

FAMILY: Labiatae

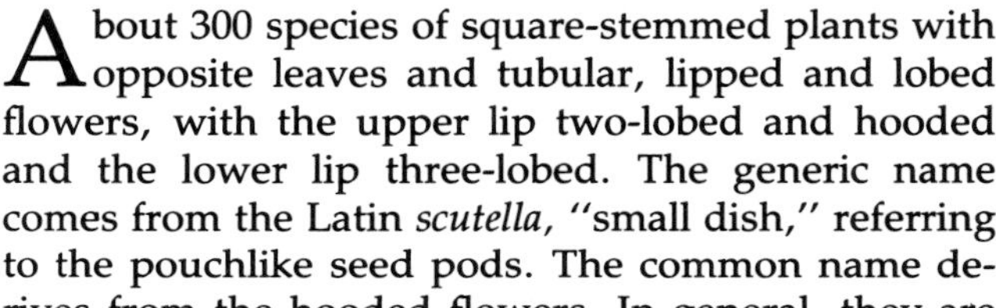

About 300 species of square-stemmed plants with opposite leaves and tubular, lipped and lobed flowers, with the upper lip two-lobed and hooded and the lower lip three-lobed. The generic name comes from the Latin *scutella,* "small dish," referring to the pouchlike seed pods. The common name derives from the hooded flowers. In general, they are sun-lovers blooming in summer.

CULTIVATION: Grow in well-drained soil in sun or partial shade.

LANDSCAPE USE: Attractive rock-garden and border plants useful for their purple-blue, white, or yellow flowers. The pouchlike seed pods are attractive enough to be ornamental in their own right.

PROPAGATION: Divide in spring, take cuttings in midsummer, or sow seed in spring or autumn.

S. alpina. Central and southern Europe. Height 6–9 in.; spread 18 in. (15–22.5 × 45 cm). A mat-forming skullcap with 1-in.- (2.5-cm-) wide, egg-shaped, sometimes toothed leaves on procumbent stems. Erect stems bearing 1½-in.- (3.8-cm-) long purple flowers with a yellow lower lip are produced in late summer. The variety ***alba*** has pure-white flowers. Zones 5–8.

S. baicalensis. Asia. Height 12 in.; spread 18 in. (30 × 45 cm). A clump-forming plant with stems that lie along the ground at their base and turn upward into erect stems. The rounded lance-shaped leaves are edged with small hairs. Purple-blue hooded flowers are produced in summer. Zones 6–8.

Scutellaria orientalis

S. incana. North America. Height 3 ft; spread 2 ft (90 × 60 cm). An upright perennial with branching stems and gray-green, toothed, egg-shaped leaves up to 4 in. (10 cm) long. Small panicles of pale-blue, hooded flowers are produced in midsummer, followed by attractive and noticeable pouchlike seed pods in late summer. Zones 3–8.

S. indica* var. *parviflora. Eastern Asia. Height 6–12 in.; spread 12 in. (15–30 × 30 cm). A tufted plant with procumbent stems and 1-in.- (2.5-cm-) long, egg-shaped, toothed, and finely hairy leaves. Dense spikes of purple-blue, hooded, and conspicuously lipped flowers appear in summer. Zones 6–8.

S. orientalis. Southern Europe, Asia Minor. Height 4 in.; spread 12 in. (10 × 30 cm). A spreading, sometimes invasive, species with hairy stems, toothed oblong leaves about ¾ in. (1.8 cm) long, and tubular, purple-lipped, yellow flowers throughout the summer and into autumn. Its invasive nature is balanced by its long blooming period. Zones 5–9.

S. scordiifolia. Korea. Height 6–8 in.; spread 8 in. (15–20 × 20 cm). A mat-forming plant with oblong, serrated, and wrinkled leaves up to 1 in. (2.5 cm) long. White-lipped purple flowers are produced in late summer. Zones 6–8.

SEDUM

(Stonecrop)

FAMILY: Crassulaceae

Sedum 'Autumn Joy'

Sedum kamtschaticum

A large genus of about 600 species of drought-tolerant annual, biennial, herbaceous perennial, and shrubby plants native to the northern temperate regions of the world. They are fleshy, succulent plants with alternate, opposite, or whorled stemless leaves and terminal clusters of starry flowers, commonly yellow or white but sometimes pink or red. The majority cultivated in gardens are excellent rock-garden plants, while a few are now widely grown in the herbaceous border. Most are easily cultivated succulents with few problems, although hot and humid summers may exacerbate fungal diseases. The generic name comes from the Latin *sedo,* "to sit," referring to the ground-hugging habits of many species. The common name is indicative of the natural habitat of many species.

CULTIVATION: Grow in well-drained, fertile soil in full sun or partial shade. Deadhead faded flowers. Fungal diseases may occur in some species in wet summers; good drainage and, if necessary, an application of a fungicide help in preventing any damaging diseases.

LANDSCAPE USE: The taller species are stalwart plants for the herbaceous border. Most of those cultivated are excellent plants for the rock garden, dry wall, or between paving stones.

PROPAGATION: Divide in spring or take stem cuttings throughout the summer.

S. acre. Gold moss stonecrop. Widely distributed. Height 2 in.; spread 12–18 in. (5 × 30–45 cm). An evergreen, mat-forming plant with alternate, light-green, overlapping, and pointed leaves about ¼ in. (0.6 cm) long on spreading stems. Tiny, flat heads of bright-yellow flowers are produced in early summer. This is an invasive species that is very useful in colonizing hot, dry areas but should be kept away from less vigorous plants. Variety ***aureum*** has yellow-tipped, pale-green leaves; var. ***elegans*** has silver-tipped leaves in spring. Both cultivars lose their tinted tips in summer. 'Minor' grows to 1 in. (2.5 cm) in height and has smaller leaves and flowers. Zones 3–9.

S. aizoon. Europe, Asia. Height 12 in.; spread 18

in. (30 × 45 cm). A compact, clump-forming plant with upright, unbranched stems and shiny, alternate, light-green, sharply toothed, 2-in.- (5-cm-) long, oblong to lance-shaped leaves. The flat, terminal clusters of ½-in.- (1.2-cm-) wide starry yellow flowers are borne on short stems just above the leaves in summer. Variety ***euphorbioides*** grows to about 10 in. (25 cm) and has larger flower heads. 'Aurantiacum' has red stems and dark-yellow flowers followed by red fruits in early autumn. Zones 4–9.

S. album. White stonecrop. Widely distributed. Height 3–6 in.; spread 12–18 in. (7.5–15 × 30–45 cm). An evergreen, invasive, mat-forming plant, with spreading stems and alternate, bright-green, cylindrical leaves up to ½ in. (1.2 cm) long. Flat heads of starry white flowers are borne on thinly leaved 6-in. (15-cm) stems in early to midsummer. 'Coral Carpet' has bright-green foliage tinged salmon-pink; 'Nigra' has dark-brown leaves. The species and its cultivars are grown chiefly for their attractive foliage. Zones 3–9.

S. × 'Autumn Joy' (*'Herbstfreude'*). Height 1–2 ft; spread 2 ft (30–60 × 60 cm). A popular border stonecrop, a hybrid between ***S. spectabile*** and ***S. telephium.*** It is a clump-forming plant with fleshy stems and alternate, sharply toothed, gray-green, blunted egg-shaped leaves up to 3 in. (7.5 cm) long. The 4–6-in. (10–15-cm) rounded heads comprising masses of starry flowers begin pale pink in early summer, mature to red-pink in mid- to late summer, and become rust-red in early to late autumn and into winter. It is easily grown and performs best in poor soil in full sun. Staking is usually necessary in overly fertile soil or in a shaded site. Aphids sometimes enjoy it, and spraying with water may be required to remove the insects. It is certainly enjoyed by bees and butterflies. 'Autumn Joy' is easily propagated by division in spring or autumn or by stem cuttings in summer. Pieces of stem or root can be plunged into the soil without any preparation. A useful hybrid for mass plantings, it is often associated with ornamental grasses and is swiftly becoming ubiquitous in the corporate and municipal landscape. It is at its best in the mixed border. Zones 3–9.

S. cauticolum. Japan. Height 2–4 in.; spread 8 in. (5–10 × 20 cm). A deciduous species with purplish, woody stems and mostly opposite, blue-gray, oblong to oval leaves on short stems. Branching, flattened heads of purplish pink flowers are borne on short, leafy stems in late summer to early autumn. Tolerant of moist soil. 'Robustum' has reddish pink flowers and grows to a height of 8 in. (20 cm). ***S.*** × 'Ruby Glow,' height 10–12 in.; spread 12 in. (25–30 × 30 cm), is a popular hybrid of this species and ***S.*** × 'Autumn Joy.' It has blue-gray, red-tinged, egg-shaped leaves and ruby-red flowers in late summer. It is becoming a popular plant, but it has an unfortunate habit of opening up in the center, exposing its almost woody stems. Annual division and cultivation in lean soil helps prevent this rather ugly habit. Zones 5–9.

S. dasyphyllum. Thick-leaved stonecrop. Europe, North Africa. Height 2–3 in.; spread 12 in. (5–7.5 × 30 cm). A mat-forming plant with wiry stems and mostly opposite, crowded blue-green leaves just ⅛ in. (0.3 cm) long. In early summer ½-in.- (1.2-cm-) wide clusters of white-tinged pink flowers appear.

S. ellacombeanum. Japan. Height 4 in.; spread 12 in. (10 × 30 cm). Often regarded as subspecies of ***S. kamtschaticum*** but distinct enough to be listed as a separate species by some taxonomists. The pale-green leaves are mostly opposite, spoon-shaped with scalloped edges. Terminal clusters of lemon-yellow, ½-in.- (1.2-cm-) wide flowers are produced in early summer. Zones 3–9.

S. kamtschaticum. Eastern Asia. Height 6 in.; spread 12 in. (15 × 30 cm). A sprawling, spreading plant with dark-green, alternate, toothed leaves up to 1½ in. (3.8 cm) long and unbranched flower stems bearing clusters of ½-in.- (1.2-cm-) wide, deep-yellow flowers in mid- to late summer. 'Variegatum' has leaves edged cream. Variety ***floriferum,*** height 8 in.; spread 12 in. (20 × 30 cm), is a spreading mat-forming variety with sprawling stems and alternate, dark-green, toothed leaves up to 1½ in. (3.8 cm) long. The flowering shoots are produced from the whole length of the stem and bear a profusion of bright-yellow flowers in summer. 'Weihenstephaner Gold' has rust-red buds and golden yellow flowers and makes an excellent groundcover in a sunny site. Zones 3–9.

S. middendorfianum. Manchuria. Height 6 in.; spread 12 in. (15 × 30 cm). Similar to ***S. kamtschaticum*** and often listed as a subspecies; however, it is a more compact and delicate plant, with dense tufts of tiny linear to lance-shaped, bronze-green leaves and masses of flat clusters of bright-yellow flowers in mid- to late summer. Variety ***diffusum*** is a coarser plant with yellow flowers that turn reddish brown in autumn. Zones 3–9.

S. reflexum. Yellow stonecrop. Europe. Height 10 in.; spread 12 in. (25 × 30 cm). A spreading, mat-forming plant with sprawling, tangled stems and alternate, linear, and cylindrical blue-green leaves up to ½ in. (1.2 cm) long. In early summer 8–10-in. (20–25-cm) stems bear terminal clusters of bright-yellow flowers. This is an outstanding groundcover for a sunny site. It is a vigorous, only slightly invasive plant. The flowers last for about a month, and the blue-green foliage is flushed purple-pink in winter. Often self-sows. 'Chameleon' has variegated foliage.

S. sieboldii. Siebold's stonecrop. Japan. Height 6 in.; spread 12 in. (15 × 30 cm). An evergreen, spreading plant with fleshy stems and rounded, slightly wedge-shaped, faintly toothed, blue-green leaves up to 1 in. (2.5 cm) long borne in whorls of three. Clusters of star-shaped, bright-pink flowers are produced in late summer and autumn. It used to be regarded as half-hardy, but it is a perfectly tough and hardy plant for the zones listed below. 'Medio-Variegatum' has blue-green leaves with a cream-splashed center and pink margins. 'Silvermoon' has variegated leaves of blue-green and white. Zones 6–9.

S. spathulifolium. Western North America. Height 2–4 in.; spread 12 in. (5–10 × 30 cm). An evergreen, mat-forming species with fleshy rosettes of alternate, spoon-shaped, gray-green leaves often brightly tinged purple-red. Short stems produce branched heads of clear-yellow flowers in summer. 'Cape Blanco' has silver-green, almost white leaves tinged purple, 'Carnea' has gray-green leaves heavily tinged red; 'Purpureum' has wine-colored leaves. Afternoon shade is necessary in areas with hot summers. Zones 5–9.

S. spectabile. Showy stonecrop. Eastern Asia. Height 18–24 in.; spread 18 in. (45–60 × 45 cm). A stonecrop for the herbaceous border, with upright, fleshy stems and pale-green, egg-shaped, opposite, and faintly toothed leaves up to 3 in. (7.5 cm) long. Flat, terminal clusters of pale-pink flowers are produced in late summer. 'Brilliant' has dense heads of rose-pink flowers; 'Carmen' has soft-pink flowers; 'Star Dust' has white flowers tinged pale pink; 'Variegatum' has foliage that is gray-green and cream. Zones 4–9.

Sedum spectabile 'Brilliant'

S. spurium. Caucasus. Height 2–6 in.; spread 12–18 in. (5–15 × 30–45 cm). A spreading, semievergreen, matt-forming plant with hairy red stems and opposite, oblong to wedge-shaped, toothed leaves up to 1 in. (2.5 cm) long. Terminal clusters of purplish pink, orange-centered flowers are produced on 4-in. (10-cm) stems in summer. It is an invasive plant grown for its bright flowers and apple-green foliage. 'Coccineum' has flowers of bright scarlet; 'Dragon's Blood' has purplish bronze leaves and brilliant-red flowers. It performs poorly in hot and humid summers. 'Green Mantle' is a nonflowering form with bright-green foliage; 'Red Carpet' has bronze foliage and red flowers; 'Royal Pink' has green leaves and pink flowers; 'Ruby Mantle' has purple-red foliage and deep-pink flowers; 'Tricolor' has green-, cream-, and deep-pink leaves; 'Variegatum' has green-and-cream leaves. Zones 3–9.

S. telephium. Orpine. Europe. Height 12–18 in.; spread 18 in. (30–45 × 45 cm). A long-lived, tuberous-rooted, clump-forming plant with fleshy, upright stems and alternate, flat, toothed, oblong to egg-shaped leaves up to 3 in. (7.5 cm) long. Terminal clusters of reddish purple flowers appear in late summer and early autumn. Variety ***maximum*** has mostly opposite or whorled egg-shaped leaves and greenish white or pale-pink flowers. ***S. telephium*** var. ***maximum*** 'Atropurpureum' has purple foliage and pink flowers. It is an attractive plant, although the stems tend to fall over in fertile soil; 'Munstead Dark Red' has purple foliage and dark-red flowers. Zones 3–9.

S. × 'Vera Jameson'. Height 9–12 in.; spread 12 in. (22.5–30 × 30cm). A hybrid between ***S. telephium*** var. ***maximum*** 'Atropurpureum' and ***S. cauticolum*** crossed with ***S.*** × 'Ruby Glow.' The egg-shaped leaves are deep purple and about 1 in. (2.5 cm) long. Short stems bear 2–4-in.- (5–10-cm-) wide heads of pink flowers in early autumn. It is a plant useful for its diminutive stature, bright flowers, and dark leaves. Zones 5–9.

SEMPERVIVUM

(Hens and Chicks, Houseleek)

Family: Crassulaceae

About 25 species of hardy and tender evergreen succulents native to the mountainous regions of Europe, North Africa, and Asia. The thick, alternate leaves are produced in rosettes and are often brightly colored, particularly at the tips. Thick, leafy, almost phallic stems bear compact clusters of starry flowers in summer. The central, flowering rosette is often surrounded by smaller plants that remain after the rosette has died; hence the common name hens and chicks. The naming of the species and the many hybrids and cultivars is considerably confused. The name houseleek comes from the Anglo-Saxon *leac,* "plant," and means "plant of the house." Sempervivums were highly prized as medicinal plants, particularly for skin diseases, and were grown in pots by the Romans. Sempervivums were also grown on house roofs to guard against lightning and witches. Other names for this genus are Jupiter's eye and Thor's beard, names derived from the appearance of the flowers. There are a great many natural and cultivated hybrids of differing qualities. A few of the more easily cultivated are listed here.

Cultivation: Grow in well-drained soil in full sun. They are tolerant of very light shade. Rust disease is a common problem in areas of humid summers and wet winters. Even slightly poor drainage will kill sempervivums.

Landscape Use: Excellent rock-garden plants either as single specimens or in a large, sweeping mass. Easily grown on roof tiles, rock walls, and in paving stone crevices.

Propagation: Detach the young plants (chicks) and replant during early autumn or spring. Sow seeds in spring and plant in autumn.

S. arachnoideum. Cobweb houseleek. Europe. Height 6–8 in.; spread 12 in. (15–20 × 30 cm). A beautiful, evergreen, mat-forming succulent 3–4 in. (7.5–10 cm) high, with densely crowded rosettes of fleshy green leaves up to ¾ in. (1.8 cm) wide, tinged red at the tips. The leaf tips are connected by fine, cobweblike hairs. Fleshy stems up to 6 in. (15 cm) long bear bright rose-red star-shaped flowers in summer. Subspecies ***tomentosum*** has rosettes twice as large as the species and

Sempervivum arachnoideum

carmine-red flowers. There are a number of hybrids produced from the crossing of this and other species. Zones 5–9.

S. montanum. Europe. Height 4–6 in.; spread 9 in. (10–15 × 22.5 cm). A highly variable specie forming mats of dull green and hairy, 2-in.-(5-cm-) wide, 2–3-in.- (5–7.5-cm-) high rosettes. Stems approximately 4 in. (10 cm) long bear hairy, reddish purple flowers in terminal clusters in summer. A parent of many hybrids. Zones 5–9.

S. tectorum. Houseleek. Europe. Height 12–18 in.; spread 8 in. (30–45 × 20 cm). Densely crowded rosettes up to 6 in. (15 cm) in height, with bright-green, red-tipped leaves up to 3 in. (7.5 cm) long. Branching, leafy, and hairy stems up 12 in. tall with terminal clusters of rose-purple flowers are produced somewhat infrequently in summer. This species has been widely cultivated since the 16th century. Variety ***alpinum*** has smaller rosettes of green leaves with a red base; var. ***calcareum*** has sharply pointed brown-tipped leaves. Zones. 5–9.

Hundreds of hybrids and cultivated varieties have been produced from the above species and others not described here. A few are listed below. For further information contact the relevant alpine and rock-garden societies, or consult garden centers and nurseries that specialize in ***Sempervivum.***

'Alpha' has bronze-green leaves flushed red and tufts of silver hairs at the leaf tip; 'Bloodtip' has rosettes of green leaves with sharply pointed and upturned, blood-red tips; 'Commander Hay' has large rosettes of reddish brown leaves with green tips; 'Emerald Giant' has large green rosettes that turn pink in winter; 'Hot Shot' has gray-green leaves with rusty-red edges; 'Laura Lee' has hairy bronze-purple leaves; 'Lavender and Old Lace' has green leaves tinged lavender and edged with silver hairs; 'Ohio Burgundy' has burgundy-red rosettes; 'Othello' has flat rosettes of deep-red leaves; 'Pekinese' has light-green leaves with pink tips; 'Royal Ruby' has deep ruby-red leaves; 'Shirley's Joy' has green leaves frosted with silvery hairs; 'Snowberger' has blue-green leaves with a white sheen; 'Wolcott's Variety' has green leaves toned silver-pink; 'Zenobia' has emerald-green leaves with dark-purple markings. Zones 5–9.

SENECIO

(Groundsel)

Family: Compositae

Senecio aureus

An enormous genus of over 3,000 species of annuals, perennials, subshrubs, shrubs, and trees native around the world, although primarily indigenous to temperate regions. Those herbaceous perennials grown in gardens have basal or alternate leaves and daisylike flowers. The generic name supposedly comes from the Latin *senex,* "old man," referring to the grizzled whorl of the flowers (pappus). The common name comes from the Anglo-Saxon and means "ground-swelling," a description of the common groundsel's ability to seed itself widely.

Cultivation: Grow in ordinary garden soil in full sun.

Landscape Use: Most herbaceous species are not of great ornament, but the divided foliage and daisylike flowers are sometimes useful in the herbaceous border or in the woodland or meadow garden.

Propagation: Divide in spring or autumn. Sow seeds in spring or autumn.

S. ***abrotanifolius.*** Europe. Height 18 in.; spread 12 in. (45 × 30 cm). A lax, sprawling plant with woody stems and dark-green leaves divided into linear segments. Flower heads up to 2 in. (5 cm) wide bear orange-red flowers in summer. Zones 4–8.

S. ***aureus.*** Golden groundsel. United States. Height 18 in.; spread 18 in. (45 × 45 cm). A clump-forming plant with long-stemmed, egg-shaped, toothed basal leaves becoming stemless and divided upon the flower stem. Clusters of golden yellow daisy flowers are produced in late spring. Not an outstandingly ornamental species, but it grows well in light shade in damp soil and is a good candidate for the woodland or bog garden, where its flowers introduce a warm summer color to the spring landscape. Zones 5–8.

S. bicolor var. ***cineraria (S. cineraria, S. maritima).*** Dusty miller. Mediterranean. Height 1 ft; spread 18 in. (30×45 cm). A subshrub with a woody base and oval, silver-woolly leaves deeply cut into bluntly lobed segments. Terminal clusters of greenish yellow daisies are produced in summer, but these are of little consequence and, in fact, deter from the bright foliage and should be removed. It is a plant for dry climates and performs badly in humid conditions and when it is subject to continual winter wet. In such climates it is widely grown as an annual. 'Silver Dust' has leaves that are deeply cut into silver lace; 'White Diamond' has coarsely lobed bright-white leaves. Zones 8–9.

S. doronicum. Europe, North Africa. Height 2 ft; spread 1 ft (60×30 cm). A clump-forming plant with roundly heart-shaped, dark-green leaves and slender stems bearing lemon-yellow daisies in early summer. Zones 6–9.

S. pulcher. South America. Height 2 ft; spread 18 in. (60×45 cm). An unusual plant with yellow-centered, purplish pink daisies about 2 in. (5 cm) wide that bloom in autumn. The leathery, dark-green leaves are hairy, lance-shaped, and toothed. Requires well-drained soil. Zones 8–9.

SERRATULA

FAMILY: Compositae

A genus of about 70 species of sun-loving perennials native to Europe, Asia, and North Africa not widely grown in gardens but of some value for their thistlelike flowers in summer and autumn. The generic name comes from the Latin *serrula,* "little saw," referring to the saw-edged leaves.

CULTIVATION: Grow in ordinary, well-drained soil in full sun.

LANDSCAPE USE: Plant in a sunny border or rock garden for summer display.

PROPAGATION: Sow seed or divide in spring.

S. seoanei (S. shawii). Southern Europe. Height 9 in.; spread 6 in. (22.5×15 cm). A variable plant with dark-green, deeply cut, serrated, and bristly egg-shaped to lance-shaped leaves and branching stems bearing terminal purple-pink thistlelike flowers in summer and autumn. Zones 5–8.

S. tinctoria. Europe. Height 3 ft; spread 18 in. (90×45 cm). A clump-forming, many-branched plant with egg-shaped to lance-shaped, dark-green leaves divided into narrow, serrated, and bristly segments. Cylindrical heads of reddish purple flowers are borne on branching stems in late summer. Variety ***macrocephala*** grows to about 2 ft (60 cm) and has larger flowers. Zones 5–8.

SESLERIA

(Moor Grass)

FAMILY: Graminae

Widely distributed grasses, some of which are of ornamental value for their dwarf habit and attractive flowers and foliage.

CULTIVATION: Grow in full sun to partial shade in well-drained soil.

LANDSCAPE USE: Pleasant but not overwhelmingly

ornamental grasses for use as accent plants or as a contrast to more dramatic herbaceous plants.

Propagation: Divide in spring or autumn.

S. autumnalis. Autumn moor grass. Europe, Asia. Height 2 ft; spread 1 ft (60 × 30 cm). A clump-forming grass with light-green leaves forming a spiky hummock up to 16 in. (40 cm) high. Upright stems bear feathery panicles of rather dull silvery white flowers from midsummer to late summer. Evergreen in mild areas. Performs well in hot summers. Zones 5–8.

S. heufleriana. Europe. Height 20 in.; spread 18 in. (50 × 45 cm). A clump-forming grass with blue-green leaves forming a hummock about 16 in. (40 cm) tall. Feathery panicles of dark purple-brown flowers are produced in early spring. Drought tolerant. Zones 5–8.

Sesleria autumnalis

SHORTIA

Family: Diapensiaceae

Eight species of evergreen woodland plants native to eastern North America and Asia, with creeping rootstocks; glossy, heart-shaped basal leaves; and nodding white, pink, or pale-blue flowers in spring. Named after Dr. Charles Short (1794–1863), a Kentucky botanist.

Cultivation: Grow in moist but not boggy, acid soil in shade.

Landscape Use: Handsome woodland plants for the shaded garden.

Propagation: Divide in spring.

S. galacifolia. Oconee-bells. North and South Carolina. Height 6–8 in.; spread 12 in. (15–20 × 30 cm). A clump-forming evergreen with round, toothed, glossy, and leathery leaves up to 2 in. (5 cm) wide often tinged bronze in winter. The leaves are reminiscent of those of ***Galax urceolata,*** hence the specific name. Nodding, bell-shaped, white flowers up to 1 in. (2.5 cm) across, flushed with pink, with serrated petals are borne singly on short stems in mid- to late spring. Zones 4–8.

S. soldanelloides. Fringe-bells. Japan. Height 6–8 in.; spread 12 in. (15–20 × 30 cm). Evergreen clumps of rounded, heart-shaped, deeply toothed glossy leaves up to 2 in. (5 cm) wide. Nodding, bell-shaped, strongly fringed flowers are deep pink to bluish white and are produced in late spring. Variety ***illicifolia*** has leaves more coarsely toothed. Var. ***minima*** is a shorter, more compact plant; var. ***magna*** has larger-toothed leaves and rose-pink flowers. Zones 4–8.

S. uniflora. Nippon-bells. Japan. Height 6–8 in.; spread 12 in. (15–20 × 30 cm). Very similar to ***S. galacifolia*** but with glossy green leaves that are heart-shaped with wavy edges. White or pinkish white flowers with serrated to fringed petals appear in mid- to late spring. 'Grandiflora' has 2-in.-(5-cm-) wide, pinkish white flowers. Zones 4–9.

SIDALCEA

(False Mallow)

FAMILY: Malvaceae

Sidalcea malviflora 'Starks Hybrids'

A small genus of flowering plants native to western North America with rounded, often lobed basal leaves and deeply cut stem leaves. Cup-shaped, five-petaled flowers are produced on long stems in summer. The cultivars and hybrids available are often products of the crossing of ***S. candida*** and ***S. malviflora.*** They are generally listed under ***S. malviflora.*** The Latin name is a combination of two related genera, ***Sida*** and ***Alcea.***

CULTIVATION: Grow in full sun or light shade in well-drained soil in climates with temperate summers. Cut back faded flower stems for repeat bloom. Stake where necessary. Control Japanese beetles, which take an almost lascivious delight in devouring the flowers.

LANDSCAPE USE: Upright perennials for the summer border. The range of pink flowers is very satisfactory, particularly in combination with blue campanaulas and the silvery foliage of ***Artemisia*** species.

PROPAGATION: Sow seed in spring, planting into permanent position in autumn. Divide in spring.

S. candida. Western United States. Height 3 ft; spread 18 in. (90 × 45 cm). Although not widely grown, it is an important contributor to the more ornamental cultivars. It is a clump-forming plant with rounded, coarsely lobed, and toothed basal leaves up to 8 in. (20 cm) long. The alternate stem leaves are finely divided into five to seven segments. Spikes of small, cup-shaped, bluish white flowers are produced in summer. Zones 4–7.

S. malviflora. Prairie mallow. Western North America. Height 2–4 ft; spread 18 in. (60–120 × 45 cm). A clump-forming plant with rounded midgreen basal leaves with seven to nine shallow lobes. The stem leaves are alternate and deeply divided into five to seven fingerlike segments. Spikes of 1–2-in.- (2.5–5-cm-) wide, lilac-pink flowers are produced in summer. The species has been superseded by the following cultivars.

'Brilliant'; height 2½ ft (75 cm,) deep rose-red flowers

'Croftway Red': height 3 ft (90 cm,) rich red flowers

'Elsie Heugh': height 3–4 ft (90–120 cm), pale-pink-fringed flowers

'Jimmy Whittet': height 4 ft (120 cm), purplish pink flowers

'Loveliness': height 2½ ft (75 cm), shell-pink flowers

'Mrs. T. Alderson: height 4 ft (120 cm), rose-pink flowers

'Nimmerdor': height 6 ft (180 cm), rich-pink flowers, a vigorous variety

'Oberon': height 2½ ft (75 cm), deep-pink flowers

'Puck': height 2 ft (60 cm), clear-pink flowers, a dwarf variety
'Rose Queen': height 4 ft (120 cm), rose-pink flowers
'Stark's Hybrids': height 3–4 ft (90–120 cm), range from pale-pink to almost red flowers
'Sussex Beauty': height 3 ft (90 cm), pale rose-pink flowers
'William Smith': height 3½ ft (105 cm), salmon-pink flowers
Zones 5–7.

SILENE

(Campion, Catchfly)

FAMILY: Caryophyllaceae

Silene schafta 'Robusta'

Silene vulgaris ssp. *maritima*

A large genus of annual, biennial, and perennial plants, a few of which are grown as rock-garden or edging plants or, occasionally, in the woodland garden. The leaves are basal or opposite, and the pink, white, or red, five-petaled flowers are borne either singly or in one-sided sprays. The group of sepals often expands, giving the base of the flower a balloon- or bladderlike appearance. A number of species have sticky stems and "bladders," giving rise to the common name of "catchfly" and the Latin name of *Silene,* from *sialon,* "saliva."

CULTIVATION: Grow in well-drained soil in full sun to partial shade.

LANDSCAPE USE: Rock-garden or front-of-border plants. The taller species have value in a partly shaded site.

PROPAGATION: Carefully divide in spring or autumn. Sow seeds in spring. Take stem cuttings in midsummer.

S. acaulis. Moss campion. Europe, Asia, North America. Height 1 in.; spread 6 in. (2.5 × 15 cm). A densely tufted, mat-forming, evergreen plant with ¼–½- in.- (0.6–1.2-cm-) long, linear green leaves and stemless five-petaled, flat, pink flowers up to ½ in. (1.2 cm) wide, blooming in spring. Requires poor, gritty soil for good flowering and cool climates for healthy growth. 'Flore Pleno' has double pink flowers. Zones 3–5.

S. alpestris. European Alps. Height 4–6 in.; spread 8 in. (10–15 × 20 cm). A tufted plant with linear, lance-shaped, glossy leaves ½ in. (1.2 cm) wide and branching stems with rounded and fringed white flowers in late spring. Zones 4–7.

S. caroliniana. Eastern United States. Height 8 in.; spread 12 in. (20 × 30 cm). A short-lived, mound-forming perennial with bluish green, roundly lance-shaped leaves up to 5 in. (12.5 cm) long. Clusters of 1-in.- (2.5-cm-) wide, deep-pink, notched flowers are produced in early summer. Zones 5–8.

S. fimbriata. (S. multifida). Caucasus. Height 2 ft; spread 18 in. (60×45 cm). A clump-forming plant with hairy, dark-green, elliptical basal leaves becoming narrow up on the stem. Deeply fringed white flowers with a conspicuous bladder are borne on sticky stems in summer. Zones 5–8.

S. hookeri. California. Height 2 in.; spread 8 in. (5×20 cm). A short-lived plant with procumbent stems and grayish, hairy, roundly lance-shaped leaves up to 4 in. (10 cm) long. Pink, salmon, or orange-pink deeply cleft flowers are borne on short stems in late summer. Not an easy plant to grow, it requires well-drained, lime-rich soil and protection from winter wet. Zones 4–6.

S. polypetala. Southeast United States. Height 4–6 in.; spread 18 in. (10–15×45 cm). A rare and endangered plant that I hope will be widely propagated and available to the interested gardener. It is a clump-forming plant with dark-green, narrowly egg-shaped leaves and delightful fringed 1¼-in. (3.2-cm) wide flowers of lavender-pink that appear in late spring. It requires part to full shade in well-drained soil. I have made the mistake of growing this in too much sun, and it did not prosper. However, in the right place it is an extraordinarily pretty plant. Zones 6–8.

S. schafta. Caucasus. Height 6 in.; spread 12 in. (15×30 cm). A mat-forming plant with a woody rootstock and rosettes of narrowly egg-shaped light-green leaves. Magenta-pink, notched flowers appear from mid- to late summer. Prefers a well-drained soil in full sun. Zones 5–7.

S. virginica. Fire pink. Eastern United States. Height 2 ft; spread 1 ft (60×30 cm). This species wanders between ***Melandrium*** and ***Silene*** but is currently resting in this genus. It has basal clumps of roundly lance-shaped mid-green leaves up to 4 in. (10 cm) long and sticky stems with longer, stemless leaves. Axillary and terminal clusters of 2-in.- (5-cm-) wide crimson flowers with notched petals are produced in late spring to early summer. Grow in light to partial shade. It is a relatively short-lived plant requiring propagation every couple of years. Zones 3–8.

S. vulgaris. Bladder campion. Widely distributed. Height 2 ft; spread 1 ft (60×30 cm). An erect plant with branching stems and egg-shaped to linear, gray-green leaves up to 2 in. (5 cm) long. The deeply notched flowers appear in summer and are generally white, with a marked bladderlike base. Subspecies ***maritima*** is a trailing plant growing to a height of 12 in. (30 cm), with light-green leaves and white flowers on erect stems. Variety ***rosea*** has rose-pink flowers, 'Flore Pleno' has densely double white flowers; 'White Bells' has slightly nodding, white tubular flowers. Zones 4–8.

SILPHIUM

(Rosinweed)

Family: Compositae

A small genus of about 20 to 25 species of coarse, large-leaved, late-flowering daisies native to eastern North America. The leaves are opposite, alternate, or whorled. The flowers are daisylike, mostly yellow, blooming in mid- to late summer. The common name refers to the resinous secretions from some species.

Cultivation: Grow in moist but not boggy soil in full sun.

Landscape Use: Coarse, bold plants for the back of the border or on the edge of a bog garden.

Propagation: Divide in spring or sow seed in autumn.

S. laciniatum. Compass plant. Eastern United States. Height 6–8 ft; spread 3 ft (180–240×90 cm). A coarse perennial with stout and rough, hairy stems and ferny, finely divided leaves up to 18 in. (45 cm) long at the base of the stem becoming narrower and smaller up on the stem. The leaves grow vertically on the stem, with the leaf edges pointing north and south. Clusters of showy yellow flowers are up to 5 in. (12.5 cm) wide and bloom in mid- to late summer. Zones 3–9.

S. perfoliatum. Cup plant. Eastern North Amer-

Silphium perfoliatum

ica. Height 6–8 ft; spread 3 ft (180–240 × 90 cm). Stout square stems and coarsely toothed, opposite, wedge-shaped to heart-shaped leaves up to 14 in. (35 cm) long. The bases of the leaf stems grow together to form a cup. In late summer masses of 3-in.- (7.5-cm-) wide yellow daisies are produced on thick stems above the leaves. Zones 3–9.

S. terebinthaceum. Prairie dock. Eastern North America. Height 6 ft; spread 3 ft (180 × 90 cm). A large, clump-forming plant with basal egg-shaped to elliptical, toothed or lobed, light-green leaves up to 2 ft (60 cm) in length. The mostly leafless stems bear 3-in- (7.5-cm-) wide yellow daisies in mid- to late summer. Zones 3–9.

SISYRINCHIUM

(Blue-eyed Grass)

Family: Iridaceae

Sisyrinchium striatum

About 75 species of irislike perennials native to North America. The leaves are grasslike or linear, the flowers star-shaped and blue, white, yellow, or purple and bloom in spring and summer. In general, they are plants for cool climates.

Cultivation: Grow in well-drained, moist soil in full sun. Remove faded flower heads to prevent self-seeding.

Landscape Use: Attractive grassy plants for the front of the border or rock garden.

Propagation: Divide in spring or autumn every three years. Sow seed in autumn.

S. angustifolium (S. graminoides, S. bermudiana). Blue-eyed grass. Eastern North America. Height 12 in.; spread 4 in. (30 × 10 cm). A tufted semievergreen plant with deep-green grasslike leaves and branched, winged flower stems bearing starry purple-blue flowers in late spring and early summer. Zones 2–9.

S. bellum. California. Height 6 in.; spread 4 in. (15 × 10 cm). A smaller, less hardy version of ***S. angustifolium,*** with purple-blue flowers with yellow throats. Blooms in summer along with other California natives such as ***Escholzia californica*** and ***Limnanthes douglasii.*** Zones 7–9.

S. californicum. Golden-eyed grass. Northwestern North America. Height 1–2 ft; spread 1 ft (30–60 × 30 cm). A semievergreen, tufted plant with light-green grassy leaves and bright-yellow, 1-in.-(2.5-cm-) wide flowers in late spring and early summer. A beautiful plant when well grown. Zones 8–9.

S. douglasii. Purple-eyed grass. Northwestern North America. Height 8–10 in.; spread 6 in. (20–25 × 15 cm). A spring-flowering plant with grassy foliage and starry, nodding, bell-shaped reddish purple flowers. The plant dies down in midsummer. Variety ***album*** has white flowers. The cultivar 'Quaint and Queer' (which, in truth, may not be connected to this species) is a tufted plant with mid-green grasslike leaves and summer-blooming, open-faced and starry, apricot flowers with a maroon throat. It is a pretty plant that combines wonderfully well with dark foliage plants. Zones 6–8.

S. striatum. South America. Height 1–2 ft; spread 1 ft (30–60 × 30 cm). A clump-forming plant with irislike gray-green leaves up to 18 in. (45 cm) long and unbranched, winged stems with summer spikes of creamy yellow flowers with darker yellow throats and purple veins. The most "garden worthy" of the genus, this species is very handsome in flower. After flowering the shoot producing the flower stem dies, causing the plant to look very messy. Dead stems should be removed and the plant fed (and watered if necessary) to provide vigor. 'Aunt May' (Variegatum) has gray-green leaves longitudinally striped creamy white. Zones 6–8.

SMILACINA

(False Solomon's-seal)

Family: Liliaceae

About 25 species of woodland plants native to North America and Asia with alternate leaves and arching stems. They are similar to ***Polygonatum*** species but differ by having feathery clusters of white flowers at the end of the stems rather than having small, bell-shaped flowers borne from the leaf axils. While only one species is of ornamental value, a number of others are worth growing. The generic name refers to the resemblance to ***Smilax,*** a genus of woody vines.

Cultivation: Grow in humus-rich, moist soil in shade.

Landscape Use: Handsome foliage plants for the shaded border or woodland garden, where the dappled sunlight illuminates the masses of white flowers.

Propagation: Divide in spring or autumn. Seed is very slow to germinate.

S. racemosa. False Solomon's-seal. North America. Height 2–3 ft; spread 18–24 in. (60–90 × 45–60 cm). A clump-forming plant with arching stems and pointed, light-green, conspicuously veined, narrowly egg-shaped leaves up to 9 in. (22.5 cm) long. Feathery and fragrant, almost pyramidal panicles of creamy white flowers are borne at the end of the stems in spring and summer. The flowers are followed by red berries with purple spots.

While not a flashy plant, it does have an elegant grace that lends an air of refinement to the right spot. Zones 4–9.

S. ***stellata.*** North America. Height 1–2 ft; spread 18 in. (30–60 × 45 cm). Arching stems with pale-green, sharply lance-shaped leaves up to 6 in. (15 cm) long and terminal sprays of star-shaped white flowers in late spring and early summer. The flowers are followed by dark-red berries. Zones 3–8.

S. ***trifolia.*** North America. Height 1 ft; spread 18 in. (30 × 45 cm). An inhabitant of boggy ground with erect, arching stems and three alternate, elliptical and stemless leaves up to 5 in. (12.5 cm) long. Terminal clusters of creamy white flowers are produced in late spring and early summer, followed by red berries. Zones 3–8.

SOLIDAGO

(Goldenrod)

FAMILY: Compositae

Solidago 'Peter Pan'

About 130 species of flowering plants mostly native to North America with some species indigenous to Europe, Asia, and South America. They are generally upright plants with alternate leaves and plumed clusters of tiny yellow flowers in late summer and autumn. They are valued for their golden yellow flowers in a season when the sun is golden yellow, too. They are common to open fields and meadows, light woodland, and roadsides of much of North America. Perhaps they are more beautiful in the wild, where they can be seen in combination with asters, joe-pye-weed, and other autumnal beauties. They are beginning to be acknowledged as good garden plants for North America, throwing off the bad and unfounded publicity as rank weeds that cause allergies. The garden hybrids are a mix of crosses between species. The genus as a whole is a taxonomic tumble. We can leave taxonomists to battle it out while we enjoy the beauty of the plants themselves.

The cultivars have been produced for better flowers and for a more compact habit. Their parentage is complex but involves ***S. canadensis, S. virgaurea, S. virgaurea*** var. ***minutissisma,*** and others. There are more and better garden plants to come from the development of ***Solidago.*** The generic name is said to be derived from the Latin *solidus* and *ago,* "to make solid," a reference to its supposed power to heal wounds.

CULTIVATION: Grow in well-drained soil in full sun or, if you must, in light shade. Staking the taller species is necessary.

LANDSCAPE USE: Effective late-flowering plants for the sunny border or rock garden. They have great beauty when combined with autumn-flowering asters.

PROPAGATION: Divide in spring or autumn. Take stem cuttings of named hybrids. Sow seed in the autumn.

S. caesia. North America. Wreath goldenrod. Height 2–3 ft; spread 1 ft (60–90 × 30 cm). Erect and unbranched purplish stems with sharply toothed, stemless, lance-shaped flowers are borne in the upper leaf axils in midsummer to autumn. Tolerant of partial shade. This is a handsome goldenrod because of its single stem and the tight clusters of yellow flowers blooming along it. Zones 4–9.

S. canadensis. North America. Height 3–5 ft; spread 1 ft (90–150 × 30 cm). A coarse and weedy plant with great natural beauty. From a substantial rhizomatous rootstock rise somewhat hairy, erect stems with variously linear to lance-shaped to elliptical, serrated leaves up to 6 in. (15 cm) long. One-sided, branching panicles of tiny golden yellow flowers are produced in autumn. Zones 3–9.

S. odora. Sweet goldenrod. North America. Height 3–4 ft; spread 1 ft (90–120 × 30 cm). Erect stems with anise-scented, linear to lance-shaped leaves up to 4 in. (10 cm) long and one-sided panicles of golden yellow flowers in autumn. Zones 3–9.

S. rugosa. Wrinkled goldenrod. North America. Height 5–8 ft; spread 1–2 ft (150–240 × 30–60 cm). A clump-forming plant with rough, hairy stems, egg-shaped leaves, and one-sided panicles of golden yellow flowers in late summer and autumn. Zones 3–9.

S. sempervirens. Seaside goldenrod. Eastern North America. Height 6 ft; spread 1–2 ft (180 × 30–60 cm). A useful plant for poor soil and salty air. The basal leaves are spoon-shaped up to 16 in. (40 cm) long. The stem leaves are are lance-shaped and smaller. One-sided panicles of golden yellow flowers are produced in late summer through to late autumn. Zones 4–9.

S. spathulata. Western North America. Height 2 ft; spread 1 ft (60 × 30 cm). A clump-forming plant with a woody rootstock and strongly aromatic stems with spoon-shaped to egg-shaped, sharply toothed leaves up to 6 in. (15 cm) long. Densely plumed panicles of golden yellow flowers are produced in autumn. Variety ***neomexicana*** is a little taller and has lance-shaped leaves with rounded tips. Tolerates dry soil. Zones 4–9.

Solidago sphacelata 'Golden Fleece'

S. speciosa. North America. Height 6 ft; spread 1–2 ft (180 × 30–60 cm). Clumps of erect stems and narrow lance-shaped, untoothed leaves, with arching panicles of showy golden yellow flowers in late summer to autumn. Tolerates light shade. Zones 5–9.

S. sphacelata. North America. Height 18 in.–3 ft; spread 2 ft (45–90 × 60 cm). A branching, clump-forming species notable for the cultivar 'Golden Fleece,' which grows to a height of 18 in. (45 cm) and produces masses of bright-yellow flowers in autumn. It is particularly ornamental and has the added advantage of being quite tolerant of dry soils. Zones 5–9.

Hybrids and Cultivars. There are many worthwhile cultivars, a few of which are:

'Baby Gold': height to 2 ft (60 cm), bright-yellow flowers
'Cloth of Gold': height about 18 in. (45 cm), deep-yellow flowers
'Crown of Rays': height 2 ft (60 cm), large panicles of bright-yellow flowers
'Goldenmosa': height 2–3 ft (60–90 cm) and blooms in late summer
'Golden Showers': height 2½ ft (75 cm); arching plumes of deep yellow
'Golden Thumb': height 1 ft (30 cm)
'Lemore': height 2½ ft (75 cm), soft-yellow flowers
'Mimosa': height 3½ ft (105 cm), golden yellow flowers
'Laurin': height 2 ft (60 cm), deep-yellow flowers in late summer
'Peter Pan': height 3 ft (90 cm), flowers in autumn. Zones 3–9.

SOLIDASTER

Family: Compositae

A bigeneric hybrid between ***Aster ptarmicoides*** and possibly ***Solidago missouriensis.*** It is a pretty plant with small yellow daisies on arching stems.

Cultivation: Grow in full sun in humus-rich soil.

Landscape Use: A good border plant for late-flowering display.

Propagation: Divide in spring or autumn or take stem cuttings in early summer.

× *S. luteus.* Height 2 ft; spread 1 ft (60 × 30 cm). An erect plant with lance-shaped, slightly toothed leaves up to 6 in. (15 cm) long. Many-branched heads of ½-in.- (1.2-cm-) wide, canary-yellow, daisylike flowers are produced in late summer and early autumn. The flowers fade to a pale, silvery yellow. Zones 4–8.

SORGHASTRUM

(Indian Grass)

Family: Graminae

A small genus of grasses native to North America and Africa. One species is of value in the garden for its upright habit, late-summer flowering, and autumn color. The generic name is a reference to its similarity to sorghum ***(Holcus).***

Cultivation: Grow in ordinary, well-drained soil in full sun. Cut back faded foliage in early spring. Staking is unnecessary.

Landscape Use: A handsome prairie grass for the meadow or large border either en masse or as a specimen.

Propagation: Divide in spring or autumn, or sow seed in spring.

S. nutans (S. avenaceum). Indian grass. North America. Height 6 ft; spread 2 ft (180 × 60 cm). An upright grass with erect, gray-green leaves about ¼ in. (0.6 cm) wide, arching at the tips, forming a clump about 3 ft (90 cm) high. In late summer 8-in.- (20-cm-) long, reddish pink plumes appear on 6-ft (180-cm) stems. The flowers turn to gold in autumn, the foliage bright orange. 'Sioux Blue,' a form selected at Longwood Gardens in Pennsylvania, has blue foliage and a more upright form. Zones 3–9.

Sorghastrum nutans

SPARTINA

(Cord Grass)

Family: Graminae

A small genus of stout and erect grasses native to North and South America, Europe, and North Africa. Only one species, and its variegated form, is grown in gardens. The name comes from the Greek *spartine,* "cord," referring to the stiff, leathery leaves.

Cultivation: Grow in moist, even boggy soil in full sun. Spreads fairly rapidly and can be aggressive. Despite its native habitat, it is tolerant of dry soils.

Landscape Use: An architectural grass used for its stiff but arching form, variegated leaves, and autumn color.

Propagation: Divide in spring.

S. ***pectinata.*** Prairie cord grass. North America. Height 6 ft; spread 2–3 ft (180 × 30–60 cm). A stiff, coarse grass native to bogs and marshes of North America, with arching, mid-green, leathery leaves with rough edges, forming a clump up to 5 ft (150 cm) tall. Insignificant, light-green flowers are produced on 6 ½-ft (195-cm) stems in late summer.

Spartina pectinata

The variegated form 'Aureomarginata' is more interesting for its mid-green, glossy leaves and narrow, gold edges. Autumn color is golden yellow. Zones 5–9.

SPIGELIA

(Pinkroot)

Family: Loganiaceae

About 30 species of herbaceous perennials native to southeastern and south-central United States and South America with opposite leaves and tubular flowers. The one species grown in gardens is still not as widely cultivated as it should be. It is to be hoped that discerning growers will identify strong traits in the variation of the species and start producing cultivated varieties we can be proud of. Named after Adrian von der Spigel (1578–1625), professor of Botany at Padua University.

Cultivation: Grow in full sun in mild climates, partial shade in hot climates, in moist but well-drained soil. Protection from hot afternoon sun is generally necessary.

Landscape Use: An elegant plant, useful for its upward-facing red and yellow funnels in early summer and occasionally in autumn. Dramatic in large masses or delicate in lightly shaded woodland.

Propagation: Divide the fleshy roots with a razor blade in spring, or sow seed in autumn.

S. ***marilandica.*** Pinkroot. Southeastern United

Spigelia marilandica

States. Height 1–2 ft; spread 1 ft (30–60 × 30 cm). A highly attractive plant with a variable habit but with generally erect stems and dark-green, opposite, egg-shaped, stemless leaves 2–4 in. (5–10 cm) long. The 2- in.- (5-cm-) long, trumpet-shaped red flowers have yellow throats. They appear in early summer and often again in the autumn. It is a sadly underused plant. Zones 6–9.

SPODIOPOGON

FAMILY: Graminae

An attractive cool-season grass with pointed leaves held at right angles to the stem, late-summer flowers, and fine autumn color that is often wine-red.

CULTIVATION: Grow in light shade in moist, well-drained soil. Requires summer irrigation when grown in full sun. Cut back after frost.

LANDSCAPE USE: A specimen grass for the shaded border.

S. sibiricus. Europe. Height 4–5 ft; spread 18 in. (120–150 × 45 cm). A stiff, clump-forming grass with short, pointed leaves held perpendicular to the stem, making a bamboolike bundle up to 3 ft (90 cm) tall. Feathery panicles of silvery flowers are produced in midsummer on 4–5-ft (120–150-cm) stems. The foliage turns burgundy-red in the autumn but quickly turns to brown after the first major frost. Zones 4–8.

Spodiopogon sibiricus

STACHYS

(Betony)

Family: Labiatae

Over 300 species of herbaceous perennials and subshrubs widely distributed throughout the temperate and subtropical regions of the world. Few of the temperate species are cultivated in gardens. Two species are widely grown for foliage and flower. The stems are square, the leaves opposite and sometimes toothed, the hooded flowers mostly held in whorled spikes in spring and summer. The generic name is derived from the Greek word for "spike," referring to the flowers. The curious common name comes from ***S. officinalis*** and is said to originate from a Celtic language from the words for "head" and "good," it being widely used in ancient times for problems with the head.

Cultivation: In general, well-drained but not dry soils in full sun or partial shade suit those species grown in gardens. The silver-leaved species does best in well-drained soil in areas with low heat and low humidity.

Landscape Use: Stalwart groundcovers and border plants.

Propagation: Divide in spring or autumn.

S. byzantina (S. lanata, S. olympica). Lamb's ears, lamb's tongue. Turkey, southwestern Asia. Height 12–18 in.; spread 12 in. (30–45 × 30 cm). A mat-forming plant with white, woolly, elliptical to oblong, lightly toothed leaves 4–6 in. (10–15 cm) long. Woolly spikes of purple flowers are borne in whorls in late spring and sporadically throughout the summer. The flowers can be quite ugly, as the stems rarely stay erect but flop all over the place. They should be removed before making their presence felt. In hot and humid climates this species and its cultivars often rot and can look truly disgusting. This can partly be prevented by numerous applications of fungicide and the cessation of overhead watering. However, it is a plant for mild climates and in hot summers performs well in spring, badly in summer, and recovers in autumn. 'Primrose Heron' has yellow-green foliage in the spring that turns gray-green in the summer. Purple flowers are produced in late spring. It is a dangerous combination. 'Sheila McQueen' is a compact plant with gray-green, felted leaves and purple spikes up to about 12 in. (30 cm) high; 'Silver Carpet' is now widely grown because of its almost sterile habits. A low, mat-forming plant that rarely produces flowers, it is the least successful cultivar for hot climates, possibly because the growth is so compact and clustered. Zones 4–8.

Stachys macrantha

S. macrantha (S. grandiflora). Asia Minor. Height 1–2 ft; spread 18 in. (30–60 × 45 cm). A clump-forming species with rosettes of dark-green, egg-shaped to heart-shaped, wrinkled and hairy, coarsely serrated leaves and spikes of violet-pink, lobed and lipped flowers held in widely spaced whorls in late spring to early summer. Variety ***rosea*** has pink flowers; var. ***superba*** is a vigorous plant with purple-violet flowers. 'Nivea' has white flowers; 'Robusta' has rosy-pink flowers and grows to 2 ft (60 cm). Grows well in partial shade. Zones 4–8.

S. nivea. Syria. Height 6–12 in.; spread 8 in. (15–30 × 20 cm). A curious rock-garden plant with a woody rootstock and gray-green, coarsely toothed, and wrinkled lance-shaped, almost tonguelike, leaves, and small spikes of white flowers in late spring and early summer. Requires a well-drained site in full sun. Zones 4–7.

S. officinalis. Betony. Europe. Height 2 ft; spread 18 in. (60 × 45 cm). A clump-forming plant with erect stems. The roundly heart-shaped leaves are toothed, wrinkled, and generally hairy, up to 4–5 in. (10–12.5 cm) long. Spikes of whorled, violet-pink flowers are produced in late spring and summer. Variety ***alba*** has creamy white flowers. 'Rosea Superba' has rosy-pink flowers. Zones 4–8.

STIPA

(Needlegrass, Feathergrass)

Family: Graminae

A small genus of grasses with narrow, rolled leaves and feathery, open panicles of flowers in summer. Three species are superb ornamentals that, although not the easiest of ornamental grasses to grow, deserve wider attention. The name comes from the Greek *stipe,* "tow" (fiber), from the feathery flowers.

Cultivation: Grow in well-drained soil in full sun in a mild climate. Both cold winters and hot and humid summers are detrimental.

Landscape Use: A large but delicate grass that is at its best in early summer.

Propagation: Divide in spring or autumn, or sow seed in spring.

S. arundinacea. Pheasant grass. New Zealand. Height 5 ft; spread 4 ft (150 × 120 cm). An evergreen grass with arching green leaves tinged brown, forming a mound about 2 ft (60 cm) high. Feathery panicles of glistening, purple-green, drooping flowers are produced in summer. Zones 5–8.

S. gigantea. Giant feather grass. Southern Europe. Height 5 ft; spread 3 ft (150 × 90 cm). A mound-forming plant with gray-green, rolled leaves making a 2-ft- (60-cm-) high hummock and 5-ft- (150-cm-) tall flowering stems bearing clouds of airy, silvery yellow flowers from early to late summer. Does not require staking. Performs poorly in hot climates. Zones 7–8.

S. pennata. Feather grass. Europe, Siberia. Height 3 ft; spread 2 ft (90 × 60 cm). A short-lived perennial grass with thin, rolled leaves forming a clump about 2 ft (60 cm) tall and feathery panicles of silvery white flowers in summer. Zones 5–8.

STOKESIA

(Stoke's Aster)

Family: Asteraceae

One species native to South Carolina, Florida, and Louisiana, with dark-green alternate leaves and blue cornflowerlike flowers in summer. Named after Jonathan Stokes, an English botanist.

Cultivation: Grow in well-drained, fertile soil in full sun or partial shade. Mulch in the colder limits of its range.

Landscape Use: An underused plant for the front of the border, where the blue or white flowers can be seen to best advantage.

Propagation: Divide in spring.

S. laevis. Southeastern United States. Height 1–2 ft; spread 18 in. (30–60 × 45 cm). Stiff, branching stems bear 8-in.- (20-cm-) long, dark-green, lance-shaped leaves with a prominent white midrib. The leaves become smaller and stalkless higher on the flower stem. In the wild the flowers are borne two to four on a single stem with the individual flowers about 1 in. (2.5 cm) wide. Cultivation and breeding produce blooms that are about 3–4 in. (7.5–10 cm) wide. The flowers consist of two types of ray florets. The inner florets are short and tubular, the outer are longer, flat, and deeply cut into five lobes. They flower for a considerable time in sum-

Stokesia laevis 'Rosea'

mer. Good drainage is the key to cultivating this plant. 'Alba' has dull white flowers; 'Blue Danube' has large lavender-blue flowers; 'Blue Moon' has pale-blue flowers; 'Blue Star' has light-blue flowers; 'Bluestone' flowers in early summer with clear-blue blossoms; 'Rosea' has rosy-pink flowers; 'Silver Moon' has creamy white flowers; 'Wyoming' has deep-blue flowers. Zones 5–9.

STYLOPHORUM

(Wood Poppy)

FAMILY: Papaveraceae

A small genus of woodland plants native to eastern Asia and eastern North America. The North American species has yellow sap, deeply lobed pale-green leaves, and bright-yellow flowers in spring. It is one of the loveliest of North American wildflowers.

CULTIVATION: Grow in rich, leafy, moist but not wet soil in partial shade. Self-seeds successfully.

LANDSCAPE USE: An excellent woodland or shade-garden perennial that is outstanding in conjunction with Virginia bluebells (***Mertensia virginica***).

PROPAGATION: Carefully divide in spring. Sow seed in autumn.

S. diphyllum. Wood poppy. Eastern North America. Height 18 in.; spread 12 in. (45 × 30 cm). A woodland native with bright-yellow sap and pale-green, hairy leaves deeply cut into five to seven lobed segments. The leaves reach a length of about 12 in. (30 cm) and are borne in basal rosettes. Bright-yellow, four-petaled, 2-in. (5-cm) wide, poppylike flowers are produced in spring. This species is largely summer dormant but may persist into late summer and autumn if grown in moist soil. Zones 4–9.

Stylophorum diphyllum

SYMPHYANDRA

(Bellflower)

Family: Campanulaceae

Symphyandra wanneri

A small genus of short-lived campanulalike perennials with alternate leaves and bell-like flowers, native to the eastern Mediterranean and Asia. They are distinguished from ***Campanula*** by having the anthers fused into a tube. The generic name comes from the Greek *Symphuio* and *aner* meaning "anthers growing together."

Cultivation: Grow in full sun in well-drained soil in a mild climate. So short-lived is this genus that they are generally grown as biennials.

Landscape Use: Pretty bell-shape flowers for the sunny border or rock garden.

Propagation: Sow seed in autumn.

S. hofmannii. Yugoslavia. Height 2 ft; spread 18 in. (60 × 45 cm). A hairy plant with erect, branching stems and coarsely toothed, pale-green, lance-shaped leaves with winged leaf stems. The basal leaves are up to 7 in. (17.5 cm) long, becoming smaller and stemless up on the flower stem. Nodding, bell-shaped, white flowers are borne on leafy stems in summer. Zones 6–8.

S. pendula. Caucasus. Height 2 ft; spread 1 ft (60 × 30 cm). Similar to the above species but with heart-shaped to oval, pale-green, hairy leaves, wingless leaf stems, and nodding creamy white flowers in summer. Zones 6–8.

S. wanneri. Alps. Height 12–18 in.; spread 12 in. (30–45 × 30 cm). A clump-forming plant with erect stems and basal rosettes of oval to lance-shaped toothed and hairy leaves becoming smaller up on the stem. Nodding, bell-shaped, violet-blue flowers are produced in summer. Zones 6–8.

SYMPHYTUM

(Comfrey)

Family: Boraginaceae

Twenty-five species of coarse, hairy perennials native to Europe and Asia with alternate leaves and blue, white, pink, or yellow flowers in nodding, branched clusters in spring and summer. While not the most refined of garden plants, they have been unfairly relegated to the wild garden. Now that we have discovered that not all plants need to be primped and polished to look their best, perhaps the comfreys will be better appreciated. The common comfrey, ***S. officinale,*** was widely used as a medicinal herb; in fact, the common name is derived from the Latin *con forma,* "to join together," an allusion to its supposed bone-setting properties. The generic name repeats the healing theme by being derived from the Greek *symphyo,* "to unite."

Cultivation: Grow in rich, moist soil in sun to partial shade.

Landscape Use: Coarse plants for the border or informal garden. Their soft, drooping flowers are particularly attractive.

Propagation: Divide in spring or autumn.

S. caucasicum. Caucasus. Height 2 ft; spread 2 ft (60 × 60 cm). A clump-forming hairy plant with pale grayish green, egg-shaped to lance-shaped, rough leaves up to 8 in. (20 cm) in length. Nodding clusters of ¾-in.- (1.8-cm-) long, bell-shaped flowers open pinkish purple but quickly turn to azure blue in spring. Grow in partial shade in moist soil. Zones 3–8.

S. grandiflorum. Caucasus. Height 10–12 in.; spread 12 in. (25–30 × 30 cm). Dark-green, wrinkled and hairy, egg-shaped leaves about 4–7 in. (10–17.5 cm) form substantial basal clumps with sterile stems lying on the ground and pointing upward. The fertile stems bear tubular, pale-yellow flowers with reddish tips in spring. A tough plant that even grows in that gardener's nightmare, dry shade. The species is more vigorous in moist soil, as are the following cultivars. 'Hidcote Blue': height 20 in. (50 cm), pink buds turn to pale-blue flowers that eventually fade to white, 'Hidcote Pink': height 20 in. (50 cm), pink buds and pink flowers; 'Variegatum': leaves edged creamy white. Zones 3–8.

Symphytum x *uplandicum* 'Variegatum'

S. × uplandicum. Height 3–4 ft; spread 3 ft (90–120 × 90 cm). A large clump-forming perennial with branching stems and 10-in.- (25-cm-) long, hairy, egg-shaped to lance-shaped, gray-green leaves. Leafy stems bear nodding clusters of violet-blue flowers in late spring and early summer. It is a hybrid between ***S. asperum*** and ***S. officinale.*** 'Variegatum' is by far the best comfrey for the garden. It has gray-green leaves with broad, creamy yellow margins. The violet-blue flowers make an odd contrast to the leaves, and the flowering stems should be removed to enhance this excellent foliage plant. Requires rich, moist soil in light shade. Zones 4–8.

SYMPLOCARPUS

(Skunk Cabbage)

Family: Araceae

Not to be confused with the other skunk cabbage, ***Lysichiton americanum,*** which is native to western North America and has a yellow spathe. The single species is a swamp-loving plant native to northeastern North America and Asia.

Cultivation: Grow in constantly moist soil in shade.

Landscape Use: A large planting of skunk cabbage gives an extraordinary, 'prehistoric" look to the landscape.

Propagation: Divide the long, fleshy roots in spring. Sow seed in autumn.

S. foetidus. Skunk cabbage. Eastern North Amer-

Symplocarpus foetidus

ica, Asia. Height 3 ft; spread 2 ft (90 × 60 cm). A wonderfully reptilian plant that produces hoodlike spathes mottled purplish red and yellow-green in late winter and early spring. The spathes wrestle themselves out of the often-frozen ground and expand to about 6 in. (15 cm) tall. They surround a black, oblong spadix. The glossy-green leaves emerge after the flowers and grow up to 3 ft (90 cm) long and 1 ft (30 cm) wide. The plant stinks only if the leaves are bruised. Zones 3–9.

TANACETUM

(Tansy)

FAMILY: Compositae

Tanacetum densum var. *amani*

A large genus of annual and perennial plants with aromatic, alternate leaves and daisylike flowers. A number of species have been batted about between this genus and ***Chrysanthemum*** and have reached their current resting place here. The common name is derived from the Greek *athanaton,* "immortal," referring either to the long-lasting flowers or to its use as a preservative for dead bodies.

CULTIVATION: Grow in well-drained soil in full sun.

LANDSCAPE USE: Many species make excellent cut flowers as well as good summer-flowering plants for border or rock garden.

PROPAGATION: Divide in spring or autumn.

T. cinerarifolium (Chrysanthemum cinerarifolium). Dalmation insect flower. Yugoslavia. Height 18 in.; spread 12 in. (45 × 30 cm). Deeply divided, ferny foliage, green above, silvery underneath, with white flowers 1½ in. (4 cm) across in summer. An attractive perennial noted for being the primary source of the insecticide pyrethrum. Zones 3–9.

T. coccineum (Chrysanthemum coccineum). Pyrethrum. Europe, Asia. Height 2 ft; spread 18 in. (60 × 45 cm). Widely grown for cut flowers, pyrethrum is also a good plant for the border. The bright-green leaves are finely cut, almost like carrot leaves. The usually single flowers are 2–4 in. (5–10 cm) wide, golden-eyed, with ray flowers of various colors. They bloom in late spring and early summer with occasional flowering in autumn. They are best divided in early autumn. 'Eileen May Robinson' grows to 2 ft (60 cm) and has pink flowers; 'Helen' has double light-pink flowers; 'Mrs. C. E. Beckwith' has double white flowers; 'Pink Bouquet' has double pink flowers with white centers; 'Robinson's Red' has dark-red single flowers. Zones 5–9.

T. corymbosum (Chrysanthemum corymbosum). Caucasus. Height 4 ft; spread 1 ft (120 × 30 cm). A clump-forming plant similar to ***T. coccineum*** but more vigorous and with branching stems. The white, yellow-eyed flowers are up to 1 in. (2.5 cm) across and are carried in clusters in summer.

T. densum subsp. ***amani (Chrysanthemum densum amanum).*** Turkey. Height 8 in.; spread 8–12 in. (20 × 20–30 cm). An attractive plant more interesting for its foliage than for its flowers, forming clumps with finely dissected, silvery, 1-in.- (2.5-cm-) long leaves and small daisylike, yellow flowers in summer. Requires neutral to lime-rich soil and protection from winter wet. Zones 6–8.

T. haradjanii (Chrysanthemum haradjanii). North Africa. Height 9 in.; spread 12 in. (22.5 × 30 cm). Delicate in appearance, this tough rock-garden plant has feathery leaves up to 2 in. (5 cm) long and is covered in white woolly hairs, giving the entire plant a frosted look. The flowers are small, yellow, and rayless, appearing in late spring and summer. Prefers lime-rich soil. Zones 7–9.

Tanacetum macrophyllum

T. macrophyllum (Chrysanthemum macrophyllum). Hungary. Height 4 ft; spread 2 ft (120 × 60 cm). Feathery, coarsely toothed, dark-green leaves up to 8 in. (20 cm) long and dense, terminal clusters of off-white flowers in summer. While not the most dramatic species of the genus, this is a handsome plant that has great presence when grown at the back of a border against a dark-green backdrop. Zones 5–8.

T. parthenium (Chrysanthemum parthenium). Feverfew. Europe. Height 18 in.; spread 12 in. (45 × 30 cm). Formerly used for its fever-dispelling properties, this is a short-lived species occasionally grown in the ornamental garden. It is a bushy plant with woody stems and strongly aromatic, deeply divided leaves oblong in outline. Masses of single, white, yellow-eyed daisies ¾ in. (2 cm) across are borne in dense clusters in summer and again in autumn. 'Aureum' has lime-yellow foliage and white flowers; 'Goldbutton' reaches a height of 12 in. (30 cm) and has double yellow flowers; 'Snowball' grows to 6 in. (15 cm) and has white flowers; 'White Bonnet' has double white flowers. The single-flower forms seed themselves widely and can be a benefit or a nuisance, depending on your point of view. Zones 4–9.

T. vulgare. Common tansy. Europe. Height 3–4 ft; spread 18 in. (90–120 × 45 cm). A vigorous clump-forming plant with grooved and angled stems and bright-green, finely divided, toothed leaves up to 8 in. (20 cm) long. Dull-yellow, rayless flowers are borne in dense clusters in summer. 'Crispum' has wavy, crisped leaves. Zones 3–9.

TELLIMA

(False Alumroot)

FAMILY: Saxifragaceae

One species of a semievergreen, shade-loving plant with basal clumps of rounded and toothed leaves and spikes of small, bell-shaped, fringed flowers in late spring and early summer. The generic name is an anagram of the bishop's-cap, ***Mitella,*** which it resembles.

CULTIVATION: Grow in partial shade in moist, rich soil.

LANDSCAPE USE: A handsome groundcover for the woodland garden or for under trees and shrubs.

PROPAGATION: Divide in spring or autumn. Sow seed in autumn.

Tellima grandiflora

T. grandiflora. Fringe-cup. Western North America. Height 2 ft; spread 2 ft (60 × 60 cm). A rhizomatous plant with hairy, heart-shaped to kidney-shaped, slightly toothed leaves up to 4 in. (10 cm) long and with five to seven shallow lobes. Erect stems produce spikes of greenish white, ¼-in- (0.6-cm-) long flowers with upturned, fringed petals in late spring and early summer. The flowers mature to pinkish red. Remove faded flower stems. Variety ***rubra*** ('Purpurea') has reddish purple leaves. Zones 4–8.

TEUCRIUM

(Germander)

FAMILY: Laviatae

A large genus of approximately 300 species. Many of which are native to the Mediterranean region. A few are grown in gardens for their sagelike flowers and aromatic foliage. They are generally bushy subshrubs with erect stems and opposite leaves. The flowers are pink, purple, or yellow, lobed and lipped, and appear in mid- to late summer. Named after King Teucer, king of Troy, or after Dr. Teucer, a botanist. Take your pick. "Germander" is derived from the Greek for "ground-oak."

CULTIVATION: Grow in well-drained, not-too-fertile soil in full sun.

LANDSCAPE USE: Attractive plants for the sunny border.

PROPAGATION: Divide in spring or take stem cuttings of the shrubby species in midsummer.

T. aroanium. Greece. Height 4 in.; spread 12 in. (10 × 30 cm). A shrubby rock-garden plant with many-branched stems lying along the ground, with ¼-in.- (0.6-cm-) long, silver-hairy, egg-shaped leaves and whorls of soft-purple flowers in summer. Zones 7–9.

T. canadense. North America. Height 3 ft; spread 1 ft (90 × 30 cm). An erect plant with egg-shaped to lance-shaped leaves up to 3 in. (7.5 cm) long, hairy underneath. Unbranched spikes of purplish pink flowers are produced in summer. Does best in moist soil. Zones 3–9.

T. chamaedrys. Germander. Europe. Height 1 ft; spread 1 ft (30 × 30 cm). A woody subshrub with erect stems and dark-green, scalloped, egg-shaped leaves about 1 in. (2.5 cm) long. In mid- to late summer ¾-in.- (1.8-cm-) long, rosy purple flowers are produced. It can be used as a low hedge, but clipping generally inhibits flowering. It is best used toward the front of a sunny border, mixed in with coarse-leafed plants. 'Variegatum' has cream-splashed foliage. Zones 4–9.

T. pyrenaicum. Southern Europe. Height 4 in.; spread 12 in. (10 × 30 cm). A spreading, woody plant with trailing stems and toothed, round, gray-green leaves up to 1 in. (2.5 cm) long. Densely crowded heads of purple-and-cream flowers are produced in summer. Requires well-drained soil in full sun. Zones 4–9.

T. scorodinia. Wood germander. Europe. Height 12 in.; spread 12 in. (30 × 30 cm). A woody-based subshrub with erect stems and heart-shaped, toothed leaves 1–2 in. (2.5–5 cm) long. Branched stems bear tiny greenish yellow flowers in mid- to late summer. A useful plant for "cooling down" the brighter colors of a border. 'Crispum' has wavy leaves but often reverts to the straight leaf form; 'Crispum Marginatum' has white-edged, wavy leaves. Zones 5–9.

THALICTRUM

(Meadow Rue)

FAMILY: Ranunculaceae

Thalictrum flavum var. *glaucum*

Thalictrum minus

A genus of about 100 species of widely distributed plants with mostly basal foliage two to three times divided into toothed or lobed leaflets and large, often fluffy panicles of purple, pink, or yellow petalless flowers in spring and summer. They are easily cultivated in mild climates and deserve to be more widely grown. The common name is a reference to the ruelike blue-green foliage.

CULTIVATION: Plant in rich, moist but well-drained soil in sun or partial shade, preferably in climates without excessively hot summers.

LANDSCAPE USE: Both foliage and flowers are beautiful. The taller species are excellent plants for the border or woodland garden.

PROPAGATION: Divide in spring. Most species are slow to recover after division. Sow seed in spring.

T. aquilegifolium. Europe, Asia. Height 3 ft; spread 1 ft (90 × 30 cm). The species name describes the leaves well. Blue-green leaves two to three times divided into round to oblong toothed or lobed leaflets, like those of ***Aquilegia,*** are borne in basal clumps as well as on the hollow stems. Terminal, almost flat-topped, 8-in.- (20-cm-) wide clusters of delicate, lilac-purple flowers are produced for a couple of weeks in late spring or early summer, followed by clusters of drooping, winged seeds. Grows best in moist soil in light shade. Reasonably heat tolerant in partial shade. Variety ***album*** has white flowers. 'Purpureum' has dark-purple stems and flowers; 'Thundercloud' has deep-purple flowers; 'White Cloud' has fluffy clusters of bright-white flowers. Zones 5–8.

T. chelidonii. Himalayas. Height 3–5 ft; spread 2 ft (90–150 × 60 cm). A tall, clump-forming plant with green leaves divided into 1-in.- (2.5-cm-) wide, egg-shaped leaflets with seven to 13 teeth per leaflet. Open clusters of lilac flowers are produced in summer. This species grows well only in mild climates in moist soil. Zones 6–9.

T. delavayi (T. dipterocarpum). Western China. Height 4–5 ft; spread 2 ft (120–150 × 60 cm). An upright plant with foliage divided three to five times, the leaflets being ½ in. (1.2 cm) wide and three-lobed. Large, branching panicles of petalless, nodding flowers with lilac sepals and soft yellow stamens are produced in summer. 'Album' has white flowers; 'Hewitt's Double' has double lilac flowers and lasts longer in flower than the single species. Zones 5–8.

T. flavum. Europe, Asia. Height 4–5 ft; spread 2 ft (120–150 × 60 cm). A clump-forming plant with stout stems and dark-green leaves, blue-green underneath, divided into three-lobed, rounded leaflets. Fluffy heads of pale-yellow flowers are produced in summer. Variety ***glaucum (T. speciossimum)*** has blue-green foliage. 'Illuminator' has pale-yellow flowers and bright-green leaves. Zones 5–9.

T. kiusianum. Japan. Height 4–6 in.; spread 6 in. (10–15 × 15 cm). A delightfully delicate plant with ferny, gray-green leaves divided into three-lobed, egg-shaped leaflets. Clusters of pale-purple flowers with darker stamens are produced in summer. Grow in moist but well-drained soil in partial shade. A little temperamental at times, it does not grow well in hot climates. Zones 5–7.

T. minus (T. adiantifolium). Europe, Asia. Height 1–3 ft; spread 1–2 ft (30–90 × 30–60 cm). A highly variable plant with delicate, ferny foliage like that of the maidenhair fern, ***Adiantum pedatum.*** The triangular blue-green leaves are divided three to four times into three-lobed leaflets. The blooms are the least interesting of the ornamental species, being greenish yellow and appearing in summer. Grow this as a foliage plant and forget the flowers. The smaller forms are more compact and more delicate in appearance. Zones 3–8.

T. rochebrunnianum. Japan. Height 4–6 ft; spread 2 ft (120–180 × 60 cm). Similar to ***T. delavayi*** but with purple-blue stems and blue-green foliage divided into ferny leaflets. Open panicles of lavender-pink flowers with pale-yellow stamens are produced in mid- to late summer. 'Purple Mist' has darker, almost purple flowers. This wonderful plant grows best in mild climates. It definitely dislikes hot summers and needs shade from the afternoon sun. Zones 5–8.

T. thalictroides. (Anemonella thalictroides). Rue anemone. North America. Height 6 in.; spread 8 in. (15 × 20 cm). A tuberous-rooted wildflower with delicate clumps of tiny, three-parted, rounded leaves and solitary, upward-facing, saucer-shaped, white or pink flowers in spring. 'Schoeff's Double Pink' has longer-lasting double pink flowers. The species is a wonderful flower for the woodland garden or shaded border. Zones 4–9.

THELYPTERIS

(Beech Fern)

FAMILY: Polypodiaceae

Greater than 500 species of deciduous ferns primarily native to tropical areas, with a handful of species indigenous to temperate parts of the world. The leaves of the Thelypteris are generally triangular to lance-shaped in outline with alternately spaced leaf segments narrowing toward the base of the leaf stem.

CULTIVATION: Grow in moist to wet soil in partial to full shade.

LANDSCAPE USE: Not the most ornamental of ferns but still useful as groundcovers in shade or in the woodland garden.

PROPAGATION: Divide in spring, or sow spores when ripe in late summer.

T. hexagonoptera. Broad beech fern. Eastern North America. Height 1–2 ft; spread 1 ft (30–60 × 30 cm). A rapidly spreading fern with a creeping rhizome and slightly hairy, triangular, yellow-green leaf blades divided into oblong leaf segments. Grows best in wet, acid soil in partial shade. Zones 3–8.

T. novaboracensis. New York fern. Eastern and central North America. Height 1–2 ft; spread 1 ft (30–60 × 30 cm). A rapidly spreading fern with yellowish green, elliptical to lance-shaped leaves with 20 to 40 deeply segmented leaflets. The fronds turn brown at the first touch of frost in autumn. Grow in full sun to partial shade. Zones 2–8.

T. palustris. Marsh fern. Widely distributed. Height 2–3 ft; spread 1 ft (60–90 × 30 cm). Growing in marshy ground, this is a fern with long leaf stems, pale-green lance-shaped leaves, and widely spaced, deeply cut leaflets. The sterile leaves are the first to appear in spring, followed by fertile leaves in summer. A spreading fern for wet ground. Zones 4–8.

Thelypteris novaboracensis

THERMOPSIS

(False Lupin)

FAMILY: Fabaceae

Thermopsis montana

Twenty species of lupinlike plants with alternate fan-shaped leaves with three leaflets and two leaflike appendages at the base of the leaf stem. Bright-yellow pealike flowers appear in late spring and early summer. Although they do not bloom for long, they are very attractive. The generic name comes from the Greek *thermos,* "lupin," and *opsis,* "like."

CULTIVATION: Grow in full sun in mild climates, partial shade in hot climates, in well-drained soil. Stake when necessary. Sometimes subject to leafhopper damage. Remove faded flower spikes for secondary bloom.

LANDSCAPE USE: Bright plants for the border contrasting well with some of the mound-forming blue-flowered geraniums.

PROPAGATION: Sow seed in late summer. Division is difficult but not impossible.

*T. **lupinoides (T. lanceolata).*** Alaska, Siberia. Height 1 ft; spread 18 in. (30 × 45 cm). A clump-forming plant with a rather lax habit and blue-green leaves divided into stemless, egg-shaped to lance-shaped, silky leaflets up to 1½ in. (3.8 cm) long and whorled spikes of bright-yellow flowers in summer. Zones 3–8.

*T. **montana.*** Western United States. Height 2–3 ft; spread 18 in. (60–90 × 45 cm). Stout hairless stems with linear, lance-shaped blue-green leaflets up to 4 in. (10 cm) long. In spring and early summer 8-in. (20-cm) spikes of bright-yellow flowers are produced. Zones 3–8.

*T. **villosa (T. caroliniana).*** Southern lupin. Eastern United States. Height 3–4 ft; spread 2 ft (90–120 × 60 cm). A straggling plant that often needs support. The blue-green leaves are divided into three roundly egg-shaped leaflets, softly hairy underneath, up to 3 in. (7.5 cm) long. Up to 12-in.-(30-cm-) long spikes of bright-yellow pealike flowers appear in late spring and early summer. Zones 3–9.

TIARELLA

(Foamflower, False Mitrewort)

FAMILY: Saxifragaceae

About six species of generally low-growing, spring-flowering plants with five species native to North America, one native to Asia. The basal leaves are lobed or divided, the flowers foamy white. The individual flowers are tiny and delicate, giving rise to the generic name, derived from the Latin, meaning, "little tiara."

CULTIVATION: Grow in rich, well-drained but moisture-retentive woodland soil in partial shade.

LANDSCAPE USE: Foamflower is one of the best groundcovers for partial shade. Not only is the foliage evergreen in mild climates, but the white flowers create a wonderful white carpet in spring.

PROPAGATION: Easily divided in spring and autumn. Sow seed in early spring.

*T. **cordifolia.*** Foamflower. Eastern North America. Height 12 in.; spread 18 in. (30 × 45 cm). An evergreen, spreading plant with a rapidly spreading habit and hairy, heart-shaped, and lobed, light-green leaves up to 4 in. (10 cm) wide. In mid- to late spring 3–4-in.- (7.5–10-cm-) long spikes of delicate white flowers, sometimes tinged pink, appear. Spreads rapidly in good soil and can be divided at almost any time during the growing season if given adequate water. Variety ***collina (T. wherryi)*** is similar to the species but is distinctly clump-forming, with almost triangular leaves. There is considerable leaf variation in foamflower, and we can expect more distinct foliage types to become increasingly available. Var. ***purpurea*** has purple-mottled leaves and pink flowers. Var. ***varie-***

Tiarella cordifolia

gata is a rather poor plant with pale-green leaves splashed yellow. Zones 3–8.

T. laciniata. Northwestern North America. Height 12 in.; spread 18 in. (30 × 45 cm). Basal clumps of heart-shaped leaves very deeply divided into three-lobed and toothed leaflets. Panicles of foamy white flowers are produced in summer. Zones 4–7.

T. polyphylla. Himalayas. Height 1–2 ft; spread 1 ft (30–60 × 30 cm). A clump-forming plant with hairless, mid-green, heart-shaped, three-lobed, and toothed leaves. In mid- to late summer 9-in. (22.5-cm) spikes of white-tinged pink flowers appear. Zones 5–8.

T. trifoliata. Western North America. Height 10–20 in.; spread 24 in. (25–50 × 60 cm). A clump-forming plant with ivylike leaves consisting of three leaflets, with the middle leaflet having three lobes, the outer leaflet two lobes. Panicles of white flowers are produced in summer. Zones 4–7.

TOLMIEA

(Piggyback Plant)

FAMILY: Saxifragaceae

Tolmiea menziesii 'Taff's Gold'

One species of semievergreen perennial native to the western United States, with maplelike leaves and greenish white flowers in early summer. The curious common name describes the fact that young plantlets are produced from on top of the leaf. Named after Dr. William Tolmie (1830–1886), a Scots botanist.

CULTIVATION: Grow in well-drained, rich soil in partial shade.

LANDSCAPE USE: An attractive woodland plant that makes a good groundcover for a shady border.

PROPAGATION: Root plant-bearing leaves in moist soil. Divide in spring.

T. menziesii. Piggyback plant. Western United States. Height 18 in.; spread 18 in. (45 × 45 cm) A mat-forming plant with long-stemmed, hairy, maplelike leaves up to 4 in. (10 cm) across forming a mound up to 6 in. (15 cm) high. The leaves frequently bear young plantlets at the base of the leaf blade. Tall stems bearing ½-in.- (1.2-cm-) long, tubular, greenish white flowers tinged brown appear in late spring and early summer. 'Taff's Gold' has yellow-splashed green leaves. Zones 6–9.

TRACHELIUM

(Throatwort)

Family: Campanulaceae

A small genus of woody-based herbaceous perennials and subshrubs native to the Mediterranean region with alternate leaves and blue or white flowers in summer. The generic name comes from the Greek *trachelos*, "neck," in reference to the supposed healing properties for diseases of the throat. Sometimes still listed under ***Diosphaera.***

Cultivation: Plant in well-drained soil in full sun. Protect against winter wet.

Landscape Use: Rock-garden or border plants particularly for dry climates. The rock-garden forms can also be successfully cultivated in an alpine house.

Propagation: Divide in spring or sow seed in autumn.

T. asperuloides. Greece. Height 3 in.; spread 6 in. (7.5 × 15 cm). A cushion-forming plant that requires good drainage and protection from winter wet. The thin stems bear tiny, egg-shaped, mid-green leaves and masses of upward-facing, pale-blue flowers in summer. Gently trim back older growth after flowering. Zones 5–7.

T. caeruleum. Throatwort. Mediterranean. Height 3 ft; spread 18 in. (90 × 45 cm). An erect plant with egg-shaped, toothed, and pointed leaves and dense clusters of lavender-blue flowers in summer. It is grown as an annual in the southern United States but is a short-lived perennial that overwinters in Zone 8. Grow in moist but well-drained, lime-rich soil in full sun. Zones 8–9.

T. jacquinii var. ***rumellianum.*** Greece. Height 6 in.; spread 12 in. (15 × 30 cm). A spreading, carpeting plant with mid-green, egg-shaped, toothed leaves and starry, bright-blue flowers in summer. Requires the shelter of a rock crevice or rock-garden trough. Zones 6–8.

TRACHYSTEMON

Family: Boraginaceae

Two species of coarse-leaved plants with large basal leaves and purple-blue flowers in spring. One species is grown as an effective groundcover in shade.

Cultivation: Grow in moisture-retentive but not wet soil in partial to full shade. Tolerates a wide variety of conditions.

Landscape Use: A good groundcover for large areas. Contrasts well with spring bulbs.

Propagation: Divide in spring or autumn.

T. orientalis. Asia Minor. Height 2 ft; spread 2 ft (60 × 60 cm). Branched and hairy stems bear purple-blue, white-throated starry flowers in spring followed by large basal clumps of 1-ft- (30-cm-) long, coarsely hairy, heart-shaped leaves. An invasive perennial that grows well in almost every soil type. Zones 5–9.

TRADESCANTIA

(Spiderwort)

Family: Commelinaceae

Tradescantia x *andersoniana* 'Purple Dome'

Tradescantia x *andersoniana* 'Iris Pritchard'

About 100 species of flowering plants native to North and South America. The tender species are widely grown as pot plants or in greenhouses and may often be listed under ***Setcresea.*** The hardy species are less widely grown except for the hybrid ***T. × andersoniana*** and its cultivars. The genus is named after John Tradescant, gardener to the English King Charles I.

Cultivation: Grow in moist but well-drained, preferably poor soil in full sun to light shade.

Landscape Use: Although somewhat straggling in habit, these are beautiful plants for the wildflower garden or sunny border, particularly when closely planted with more elegant perennials.

Propagation: Divide every two to three years in spring.

T. × andersoniana. Spiderwort. Height 1–2 ft; spread 2 ft (30–60 × 60 cm). A hybrid between ***T. ohiensis, T. subaspera,*** and ***T. virginiana,*** with generally floppy stems and up to 18-in.- (45-cm-) long, dull-green, linear to lance-shaped, veined leaves that clasp the stem. The 1–3-in.- (2.5–7.5-cm-) wide, blue, purple, to red flowers with hairy centers are borne in the axils of the leaflike bracts in summer. The individual flowers last for one day, but a succession of opening flower buds provides a floral display for over two months. Well-drained soil in full sun is the optimum site, although partial shade will do if decreased flowering is acceptable. Cut the plants back to about 12 in. (30 cm) after flowering to stimulate fresh growth. Variety ***caerulea plena*** has dark-blue double flowers. There are many cultivars, including: 'Bluestone,' with medium-blue flowers; 'Iris Pritchard,' with white flowers tinged violet; 'Isis,' with deep-blue flowers; 'J. C. Wueglin,' with sky-blue flowers; 'Leonora,' with violet-blue flowers; 'Osprey,' with white flowers with a blue eye; 'Pauline,' lilac-pink flowers; 'Purewell Giant,' with purple-red flowers; 'Purple Dome,' with rosy purple flowers; 'Red Cloud,' with deep-pink flowers; 'Snowcap,' with pure-white flowers; 'Taplow Crimson,' with deep-red flowers; 'Valor,' with purple-red flowers; 'Zwanenburg Blue,' with deep-blue flowers. They are often listed under ***T. virginiana.*** Zones 4–9.

T. bracteata. Eastern and central United States. Height 18 in.; spread 2 ft (45 × 60 cm). A lax, straggling plant with fleshy stems and linear to lance-shaped light-green leaves up to 12 in. (30 cm) long. The sticky flowers are pink-blue in summer. Variety ***alba*** has white flowers. Zones 4–9.

T. ohiensis. Eastern and central United States. Height 3 ft; spread 2 ft (90 × 60 cm). Blue-green, linear to lance-shaped leaves up to 18 in. (45 cm) long and blue, pink, or white, hairless flowers in summer. This species tends to die down by midsummer. Zones 4–9.

T. subaspera. Southeastern United States. Height 3 ft; spread 2 ft (90 × 60). Hairy, markedly zigzagging stems with elliptical lance-shaped leaves up to 10 in. (25 cm) long and hairy blue flowers in summer. Zones 6–9.

TRICYRTIS

(Toad-lily)

Family: Liliaceae

Tricyrtis formosana var. *stolonifera*

A small genus of late-summer- and autumn-flowering plants with alternate leaves and curious, spotted flowers, native to eastern Asia. They are a genus particularly beloved by horticulturists because of their general unavailability, gangling habit, and sporadic flowering. Professional gardeners love a challenge, and, except when grown in full sun or light shade, many species reward the diligent gardener with one rather small flower and long stems that often flop to the ground. The common name comes from the spotted flowers, although there are more imaginative derivations listed.

Cultivation: Grow in moist but well-drained soil in a sunny location in mild climates and in partial shade in areas with hot summers. The tall stems may need staking.

Landscape Use: Of greatest effect when planted in large masses. Single specimens always look thin.

Propagation: Divide in early spring.

T. flava. Yellow toad-lily. Japan. Height 12–18 in.; spread 12 in. (30–45 × 30 cm). A clump-forming plant with erect stems and elliptical, slightly hairy, green-spotted purple leaves up to 6 in. (15 cm) long. In autumn 2-in.- (5-cm-) wide, upward-facing, and unspotted yellow flowers are borne in the axils and stem terminal. Zones 6–9.

T. formosana (T. stolonifera). Taiwan. Height 2 ft; spread 18 in. (60 × 45 cm). A slowly spreading plant with arching stems and glossy, dark-green, stem-clasping, egg-shaped leaves about 5 in. (12.5 cm) long, hairy underneath. The funnel-shaped flowers are pale pink, heavily spotted with reddish purple, and with a yellow throat. They appear over many weeks in autumn. Variety ***amethystina*** has purplish blue flowers with a white-spotted red throat. Var. ***stolonifera*** is the current name for a group of varieties that are generally 1–2 ft (30–60 cm) taller than the species and spread more rapidly. 'Sinonome' is probably a hybrid between ***T. formosana*** var. ***stolonifera*** and ***T. hirta*** and is similar to the first species, with raspberry-speckled flowers. 'Variegata' has cream-yellow variegated leaves. Zones 5–9.

T. hirta. Hairy toad-lily. Japan. Height 2–3 ft; spread 18 in. (60–90 × 45 cm). This is an erect plant with hairy, arching stems and dark-green, hairy, oblong, stem-clasping leaves up to 6 in. (15 cm) long. Pale-purple, 1-in.- (2.5-cm-) wide flowers speckled deep purple are produced from the upper leaf axils in early autumn. The flowers are exquisite when viewed through a magnifying glass but are not impressive when seen from even a short distance. Variety ***alba*** has white flowers with a pink throat. 'Miyazaki' may be a hybrid. It has purple-blotched flowers along arching stems in autumn. 'Variegata' has cream-yellow-edged leaves; 'White Towers' has ivory-white flowers. Zones 5–9.

T. latifolia (T. bakeri). Japan, China. Height 2 ft; spread 1 ft (60 × 30 cm). An erect perennial with heart-shaped, mid-green, stem-clasping leaves up to 6 in. (15 cm) long and 4 in. (10 cm) wide. Branched flower stems bear 1-in.- (2.5-cm-) wide, purple-spotted yellow flowers in late summer and early autumn. Zones 6–9.

T. macrantha. Japan. Height 2 ft; spread 18 in. (60 × 45 cm). An upright, slowly spreading plant with dark-green, egg-shaped leaves up to 4 in. (10 cm) long and yellow flowers spotted chocolate brown, borne in autumn. Zones 7–9.

TRILLIUM

(Wake-robin)

FAMILY: Liliaceae

Trillium grandiflorum

Trillium sessile 'Rubrum'

About 30 species of low-growing, spring-flowering woodland plants with veined and wrinkled leaves, native to North America and Asia. The generic name is highly pertinent, as it is derived from the Latin *tri*, "three," and the leaves, petals, and sepals all come in threes. They are spectacular plants with large flowers in a range of colors from white and pink to yellow and red. Carpets of trillium are a wonderful sight in the deciduous woodlands of North America. Unfortunately, the North American species are not easy to propagate in the numbers the nursery industry requires, and large natural populations have been severely disturbed by unscrupulous collectors. Tissue-culture techniques are being developed to take the strain off the native populations. The sooner, the better.

CULTIVATION: Trilliums grow best in slightly acid, moist, well-drained soil in partial shade. The rhizomes should be planted 2–4 in. (5–10 cm) deep.

Landscape Use: Perfect plants for the woodland garden, where they should be planted and left alone.

Propagation: Not easy plants to propagate. Seed germination takes up to a year. Careful division in very early spring or in late summer is sometimes productive.

T. cernuum. Nodding trillium. Eastern North America. Height 12–18 in.; spread 12 in. (30–45 × 30 cm). A clump-forming plant with egg-shaped, sharply pointed leaves up to 4 in. (10 cm) long. The nodding, white, often pink- or maroon-centered flowers are borne on short stems and have outward-curving petals. The flowers are generally obscured by the large leaves. Zones 3–9.

T. chloropetalum. Western United States. Height 12–18 in.; spread 12 in. (30–45 × 30 cm). Stemless, rounded, egg-shaped, often mottled purple leaves up to 6 in. (15 cm) long and stemless pink to white upward-pointing flowers. Zones 4–9.

T. erectum. Purple trillium, Stinking Benjamin. Eastern and central North America. Height 12–18 in.; spread 12 in. (30–45 × 30 cm). Stemless, broadly egg-shaped, pointed leaves 6–7 in. (15–17.5 cm) long. Purple-red flowers are held above the foliage on short stems. The plant smells bad when bruised. Variety ***album*** has white flowers. Var. ***roseum*** has pink flowers. Zones 4–9.

T. grandiflorum. Great white trillium, white wake-robin. Eastern North America. Height 18 in.; spread 18 in. (45 × 45 cm). Perhaps the grandest of spring-flowering plants, this is also the easiest trillium to grow. It is a bold plant with stemless, often wavy, rounded to egg-shaped leaves from 3–6 in. (7.5–15 cm) long and wavy-edged, 3-in.- (7.5-cm-) wide, flaring, white flowers that fade to pink in late spring. Variety ***roseum*** has bright-pink flowers. 'Flore Pleno' has double flowers. Zones 4–9.

T. luteum. Yellow trillium. Southeastern United States. Height 18 in.; spread 12 in. (45 × 30 cm). Stemless, mostly lance-shaped leaves up to 4 in. (10 cm) long and erect yellow flowers in early spring. Zones 5–9.

T. nivale. Snow trillium. Eastern and central United States. Height 6 in.; spread 6 in. (15 × 15 cm). Uncommon in the wild and difficult in cultivation but a lovely plant nonetheless. The 2-in.- (5-cm-) long leaves are elliptical to egg-shaped. The upturned, slightly flaring white flowers appear in early spring. Zones 5–8.

T. ovatum. Coast trillium. Northwestern North America. Height 18 in.; spread 12 in. (45 × 30 cm). Similar to ***T. grandiflorum*** with egg-shaped leaves up to 6 in. (15 cm) long and white, flaring, 2-in.- (5-cm-) wide flowers with pointed petals. Zones 5–9.

T. sessile. Wake-robin. Eastern and central United States. Height 12–18 in.; spread 12 in. (30–45 × 30 cm). The egg-shaped, almost circular leaves up to 4 in. (10 cm) long are often mottled bronze and pale green. Stemless, erect, and narrow, brownish red flowers appear above the whorl of leaves in spring. Variety ***rubrum*** has purplish red flowers. Zones 5–9.

T. undulatum. Painted trillium. Eastern and central North America. Height 18 in.; spread 12 in. (45 × 30 cm). A beautiful plant that unfortunately is difficult to grow. The egg-shaped leaves are up to 7 in. (17.5 cm) long. The spectacular flowers are generally upward- and outward-facing, wavy-edged and white, marked with a red stripe at the petal base. Zones 4–9.

T. viride. Wood trillium. Central United States. Height 18 in.; spread 12 in. (45 × 30 cm). Stemless, mottled, lance-shaped to rounded leaves up to 4 in. (10 cm) long and greenish white erect flowers in early spring. Zones 5–9.

TROLLIUS

(Globe Flower)

Family: Ranunculaceae

About 20 species of large buttercups native to North America, Europe, and Asia with fan-shaped divided or lobed leaves and usually single orange to yellow, rounded flowers in spring and

Trollius europaeus

early summer. They are plants for mild climates and do not like hot and humid summers. The generic name comes from the old German *trollblume,* "round flower."

CULTIVATION: Grow in moist soil in sun or partial shade. Deadhead faded flowers for repeat bloom, and cut back fading foliage in late summer. Highly intolerant of hot conditions, these plants demand afternoon shade.

LANDSCAPE USE: Attractive flowers for the bog garden or wild border. The bright flowers contrast well with the dark foliage. Light staking is often necessary.

PROPAGATION: Divide in autumn. Globe flower is slow to recover from transplanting and may take up to a year to settle. Seed germination is erratic and generally poor.

T. chinensis (T. ledebourii). Siberia. Height 3 ft; spread 18 in. (90×45 cm). A vigorous plant with leaves deeply cut to the base and leaf segments toothed and lobed. In early summer 2-in.- (5-cm-) wide, deep-orange flowers are produced on wiry stems. 'Golden Queen' grows to 4 ft (120 cm) and has 3–4-in.- (7.5–10-cm-) wide golden orange flowers. Needs moist soil and shade from intense sun. Zones 3–7.

T. × cultorum (T. × hybridus). Height 2–3 ft; spread 18 in. (60–90×45 cm). Hybrids of ***T. asiaticus, T. europaeus,*** and ***T. chinensis,*** these are the globe flowers most commonly grown in gardens. The flowers are globular and generally yellow. The leaves are dark green and deeply divided into five to six lobed segments. 'Alabaster' has pale, creamy yellow flowers; 'Canary Bird' has pale canary-yellow flowers; 'Commander-in-Chief' has bright-orange flowers; 'Earliest of All' has orange-yellow flowers and blooms in spring; 'Etna' has dark-orange flowers; 'Fire Globe' has orange-red flowers; 'Goldquelle' has long-lasting orange flowers; 'Lemon Queen' has lemon-yellow flowers; 'May Gold' has early-blooming, pale-yellow flowers; 'Orange Globe' has golden orange flowers; 'Orange Princess' has deep-orange flowers. Zones 3–7.

T. europeus. Common globe flower. Europe. Height 1–2 ft; spread 1 ft (30–60×30 cm). A clump-forming plant with 6-in.- (15-cm-) long, dark-green leaves with pale undersides, divided into five toothed and lobed leaflets. The stem leaves are stemless and smaller. In spring and early summer 1-in.- (2.5-cm-) wide lemon-yellow globes are produced. 'Superbus' is more floriferous than the species. Zones 3–7.

T. pumilus. Dwarf globe flower. Himalayas. Height 12 in.; spread 12 in. (30×30 cm). A tufted plant with 2-in.- (5-cm-) wide leaves divided into five lobed leaflets. Bright-yellow, cup-shaped flowers about 1 in. (2.5 cm) wide are borne on almost leafless stems in late spring to early summer. Zones 5–7.

T. yunnanensis. China. Height 2 ft; spread 1 ft (60×30 cm). A clump-forming plant with broadly pentagonal, deeply lobed leaves up to 4 in. (10 cm) long and bright-yellow, orange-tipped flowers up to 2 in. (5 cm) across in early summer. Zones 5–7.

TYPHA

(Cattail, Bulrush)

Family: Typhaceae

About 15 species of deciduous, coarse, reedlike plants widely distributed in marshes, swamps, and bogs. If they are grown in gardens, it is for their decorative, cylindrical seed heads. They are often gathered in the wild to make baskets and other containers.

Culture: Grow in wet ditches, bog gardens, and streamsides in sun or shade. Invasive.

Landscape Use: Coarse plants for the large garden.

Propagation: Divide in spring.

T. latifolia. Bulrush, common cattail. North America, Europe, Asia. Height 4–6 ft; spread 2 ft (120–180 × 60 cm). A large, clump-forming plant with 1-in.- (2.5-cm-) wide, swordlike leaves and erect stems bearing a 6–8-in.- (15–20-cm-) spike of beige flowers in summer followed by a dark-brown, cylindrical seed head in late summer. Not a great ornamental but a wonderful plant for swamp enthusiasts. Zones 3–9.

Typha latifolia

T. minima. Dwarf cattail. Europe. Asia. Height 2 ft; spread 1 ft (60 × 30 cm). A more delicate plant than the species described above. The swordlike leaves are narrow, to about ¼ in. (0.6) wide. The thin spikes are rusty brown in summer, darkening to deep brown in late summer. A useful plant for the ornamental pool. Zones 6–9.

UVULARIA

(Merrybells)

Family: Liliaceae

A small genus of rhizomatous perennials native to eastern North America with light-green, alternate leaves and yellow, nodding, bell-shaped flowers in spring. The name comes from the Latin *uvula*, "palate," from the shape of the hanging flowers.

Cultivation: Grow in moist but well-drained woodland soil in partial shade.

Landscape Use: Elegant plants for the front of the border, the wild garden, or the shade border.

Propagation: Divide in early spring before flowering. Sow seed in autumn.

U. grandiflora. Merrybells. Eastern and central North America. Height 18–24 in.; spread 12 in. (45–60 × 30 cm). A clump-forming plant with clusters of slender, pale-green stems with oblong to egg-shaped leaves up to 4 in. (10 cm) long. In spring 1 ½-in.- (3.8-cm-) long, single pale-yellow, bell-shaped flowers with twisted petals hang down from the ends of the stems. While not a dramatically ornamental plant, it has great elegance and should be widely cultivated in gardens. Zones 4–9.

Uvullaria grandiflora

U. perfoliata. Strawbells. Eastern North America. Height 18 in.; spread 12 in. (45 × 30 cm). Very similar to the above species but with slenderer stems and smaller leaves that completely surround the stem (perfoliate), and pale-yellow, bell-shaped flowers to 1 in. (2.5 cm) long with glandular hairs inside the flower. Zones 4–9.

U. sessilifolia. Eastern North America. Height 16 in.; spread 12 in. (40 × 30 cm). Smaller than the other species described, with stemless, lance-shaped leaves up to 3 in. long and greenish yellow flowers in spring. Zones 4–9.

VALERIANA

Family: Valerianaceae

A large genus of about 200 species of herbaceous perennials, subshrubs, and shrubs closely related to ***Centranthus,*** few of which are cultivated in gardens. The roots are strongly aromatic, the leaves opposite, and the white or pink flowers borne in dense, domed clusters in summer. The common valerian, ***V. officinalis,*** has been widely used since ancient times as a sedative. The generic name is said to be derived from the Latin *valere,* "to be in good health."

Valeriana pyrenaica

Cultivation: Grow in full sun in rich, moist but well-drained soil. Stake the taller species.

Landscape Use: Slightly weedy rock-garden and border plants.

Propagation: Divide in autumn or spring.

V. arizonica. Southwestern United States. Height 3 in.; spread 8 in. (7.5 × 20 cm). A spreading, mat-forming plant with fleshy, dark-green, egg-shaped, long-stemmed leaves up to 2½ in. (6.2 cm) long and soft-pink, rounded flower heads up to 6 in. (15 cm) wide in late spring or early summer. Zones 5–9.

V. officinalis. Common valerian, all-heal. Europe,

Asia. Height 3–4 ft; spread 3 ft (90–120×90 cm). A clump-forming plant with grooved and hollow stems; egg-shaped, deeply lobed basal leaves; and stem leaves divided into seven to ten pairs of lance-shaped, coarsely toothed leaflets about 2–3 in. (5–7.5 cm) long. Round, domed heads up to 4 in. (10 cm) across of delicate white to pink flowers are borne on long stems in summer. The whole plant smells unpleasant but has the distinct advantage of being highly attractive to cats. Zones 4–9.

V. phu. Caucasus. Height 2–3 ft; spread 2 ft (60–90×60 cm). Similar to ***V. officinalis,*** with egg-shaped, unlobed basal leaves and stem leaves divided into three to four pairs of oblong leaflets. White flowers in panicles up to 6 in. (15 cm) across are produced in summer. The species is rarely grown, being superseded by the cultivar 'Aurea,' which has bright-yellow foliage in spring that turns to midgreen by summer. The whole plant has an unpleasant odor, and the species name is supposedly a common response to the smell. Zones 5–9.

V. pyrenaica. Pyrenees. Height 2–3 ft; spread 2 ft (60–90×60 cm). A clump-forming plant with midgreen, heart-shaped, toothed leaves up to 8 in. (20 cm) wide becoming narrower and egg-shaped, divided up on the stem. Rounded heads of pink flowers are produced in summer. Zones 5–9.

VANCOUVERIA

FAMILY: Berberidaceae

Vancouveria hexandra

Three species of woodland groundcovers native to the northwestern coast of North America with leaves divided into threes and usually leafless stems bearing tiny, drooping white flowers in spring. The genus is closely related to ***Epimedium,*** but the flowers have six petals rather than four. Named after the explorer Captain George Vancouver. (1758–1798).

CULTIVATION: Grow in moist well-drained and acid, woodland soil in partial to full shade.

LANDSCAPE USE: Delicate-looking but robust groundcovers for shade.

PROPAGATION: Divide in spring or early autumn.

V. chrysantha. Oregon. Height 12 in.; spread 12 in. (30×30 cm). A spreading, rhizomatous evergreen, with wiry stems and leathery leaves divided into three-lobed, undulating leaflets up to 2 in. (5 cm) long. Wiry, leafless stems bear ½-in. (1.2-cm-) long yellow flowers just above the foliage in late spring. Spreads slowly. Zones 6–8.

V. hexandra. Washington, California. Height 12 in.; spread 12 in. (30×30 cm). The most vigorous species with leathery leaves divided into 1–2-in.- (2.5–5-cm-) long, lobed almost hexagonal, fernlike leaflets, mid-green above, blue-green underneath.

In late spring ½-in.- (1.2-cm-) long, bell-shaped flowers are borne on wiry, leafless stems. This is a deciduous species that is more valuable for its ferny foliage and ability to colonize large areas than for its flowers. It does best in moist soil but does spread even in dry, shady areas. While it spreads well, it is not invasive. Zones 5–8.

V. planipetala. Redwood ivy. Oregon, California. Height 12 in.; spread 12 in. (30 × 30 cm). An evergreen, woodland plant with dark-green, glossy leaves divided into leathery leaflets with thick, undulating edges. Thin spikes of white or pale-purple flowers are produced in late spring. Spreads slowly. Zones 6–9.

VERATRUM

(False Hellebore)

FAMILY: Liliaceae

Veratrum viride

A genus of about 20 species native to North America, Europe, and Asia. For some reason they are not widely grown in gardens, which is a pity, as they are handsome, easy-to-cultivate plants. They are stout-stemmed plants with alternate leaves that clasp the stem and tall panicles of greenish white, yellow-green, or dark-purple flowers in summer. All parts of the plants are poisonous, and extracts from the white false hellebore, ***V. album,*** were used in Europe to coat the tips of daggers and swords to effect a speedier death. The generic name comes from the Latin *vere atrum,* "true black," referring to the color of the roots.

CULTIVATION: Grow in moist soil in full sun to partial shade in a mild climate. Protect from slugs.

LANDSCAPE USE: Handsome plants for the wild garden, border, or stream edge.

PROPAGATION: Divide in autumn or spring.

V. album. White false hellebore. Europe. Height 4–6 ft; spread 2 ft (120–180 × 60 cm). A large, clump-forming plant with softly hairy stems and leaf undersides. The leaves are dark green, heavily pleated, oblong to elliptical, up to 1 ft (30 cm) long and 6 in. (15 cm) wide. Tall panicles of greenish white flowers are borne high above the foliage in summer. Zones 4–8.

V. nigrum. Europe, Asia. Height 4–6 ft; spread 2 ft (120–180 × 60 cm). The leaves of this species are mid- to dark green, narrowly oval and ribbed, up to 1 ft (30 cm) long. The flowers are produced in summer in narrow spikes well above the foliage and are a smoky chocolate-purple color. Zones 3–8.

V. viride. Indian poke. North America, Height 4–6 ft; spread 2 ft (120–180 × 60 cm). Stout, leafy stems with oval, pleated, light-green leaves up to 1 ft (30 cm) long becoming smaller and narrower up on the stem. Tall panicles of yellow-green flowers are produced in summer. Zones 3–7.

VERBASCUM

(Mullein)

FAMILY: Scrophulariaceae

A genus of about 300 species of biennials, perennials, and subshrubs native to Europe and Asia with several species naturalized in North America. The common mullein, ***V. thapsus,*** is a widespread biennial weed. ***V. bombyciferum*** is a wonderful biennial with silvery foliage and sulfur-yellow flowers. All mulleins hybridize freely, giving the gardener a wonderful range of elegant plants for the summer border. Verbascums are mostly hairy plants with erect stems, leaves in basal rosettes as well as alternate stem leaves, and tall spikes bearing mostly yellow or white flowers in summer. The name ***Verbascum*** is said to be derived from the Latin *barba (barbascum),* "beard," in reference to the hairy foliage. *Mullein* comes from the Latin *malandrium,* "malanders" or "leprosy," a term applied to diseases of cattle for which the plant was used as a cure.

Verbascum 'Gainsborough'

CULTIVATION: Grow in well-drained soil in full sun. Stake when necessary, and remove faded flower spikes for repeat bloom. The smaller species need protecting from winter wet. Many species require one to two years to develop their true habit. Prone to spider-mite damage in hot climates.

LANDSCAPE USE: The alpine species are attractive rock-garden plants. The taller species are excellent at the back of a sunny border or grouped en masse.

PROPAGATION: Sow seed in spring. Take root cuttings in late winter/early spring.

V. chaixii. Southern Europe. Height 3 ft; spread 2 ft. (90 × 60 cm). Large rosettes of 6-in.- (15-cm-) long, gray-green and woolly, coarsely toothed and veined, oval leaves with a wedge-shaped base. Pithy stems bear tall spikes of 1-in.- (2.5-cm-) wide, five-lobed, purple-centered yellow flowers in summer. 'Album' has purple-centered white flowers and is an outstanding garden plant. Zones 5–9.

V. densiflorum (V. thapsiforme). Europe. Height 4–5 ft; spread 2 ft (120–150 × 60 cm). Large rosettes of mid-green, oval to oblong, crinkled leaves up to 6 in. (15 cm) long and stout stems bearing spikes of flat, 2-in.- (5-cm-) wide, saucer-shaped yellow flowers in summer. The stems and leaves are densely covered in fine yellowish hairs. Zones 5–9.

V. dumulosum. Asia Minor. Height 6–12 in.; spread 12 in. (15–30 × 30 cm). A subshrubby, evergreen plant with woody stems and gray-green and woolly egg-shaped leaves. Short spikes of purple-eyed bright-yellow flowers are produced in summer. 'Letitia,' a natural hybrid between this species and ***V. spinosum,*** grows to about 8 in. (20 cm) in height with woody stems branched from the base; woolly, gray-green, lance-shaped leaves; and 3–4-in.- (7.5–10-cm-) spikes of bright-yellow flowers in summer. Zones 8–9.

V. × hybridum. Height 3–5 ft; spread 2 ft (90–150 × 60 cm). A group name for a number of cultivated varieties produced from crossing ***V. phoenicum, V. olympicum,*** and other species. They are generally short-lived plants with hairy foliage and tall flower spikes. 'Cotswold Beauty' has yellow flowers with a lilac eye; 'Cotswold Gem,' height about 4 ft (120 cm), has pink-purple flowers with a darker center; 'Cotswold Queen' height 4 ft (120 cm), has buff-orange flowers with a purple eye; 'Gainsborough,' height 4–5 ft (120–150 cm), has light-yellow flowers and gray-green foliage; 'Hartleyi,' height to 4 ft (120 cm), has buff-yellow flowers with a purple eye; 'Mont Blanc,' height 3 ft (90 cm), has pure white flowers above woolly gray foliage; 'Pink Domino,' height about 3½ ft (105 cm,) has rose-pink flowers. Zones 6–9.

V. nigrum. Europe, Asia. Height 2–3 ft; spread 18

in. (60–90 × 45 cm). A short-lived plant with basal rosettes of mid- to dark-green oblong leaves, hairy beneath. In summer 18–24-in.- (45–60-cm-) long, branching spikes bear small yellow flowers with reddish brown centers. Zones 5–8.

V. olympicum. Southern Europe. Height 6 ft; spread 2 ft (180 × 60 cm). A short-lived perennial or biennial with 6–8-in.- (15–20-cm-) long, broadly lance-shaped, densely felted gray basal leaves, becoming smaller and narrower up on the stem. Branched stems bear spikes of golden yellow flowers in midsummer. A dramatic plant for the back of the border. Zones 6–8.

V. phoenicum. Europe, Asia. Height 3–4 ft; spread 2 ft (90–120 × 60 cm). A clump-forming plant with basal rosettes of lobed, dark-green, crinkled leaves and unbranched stems bearing spikes of mostly purple but sometimes pink, red, or white flowers in early summer. Although a worthy garden plant, it is seen at its best as a contributor to ***V. × hybridum.*** Zones 6–8.

V. spinosum. Crete. Height 9–12 in.; spread 12 in. (22.5–30 × 30 cm). A subshrub with woody stems and toothed and spiny, narrowly lance-shaped, gray-green leaves. Small spikes about 4 in. (10 cm) long produce bright-yellow flowers in early summer. Zones 5–8.

VERBENA

FAMILY: Verbenaceae

Verbena bonariensis

A large genus of generally subtropical or tropical annuals, herbaceous perennials, and subshrubs with angled stems, opposite, toothed, or dissected leaves and mostly pink or purple flowers in summer. By far the majority cultivated are annuals or tender perennials that are treated as annuals.

CULTIVATION: Grow in a well-drained soil in full sun. Susceptible to powdery mildew in wet summers.

LANDSCAPE USE: *V. bonariensis* is an excellent plant for the back of the border or in a large, tight mass as a summer hedge. The smaller species are colorful edging or rock-garden plants. All associate well with silver-foliage plants.

PROPAGATION: Take root cuttings in early spring or stem cuttings in spring or summer. Sow seed in spring.

V. bonariensis. South America. Height 3–6 ft; spread 2 ft (90–180 × 60 cm). An upright plant with wiry and hairy, branching stems and basal clumps of 4-in.- (10-cm-) long, stem-clasping, sharply toothed, elliptical leaves. The 2-in.- (5-cm-) wide heads of tiny purple-blue flowers are produced throughout the summer and into autumn. Staking is rarely necessary. Self-sown seedlings appear to grow more easily and more vigorously than seedlings grown in pots. An outstanding species for climates with hot summers. Zones 7–10.

V. canadensis. North America. Height 12–18 in.; spread 2–3 ft (30–45 × 60–90 cm). A coarse and hairy plant widely grown as an annual. It is a clump-forming plant with many-branched stems growing along the ground with the stem ends growing upward (decumbent). Deeply cut and lobed, egg-shaped leaves grow 3–4 in. (7.5–10 cm) long and have a wedge-shaped base. Clusters of purplish pink flowers are produced throughout the summer and autumn. A useful plant for the rock garden or in large containers. 'Glowing Violet' has violet-purple flowers; 'Rosea' has rose-red flowers. Zones 6–10.

V. rigida (V. venosa). Rigid verbena. South America. Height 1–2 ft; spread 18 in. (30–60 × 45 cm). A drought-tolerant plant that performs well in areas with hot climates. It is a spreading species with hairy, oblong to lance-shaped, stem-clasping, irregularly toothed and stiff leaves up to 4 in. (10 cm) long. Spikes of bright-purple flowers are produced throughout the summer and into autumn. Zones 8–10.

V. tenuisecta (Glandularia tenuisecta). Moss verbena. South America. Height 8–12 in.; spread 12–18 in. (20–30 × 30–45 cm). A spreading plant with decumbent stems and bright-green leaves triangular in outline but finely divided into narrow, linear segments. Solitary heads of lilac-lavender flowers are produced from early summer to hard frost. A wonderful plant that should be widely grown in climates with hot summers. It self-sows freely and is so easy to propagate by cuttings that it is easy to become too enthusiastic and be inundated with the plant. Moss verbena tends to get straggly by midsummer, but this can be rectified by shearing to about 6 in. (15 cm) from the ground. In areas where it is not winter hardy, it is an excellent, trouble-free annual. 'Alba' is a less vigorous white-flowered form. Zones 8–10.

Verbena tenuisecta

VERNONIA

(Ironweed)

FAMILY: Compositae

A large genus of almost 1,000 species of herbaceous perennials, subshrubs, shrubs, and trees mostly native to the subtropical regions of the world. A number of species are native to temperate North America. One species, the New York ironweed, is native from Massachusetts to Mississippi and is beloved by native plant enthusiasts. The genus is named after William Vernon, a British botanist.

CULTIVATION: Grow in a rich, moist soil in full sun.

Landscape Use: A tall, late-blooming plant for the wet meadow, wildflower garden, or herbaceous border.

PROPAGATION: Divide in spring.

V. altissima. Eastern North America. Height 4–8 ft; spread 2–3 ft (120–240 × 60–90 cm). A stiff, erect plant with lance-shaped leaves up to 12 inches (30 cm) long and purple flowers in a flattened cluster in late summer and early autumn. Zones 5–8.

V. noveboracensis. New York ironweed. Eastern United States. Height 6 ft; spread 2–3 ft (180 × 60–90 cm). A common species in moist meadows

Vernonia noveboracensis

of the eastern United States, with stout stems and lance-shaped, serrated, and stemless leaves up to 8 in. (20 cm) long that are rough to the touch. Broad clusters of deep-purple flowers are borne on leafy stems in late summer and autumn. Zones 4–9.

VERONICA

(Speedwell)

Family: Scrophulariaceae

Veronica austriaca ssp teucrim 'Crater Lake Blue'

Almost 250 species of spring- and summer-flowering herbaceous perennials, subshrubs, and shrubs widely distributed throughout the temperate world. The shrubby species are largely placed in the genera ***Hebe*** and ***Parahebe.*** The herbaceous species range from prostrate, creeping, rock-garden plants to erect border plants. The leaves are opposite, and the small, often saucer-shaped flowers are held in dense, unbranched spikes. The genus is named after St. Veronica, and the common name possibly refers to the lightly attached petals that drop at the slightest touch, quickly losing their beauty.

Cultivation: Grow in moist but well-drained soil that does not dry out in summer, in full sun. Deadhead for repeat bloom and stake when necessary.

Landscape Use: The taller species are long-lasting border plants while the smaller species are attractive in the rock garden or wall garden.

Propagation: Divide in early autumn or spring, or take cuttings in midsummer.

V. alpina. Alpine speedwell. Northwestern North America, Europe, Asia. Height 8 in.; spread 12 in. (20 × 30 cm). A low-growing, mat-forming plant with oblong, untoothed, shiny green leaves up to 1½ in. (3.8 cm) long and small, dense spikes of dull-blue flowers in late spring. 'Alba' has white flowers. An unassuming plant but one with considerable charm. Zones 3–8.

V. austriaca. Europe, Asia Minor. Height 12 in.; spread 12 in. (30 × 30 cm). A mat-forming plant with variably shaped leaves up to 1½ in. (3.8 cm) long, lance-shaped to egg-shaped, toothed, and sometimes lobed to deeply cut and fernlike. The bright-blue flower spikes appear in early summer. Subspecies ***teucrium*** (***V. teucrium, V. latifolia***) has gray-green, hairy leaves and bright-blue flowers. There are a number of cultivars. 'Blue Fountain' grows to 2 ft (60 cm) and has bright-blue flowers; 'Crater Lake Blue' grows to about 12 in. (30 cm) and has bright-blue flowers; 'Kapitan' grows to about 10 in. (25 cm) and has short spikes of bright-blue flowers; 'Royal Blue' grows to about 12 in. (30 cm) and has deep-blue flowers. Zones 5–8.

V. cinerea. Asia Minor. Height 4 in.; spread 12 in. (10 × 30 cm). A mat-forming, sometimes invasive species with hairy, silver-green, narrowly lance-shaped leaves and white-eyed, dark-blue flowers on 2-in.- (5-cm-) long spikes in early summer. Zones 5–8.

V. gentianoides. Caucasus. Height 18 in.; spread 18 in. (45 × 45 cm). A mat-forming plant with basal rosettes of dark-green, oblong, untoothed leaves up to 3 in. (7.5 cm) long and leafy stems bearing 10-in.- (25-cm-) long spikes of pale-blue to white flowers in early summer. A gorgeous plant that deserves wider attention. 'Nana' is a dwarf form growing to 8–10 in. (20–25 cm); 'Variegata' has leaves with white edges. Zones 4–8.

V. longifolia. Europe, Asia. Height 2–4 ft; spread 1 ft (60–120 × 30 cm). A clump-forming perennial with 3-in.- (7.5-cm-) long, toothed and pointed, egg-shaped leaves and stiff stems bearing 12-in.- (30-cm-) long spikes of lilac-blue, ¼-in.- (0.6-cm-) wide flowers in early summer. Variety ***subsessilis*** grows to about 3 ft (90 cm) and has slightly larger violet-blue flowers. 'Blue Giant' grows to 4 ft (120 cm) and has pale-blue flowers; 'Foerster's Blue' grows to about 2 ft (60 cm) and has deep-blue flowers that last for up to two months; 'Romiley Purple' grows to about 4 ft (120 cm) and has purple flowers. Zones 4–8.

V. pectinata. Asia Minor. Height 8 in.; spread 12 in. (20 × 30 cm). A mat-forming species with egg-shaped, toothed, gray-green and hairy leaves ½ in. (1.2 cm) long and white-centered, violet-blue flowers in early summer. 'Alba' has white flowers; 'Rosea' has rose-pink flowers. Tolerant of dry soil. Zones 4–8.

V. prostrata. Europe, Asia. Height 8 in.; spread 12–18 in. (20 × 30–45 cm). A spreading, mat-forming plant with mid-green, toothed, egg-shaped to linear leaves up to 1½ in. (3.8 cm) long and short spikes up to 3 in. (7.5 cm) long of deep-blue flowers in early to midsummer. 'Heavenly Blue' grows to about 4 in. (10 cm) high and has deep-blue flowers; 'Mrs. Holt' grows to about 6 in. (15 cm) and has pink flowers; 'Spode Blue' grows to a height of 8 in. (20 cm) and has china-blue flowers; 'Trehane' grows to a height of 8 in. (20 cm) and has golden-green foliage and deep-blue flowers. Zones 4–8.

V. spicata. Spiked speedwell. Europe, Asia. Height 1–2 ft; spread 18 in. (30–60 × 45 cm). A highly variable plant with glossy, mid-green, oblong to lance-shaped, toothed leaves up to 2 in. (5 cm) long and dense, 3-in.- (7.5-cm-) long spikes of deep- to pale-blue flowers in summer. 'Goodness Grows' is a hybrid between this species and ***V. alpina*** and grows to about 12 in. (30 cm) with long-lasting, deep-blue flowers. A superior hybrid. Subspecies ***incana*** (***V. incana***), the woolly speedwell, has silver-gray leaves and violet-blue flowers. It was formerly thought of as a separate species and is often listed as such. Although there is considerable crossing between the species and subsp. ***incana,*** the following cultivars should be thought of as being varieties of ***V. spicata.*** 'Alba': white flowers and glossy green foliage; 'Blue Fox': height about 18 in. (45 cm), lavender-blue flowers and green leaves; 'Blue Peter' height 2 ft (60 cm), dark-blue flowers and green foliage; 'Blue Spires': height 18 in. (45 cm), green foliage and deep-blue flowers; 'Heidekind': height 10 in. (25 cm), rose-pink flowers; 'Icicle': height 18 in. (45 cm), dark-green, glossy foliage and white flowers; 'Red Fox': height 12–18 in. (30–45 cm), glossy green leaves deep rose-pink flowers.

The following are cultivated varieties of ***V. spicata*** subsp. ***incana.*** 'Barcarolle': height about 12 in. (30 cm), rose-pink flowers and gray-green foliage; 'Minuet': height 12 in. (30 cm), silvery leaves and bright-pink flowers; 'Nana': height 8 in. (20 cm), gray-green leaves, violet-blue flowers; 'Wendy': height 2 ft (60 cm), gray-green leaves, lavender-blue flowers. Zones 4–8.

V. 'Sunny Border Blue.' Height 18–20 in.; spread 12 in. (45–50 × 30 cm). A hybrid of unknown parentage introduced by Robert Bennerup in the late 1940s. It is a clump-forming plant with egg-shaped and crinkled, dark-green and glossy leaves and erect spikes of violet-blue flowers throughout the summer and into autumn. An outstanding plant with a long flowering period, it does not need staking and has no apparent pest problems. It is easily cultivated and is particularly good with silver foliage plants or in contrast to the flat plates of yellow daisies. Zones 4–8.

Veronica 'Sunny Border Blue'

VERONICASTRUM

(Bowman's Root, Culver's Root)

FAMILY: Scrophulariaceae

Veronicastrum virginicum

Two species, one native to North America, the other endemic to northeast Asia. The North American species is the one cultivated in gardens. Taxonomists move ***Veronicastrum virginicum*** backward and forward between this genus and ***Veronica.*** Perhaps this will be its final resting place. The roots of this plant have been used for a number of medicinal purposes, including "torpidity of the liver."

CULTIVATION: Easily grown in moist but well-drained soil in full sun. May need staking if grown in partial shade. Leave undivided for three to five years to establish.

LANDSCAPE USE: A tall border plant that combines well with other late-flowering plants.

PROPAGATION: Carefully divide in spring. Take stem

cuttings in midsummer or sow seed in spring or autumn.

V. virginicum. (Veronica virginica). Eastern United States. Height 4–6 ft; spread 2 ft (120–180 × 60 cm). An erect plant with strong stems and lance-shaped, sharply toothed leaves up to 4 in. (10 cm) long. The leaves are arranged in whorls around the stems. The 9-in.- (22.5-cm-) long terminal spikes of pale-blue to white flowers are produced in late summer and autumn. Variety ***alba*** has white flowers, var. ***rosea*** has pale-pink flowers. Zones 3–8.

VIOLA

(Violet)

FAMILY: Violaceae

Viola cornuta 'Boughton Blue'

About 500 species of widely distributed, tufted or stemmed plants with generally heart-shaped basal or alternate stem leaves and multicolored flowers consisting of five sepals and five rounded petals. The lower petal is often spurred. True violets have two different kinds of flowers, infertile often showy flowers in spring and fertile, petalless flowers that are often hidden in the soil. Most species are highly promiscuous and hybridize with great frequency and enthusiasm. This hybridizing often makes identification difficult. The garden pansy is a product of much crossing and is listed under the collective name ***V. × wittrockiana.*** Although a short-lived perennial, the garden pansies are usually grown as annuals or biennials. The true violets are more delicate perennials that are generally evergreen except in the coldest climates. Despite their delicate appearance, they are robust plants thriving in a great variety of environments, from the sides of mountains to woodland bogs. The name Viola is said to be the Latin form of the Greek Ione. When Zeus turned Io into a white cow, to hide her from Juno's jealousy, he created the violet as food for her.

CULTIVATION: In general, violas are best grown in moist but well-drained soil in full sun to partial shade. Deadhead faded flowers for repeated bloom.

LANDSCAPE USE: Most are excellent rock-garden plants, crevice or trough plants, or edging plants for the border.

PROPAGATION: Sow seeds in spring and summer. Take cuttings in spring and summer or divide in early spring or autumn.

V. adunca. Western dog violet. North America. Height 4 in.; spread 8 in. (10 × 20 cm). A compact, tufted plant with finely toothed, egg-shaped leaves up to 1½ in. (3.8 cm) long on leafy stems up to 2 in. (5 cm) long. White-eyed violet flowers turning purple-red are produced in spring and summer. Zones 4–8.

V. aetolica. Balkans. Height 3 in.; spread 6 in. (7.5 × 15 cm). A delicate, clump-forming plant with egg-shaped, toothed leaves up to ¾ in. (1.8 cm) long and short-stemmed, 1-in.- (2.5-cm-) wide, clear-yellow flowers occasionally with the upper petals violet. Needs sun. Zones 5–7.

V. biflora. Twin-flower violet. Northern hemisphere. Height 3–6 in.; spread 6 in. (7.5–15 × 15 cm). A spreading plant with 6-in.- (15-cm-) long stems and bright-green, kidney-shaped leaves. The bright-yellow flowers are usually borne in pairs and have the lower petals striped with chocolate-brown veins. Needs shade. Zones 4–8.

V. canadensis. Canada violet. North America. Height 12 in.; spread 12 in. (30 × 30 cm). A tall, spreading violet with weak, leafy stems and heart-shaped leaves up to 4 in. (10 cm) long. White-tinged purple flowers have a yellow throat and lower petals veined purple, and are produced from the leaf axils. Zones 3–8.

V. cornuta. Horned violet. Pyrenees. Height 4–12 in.; spread 12 in. (10–30 × 30 cm). A vigorous, tufted plant with egg-shaped, round-toothed, pointed leaves 1–2 in. (2.5–5 cm) long with leaflike appendages on the nodes of the leaf stem. The 1-in.- (2.5-cm-) wide, slightly fragrant, spurred and starlike violet flowers are produced on 2–4-in.- (5–10-cm-) long stems in late spring. Cut back in summer for repeat bloom in the autumn. Variety ***alba*** has white flowers; var. ***lilacina*** has lilac-blue flowers, blooms throughout the summer, is tolerant of heat, and is undoubtedly the most floriferous variety; var. ***purpurea*** has purple-violet flowers. 'Arkwright Beauty,' probably a hybrid, has ruby-red flowers with a black center and yellow eye; 'Boughton Blue' has light-blue flowers; 'Blue Perfection' has light-blue flowers with a white eye; 'Chantreyland' has apricot flowers; 'Jersey Gem' has purple-blue flowers; 'White Perfection' has clear-white flowers; 'Yellow Perfection' has bright-yellow flowers. Tolerates full sun in mild areas, partial shade in hot summer climates. Zones 6–9.

Viola canadensis

V. corsica. Corsica. Height 4 in.; spread 8 in. (10 × 20 cm). A clump-forming viola with leafy stems. The basal leaves are rounded, the stem leaves lance-shaped. The violet-blue flowers have a central yellow eye and yellow-flushed lower petals veined dark purple. An excellent viola for full sun to partial shade in areas with hot summers. Flowers from spring to late summer and seeds itself readily. Zones 6–9.

V. hederacea. Ivy-leaved viola. Australia. Height 2–4 in.; spread 8 in. (5–10 × 20 cm). A spreading, stemless, tufted plant with ivylike, heart-shaped leaves and white-tipped, pale-violet flowers. Needs a sheltered site in partial shade. Zones 7–9.

V. labradorica. Labrador violet. North America. Height 2 in.; spread 8 in. (5 × 20 cm). A clump-forming plant with mid-green, egg-shaped, and finely toothed leaves up to 1 in. (2.5 cm) wide. The mauve-purple flowers appear sporadically throughout spring and early summer. Variety ***purpurea*** is the form more commonly seen in gardens. The leaves are dark purple-green, the flowers mauve-purple. This is an excellent plant as a groundcover among hellebores and primulas. Grow in moist but well-drained soil in shade. Self-seeds readily. Zones 3–8.

V. obliqua. (V. cucullata). Marsh blue violet. Eastern North America. Height 3–6 in.; spread 12 in. (7.5–15 × 30 cm). An evergreen, spreading, stemless viola with pale-green, basal, variably rounded, toothed leaves up to 4 in. (10 cm) wide and nodding, ½-in.- (1.2-cm-) wide violet flowers with the lower petal striped with purple veins and the lateral petals hairy. 'Freckles' has purple flowers flecked light blue; 'Red Giant' grows to 8 in. (20 cm) and has maroon flowers; 'Royal Robe' grows to 8 in. (20 cm) and has dark violet-blue flowers; 'White Czar' has yellow-eyed white flowers. Zones 4–9.

V. odorata. Sweet violet. Europe, Asia. Height 8 in.; spread 12 in. (20 × 30 cm). A stoloniferous plant with tufted, mid- to dark-green, egg-shaped to heart-shaped toothed leaves up to 2 in. (5 cm) long. The ½-in.- (1.2-cm-) wide violet flowers are borne on 8-in.- (20-cm-) long stems in winter and spring in mild climates and in spring in cold. 'Alba' has white flowers; 'Semperflorens' has violet flowers in spring to early summer. Needs well-drained soil in full sun to partial shade. Zones 5–8.

V. pedata. Bird's-foot violet. Eastern North America. Height 6 in.; spread 12 in. (15×30 cm). A stemless, clump-forming plant with fan-shaped leaves divided into three to five narrow, toothed segments. The leaves are reminiscent of a bird's foot. The 2–6-in.- (5–15-cm-) long stems bear white-throated lilac-blue flowers in spring. Variety ***alba*** has white flowers; var. ***bicolor*** has flowers with the two upper petals dark violet and the three lower petals pale lilac. Grow in well-drained woodland soil in partial shade. Zones 3–8.

WALDSTEINIA

(Barren Strawberry)

Family: Rosaceae

Waldsteinia fragrarioides

A small genus of strawberrylike plants with leaves divided into three. The yellow, five-petaled flowers appear in late spring and early summer. Named after the Austrian botanist Count Franz Adam Waldstein-Wartenburg (1759–1823).

Cultivation: Grow in full sun to partial shade in well-drained soil.

Landscape Use: Good groundcovers for a sunny site, particularly effective with ***Brunnera macrophylla.***

Propagation: Divide in spring or early autumn.

W. fragrarioides. Barren strawberry. Eastern United States. Height 4–6 in.; spread 12 in. (10–15×30 cm). An attractive mat-forming plant with three-parted, 2-in.- (5-cm-) long, softly hairy, evergreen, and wedge-shaped, glossy leaves toothed at the tip. The ¾-in.- (1.8-cm-) wide, saucer-shaped yellow flowers are produced on almost horizontal stems in late spring and early summer. Zones 4–7.

W. ternata. Siberian barren strawberry. Europe, Siberia, Japan. Height 4–6 in.; spread 12 in. (10–15×30 cm). Similar to the above species with a more compact habit. The leaves are about 1 in. (2.5 cm) long, three-parted and irregularly toothed. The yellow, saucer-shaped flowers are held on upright stems above the foliage. Zones 4–7.

WOODSIA

Family: Aspleniaceae

About 40 species of deciduous ferns widely distributed throughout the temperate regions of the world. Named after Joseph Woods (no relation), an English botanist.

Cultivation: Grow in moist but well-drained, preferably rocky soil in open shade.

Landscape Use: Fine-textured ferns for the rock garden.

Propagation: Divide in early spring or sow spores in late summer.

W. ilvensis. Rusty woodsia. Europe, Asia, northern North America. Height 6 in.; spread 6 in. (15 × 15 cm). A clump-forming, deciduous fern with gray-green, lance-shaped leaves with bluntly lobed leaf segments. The leaf undersides start gray-green in spring but quickly develop to a rusty brown color. A handsome fern for the shaded rock garden. Zones 4–8.

W. obtusa. Blunt-lobed woodsia. Eastern and central North America. Height 12–16 in.; spread 12 in. (30–40 × 30 cm). Similar to the rusty woodsia but semievergreen and larger, with gray-green, lance-shaped leaves up to 3 in. (7.5 cm) wide, divided into blunt-lobed segments. Grows best in partial shade. Zones 4–9.

XEROPHYLLUM

(Turkey Beard)

Family: Liliaceae

Xerophyllum asphodeloides

Two species of herbaceous perennials native to North America, with grasslike foliage and white flowers borne in a dense, terminal spike in summer. They are not easily cultivated, requiring the right mix of soil and climate to do well in the garden.

Cultivation: Grow in acid, moist but well-drained soil in partial shade. They are difficult plants to grow, and if well established in a particular site should be left alone.

Landscape Use: Unusual American natives for

the wild garden and rock garden.

Propagation: Carefully divide the woody rhizomes in spring, or sow seed in autumn. Never take from the wild.

X. asphodeloides. Turkey beard. New Jersey to North Carolina. Height 2–5 ft; spread 2 ft (60–150 × 60 cm). A clump-forming plant with woody roots and stiff, grasslike basal leaves up to 18 in. (45 cm) long. The leaves become smaller up on the stem. An erect stem, sometimes up to 5 ft (150 cm) in length, bears a 6–12-in.- (15–30-cm-) long oblong spike of starry, creamy white flowers in summer. It is a wonderful sight in the pine barrens of New Jersey or along the Blue Ridge Parkway in Virginia. Zones 6–8.

X. tenax. Bear grass. Western North America. Height 2–6 ft; spread 3 ft (60–180 × 90 cm). Similar to the above species but with leaves up to 3 ft (90 cm) long and white flowers in a pyramidal spike up to 2 ft (60 cm) long. Zones 7–9.

ZANTEDESCHIA

(Calla Lily)

Family: Araceae

Zantedeschia aethiopica 'Crowborough'

A small genus of stemless plants with long-stalked basal leaves with a clublike yellow, white, or purple spadix surrounded by a white, yellow, or pink spathe. They are tender, tuberous-rooted perennials that, except for one species, are grown outside in subtropical and tropical climates or inside a greenhouse. They are a common flowering plant in parts of California. The one species that tolerates a small degree of frost is root hardy to Zones 8–10.

Cultivation: Grow in moist to wet soil in full sun to light shade. The common calla lily can be grown in 6 in. (15 cm) of water at a pond's edge.

Landscape Use: A dramatic aquatic.

Propagation: Divide the rhizomes in spring.

Z. aethiopica. Calla lily. South Africa. Height 1½–3 ft; spread 18 in. (45–90 × 45 cm). An arresting plant with deep-green, glossy, arrow-shaped, triangular leaves up to 18 in. (45 cm) long. The clublike spadix is yellow and fragrant, the milky white spathe is up to 10 in. (25 cm) long and flaring. 'Crowborough' grows to 3 ft (90 cm) and is listed as being slightly hardier than the species; 'Green Goddess' is an undramatic plant with green spathes splashed with a white center. Zones 8–10.

Bibliography

Aden, Paul. *The Hosta Book.* Portland, Ore.: Timber Press, 1988.

Armitage, Allan M. *Herbaceous Perennial Plants.* Athens, Ga.: Varsity Press, 1989.

Bailey Hortorium. *Hortus Third.* New York: Macmillan, 1976.

Bailey, L. H. *The Standard Cyclopedia of Horticulture.* New York: Macmillan, 1977.

Bloom, Alan. *Making the Best of Alpines.* Norwich: Jarrold & Sons, 1975.

———. *Perennials for Your Garden.* Chicago: Floraprint U.S.A. 1981.

Brickell, Christopher, and Fay Sharmon. *The Vanishing Garden.* London: John Murray, 1986.

Brickell, Christopher, ed. *The American Horticultural Society: Encyclopedia of Garden Plants.* New York: Macmillan, 1989.

Brown, Emily. *Landscaping with Perennials.* Portland, Ore.: Timber Press, 1986.

Bruce, Hal. *How to Grow Wildflowers and Wild Shrubs and Trees in Your Own Garden.* New York: Alfred A. Knopf, 1976.

Chatto, Beth. *The Dry Garden.* London: J. M. Dent & Sons, 1978.

Cobb, James L. S. *Meconopsis.* Portland, Ore.: Timber Press, 1989.

Ekstrom, Nicholas H., and Ruth Rogers Clausen. *Perennials for American Gardens.* New York: Random House, 1989.

Everett, Thomas H. *The New York Botanical Garden Illustrated Encyclopedia of Horticulture.* New York: Garland Publishing, 1981.

Fish, Margery. *Cottage Garden Flowers.* London: Faber & Faber, 1980.

Foerster, Karl. *Rock Gardens Through the Year.* New York: Sterling Publishing, 1987.

Foster, F. Gordon. *Ferns to Know and Grow.* Portland, Ore.: Timber Press, 1984.

Foster, H. Lincoln. *Rock Gardening.* Boston: Houghton Mifflin, 1968.

Harkness, Mabel G., and Deborah D'Angelo. *The Bernard E. Harkness Seedlist Handbook.* Portland, Ore.: Timber Press, 1986.

Harper, Pamela, and Frederick McGourty. *Perennials: How to Select, Grow and Enjoy.* Tucson, Ariz.: HP Books, 1985.

Hudak, Joseph. *Gardening with Perennials.* Portland, Ore.: Timber Press, 1985.

Ingwersen, Will. *Manual of Alpine Plants.* London: Collingridge Books, 1986.

Jellito, Leo, and Wilhelm Schact. *Hardy Herbaceous Perennials.* Portland, Ore.: Timber Press, 1990.

Kartesz, John T., and Rosemarie Kartesz. *A Synonymized Checklist of the Vascular Flora of the United States, Canada and Greenland.* Chapel Hill: University of North Carolina Press, 1980.

Kohlein, Fritz. *Saxifrages and Related Genera.* London: B. T. Batsford, 1984.

Lacy, Allen. *The Garden in Autumn.* New York: Atlantic Monthly Press, 1990.

Lancaster, Roy. *Garden Plants for Connoisseurs.* Portland, Ore.: Timber Press, 1987.

Lellinger, David B. *A Field Manual of the Ferns & Fern-Allies of the United States and Canada.* Washington, D.C.: Smithsonian Institution Press, 1985.

Lewis, Peter, and Margaret Lynch. *Campanulas.* Portland, Ore.: Timber Press, 1989.

McGourty, Frederick. *The Perennial Gardener.* Boston: Houghton Mifflin, 1989.

Matthew, Brian. *The Genus Lewisia.* Portland, Ore.: Timber Press, 1989.

Ottesen, Carole. *Ornamental Grasses: The Amber Wave.* New York: McGraw-Hill, 1989.

Philip, Chris. *The Plant Finder,* 4th ed. Whitbourne, England: Headmain, 1990.

Robinson, William. *The English Flower Garden,* 15th ed. London: John Murray, 1934.

Schacht, Willhelm. *Rock Gardens.* New York: Universe Books, 1981.

Schmidt, Marjorie G. *Growing California Native Plants.* Berkeley: University of California Press, 1980.

Snyder, Leon C. *Flowers for Northern Gardens.* Minneapolis: University of Minnesota Press, 1983.

Still, Steven. *Manual of Herbaceous Ornamental Plants,* 3rd ed. Champaign, Ill.: Stipes Publishing, 1987.

Thomas, Graham S. *Plants for Ground-Cover.* London: J. M. Dent & Sons, 1970.

———. *The Art of Planting.* London: J. M. Dent & Sons, 1984.

———. *Perennial Garden Plants,* 3rd edition. Portland, Ore.: Sagapress Inc./Timber Press, 1990.

Trehane, Piers. *Index Hortensis: Volume 1.* Wimborne, Dorset: Quarterjack Publishing, 1989.

Walters, S. M., ed. *The European Garden Flora.* Cambridge: Cambridge University Press, 1986.

Webb, D. A., and R. J. Gornall. *A Manual of Saxifrages.* Portland, Ore.: Timber Press, 1989.

Wister, John. *The Peonies.* Washington, D.C.: American Horticultural Society, 1962.

Wyman, Donald. *Wyman's Gardening Encyclopedia.* New York: Macmillan, 1986.

Yeo, Peter. *Hardy Geraniums.* Portland, Ore.: Timber Press, 1985.

Appendix A:

Index of Societies

The following is a short list of plant societies and related organizations specializing in information on herbaceous perennials or on gardens open to the public.

Alpine Garden Society
E. Michael Upward
Lye End Link, St John's
Woking, Surey GU21 1SW
England

American Association of Botanic Gardens and Arboreta
786 Church Road
Wayne, PA 19087

American Fern Society
James D. Caponetti, Treasurer
Dept. of Botany, University of Tennessee
Knoxville, TN 37916

American Hemerocallis Society
Elly Launius
1454 Rebel Drive
Jackson, MS 39211

American Hosta Society
Warren I. Pollock, Chair
202 Hockney Circle
Wilmington, DE 19803

American Iris Society
Jeane Stayer, Secretary
7414 East 60th Street
Tulsa, OK 74145

American Penstemon Society
Orville M. Steward, Membership Secretary
P.O. Box 33
Plymouth, VT 05056

American Peony Society
Greta Kessenich
250 Interlachen Road
Hopkins, MN 55343

American Primrose Society
Brian Skidmore, Treasurer
6730 W. Mercer Way
Mercer Island, WA 98040

American Rock Garden Society
Buffy Parker
15 Fairmead Road
Darien, CT 06820

Hardy Plant Society
Connie Hanni
33530 S.E. Bluff Road
Boring, OR 97009

Hardy Plant Society
Simon Wills
The Manor House
Walton-in-Gordano
Clevedon, Avon BS21 7AN
England

Herb Society of America
Leslie Rascan, Executive Secretary
9019 Kirtland Chardon Drive
Mentor, OH 44060

The Perennial Plant Association
Steven Still, Secretary
3383 Scirtzinger Road
Columbus, OH 43026

The Royal Horticultural Society
80 Vincent Square
London SW1P 2PE
England

Sources of Herbaceous Plants

The following is a brief list of the more prominent nurseries in the United States specializing in the sale of herbaceous perennials. Smaller nurseries may well carry uncommon collections or plants that are unavailable elsewhere.

Kurt Bluemel Inc.
2740 Green Lane
Baldwin, MD 21013

Bluestone Perennials Inc.
7211 Middle Ridge Road
Madison, OH 44057

Busse Gardens
635 East 7th Street
Route 2, Box 13
Cokato, MN 55321

Canyon Creek Nursery
3527 Dry Creek Road
Oroville, CA 95965

Carroll Gardens Inc.
Box 310, 444 East Main Street
Westminster, MD 21157

High Altitude Gardens
P.O. Box 4238
Ketchum, ID 83340

Holbrook Farm & Nursery
Route 2, Box 223B
Fletcher, NC 28732

Klehm Nursery
Route 5, 197 Penny Road
South Barrington, IL 60010

Milaeger's Gardens
4838 Douglas Avenue
Racine, WI 53402

Plants of the Southwest
1812 Second Street
Santa Fe, NM 87501

Prairie Nursery
P.O. Box 365
Westfield, WI 53964

Siskiyou Rare Plant Nursery
2825 Cummings Road
Medford, OR 97501

Sunny Border Nurseries
1709 Kensington Avenue
P.O. Box 86
Kensington, CT 06037

Andre Viette Farm & Nursery
Route 1, Box 16
Fisherville, VA 22939

Walters Gardens Inc.
P.O. Box 137
Zeeland, MI 49464

Wayside Gardens
Hodges, SC 29695

Western Hills Nursery
16250 Coleman Valley Road
Occidental, CA 95465

White Flower Farm
Litchfield, CT 06759

Woodlanders Inc.
1128 Colleton Avenue
Aiken, SC 29801

Appendix B:

Categorical Index

Perennials Native to or Naturalized in North America

Aconitum columbianum
Aconitum unciniatum
Acorus calamus
Actaea pachypoda
Actaea rubra
Adiantum pedatum
Agastache foeniculum
Agastache nepetoides
Agastache urticifolia
Agave americana
Amsonia ciliata
Amsonia tabernaemontana
Anaphalis margaritacea
Andropogon gerardii
Andropogon virginicus
Anemone canadensis
Anemone caroliniana
Anemone deltoidea
Anemone narcissiflora
Angelica atropurpurea
Antennaria dioica
Antennaria plantaginifolia
Aquilegia caerulea
Aquilegia canadensis
Aquilegia chrysantha
Aquilegia formosa
Aquilegia longissima
Arisaema dracontium
Arisaema triphyllum
Artemisia ludoviciana
Artemisia stelleriana
Asarum canadense
Asarum caudatum
Asclepias incarnata
Asclepias speciosa
Asclepias syriaca
Asclepias tuberosa
Asplenium platyneuron
Asplenium ruta-muraria
Asplenium trichomanes
Aster divaricatus
Aster dumosus
Aster ericoides
Aster laevis
Aster lateriflorus
Aster linariifolius
Aster novae-angliae
Aster novi-belgi
Aster praealtus
Aster puniceus
Aster spectabilis
Astilbe biternata
Athyrium filix-femina
Athyrium pycnocarpon
Baptisia alba
Baptisia australis
Baptisia leucophaea
Baptisia pendula
Baptisia perfoliata
Baptisia tinctoria
Boltonia asteroides
Botrychium virginianum
Boykinia aconitifolia
Calla palustris
Callirhoe involucrata
Callirhoe triangulata
Caltha biflora
Caltha leptosepala
Caltha palustris
Campanula rotundifolia
Caulophyllum thalictroides
Chasmanthium latifolium
Chelone glabra
Chelone lyonii
Chelone obliqua
Chrysogonum virginianum
Chrysopsis bakeri
Chrysopsis mariana
Chrysopsis villosa
Cimicifuga americana
Cimicifuga racemosa
Clintonia borealis
Clintonia umbellulata
Convallaria majalis
Coreopsis auriculata
Coreopsis grandiflora
Coreopsis lanceolata
Coreopsis tripteris
Coreopsis verticillata
Cornus canadensis
Coronilla varia
Cypripedium acaule
Cypripedium calceolus
Cypripedium reginae
Cystopteris fragilis
Delphinium cardinale
Dennstaedtia punctilobula
Dentaria diphylla
Dentaria laciniata
Deschampsia caespitosa
Dicentra canadensis
Dicentra cucullaria
Dicentra eximia
Dicentra formosa
Dicentra uniflora
Diphylleia cymosa
Disporum flavum
Disporum hookeri
Disporum lanuginosum
Disporum maculatum
Dodecatheon alpinum
Dodecatheon clevelandii
Dodecatheon cusickii
Dodecatheon jeffreyi
Dodecatheon meadia
Dodecatheon pulchellum
Dryopteris cristata
Dryopteris dilatata
Dryopteris intermedia
Echinacea angustifolia
Echinacea pallida
Echinacea purpurea
Epilobium latifolium
Eragrostis curvula
Eragrostis trichodes
Erigeron aureus
Erigeron glaucus
Erigeron philadelphicus
Eryngium yuccifolium

Eupatorium coelestinum
Eupatorium hyssopifolium
Eupatorium fistulosum
Eupatorium perfoliatum
Eupatorium rugosum
Euphorbia corollata
Festuca ovina var. *glauca*
Gaillardia aristata
Galax urceolata
Gentiana andrewsii
Geranium maculatum
Gymnocarpium dryopteris
Hedyotis caerulea
Helenium autumnale
Helenium bigelovii
Helenium flexuosum
Helianthus helianthoides
Helonias bullata
Hepatica nobilis
Hexastylis shuttleworthii
Hexastylis virginiana
Hieracium lanatum
Heuchara americana
Heuchera cylindrica
Heuchera micrantha
Heuchera sanguinea
Hieracium aurantiacum
Hieracium venosum
Inula helenium
Iris brevicaulis
Iris cristata
Iris missouriensis
Iris setosa
Iris versicolor
Jeffersonia diphylla
Leucanthemum vulgare
Lobelia cardinalis
Lobelia siphilitica
Liatris aspera
Liatris gramnifolia
Liatris pycnostachya
Liatris spicata
Luzula pilosa
Lychnis alpina
Lychnis flos-cuculi
Lysichiton americanus
Maianthemum canadense
Malva moschata
Marshallia grandiflora
Matteucia struthiopteris
Mertenisa paniculata
Mertensia virginica
Mertensia viridis
Millium effusum
Mimulus cardinalis
Mimulus ringens
Mitella diphylla
Monarda didyma
Monarda fistulosa
Oenothera missouriensis
Oenothera perennis
Oenothera pilosella
Oenothera speciosa
Oenothera tetragona
Onoclea sensibilis
Pachysandra procumbens
Peltiphyllum peltatum
Penstemon barbatus
Penstemon confertus
Penstemon digitalis
Penstemon smallii
Phalaris arundinacea var. *picta*
Phlox adsurgens
Phlox bifida
Phlox carolina
Phlox divaricata
Phlox douglasii
Phlox glaberrima
Phlox maculata
Phlox nivalis
Phlox ovata
Phlox paniculata
Phlox pilosa
Phlox stolonifera
Phlox subulata
Physostegia virginiana
Phytolacca americana
Podophyllum peltatum
Polemonium carneum
Polemonium foliosissimum
Polemonium reptans
Polygonatum biflorum
Polypodium virginianum
Polystichum acrostichoides
Pontederia cordata
Porteranthus stipulata
Porteranthus trifoliata
Potentilla tridentata
Pycnanthemum flexuosum
Pycnanthemum pilosum
Pycnanthemum tenuifolium
Pycnanthemum virginianum
Ratibida columnifera
Ratibida pinnata
Rudbeckia fulgida
Rudbeckia laciniata
Rudbeckia maxima
Rudbeckia nitida
Salvia azurea
Salvia farinacea
Salvia greggii
Sanguisorba canadensis
Saxifraga aizoides
Saxifraga oppositifolia
Saxifraga paniculata
Saxifraga pensylvanica
Scutellaria incana
Sedum spathulifolium
Senecio aureus
Sidalcea candida
Sidalcea malviflora
Silene acaulis
Silene caroliniana
Silene polypetala
Silene virginica
Silphium laciniatum
Silphium perfoliatum
Silphium terebinthaceum
Sisyrinchium angustifolium
Sisyrinchium californicum
Sisyrinchium douglasii
Smilacina racemosa
Smilacina trifolia
Solidago caesia
Solidago canadensis
Solidago odora
Solidago rugosa
Solidago sempervirens
Solidago spathulata
Solidago speciosa
Solidago sphacelata
Sorghastrum nutans
Spartina pectinata
Spigelia marilandica
Stokesia laevis
Stylophorum diphyllum
Symplocarpus foetidus
Tellima grandiflora
Teucrium canadense
Thalictrum thalictroides
Thelypteris hexagonoptera
Thelypteris novaboracensis
Thermopsis montana
Thermopsis villosa
Tiarella cordifolia
Tolmeia menziesii
Tradescantia × andersoniana
Tradescantia bracteata
Tradescantia ohiensis
Tradescantia subaspera
Trillium cernuum
Trillium chloropetalum
Trillium erectum
Trillium grandiflorum
Trillium luteum
Trillium nivale
Trillium ovatum
Trillium sessile

Trillium undulatum
Trillium viride
Typha latifolia
Uvullaria grandiflora
Uvullaria perfoliata
Uvullaria sessilifolia
Valeriana arizonica
Veratrum viride
Verbena canadensis
Vernonia altissima
Vernonia noveboracensis
Veronica alpina
Veronicastrum virginicum
Viola adunca
Viola canadensis
Viola labradorica
Viola obliqua
Viola palmata
Viola pedata
Waldsteinia fragrarioides
Woodsia ilvensis
Woodsia obtusa
Xerophyllum asphodeloides
Xerophyllum tenax

Perennials Suitable for the Rock Garden

Acaena spp.
Acanthus dioscoridis var. *perringii*
Achillea chrysocoma
Achillea clavennae
Achillea tomentosa
A. × *wilczeckii*
Adenophylla tashiroi
Adiantum spp.
Adonis spp.
Aethionema spp.
Alchemilla spp.
Alyssum spp.
Anacyclus spp.
Anagallis spp.
Anchusa angustissima
Anchusa caespitosa
Androsace spp.
Antennaria spp.
Anthemis spp.
Aquilegia spp.
Arabis spp.
Armeria spp.
Artemisia spp.
Asperula spp.
Asplenium spp.
Aster alpinus
Aster amellus
Aster spathulifolius
Aubrieta spp.
Aurinia spp.
Ballota spp.
Bellis spp.
Briza spp.
Bupleurum angulosum
Bupleurum ranunculoides
Calandrinia spp.
Calceolaria spp.
Callirhoe spp.
Campanula betulifolia
Campanula caespitosa
Campanula carpatica
Campanula cochlearifolia
Campanula garganica
Campanula portenschlagiana
Campanula poscharskyana
Campanula simplicaulis
Centranthus spp.
Cerastium spp.
Codonopsis clematidea
Convolvulus spp.
Corydalis spp.
Crepis spp.
Cyananthus spp.
Cystopteris spp.
Deschampsia spp.
Dianthus spp.
Diascia spp.
Dodecatheon spp.
Draba spp.
Edraianthus spp.
Epilobium canum
Epilobium glabellum
Epimedium spp.
Erinus alpinus
Erodium spp.
Euphorbia myrsinites
Gentiana scabra
Gentiana sino-ornata
Gentiana verna
Geranium argenteum
Geranium cinereum
Geranium dalmaticum
Geranium endressii
Geranium macrorrhizum
Geranium renardii
Geranium × *riversleianum*
Geranium sanguineum
Geranium wallichianum
Geum spp.
Glaucidium spp.
Glaucium spp.
Globularia spp.
Gypsophila repens
Helictotrichon sempervirens
Helichrysum spp.
Hepatica spp.
Hieracium spp.
Iberis spp.
Inula acaulis
Iris chrysographes
Iris douglasiana
Iris pumila
Iris tectorum
Leontopodium spp.
Lewisia spp.
Linaria spp.
Mazus spp.
Monardella spp.
Myosotis spp.
Omphalodes spp.
Origanum spp.
Ourisia spp.
Oxalis spp.
Penstemon spp.
Persicaria spp.
Petrorhagia spp.
Phlox spp.
Phuopsis spp.
Physoplexis spp.
Phyteuma comosa
Polygala caerulea
Potentilla spp.
Primula spp.
Prunella spp.
Pulsatilla spp.
Ramonda spp.
Ranunculus spp.
Raoulia spp.
Roscoea spp.
Sagina subulata
Saponaria spp.
Saxifraga spp.
Scutellaria spp.
Sedum spp.
Sempervivum spp.
Serratula spp.

Silene spp.
Sisyrinchium spp.
Stachys nivea
Symphyandra spp.
Tanacetum spp.
Teucrium spp.
Thymus spp.
Trachelium asperuloides
Trachelium jacquinii var. *rumelianum*
Valeriana spp.
Vancouveria spp.
Verbascum dumulosum
Verbascum spinosum
Verbena spp.
Veronica spp.
Viola spp.
Woodsia spp.

Perennials Suitable for Meadows

Achillea spp.
Andropogon spp.
Asclepias spp.
Aster spp.
Coreopsis spp.
Chrysopsis spp.
Delphinium spp.
Echinacea spp.
Epilobium spp.
Eupatorium spp.
Filipendula spp.
Gaillardia spp.
Geranium pratense
Hedyotis spp.
Helianthus spp.
Heliopsis spp.
Leucanthemum spp.
Liatris spp.
Miscanthus spp.
Panicum spp.
Penstemon spp.
Phlox spp.
Primula spp.
Pycnanthemum spp.
Ratibida spp.
Rudbeckia spp.
Salvia spp.
Senecio spp.
Solidago spp.
Sorghastrum spp.
Thalictrum spp.
Vernonia spp.

Perennials Suitable for Wet Sites

Acorus spp.
Anagallis tenella
Anemone × *hybrida*
Aruncus spp.
Astilbe spp.
Astilboides tabularis
Butomus umbellulatus
Calamagrostis spp.
Calla spp.
Caltha spp.
Campanula glomerata
Carex elata
Chelone spp.
Diphylleia cymosa
Equisetum spp.
Euphorbia palustris
Filipendula spp.
Glyceria spp.
Gymocarpium dryopteris
Helianthus angustifolius
Helonias bullata
Heracleum spp.
Houttuynia spp.
Iris fulva
Iris hexagona
Iris laevigata
Iris pseudacorus
Iris versicolor
Juncus spp.
Ligularia spp.
Lobelia spp.
Lysichiton spp.
Lysimachia spp.
Lythrum spp.
Meconopsis spp.
Mertensia spp.
Mimulus guttatus
Monarda spp.
Osmunda spp.
Peltiphyllum peltatum
Peltoboykinia tellimoides
Pontederia cordata
Phragmites spp.
Primula spp.
Ranunculus spp.
Rheum spp.
Rodgersia spp.
Sanguisorba spp.
Scirpus spp.
Silphium spp.
Smilacina spp.
Spartina spp.
Symplocarpus foetidus
Thelypteris spp.
Trollius spp.
Typha spp.
Zantedeschia spp.

Perennials Suitable for Dry Sites

Acantholimon spp.
Achillea spp.
Aethionema spp.
Agave spp.
Alyssum spp.
Anaphalis margaritacea
Antennaria spp.
Anthemis spp.
Arabis spp.
Arenaria spp.
Aster spp.
Callirhoe spp.
Carex spp.
Centranthus spp.
Chrysopsis spp.
Convolvulus sabatius
Coreopsis spp.
Coronilla spp.
Cortaderia spp.
Disporum spp.
Echinops spp.
Elymus spp.
Epilobium canum
Erigeron compositus
Erinus alpinus
Euphorbia amygdaloides
Filipendula vulgaris
Gaillardia spp.
Gaura lindheimeri
Geranium macrorrhizum
Glaucium spp.
Helianthus salicifolius
Helictotrichon sempervirens
Heliopsis spp.
Helleborous argutifolius
Hieracium spp.
Lathyrus spp.
Lespedeza spp.
Lewisia spp.
Linum spp.
Liriope spp.
Luzula spp.
Lychnis coronaria
Marrubium spp.
Miscanthus spp.
Nepeta sibirica
Origanum spp.
Panicum spp.
Perovskia spp.
Petrorhagia spp.
Saponaria spp.
Saxifraga spp.
Sedum spp.
Sempervivum spp.
Solidago spathulata
Solidago sphacelata
Symphytum grandiflorum
Trachelium spp.
Vancouveria hexandra
Veronica pectinata

Perennials Tolerant of Substantial Shade

Asarum spp.
Asplenium spp.
Astilbe spp.
Athyrium spp.
Begonia grandis
Blechnum spp.
Boykinia spp.
Carex conica
Caulophyllum thalictroides
Chasmanthium latifolium
Chelone spp.
Cornus canadensis
Cypripedium spp.
Cystopteris spp.
Deschampsia spp.
Dicentra spp.
Digitalis spp.
Disporum spp.
Dodecatheon spp.
Dryopteris spp.
Eomecon spp.
Epimedium spp.
Equisetem spp.
Eranthis spp.
Euphorbia amygdaloides
Galax urceolata
Geranium × *oxonianum*
Geranium maculatum
Geranium phaeum
Hakonechloa macra
Helleborous spp.
Hepatica spp.
Hesperis spp.
Hexastylis spp.
Hosta spp.
Jeffersonia spp.
Lamium galeobdolon
Lamium maculatum 'Aureum'
Lobelia spp.
Luzula spp.
Matteucia spp.
Mertensia spp.
Mitella spp.
Myosotis spp.
Omphalodes spp.
Osmunda spp.
Ourisia spp.
Pachysandra spp.
Paris spp.
Peltiphyllum spp.
Phlox spp.
Phyllitis spp.
Podophyllum spp.
Polystichum spp.
Ramonda spp.
Rumex scuttatus
Shortia spp.
Smilacina spp.
Stylophorum spp.
Symplocarpus foetidus
Tellima spp.
Thelypteris spp.
Tiarella spp.
Trachystemon spp.
Trillium spp.
Vancouveria spp.
Woodsia spp.
Viola spp.

Perennials Tolerant of Full Sun

Acaena spp.
Achillea spp.
Aconitum spp.
Adenophora spp.
Aethionema spp.
Agapanthus spp.
Alopecurus spp.
Amsonia spp.
Anagallis spp.
Anchusa spp.
Andropogon spp.
Anemone canadensis
Anemone × hybrida
Angelica spp.
Antennaria spp.
Arenaria spp.
Armeria spp.
Arrhenatherum spp.
Artemisia spp.
Arundo spp.
Asclepias spp.
Aster spp.
Ballota spp.
Baptisia spp.
Boltonia spp.
Briza spp.
Buphthalmum spp.
Bupleurum spp.
Calamagrostis spp.
Calamintha spp.
Calandrinia spp.
Callirhoe spp.
Campanula spp.
Catananche spp.
Centranthus spp.
Cephalaria spp.
Cerastium spp.
Ceratostigma spp.
Chrysanthemum spp.
Chrysopsis spp.
Convolvulus spp.
Coreopsis spp.
Coronilla spp.
Cortaderia spp.
Crambe spp.
Crepis spp.
Cyananthus spp.
Dictamnus spp.
Dracocephalum spp.
Elymus spp.
Epilobium spp.
Eragrostis spp.
Erianthus spp.
Eryngium spp.
Eupatorium spp.
Euphorbia spp.
Festuca spp.
Foeniculum spp.
Gaillardia spp.
Galega spp.
Gaura spp.
Geranium spp.
Geum spp.
Glaucium spp.
Glyceria spp.
Gypsophila spp.
Helianthus spp.
Helictotrichon sempervirens
Helichrysum spp.
Heliopsis spp.
Hemerocallis spp.
Hieracium spp.
Hyssopus spp.
Iberis spp.
Imperata spp.
Incarvillea spp.
Inula spp.
Iris spp.
Knautia spp.
Kniphofia spp.
Lathyrus spp.
Leonotis spp.
Leucanthemum spp.
Lewisia spp.
Liatris spp.
Limonium spp.
Lupinus spp.
Lychnis spp.
Lythrum spp.
Malva spp.
Marrubium spp.
Melissa spp.
Mentha spp.
Miscanthus spp.
Molinia spp.
Oenothera spp.
Paeonia spp.
Panicum spp.
Papaver spp.
Penstemon spp.
Perovskia spp.
Petrorhagia spp.
Phlomis spp.
Phlox bifida
Phlox douglasii
Phlox subulata
Phormium spp.
Phragmites australis
Platycodon spp.
Polygala spp.
Pontederia spp.
Pycnanthemum spp.
Raoulia spp.
Ratibida spp.
Romneya spp.
Ruta spp.
Salvia spp.
Saponaria spp.
Saxifraga spp.
Scabiosa spp.
Sedum spp.
Sempervivum spp.
Serratula spp.
Silphium spp.
Sisiyrinchium spp.
Solidago spp.
× Solidaster
Sorghastrum spp.
Spartina spp.
Symphyandra spp.
Tanacetum spp.
Teucrium spp.
Trachelium spp.
Verbascum spp.
Verbena spp.
Vernonia spp.
Veronica spp.

Perennials with Fragrant Flowers or Foliage

Acorus spp.
Adenophora lilifolia
Aethionema spp.
Agave americana
Alyssum montanum
Anemone sylvestris

Arabis spp.
Artemisia lactiflora
Centranthus ruber
Cimcifuga simplex
Clintonia umbellulata
Convallaria majalis
Crambe cordifolia
Crambe maritima
Dianthus spp.
Dicentra canadensis
Dictamnus albus
Filipendula ulmaria
Foeniculum vulgare
Galium odoratum
Geranium dalmaticum
Helonias bullata
Hemerocallis spp.
Hieracium villosum
Hosta spp.
Iris spp.
Lunaria spp.
Lysichiton spp.
Lysimmachia nummularia
Maianthemum canadense
Malva moschata
Melissa officinalis
Menta spp.
Myrrhis odorata
Oenothera odorata
Papaver spp.
Petasites fragrans
Phlox divaricata
Phlox maculata
Polygonatum odoratum
Primula spp.
Rodgersia aesculifolia
Romneya coulteri
Ruta graveolons
Salvia spp.
Saxifraga × *apiculata* 'Pungens'
Smilacina racemosa
Solidago odora
Viola spp.
Zantedeschia aethiopica

Summer-flowering Perennials with Long Blooming Periods (cvs. = cultivars)

Achillea millefolium cvs.
Anthemis tinctoria cvs.
Aquilegia 'McKana Hybrids'
Aster × *frikartii* cvs.
Centranthus ruber cvs.
Chrysogonum virginianum
Chrysopsis mariana
Chrysopsis villosa cvs.
Coreopsis grandiflora cvs.
Corydalis lutea
Dicentra eximia cvs.
Geranium sanguineum var. *striatum*
Helianthus helianthoides cvs.
Hemerocallis cvs.
Lythrum virgatum 'Morden's Pink'
Nepeta × *faassenii* cvs.
Phlox paniculata cvs.
Rudbeckia fulgida var. *sullivantii* 'Goldsturm'
Rudbeckia nitida 'Autumn Glory'
Salvia × *superba* cvs.
Sedum 'Autumn Joy'
Sidalcea malviflora cvs.
Veronica 'Sunny Border Blue'.

Herbaceous Perennials for Foliage

Acanthus spp.
Adiantum spp.
Ajuga reptans
Andropogon spp.
Artemisia spp.
Arum spp.
Arundo donax
Asarum spp.
Asplenium spp.
Athyrium spp.
Botrychium spp.
Briza spp.
Calamagrostis spp.
Carex spp.
Chasmanthium latifolium
Cortaderia sellona cvs.
Dennstaedtia punctilobula
Dryopteris spp.
Elymus glaucus
Erianthus ravennae
Festuca spp.
Foeniculum vulgare purpureum
Galium odoratum
Helictotrichon sempervirens
Heuchera spp.
Houttuynia cordata 'Variegata'
Imperata cylindrica 'Rubra'
Iris spp.
Lamium spp.
Liriope spp.
Macleaya spp.
Marrubium spp.
Matteucia spp.
Miscanthus spp.
Molinia spp.
Onoclea sensibilis
Osmunda spp.
Panicum virgatum
Peltiphyllum peltatum
Pennisetum spp.
Phalaris arundinacea var. *picta*
Polygonatum spp.
Polypodium spp.
Polystichum spp.
Pulmonaria spp.
Rheum spp.
Rodgersia spp.
Salvia spp.
Sempervivum spp.
Stachys byzantina
Stipa spp.

INDEX